The Ranger Book

Visit www.booksurge.com to order additional copies.

ROSS HALL

THE RANGER BOOK

A HISTORY 1634 - 2006

2007

The Ranger Book

CONTENTS

Acknowledgements xvii

Introduction xxiii

Foreword. xxvii

The Ranger Book 1

1634—Present Day. 1

   Up In The Air 1

Ranger Creed 3

   Ranger Thoughts On the Creed 3

   Keith Nightingale 3

   Wayne Downing 5

   Kenneth Leuer. 5

   William F. "Buck" Kernan. 6

   Ron Rokosz 6

   Keith Antonia 7

   Steve Hawk 7

   Edison Scholes 7

Validation of the Concept—Colonial Era 9

   Benjamin Church. 10

   Pre-Revolutionary War Ranger Units 13

French and Indian War—1754-1763 17

   Who Was Robert Rogers? 18

   Rogers' 19 Standing Orders?. 24

   Rogers' Rules of Discipline—The Real Version 25

Revolutionary War 29

   Thomas Knowlton 32

   Nathan Hale 33

   Francis Marion—Swamp Fox 33

   Daniel Morgan. 35

War of 1812—Indian Wars 37

Civil War 41

   Mosby, Ashby, Morgan—Confederate Rangers 43

Unit History and Lineage 47

   Quick Lineage Reference 52

World War II 55

World War II—Ranger Style. 59

   About Lucian King Truscott 61

   The Man: William Orlando Darby 61

John Raaen, Jr. 62

The First of the 1st—Darby's Rangers 65

Achnacarry 68

Dieppe. 71

2nd Army Ranger School. 74

North Africa 77

TORCH 77

The Attack—The Rangers' First Test 78

St. Cloud—LeMacta. 79

Tunisia 81

Sened Station. 81

Dernaia Pass 83

Djebel el Ank—El Guettar 84

Trained But Not Used—29th Infantry Division Rangers. 87

3rd and 4th Ranger Battalions Come On Line 89

Raymond Noel Dye 90

Sicily and Beyond. 92

Noel Dye. 95

Butera 98

Italy—The Bloody Boot 102

Salerno—Maori 102

Anzio—The End of the Beginning .111

The Hell of Cisterna. 113

Noel Dye 115

Darby's Rangers Spread Their Skills Without Him 119

Birth of the 2nd and 5th Battalions .121

Camp Forrest. 122

Rudder—A Short Biography 123

The Mission—D-Day 137

Omaha Beach—Dog Red—Dog White—Dog Green—Charlie. 143

Operation Overlord Becomes Reality 143

Ike Eikner 145

John Raaen 145

Charlie Beach—Vierville Draw. 147

Thomas Herring—5th Ranger Battalion. 149

Was General Norman Cota Responsible For The Phrase, "Rangers Lead
    The Way?" 150

Keith Nightingale 150

Tom Herring 151

The Assault On Pointe du Hoc 153

John Raaen 153

Ike Eikner 154

Leonard Lomell at the Pointe 159
Relief Heads For The Pointe. 165
John Raaen 166
Casualties—D-Day 168
Frank South—Medic, 2nd Battalion 169
John Raaen 170
Maisy 170
Rest, Then Brest 171
5th Battalion—Brest Campaign 173
Lochrist Battery. 176
Edlin's Patrol Takes The Prize 177
Saar Campaign—5th Battalion Trains, Fights, Rests 181
Hurtgen Forest—Hill 400 181
Vossenack—Germeter 183
Bergstein—Castle Hill. 185
2nd and 5th Battalions Invade Germany 193
Crossing the Rhine 193
5th Battalion at Irsch-Zerf. 194
Harry Herder. 198
6th Ranger Battalion—Pacific Theater 203
Henry Mucci—The Story of a Slave-Driving Man 204
Leyte Gulf Mission. 204
Leo Strausbaugh. 205
Cabanatuan 212
Robert Prince 215
Leo Strausbaugh—Mucci Leaves. 219
GALAHAD—5307th Composite Unit (Provisional)—Merrill's Marauders 221
The New GALAHAD. 227
Myitkyina, 475th, MARS, and China 229
Howard Garrison. 229
Korean War History—Ranger Training Center—1950-51 235
Birth of the Korean Ranger 237
The Great Debate 243
From Center For Military History—TO&E, TDA History. 247
Ranger TO&E 7-87 247
Korean War Ranger Units. 249
Eighth Army Rangers 250
Ralph Puckett 251
Origin and Formation 251
8 ARCO Speaks—Puckett, Walls, Summers, Cassat, Anderson, Bunn, Ross, et al.253
Hill 205 265
Korean War Airborne Rangers Training and Action. 275

Ranger Infantry Companies (Airborne) 279
   RICA Battle High Points. 279
   History—1st—15th RICA 279
   Changmal Raid 281
   Al Bukaty 282
   Chipyong-ni. 283
   May Massacre 284
   Majori-ri to Chechon 287
   Musan-ni—First Ranger Combat Jump 288
   2nd RICA—Queen, Payne, Allen, Lyles 289
   Bloody Nose Ridge 298
   Musan-ni. 301
   Ed McDonough 301
   Hwachon Dam. 302
   Hill 383 307
   Objective Sugar 308
   299 Turkey Shoot. 310
   Hill 628 310
   Topyong-ni 313
   Who Fought In Korea? 314
LRP Foundation—Cold War Europe 317
   Mike Martin 317
   Jack Daniel 320
   Steve Melnyk 321
   Bob McMahon. 323
   Bill Spies—157H 324
   V Corps LRRPs to Company A, 75th Infantry (Ranger) 324
Vietnam 329
   Sacrifice and Success—A New Day for Rangers. 329
   White Star—1959-62 331
LRRP, LRP, Ranger 333
Vietnam Ranger Evolution 339
   The First of the First—1st Brigade, (LRRP), 101st Airborne Division 340
   Company F (LRP), 58th Infantry, 101st Airborne Division 341
   Darol Walker, Division LRP Company First Sergeant 341
   Company L, 75th Infantry (Ranger), 101st Airborne (Airmobile) 346
   Steve Pullen and Robert Suchke. 350
   Training and Preparation Influence Mission Outcome 358
   Bob McMahon. 361
LRRP/LRP/Ranger Units of the Vietnam Era. .363
Lineage, Linkage, and Acceptance 365
Rangers In Non-Ranger Units And As Advisors 369

Edison Scholes 370

John (Jack) Daniel 371

William Spies 373

Ken Bonnell 375

Mike Martin 377

Doug Perry 379

Earl Singletary 387

Suchke—My First Mission 393

Roger McDonald 396

The Near Miss at Son Tay 407

Sydnor—Ground Forces Commander—Son Tay Raid 412

In-Country Training 421

MACV Recondo 421

Steve Pullen 422

Stateside Recondo 423

Roger McDonald 423

Earl Singletary 424

Howard Denton—82nd Recondo 424

State-Side Ranger Training During Vietnam 425

Bill Spies 425

The Big Jump—War and Peace—And War 427

Alpha, Bravo and Charlie Companies—Pre-Battalion Days 427

David Cress 427

Formation of the 1st Ranger Battalion—1974 429

Keith Nightingale—Standing Up A Ranger Battalion 429

Kenneth Leuer 434

Ron Rokosz 443

Bill Spies—Abrams and the Creation of 1st Ranger Battalion TO&E 445

Steve Hawk 446

David Hill 455

Steve Bishop 459

Eagle Claw—Desert One 463

Grenada 467

Brendan "Duke" Durkan 470

Richmond Hill Prison 474

Gary Curtis 474

Securing The Students 475

Bill Kinsland 475

Grand Anse 476

Tragedy At Calvigny Barracks 477

Perry Doerr 478

Special Operations—How It All Fits Together 479

The 75th Ranger Regiment 481
    Ron Rokosz 486
    Keith Antonia 487
    Why Rangers Are Elite 487
    75th Ranger Regiment Honors 487
    Keith Antonia—Changes in Regimental Support Forces and Training 448
    Regimental Reconnaissance Detachment 490
    Wayne Downing—Bio 491
    Wayne Downing 493
    Tools of the Trade—Modern Era 494
    Standard Weapons Systems per battalion 494
    At The Armory—Kazziah, Brown, Burkhead 494
Panama 501
    Steve Pullen 507
    Rio Hato 509
    Torrijos-Tocumen 511
    Leader of the Pack—Kernan Biography 513
    William "Buck" Kernan 514
    Wayne Downing 519
    Michael Kelso 520
    Keith Antonia—Grenada To Panama 520
    Duke Durkan—MIA 523
    Ed Scholes 523
Operation Desert Storm 529
    Perry Doerr F/51 LRSC 529
    Rangers In Other Times and Places 531
Task Force Ranger—Somalia 533
    The Battle of Mogadishu 534
War In The Middle East 539
Afghanistan—Operation Enduring Freedom 541
    The First Drop 543
    Order of Battle 544
    Rangers In Operation Anaconda 545
    Takur Ghar 545
    Strykers in Afghanistan 549
IRAQ 551
    Tony Torres 552
    The Deaths of Odai and Qusai 556
    Brad Bonnell 557
    Rangers Help Rescue POW 560
    How Hot Is Iraq? 560
    The War Is Over, But Not Over 561

Coalition Support. 564
Ranger School. 565
    The Ranger Tab. 565
    The Ranger Training Brigade's Mission 566
    Why Go To Ranger School? 567
    Barry Blackmon. 567
    Keith Antonia 568
    Ed Scholes. 568
    David Cress 568
    Perry Doerr 569
    Steve Bishop 569
    Doug Perry 569
    Ken Bonnell 569
    Pre-Ranger, RIP, and ROP(e) 569
    Keith Antonia—Ranger Training Elsewhere. 571
    Jack Daniel—ROTC Ranger Training 571
    Luca Bertozzo—Italian Ranger. 571
    Patrick Corcoran 573
    Three Phase Memories 574
    Ranger School 1972—City Phase 575
    Howard Denton. 575
    Mountain Phase Memories 582
    The Swamp Phase 590
    Jack Daniel 597
    Mountain Ranger Students 2004 598
    Bob McMahon. 602
    Earl Singletary. 604
Evolution of Ranger Training Camps. 605
    Keith Nightingale 606
    Jack Daniel 606
    Bill Spies—Walking Lanes. 607
    John Lange 609
    Daniel Barnes 614
    Doug Perry 615
    OPFOR (Opposing Forces—Aggressors) 616
    Barry Blackmon. 616
    Tony Torres 617
    Brian Cunningham 619
    Camp Frank D. Merrill 620
    Johnny Burt 1948-1953 620
    Steve Hawk 623
    Perry C. Doerr. 624

Ken Bonnell 626
Douglas Flohr and Glenn Legg. 626
Brian Cunningham 634
Greg Jolin 635
Steve Bishop 636
Keith Antonia 637
Steve Hawk 638
An Afternoon Raid in North Georgia. 639
General Ranger-Related Information 643
CSM Kelso—The Top Non-Com of USAIC .643
Michael Kelso 644
Bonnells—A Family of Rangers 648
Brad Bonnell 649
Mike Martin Marches On 652
The Black Beret. 653
The History of the Ranger Black Beret By Robert Black. 654
Just How Many Rangers Are There?. 656
Bibliography 659

Companion CD

For more than five years, I gathered information and recorded interviews until it became obvious I had more than I could ever use. To that end, nearly 90,000 words had to be cut to meet publishing demands. That hurt. Short sections on Delta, 160th SOAR, weapons, food, aircraft and miscellaneous pieces had to be cut—but they are not gone for good. I even had to cut passages from Ranger interviews—mostly stories—but, again, they are not lost.

Having said that, the history of the Rangers does reside within these pages—there is just so much more to add. No single, or even double volume can contain all the stories and photographs we've got. To that end we offer the "extras" the only way we can.

There is a companion CD that goes with this book. It contains those stories and all the sidebar articles that had to be cut. It also contains dozens of miscellaneous photographs dating from WWII forward. There are a lot of past and present Ranger faces in those shots.

More than 170 pages of extra information and great stories reside in this form only.

The CD can be obtained by sending $10 (checks only, please) to:

Ross Hall
2557 Jay Bridge Road
Dahlonega, Georgia 30533

ACKNOWLEDGEMENTS

This project is not a one-man show. Many people have contributed information, time, expense and expertise to create this unique document. There is no way to thank them all except to say THANKS!

Michael Thompson

C/2/5 1ˢᵗ Cav, Vietnam

My good friend acted as researcher, photographer, computer wizard and mentor, especially in the first half or so of the project, while I was still learning.

Michael was kind enough to do the graphics for the book cover.

Terri McCamish

Personal secretary to the Lt. Colonel Commanding 5ᵗʰ RTB. Terri was a real door opener, especially in the beginning, when I didn't even know which doors to open.

Randy White

Webmaster for L Co (Ranger) 75ᵗʰ Infantry

Randy provided information and clarification on several subjects.

Larry Ivers

Military historian

Ranger

Larry was the first real historian to offer help, which focused on early Rangers.

Colonel (Ret) Ralph Puckett

He helped me with personal archives and information about the Korean War and several other things.

William Spies

My friend, Bill, has more energy than a Cub Scout troop.

He opened more doors than I knew existed. He knows everybody.

Major General (Ret) Kenneth Leuer

He contributed large amounts of information on several subjects.

SFC Daniel Barnes

Public Affairs, Camp Frank D. Merrill, 2004-2005

Dan was always there when I needed him.

Thanks also to many other CFM soldiers, including 1SGT **Austin Stoeffel; Lt. Colonels Dochnal, Antonia, Flynn, Flohr and Pemrick; 1SGTs Corcoran and Orear; CSM Legg; SMJ Durkan and CSM Byron Barron.** There are too many good guys to name them all.

Steve Hawk and Doug Perry of the US Mountain Ranger Association

Rangers and friends who helped pave the way.

Several members of the Mountain Ranger Association stepped up to help in this project, including **Brian Cunningham, J. D. Kirby, Bob Suchke and Jack Daniel.**

Steve Pullen
Wisdom—library—friendship. What more can I say?

Keith Nightingale
He gave me lots of information in general, especially concerning the Ranger Creed.

Robert Black
Bob contributed a couple of items to the project, notably an essay on the black beret. His own written histories of Civil War, WWII and Korean War Rangers are excellent.

Edison Scholes
Major General (Ret) Scholes contributed a wealth of information on Panama.

Editors
Kenneth Leuer
Edited formation of 1st Battalion and Ranger Creed

John Raaen
Lester Kness
Thomas Herring
Frank South
Leo Strausbaugh
Editors, WWII section

Ralph Puckett—Korea, particularly Eighth Army Ranger Company sequence
Brian Cunningham—Vietnam
J. D. Kirby—Vietnam
Several other Rangers signified copies of their interviews as being accurate. Some clarified points, and/or added to what was recorded.

Sharon Hall—full print edit
Alix Neel—proofreader

This Book Is Dedicated To All Rangers, Past And Present,
Especially Those Who Thought
I'd Never Finish.

INTRODUCTION

*M*ajor *(Ret) William Spies is a member of the Ranger Hall of Fame—a man with tours in Korea and Vietnam who became Chief of the Benning Phase of Ranger Training. This project would not have been possible without him.*

I am deeply humbled, yet highly honored to have been invited to introduce this impressive, easy to read history of American/US Army Rangers—who they are, and what makes them famous.

This is writing that warrants your reading—reading by military historians and those who enjoy learning history when taught by those who have lived it, and by a most able historian. *The Ranger Book* should be required reading in every Junior and Senior ROTC program and in all of the military academies—including the Coast Guard and the Merchant Marines.

Study this book. Learn from those who lived this history and learn from the extensive and meticulous research of this gifted author. Not only will you meet true heroes in this book, you will also be pleasantly surprised, deeply impressed and much better informed.

Ross Hall spent over five years, countless trips and hours upon hours researching and interviewing. It is anyone's guess how much time he spent writing and re-writing, knowing him to be the perfectionist that he is. Ross wasted no time or effort—and all for our gain.

He has taken a unique and very detailed approach in recording the long and colorful history of the American Rangers. As Ross vividly points out, the history of the American Army Ranger goes back to at least 1634, when Ed Backler was commissioned by the Virginia Colony to "Rainge (sic) among the Indians on Kent Island to larn (sic) their disposition and intentions."

The American Ranger served on this continent some 150 years in many armed conflicts and six major wars before there were US Marines or a US Army. Since the 1630s, many Rangers have served this great nation with clear distinction, exceptional bravery and much sacrifice.

To list a few that are well known, and some not so well known: Ben Church of the 1690 era; Robert Rogers of the 1750 era; Nathan Hale; Francis Marion the Swamp Fox; Abraham Lincoln; Daniel Morgan; John Mosby; and Bill Darby.

The experiences of more modern Rangers are relayed by themselves. I will mention several whom I know personally that Ross has included in this work: Colonel Bud Sydnor, the Ground Commander during the Son Tay Raid in Vietnam; Major General Ken Leuer, the first Commander of the 1ˢᵗ Battalion, 75ᵗʰ Rangers when activated in 1974; General Wayne Downing—the Army claims he was the third Colonel of the 75ᵗʰ Ranger Regiment when it was re-activated 1984—to us, Rangers he is the first Colonel; and General Buck Kernan, a Rangers' Ranger in every sense of the saying, commander of the 75ᵗʰ Ranger Regiment during the daring and complicated Airborne/Parachute Assault during Operation Just Cause into Panama

In addition to the General Officers, you will read Ranger history as experienced and seen by Field and Company Grade Ranger officers, Ranger Non-commissioned Officers, Ranger Instructors, Ranger Class students, and several enlisted men, both Rangers and non-Rangers of Long Range Patrols/Long Range Surveillance Units (LRPs/LRSUs).

The soldiers and Rangers who served in the LRPs of Germany and Vietnam, and today's LRSUs and Army Rangers, do exactly what Ed Backler was commissioned to do back then—learn the enemy's disposition and intentions. They do it adhering to the very same principles used by the earliest Rangers and other Rangers since those times.

This book allows you to learn firsthand Ranger history through the actual experiences of some who were there. Here are a few more whom I know very well: 1SGT Lenny Lomell, who actually destroyed the big guns on Point du Hoc; Colonel Ralph Puckett, who was awarded two of the nations second highest awards for valor; 1SGT Doug Perry, a renowned Ranger Instructor; Steve Hawk, a Private in the original 1/75; Steve Melnyk, who served as an E-4 Specialist in a LRP in Germany during the late 1950s; and Command Sergeant Major (CSM) Mike Kelso, who fought in Rhodesia, was CSM of the Ranger Training Brigade, then the US Infantry School, and retired as the CSM of the Infantry Center.

There are many more included in this book—every one a true hero! Read the words from their mouths and enjoy! Not only does Ross expose us to many Rangers, he has included, in great depth, history they made and were surrounded by during their service. You will learn much about how and why Army Rangers are what they are. You will learn about the Army Ranger ethos and how it has shaped the US military. That ethos includes excellence in all they do, plus leadership, loyalty, daring and dependability.

The Ranger Book presents much detail about Ranger Tables of Organization & Equipment, combat loads, Ranger training, how Rangers were employed and capabilities of various Ranger units.

This work will have a major impact in clarifying just what an Army Ranger is, how he operates, and how he is best employed during combat.

Ross has done well in relating the following: Rangers are famous for operating deep into the enemy's territory to reconnoiter, or by violent, swift action, ambush and raid strategic targets. They operate independently. Their security comes from their speed and ability to infiltrate and ex-filtrate clandestinely by land, sea and air through areas and by means that most consider unreasonable or impossible. Unlike the Green Berets/Special Forces who usually rely on indigenous forces for security, housing and food, Rangers rely on secrecy, stealth, speed and only their own resources. They are highly skilled in navigation, demolitions, weaponry, hand-to-hand combat and survival.

You will be fascinated by the experiences related here by the individuals themselves who have trained and fought as Army Rangers, one segment of this world's most elite warriors. You will learn history as it has rarely, if ever, been written. This book is factual and intriguing. Yet, there are no plots or subplots, just the historical facts as presented by Ross and by some of those who actually made the history. It is full of detail and amazingly captivating.

I highly recommend this book to all who enjoy history, both civilian and military, and to all who are serious historians.

I would be remiss if I failed to enlighten you to some degree about Ross Hall, the author of this captivating historical work, and a very special close friend of mine. Several years ago, Ross and I drove from his home in north Georgia to Atlantic City, New Jersey to meet with a bunch of Rangers. It was there he first met Lenny Lomell of Point du Hoc fame. Since then, we have remained in close contact.

Claiming that Ross is one unique human being is a gross understatement. In plain language, he is an odd sort of character. Just spend a couple of hours with him and it sneaks up on you that he is not your average man stumbling around on our mother earth.

He has a way with words that belies a keen and dry sense of humor, while inculcating you with a genuine sense of concern—about our environment, about humanity, and about Army Rangers.

He was born in 1950 in the Arkansas Ozarks. He is the son of a minister who served as a missionary with the Lakota Sioux. His deep respect of those people still surfaces. Since 1962, he has spent most of his life in the Deep South.

Some of his experiences include, not necessarily in this order: was a Boy Scout; attended college; sailed as a Mate on an excursion schooner to the Bahamas and points south; got run off by Cuban gunboats and scudded through a hurricane; was a SCUBA diver; dodged sharks; earned trophies in the martial arts; hitch-hiked up and down the eastern seaboard from Key West to New York; taught self defense; built a house back in the woods of north Florida; played the guitar for a living; became an EMT and then an RN working ER and ICU; saw lives end too many times; built his second house in Dahlonega; farmed a nursery and did landscaping; became a reporter; and finally remarried his true love, Sharon, whom he fondly refers to as "My Lady." They have five sons and five grandkids.

While reporting for a weekly newspaper in Dahlonega, Georgia, home of the 5th Ranger Training Battalion, he became aware of this human breed known as Army Rangers. Having several in his family who have served in various Branches of the military, he is most impressed with Rangers.

He writes, "Nothing before my time with Rangers has given me greater pleasure and greater respect for integrity, commitment and excellence. No matter where I go from here I will always be involved. You guys are tops in my book."

His work, *The Ranger Book*, is tops!

Drive On!

Ranger Bill Spies

FOREWORD

This project started out to be a short, concise history of Camp Frank D. Merrill—home of the 5th Ranger Training Battalion in Lumpkin County, Georgia.

Needless to say, it got away from me.

I realized that learning about the Mountain Camp meant learning about the men in it, which led to Ranger actions. Drilling deeper, I discovered an organization with a long and rich history, populated by extraordinary soldiers. I was hooked.

Over time I've been made an Honorary member of the US Mountain Ranger Association, and by extension, a member of Worldwide Army Rangers, Inc. At this time I write a monthly Ranger column for the Static Line newsmagazine, and edit WAR's newsletter. I've been immersed in the Ranger concept and culture for years. I guess I know as much about them as any civilian can.

However, that is as close as I get. I have never worn the Tab. For purposes of this project, that is both good and bad. Because I am not a Ranger, I feel I can be more objective. The flip side of that is, there are some things I can never know or experience. That's why there are more than 70 Ranger voices inside these pages.

When beginning this project, I sent feelers in all directions trying to link up with someone who knew more than me. Since at the time I knew just about nothing, it wasn't difficult to find someone to educate me.

As I brought myself up to speed I read everything Ranger I could get my hands on. That's when I found out there was no complete history out there. There are fragments based on time and unit, but nothing close to what I felt must be produced. Even the fragments were suspect. Often, no two accounts are the same. Memories are bound to be somewhat flawed, and sometimes writers slant history a little to make it fit better.

A major point was made by Ranger historian Larry Ivers, who warned me by saying, "People have played fast and loose with Ranger history." To my dismay I soon found out how right he was. There are wannabees and pretenders, written "histories" that are so far off it's ludicrous, and last but not least, information from the Army itself. There are miles of stacks of millions of bits of information put down in the Army's exacting style—sometimes by people who were not there when the action occurred. Even when an actual participant wrote After Action Reports, some things got left out or were ambiguous. In most cases it is impossible to know *exactly* what happened in a given event, except in a broad overview.

I met people and listened to them. I began to show up at Mountain Ranger Association meetings and 0600 in-walker briefings and Change of Command ceremonies. Before long the Rangers got tired of seeing me just standing there watching, and started inviting me to doings at the Camp.

On my 50th birthday, they put me on a Black Hawk helicopter and tried to make me throw up all over the Tennessee Valley Divide. They let me shoot their weapons, eat their food, and watch them train.

There is so much to present there is no room for photographs, or even maps—not to mention the interviews I wanted and couldn't get—yet. Ample quantities of history await.

To deal with pertinence and accuracy a researcher must look at corroborating evidence as often as possible. Sadly, it is not always available. Sometimes you just have to take someone's word for what happened and report what was said about a particular place and time.

While perusing my share of official documents for truth, I also crosschecked as much as possible by simply talking to Rangers. Some of them edited pieces of which they were a part. If something was very wrong it raised flags when reviewed by those who were there when it happened—and they had no trouble telling me about it.

The driving forces behind my simple narrative are the confident voices of men who were there, men who raced frantically across Omaha Beach, stalked the jungle stillness, or fired frozen weapons with frozen hands in the mountains of Korea. Those memories are the real history of those men in those times—quite apart from the overall picture presented as "official" history. My job was to put official and personal histories together in a chronological, easily read format.

This is a long look at the Rangers, dealing with their portion of military history in context with the overall picture. To achieve that context there are mini-histories of events leading up to Ranger actions in major conflicts. Not everybody knows why we were in Vietnam, or Panama. World happenings influence military happenings. To me, it's all part and parcel.

This is not intended to be a scholarly work with footnotes on every page, nor is it an in-depth analysis. What I have done is gather information pertinent to Rangers, support it with interviews where possible, and present it in an easily read chronological format. The whole idea was to produce a document acceptable to both military and civilian readers.

Throughout this project I have interjected my own comments, which are usually presented in italics. I have tried to keep it down. During the many re-writes, my editor succeeded in getting rid of the more personal ones, such as when I referred to Hitler as an idiot. Well, he was.

Still, it is not the function of this work to expose or speculate about individual, governmental or military misdoings unless it relates to the Rangers, and even then it's usually a case of he said/he said. I have tried to report those issues in that way.

Besides, the Rangers have their own particular set of issues, including misuse in battle, constant deactivation after conflicts—until fairly recently—the loss of the Black Beret and several others.

The men profiled here are of a slightly higher caliber, men who always seem to be out front bringing it to the enemy, whether in the hardwood forests of North America more than 350 years ago or in the sandy heat of the Iraqi desert. These men tell stories of courage and incredible acts of physical and mental toughness, but they also share a deep brotherhood and talk about each other like family.

To quote Ranger David Cress, "I loved them all, even the ones I didn't like."

During the years this project has consumed, I have been privileged to spend a great deal of time among Rangers of all ages, and it is plain to see that brotherhood, especially when conceived in danger, does not go away. There are several major Ranger Associations, and the overriding message of each one is brotherhood and the promotion of Rangers, past and present.

Many men have spoken to me about that bond, and about the myriad other things that make up the Ranger experience. Some of them were squad members; some were Generals. They told me of their combat experiences, but that is only a small part of what they had to say. They emphasized training, leadership, and excellence in all things. They are proud to be Rangers, and rightly so.

Rangers don't just fight; they live the philosophy. They are highly intelligent, well organized and superbly trained. They are motivated. They have the right equipment and support. They can fall out of the sky and wreak havoc anywhere in the world in a matter of hours.

Rangers are not supermen—indeed, on average, many of them appear a little undersized for fighting men, but up close they seem to be made of wood and stone. They can climb anything or cross any barrier. They are soldiers doing what soldiers do—they just do it a little better, faster and more effectively. They don't make a big deal out of it. They know what is expected of them and they go forward.

It has been a genuine pleasure being among them, and I will stay among them as long as they will have me. There is a lot of history being made just now in the east, and much more history and stories of the past still to be chronicled and kept safe for future Rangers.

This work is for those good men; ready to go down the danger trail to protect something they believe in.

I believe in them. They are for real.

THE RANGER BOOK

1634—Present Day

Up In The Air

From the portside gunner's window of a Black Hawk helicopter I watched a section of woods in the north Georgia mountains, seeing nothing but wildly blowing foliage as the big bird lightly touched down in a small meadow at the edge of some trees.

Then suddenly there were men coming toward us, hard-looking men, heavily camouflaged and just as heavily armed. Two soldiers turned their weapons to the forest while the rest threw their gear through the wide-open door, following it in seconds, and we went straight up out of there like a runaway express elevator, topped the trees, and banked hard to starboard. As we juked around through valleys, flying low, banking this way and that, I saw ground in my little window, then sky. My stomach and sense of wonder were vying for first place in my astonished mind, as the UH-60 became the world's greatest roller coaster.

The Ranger students and Instructors in the back didn't seem to mind at all. I was wondering how they could be so nonchalant about being turned six directions every couple of seconds when I glanced right and saw my camera floating about two feet off the deck, easing toward the window, my sense of balance right behind it.

Please, God, I prayed, don't let me lose it in front of these guys.

Anybody but them.

A Quick Word

There are more than 80 Ranger voices in this project, about 70 of which are presented in the form of an interview. Some of those interviews were conducted face-to-face, some were done over the telephone, some given through email exchanges. In most cases of conversational interview, the contributor's words were recorded for accuracy.

Some of the men have their words listed in more than one place in the project, so their biographical information is not listed with each entry.

A decision was made not to list rank in the heading of each offering, as all Ranger words in the project have the same value. Ranks are delineated in each man's biography, which generally precedes the first appearance of his name, except in the case of the Ranger Creed statements and a very few other instances.

In most cases, words in italics are the comments or questions of the author. In the interviews, clarifications by the author are in brackets, while clarifications by Rangers are in parentheses.

Certain words will be capitalized or not depending on how the author feels about them. Examples are: communism, Cadre (Rangers only), Sergeant, officer, Instructor (Rangers only), Platoon Leader, Non-Com and others.

First Things First

This project has to open with the Ranger Creed, even though it didn't appear until after the Vietnam War. The Creed embodies the overall philosophy that has guided these excellent warriors through 375 years of service. As with the rest of the book—from WWII forward—we'll let them tell you about it.

RANGER CREED
By CSM Neal R. Gentry and Others

Recognizing that I volunteered as a Ranger, fully knowing the hazards of my chosen profession, I will always endeavor to uphold the prestige, honor and high "esprit de corps" of my Ranger Regiment.

Acknowledging the fact that a Ranger is a more elite soldier who arrives at the cutting edge of battle by land, sea or air, I accept the fact that as a Ranger my country expects me to move further, faster, and fight harder than any other soldier.

Never shall I fail my comrades. I will always keep myself mentally alert, physically strong and morally straight, and I will shoulder more than my share of the task, whatever it may be, one hundred percent and then some.

Gallantly will I show the world that I am a specially selected and well-trained soldier. My courtesy to superior officers, neatness of dress and care of equipment shall set the example for others to follow.

Energetically will I meet the enemies of my country. I shall defeat them on the field of battle for I am better trained and will fight with all my might. Surrender is not a Ranger word. I will never leave a fallen comrade to fall into the hands of the enemy, and under no circumstances will I ever embarrass my country.

Readily will I display the intestinal fortitude required to fight on to the Ranger objective and complete the mission, though I be the lone survivor.

Rangers Lead The Way

Ranger Thoughts On the Creed

Some of the following emails were written in May/June 2004. They constitute a discussion between participants as well as comments from other individuals. Other offerings came during interviews.

Keith Nightingale

For the last year I have been compiling the history of the Creed for the Ranger Association. I was an "original" Ranger commanding HQ Co for [Colonel] Leuer and was intimately involved in the Ranger Creed development.

Ken Leuer felt the Rangers must have a simple encompassing Creed that could put everything together for all ranks and be the foundation of the organization. He tasked Neil Gentry, the CSM [Command Sergeant Major], with putting together a draft. I have a copy of that original draft.

Leuer thought it a good start but needed work. It was heavily airborne-oriented. My impression was that it was almost a carbon copy of the Airborne Creed posted around the Fort Benning Airborne Training area. He passed it to Rock [Hudson] for refinement.

The refined version was reviewed at a Commander's Call with Leuer, staff and commanders and became final to what we have today.

We began the Creed at Battalion PT [physical training] with each commander reciting a stanza. Each squad was required to memorize it and this was constantly reinforced daily with required stanza repetitions for virtually everything we did in the field and garrison until everyone had it down cold. This was ALWAYS redone at PT with Leuer picking out positions to lead a stanza before each exercise, e.g.: "2nd Platoon Leader, Co B, repeat the third stanza of the Ranger Creed."

It is pretty clear in my mind that the editors/authors were: Whoever wrote the Airborne Creed (the base document), CMS Gentry (original modifications) with discussions with Ken Leuer (I think Leuer grew frustrated with Gentry's inability to reform the document), Rock Hudson (major modifications) with discussions with Ken Leuer, and commanders in session on the final (primarily small wordsmithing—Rock's version was pretty much there).

I think the takeaway regarding the Creed is not so much exactly what it says or how it is interpreted but the inclusion process and assimilation of the spirit and solidarity of the speaker with the group. It is the one thing that bonds all Rangers and is unique to them. The belief in uniqueness is a very critical part of the Rangers' inner being in terms of demonstrated performance. It is less important that a Ranger is truly better than the enemy than that he believes he is. The Creed is a foundation piece to that belief.

Excerpts From Nightingale's History of the Creed

Every living Ranger knows and understands the Ranger Creed. It is a living embodiment of a personal and organizational philosophy. It sustains the individual and the unit in its darkest hours and most perilous exposures. It is posted on walls of living quarters around the world where Rangers live and have lived. It is referred to by many non-Rangers as a secret basis for their own existence and personal beliefs. It transcends all other motivations of the individual. It defines the person and the organization. It is what is and what all believe.

Webster defines a creed as "a set of fundamental beliefs;" also: "a guiding principle." The Ranger Creed states what a Ranger as an individual stands for, what he will do; and for the unit, what it must do. It is simple, clear and unambiguous and that is both its strength and its glory.

Throughout recorded history, every great Nation has had a small military organization that was utterly reliable and totally dependable to accomplish the mission of the moment or disintegrate itself trying. It was both the model of the best that military structure possessed as well as its last resort. The Greek Hoplites, Caesar's Tenth Legion, Napoleon's Old Reliables, the British Household Guards and the American Ranger—each had a Creed as the basis for binding and bonding their membership into a cohesive mass that thought and acted alike, shared common values and forsook privations while relegating personal desires for the greater good. In the darkest of moments and in the most tenuous of times, the Creed focused the members and caused ordinary people to achieve extraordinary things. It was the foundation of the organizational soul.

The Ranger Creed has grown from a memorized set of stanzas uncertainly repeated on a dark humid PT field at Ft Stewart, Georgia to a near universal guide to life, duty and performance for any person exposed to its words. The Creed is posted on walls around the world wherever Rangers have been and do their work. It is carefully folded and carried in thousands of rucksacks and notebooks. It resides on plaques and mementoes of retired Rangers and is indelibly etched in the mind of any soldier, sailor, airman or Marine who has worn the Tab or been associated with the Regiment or Ranger Training Brigade [RTB].

The Creed is the first thing spoken in the morning and the last at night. It is the last non-operational item a Ranger will discuss before executing his assigned Ranger mission or jumping out the door into hostile territory.

The Ranger Creed is both the comfort and the courage that opens the wellsprings of the individual soldier and converts him from an ordinary to an extraordinary soldier and makes him truly the glory of our Nation.

Wayne Downing

The Ranger Creed was believed by every man in the unit. We subscribed to its philosophy in every thing we did. It made us unique because it was a living guide to our actions.

Kenneth Leuer

I was looking for something that I could put on the backs of the Non-Commissioned Officers that could bring them to buy in. I wasn't sure, with what we brought out of Vietnam and everything, that I could get the stimulus going that people wanted to be in the Gold Medal ring.

Neal Gentry was the Sergeant Major I selected. There was a lot of discussion, why Gentry…and Gentry probably wasn't the one, but he was the best one for me. He was loyal, he was honest, supported me a thousand percent. We were flying over to Fort Stewart a few days after I'd met with General DePuy, and I said, "Sergeant Major, one of the items on the Charter I got from General DePuy is we got to have a Creed. I want you to put together the Ranger Creed. I will edit it, I will approve it, and I will pass on it. You put it together. That Creed is to be supported, maintained, guarded, and lived up to as an example by the Non-Commissioned Officer corps. Officers will certainly be a part of the Creed, but that is the Non-Coms'…to take care of, and imbue in every soldier in the battalion."

I said, "Take a look at the Code of Conduct, to look at some of these things and see what you might want to come up with. What might be neat, maybe you could do something with the word 'Ranger.'"

At that time we weren't sure we were going to be called Rangers. We were looking at Commandos and…some other things.

He chose "Ranger" and worked with it, and then as we started bringing Cadre in, other NCOs, they started working with him, and about once a week he would bring it in to me and I'd probably keep it over the weekend. We worked on it and worked on it and we thought we had it standing up fairly well.

Morning PT was a daily affair, and Leuer was often present. When the Creed was ready it was implemented as part of the drill.

We started what would become a weekly activity when we were in garrison. Monday was my PT day, when I would run PT for the whole battalion. I would say, "Squad Leader, 3rd Squad, 2nd Platoon, A Company, first stanza of the Ranger Creed!" And he would pump it out, loud and clear. If he couldn't do it, the Platoon Sergeant, then the Platoon Leader, then the Company Commander. I tell you what—they knew the Ranger Creed.

William F. "Buck" Kernan

As did most Rangers, I first learned the Ranger Creed when I was assigned to the 2nd Ranger Battalion in February 1976. At first I did not have an appreciation for how much the words in the verses would mean in my professional development. I was more concerned about committing it to rote memory for fear of professional embarrassment should I fail to remember the stanzas or not get the wording precisely correct.

Once I had fully committed it to memory, I found myself dwelling on the meaning of the words and routinely found them inspiring during difficult times. The Creed was always there to remind me of what I had volunteered to do, what my purpose was, and what values other Rangers and myself expected. It gave meaning, purpose, and standards to what I was tasked to do. Even today, I find myself mentally repeating a stanza if it fits the occasion.

The old saying that "the Tab was an award, but the Scroll was a way of life" is very true. The foundation or touchstone to that way of life is The Creed. Rangers routinely do the routine things well and [commit] courageous acts because of their determination to fulfill The Creed. Witness Somalia or Operation ANACONDA …as well as numerous other examples.

During Operation JUST CAUSE, as the Regimental Commander, I had each aircraft recite the Ranger Creed at the three-minute warning. Each C-130 was packed with 64 combat-equipped Rangers. The jumpmasters started the Creed with the sticks reciting as normal. It was deafening in my aircraft, as I am sure it was in all others. Several USAF crew members later told me in addition to being very inspirational to them, they thought the battle had already been joined inside the aircraft. The Rangers were pumped, knew what this meant, and the Creed reminded them of their duty. Despite receiving effective ground fire 30 seconds out, all Rangers unhesitatingly jumped and successfully completed their missions.

Ron Rokosz

I believe Leuer, based on his background, had in mind the need for a creed of some sort that would pull Rangers together. I believe that from the start, he wanted it to be more than something one could quote, and more something Rangers could live by and feel bonded to. My recollection is similar to yours [Nightingale]. He gave the mission to CSM Gentry, was frustrated by the results, turned it over to Hudson for revision, then pulled us all in for input prior to the final result. I also agree with Buck's view that initially it was something we "had" to learn; but over time, became something that was internalized by all Rangers.

Leuer started to inculcate it by reciting it at Battalion PT sessions; then it became something that was recited daily at PT sessions down to squad level. Over time, I am sure it was something often quoted as a measurement of how we should conduct ourselves.

I was original B Co Commander in 1/75. Other original company commanders were Clark, Barnhill and Nightingale. So, I was there when we formed the battalion, moved to Stewart; was there when Leuer launched the Ranger Creed.

A great story that I will always remember. We had battalion PT, I think monthly. Leuer would get up on the PT platform and lead exercises. After the Ranger Creed was written and put out, we were in battalion formation and Leuer asked A Co Commander to lead the battalion in the first stanza of the Ranger Creed. As soon as he did that, I was sweating bullets because I had not memorized it. Luckily, A Co commander hadn't either and said he did not know it. Then Leuer asked me to recite it and I replied the same. Then he went to Nightingale, and Keith obviously was smarter than us and assumed it was coming and he knew the first stanza. After that PT formation, we all swore we wouldn't be caught short again, and began having all the soldiers learn it.

Later, I was Regimental Deputy Commander under Downing. So, I was part of group that initially formed the Regiment. Of interest, while Deputy, both 2/75 and 3/75 Battalion Commanders were relieved, and I went to both as interim battalion commander. I "believe" I was the first individual to be assigned to all three battalions and the Regimental Hqs. I later commanded 1-509th in Italy, and 2nd Brigade, 82nd Airborne, during Desert Storm. I was J3 at JSOC, Commander, SOCPAC in Hawaii, then Assistant Division Commander, 25th ID. I retired when I was working in DCSOPS in the Pentagon.

Keith Antonia

Keith Antonia sent this email in response to his seeing a photo Sharon Hall took of him reciting the Creed at Pine Valley in April 2003, with Ralph Puckett in the background.

I get choked up looking at it. I was really proud to recite the Ranger Creed with such distinguished Rangers present. Colonel Ralph Puckett was the Honorary Colonel of the Regiment in 1997-1999, when I was the S-3 of the 75th Ranger Regiment at Fort Benning. Colonel Puckett would wander into my office and chat with me every once in a while at our headquarters at Benning. I felt humbled in his presence and I never thought I deserved a visit from such a man.

I was really afraid that I might screw up the Ranger Creed that day at Pine Valley. Back in the Regiment, if you screwed up the sacred Ranger Creed by one word, you paid a price. I found out what the SOP of the Ranger Regiment S-3 shop was—the hard way—after I messed up one of the stanzas. My subordinates ordered me to the "rock" out back and I had to do "elevated" pushups (feet up on the rock, hands on the ground) while they poured cold water on me—in the winter after PT. You don't mess up the Ranger Creed. I felt if I messed it up at Pine Valley, some of the guys would throw me into the river after the ceremony.

Steve Hawk

When I first got in the battalion I don't think the Creed was fully formulated. I can remember sitting at the breakfast table in the mess hall with Sergeant Major Gentry and a guy named Johnny Newhouse. He was one of the few people that was a Ranger-enlisted option and graduated and came to the battalion. He was also an Eagle Scout. There's a lot of things about the Ranger Creed that's a lot like the Boy Scouts.

The Sergeant Major would take paper and pen and write it out and try to change words around. Initially it was real hard to recite the Creed because it wasn't written...with any pauses or breaks. You had to go a long, long distance before a pause, and half the people would forget it. I remember him writing it so there would be pauses so you could recite it. It was constantly drilled into your head.

Edison Scholes

It's just a shame we didn't adopt something like that for the bigger battalions. It really nails down some things that troops can understand and be loyal to and relate to. It's sort of like Semper Fi that the Marines have. It goes from one end of the Marines to the other. Semper Fi is their watchword.

To me the Ranger Creed really gives something a young soldier can understand and lay out before him and say, "This is what I live by."

VALIDATION OF THE CONCEPT—COLONIAL ERA

The deep roots of Ranger heritage were established in the Colonial Era more than a century before the Revolutionary War when a new type of fighting man was needed to counter expanding threats against the colonists. The men who were selected were able to handle the job well because it wasn't really new to them. The first Rangers could be characterized as half-wild—a good thing—because the Indians they fought were the same. Conventional tactics of overwhelming force on an open battlefield were not sufficient to tame the minor allies of major nations such as France and Spain.

The first Rangers were trappers, hunters and trackers, and many had experience fighting Indians. In a way they were character actors in a play being written as they worked. Such men were perfectly suited for the job, considering they could track anything anywhere, live outside with no supply train, and knew their enemies well. Accordingly, very little, if any, training was needed or performed in the beginning.

Men were needed to go where the Indians went—men with courage and knowledge of woodcraft, plus a willingness to endure physical hardship to complete the mission.

There were no training centers, no Ranger Instructors. The men who became the first Rangers already knew how to do the job, and they usually did it alone or in small groups, working under private authority instead of governmental protocols.

Why "Ranger"?

The name comes from the Frankish "hring," meaning circle, or ring, a fitting term because patrols and flanking movements are often curved, putting the Ranger behind his enemy. It's probable the origin of the word came from England, where it was used to describe keepers of the royal forest, which included routing out poachers. The keepers often used a widening circular movement to locate intruders, ranging outward in widening circles. That method of approach continued in the New World. The colony of Virginia relied on private land owners to furnish men with weapons to defend the mandated palisade walls around family holdings and to use some of those men to act as scouts, ranging out in circular patrols to try and locate hostile Indians.

First Rangers

The first Ranger acknowledged by historians was Edward Backler (could be Blackler) working mostly alone in 1634, though it is probable there were other men doing the same work, but are not documented. Backler worked for William Claiborne in the area of Virginia that sits next to Maryland. Claiborne lists him for two years as a "rainger," which is apparently the old English spelling. In Claiborne's case there were also some hostile Marylanders trying to horn in on his lucrative trading post on Kent Island on Chesapeake Bay. He used Backler to provide information on the movements of his enemies.

The practice of privately funded Rangers was generally at an end by mid-century when government-sanctioned "Parties of Rangers" began to broaden the effects of the militiamen. Between Virginia and Maryland there were several parties of men patrolling the edges of civilization, much of the time in hostile territory, acting as the first line of defense for the colonists.

Small forts—outposts, really—were built along the frontier as a means of deterring hostile Indians, but they were highly inefficient at doing so, and they cost too much to maintain. A decade and more before the turn of the century they were gone, replaced by men on horseback who could keep track of the enemy. Between duties, which could be weekly or monthly, those men worked the farms.

Around 1700 there were at least two companies of Rangers patrolling between what are now Washington and Baltimore, keeping touch between two large holdings (forts) about 75 miles apart.

Rangers of the day dressed like what they were; woodsmen, horsemen, rough-and-ready fighters. They wore no uniforms, no fine clothing or shine on their shoes. They were also made to supply everything a horseman would need, including food for himself and his mount. Weapons were supplied by the fighting man who would use them, generally consisting of a flintlock musket, often featuring a sawed-off barrel for use on horseback.

These days Ranger weapons have gotten smaller for the same reasons—not horseback exactly—but for close encounters in quick actions.

A couple of pistols sat in front of the rider, and a sword previously carried evolved into a hatchet which could be thrown, wielded, or used as a tool. Payment was in the currency of the day, whether it be tobacco, foodstuffs, or local currency.

The use of Ranger units continued almost without cease during the 1700s. It is important to note that though the units were under British authority they were technically Continental Militia and did not work for the British Army as regular troops. However, the British often paid them.

Benjamin Church

Ben Church is significant in Ranger history because he was one of the first recognized Ranger leaders, and because he was very effective at gathering information and raiding enemy positions. Though there were many men acting as scouts and fighters for the colonial settlements, Captain Benjamin Church and his men populated the earliest company-sized unit of Rangers, circa 1675-76. Other organizations were known as "Parties of Rangers" or "Troops" during the last of the 17th Century.

The conflict of the day was called King Philip's War, after the chief of the Wampanoag, which pitted Church's men—including Indians—and others like them against the French, as well as King Philip and other Indian tribes.

Research into Church's actions reveals he was powerful and effective enough to gain him fame both as a God-fearing Loyalist who got the job done against the Crown's enemies and a leader who went just a tad too far at times. It really depends on which side is telling the story.

He fought against Indians and recruited Indians and in between he dealt with the British and the French. Church had nothing against Indians—as long as they were in his employ and/or Christian—and had many surrender to him under the promise of mercy. Unfortunately, Church's influence only spread so far and some Indian prisoners he may have made promises to suffered or were sold as slaves. He objected to no avail.

Ben Church was active long after King Philip's War. In 1689 men under his authority could get eight pounds (British) for a dead Indian.

Church continued in service although his career appears to have been on the edge of destruction several times for things done to Indians by men under his command, but evidently not with his knowledge. Either way he was back in 1692 as second under Governor Phips. Orders were given to secure the safety of any Indian captives.

French captives weren't treated much better, if any.

He was still very active in 1704, though he was in his sixties and quite fat. While he had been somewhat compassionate toward his enemies earlier, that seems to have changed, at least in terms of psychological interrogation. The story goes that he would let his captives think he was going to give them to his Indian allies, right up to the last minute, thinking they would be tortured beyond endurance, then ask them again whatever it was he wanted to know. There are no details about what happened if the captives didn't talk.

Captain Church died in 1718.

Southern Rangers

Wide open in 1700, Georgia was nearly unpopulated except for Indians. It was considered to be outside the Colonial frontier, which ended at South Carolina—not yet a Royal Colony. With the Spanish in Florida and the French in Louisiana, Georgia became an avenue for hostiles to attack the southern reaches of the colonies. For years the job of defense was given mostly to the Indians of the area, with colonists occasionally leading raiding parties against the Spanish.

One thing led to another over the years, and friends became enemies. Soon South Carolina found itself in charge of its own defense and that of the colonies to the north.

In South Carolina the Ranging System was set up as the Northward, Westward, and Southward Companies, based at forts along the Santee, Edisto, and Ashepoo Rivers.

The three companies stood down in June 1718, but a separate company took shape a month later and was based near Columbia, South Carolina.

There were never enough volunteers for the highly hazardous duty and men had to be drafted from regular militia units to fill the gaps. After 1717 even indentured servants could be called to duty. Finding men was a definite hardship, enough so that Charles Town harbor could not relinquish any ship to the sea while drafts for fighting men were under way. Still, the use of Rangers saved the militia from having to do the job, and the job was done somewhat better for that.

In 1730 things began to happen along the short Georgia coastline when Britain and the locals decided to build around Savannah and along the lower Altamaha River. This expansion marked the beginning of the push south and west from South Carolina, and caused the Spanish and the local Indians serious worries.

At first, home defense was left to the people at home. A Tythingman led loosely organized militias made of squads of ten men each, called Tythes. Those groups stayed very close to home. Fear of a slave uprising took root, and Georgia went so far as to ban slavery, mostly so there would be more white men on hand for defense.

As the colony expanded, people began to settle outside of towns with their stockade walls and were thus open to attack. At first the new Georgians built a few small forts, relying heavily on advice and help from the more experienced South Carolinians. Quickly they learned that Indians didn't mind going around them to get to the settlers. Someone was needed to interdict the hostiles, someone who understood them and could fight the way they fought, find them before an attack, and stay out in the wilderness for long periods. It was time for Rangers in the new territory.

By 1716, as had been the case in Virginia, the idea of forts doing the job was discarded in favor of Ranger parties. North Carolina also took advantage of the experience of Virginia's colonists and employed Rangers during the Yamasee (Indian) War.

In Georgia, James Oglethorpe used Rangers for the same purpose the colonies did—to track Indian movements. Such units were staffed by one-or-two-dozen men on horses who provided Intelligence and did such fighting as was necessary when the territory was encroached upon by Indians or Spanish forces out of Florida. Oglethorpe's victory at Bloody Marsh in 1742 was due in part to his Ranger units.

During the War of Jenkin's Ear (King George's War), 1739-1748, the French, Spanish, and various Indian tribes all faced Ranger elements from Nova Scotia to Georgia.

As the country continued to expand and develop, such men honed their skills on raids and patrols for decades, though Georgia's Rangers were disbanded in 1749.

The next noteworthy example of the Ranger concept arose in the French and Indian War, (1754-1763) fought parallel with the Seven Year's War in Europe. The use of line infantry and massed firepower into massed bodies stacked European battlefields with wasted lives, but that was what the military minds of that era considered practical warfare. The idea of firing from cover was considered unmanly. But then, they didn't have to contend with the guerilla tactics of the Native Americans.

Someone was needed to start the ball rolling, and a rugged frontiersman named Robert Rogers filled the bill nicely. Tough, very strong, with excellent woodcraft and no shortage of courage, Rogers came running when a call was made in 1755 for volunteers.

He did well enough as a scout around Lake George that Governor William Shirley of Massachusetts made him a captain of a Company of Rangers. Part of the military from a young age, Rogers knew the ropes, and knew what he wanted to do with the opportunity. He was very persuasive and personable, but he had a set of ideas strongly enough embedded that he wrote them down, and they still apply today. Called Rogers' Rules of Discipline, they are being taught to new Ranger students nearly 250 years later.

The numbers for that first unit run from 60 to 56, but it is generally agreed there was one Captain, one Lieutenant, and one Ensign, with three Sergeants to run the show.

Rogers' company came alive on March 23, 1756, originally designated as the Ranger Company of the New Hampshire Provincial Regiment, but later changed to His Majesty's Independent Company of American Rangers. Before long it was simply Rogers' Rangers.

The Rangers went to work harassing the French, moving deep into enemy territory and wreaking havoc on supply lines. They also gathered information, an action perhaps even more important than raiding Indian villages and disrupting the French. In larger actions the Rangers acted as flankers and scouts for the British around Lake Champlain. Rogers' men traveled on foot or on horseback, but they also made raids using small boats to infiltrate enemy lines, making some of the first Ranger amphibious assaults.

Rogers wanted his men to be ready for anything, and he conducted live-fire exercises to get them that way. He also kept them going when the rest of the army was dug in for winter, using snowshoes and sleds to travel.

At one point, Rogers took 200 Rangers by boat and by land in a move against the Abenaki Indians. The intrepid frontiersmen covered about 400 miles in two months, going deep into enemy lands. The trek took its toll on the force, but they arrived undetected and attacked the Abenaki settlement September 29, 1759, destroying the village and killing several hundred warriors.

Rogers and his men gained fame for their daring exploits and rough-and-tumble attitude, but there were some who saw them as undisciplined and uncontrollable. Rogers himself became known as a fine soldier, but an inept administrator, sometimes given to corruption and drink.

For more about Robert Rogers, see his biography in the French and Indian War section.

Pre-Revolutionary War Ranger Units

Before the Revolution began in 1775, there were many Ranger units and Ranging Parties scattered north and south among the eastern coastal states. Though there is no hard-and-fast list of such units, many of them have been identified and some are listed below.

The condensed information in this particular list is taken in part from Ranger historian Larry Ivers' more complete work. Ivers used two criterions to decide which was which among the various "Ranger" groups. One, the unit must have been called or characterized as a Ranger unit by its contemporaries. Two, the unit must have participated in Ranger-type missions such as reconnaissance, ambush, raid, or as spearheaders.

Considering earlier units worked in the forests and did a fair amount of stealthy missions in enemy territory, they are more likely to have earned the name Ranger than some of the units to come, particularly in the 1800s when most units bearing the name were more like light infantry, both mounted and dismounted.

1634-1754

This is where it all started. The earliest colonial Rangers were out there by themselves, without fire support, communications, or medevac. They used single-shot weapons or hatchets and knives. Most often they hunted and foraged for their own food and supplied their own horses and gear. In many ways the first Rangers are very close in spirit to the men of the 75th Ranger Regiment. For their day and time they were special operations soldiers.

As previously noted, Ranger history began—more or less—with Ed Backler in the years 1634-35. Backler was in Virginia, and though he may have been alone in the beginning, there were many more like him to come, and they came in groups.

Within the next 43 years there were some 34 Ranger units in the Maryland and Massachusetts areas alone. Some of them are listed as simply "Parties of Rangers" and some are listed by commander or location. There were frequently Indians involved as either scouts or fighting men.

Some examples of the variety seen are the Susquehanna Indian Ranging Parties of 1666, John Douglas's Party of Rangers of 1675, John Allen's Troop of Rangers of 1676, Richard Owen's Party of Rangers of 1698-1700, and Benjamin Church's Ranging Company of 1675-76.

Benjamin Church has become the focus of Ranger history as one of the first "real" Ranger ancestors.

With all apologies to Ed Backler, Ben Church is featured in Ranger literature as something of a founding father, where Backler is more a "line of descent" person. Church went on for more than 25 years as a Ranger in one group or another, and got several of his family members involved. For instance, a 1704 expedition from Massachusetts listed 12 companies, three of which were commanded by Church or his relatives, Constant and Edward.

During the first 10 years of the 18th century there were at least a dozen more companies just in Massachusetts, with more to come.

In the 50 years or so between 1671 and 1718 there were 53 Ranger units in Virginia—which may have included parts of modern West Virginia. That is a lot of Rangers, even given the half-century to cover them all. Some few are listed as garrisons, but the rest are noted as "parties" or "troops." Though the term "Company of Rangers" has been used several times before this, there is still no mention of a "Ranger Company".

Some examples of Virginia Ranger units are the Appomattox River Garrison of Rangers, 1676-79; Pomunkey River Garrison of Rangers of the same time frame; Thomas Owsley's Party of Rangers, 1692; and Hughes' Party of Volunteer Rangers, 1717. Connecticut and New Hampshire fielded a Party of Rangers or two, and New York featured several Troops of Horse Militia (Ranger) between 1724 and 1748.

In the south, North Carolina, South Carolina, and Georgia all had Ranger units roaming the countryside, though North Carolina's were few and essentially confined to the earlier part of the century.

South Carolina could boast nearly 20 units between 1716 and 1751, again divided into parties, troops, and garrisons, and for the first time, divisions and companies. John Jones' Division of Westward Rangers—Company of Western Rangers—was on duty from 1716-1718, and James McPherson's Company of Southern Rangers had a long history beginning with a nine-year stint from 1727 to 1736, then resurrected in 1744, 1746, and 1751.

Between 1734 and 1747 the great state of Georgia had at least 20 Ranger units running around, including an English unit, a Highlander unit, and a couple of units raised in South Carolina and Virginia. Fort Augusta had a Garrison of Rangers for a decade ending in 1747, and Savannah barracked a garrison in 1741. Units were listed as parties, garrisons, companies, or troops.

1754-1763

This was the time of the French and Indian War, pitting the English, colonists and Indians against the French and Indians. For the first time there are units listed directly under British Army control. Also, there is a shift in geographical location for a majority of units, with very few units in the south and many in the north. Units from Pennsylvania are listed for the first time —13 of them—all companies, beginning in 1755. Even New Jersey created a few units during that hard time of terrible Indian attacks and French cannon.

Interestingly, South Carolina and Georgia had far fewer Ranger units—all called troops—in the mid-50s than in the first half of the century. That would change again in the coming revolution.

By far the greatest concentration of Rangers was in Virginia—and West Virginia to be—between 1754 and 1764. There were more than 40 companies, and for the first time four of them were formed into a battalion.

Every one of the listed companies carries the name of its commander or sponsor. A few of the names ahead of "Company of Rangers" are John Ashby, Buchanan, David Lewis, Thomas Waggoner, Stewart (Light Horse), Robert Breckenridge, James McGavok, and Spottswood.

The British Army—it was their fight—fielded some 25 companies, mostly from the north (Massachusetts, New Hampshire, New Jersey, and others). It was from this mix of British, colonials and Indians that Robert Rogers emerged. There were Independent Companies—paid by the British—and British Provincial Regulars, as well as large bodies of "sympathetic" Indians who acted as scouts, guides, and combat soldiers.

Robert Rogers' Company of Rangers—His Majesty's Independent Rangers—was raised in New Hampshire in 1756. At times, some of the companies of that area came under the overall command of Rogers.

Since many of the units of that time worked for the British, it is important to note that the British Army itself denies ever fielding a Ranger unit of its own.

Included were units such as Joseph Gorham's Company of North American Rangers, James Rogers' (brother of Robert) Company, Lotridge's Company of Mohawk Indian Rangers from New York, and Moses Hazen's Company.

Hazen would become a Major General in the Revolution.

In the intervening years between the defeat of the French and the beginning of the revolution, many of the Indian tribes continued fighting the westward expansion of the white man. For that matter, some of them weren't too happy about the new guys being there on the coast.

Few men had ever heard of the Sioux or the Apache, yet Indian Wars raged along the eastern frontier during the 16 years between one war and another.

There weren't as many Ranger units then, but they still operated. The British Army had several units out there working, including Moses Hazen's and Joseph Gorham's Companies, still intact from the previous war, and Joseph Hopkins' Company of Queen's Royal American Rangers.

In South Carolina a regiment is listed for the first time, under the overall command of William Thompson, and featuring eight Ranger Troops. Most of those were gone by 1768.

Pennsylvania and Virginia offered several companies each from 1763 to 1774, including Crockett's Company of Rangers from Virginia, and Barritt's Detachment of Lancaster County Rangers from Pennsylvania.

Georgia threw in a couple of Light Horse Ranger units between 1773-1776.

One reason the Indian Wars came to an end—sort of—was because of the beginning of the Revolutionary War in 1775. Quite suddenly, tribes that had been persecuted by the British were being wooed to fight against the independence-minded colonials. Of course, the colonials had their own Indian friends.

For eight years, Rangers of both sides fought bravely and well, sometimes against each other. Units flourished under the impressive guidance of people such as Francis Marion and Thomas Knowlton.

For more on units of the Revolutionary War and the War of 1812, see the sections under those headings.

FRENCH AND INDIAN WAR—1754-1763

In the mid-1700s the population in North America was still bordered by the Atlantic Coast and the Appalachians. America's colonies were expanding, and since the Spanish held Florida and the French held Canada, the way west over the mountains was the most desirable way to move.

The French, claiming the watersheds of the St. Lawrence and Mississippi Rivers, including the Great Lakes and the Ohio River Valley, did not take kindly to British subjects coming into their territory, something that local governments were encouraging people to do.

The French decided to draw the line, and they drew it north to south in a strange kind of diagonal thrust from Lake Champlain to the Gulf of Mexico. France put together a line of forts from eastern Canada to New Orleans and dared England to pass them. The British, not to be outdone, built a few forts in response, but it was obvious the bar had been set, and must be raised.

Robert Dinwiddie, Lt. Governor of Virginia, upon hearing of the new French forts, sent junior officer George Washington out to deliver a message telling them to vacate the premises. Of course, they laughed politely and let Washington live.

On the way home, Washington noticed a great place to build a fort near the headwaters of the Ohio River. His vision became Fort Prince George, but when it was near completion the French decided it was indeed a very good place for a fort. They came April 18, 1754, and took it over, renaming it Fort Duquesne, after the Governor-General of New France.

Washington had a temper, and this was a good time to use it.

Washington is said to have generated the first fight between Britain and France in the French and Indian War—still two years from being declared—in the fields south of the fort. As the story goes, he won the first round and lost the second when French reinforcements poured out of the fort.

The presence of the forts and the incoming French troops made war inevitable, and that first fight got the ball rolling. The two countries had been in conflict for nearly 20 years, and it seemed inevitable that they would again do battle because France's claims were in the way of England gaining the whole of the North American continent, or at least more of it than they had.

There was plenty of government intrigue and religious righteousness, but that is another story. Suffice to say the two countries, along with their various Indian allies and the inhabitants of the colonies, were set to fight again. Probably neither side realized all the ramifications of victory and loss.

But, it wouldn't be one war in one place fought by two forces. The French and Indian War was actually a series of conflicts ranging over nine years. In Europe the conflict was called the Seven Years' War as it was known by English Canadians. French Canadians referred to it as the War of the Conquest because the British conquered New France.

Though the war began in the colonies it soon spread to Europe, Canada, and even into the Caribbean. Indian tribes were divided in their allegiances, but fought more for the French than against them.

Several men who would become Revolutionary War heroes got their start in this conflict. The best known—a Ranger ancestor—is Robert Rogers.

Who Was Robert Rogers?

Considered by many to be one of the founding fathers of Rangerdom—almost a Patron Saint—Robert Rogers led an interesting, though somewhat checkered life.

Many Ranger leaders have short biographies in this project, but none of them go into any detail about the man's private life except to say he did well in endeavors after the military. However, while researching Rogers it became quite evident that here was a man who was really two men—the excellent soldier and the opportunistic mercenary.

Rogers occupies a narrow space in Ranger history, albeit an important one for what he did militarily, therefore his exploits during the French and Indian War are our main focus.

Depending on which history one believes, Rogers was Scots-Irish and was born either in 1727 or 1731 in Londonderry, New Hampshire.

He had only a small amount of "book learning" and spent much time in the forests alone or with hunters. He became an accomplished woodsman and hunter and traveled between French and English settlements, learning their ways as well as intermingling in the societies of the various local Indian tribes. In short, he knew the lay of the land and the inhabitants well. Included in his worldly education were parts of the French and Indian languages and customs along with the locations of river fords and mountain passes.

His early years gave him the skills to add to his considerable physical prowess—he was a big man—and it wasn't long before he was gaining the military knowledge he would need to lead.

He started in the military (militia) early, serving on scouting duty in 1746 at the age of 19. He is seen again three years later, and again in 1753, when the muster rolls place him under Captain John Goff.

As the most famous Ranger of the early days, he should be given a strong seat in the ranks of Ranger ancestors for his military successes and his establishment of order and discipline among unruly ranks of men like himself.

Rogers in the French and Indian War

During that time, the colonies had about a million and a half people and French Canada less than 100,000. England claimed territory from the Atlantic—Newfoundland in the north—to Florida in the south, all by (arguable) right of discovery, and the rest of the country by grants. France claimed Canada, much of New England and the basins of the Ohio and Mississippi Rivers, plus large tracts relating to those rivers.

Over the course of 1755, the British attacked a few French-held forts, but the main thrust was in the far north. General Moncton rode against the French along the Bay of Fundy in Canada. Another major event of that year was the movement of General William Johnson's forces against Crown Point, a major fortification in New York, on Lake Champlain. A large number of Indians bolstered his capabilities.

Gathering troops, Johnson took on—among others—nine or 10 companies from New Hampshire, one of which was a Ranger Company commanded by Robert Rogers. Rogers made Captain in 1755 and was working for the government of New Hampshire building a fort at the mouth of the Ammononusuc River when he was ordered to join General Johnson's army. He led different-sized units doing several different things, but his main thrust was reconnaissance (recon) along rivers and anywhere else the French had put their forts, getting close to Crown Point at one stage of his travels.

Previous wars on the continent had taught the British that Rangers were the only ones capable of fighting Indians in their natural environment with any chance of success. Lines of massed red coats chasing highly mobile Indians wasn't going to work and they knew it. From the beginning Rangers had a niche, much the same as today—small, light units, working quickly, gathering information, striking with fury and precision. Not much has changed.

The early Ranger units were capable of traveling long distances on foot or horseback—at times using snowshoes or boats—sleeping under the stars, continuing for days on small rations and second-guessing a people who had lived in the same forests for centuries.

Rogers was tailor-made for such a life, and thrived on it. It was here, during the mid-1700s, that Rangers became more than just a band of hardy militia without organization. Rogers made rules and wrote them down. He put together an out-front unit that did its job better than expected and gave the name "Ranger" legitimacy.

Excerpt from a history of Robert Rogers by Joseph B. Walker, 1885

Walker was British.

"Stand such a man in a pair of stout shoes or moccasins; cover his lower limbs with leggings and coarse small clothes; give him a close-fitting jacket and a warm cap; stick a small hatchet in his belt; hang a good-sized powder-horn by his side, and upon his back buckle a blanket and a knapsack stuffed with a moderate supply of bread and raw salt-pork; to these furnishings add a good-sized hunting knife, a trusty musket and a small flask of spirits, and you have an average New Hampshire Ranger of the French and Indian War, ready for skirmish or pitched battle; or for the more common duty of reconnoitering the enemy's force and movements, of capturing his scouts and provision trains, and getting now and then a prisoner, from whom all information possible would be extorted; and, in short, for annoying the French and Indian foe in every possible way.

"If you will add three or four inches to the average height of such a soldier, give him consummate courage, coolness, readiness of resource in extremities, together with intuitive knowledge of the enemy's wiles, supplemented with a passable knowledge of French and Indian speech, you will have a tolerable portrait of Captain Robert Rogers at the beginning of our Seven Year's War."

Rogers' Best Years

The British weren't very organized at first, changing overall command three times by 1756, until Lord Londown held control—though not very well. Hostilities overseas had escalated to the point of a formal declaration of war, though fighting had been going on in the colonies for nearly two years at that point. In 1756 Rogers led men on recon missions, some of which brought exchange of fire, moving on foot, by boat and on snowshoes.

Rogers' now-famous journal gives us a look at a handful of tough men, each carrying his own supplies on long journeys in hostile territory, executing Ranger missions, including prisoner snatch, ambush and raid, along with a lot of silent recon. There are 13 such forays listed in his journal for that year. He wrote that in January, he and 17 men crossed Lake George on the ice and captured two prisoners and two sledges loaded with supplies.

A month later, he took 50 men to the French stronghold at Crown Point to gain some information, but was discovered and made to withdraw when the French troops came out in force. Before Rogers and his men left they burned a number of houses and barns, destroyed stores of wheat, and killed livestock. Rogers had little choice in the matter of making war on civilians because he was so ordered. In those days people were on one side or the other, and if not actually fighting, there was the question of supply.

British Major General Shirley gave him orders in 1756 and Rogers duly noted them in his journal.

"From time to time, to use your best endeavors to distress the French and allies by sacking, burning and destroying their houses, barns, barracks, canoes and battoes, and by killing their cattle of every kind; and at all times to endeavor to way-lay, attack and destroy their convoys of provisions by land and water in any part of the country where you could find them."

In March, Rogers was re-commissioned as a Captain of an independent Company of Rangers with wages provided by the Crown. That began what we think of today as Rogers' Rangers.

In June he and his men came across two small boats loaded with supplies on Lake Champlain. The Rangers killed four of the 12 accompanying men. In his journal, Rogers wrote, "We sunk and destroyed their vessels and cargoes, which consisted chiefly of wheat and flour, wine and brandy; some few casks of the latter we carefully concealed."

In October, British General Abercrombie was at Fort Edward watching over the army for Lord Londown, who was due any time. When he did show up it was decided winter was too far along for much maneuvering and the British went into winter quarters, hoping the French would do the same.

However, hostilities did not cease entirely, as noted in Rogers' journal for October 22, 1756. The following is an excellent example of just how cheeky he was.

"This morning we embarked in two whale boats, with a party of twenty men, being ordered to bring a prisoner from Ticonderoga.

"We continued on course, landed on the night of the 27th on the west shore, concealed our boats, and traveled by land within a mile of the Fort. The next day we discovered two videttes to the piquet guard of the French Army, one of whom was posted on the road leading into the woods. I marched directly down the road in the middle of the day, with five of my party, until we were challenged by the sentry. I answered in French signifying friends; he was thereby deceived, till we came close to him, when perceiving his mistake, in great surprise he called out 'Qui etes vous?' I answered, 'Rogers,' and led him from his post in great haste, and with our party reached (Fort) William Henry October 31."

During that year he apparently led however many men were deemed necessary at the time, from a large squad to two companies. Later in the year he was promoted to Major of Rangers and given command of a blossoming corps eventually containing nine companies. By year's end there were four companies, two based at Fort William Henry and two at Fort Edward for the winter.

His fame grew along with his command and he was being noticed by high-rankers. In January 1757, an event occurred which elevated him even further.

In the dead of the northern winter Rogers and 74 men took off over the ice of Lake George to have a look at a few French forts. At times they took short cuts overland by wearing snowshoes, and in a week they were halfway between Fort Ticonderoga and Crown Point. There they came upon a supply train, sledges packed with food and other necessities for the French. The Rangers captured three of the sledges, a few horses, and about seven men.

The remaining men made it to Ticonderoga and stirred up the garrison, which soon began sending troops after Rogers. The Rangers didn't get far before a large force—perhaps 250—of French and Indians found them and tried to surround them. Rogers and his men fought hard through the afternoon. He was wounded and lost more than a quarter of his men, though enemy losses were reported at more than 100. Breaking off the fight, he and his remaining men retired to the forest for nightfall and made good their escape back to Fort William Henry.

Rogers was given credit for a great victory and for getting most of his men back safely. So favored was he that Lord Londown commissioned him to train a company of British Regulars how to perform like Rangers.

That doesn't mean they became British Rangers.

Having scant chance of making woodsman and Indian fighters out of Regulars, Rogers nevertheless set to it with a will. It was there the 28 Rules originated, actually written for British Regulars trying to emulate American Rangers.

Rogers' Rules appear in this section.

Lord Londown, not greatly renowned for his military prowess, sailed on Halifax with some 6,000 men in June 1757. Rogers and four companies of Rangers were also aboard. On landing, Londown's force was reinforced by another 5,000 men—giving him a large group of soldiers for that day—and making him ready for the assault on Louisburg. However set he was to make a telling blow against the French, Lord Londown apparently decided battle was bad business and turned everybody around for home. When the Rangers arrived back at Fort William Henry they found it didn't belong to the British any more. Had they not been gone with Londown, four companies of Rangers may have made a crucial difference in the fight.

Londown's inactions, and those of others, had the British reeling by the end of 1757. Power in England changed hands at that time, bringing the government of William Pitt into the decision-making process. Changes were made, and General Abercrombie took over from Londown and began to make things happen.

In short succession, several French river forts were taken, including DuQuesne and Louisburg. Rogers' Rangers were in the front when an assault on Ticonderoga failed, and at the rear during withdrawal, making them the first line of offense and defense in the same battle.

There were many battles, large and small, as the two great powers vied for the new land. Rogers and about 180 men were met on the shores of Lake George by a much larger group of French and Indians and took 60 percent casualties. That Rogers returned with any men at all was something of a miracle, and again his stature increased when General Abercrombie commended him.

The British were swinging the pendulum the other way by 1759 and the French no longer held Ticonderoga and Crown Point. Quebec fell in September and Canada belonged largely to the British.

Having held the French down for the time being, British HQ, specifically Major General Amherst, ordered Rogers to go after the Abenaki—aka St. Francis—Indians in their village. Rogers had orders to take 200 men, but he ended up attacking with less than 150. They were to travel some three weeks inland to find and do whatever necessary to "disgrace the enemy." The same orders also contained the codicil that women and children were not to be harmed—and the record says they weren't, but some 200 braves were killed.

The Rangers came screaming in just before dawn and caught the tribe asleep, making short work of the men before they could get organized. As the story goes all the buildings were burned except a few storehouses with provisions for the women and children.

Either way, that particular tribe was out of the running and would not be ambushing colonists anymore—an action attested to by the presence of hundreds of scalps found by the Rangers.

The French had about had it, too, especially when they failed to retake Quebec in 1760. British General Amherst moved on Montreal with a large body of troops including some 600 Rangers in boats commanded by Rogers. Montreal fell in early September without a real fight and the war was all but over.

Rogers was ordered to take some men and spread the news to the outlying French forts that they were no longer under French rule. In November, they reached the approximate area where Cleveland stands and were met by the great Ottawa Chief, Pontiac, who upon hearing of the French surrender, let them pass. The Rangers continued to Detroit where quick negotiations resulted in the fort changing hands.

Rogers fulfilled his mission at other forts along the chain until a harsh winter made travel impossible. He was back in New York by mid-February. Except for taking a handful of Rangers and aiding in the defense of Detroit when Indians attacked it in 1763, Rogers was through with military life for a while.

By 1765, Rogers was probably in England turning out publications. It was there he published the multitude of observations made during his Ranger days, titled: *The Journals of Major Robert Rogers; containing an account of the several excursions he made under the generals who commanded upon the continent of North America, during the late War. From which may be collected the material circumstances of every campaign upon that continent from the commencement to the conclusion of the war.*

The original edition was printed and sold by J. Millan, a bookseller near Whitehall, but a second edition published in 1883 by American Dr. F. B. Hough contains more information. A separate book was titled: *A Concise View of North America*—also with a longer title—but did not deal with the military.

In these books, Rogers shows good style and use of language, in no way fitting the view he was a nearly illiterate woodsman with little knowledge.

It is possible another book was at least partially written by Rogers—"Ponteach;" or "The Savages of America." This is now a very rare book with few copies remaining—if any.

Ponteach has gradually become Pontiac (Pon-te-ach). It is said Kenneth Roberts used the book as a resource when writing "Northwest Passage."

Rogers' Last Years

To say Rogers was a military genius, but also an inept administrator is an overstatement of the first and an understatement of the second. When he spent any time around civilization he got in some kind of trouble or another—often serious trouble. Evidently he could not manage money and bounced back and forth between fame and notoriety, making deals with whoever was at hand. That kind of unethical conduct carried over into his military life as he got older and earned him both arrest and censure. Although a big success during the French and Indian War, Rogers didn't do so well in the following years.

He is on record in New Hampshire for buying and selling tracts of land for a few years. In 1764 the Governor gave him as "a reduced officer," some three thousand acres in Vermont. With that land and what he had acquired on his own he should have been set for life. However, some years later his wife divorced him for "infidelity and desertion" and took much of the land. That, combined with bad management and some not-so-clean deals, took most of the rest. In early 1766—between wars—a letter from Sir William Johnson to General Thomas Gage says this of Rogers: "He was a soldier in my army in 1755, and, as we were in great want of active men at that time, his readiness recommended him so far to me that I made him an officer and got him continued in the Ranging service, where he soon became puffed up with pride and folly from the extravagant encomiums and notices of some of the Provinces. This spoiled a good Ranger, for he was fit for nothing else—neither has nature calculated him for a large command in that service."

His reputation and tenure kept him going for a while, though. In June 1766, Rogers was appointed Captain Commandant of the garrison at Michilimackinac by General Gage. He took charge of Indian affairs there, but did not do well. In a relatively short time he was engaging in black market trade and became indebted. He became argumentative with his superiors and was deeply mired in trouble. Finally he pushed too hard and was arrested for treason—he had allegedly corresponded with a French officer—and taken in irons to Montreal to be court-martialed. Luckily for him he wasn't convicted, and took ship for England about 1770.

England was a different story. In serious trouble and debt in the new world, back in England he was a hero. His books had certainly helped make him seem the part, and the higher-ups treated him with due respect, as did the common folk who looked at him as a legend. Rogers was able to get a hefty chunk of back pay from the government, but when he aspired to honorary nobility the same higher-ups backed away and he began to slide again.

Several years later, Rogers was back in North America as a retired British officer on half pay. He is reported to have traveled a good bit talking to this person and that, but the whole effect of his presence seems to have been one of suspicion on the part of those who knew him.

Desperate for a command—and an income—Rogers applied first to the Continental Army and then the British Army for a commission. George Washington wouldn't even grant an audience when he came looking for a commission at the start of the Revolutionary War because he was thought by many to be a spy. The British asked him to state his intentions more fully and hired him on—again.

Some time in 1776, the British ranked him as Lt. Colonel Commandant and told him to raise a company of Rangers for the British effort against the Colonies. This he apparently did, but did not last long in command and did not do especially well as commander.

A year later, he was back in England where he lived out his life, dying virtually alone. His remaining funds went to a creditor.

That sad story aside, one has only to imagine this brawny woodsman howling in battle, wielding a hatchet and sawed-off musket against equally wild Indians—the intrepid leader of an elite group of men—to see why he is part of the Ranger legend.

Robert Rogers remains a large rock in the Ranger foundation—strong, brave and true—as long as he had a war to fight.

Rogers' 19 Standing Orders?

Taken from FM 7-85—Appendix D

Though the Rangers still display these orders, it is fairly certain that Robert Rogers did not write them. They are the product of the book/movie, "Northwest Passage," and were given out by a Sergeant McNott. Rogers wrote a lot of things, including his 28 Rules of Discipline, and he was generally eloquent and well written. To be sure, the following Standing Orders are concise and to the point, but when one looks over the real thing it is obvious the same man did not write both.

1. Don't forget nothing.

2. Have your musket clean as a whistle, hatchet scoured, sixty rounds powder and ball, and be ready to march at a minute's warning.

3. When you're on the march, act the way you would if you was sneaking up on a deer. See the enemy first.

4. Tell the truth about what you see and what you do. There is an Army depending on us for correct information. You can lie all you please when you tell other folks about the Rangers, but don't ever lie to a Ranger or officer.

5. Don't never take a chance you don't have to.

6. When you're on the march we march single file, far enough apart so one shot can't go through two men.

7. If we strike swamps or soft ground, we spread out abreast, so it's hard to track us.

8. When we march, we keep moving till dark, so as to give the enemy the least possible chance at us.

9. When we camp, half the party stays awake while the other half sleeps.

10. If we take prisoners, we'll keep 'em separate till we have time to examine them, so they can't cook up a story between 'em.

11. Don't ever march home the same way. Take a different route so you won't be ambushed.

12. No matter whether we travel in big parties or little ones, each party has to keep a scout twenty yards on each flank and twenty yards in the rear, so the main body can't be surprised and wiped out.

13. Every night you'll be told where to meet if surrounded by a superior force.

14. Don't sit down to eat without posting sentries.

15. Don't sleep beyond dawn. Dawn's when the French and Indians attack.

16. Don't cross a river by a regular ford.

17. If somebody's trailing you, make a circle, come back onto your tracks, and ambush the folks that aim to ambush you.

18. Don't stand up when the enemy's coming against you. Kneel down, lie down, hide behind a tree.

19. Let the enemy come till he's almost close enough to touch. Then let him have it and jump out and finish him up with your hatchet.

Rogers' Rules of Discipline—The Real Version

Michael Thompson proofed this transcript against a copy from the original 1769 Dublin edition of Rogers' Journals. Punctuation and spelling are exactly as they were in the original publication, including the words roll-call, fire-lock, draughted, centries, reconnoitre, favours, surprize, chuse, endeavour, sternmost, shew, and the one apparent typo in the epilog, "which which."

While most of the text is here, there are a few "wordy" spots left out, such as the first statement of the first rule "All Rangers are to be subject to the rules of articles of war..." which consists of 111 Articles in 20 sections on 32 pages. The 20th Article says "These Articles Should Be Read Once Every Two Months."

Preface

"These volunteers I formed into a company by themselves, and took the more immediate command and management of them to myself, and for their benefit and instruction reduced into writing the following rules or plan of discipline, which on various occasions I had found by experience to be necessary and advantageous."
Robert Rogers

I. All Rangers are to be subject to the rules and articles of war; to appear at roll-call every evening on their own parade, equipped each with a fire-lock, sixty rounds of powder and ball, and a hatchet, at which time an officer from each company is to inspect the same, to see they are in order, so as to be ready on any emergency to march at a minute's warning; and before they are dismissed the necessary guards are to be draughted, and scouts for the next day appointed.

II. Whenever you are ordered out to the enemies forts or frontiers for discoveries, if your number be small, march in a single file, keeping at such a distance from each other prevent one shot from killing two men, sending one man, or more, forward, and the like on each side, at the distance of twenty yards from the main body, if the ground you march over will admit of it, to give the signal to the officer of the approach of an enemy, and of their number, &c.

III. If you march over marshes or soft ground, change your position, and march abreast of each other, to prevent the enemy from tracking you (as they would do if you marched in a single file) till you get over such ground, and then resume your former order, and march till it is quite dark before you encamp, which do, if possible, on a piece of ground that may afford your centries the advantage of seeing or hearing the enemy at some considerable distance, keeping one half of your whole party awake alternately through the night.

IV. Some time before you come to the place you would reconnoitre, make a stand, and send one or two men, in whom you can confide, to look out the best ground for making your observations.

V. If you have the good fortune to take any prisoners, keep them separate, till they are examined, and in your return take a different route from that in which you went out, that you may the better discover any party in your rear, and have an opportunity, if their strength be superior to yours, to alter your course, or disperse, as circumstances may require.

VI. If you march in a large body of three or four hundred, with a design to attack the enemy, divide your party into three columns, each headed by a proper officer, and let these columns march in single files, the columns to the right and left keeping at twenty yards distance or more from that of the center, if the ground will admit, and let proper guards be kept in the front and rear, and suitable flanking parties at a due distance as before directed, with orders to halt on all eminences, to take a view of the surrounding ground, to prevent your being ambushed, and to notify the approach or retreat of the enemy, that proper dispositions may be made for attacking, defending, &c. And if the enemy approach in your front on level ground, form a front of your three columns or main body with the advanced guard, keeping out your flanking parties, as if you were marching under the command of trusty officers, to prevent the enemy from pressing hard on either of your wings, or surrounding you, which is the usual method of the savages, if their number will admit of it, and be careful likewise to support and strengthen your rear guard.

VII. If you are obliged to receive the enemy's fire, fall, or squat down, till it is over, then rise and discharge at them. If their main body is equal to yours, extend yourselves occasionally; but if superior, be careful to support and strengthen your flanking parties, to make them equal with theirs, that if possible you may repulse them to their main body, in which case push upon them with the greatest resolution, with equal force in each flank and in the center, observing to keep at a due distance from each other, and advance from tree to tree, with one half of the party before the other ten or twelve yards. If the enemy push upon you, let your front fire and fall down, and then let your rear advance thro' them and do the like, by which time those who before were in front will be ready to discharge again, and repeat the same alternately, as occasion shall require; by this means you will keep up such a constant fire, that the enemy will not be able easily to break your order, or gain your ground.

VIII. If you oblige the enemy to retreat, be careful, in your pursuit of them, to keep out your flanking parties, and prevent them from gaining eminences, or rising grounds, in which case they would perhaps be able to rally and repulse in their turn.

IX. If you are obliged to retreat, let the front of your whole party fire and fall back, till the rear hath done the same, making for the best ground you can; by this means you will oblige the enemy to pursue you, if they do it at all, in the face of a constant fire.

X. If the enemy is so superior that you are in danger of being surrounded by them, let the whole body disperse, and every one take a different road to the place of rendezvous appointed for that evening, which must every morning be altered and fixed for the evening ensuing, in order to bring the whole party, or as many of them as possible, together, after any separation that may happen in the day; but if you should happen to be actually surrounded, form yourselves into a square, or if in the woods, a circle is best, and, if possible, make a stand till the darkness of the night favours your escape.

XI. If your rear is attacked, the main body and flankers must face about to the right or left, as occasion shall require, and form themselves to oppose the enemy, as before directed; and the same method must be observed, if attacked in either of your flanks, by which means you will always make a rear of one of your flank-guards.

XII. If you determine to rally after a retreat, in order to make a fresh stand against the enemy, by all means endeavor to do it on the most rising ground you can come at, which will give you greatly the advantage in point of situation, and enable you to repulse superior numbers.

XIII. In general, when pushed upon by the enemy, reserve your fire till they approach very near, which will then put them into the greater surprize and consternation, and give you an opportunity of rushing upon them with your hatchets and cutlasses to the better advantage.

XIV. When you encamp at night, fix your centries in such a manner as not to be relieved from the main body till morning, profound secrecy and silence being often of the last importance in these cases. Each centry, therefore, should consist of six men, two of whom must be constantly alert, and when relieved by their fellows, it should be done without noise; and in case those on duty see or hear anything, which alarms them, they are not to speak, but one of them is silently to retreat, and acquaint the commanding officer thereof, that proper dispositions may be made; and all occasional centries should be fixed in like manner.

XV. At the first dawn of day, awake your whole detachment; that being the time when the savages chuse to fall upon their enemies, you should by all means be in readiness to receive them.

XVI. If the enemy should be discovered by your detachments in the morning, and their numbers are superior to yours, and a victory doubtful, you should not attack them till the evening, as then they will not know your numbers, and if you are repulsed, your retreat will be favored by the darkness of the night.

XVII. Before you leave your encampment, send out small parties to scout round it, to see if there be any appearance or track of an enemy that might have been near you during the night.

XVIII. When you stop for refreshment, chuse some spring or rivulet if you can, and dispose your party so as not to be surprised, posting proper guards and centries at a due distance, and let a small party waylay the path you came in, lest the enemy should be pursuing.

XIX. If, in your return, you have to cross rivers, avoid the usual fords as much as possible, lest the enemy should have discovered, and be there expecting you.

XX. If you have to pass by lakes, keep at some distance from the edge of the water, lest, in case of an ambuscade, or an attack from the enemy, when in that situation, your retreat should be cut off.

XXI. If the enemy pursue your rear, take a circle till you come to your own tracks, and there form an ambush to receive them, and give them the first fire.

XXII. When you return from a scout, and come near our forts, avoid the usual roads, and avenues thereto, lest the enemy should have headed you, and lay in ambush to receive you, when almost exhausted with fatigues.

XXIII. When you pursue any party that has been near our forts or encampments, follow not directly in their tracks, lest you should be discovered by their rear guards, who, at such a time, would be most alert; but endeavor, by a different route, to head and meet them in some narrow pass, or lay in ambush to receive them when and where they least expect it.

XXIV. If you are to embark in canoes, bateaux, or otherwise, by water, chuse the evening for the time of your embarkation, as you will then have the whole night before you, to pass undiscovered by any parties of the enemy, on hills, or other places, which command a prospect of the lake or river you are upon.

XXV. In paddling or rowing, give orders that the boat or canoe next the sternmost, wait for her, and the third for the second, and the fourth for the third, and so on, to prevent separation, and that you may be ready to assist each other on any emergency.

XXVI. Appoint one man in each boat to look out for fires, on the adjacent shores, from the numbers and size of which you may form some judgment of the number that kindled them, and whether you are able to attack them or not.

XXVII. If you find the enemy encamped near the banks of a river, or lake, which you imagine they will attempt to cross for their security upon being attacked, leave a detachment of your party on the opposite shore to receive them, while, with the remainder, you surprise them, having them between you and the lake or river.

XXVIII. If you cannot satisfy yourself as to the enemy's number and strength, from their fire, &c. conceal your boats at some distance, and ascertain their number by a reconnoitring party, when they embark, or march, in the morning, marking the course they steer, &c. when you may pursue, ambush, and attack them, or let them pass, as prudence shall direct you. In general, however, that you may not be discovered by the enemy on the lakes and rivers at a great distance, it is safest to lay by, with your boats and party concealed all day, without noise or shew, and to pursue your intended route by night; and whether you go by land or water, give out parole and countersigns, in order to know one another in the dark, and likewise appoint a station for every man to repair to, in case of any accident that may separate you.

Epilogue

Such in general are the rules to be observed in the Ranging service; there are, however, a thousand occurrences and circumstances which which may happen, that will make it necessary, in some measure, to depart from them, and to put other arts and stratagems in practice; in which cases every man's reason and judgment must be his guide, according to the particular situation and nature of things; and that he may do this to advantage, he should keep in mind a maxim never to be departed from by a commander, viz. to preserve a firmness and presence of mind on every occasion.

REVOLUTIONARY WAR

Timeline 1775—1783
1775

April 19—The first shots of the Revolutionary War are fired at Lexington and Concord, Massachusetts.

June 17—Americans lose at Bunker Hill (aka Breed's Hill). Ranger ancestor Thomas Knowlton distinguishes himself in the action.
1776

January 1—Americans attempt to take Quebec City. Ranger ancestor Daniel Morgan is captured, but is exchanged and re-enters the fight.

August—Several large and small battles with the Cherokee result in the Indian town of Tamassy, South Carolina, being burned by Andrew Pickens. The Cherokee are substantially defeated during this month, though they continue to fight.

At Long Island, New York, Washington is defeated and withdraws during a foggy night.

September 16—At Harlem Heights, New York, Nathaniel Greene defeats British and Hessians. Ranger ancestor Thomas Knowlton is killed in this battle.

December 26—In the historic Battle of Trenton, George Washington crosses the Delaware River under cover of darkness and fog and surprises a Hessian Brigade, decisively defeating it. Sagging morale soars after the quick victory.
1777

September 19-October 17—Winter—Burgoyne surrenders his army to American Major General Horatio Gates at Saratoga, New York.

The Spartan encampment at Valley Forge torments the freezing and hungry Continentals. Washington's army is hard put to make it through the winter.
1778

February—France signs a treaty with the Continental Congress and agrees to get into the fight.

December 29—In the last of the year, events in Savannah, Georgia, open the southern campaign.
1779

July 16—At Stony Point, New York, Americans inflict heavy casualties on the British by attacking with bayonets only.

August 29—Iroquois and Seneca Indians have been repeatedly attacking settlements as well as armed units, so American forces gather and repay the compliment by burning their villages and killing their warriors. Indian power in that region was somewhat curtailed after that.

1780

April-May—Lt. Colonel Banastre Tarleton enters the fight in the south and has immediate success against local militia and cavalry. He is not a good guy. In late May in Waxhaws, South Carolina, his men, known as the Loyalist Legion, capture and execute—by bayonet—more than 100 men of Colonel Buford's Virginia unit, thereafter known as Buford's Massacre.

July 25—Lord Cornwallis is countered by American General Horatio Gates taking command of the Southern Continental Army.

August 25—Francis Marion, a Ranger ancestor, attacks a guard unit at Nelson's Ferry, South Carolina, and liberates some 150 men who had been captured at Camden.

September—On the fourth at Blue Savannah, South Carolina, Marion entices Loyalists too near the swamps and defeats them soundly. Through the rest of the month Marion, Lt. Colonel Davie and a man named Clarke hit the Loyalists and Tarleton hard at every opportunity. The British have little luck finding any of them when they want to.

October 7—Militia from North and South Carolina, Virginia, and Georgia catch a large British force at King's Mountain and take the day. This action was an important step in the turning of the tide.

December 2—General Nathanael Greene becomes head of the Southern Continental Army.

Ranger ancestor Brigadier General Daniel Morgan sends Colonel William Washington to attack Georgia Loyalists, who suffer 150 casualties at Hammond's Store, South Carolina.

1781

January 17—The hated Tarleton, at the head of British Regulars, is defeated by Morgan at Cowpens, South Carolina, taking enough damage to change the direction of the war in the south. Between the recent British loss at King's Mountain and Cowpens, Redcoats are getting scarce.

January 24-25—Marion and "Light Horse" Harry Lee (father of Robert E. Lee) accept the surrender of Georgetown, South Carolina.

February—The British fight back in North Carolina. At Tarrant's Tavern, militiamen are butchered by Tarleton's Legion, using sabers. Less than a month later Lee tricks some Loyalists into coming close and returns the favor, also using sabers. North Carolina Loyalists begin to get hard to come by.

March-April—Marion is being chased by various British officers and giving them a tough time. While he is away his camp at Snow's Island is attacked.

October 19—After nearly three weeks of siege by Washington, Cornwallis surrenders at Yorktown.

1782

February—Marion's Brigade loses twice in short fights in South Carolina, but the end is near for the British, and everybody knows it.

December 14—Charleston, the last British stronghold in the south, is evacuated. Nearly 4,000 Loyalists and 5,000 slaves go with what's left of the army.

1783

April 15—The Second Treaty of Paris changes the British role in the western hemisphere forever.

Ranger Ancestors Everywhere

There were men with a lot of experience fighting in the Revolutionary War. Men who were trained and blooded in former conflicts with the French and Indians—men such as Moses Hazen, John Stark, and Israel Putnam. Those men had organized and led units designated as Ranger Parties or Companies and knew much about the advantages of such groups. However, General Washington was of the opinion that protecting the states from marauding Indians was a matter for the states and so few American Army (Continental) Ranger units were formed.

Though the British had begun to bend slightly in their rigid military philosophy, they still favored the use of ranks of infantry, marching and firing in order. To an American sharpshooter hidden in the bushes a couple of hundred yards off, those formations were nothing short of target practice.

Another problem for both sides was the knowledge shared between them of tactics, important commanders, and logistics problems. The Revolutionary War was much like the Civil War in that neighbor fought against neighbor, father against son, cousin against cousin. Some chose the "safe" side of British power and stayed loyal to the Crown, while others chose a new destiny—that of liberty and freedom from outside rule.

The divided factions conjured violence throughout the fledgling nation. Fighting could break out almost anywhere, any time, because of the division of loyalties.

The Continental Congress decided on June 14, 1775, that "six companies of expert riflemen be immediately raised in Pennsylvania, two in Maryland, and two in Virginia." Those companies were composed of very tough frontiersmen, trappers and Indian fighters, and made a name for themselves in the history of unconventional warfare.

One unit, formed under Daniel Morgan in June, 1775, was called "The Corps of Rangers" by George Washington, and drew the comment from British General John Burgoyne that it was "the most famous corps of the Continental Army, all of them crack shots."

The term "Corps" was almost interchangeable with "Company" or "Party." The number of men could vary greatly and was nothing like the modern-day Corps, which is composed of at least three divisions.

The company was raised from men of the Shenandoah Valley region of Virginia, and sent on their way to join the Army in Boston. Unfortunately, the group was about as rowdy as Rogers' Rangers of the previous years, so even though they caused the British a lot of trouble, leading them was no easy task. Colonel Dan Morgan was up to it, combining sheer grit and tact to keep his men in line.

Morgan's company took part in the invasion of Canada, but a foul-up brought his capture, with many of his men, in Quebec. He was eventually exchanged and given a 600-man rifle corps, which fought with distinction at Saratoga. Morgan was elevated to Brigadier General after that, and his company dispersed, absorbed by the whole.

Lt. Colonel Thomas Knowlton led another Ranger unit of the time. Such units spent much time patrolling and doing reconnaissance work, but also did some toe-to-toe fighting. Knowlton's Connecticut Rangers, about 150 hand-picked men, took part in the action at Harlem Heights, but lost their Colonel in the process.

Perhaps the best-known light (horse) infantry belonged to Francis Marion, known as the "Swamp Fox." His exploits were famous enough to inspire a television series in the 1960s, but the truth is, he was an independent man. Sometimes he worked with Washington, sometimes not.

Late in the war, Marion operated out of the South Carolina swamps, getting in behind the British and cutting supply lines and generally disrupting continuity. He also gave British sympathizers a hard time by routing their livestock and burning their homes, even killing some.

Marion and small groups of men did a lot of damage with surprise raids and well-planned interdiction actions, acting very much like the Rangers of today. But they, as with Rogers' men in the French and Indian War, were volunteers—hardy individuals who brought considerable toughness and skill to the table, then disbanded when the fighting was over. They were militia, not Continental Army, though they sometimes acted in accord.

Robert Rogers was also in the mix during the Revolutionary War, but unfortunately fought on the wrong side—when he was allowed to do anything at all. By that time the Continentals didn't trust him since he spent so much time working for the British. His story can be found under "Who Was Robert Rogers"?

A look at Ranger history so far points out the quality of the men and their leadership as being the primary reasons for success of the early units. Though the units were under military authority, they often ranged freely for long periods, doing pretty much as they pleased until given direct orders for a mission. As time passed, bringing conflicts from other quarters, Ranger units were again formed to perform tasks impossible for—and foreign to—the main body of the Army, whether American or British.

Thomas Knowlton

Born in 1740, Thomas Knowlton followed his brother, Daniel, on several scouting missions during the French and Indian War, though he was but 14 when it started. Daniel was a well-known officer and scout so Thomas was in the right place to learn.

Like Robert Rogers, Knowlton was a big man, handsome and charismatic—a natural leader who looked after his men and used his military knowledge well.

By the summer of 1775, Knowlton commanded some 200 Connecticut Volunteers. He led those men onto Bunker Hill on June 16 to meet greatly superior British forces under General Howe. Knowlton saw at once the hill was all but indefensible, open to attack from all sides, including the sea. He quickly erected a series of obstacles for the British to pass over or around, thus slowing their attack and making them easier targets for the American long rifles.

The historic battle cost the Americans nearly 500 casualties, but the British lost twice that many. Knowlton's actions on Bunker Hill distinguished him enough for Washington to pay attention and expand his capabilities.

Men from Connecticut, Rhode Island and Massachusetts were carefully chosen and gathered under Knowlton's command to be given the designation "Ranger." Knowlton's Rangers operated directly under Washington, performing scouting missions, raids and ambushes. It is said the unit became quite adept at stinging the British from ambush.

On the morning of September 16, 1776, while on patrol near the British camp at Harlem Heights, New York, the Rangers were seen and taken under attack by the feared Black Watch—large men all, mostly Highlanders.

The Black Watch is still around. Their motto is, "No one wounds me with impunity."

Accurate fire from the Americans held the Black Watch off long enough to affect their escape without being badly hurt in the lop-sided fight.

Later that day, Knowlton's Rangers were part of the larger Battle of Harlem Heights in which the Americans were able to lure the British into attacking, then tried to ambush them and use the Rangers to cut their rear. Unfortunately, American flankers fired too soon and all of the British force wasn't within the containment zone. In an effort to reach the British rear the Rangers had to fight an aroused and recovering British line.

Though that part of the plan was a failure, the Americans won the rest of the battle—barely.

It cost them Lt. Colonel Thomas Knowlton, shot in the back. It was a large loss. Had he lived he may well have become one of America's best Generals.

Nathan Hale

Knowlton's Connecticut Rangers held another outstanding American in the ranks. Nathan Hale, a courageous young man of 21, was given command of a company of Knowlton's Ranger Battalion. He didn't get to stay with them long, however, because General Washington needed a man to go behind enemy lines and gather Intelligence on the British and their Allies in the New York area. Hale volunteered and was chosen to go alone, disguised as a schoolteacher, which he was in civilian life.

He got through enemy lines and was doing his job well, writing down information and making drawings of defenses, but his youthful inexperience got him into trouble. He told the wrong person what he was doing and was quickly arrested after about a week on his mission. A search of his clothing produced damning evidence of his actions in the form of drawings and notes. He had no recourse but to stand tall and admit his mission.

Hale was sentenced to be hanged the next day, September 22, 1776. He met his fate well, by all accounts, and even gave a short speech before the end. There are several accounts of what he said, but the most famous line—true or not—survives as a rallying cry to this day.

"I only regret that I have but one life to lose for my country!"

Francis Marion—Swamp Fox

Though he figures large in early Ranger history, Francis Marion never had the title "Ranger" applied to himself or his eventual unit, known as Marion's Brigade. However, the actions of the relatively small organization against the British at a time when South Carolina was teetering under the English thumb were more in line with current Ranger doctrine than other "light horse" units of the time. Indeed, Marion used boats often, getting behind British lines unseen and attacking in small unit actions. Whether by horse, boat or foot, Marion's men gave the British a hard time in a small area mostly in the south of the state.

A South Carolina boy from the beginning, Marion was born in 1732 near Georgetown and spent his early life in the forests and swamps of that area. Much like men of an earlier era who took naturally to a Ranger-type lifestyle, Marion was part of his environment and knew how to function well within it. In 1753, with the French and Indian War on the horizon, he joined a militia company headed by his brother, Gabriel. Though his military training began there, that unit didn't see action.

During the Cherokee War—actually an extension of the French and Indian War—Marion perfected his horsemanship and military skills while part of Captain William Moultrie's unit. He was a natural leader, which, along with his growing skills, allowed him to rise to prominence within the ranks.

He was promoted in late 1776 to Lt. Colonel and two years later took command of the Second State Regiment, the unit he had been with for three years. That occurred when Moultrie left the militia for a place in the Continental Army.

In Charleston he jumped from a second-story window and broke his ankle—so the story goes—while trying to escape a friend's drinking party. That action caused him to be absent from Charleston when the end came on May 12, 1780, allowing him continued freedom.

In July of that year, Marion briefly joined Major General Horatio Gates, who sent him to gather Intelligence on British movements and burn any boats he could find along the Santee River to keep the enemy from using them. Gates then marshaled his forces—not enough—and marched on Camden, where General Cornwallis defeated him.

Upon learning of Gates' loss at Camden, Marion continued on his mission of boat-burning until he got wind of some 150 Marylanders (POWs from Camden) being held by the British at the home of his old friend, Thomas Sumter.

In what came to be called the battle of Nelson's Ferry, or Great Savannah, Marion attacked August 24 and routed about 90 British guards, liberating the prisoners and taking some of his own.

That particular action, coupled with Gates' defeat, put Marion in an untenable position. Cornwallis now knew Marion was there and considered him a threat to his supply lines. British Regulars were sent to destroy that threat. Marion had few men at that point and there was little or no organized resistance against the British in South Carolina.

Little Francis Marion, barely five feet tall, was on his own when he and about 60 men faded away into the swamps.

The name "Swamp Fox" reportedly came from Tarleton, who was just giving up on one particular chase into Ox Swamp and said words to the effect of, "The devil himself couldn't catch that old fox (or swamp fox)."

Major James Wemyss, who chased Marion down the Pee Dee River while simultaneously brutalizing the locals, made the first try. Wemyss didn't trap the Swamp Fox, but he probably gave him some new recruits.

At about the same time (September-October), Marion gained more victories at Blue Savannah, Black Mingo Creek, and Tearcoat Swamp, all against Loyalists. At Tearcoat the Tory militia gave up a number of new muskets and other supplies for use by Marion's men.

The British were incensed and stepped up efforts to find him. Cornwallis sent about 1500 soldiers to round up less than a hundred militiamen, with Lt. Colonel Tarleton as the main British officer after Marion at the time. He couldn't catch him, either.

After a few more skirmishes with both Regulars and Loyalists, Marion was promoted to Brigadier General in December. Things were swinging a little more toward the good guys at that point, and a new commander of Continental troops, Major General Nathanael Greene, took over to try and get things moving.

Marion raised a brigade-sized unit and retired to his base on Snow's Island. From there he continued to harass the British in several small, and a few large skirmishes, notably Halfway Swamp and Wyboo Swamp.

By March 1781, British interest in Marion was peaking. Two Colonels, Watson and Doyle, were dispatched to get the Swamp Fox once and for all. They were not successful. At one point the two British Colonels were separated and trying to get back together. Watson ran into Marion at Mount Hope Swamp first, but then had to fight him all the way back to Georgetown through ambushes and sharpshooters. The British got to Georgetown with many wounded, having left their dead.

During the siege of Fort Watson in April 1781, Colonel "Light Horse" Harry Lee joined Marion. The two forces, Marion's Brigade and Lee's Legion, joined on the Black River on April 14. The leaders decided to capture Fort Watson, though Sumter had tried and failed.

The fort was relatively new, built on top of a huge Indian mound. It is now an historic site.

After surrounding the fort, Marion and Lee were forced to wait for large enough cannon to do damage. While they waited it was suggested they build a tower tall enough to allow sharpshooters to fire down into the fort. This was accomplished quickly with materials on hand and the British found themselves exposed to the long rifles. They didn't last long after that, surrendering the fort on April 23.

The Swamp Fox finished up his memorable battles when he commanded the militia at Eutaw Springs in September. He then took on duties as a State Senator, at least for a time, and again went back to battle. He took command of his brigade and the British at Fair Lawn in August.

Marion continued his political interests after the war, and for a time was commander of Fort Johnson. He was South Carolina's representative at the Constitutional Convention in 1790 and lived to see his home territory become part of the new Union of States. He died five years later at his plantation home, Pond's Bluff.

Daniel Morgan

A leader of Rangers for a relatively short time, Daniel Morgan became one of the best known names of the Revolutionary War as commander of larger bodies of men. It figures he began as a scout and a Ranger.

Born in Hunterdon County, New Jersey, in 1736, Morgan was often in trouble for being an aggressive male—good Ranger characteristics—and left for Virginia when he was 17. Two years later he worked as a wagoneer with General Braddock when Fort Duquesne was tried, but held.

Several years after that he joined the British forces as a Ranger fighting the French and Indians, then after the main conflict he was part of the move against the Indian chief, Pontiac. Morgan also commanded militia during Lord Dunmore's War.

When the Revolution began Morgan was given command of a Virginia rifle regiment and joined George Washington in August in his siege of Boston. In late September, he left Boston and traveled with Benedict Arnold to Canada with the ultimate aim of reducing Quebec.

The name Benedict Arnold conjures up visions of treachery, and rightly so, but before all that, Arnold was a veteran soldier, a fighting man who could have ended up as one of America's heroes.

After the terrible hardships endured during the Canadian winter the battle for Quebec went badly for the Continentals. Arnold was wounded and Morgan took command briefly, but was then cornered and captured on December 31, 1775. It would be another year before Morgan was exchanged for a British prisoner and able to return to war. By April, he was back with Washington, who ordered him to join General Gates near Saratoga, New York with his rifle "company."

Unit designation was not what it is today. A company could equal a large platoon or have 200 men. Accordingly, a corps could be company-sized or regiment-sized. So, it is difficult to know the exact number of men in any given "company," though Morgan probably had a few hundred.

Morgan went on to fight at Saratoga and Cowpens, putting British Colonel Tarlton down in several hard-fought battles. His star continued to rise, bringing a promotion to Brigadier General.

He was elected to the Congress in 1797 after commanding militia in the Whiskey Rebellion three years earlier. He retired to his home, named "Saratoga," and died in Virginia in the summer of 1802.

WAR OF 1812—INDIAN WARS

There are differing schools of thought about Ranger participation in this war. Essentially they are divided into two opposing factions.

One, there were Ranger units doing government work during the War of 1812, but they didn't do much in the way of Ranger missions, and so can be at least partially discounted as legitimate Ranger ancestors.

Two, there were genuine Ranger units—on horseback for the most part—and they should be considered for a place in the ancestral roles mainly because they bore the name.

The author thinks both are correct, yet it is not the function of this project to decide such things, but merely report the findings. As always, we begin with a little history.

Less than a half-century after winning independence, America fought the British again in the War of 1812. The conflict lasted three years and ran concurrently with the British fight against Napoleon's France in Europe. America and Canada got involved because of trade disagreements between the British, French and North America, and because the British had the bad habit of going aboard American ships at sea and pressing men into service.

That was an old tradition, but to liberty-minded Americans, it was intolerable. When such men came into power along with President James Madison in 1809 they focused their wrath on the British so fiercely they became known as the War Hawks.

The War Hawks thought everything north of the Gulf of Mexico should be part of the United States, and that meant Canada. This brought on 10 American thrusts into Canada, all of which were repelled. Canada actually prospered from the war. The greatest losers, of course, were the Indians on both sides.

In the end, the War Hawks pushed hard enough to bring about war with Britain, which also meant against the united Indian tribes under the great Chief Tecumseh.

The "new" frontier had become a great deal larger in 1803 when Napoleon sold the Louisiana Territory to America, stretching the frontier all the way to the Rocky Mountains. Besides the Indian problems in the Ohio Valley, there were a lot of hostiles between the Mississippi River—the previous boundary—and the Rockies. As settlers pushed through the Ohio Valley and began to cross the Mississippi, the Indian tribes feared the loss of their lands and began to fight the expansion with hit-and-run raids and ambushes. They were very good at it.

During the period 1812-1815, the British also used Indian forces against Americans. As before, someone with mobility and unconventional tactics and training was needed to counter the threat of roaming Indian parties. Who better to deal with an elite enemy than elite soldiers? Once more, Congress called for the formation of Ranger units. By December 28, 1813 the Army Register listed officers for 12 companies, but 17 volunteer companies were authorized.

United States Rangers were put together from frontier settlements as part of the Regular Army, and used horses and boats to travel and fight from Ohio to Missouri. As with any war there were many skirmishes and fights, both large and small. There were also some independent companies raised by states to cover local problems.

That is not a lot of units considering the proliferation of Rangers both before and after this war. Robert Rogers raised nine companies by himself during the French and Indian War. In the Civil War there were Ranger units all over the place in the South. Still, this time they worked for the Army and were not independent state militia.

From Ranger beginnings in the 1600s to the late 1800s it was tradition for Rangers to furnish and carry their own gear. For that, they made more money than regular soldiers, which wasn't much.

In those days, a US Ranger made one dollar a day, three times the norm. They didn't usually wear regular uniforms, but weapons were the best they could get, and often the same within a unit (company). A favorite weapon of the Rangers was the .69 caliber musket, more accurate and more quickly loaded than the British-issue .70 caliber Brown Bess.

Imagine the damage caused by a .70 caliber round! It is almost twice the size of a standard 7.62mm bullet used today, though it travels much more slowly.

Daniel Boone is listed as a Ranger for North Carolina around 1759, more than 50 years earlier, stationed at Fort Waddell on the Yadkin River. He was gone, but his legend lived on when three of his sons commanded Ranger Companies during the War of 1812.

One prominent Ranger leader during that era was Nathan Boone, a man who rose to the rank of Lt. Colonel in the military, and then served as a legislator for Missouri, where he was one of the first settlers. At the start of the war he raised and commanded a Company of Horse Rangers that became part of the Missouri militia. Boone's Rangers did good service between the mighty Mississippi and the Missouri Rivers, helping keep Missouri safe.

Later, in the 1830's, Boone led troops in the Black Hawk War and the Mexican War.

The Battle of New Orleans put Andrew Jackson and his riflemen in the spotlight. Composed of men from Kentucky and Tennessee, the unorthodox unit drew praise from some, criticism from others, but they generally got the job done.

During the war with the Seminole nation in 1818, Jackson used a couple of Ranger companies against an elusive enemy, a mission more suited to the men's abilities.

Jackson was a proponent of unorthodox tactics and often used woodsmen as scouts. Otherwise, the riflemen at New Orleans were just that: riflemen. Still, he was known to like the idea of an elite, quick-striking force.

Abraham Lincoln was part of the Illinois frontier guard—often called Rangers—in the Black Hawk War of 1832, and provided his own weapon and horse. He was in a couple of units, including Jacob Early's Company, which covered northwestern Illinois and southern Wisconsin, looking for hostiles. His *recorded* service was short, just over a month between the two units, but Lincoln is an acknowledged Ranger ancestor and is in the Ranger Hall of Fame.

The main thrust of the Ranger concept changed somewhat when the country expanded to the prairies, and mounted men were needed to cover the large distances and pursue enemies on horseback. Congress knew the drill, and in 1832 gave authorization to form a battalion of Mounted Rangers. If you had your own arms and a good horse, you could enlist for a year and go chase Indians. A lot of bold men did just that, and the Ranger phenomenon grew. By 1860, there were more than 70 units calling themselves Rangers. The proliferation of such units before the Civil War had much to do with the number of Ranger units during the war. Many men had some experience riding and fighting and were perfect recruits for the Ranger and guerilla organizations that popped up when the war began.

How many of those units actually did Ranger-type missions is open to question, but the concept and the name stayed alive.

CIVIL WAR

The Civil War featured Ranger units on both sides, but not all of them were the real deal. The term generally referred to partisan units raiding behind the lines, and not trained-for-the-task units. The term "Partisan Ranger" was widely used, but had at least two different meanings.

Generally speaking, the "genuine" Ranger units were authorized by the Army, but raised by the states, and most worked in the eastern theater. The guerilla-type units, such as Quantrill's Raiders, were not always authorized and worked mostly in the western theater (Arkansas, Missouri) as more-or-less independent groups. Some of those groups were loosely organized bands of "guerillas" that were really no more than out-of-control bandits and killers hiding behind a façade of patriotism. Other units used the name just to attract recruits, and ended up fighting alongside the regular Army.

The problem of who was which became prominent enough to cause legislation to be passed, giving authorities some control over the runaway raiders, and allowing more uniformity of rank, pay and mission to authorized Ranger units.

In the beginning, the call went out for partisan guerilla fighters to "swarm the Federals" and cause great harm in their rear areas. Governor John Letcher of Virginia acted first and commissioned the activation of ten companies of Partisan Rangers. They would operate independently, but they would be working for the state. This action was followed quickly by several states.

Unfortunately, the Rangers of the day were not the well-trained, disciplined troops of today. More than a few of them got the idea they could do anything they pleased. Complaints began to pour in. It was suggested all Partisan Ranger units be dissolved and the men conscripted into the Army. The original Act giving rise to the Virginia Partisan Rangers was set in April 1862, but repealed in February 1864.

In Arkansas, General Thomas C. Hindman looked upon them somewhat differently. A staunch proponent of guerilla warfare, he went so far as to publish his own rules in July 1862.

Hindman's Guerilla Act

I. For the more effectual annoyance of the enemy upon our rivers and in our mountains and woods all citizens of this district who are not subject to conscription are called upon to organize themselves into independent companies of mounted men or infantry, as they prefer, arming and equipping themselves, and to serve in that part of the district to which they belong.

II. When as many as 10 men come together for this purpose they may organize by electing a captain, 1 sergeant, 1 corporal and will at once commence operations against the enemy without waiting for special instructions. Their duty will be to cut off federal pickets, scouts, foraging parties, and trains, and to kill pilots and others on gunboats and transports, attacking them day and night, and using the greatest vigor in their movements. As soon as the company attains the strength required by law it will proceed to elect the other officers to which it is entitled. All such organizations will be reported to these headquarters as soon as practicable. They will receive pay and allowances for subsistence and forage for the time actually in the field, as established by the affidavits of their captains.

III. These companies will be governed in all respects by the same regulations as other troops. Captains will be held responsible for the good conduct and efficiency of their men, and will report to these headquarters from time to time.

From Alabama a request was sent to the Confederate Secretary of War, Leroy Pope Walker, to allow guerilla companies to be formed to fight the way they wanted to, unencumbered by the restraints of government sanction, and to keep whatever they captured.

In the ocean war they were called Privateers.

The Confederacy replied that organizations of that ilk would be regarded as outlaws, and furthermore, that only state-sponsored, government-authorized, go-by-the-rules units would be allowed.

The Partisan Ranger Act

There was so much debate on the pros and cons of guerillas and Partisan Rangers that the Confederate Congress finally passed the Partisan Ranger Act of April 21, 1862.

In part, it read:

Sec.1. The Congress of the Confederate States of America do enact, That the President be, and he is hereby authorized to commission such officers as he may deem proper with authority to form bands of partisan rangers, in companies, battalions or regiments, to be composed of such members as the President may approve.

Sec. 2. Be it further enacted, That such partisan rangers, after being regularly received in the service, shall be entitled to the same pay, rations, and quarters during their term of service, and be subject to the same regulations as other soldiers.

Sec.3. Be it further enacted, that for any arms and munitions of war captured from the enemy by any body of partisan rangers and delivered to any quartermaster at such place or places as may be designated by a commanding general, the rangers shall be paid their full value in such manner as the Secretary of War may prescribe.

So, considering Section 3, men able to tow the line with the Rangers had a pretty good incentive to go fight and capture arms so they could be paid for them. It wasn't long before word got around and men who would normally have joined the Army were joining the Partisan Rangers because they made more money, or at least the possibility existed.

One problem with recognition of who was, and was not, an actual Ranger, lies in the form of designations for units of the time. There is no complete list of all "Ranger" units during the Civil War. The existing list is quite long, but it is by no means complete, and it is plagued with the above problems as far as telling for certain which units were "real."

Cavalry units often called themselves Rangers but were listed as cavalry. Similarly, rifle units were sometimes listed as Battalions of Partisan Rangers, but fought with the army. To make matters of recognition worse, several units were absorbed or merged with others during the war.

In the South alone there were more than 150 Partisan Ranger units of various sizes, and more than 100 guerilla organizations. Of those, just five are listed as Confederate.

Of the guerilla units, 62 were from Missouri.

There were some tough things happening in Missouri, Arkansas, and into Kansas during those dark days. People like William "Bloody Bill" Anderson and William Quantrill were on the warpath. Raids into Kansas provoked the Federals to retaliate in kind in Missouri.

There were other Partisan Rangers/guerillas in Missouri that did quite well and remained respectable while doing so.

Mosby, Ashby, Morgan—Confederate Rangers

There were some well-known leaders and organizations, particularly those of Confederate Colonels John Singleton Mosby and Turner Ashby, and General John Hunt Morgan.

Mosby's Rangers worked against Union forces south of the Potomac River, cutting supply lines, intercepting communication attempts, and assaulting small outposts. Mosby usually attacked with 20 to 50 men and faded away before larger forces could be brought to bear, mirroring the tactics of Francis Marion.

The Ranger leader was a small man given to fits of temper, but led his forces aggressively, commanding respect from his men and his enemy. From modest beginnings in 1862, Mosby's forces grew to eight companies by 1865. The growth began when Mosby, then an officer with the 1ˢᵗ Virginia Cavalry, requested permission to conduct raids with a small force (nine men) behind enemy lines. His commander, Major General J. E. B. Stuart, let Mosby go forward with his ideas, and his success earned him a Captain's commission in 1863.

Stuart was a cavalryman with much experience making dashing raids and forays in Virginia under Stonewall Jackson, when not protecting the flanks.

With that authority, Mosby raised a company of partisans, including some too young, some too old, some just out of the hospital, and even a few deserters to go with a core of regulars. The bold leader figured if he could cause enough problems for the Union Army, troops would have to be withdrawn from other places to guard against raids. Mosby would then calculate weak spots in the Union holdings and attack them. The unit got so good and knew the country so well that they became one of the first to carry out night raids.

One story—unsubstantiated—states that Mosby and nine men once routed an entire Union regiment in its bivouac.

A famous exploit occurred in 1863 when Mosby and 29 Rangers kidnapped a Union Brigadier General from Fairfax Courthouse, Virginia, under the noses of the Regimental Guard. Mosby had been incensed when he heard a Union Colonel, Percy Wyndham, had called he and his men criminals. He resolved to teach the Colonel a lesson by kidnapping him from the courthouse deep behind enemy lines. Going in at night after cutting telegraph wires, Mosby by-passed the Union sentries and arrived at what he mistakenly thought was Wyndham's house. The prisoners he did get told him the Colonel was gone anyway, but there was a Union General named Edwin Stoughton in town. That was good enough for Mosby.

Disguised as Federal messengers, the Southerners got to General Stoughton and escorted him and several other prisoners in quick fashion out of there and back to their camp, arriving in good form and with not a single casualty.

Mosby spent time studying the exploits of Francis Marion—the Swamp Fox of the Revolutionary War—and used them well. Union forces tried everything to catch Mosby and his men, even resorting to "scorched earth policy," but the unorthodox fighters were able to fade into the population and the forests and become invisible.

Shades of Vietnam and Iraq.

Mosby kept it up until the Confederate surrender, and then disbanded his troops rather than give up.

Another Virginian, Turner Ashby, had good success with raiding and harassing Union troops, keeping large numbers occupied. Ashby served for a long time under Thomas "Stonewall" Jackson during the Virginia campaign of 1861-62 and became a valuable commander and ferocious fighter until his untimely death in battle. Unfortunately, he had difficulty controlling his troops when in garrison (or occasionally in battle) and was often unable to be located by Jackson. Still, Ashby's cavalry provided Intelligence, mostly correct, and protected Jackson's flank, as well as scaring Union pickets to death. Though not technically designated as a Ranger unit, Ashby's cavalry did much of what Rangers are designed to do—establish recon, infiltration and quick-strike protocols, and carry them out.

There is a definite parallel between the thunder of charging cavalry and the thunder of assaulting Black Hawks.

Ashby, elevated by Jackson to a generalship just before he was killed, and Jeb Stuart, who replaced him as Stonewall's commander of cavalry, were hard fighters and good at what they did, but they were never termed "Rangers" at any point in the Civil War.

Mosby was also involved in the Virginia campaigns, but later he led a partisan group doing a job that ran more in line with the current raider philosophy.

Generals used cavalry for far-reaching eyes and ears, so men on horseback were often the first to fire on one another as forces converged. Some of the later brigades of horse could count nearly 2,000 men—enough to either turn an enemy's flank or reinforce one of their own.

The Ranger cavalry of General John H. Morgan began in late 1861 and caused problems for the Union until the summer of 1863 when they got serious. An attack at Green River Bridge, Kentucky, failed, but while withdrawing Morgan captured the Union garrison at Lebanon, Kentucky, and stole two ships. Ferrying his men across the Ohio River, he then captured the town of Corydon, Indiana. Federal troops and gunboats came arrowing to that point and Morgan was on the run again—this time almost as far north as Lake Erie, the deepest Confederate thrust of the war. Hunt and his men were finally caught near East Liverpool, Ohio, and made to surrender.

That Rangers honor such men as ancestral heroes is testimony to their dedication and abilities, as well as an acknowledgement of their accomplishments.

Union Rangers

Though men of the South seemed more naturally inclined to fill Ranger boots and saddles, Union Rangers also played a part in the Civil War. Mean's Rangers, who captured part of an ammunition train from Confederate General Longstreet, were given the mission of eliminating Mosby, but could never do it.

Supply trains (wagons) for huge armies were often many miles long. Cavalry on both sides harassed and plundered whenever the opportunity arose.

Western Rangers

In the west, Indians were rising up because all the soldiers had gone to war, so the states put together Ranger units for defense. An active Minnesota unit, the First Regiment of Mounted Rangers, had 12 companies, and helped oust the Santee Sioux in 1862-63.

UNIT HISTORY AND LINEAGE

Despite the number of pre-20th Century Ranger units, present day Rangers trace their unit history and lineage back to WWII. That doesn't mean some of the individual companies don't have roots going farther back, especially the National Guard Companies. It also doesn't mean Rangers have forgotten where they came from. However, the Ranger Regiment flag sports colors back to the Ranger Battalions of WWII and that is what the following section details.

A close look at Ranger history reveals a pattern of activation and inactivation according to whatever crisis was happening at the time. This has been true since before Francis Marion wandered around in the swamps of South Carolina, and then went home when it was all over.

Not until the 1940s did Rangers gain battalion strength, but still went through inactivity between WWII and Korea, then again in the years before Vietnam. Finally recognized as necessary on a permanent basis, Rangers regained battalion strength in 1974.

Many heroic units have come and gone in the long years since Colonel William Darby in 1942, with reorganization rampant as the Rangers steadily made their mark and began to put down roots. The 75th Ranger Regiment was born in 1986, the first permanent unit of these unique soldiers, supported by a Ranger Department and the four (now three) Ranger Training Battalions.

The following text traces the lineage of the 75th Ranger Regiment back to a nailed-together unit that consistently managed the improbable against superior forces in Burma in 1943—Merrill's Marauders.

Though the lineage of the 75th Ranger Regiment is the main focus here, Ranger units from the National Guard, (425th Infantry, 143rd Infantry, 65th Infantry), the 8213th known as the Eighth Army Ranger Company, and the short-lived 29th Ranger Battalion of WWII (originally a National Guard unit) are included.

Bear in mind that many of the recorded changes of one unit to another, or the consolidation of several inactive units, was often done on paper to create a suitable organization before staffing it with new men, taking the line further into history.

75th Ranger Regiment

Modern Rangers follow a lineage dating back to Merrill's Marauders, the 5307th Composite Unit (Provisional), which was organized in the Army of the United States (AUS) in 1943. They were activated and fought in the China-Burma-India Theater of Operations. In 1944 that unit and several others came together and were re-designated the 475th Infantry Regiment, assigned to the 5332nd Brigade (Prov). A year later they were inactivated in China.

For more on Merrill's Marauders see the WWII section.

Post-Korea, troops were needed abroad, so the inactive 475th became the 75th Infantry in 1954, and worked under the Regular Army after becoming active in Okinawa. Two years later it was over again.

It was 1969 before the 75th was put back together and given status as a parent regiment under the Combat Arms Regimental System. It was at that point the Vietnam Rangers came into being.

In 1984 another reorganization at Fort Benning, Georgia, led to an assignment to the 1st Special Operations Command. By 1986 the 75th Ranger Regiment was born of a marriage of the former 1st, 3rd, 4th, 5th and 6th Ranger Infantry Battalions of WWII and the 2nd Infantry Battalion.

The unit was subsequently withdrawn from Combat Arms (CARS) and became a parent regiment under the Army Regimental System.

1st Battalion, 75th Ranger Regiment

In 1960, former Company A of the 1st Ranger Infantry Battalion consolidated with 1st Company, 1st Battalion, 1st Regiment, 1st Special Service Force, and was named Headquarters and Headquarters Company (HHC), 7th Special Forces Group. It was then part of the 1st Special Forces Group, a parent regiment under CARS. Further mixing with HHC, 77th SFG, and 1st Special Forces brought about HHC, 7th SFG, and 1st Special Forces.

The birth of HHC, 1st Battalion, 75th Infantry (Ranger) came at Fort Stewart, Georgia, in 1974, made up of Company C (Ranger), 75th Infantry, which was inactivated in Vietnam in 1971. That group was assigned to the 1st Special Operations Command (Airborne) in 1982.

Former Company A was withdrawn from CARS in 1986, left the 1st Special Forces, and was put together with HHC, 1st Battalion, 75th Infantry, with the whole being designated 1st Battalion, 75th Ranger Regiment.

2nd Battalion, 75th Ranger Regiment

Former Company A, 2nd Infantry Battalion, joined with 4th Company, 2nd Battalion, First Regiment, 1st Special Service Force in 1960, with the whole being called HHC, 10th SFG, part of 1st Special Forces.

In 1974 Company H (Ranger), 75th Infantry, inactive since 1972, was brought back to life as HHC, 2nd Battalion, 75th Infantry at Fort Lewis Washington.

The group was assigned to the 1st Special Operations Command (Airborne) in 1982. Four years later Company A was withdrawn from the 1st Special Forces and melded with HHC, 2nd Battalion, 75th Infantry, becoming the 2nd Battalion, 75th Ranger Regiment.

3rd Battalion, 75th Ranger Regiment

A consolidation of former Company A, 3rd Ranger Infantry Battalion, and 1st Company, 1st Battalion, Second Regiment, 1st Special Service Force brought about HHC, 13th Special Forces Group, part of the 1st Special Forces. At that point the unit was withdrawn from the Regular Army and placed in the Army Reserve.

1984 saw the re-designation of Company F (Ranger), 75th Infantry as HHC, 3rd Battalion, 75th Infantry. The group was activated at Fort Benning, Georgia and assigned to the 75th Infantry Regiment, which was given to the 1st Special Operations Command.

Company A was withdrawn from 1st Special Forces in 1986 and mixed with HHC, 3rd Battalion, 75th Infantry, coming into the 75th Ranger Regiment as the 3rd Battalion.

World War II

1ˢᵗ Ranger Infantry Battalion

The 1ˢᵗ Ranger Battalion was put together overseas and taken to Carrickfergus, Northern Ireland, where it was activated in 1942. From that core and plenty of new volunteers came the 1ˢᵗ (E and F Companies), 3ʳᵈ (A and B Companies), and 4ᵗʰ (C and D Companies) Ranger Battalions in 1943. A year later all were disbanded after the debacle at Cisterna, Italy. The least experienced survivors of the battalions were absorbed into the new 474ᵗʰ Infantry, and the best of the bunch became Instructors and administrators in the U. S.

Quite a few ended up in the First Special Service Force.

In 1948, the whole was put back together as the 1ˢᵗ Infantry Battalion in the AUS, but activated in the Panama Canal Zone. Two years later the group was inactivated, also in the Canal Zone, with Company A becoming the 1ˢᵗ Ranger Infantry Company and attached to the 2ⁿᵈ Infantry Division in Korea.

Company B also went to Korea as the 5ᵗʰ Ranger Infantry Company. That group was put with the Eighth Army Ranger Company and attached to the 25ᵗʰ Infantry Division.

The 1ˢᵗ and 5ᵗʰ Ranger Companies were inactivated in 1951, but a year later the 1ˢᵗ Ranger Infantry Battalion was restored.

The formation of the 1ˢᵗ Special Forces came in 1960 when the 2ⁿᵈ Infantry Battalion and the 3ʳᵈ, 4ᵗʰ, 5ᵗʰ, and 6ᵗʰ Ranger Infantry Battalions were put together. That lasted until 1986 when all were withdrawn from the 1ˢᵗ Special Forces and consolidated with the 75ᵗʰ Infantry, becoming part of the 75ᵗʰ Ranger Regiment.

2ⁿᵈ Ranger Infantry Battalion

The 2ⁿᵈ Ranger Battalion was put together at Camp Forrest, Tennessee, where it was activated in 1943, its name changed to 2ⁿᵈ Ranger Infantry Battalion. The 2ⁿᵈ went to Europe until the war was over, and was then made inactive at Camp Patrick Henry, Virginia in 1945.

In 1949, the group became the 2ⁿᵈ Infantry Battalion, and Companies E and F were disbanded. The unit was activated in the Panama Canal Zone.

A general reshuffling of elements over the next two years sent parts of the 2ⁿᵈ to many different places. Companies E and F were restored when the 2ⁿᵈ Infantry Battalion was inactivated in the Canal Zone in 1950, and those companies and Companies A and B were activated at Fort Benning.

Company A became the 2ⁿᵈ Ranger Infantry Company and went to the 7ᵗʰ Infantry Division in Korea. Company B became the 6ᵗʰ Ranger Infantry Company and went to Germany as part of VII Corps. Company E became the 9ᵗʰ Ranger Infantry Company and stayed in-country at Fort Benning's US Army Infantry Center. Company F went to Japan as the 10ᵗʰ Ranger Infantry Company.

In 1951, Companies C and D came on line at Fort Benning, with Company C becoming the 14ᵗʰ Ranger Infantry Company, reporting to Camp Carson, Colorado. Company D stayed at Benning as the 15ᵗʰ Ranger Infantry Company.

At that point, Companies A-F were inactivated. The whole was re-designated as the 2nd Ranger Infantry Battalion in 1952, with all elements restored, and became part of the Regular Army. On paper.

Three years later the Ranger name went away once again, with the change making the group the 2nd Infantry Battalion, activated in Iceland.

In 1960, the 2nd was inactivated at Fort Hamilton, New York, and became part of the 1st Special Forces, along with the 1st Special Service Force and the 1st, 3rd, 4th, 5th and 6th Ranger Infantry Battalions.

The group was withdrawn from the 1st Special Forces in 1986, mixed with the 75th Infantry, and was reborn as part of the 75th Ranger Regiment.

3rd Ranger Infantry Battalion

The 3rd Ranger Infantry Battalion was a mix of Companies A and B, 1st Ranger Battalion and the 3rd Ranger Battalion, which was organized in North Africa. The unit was named the 3rd Ranger Battalion at first, but became the 3rd Ranger Infantry Battalion. All of that happened in 1943, a good year compared to 1944, when the unit was disbanded after losing much of its strength in Italy. It was 1950 before Companies A-E were put back into the Regular Army, becoming active at Fort Benning. Company A became the 3rd Ranger Infantry Company (Airborne) and was sent to Korea as part of the 3rd Infantry Division.

Company B became the 7th Ranger Infantry Company, and stayed at Fort Benning. Company C went to Japan as the 11th Ranger Infantry Company, and Company D became the 12th Ranger Infantry Company, relocating at Camp Atterbury, Indiana. Company E went to Camp Pickett, Virginia, as the 13th Ranger Infantry Company.

The 3rd, 7th, 11th, 12th and 13th were inactivated in 1951, but the whole became part of the Regular Army in 1952, with all elements restored as the 3rd Ranger Infantry Battalion.

The formation of the 1st Special Forces in 1960 put the 3rd together with the 1st, 4th, 5th and 6th Ranger Infantry Battalions, along with the 1st Special Service Force and the 2nd Infantry Battalion.

That group was extracted from the 1st Special Forces in 1986 and consolidated with the 75th Infantry, with the result being the birth of the 75th Ranger Regiment.

4th Ranger Infantry Battalion

In 1943, Companies C and D of the 1st Ranger Battalion, and the 4th Ranger Battalion were put together in North Africa to form the 4th Ranger Battalion, which soon became the 4th Ranger Infantry Battalion. The battalion fought at Anzio, lost too many men trying to relieve other Rangers at Cisterna, and was disbanded at Camp Butner, North Carolina, in 1944.

Companies A and B went back to the Regular Army in 1950 and were activated at Fort Benning, Georgia. Company A became the 4th Ranger Infantry Company and went to Korea as part of the 1st Cavalry Division. Company B turned into the 8th Ranger Infantry Company and fought with the 24th Infantry Division in Korea.

About a year later, the 4th and 8th were inactivated, but in 1952 they were brought back into the Regular Army as the 4th Ranger Infantry Battalion with all elements restored.

The 1st Special Forces was formed in 1960, composed of the 1st, 3rd, 4th, 5th and 6th Rangers, the 2nd Infantry Battalion, and the 1st Special Service Force. That lasted until 1986, when all were withdrawn from the 1st Special Forces and consolidated with the 75th Infantry, with the whole being named the 75th Ranger Regiment.

5th Ranger Infantry Battalion

The 5th Ranger Battalion began life in the AUS, was renamed the 5th Ranger Infantry Battalion, trained in the US at Camp Forrest, and was sent for more training in Carrickfergus, Northern Ireland, in 1943. They were disbanded in Austria in 1945, taken to the US, and inactivated at Camp Miles Standish, Massachusetts.

1960 saw the formation of the 1st Special Forces, a composite of the six Ranger Infantry Battalions, the 2nd Infantry Battalion, and the 1st Special Service Force.

The whole was withdrawn in 1986, mixed with the 75th Infantry, and called the 75th Ranger Regiment.

6th Ranger Infantry Battalion

The 6th began life in the Regular Army as the 98th Field Artillery Battalion in 1940, and was activated at Fort Lewis, Washington, in 1941. Toward the end of WWII the group was changed to the 6th Ranger Infantry Battalion, fought in the Pacific Theater as perhaps the only Ranger group to be successfully utilized in the capacity for which it, and the other battalions, were designed. The battalion was inactivated a year later, in 1945, in Kyoto, Japan.

As with the rest of the Ranger Battalions, the 6th was integrated with the 1st Special Service Force in 1960, along with the 2nd Infantry Battalion, and re-designated as the 1st Special Forces.

1986 saw the removal of those groups from the 1st SF. They were put together with the 75th Infantry, giving rise to the 75th Ranger Regiment.

It should be noted that other units performing Ranger-type missions existed within WWII Army structures. One such was the 1st Special Service Force, which came into being in July 1942. With men from Canada and the US it was an unusual, but successful unit in the European Theater. It was disbanded in January 1945, with most personnel going into the 474th Infantry Regiment, a new unit made up of several components, including men from 1st, 3rd and 4th Ranger Battalions, and the entire 99th Infantry Battalion, a similarly trained unit of Norwegian-Americans.

The Alamo Scouts are another Ranger-type unit that ended up in SF lineage, and very nearly became the heritage of present-day Rangers.

The Companies

Each battalion is made up of companies, the core of the unit. Many Ranger companies were activated for specific reasons, such as war, and then inactivated when hostilities ceased. Some have short histories; some long. Individual companies may have been assigned several different places as parts of several different organizations. Whatever the lineage or linkage, from Darby's Rangers and Merrill's Marauders in WWII to the present day 75th Ranger Regiment, the companies have been the building blocks for the solid structure that has become the modern Rangers.

Each company was inactivated after WWII, no longer deemed necessary, but reactivated for the Korean War when the need arose. Before the Korean War was over, the companies, no longer able to stand with battalion status, were deactivated yet again. Incredibly, the Korean War companies saw their status and designation revert back to WWII company designations.

On close examination of the lineage/linkage section, the reader will see how the Ranger Companies have been shuffled to meet the needs of the overall military picture, much to the detriment of direct heritage and traditions.

Today's Rangers come from—at least on paper—Merrill's Marauders, who were not Rangers. WWII and Korean War Ranger units were not available during the selection of a proper ancestor, so the Marauders were chosen.

There is controversy to this day about Ranger lineage, and about who is really entitled to the Ranger name and the history of WWII and Korean War Ranger units. Commenting on the Marauders as the point of current Ranger lineage, Ranger author/historian Robert Black said, "The Army said it was done to preserve Ranger history. How can you lose history? What was done to the Rangers of WWII and the Korean War was the same thing as having your children stolen from you."

The current Ranger Regiment bears the history of almost all Rangers, at least as far as the layman can tell, but there have been numerous fights to re-align certain units in the family tree.

Quick Lineage Reference

As an easy reference, Ranger units from WWII to present are listed below

75th Infantry Regiment (5307th Composite Unit, Provisional), U. S. Regular Army, 1943-1945 (Merrill's Marauders)

Ranger Infantry Battalions (six companies each), U. S. Regular Army 1942-1945
    1st (Darby)   1942-1944
    2nd (Rudder)   1943-1945
    3rd (Dammer) 1943-1944
    4th (Murray)   1943-1944
    5th (Schneider) 1943-1945
    6th (Mucci)   1944-1945
    29th (Provisional Battalion of 29th Infantry Division) (Milholland) 1943

Ranger Squads (Provisional) (formed from several large units) 1944-1945

8213th (Provisional) (Eighth Army Ranger Company) 1950

Ranger Training Center (Airborne), Ranger Training Command (RTC) 1950-1951
    Company A, RTC 1951 (training company)
    Company B, RTC 1951 (training company)

Ranger Infantry Companies (Independent Airborne Companies attached to Regular Army Divisions) 1950-195

    1st (2nd Infantry Division) 1950-1951

    2nd (7th Infantry Division) 1950-1951

    3rd (3rd Infantry Division) 1950-1951

    4th (1st Cavalry Division) 1950-1951

    5th (25th Infantry Division) 1950-1951

    6th (1st Infantry Division) 1950-1951

    7th (RTC) 1950-1951

    8th (24th Infantry Division) 1950-1951

    9th (31st Infantry Division) 1951

    10th (45th Infantry Division) 1951

    11th (40th Infantry Division) 1951

    12th (28th Infantry Division) 1951

    13th (43[rd]Infantry Division) 1951

    14th (4th Infantry Division) 1951

    15th (47th Infantry Division) 1951

Ranger Department, U. S. Army Infantry School, Regular Army 1952-Present

    Ranger Training Brigade, Fort Benning, Georgia

    4th Ranger Training Battalion, Fort Benning, Georgia

    5th Ranger Training Battalion, Dahlonega, Georgia

    6th Ranger Training Battalion, Eglin Air Force Base, Florida

75th Infantry (Ranger) Independent Companies attached to Divisions and Corps 1969-1974

A Company (197th Infantry Brigade and V Corps, Germany) 1969-1974

B Company (VII Corps, Germany) 1969-1974

C Company (I Field Force) 1969-1971

D Company (II Field Force) 1969-1971

E Company (9th Infantry Division) 1969-1970

F Company (25th Infantry Division) 1969-1971

G Company (23rd Infantry Division) 1969-1971

H Company (1st Cavalry Division) 1969

I Company (1st Infantry Division) 1969-1970

K Company (4th Infantry Division) 1969-1970

L Company (101st Abn Division) 1969-1971

M Company (199th Brigade) 1969-1970

N Company (173rd Abn Brigade) 1969-1971

O Company (US Army-Alaska) 1967-1969 (82nd Abn Division) 1969

P Company (5th Infantry Division) 1969-1971

Airborne Ranger Companies of the Army National Guard 1981

    D Company (151st) Indiana 1970

    E Company (65th) Puerto Rico

    F Company (42nd) Michigan

    G Company 143rd) Texas

    H Company (175th) Maryland

75th Infantry (Ranger) Regiment

Contains HHC and three line battalions of three companies each. It was formally designated October 3, 1984, but by February 1986 the whole was changed to the 75th Ranger Regiment, which it remains today.

    1st Battalion—January 31, 1974

    2nd Battalion—October 1, 1974

    3rd Battalion—October 2, 1984

WORLD WAR II

After the Civil War there didn't seem to be any place for elite groups like the Rangers. That exclusion lasted 75 years until WWII, when there was again a need for such rugged men.

Considering the massed engagements of the Civil War and WW I, conventional military thinking had little to do with elite units that would take needed manpower from line units. Other voices said training a unit for too narrow a mission structure would have such groups waiting, idle, for the right use to present itself. Such thinking continues in some of the higher ranks to this day. Military schools focused on large-unit tactics, and tried to get all of their students to follow that line of thinking, discouraging unorthodox directions.

As the Army downsized between wars, funding was hard to come by, and what was available was used to further the concept of Line Infantry Wins Wars. The general public, however, loved the idea of the loner, fighting it out against overwhelming odds, defiant and energetic to the last. It was all very romantic, with the public looking for heroes, even if they weren't from the present century.

The novel, *Northwest Passage,* written by Kenneth Roberts, became a best seller in 1937. It depicted the life of a young man in the service of Robert Rogers' Rangers during the French and Indian War. Eventually the story made the big screen, with Spencer Tracy playing the part of Rogers.

With WWII looming large, the idea of a special force like the Rangers was way back in the minds of military planners. The lessons of the Civil War and earlier periods had faded into obscurity except in cinema and novels. Conventional thought had great powers slugging it out toe to toe on a level playing field, and the exploits of previous Rangers were—what was thought to have been—mere pinpricks, not enough to justify the existence of such units, let alone give them the best soldiers in the service to fill their ranks.

Ironically, it was the courage and daring of British Commandos that brought the idea of elite units into the line of sight of the United States military hierarchy.

Timeline

This section begins with a timeline to give context to Ranger activities. The following is a brief summary of pertinent events of WWII. Where the six Ranger Battalions came awake and where they went to sleep is interspersed with political and military occurrences, including major events within the Ranger ranks. The war had been going on since 1939, but we begin with pre-Rangers in 1941.

1941

While simultaneously fighting the British in Libya and Egypt and pounding Britain, Hitler makes a huge mistake when he decides to humble Russia. Late in the year, December 7, America is forced out of neutrality by Japan's smashing blow at Pearl Harbor, which brings a declaration of war on Japan and Germany; young men march to the recruiters (and some young women, too).

There are still no Rangers, but the raw materials are forming.

1942

January finds American soldiers in England.

The British lose 25,000 men as prisoners at Singapore in February. At this time the Japanese appear invincible, but the Germans are already beginning to fray at the edges. The British begin to advance and retreat several times in the coastal fight in North Africa, ending with control of El Alemein in Egypt. Tobruk, in Libya, is taken and lost by both sides.

In the north, the Russian winter is helping chew up the Germans at Stalingrad.

Britain and Germany are bombing each other without pause while Germany starts systematically murdering people in concentration camps.

The Japanese lose a chunk of their Navy in the Pacific and their decline begins.

Finally, there are Rangers. The 1st Ranger Battalion is formed under Lt. Colonel William O. Darby, and activated June 19.

1943

Operation TORCH—the Allied invasion of North Africa—is the first battle experience for the first Ranger unit since the Civil War. Landing in Algeria, the Rangers, part of a large troop movement, work east along the coast toward Tunisia while British General Bernard Montgomery pushes the Germans toward the same place from the southeast. Eventually, much of the German and Italian forces get away to Sicily and Italy, but many are taken prisoner during the surrender in May.

A few months later the Allies invade the island of Sicily, off the southwest coast of Italy. This time there are the 1st, 3rd and 4th Ranger Battalions. The 3rd and 4th were formed in North Africa and trained there by Darby and his men.

In the States, the 2nd and 5th Ranger Battalions are being formed and trained in both America (Camp Forrest) and England/Scotland.

After Sicily the Rangers join in the assault on Italy. The Italians see it coming, first kicking Mussolini out, then surrendering before the invasion. The Germans take over right away, disarming some Italians and conscripting others for the coming fight.

Three battalions of Merrill's Marauders—the basis of modern Ranger lineage—are fighting the Japanese down through Burma.

1944

In Italy, Americans land at Anzio in January after taking Salerno and have a hard time breaking out of the beachhead. A few miles inland at a place called Cisterna, the 1st and 3rd Battalions are all but eliminated by a greatly superior force and the 4th is beaten up badly trying to reach them. This disaster heralds the end of Darby's Rangers.

The 2nd and 5th Battalions participate in the landings at Omaha Beach and Pointe du Hoc on D-Day, June 6. The legendary motto, "Rangers Lead The Way" originates here.

From there, the two battalions work inland until they reach Brest on the far side of the Brittany Peninsula, then push on across Belgium and into Germany until the end of the war. There are many fights, many casualties.

The Russians are pushing the Germans back, too, and the "evil empire" is shrinking, although a big counterattack in the Ardennes forest in France nearly blows a hole in the American line. The Battle of the Bulge costs many thousands of lives, including some Rangers.

In the Pacific, America begins island hopping, and needs some recon-spearheader types. The 6th Rangers are born and get in on the invasion of Leyte by landing on three islands a few days early. Elements of the 6th lead the famous Cabanatuan prisoner rescue. This battalion also stays in service until the end of the war.

1945

Germany and Japan are failing fast. Concentration camps are being liberated by Russian and American troops and their horrors are made known.

In February, Marines storm the beaches at Iwo Jima in the Pacific.

In March, the Americans open a major road into Germany, and secure a bridge across the Rhine River at Remagen. The 2nd and 5th Rangers move forward, but things are slowing down.

Franklin Delano Roosevelt dies in April. Harry Truman becomes President of the United States. In Britain, the second old guard steps down when Clemet Attlee takes Churchill's spot.

Germany gives up on May 7. Japan says enough on August 14.

By the end of the year there are—again—no more Rangers.

WORLD WAR II—RANGER STYLE

The beginnings of WWII had military planners chasing off in all directions trying to figure out how to fight a war without properly trained and equipped troops. Axis forces were running amok in Europe and the Pacific Ocean, and most of our big Naval guns lay in smoking ruins at Pearl Harbor. The Germans, and particularly the Japanese, were not fighting the conventional static, big-front battles so much as they were conquering countries city by city, some of which lay in deep jungles or tall mountains. This was no trench war. The armies moved fast, ready and willing to use their considerable arsenals and manpower to expand their holdings. It was a new type of warfare; they were mechanized, mobile and spread out all over the place.

House-to-house combat was not unusual in Europe, even in the early days, and the Japanese were landing troops on islands and fighting through jungles, learning the ways of the native guerilla fighters and adopting those tactics. At that point, America had very few men with urban or jungle fighting knowledge, let alone amphibious operations. The thin ranks were filled with men without combat experience or up-to-date weapons and training, let alone the ability to wage urban warfare or fight in the jungles.

The Germans, having conquered most of the countries around their homeland, began branching out into southern Europe and North Africa, and also went full-tilt on an ill-fated charge into Russia, called Operation Barbarossa.

Russia and Germany had shared a non-aggression pact, and Russia had taken part of Poland and all of Finland for its own. Hitler then decided to ignore the pact.

They made wide use of radar stations along occupied coastlines, and fortified themselves against attacks by sea or air. The Allies—principally the British at that point—were keen to attack German-occupied territory, and the "eyes" of the enemy became necessary targets, but not for the main battle groups. Someone was needed to go in with a small, secretive force, take control of shore batteries, interrupt communications, and knock out radar sites, paving the way for those to come.

At the outset of hostilities, no such independent American units existed. With the Army coming into the conflict in 1942 and needing a complete overhaul, such things as elite units were not on the opening menu. The whole concept had to be redefined to fit the rising needs.

Military memories began to look back, remembering history, settling on the kind of men they would need and the kind of training necessary for success. One such memory belonged to General George C. Marshall, the Army Chief of Staff in 1939. Marshall, a graduate of Virginia Military Institute (VMI), had been an outstanding officer in WWI, and had spent time in China as well as several other postings. He knew his way around.

Though he was stern, he had an open mind, and was one of the main proponents of the birth of special operations. As a backer, he was one of the best. This propensity for new ideas dated back a decade to his time as Assistant Commandant of the Infantry School, where he encouraged alternatives to the "school solution."

Considering the lack of combat experience in America's young army, Marshall and others were faced with getting green troops in shape for upcoming battles, plus the unenviable task of re-educating stodgy WWI officers. One answer lay in the study of British Commando units, a small group of brave souls who had proven their worth and the viability of the commando concept.

They were the only units with the necessary skill and bravery to make those small, stinging thrusts across the water. Those intrepid soldiers gave much to their country, and to the formation of the American Ranger concept, patterned after their own organization.

Marshall looked hard at that organization and liked what he saw. The British had formed 440-man battalions, all volunteers selected through interviews with troop commanders. The best got in, and then the rigorous training started and the real weeding out process began. Those in top shape who showed bold resourcefulness, could swim well, and had the youthful stamina necessary to pass the training, let alone the tough missions that would follow, became the apex of British soldiery.

These battalions were trained in specialized ways, with emphasis on physical fitness, weapons, and demolitions. The exercises were made as real as possible in preparation for combat. After several misfires, the Commandos did run some missions, but they weren't spectacular enough for the top British brass. Though the Brits didn't exactly "wow" everybody, they proved the concept was worth looking into. The problem was, no one really knew how to use these special troops because everything that happened was new.

Marshall wanted what President Roosevelt wanted—American forces on European soil, and soon. The Commando concept looked valuable enough to pursue, and he did.

In 1942, Marshall implemented a plan to increase air operations and begin small raids along the enemy coast. Not only would the raids boost morale in the service and at home, but it would give a number of men the needed combat experience, which they would then spread through other units as they were reassigned.

Thus was the concept of the Force-Expander born. The idea was that one well-trained man would "expand" the capabilities of a platoon or squad just by being there for teaching and leadership.

Indeed, one of the first ideas was to put some 70-plus American soldiers through Commando training with an eye toward becoming the rock that the coming mountain would be built upon. To carry some of that great training back to the US Army, it was suggested another group—heavy with NCOs—should also train and be used as teachers for the "common" soldier.

Not only was this a great idea, it helped mollify some stubborn commanders when they figured they might get their soldiers back with a lot more education.

Marshall and Combined Operations leader British Lord Louis Mountbatten got together in April 1942, with the result being a proposal for 12 officers and 60 enlisted men to go through Commando training and become the nucleus of what was to become the American Rangers.

Marshall needed someone to spearhead the project, and settled on Colonel Lucian K. Truscott, a former cavalryman from Texas. A small, wiry man with a distinctive voice, Truscott was on his way to an outstanding career, though he had no combat experience—very few did, at that point. He was given the job of producing the first specially trained troops of the era, using the British Commandos as models and guides.

To be sure, Truscott had to pass under the gaze of several top military minds, including General Dwight D. Eisenhower, the Chief of War Department Operations. This was to be a big job and a bumpy ride. Truscott would need all the backing he could get.

The Americans wanted a cross-channel invasion as soon as possible—they hoped for 1943—and special operations was one of the first steps to gaining the necessary Intelligence.

Truscott was made head of American involvement at Combined Operations Headquarters, an inter-service organization created by Winston Churchill to oversee special operations. Marshall told Truscott what he visualized as the dispersal of specially trained troops to a wide range of other units, who "would be able to counter the fears and uncertainties which imagination and rumor always multiply in combat." Such troops were specifically thought of for the coming invasion.

Truscott took the ball and ran with it.

About Lucian King Truscott

Though not a Ranger himself, General Truscott's words and deeds very much figure in Ranger history. In 1942 General George C. Marshall gave Truscott the job of putting together a new type of organization that would be a cut above the common soldier.

He was inducted into the Ranger Hall of Fame for his endeavors leading to the formation of the Ranger Battalions, and for exemplary service to the Army in general. During WWII, Truscott held battle commands at the levels of Regiment, Division, Corps, and Field Army, with promotions to match, ranging from Colonel to Lieutenant General.

Among other battles—including North Africa—Truscott led the 3rd Division into Italy and was nearby when the original Ranger Battalions were decimated at Cisterna, near Anzio.

It is uncertain whether he originated the designation "Ranger" for the new battalions—there are others who either claim it, or have been tagged with it—but he was instrumental in choosing William O. Darby as the first Ranger Commander, and was a driving force behind getting the battalions moving and assigned.

The Man: William Orlando Darby

Bill Darby was born in Fort Smith, Arkansas, February 9, 1911. Like many small-town kids, he knew practically everybody from being a Boy Scout, delivery boy, and regular attendee of the neighborhood church. He also read a lot, putting away knowledge that would later give him ease with almost anybody, something that showed up early.

Darby was a people-person, a natural leader. Handsome and persuasive, he was friendly and didn't mind lending a hand.

He was barely in school during WWI, but grew up with the idea of a career in the military, preferably through the gates of West Point. In 1929, that was no easy feat. Named as a second alternate by local Congressman Ben Cravens, Darby sat on the sidelines watching in disbelief, as the first two didn't make the grade.

He turned out to be a top-notch Cadet, even making Cadet Company Commander, Class of 1933. Energetic and likeable, he had a knack for getting things going, but graduation was based on grades and military performance, placing him in the middle, taking the sheepskin 177th of 346.

As a 2nd Lieutenant with a B.S. degree, Darby interned at Fort Bliss, Texas as part of the 1st Battalion, 82nd Field Artillery, First Cavalry Division. The 82nd was the only horse-drawn "arty" unit left, so the young Darby got to learn some new methods of moving guns.

Darby stayed in artillery for eight years, working his way up, learning as he went. He matured into a solid officer, earning his Captain's bars in October 1940.

Perhaps because he was so well squared-away, he was given an opportunity to participate in a joint Army-Navy amphibious landing exercise in Puerto Rico a year later. He also did some time with the Caribbean Force in the New River area of North Carolina, doing ship-to-shore landing exercises. Not many officers got the chance to learn the "new" way of attacking, and Darby was to make good use of the knowledge gained.

Pearl Harbor changed everything, with Darby winding up as an aide to Major General Russell P. Hartle, commander of the 34th Infantry Division. This turn of events led Darby from a temporary posting in New York City to a ship bound for Ireland with elements of the 34th. Arriving in January, 1942, Hartle took command of the US Army in Northern Ireland.

During the three months it took to get the rest of the division overseas, Darby chafed at the relative inactivity and requested a transfer to something more to his tastes. Arrangements dragged, keeping the officer in place; a good thing for him because decisions were being made in the Planning Department he knew little or nothing about.

The likes of General George Marshall, Lord Louis Mountbatten, and Colonel Lucian K. Truscott took hold of Darby's future by declaring a need for elite troops and moving forward with the concept. The man who would come to be known to his men as "El Darbo" was assigned to lead the first Ranger unit of WWII on June 8, 1942.

John Raaen, Jr.

Major General (Retired) John Carpenter Raaen, Jr. has been a big help with this section of the project. A short biography accompanies his later comments in the section on D-Day.

My mother grew up in Fort Smith, Arkansas. Bill Darby was that little kid down the street that was such a nuisance. When Darby entered West Point, my Dad was still stationed there. One of the customs was that officers would invite any Cadets they knew to come over to the quarters and relax, take off the stiff collar, talk, listen to that new-fangled thing called a radio, and, of course, eat. Darby was one of those who visited our quarters. I don't remember him, I was only in the third grade...but over the next 10 years I heard a lot about Darby.

I was appointed to West Point by Congressman Ben Cravens, the same man who appointed Darby. Of course, when he got all that publicity about forming the Rangers and the landings at Arzew, I swore I'd get into the Rangers somehow or other.

Early in 1945, I was a patient at Walter Reed and my father was in the Pentagon. So was Darby, and in the G-3 Section of the War Department. Dad invited Darby to the Army-Navy

Country Club for dinner, and the three of us sat around talking about the invasion (D-Day). Darby wanted to know everything about it. When we finally said our adieux, Darby confided he had wangled an around-the-world trip, ostensibly to inspect worldwide units, but actually he was job hunting, anything to get back into combat, he said. He found one as Assistant Division Commander (ADC), 10th Mountain Division. He never made it around the world.

THE FIRST OF THE 1ST—DARBY'S RANGERS

Truscott was promoted to Brigadier General, giving him more authority and credibility. Working with the British he soon learned both the value and the limitations of the Commandos. He also learned they had that military niche filled and that Americans would not have much to do if they used the Commando operations as a springboard.

Separate American units were the answer—providing they were put to correct use elsewhere and not harnessed with their British counterparts.

Truscott put forth his plans for a provisional Commando unit on May 26, 1942, and Marshall approved it. Once authorized to continue, Lt. Colonel Haskell H. Cleaves and Major Theodore J. Conway were directed to put together a tentative organizational table. A couple of weeks of gathering information and touring Commando camps by Conway resulted in a system organized along British lines, containing a headquarters company of 77, and six line companies of three officers and 64 men.

There was a lot to figure out. What would this unit be? How should it be armed and equipped?

The new unit would carry standard combat arms, but also use demolitions and collapsible rubber dinghies, among other specialized items. The size of the units and their weapons were predicated on the size of the available British landing craft, as such, nothing larger than an 81-mm mortar was to be transported. The LCA (Landing Craft, Assault) had a capacity of a little more than 30 Commandos or Rangers and their arms, so in a crammed situation a full company of 68 men could be forced into two landing craft.

According to some men who were on those little boats, "crammed" is the operative word.

At that point, Truscott had everything but the men. There were troops in Northern Ireland he could draw from, but the National Guard 34th Infantry Division and the 1st Armored Division, commanded by Major General Orlando Ward, were not too hot about the idea of losing personnel. The two units had already undergone some big changes and weren't looking for more.

Major General Hartle, previously in command of the 34th, had been elevated to command of US forces in Northern Ireland, which eventually included V Corps. He was following the wishes of General Marshall, Army Chief, and there were very few who could argue against him. With that clout, he sent the word down the line, and on the other side of the grumbling came cooperation. Circulars appeared on bulletin boards across Ireland's American postings, recruiters hunted where they could, and Truscott got his men, volunteers all, *supposedly* the cream of the crop from two divisions.

Administration and other mundane tasks relating to the new unit were left to the 34th Division.

The original purpose of the unit was "training and demonstration." The men were to train with the Commandos, go on raids with them, and then be dispersed to other units to spread the gained knowledge. New men would then fill the depleted ranks.

If Darby knew that, he didn't tell his men. Fortunately, that dispersal never occurred.

Hartle communicated his desires in a letter written June 7, stating he wanted volunteers from available forces in Northern Ireland—and that Truscott and crew had just 10 days to put the organization together.

For a commander, Hartle suggested Captain William Orlando Darby, his aide when he commanded the 34th Division. Hartle knew Darby well, and knew he wanted to get involved in the action. Indeed, had even asked to be transferred out after Pearl Harbor. Darby was given command on June 8, 1942, a week after his promotion to Major. Just over two months later he was made a Lt. Colonel.

Major Darby was just what the doctor ordered, getting underway in a fury of organization that had the basic unit together in just a few weeks. He had 2,000 applicants from the 1st Armored and the 34th Infantry, as well as other units in the area, mostly from V Corps units. He decided to weed them out by use of interviews done by selected officers chosen by Darby and a Colonel Hayford from Hartle's staff, at Carrickfergus, Northern Ireland, a small town about 20 miles north of Belfast.

Though all the men were "volunteers," it soon became apparent to Darby that some commanders had taken the opportunity to unburden themselves of malcontents in their ranks, some of them "tough guys" who ultimately found themselves among even tougher guys. One of the questions asked of the new recruits was how they felt about using a knife in combat.

It was a polite way to ask if a man could look into the eyes of the person he was killing. The use of a knife is personal; not like shooting a figure in the distance.

Darby wasn't concerned with a man's size so much as his ability and stamina, but the willingness to become part of the group was also a big factor. He wasn't looking for thrill-seekers.

Truscott had discussed the new type of unit with Major General Dwight D. Eisenhower, who was then head of the War Plans Division of the War Department, using the term "Commando" to describe operations. Eisenhower suggested a different name for the unit, considering the British already used the title. Truscott took the hint, choosing instead the term "Ranger," saying later he did so because of the mantle of courage, initiative, ruggedness and fighting ability attached to the historic Ranger units, specifically Rogers' Rangers of old. He stated in his later writings that he chose the name from several offerings. Others have suggested they came up with it, and there is a possibility that Marshall came up with the name—at least Darby thought so. It is also possible Lord Mountbatten suggested it. However, it appears fairly certain that Truscott is responsible for the term "Ranger," at least insofar as implementation goes.

On June 13, the unit was openly designated 1st Ranger Battalion—and the legend continued.

By mid-month volunteers had swarmed Darby's interview teams. They began to trickle through to the battalion and some trickled right back out again. More than 100 had already been sent back to their original units.

The 1st Ranger Battalion was activated June 19, 1942 by General Order No. 7, the beginnings of a scattered force of six battalions that fought with distinction in North Africa, Sicily, Italy, the Philippines, on the beaches and cliffs of Normandy on D-Day and on into France, Belgium and Germany.

The 1st Battalion was to have a Headquarters Company of eight officers and 69 enlisted men to look after the six line companies, each with three officers and 62 enlisted men. This amounted to just 26 officers and 441 men compared to a regular rifle battalion that totaled almost 850 men, but had only 22 officers. The Rangers were officer-heavy, and would become NCO-heavy, as well, a trend that continues to this day.

The six battalions, spread through time and distance, all had the same purpose—to produce and maintain the best fighting men in the world and use them as spearheaders, infiltrators, advance recon forces, and for lightning attacks on outposts and emplacements.

Darby had the first crack at putting together such a unit, and the other battalions used many of his methods as they came on line.

The original group of 26 officers and 441 enlisted men was given a 10 percent over-man (increase) to make up for expected losses in training. The youngest man in Darby's new unit was 18, the oldest, 33—Roy A. Murray, who would later make command status—with an average age of 25. The 34th Division supplied about 50 percent of the unit's make-up, and about 40 percent came from the 1st Armored Division. The remainder was made up of volunteers from medical, quartermaster, and signal troops from the V Corps. The majority of the men were *draftees.*

Strangely, the only officer (of eight) who came from the Regular Army was Darby himself. The rest were from the National Guard or the Reserves, including the Executive Officer, Herman W. Dammer. Darby saved Dammer from the static duty of an anti-aircraft unit to become a driving force in the evolution and effectiveness of the Rangers.

The original Command Staff consisted of Darby, Dammer as Executive Officer (XO) and S-3 (Operations), an S-1 (Personnel) and S-4 (Supply). There was no S-2 (Intelligence). Additionally, there was a Medical Officer and a Communications Officer. Original Company Commanders were: 1st Lt. Gordon Klefman (Co. A), 1st Lt. Alfred H. Nelson (Co. B), Captain William Martin (Co. C), Captain Alvah Miller (Co. D), 1st Lt. Max Schneider (Co. E), and Captain Roy Murray (Co. F).

The companies were broken down into a headquarters section, two eleven-man assault sections, and a 60mm mortar section. They were heavily armed, given the small size of the 65-man units.

Initially armed with M1903 Springfield rifles, the men were issued the M1 Garand before leaving for battle. The standard sidearm for officers was the big .45 cal. pistol (M1919A4), which used the same ammunition as the Thompson submachinegun (four per company). There were eight Browning Automatic Rifles per company, the legendary BAR, .30 caliber and welcome in a firefight. Added to that punch were four A-4 light machineguns (tripod mounted). A couple of 2.36-inch rocket launchers were available, the forerunner of the 3.6-inch Bazooka. There were even authorized brass knuckles—and the Commando-favored Sykes knife, now a symbol of the Rangers.

The Fairbairn-Sykes knife was given to the men of the 1st Battalion on graduation. Several different manufacturers made this famous knife over the years. For more on the knife, see the section about it under Miscellaneous.

The "big guns"—six 81mm mortars—belonged to Headquarters Company, though the British issued the American battalion six of their .55 caliber "Boys" anti-tank weapons to boost an already considerable amount of firepower.

Many things would change during the war and flexible organizational charts were necessary to accommodate those changes. Whether adding or subtracting men or equipment, the Ranger Table of Organization and Equipment (TO&E) was—and is—amended to meet evolving purpose.

For instance, the men wore a WWI helmet in the beginning, and used a good bit of WWI-era equipment until America's manufacturing arm began to send new and better supplies.

Achnacarry

With the basic infrastructure together, Darby moved his men to Achnacarry Castle at Inverness, Scotland, the home of the Lord of the Camerons. There the Commando Training Depot was located, and there the un-christened Rangers were to become the best specialized fighting force the Americans could offer. In charge of turning the inexperienced soldiers into an elite force was Lt. Colonel Charles Vaughan, an enthusiastic British officer with experience in commando-style raids early in the war.

Vaughn met the new Rangers at the train depot and led them off to Achnacarry to the tune of bagpipers. It was all glorious and fun at first, until the Americans realized the castle wasn't just around the corner. The pipers kept up the pace, and no Ranger dared fall out.

Darby was taken with Vaughn, as well as the other Instructors and what they brought to the table.

He wrote, "The tremendous personality of Colonel Vaughan pervaded the atmosphere of the Commando Depot. A former Guards drill sergeant and an officer in WWI with later experience in commando raids, he was highly qualified for his job. He had served with distinction during the commando raids against Vaagso and Lofoten Islands in Norway. A burly man, about six-feet-two, strongly built and of ruddy complexion, he had a face that at times showed storm clouds and at other times, warm sunniness. A man of about 50 years of age, he was in excellent physical condition and remarkably agile. He was constantly in the field, participating in, observing and criticizing the training of the men. During it all he was highly enthusiastic. Observing a mistake he would jump in and personally demonstrate how to correct it. He insisted on rigid discipline, and officers and men alike respected him. He was quick to think up means of harassing the poor weary Rangers, and as he put it, 'To give all members the full benefit of the course.' The British Commandos did all in their power to test us to find out what sort of men we were. Then, apparently liking us, they did all in their power to prepare us for battle. There were British veterans who had raided Norway at Vaagso and at the Lofoten Islands, men who had escaped from Singapore, and others who had slipped from the Italians in Somaliland. As Instructors at the depot, these men were a constant source of inspiration to my Rangers and, at the same time, a vivid reminder of the difficulties of the job ahead. At the beginning of the training, in the presence of the commanding officer of the Commando Depot, I told the Ranger officers they would receive the same training as their men. Furthermore, the ranking officer present was to be the first to tackle every new obstacle, no matter what its difficulty. I included myself in this rule, believing deeply that no American soldier will refuse to go as far forward in combat as his officer."

The first group of 300 men arrived June 11.

The men were stashed eight-together in British-type Bell tents, and bathing was done in a freezing stream coursing through the rugged country. They ate as their hosts ate, consuming tea, fish, and beans for breakfast, with bully beef added for lunch, and regular beef added for dinner. Colonel Vaughn was unmoved by complaints about the food, saying it was "all part of the training."

The training was a month long and extremely rigorous, with physical fitness a primary concern. Speed marches (five miles an hour), log drills (lifting and carrying huge logs in a team effort), and hand-to-hand combat were almost daily routines. The marches, in particular, were noteworthy. As the men grew stronger, the marches grew longer, getting up to 25 miles with an average speed of four miles per hour over varied terrain. Once their feet were up to the task —blisters were a problem at first—the Rangers learned how to use long, regular strides to cover ground in a hurry. Once they made 10 miles in 87 minutes.

That converts to one mile in eight-point-seven minutes—walking. Go try it, but first put your 60-pound pack on, and do EVERY mile in that time.

Weapons training involved not only Allied weapons, but also those of the enemy. The instructors closely monitored familiarity with weapons and marksmanship. The group focused on small unit tactics, as commandos tend to work that way, and used the buddy system of covering fire while advancing to attain objectives as safely as possible. Work was also done with small boats. Obstacle courses were murderous, as were marches through freezing streams and over rugged mountains.

These days the Rangers have the Darby Queen, the longest obstacle course in the Army at a mile-and-a-half, up and down through dense woods—29 obstacles, some of which are 20 feet tall. The course is difficult enough to be featured as part of Best Ranger Competition. For more on the subject, see Best Ranger.

The 1st Battalion was trained under live fire some of the time to make things as realistic as possible, though soap bullets were also used as a painful, if not lethal, substitute. Battle preparedness was also stressed. The ability to react to tactical problems and execute solutions was paramount. To gain that ability Rangers were taught how to stalk sentries, gain information as an advance unit, excel in street fighting, and take out pillboxes and other strong points.

As today, field exercises were a major part of the course, and took the greatest toll. The Commandos believed the average soldier could march one whole day, the good soldier two whole days, but it took the best soldiers to march three days and fight at the end of the trek. After the first three-day Field Exercise the 10 percent over strength Rangers were down to 10 percent under strength.

Another weed-out phase was the rifle/bayonet course where men worked in pairs, covering each other while climbing obstacles such as a 14-foot wall just so they could leap off the top into mud so deep some had to be pulled out by the Instructors. The end of the course was a rapid climb up a steep slope while under fire. At the top, the men were supposed to bayonet a target, but many were so exhausted they would stick the dummy and fall out right there. Anyone unable to finish the course after a few tries "went away."

Today the same quality control applies. If a student doesn't make the grade he simply goes away—back to his original unit. The other students do not see him again.

As far as realism and coverage, Achnacarry was as good a course as could be found anywhere, and the Americans improved rapidly, at least the ones that didn't get sent packing. The Rangers worked against opposition forces dressed in German uniforms and using German weapons, forces that didn't mind sending a bullet close enough to a trainee to permanently implant a lesson in ducking.

It was at Achnacarry that the famous Slide for Life, or Death Slide, came into being. This test of courage and muscle is still used today. In those days the men climbed a 40-foot-tall tree and went sailing across a fast river hanging from a toggle rope that ran downhill at about 45 degrees and ended in a big muddy puddle.

The Slide For Life remains a staple of Ranger training. There are several good stories about the Slide to be found in the interviews in the training section.

Between firing at sudden pop-up targets and being taught self-reliance, the Rangers had the full-meal-deal. Or so they thought.

From that pleasant interlude the fledgling Rangers were taken to Argyle, Scotland, on August 1, for another month of training, this time mostly amphibious. On the western coast the Royal Navy used the *HMS Dorlin*, a ship that didn't float, as an amphibious training center. This would be the first time the battalion practiced such tactics as a whole rather than focusing on small-unit work.

The men were split up around the area, with HQ at Shielbridge, but the training often took place among the small islands dotting the coastline. It was perfect terrain for practicing landings, giving the Rangers a variety of topographies to work with. The islands, with names such as Mull, Rhum, Eigg, Canna and Soay, presented excellent sites to perfect techniques used to knock out coastal batteries. The Rangers were even taught basic seamanship, crosscurrents, tides and simple navigation, so as to be able to step in if the Navy men aboard an assault craft were taken out.

The ultimate Field Exercise came as a three-day problem in which the Rangers were to land on the Island of Mull and capture its biggest town, Tobermory. Lieutenant Max Schneider, who would become famous as commander of the still-to-come 5th Battalion during D-Day, was at the head of Companies E and F. He left two days early to take a look at defenses, and while doing so, got the Home Guard to help out. It was his job to keep his compatriots out. He did what he could, but ultimately found out what the Rangers could do.

Major Herman Dammer, Darby's deputy, was to hit the island with four companies, knock out a radio station, and capture the town. The "radio station" was an old fort, and not long for this world.

Soap bullets were to be used, carrying the same powder charge, and not to be fired under 200 yards. Any closer and they hurt too much.

Dammer came in the rainy dark and ran into two of Schneider's patrol boats, entangling them in a running, soapy battle that ended with Dammer taking over everything afloat. The boats continued to the beach and the assault was on. Fighting raged through the town, building-to-building, with Schneider's men, the Home Guard, and police pushed back to the center of town where they were surrounded. Mission accomplished.

From there, it was Dundee for practice in assault tactics with a Commando force. The training was stepped up toward realism and occasionally, live grenades would find their way into boats full of students.

By summer, it was known among the high-rankers that someone would be sent across the Channel. There were several options, one of which involved some Rangers. Seven officers and a dozen enlisted men were sent to train with the 2nd Canadians on June 19—the day the battalion was activated. After bad weather and German bombers disrupted the first attempt at a raid before it got started, the men returned to the Rangers by July 11.

Dieppe

September came to Scotland, and found the bulk of the Rangers ready for missions, though 50 men had already participated in an ill-fated raid on the French coastal town of Dieppe, in the very heavily defended Pas de Calais area.

The Dieppe raid was just that—a raid and not an invasion. There were no plans to hold the territory. Indeed, there was little in the way of support except to get the men to shore. Still, it was important to some in the military, notably Mountbatten, and in the civil service, no less than Winston Churchill pushed for a second try. Operation Jubilee was slated for August 19, 1942.

Attached to a Canadian and British force of some 6,100 men, six officers and 44 enlisted Rangers were drawn from all six 1st Battalion Companies to join in the assault on Dieppe. The small town was located in an area of chalk cliffs and river outlets, rocky beaches and lots of German guns. Used primarily as a shipping port, Dieppe was also a communications hub; two factors that made it a worthwhile target. The grouping of small towns was fairly well protected.

There were three coastal batteries, one on each side of town and one in the middle, inland. The outside two were 11 miles apart with Dieppe roughly in the center. There were also several thousand well-entrenched German troops.

British Commando No. 3 was to land west of town and take out the four six-inch guns at an outlying community named Berneval while No. 4 Commando was given the six 150mm guns to the east. Only four Rangers went with No. 4, but 36 went with No. 3.

The Canadian 2nd Infantry Division was allotted Dieppe itself, giving berth to six Rangers with the Queen's Own Cameron Highlanders (two Rangers), Essex Scottish Regiment (one Ranger), South Saskatchewan Regiment (one Ranger), Royal Hamilton Light Infantry (one Ranger), and the Royal Regiment of Canada. There were other units participating, including an Armored Regiment, but none carried Rangers with them.

Training hard, the Commandos and attached Rangers practiced through the first half of August. The Rangers were integrated into the group and given missions and status among their former Instructors. Unfortunately, the six men assigned to the 2nd Canadian were dropped off at their various units only hours before the actual assault, and were considered "observers" by their counterparts.

Rangers were armed with the new M1 and anything else they could carry when the landing began at 0450. They were ready, as was the main force of British and Canadians.

A landing of such scale had not been attempted before, which was the main reason for doing it in the first place, and problems immediately began to surface. Between accurate enemy fire and mechanical failure in the ships and landing craft, many of the Rangers never reached the beach.

In the west near Berneval, Yellow Beach One and Two were designated No. 3 Commando targets. As a result of carnage in the harbor by German aircraft and some E-boats, only part of No. 3 made it to shore, and only four of the 36 Rangers were still with them. The mixed group of Commando Troop survivors and the four Rangers took off across Yellow Beach One, fighting their way inland toward the guns. Lt. Edward Loustalot was killed assaulting a machinegun position during that move, and the rest soon realized they were not in a good place. Germans had moved in behind them by then and a fighting withdrawal to the beach ensued. The remaining men sought shelter in the rocks along the beach, but they were overwhelmed and had to surrender.

On Yellow Beach Two, less than 20 Commandos—no US—were able to get inland and pin down the Berneval gunners, effectively taking them out of the fight.

Number 4 Commando landed at Orange Beaches One and Two—almost a mile apart. Two Rangers were with A Troop at Orange One, making a fairly smooth landing and working inland quickly. As on Yellow Two, the men were able to fire on the gunners and stop them from pounding the ships and beaches. The Germans didn't react favorably to the intrusion and began laying mortar and machinegun fire on the Commandos and Rangers. During that fight Ranger Corporal Franklin Koons was credited, and later decorated by the US and Britain, for being the first American ground soldier to kill a German soldier in Europe.

At Orange Beach Two, elements of No. 4 Commando, with two Rangers attached, got through barbed wire entanglements to scale a 30-foot tall cliff with ladders. The group was able to block a crossroads and cut communication while taking on enemy weapons positions.

The two parts of No. 4 linked up, fixed bayonets, and took the gun emplacement. Their mission accomplished, No. 4 withdrew to the beach under fire and made it into the water and their landing craft.

The main landing by the 2nd Canadian was a disaster. Of nearly 5,000 men, some 68 percent became casualties, including 913 dead. Two thousand were taken prisoner.

The six Rangers dispersed among the units in the frontal assault fared about as well. Two never landed, one of them was wounded at sea, one was wounded and later died, one died on the beach, one was wounded trying to get out to the boats and was eventually captured, and one was wounded swimming out, but got away.

Fifty Rangers participated, but only 12 got to the beach. Of those, only eight got inland. Reports of WIA and KIA Americans vary due to the number of men hit on the boats, but there were probably less than 10 killed—a 20 percent casualty rate, not including all the wounded.

Was it worth all the death and destruction to the Allies? The debate still goes on today. On one hand, the experience was invaluable. On the other, a great many men did not return to share that experience. Did it sting the Germans? Probably some, but the Germans could only see it as a tactical victory, though the Allies were trying for a strategic victory of their own.

The main problem was lack of fire support from the ships. The British Navy wouldn't risk any ship larger than a destroyer—there were nine—and the aircraft were mostly limited to fighters, with a loss of 106—a huge hit. The enemy was not hurt or dazed when the Canadians came ashore.

There was also a lot learned about amphibious operations of that scale, and planning and training were both beefed up afterward. The landings to come at Normandy would be better because of Dieppe, but the heavy price continues to be debated.

Dieppe was important for the Rangers for the same reasons as the British, perhaps more so in terms of publicity. Rangers had become the first US ground troops to attack a European position, the first to die in Europe, the first to kill an enemy in Europe, and the first to be taken prisoner.

For all the hoopla, only a handful of men returned to the 1st Battalion to tell their battle stories.

News of the raid was certainly well received in the States, where the Rangers were hailed as heroes. Both the *New York Times* and *Newsweek* published pieces on "Truscott's Rangers." It wasn't long before real news of the desperate conditions at Dieppe began to reach the public, especially the English, and the fine stories died a natural death.

Train, Train, Train

In the States, other units were training selected men in a version of commando-style warfare, including the use of small boats, night raids, demolitions, and personal combat. But that was for the larger units, and the core of Rangers already overseas was, for the moment, the only active American group with the expertise to run raids.

The 1st moved to Dundee for coastal raiding training after Dieppe, practicing their craft against pillboxes and gun batteries in joint training with Commandos. It was during that time that "auxiliary" personnel were brought into the unit. Men who were listed on the roster as cooks sometimes ended up in the van of assaults as Tommy gunners—but at least the unit had cooks. They also got some administrative people, but everybody had the same problem of where to stay. More people meant more housing. Military infrastructure being what it was, Rangers were parceled out to local families who put them up (mostly) willingly. Some of the "family" groups became very close in that setting of common urgency against a common enemy.

Another close relationship begun in Scotland was the informal attachment of Chaplain Captain Albert E. Basil, whose formal military parent was the British Special Service Brigade. Father Basil kindly consented to do a funeral for a Ranger killed in training, and stayed about nine months.

Darby knew the merit of the inspiration and comfort Father Basil gave to his Rangers.

He wrote, "I asked if he could be permitted to stay with us until after we had landed in North Africa. In fact he stayed on with us through the Tunisian campaign until the British Army discovered they had one missing chaplain. Unfortunately for us, Father Basil was then returned to the British Army."

The chaplain went where the Rangers went, becoming more and more like them. Darby remembered, "His one unfailing exception to complete Americanization was his insistence on wearing the Commando's Green Beret and shoulder patch."

Work was a little different at Dundee, where individual responsibilities were developed. Sometimes the officers would act as enlisted men while NCOs led the unit. This was supposed to develop initiative, and it did. One challenge Darby gave his men was to get to a town 25 miles distant in five hours. Since the standard Ranger pace is five-miles-per-hour, that should do it. Darby cautioned that no hired transportation was to be used.

By the close of the allowed time frame, every Ranger was in ranks, having come by horse, buggy, cars and trucks, even by air. No one paid, so no one failed.

The men were ready, hard and sharp, and educated better than any other soldier. They had become a tight ship, sailing under the mastery of Bill Darby, who said his men followed current Army codes as well as Robert Rogers' orders to his scouts and Rangers.

Darby wrote, "The modern Rangers had heeded Rogers' orders throughout their training, paying particular attention to his final order. It was, as written in 1761: 'Having read the foregoing orders, when all else fails, the thing to do is to forget the above instructions and go ahead.'"

The Battalion Sergeant Major at that time was Warren "Bing" Evans, who, as of 2004, was Honorary Sergeant Major of the 75th Ranger Regiment. A big, rugged man, Evans kept the boys in line. He received a battlefield promotion for his actions at the upcoming raid on Sened Station in Tunisia.

2nd Army Ranger School

It is worth noting what was happening back in America at that time. With the giant call to arms going on, the Army was getting a good look at the 17-to-25-year-old American male, and didn't like what it saw. Even General Marshall was saddened by the offerings.

"The ordinary military quality is not dominant in the American any more. It is no longer the question of taking the gun off the mantle-piece and fighting the savages."

Indeed, America was changing, getting more urban all the time, and the rough-and-ready frontiersmen were gone. The ability to hike all day, make one precise shot, and hump 50 pounds of meat home was no longer necessary. As a result the United States had no ready-made Ranger force available. If Marshall and others wanted Rangers, they would have to manufacture them.

The idea of suddenly having a large group of experienced soldiers was far-fetched, considering the lack of time in combat for uniformed soldiers, and the lack of military attitude among the conscripts. To accomplish what it could, the Army—really, independent commanders—initiated a few "Ranger" programs around the U. S.

The Second Army Ranger School at Camp Forrest, Tennessee was put together by Lt. General Ben Lear, and was perhaps the best of the bunch. Lear formed his two-week course around the guidelines used by the Marines, drilling handpicked men in everything from camouflage to street fighting. The well-trained men were then used as force-expanders, teaching "Rangerism" among the common soldiers in their home units. Unfortunately, the school was short-lived, but it wouldn't be long before Camp Forrest was hosting new Rangers, anyway.

NORTH AFRICA

With plans underway for wider Ranger-type training, full units were still distant, so when the decision was made to invade North Africa Darby's men were the only raid-capable unit available outside of the Marines, most of whom were in the Pacific.

Darby's Rangers probably didn't know of the pushing and shoving in the government halls of America and England. US strategy said go straight into Europe and face the monster head on. British thinking was more conservative, figuring the enemy was too strong in France and there was not enough manpower or materials available to launch an invasion and push forward with success.

There was a lot of arguing until Churchill finally persuaded Roosevelt to go into North Africa first, which meant another year or two before the English Channel could be crossed in force.

The Italians were very sorry to hear about that decision. Many of them would die because of it, in North Africa, Tunisia, Sicily, and in their homeland.

The Germans were in North Africa in some numbers, supporting—pushing—their allies, the Italians and Vichy French. General Erwin Rommel's Afrika Korps was to the southeast, fighting a rear-guard action against Montgomery's British Eighth Army.

Rommel and Montgomery were waging an all-out brawl along the coast of Egypt and Libya, and had been for many months. The Egyptian city of El Alemein, to the east of Libya, and the Libyan city of Tobruk were hot spots a couple of times each. The Germans and the British gained and lost the same ground several times through repeated heavy counter-attacks. At one point the British gave up 30,000 men to POW status, but the Brits didn't quit, and kept up the pressure. Rommel finally had enough and withdrew westward and north, consolidating his forces in Tunisia where the Americans banged on him from the west, and the British were coming up his back trail from the southeast. Montgomery was one thing; American troops were something else.

The battle for North Africa wouldn't be another Dieppe. The US had come in force. With Allied troops and water surrounding them the Germans were caught, and they knew it.

TORCH

The operational code name was TORCH, and it involved a full-scale landing along a 70-mile front ranging from Algiers, Algeria, to Casablanca, Morocco. A combination of US and British forces would head for Algiers, then the British Navy would land and support Americans landing some 260 miles west, at Oran. Troops coming directly from America would take on Casablanca. The Rangers were to act as a spearhead force near Oran, at Arzew. They were a streamlined assault team that could go in first, fast, and furious, knocking out chosen targets to make things safer for the larger group to come. This was a big deal for the Rangers. This was no raid. They would not withdraw once on shore.

On September 24, the battalion moved to Glasgow and became part of Major General Lloyd Fredendall's II Corps and further attached to Major General Terry Allen's 1st Infantry Division. The 18th Regimental Combat Team (RCT) was their supply and administration unit.

The whole idea of the 1st Ranger Battalion being a training and demonstration unit under British control went out the window with this plan. The Rangers would go into battle under American control, and they wouldn't be looking back.

Training for the assault landing was stepped up along with planning. Darby wanted more firepower, so he made D Company into an 81mm mortar unit. Along with the 60mm crews from the other companies, they practiced moving the heavy weapons around, even developing a wheeled cart for the 81s.

One good happening was the inclusion of the mess team into the battalion. That amenity made a big difference to the American men who had been fed British fare for months.

In mid-October, the battalion boarded the HMS *Royal Scotsman*, the HMS *Ulster Monarch*, and the HMS *Royal Ulsterman*. They would stay on those ships for almost a month, practicing amphibious landings that culminated in a pre-invasion exercise code named MOSS TROOPER.

The Plan

The Americans would land on both sides of Oran and drive against the fair-sized port. The Rangers were to come ashore at the port of Arzew, about 20 miles east of Oran, with the bulk of the 1st Division.

There was a battery of four 105mm guns ensconced on the high ground behind Arzew, dominating the harbor entrance. A smaller position on a point at the harbor mouth mounted three 75mm guns. That place was appropriately called Fort de la Pointe. Darby was given both batteries to destroy, which meant he had to split his battalion. The main fort was above, but someone would have to penetrate the harbor and seal off the lower fort.

In addition to the guns, the harbor itself would be a problem. Two concrete jetties thrust into the Mediterranean—one of them almost a mile—nearly coming together across a narrow alley of water which could be blocked by a boom to keep ships out. Had that boom been closed, things may have been different. Since nobody knew whether it would be open or closed, Darby took most of his men to the heights, figuring he could come down and get the lower fort later if necessary.

The Attack—The Rangers' First Test

In the pre-dawn murk of November 8, 1942, Darby's Rangers went ashore in two groups and struck fear into the hearts of the defending French garrisons.

Companies A and B, in British landing craft led by Darby's XO, Major Herman Dammer, bypassed the boom at the entrance to the harbor and landed unseen at Arzew. This action was not as easy as it sounds because ships took many of the landing places along the breakwaters. The Rangers' guide, a British Navy officer, had problems finding a place to land, causing delay as the boats went round and round trying to find a suitable spot.

The group made its way to Fort de la Pointe, which involved getting over barbed wire and using ladders to climb a 30-foot cliff. Company A went forward to attack the fort and seize the guns while B Company created a blocking position to keep the fort from being reinforced.

One platoon of A Company went through the main gate of the fort while the second platoon moved up an embankment to hit the guns from the side. The Rangers of 2nd Platoon were inside the fort before the French knew what was happening, and 1st Platoon cut through barbed wire and took the guns without firing a shot. The whole thing took just 15 minutes and there were no Ranger casualties.

B Company was taking prisoners at their blockade, but they were also taking sniper fire that hit flesh and bone. Dammer sent men to secure the port facilities, radioed Darby, then fired the pre-arranged flare signal to the landing force to say the door was open.

Darby took HQ, C, D, E, and F Companies into the landing craft and went after the 105s on the heights. In the process of loading everyone a boat was up-ended while being lowered into the water. Rangers went into the sea, heavily weighted down with equipment, and were picked up by other craft. The major loss was Darby's radio, signal equipment, and flares. Communication dropped to nothing.

Like their brothers, they landed undetected about 0130 and made quick time up a road, even though they transported Company D's four 81mm mortars. Only one sentry saw them, but he was quickly subdued. The mortars were positioned about 500 yards from the objective and Darby put C, E, and F Companies in a line and began to move on the fort. They were cutting through a ring of barbed wire when the French found them and began firing. Darby pulled his men back a little and called his mortars into action. Unfortunately for the French, there was no overhead cover in the fort and the rounds—50 or so—ripped them up. When the Rangers renewed the ground assault the French had decided that was enough, and more than 300 were taken prisoner.

The loss of his flares set Darby back even though he accomplished his mission. He was unable to send a series of different colored flares—as arranged—and shot only green, which is all he had left. At sea the green flares were not accepted and the mass landing was postponed by two hours, during which time the Rangers were still ashore and the French were getting worked up. Too bad for the French, their main defenses had been stripped.

The 1st Infantry Division stormed ashore with a lot less resistance, thanks to the Rangers' handiwork in the darkness. Small pockets of defenders—and some snipers—were captured or killed until around noon when the French surrendered.

Arzew fell smoothly, but at Oran, just a few miles distant, Americans were dying on ships trying to get into the harbour, and a naval battle was raging off Casablanca.

Everybody was happy, most of all the Rangers themselves for having such success, but reality set in quickly when capable combat troops were needed on the expanding front lines.
St. Cloud—LeMacta

Between Oran and Arzew was a small town named St. Cloud. The 18th RCT was tasked with taking the town, but after committing two battalions with small results against the defending French Foreign Legion, it was decided to hold St. Cloud in a pocket with one battalion and drive around it toward Oran.

Company C Rangers were an added bonus in keeping St. Cloud contained. On November 9, the battalion was ordered to march—at night—around the town and block the road to keep the enemy from breaking free. When they had enough daylight to see, the Rangers found a convoy in front of them. Being Rangers, they promptly attacked with two platoons.

Suddenly, overwhelming fire pinned them to the earth. Trying to maneuver brought them only casualties from a nearby artillery emplacement, so the company dug in and held on. Hours went by before Oran was taken and orders came down for the enemy to cease fire, but three Rangers lay dead and nine more were wounded.

That afternoon a section of the 16th Infantry had taken LeMacta, east, on the coast, and ran into trouble with heavy French counter-attacks. General Terry Allen, commanding the 1st Infantry Division, needed some tough guys to get things going, and there sat the Rangers. Darby sent E Company to help. They did just that, riding a train to their destination, clearing the road to LeMacta, and riding a train back.

On the 10th, General Allen appointed Darby Mayor of Arzew. After taking the town, he then had to return it to near normal. The easiest way was to install the real Mayor in the office and let him take control, as long as Darby was satisfied with how he did things.

The Mayor probably got the idea right away, considering Darby's 1st Battalion was in II Corps reserve and providing town security at the time.

Onward

Unfortunately, there weren't a lot of Ranger-type missions available after the initial landing, and Darby's men served their time on the line in several cases. General Allen called the Rangers "a specially trained unit of high combat value," which was only a partial recognition of their abilities. In fact, the whole concept of raiding Rangers, a quick-strike force without heavy weapons, was so new that most of the field commanders had little knowledge of how to use them properly. In many cases they were fed into the mill, and did so well they kept being sent back. Darby knew better than to refuse. He knew all too well that his unit could be disbanded and absorbed into the whole if they didn't stay employed.

A three-month hiatus after the landings at Arzew made Darby nervous, and he lost some men to transfer while the brass figured out how to use the special unit. Darby knew what to do. He ran his men hard, knowing they thought they were slick after the success at Arzew.

Keeping an edge was hard, but Darby was up to it.

He had this to say. "For the next two months I marched the men for long distances on short rations, so the training in Scotland seemed easy in comparison. There were night problems, many of them, and landings were practiced again and again. They replayed the Arzew operation like a phonograph record, changing the needle though by executing it at different times under varied weather conditions and under differing conditions of the tide, wind and swell. Probably years from now old Rangers, if brought back to Arzew, could fall into position without re-instruction. I believe veteran soldiers, even between campaigns, require continual training to prepare them for new and unusual enemy tactics."

At one point the Rangers were used to demonstrate live-fire amphibious landings to help train other troops for the next round.

There was a raid on an island off Tunisia proposed and trained-up for, but the move was cancelled at the last minute.

One good thing was the addition of some 100 replacements, including a few officers. Darby asked these men if they really wanted to join the Rangers—some didn't—and then distributed among the companies until the slots were filled. The remainder was temporarily organized into an extra company (G) under newly arrived Captain Jack Street. The new men were immediately put into the training program.

Tunisia

Finally, in early February 1943, the Rangers got a job that was tailor-made for them.

The Allies were in a hurry to get to Tunisia before Field Marshall Erwin Rommel got there. Rommel was fleeing west with 70,000 men, fighting a retreat before Montgomery's forces. Should Rommel arrive first, he would link up with Generaloberst Jurgen von Arnim's forces—currently fighting the Allied advance—and cause the Allies some great unrest. In short, if the enemy controlled Tunisia, German and Italian soldiers could get away across the Mediterranean and live to fight another day.

Though they were pushed hard until the last minute that is almost exactly what happened.

The points of conflict began to narrow until Von Arnim, Rommel, Montgomery, and US General George Patton began to rub up against each other.

The Rangers were flown into Tunisia on C-47s and put to work immediately for Lt. General Fredendall's II Corps, which anchored the right. The General wanted the Rangers to open up that flank, go in there and do some harassing, gather information, and make the Italians wonder what was happening. The 1st Infantry Division had a go and couldn't get anywhere, and the Germans were holding the passes, keeping the slot open for the coming Afrika Korps to move up. Fredendall needed to know what was going on, who he was fighting, how many there were, and where they were. Who better to gather the information and give the Italians bad dreams?

Sened Station

Sened Station was a classic Ranger raid that is still being taught to students today.

There were a couple of other things the General wanted, chiefly that the Rangers would give the enemy the impression a much stronger force than Darby's 500 was moving around in the dark. The men were to capture some prisoners, while inflicting maximum casualties on the ones they didn't snatch—if they had the chance.

Darby got orders February 9 to hit Sened Station.

The targeted enemy position wasn't at Sened Station, but near it, guarding a mountain pass that led to open plains beyond—the perfect place to move armor.

To get pre-assault information Darby went forward and consulted with the British Derbyshire Yeomanry, spread out in observation posts in front of the main Allied group. From that meeting came the knowledge of what forces the enemy had in place and a look at the terrain around Sened.

When the time came for the raid the Rangers were 32 miles from Sened Station, but were able to ride in trucks for the first 20 miles on the night of February 10. The second leg, eight miles of tumbled terrain, began as soon as they unloaded and occupied Companies A, E, and F during the last hours of the night. They were traveling light, carrying only a canteen, a C-ration, and a shelter-half, moving quickly and quietly to get to the next position. Traveling with them were the 81mm mortars of HQ Company, which made it all the harder to be silent and quick. By dawn they were just four miles away.

Once in the hills overlooking the Italian outpost, which was garrisoned by elements of the Centauro Division and elite Bersaglieri mountain troops, the Rangers camouflaged themselves and spent the day observing the Italians, waiting until dark to make their stealthy advance. They went forward as they had been taught, using terrain features to mask their movement until they were about a mile from the objective. Again, they waited.

An hour before midnight they moved.

At 600 yards the unit spread out into skirmish formation and went forward. Using colored lights shone backwards to keep position, the unit moved to within 200 yards before being discovered and fired upon. The well-trained men kept their cool, continuing forward under machinegun fire until they were close enough for a bayonet assault. When they came, there was no stopping them.

The Italians couldn't stand up to the screaming Rangers, and lost 75 soldiers to the overwhelming men they called "Black Death."

Other estimates range from 50 to 80.

The Rangers went into battle wearing black watch caps together with darkened faces, and hit at night. During his editing of this section MG (ret) John Raaen wondered if the watch cap was a precursor to the Black Beret. Could be.

There was also the matter of six mortar crews blasting the rear of the Italian camp, adding to the devastation and the impression of greater strength while killing more of the enemy. Carefully planned and executed, the raid was a stellar performance, giving the Italians a bitter taste of American soldiery.

The fighting at the camp perimeter was close; hand-to-hand some of the time. One Ranger is quoted as saying, "There was some pretty intense fighting there, but a man doesn't talk about what he does with a bayonet." The assault was over in 20 minutes, with Ranger losses at one killed and about 20 wounded.

Darby remembered a conversation on the radio with Captain Max Schneider, who was on the scene of the raid. "During the action I called Captain Schneider to find out how many prisoners he had taken. The captain replied, 'I think I have two, sir'. The field radio connection was bad, and I asked for a repeat. The two Italians tried to pull a getaway, and the Captain fired two quick shots, answering in the same breath, 'Well, sir, I had two prisoners.'"

At least a dozen Rangers were awarded the Silver Star for the successful Sened Raid, but not before the companies got out of danger. With only a couple of hours of darkness left, the men were still 12 miles from any kind of safety. With the idea of pursuit in their minds, the Rangers split up for the return trip, and the guards and their prisoners—11 men of the 10th Bersaglieri—were told they had better keep up.

The success was a morale-booster for the Rangers, but it was short and sweet because the Germans pushed armor through the Kasserine Pass and things went sour for the Allies.

Dernaia Pass

On Valentine's Day Darby was getting ready for whatever was to come next when word came down for the Rangers to leave the temporary camp at Gafsa. The Rangers were to be rear guard for the withdrawal of II Corps elements being pushed by a German armor thrust.

They hunkered down and waited, knowing Axis troops were coming on, reported by outposts to be moving in three columns. Darby sent some men out to take a look. A nervous group moved out to find the "enemy" was really a large herd of camels.

Still, they knew there was real armor out there—could, in fact, hear it clanking along—and had only basic light infantry anti-tank capability.

Though we cannot absolutely vouch for the accuracy of this statement by Darby, it is just too good to leave out. With the noise of tanks close by, Darby reportedly told his men, "If we get caught by the tanks, God help the tanks."

Relieved, the battalion moved out, heading for Kasserine Pass, but were sidetracked to Dernaia Pass astride the Tebessa road. Darby said the orders were four hours late arriving, so the Rangers were stuck out front on their own, with little knowledge of the enemy's whereabouts or strength. With the Axis on their heels, the Rangers headed for comparative safety at Dernaia Pass, but kept looking back to see if the German tanks were gaining. They finally made it, only to be told they must hold the pass, a task for which they were less than suited. Lacking heavy weapons and facing German and Italian tanks, the men dug in and waited. They would wait for almost two weeks.

Darby spread them out over a two-mile line in front of the pass and was told to hold at all costs to delay the Axis advance. The main attack was figured to come right through them.

There were other units around, mostly behind the Rangers, and several miles back. Artillery was in support, though, and the Rangers were depending on it.

This is a perfect example of the misuse of the battalion as line infantry.

As it turned out, the Axis forces tricked everybody and went around Dernaia to strike at Kasserine. The 1st Infantry Division took the hit, specifically the 168th Regimental Combat Team, and was forced to commit all reserves. Many brave American soldiers died that day.

Fortunately, the Rangers stayed put at Dernaia Pass, and actually got some rest when they weren't patrolling at night, as was the enemy. Short, small actions resulted, but nothing major. The set routine was to filter six patrols out about three miles, hooked to base by telephone wire, and let them talk back and forth to each other and HQ. Each patrol had a number and a certain position to occupy, so Darby knew where they all were and what they were doing all the time.

With little else to occupy them, the Rangers set up roadblocks on the Tebessa (highway) and bagged more than a few German and Italian prisoners and vehicles. Also on the agenda was a little artillery spotting, which had good results until the Germans decided to go kill the Ranger on the hill with the binoculars. They didn't, and Lieutenant George Sunshine got away.

It wasn't all "sunshine" during those February days. The Rangers were also shelled, bombed and strafed.

The counterattack by the Axis failed, even though Rommel had charge of the whole thing. It was too little, too late.

The 1st Battalion kept it up until March 1 when they were withdrawn to a rest area at the village of La Kouif where they hid their tents from air attack. The stand-down didn't last long, and soon the Rangers were back to battle.

The next stop was with the 1st Infantry Division, still under the II Corps, but with Fredendall replaced March 7 by the hard-charging Major General George S. Patton. Much shuffling of troops took place, with II Corps containing the 1st, 9th and 34th Infantry Divisions, plus the 1st Armored Division and the 13th Field Artillery Brigade as well as other support forces. The Rangers were signed on as "auxiliary troops."

The idea was to take Gafsa back from the enemy, expand from there, and take some airfields for the use of the US Twelfth Air Force. There was a lot of movement, and the Rangers were but a small part. Still, what they accomplished was highly necessary to the success of the whole.

During the planning for the return to Gafsa, Darby was half out of his mind with sickness, and his Exec, Herman Dammer, got things going. It was only when the unit moved that Darby left the hospital, still weak, and joined them.

Djebel el Ank—El Guettar

When the Allies rolled into Gafsa they found it empty. The huge flux of men and machines and equipment tried to find a place to stay, crowding in under the few trees, getting ready for the next push toward the town of El Guettar. Thought to be still occupied by the Germans, El Guettar had to be cleared before the 1st Division could advance.

The Rangers were given the task of finding out what was there, perhaps gathering a few prisoners on the way. They set out at night, found a way around the flank and came into El Guettar the night of March 18. It, too, was empty. The "good fortune" just meant the Axis forces had consolidated into hard-to-get-at positions, beginning with the pass at Djebel El Ank. Not knowing where the enemy was, US command sent the Rangers to find out, which they did at the rocky outcropping known as the Ank.

The Rangers were to act as flank protection for the 26th Infantry in an assault on the Italian blocking force. Taking the pass would open the way for the rest of the Army to spread out into two well-defined areas of battle in the plains beyond. It also meant the road forward would be open.

The Rangers went to work plying their unique talents and found a way past the roadblock through nearly impassable terrain. On March 20, the Rangers and a 4.2-inch mortar company wound through six miles of ravines and mountains and got behind and above the Italians.

Of the 1st Battalion, Darby said there were no missteps, no clanking of equipment, just a smooth transfer of force from one place to another. Done entirely in the darkness—with a little moonlight—the journey was punctuated by stops and starts, ups and downs where equipment had to passed hand-to-hand as quietly as possible. At dawn—the attack was set for 0600—the curtain rose on a flank/rear assault by the Rangers on a surprised enemy, accompanied by a frontal charge by the 26th RCT (Regimental Combat Team). The Ranger Force was situated on a plateau to the rear of the defenders, sharply outlined, and could look down upon the roadblock. Mortars fired into the defense below, but it wasn't long before enemy artillery was hitting Darby's force along the ridge. The commander sent a couple of Ranger squads downhill to silence the guns. The big guns weren't the only ones firing at the Rangers, however, and Darby reported he was told by Corporal Robert Bevan that the man was able to silence a machinegun at a range of 1,350 yards, using a Springfield '03 and a telescopic sight.

The Rangers and attached groups came ravaging down the hill, overcoming strong points as they struck them from behind. Hit from three sides at once, some of the Italians gave up and fled, but about 900 were captured, many of them caught by the Rangers.

The worn-down holdouts listened when Father Basil called to them to give up, and many did. Some even removed mines; an act that probably saved American lives.

By about 1400 hours, Darby reported to 1st Division that the valley was secured, thus giving American forces a firm left flank. The 1st moved into the mountains connecting all the small passes and towns that covered the rough terrain. Running south from Djebel el Ank, the ridges turned westward toward Djebel Berda, cutting the road from El Guettar to Gabes. By occupying the high ground, the Americans were across the path of the advancing Afrika Korps. Having continually worked south, the Allies had isolated the two German forces, threatening to keep them from linking up. El Guettar, for which the battle was named, was slightly north of Djebel el Ank, and northwest of Gabes.

The road between El Guettar and Gabes was the main route Rommel would have to follow. Gabes, on the coast, was about 40 miles from Djebel el Ank. The Axis forces needed Djebel el Ank open, and counterattacked viciously with a large force including three Panzer Grenadier and two Italian infantry divisions. To meet that thrust the American II Corps had the 1st and 9th Infantry Divisions and the 1st Armored Division. The Rangers, who were situated just north of the Gabes road, to the right of the 3rd Battalion of the 18th RCT, were also in the mix. The other two battalions of the 18th were five miles to the southeast, at Djebel Berda.

It was March 23, only the third day of the 21-day battle of El Guettar, and things were about to explode. Said Darby, "From the heights in our segment, the Rangers looked down on a developing attack of Germans in parade-ground formation."

The Germans were in plain view, though at a considerable distance, moving forward en masse. The 10th Panzer Division sent six battalions at the Rangers, two each of tanks, infantry, and artillery. Darby said 60 tanks followed the infantry in a scene reminiscent of Civil War attacks. "The Germans took no cover, seeming not to be aware of the almost certain death trap into which they were moving. I was never so wildly excited as when watching this mass of men and vehicles inching toward us."

American artillery began taking the Germans apart at about 1,500 yards, blowing huge holes in the mass of infantry. On they came, taking fearful losses, charging forward the last few hundred yards into concentrated fire. The Americans held, and the attack was broken.

The next day the Rangers were sent to assist the two battalions of the 18th RCT at Djebel Berda. At sundown the 18th was overwhelmed by German paratroopers fighting as infantry. The Rangers, located a short distance away on Hill 772, went down to help. Ranger Company D was left on the hill. A platoon of C Company worked its way around behind the Germans and directed accurate 18th Infantry cannon fire into the enemy, six rounds each from six guns. Platoon Leader Lt. Shunstrom later said, "We really blew hell out of the Germans."

By mid-afternoon the Germans caught on and went after the Rangers, causing them to withdraw from the observation point and Hill 772, the latter because of a lack of ammunition. The commander of the 18th asked if the Rangers could hold and got the standard answer— "Yes." But Darby did ask for a battalion to help out. He got part of one, enough to bolster his small force while the remainder of the 18th filtered back a couple of miles to rest and regroup. The Ranger group held the position for three more days, virtually alone and cut off, until relief came in the form of elements of the 9th Division on March 27.

During the period March 16-27, the Rangers were usually the decided underdog in most fights—and there were some doozies—but Darby said, "Through all kinds of combat, my men had fought with skill and cunning, losing only three killed and 18 wounded."

The ability of the British Eighth Army and Patton's II Corps to link up was paramount, and the opening of the pass at Djebel el Ank allowed that to happen. A small group of determined, well-trained soldiers had ripped a hole in the fabric of the Axis forces, and their buddies were pouring through it.

The Rangers were withdrawn from combat for patrolling duties, broken up into two-company units in three different places around Gafsa. There they stayed until the battle of El Guettar was over. For their heroic efforts in the battle of El Guettar, the men of the 1st Battalion were awarded the Presidential Unit Citation. The citation came from commendations made by General Terry Allen about the Rangers' part in the battle. Darby was given the Distinguished Service Cross.

April 17 saw the Rangers move by truck and train back to Oran, in Algeria.

Another excellent set of operations for the Rangers brought more notice than just from their adoring public. General Patton offered Darby a promotion to Colonel and his own regiment, but the focused Darby chose to remain with his battalion. Perhaps Darby had something else on his mind, like the formation of a Ranger Regiment with himself in command. It wasn't a bad idea, and he would eventually get most of what he wanted, but not all. First, there was the consideration of the invasion of Italy, starting with Sicily—Operation HUSKY.

As the Allied plans got more ambitious, so did the need for first, fast, and furious in terms of amphibious landings, which were still relatively new. The success of the Rangers through their willingness to fight in the line kept them in the forefront of operations, and Darby was directed to get some more Rangers into the fight. Thus were the 3rd and 4th Battalions born in mid-1943.

But, there were other specially trained groups out there, and requests for even more. By 1943, Allied interests were crawling out of the red and into the black, which changed the focus of the war effort from defense to offense. That meant invasion, amphibious landings, and destruction of static defenses such as coastal batteries and radar sites.

The Americans were pushing for an invasion of France, wanting a cross-channel effort to put troops in Europe, but the British had a few other things in mind. Reluctantly, the Americans agreed to hit Sicily first, followed by Italy, and secure Europe from the south before hitting with everything from the west. The idea was to take Italy out of the war, draw German divisions from Russia, and maybe get Turkey on the Allied team.

Trained But Not Used—29th Infantry Division Rangers

With the 1st Rangers in North Africa, someone was needed to fill the raiding slot left open by their departure, not to mention a group to spearhead any landings. To fill the bill, ETOUSA (European Theater of Operations, U. S. Army) created a new unit made up of troops from the II Corps. On September 30, 1942, a provisional Ranger battalion was put together in order to rotate officers and men through training, and then send them back to their units to spread that training around.

The problem was most American units were going away, and only the 29th Infantry Division was left in Britain. The 29th was a National Guard unit from Maryland and Virginia, and that's where the recruits came from. By December, Major Randolph Milholland was busy organizing the new unit. Whether by design or coincidence, Milholland used Darby's techniques for interviewing and selecting his soldiers. First the officers were chosen, then they chose the enlisted men, all volunteers. To lend some experience, a few men from Darby's 1st Battalion entered the unit and led the headquarters company and the two satellite companies that made up the entire structure.

The men of the 1st Battalion who went to the 29th were in addition to the men Darby would have to use from the 1st to supplement the new 3rd and 4th Battalions. Experienced men from the original battalion were getting scarce.

Initial training in place led to five weeks at the proving grounds of Achnacarry, which led to additional training with landings and raids. That carried past the New Year, and by spring of 1943 Milholland's Rangers were ready. All they needed was a mission, but getting one was a problem.

The 29th (aka 2nd Provisional Ranger Battalion) began with only two line companies and a HQ Company and would have to be beefed up and extra-equipped, but Marshall was still in charge, giving the go-ahead on the condition the 29th would be disbanded when a replacement unit came aboard. Thus was the 29th given full strength, though it would be short-lived.

The 29th Ranger Battalion was expanded to four companies and trained for two more months until May. During that time elements of the unit went with British Commandos in three separate raids in Norway. Attempting to take out a bridge, the stealthy unit was discovered early when a guide made noise on the approach and surprise was lost. No success there, but a three-day recon expedition was successful. One more try was not only unsuccessful, but also unnecessary when the proposed target, a remote command post, was found empty.

Training continued for the 29th with the addition of amphibious deployment, getting the unit ready for anything. So new and productive was the training that a film was produced for the units back in the States to study assault methods.

With the 29th honed to an edge in September, a mission was laid on to destroy a German radar site on the Ile d' Ouessant, off the coast of Brittany. The success of the raid led to a nose thumbing by the Rangers to the Germans when a helmet and cartridge belt were left behind, just to let them know who was on their turf.

The thinking in the planning minds was that elite forces such as the Rangers would be needed as a spearhead force in the cross-channel invasion landings to come, but there weren't enough special units to go around. Darby was tied up in the Mediterranean and Milholland's men were slated to be reabsorbed into their parent unit, the 29th, before D-Day.

More Rangers were needed, and though the planners knew it as early as fall of 1942, it was December before ETOUSA made the formal request for another battalion.

Though they performed well, the 29th was inactivated in October to make way for the 2nd Battalion coming across the ocean to fill the slot. The division of the same designation took in the men of the 29th, where they spread their hard-earned knowledge among their original comrades, which improved the whole unit.

Breaking up the Ranger unit didn't do much for the morale of those highly trained men. Why a place was not made for the unit as a whole is unknown, except there were only so many Ranger units allowed. Why build a unit in the States when one was already trained overseas? Go figure.

In a memo from Major Richard Fisk, Assistant Adjutant General, ETOUSA, the rationale for another unit was plain. "Experience has proven that specially trained units of this character are invaluable in landing operations, for the reduction of coastal defenses and similar missions."

Though the truth of those words seems beyond debate, there were plenty of old soldiers to take up the task. Chief of Army Ground Forces, Lt. General Lesley McNair, had this to say, "Hell, we rehearsed trench raids in the last war, only we didn't call them Commandos."

Under McNair, special training for special units took a big hit. Commando-style training at the Amphibious Training Center was discontinued, as was the Second Army Ranger School. At a time when good men were desperately needed to fill the ranks of line units, the feeling among the old school was decidedly against the formation of any more Ranger units, which would take the best men from units already up and running.

3RD AND 4TH RANGER BATTALIONS COME ON LINE

Other things happened in 1943 to bring more Rangers to the scene, as more battalions were authorized in the Mediterranean, with Darby at the helm. With the invasion of Sicily imminent, planners knew Rangers would be needed, and asked Darby how many battalions he thought the effort would take. Ever the optimist, Darby figured 15 might do. The planners thought Darby had been in the sun too long and gave him three.

What if he had only asked for three?

The 29th was ready in Ireland, but could not be moved out of that theatre until the 2nd Battalion, forming in America, was ready to take its place. Thus, Darby had to put together two battalions virtually from scratch. Choosing officers and non-coms carefully to head the new units, he began his search for suitable talent.

For his part, Darby didn't want to go through the same process as before when he selected men in Ireland. Wanting no misfits this time, he chose to go hunting for recruits rather than have a bunch of thugs dumped on him. Darby had little choice but to start where he was, in Oran. He had posters up anywhere soldiers might be, and made speeches where he could, speaking the truth about how hard Ranger life could be. He also used a goodly dose of patriotism and pure male machismo. Still, it was a selection process, and Darby would only take those he wanted. He wrote, "…I proceeded to select the men I needed because I believed that the best men don't always volunteer."

The two new battalions, the 3rd and 4th, were commanded by Major Herman Dammer and Lt. Colonel Roy Murray, respectively. Darby, having turned down a promotion and a regimental command, stayed at the helm of the 1st Battalion, as well as overseeing the whole Ranger Force.

To form a nucleus for the new units, elements of each of the six companies of 1st Battalion were used to fill critical TO&E slots so each battalion had a core of experienced men.

Murray took some men and toured the bars and recreation areas looking for the right material, then made the pitch.

Instead of going to existing line units, or units which would soon see action, Darby focused on new men coming in, or those working in the rear in Algeria and French Morocco. Still, unit commanders of Ranger recruits had to release the men, and some of them weren't too happy about it. They complained the Rangers were taking the best men, a problem that plagued the early Rangers with each expansion, as it did in 1974 with the formation of the 1st Battalion, 75th Infantry (Ranger).

An exhaustive effort brought about 10 percent of those contacted into the training program. To most of those men, the idea of being part of an elite unit, or simply being adequately readied for combat was enough to sign on.

Of only one-in-10 who would even consider subjecting themselves to the training and the subsequent risk in combat, how many would actually do well? The type of soldier needed had to be rooted out of the general Army population, and could be stuck in any role, as is still the case. The man might be working as a cook—at least one was—but still have the physical and mental reserves to do the job, as well as the willingness to try. Today the Rangers are well known, but back then most recruits had to be told about them before they could decide to volunteer.

Darby assembled his recruits on a plateau above the port of Nemours, Algeria, where Herman Dammer set up a replica of the British Commando Depot. For six weeks, speed marches, climbing exercises, weapons familiarization, night operations, and amphibious training wore the new men down and gave Darby and his officers a chance to see what they had. The training was altered somewhat from that of the 1st Battalion because of that unit's combat experience in North Africa.

The men practiced night amphibious operations with the Navy on a beach similar to Gela on the Sicilian coast—their next port of call. The instructors liked to use a lot of live ammunition during these landings, a tactic that seemed to increase with each new battalion's training.

Darby and his officers needed tough, courageous men, and one of the ways to test the recruits was to send them down a "nearly vertical cliff slide of some 600 feet to a beach below."

That would do it.

Raymond Noel Dye

Noel Dye arrived in North Africa as a replacement and became the youngest member of the Rangers at that time. He landed at Sicily and stayed with Darby's men through several wounds, making it to the devastation near Cisterna after Anzio.

His story is broken into sections throughout this piece, taped at Uchee Creek, Fort Benning, April 25, 2004.

We came on LSTs [Landing Ship, Tank], straight from the States. Our ship got sunk just south of Bermuda. We hit a big heavy storm there and it broke our ship in half and damaged ten or fifteen others. I think we lost two or three of them. We all went into Bermuda and stayed there for a couple of weeks until they got another convoy up of LSTs. We couldn't go with a regular convoy because the LSTs are too slow. We never had any planes or any submarines or anything bother us all the way to North Africa, all the way to Oran.

At that time, I was in the Armored force. I went to the Repple-Depple and they were going to assign me to whatever. I was 18 years and four months old.

I went down the dock and over on the side was a whole bunch of tanks and armored cars and half-tracks, and they were all blown up and burned up and they were shipping them back to the States on the empty freighters to try to see what they could do with them, I don't know. They were all lined up, 50 of those damn things on that dock. And that was what I was supposed to be going into!

Old Colonel Darby and his boys came along. There was an announcement on the loudspeaker that morning. Said anybody wants to go listen to the Rangers, they were looking for volunteers. I thought, well, I didn't know anything about the Rangers, never heard of them, but I didn't want in those tanks. I went out to listen to them, and I held my hand up.

The raid on Sened Station had already happened, and Darby made sure to talk about it to the listening men. Some of the men had heard of the prowess of the Rangers, others had not. Darby told them straight out that serving with the Rangers was hazardous duty.

They were good about it [telling of hazardous duty], but after seeing those blown-up tanks it sounded pretty easy to me. I was always a good marksman, and I was in pretty good health then.

I went out to Nemours [border of Morocco and Algeria] and they put me in F Company of the 1st Ranger Battalion. At that time they had already split them up into 1st, 3rd and 4th Battalions.

When I was still in North Africa we went out and trained, climbing cliffs and stuff like that. We did a 10-mile speed march every morning [carrying everything].

I got malaria first, but I didn't go to the aid station because I didn't want to get kicked out and have to go back to the armored force. So I kept on going, then I got diarrhea, but I still kept on going. Then one day coming back from climbing the cliffs, we were marching back, I just passed out. They took me to the hospital.

Dye remembers waking up in the hospital briefly and seeing a medic insert a syrette of some kind of drug into his IV line. He was told later that his heart stopped when the drug got in his bloodstream. He has no memory of the episode.

I woke up in a weapons carrier, it was night, bouncing all over the road. I started moving around and when the two guys up front saw I was alive they stopped and came back and checked me. Then we turned around and went somewhere else.

It is probable that Dye was being taken to a graveyard. Oops!

When I woke up next I was in a big hospital. I stayed there for a while and then one day they came through and said, "Anybody here from the Rangers?" I said yes and they said to get dressed and get ready because the Rangers are moving out. They found my clothes and put me in a jeep and took me back to the Ranger camp. When we got there only two tents were left. Everything else was cleared out. They had big holes dug in the ground and they were burning everything left in there.

The only ones left there was F Company, 4th Battalion [that's how he went from 1st to 4th—by the luck of the draw]. Captain Nye was there. There was one pyramidal tent still there. The jeep driver handed him the papers. He looked at me and said, "What are we going to do with him?" I looked like crap, I was still sick. He finally said, "Altieri, you take care of him."

James Altieri, then a Buck Sergeant, went on to become the noted author of "Rangers Lead the Way," the story of Darby's Rangers.

Altieri says, "What do I do?" and Captain Nye says, "I don't know, just take care of him."

They were busy. So Altieri went out of the tent and I followed him. Got about 50 feet from the tent and I said, "What am I supposed to do?" He says, "You stay within sight or hearing of me, and that's it." He turned around and said that to me and then just went on walking and I followed him. I followed him after that clear to Italy. If it wasn't for him, I wouldn't be here. He saved my life more than once.

Sicily and Beyond

With initial training at an end, the invasion of Sicily occupied the next block of Ranger history. The three units were split up, the 1st and the 4th going to Algiers with Darby, and Dammer's 3rd joining up with 3rd Division around Bizerte, in northern Tunisia. The 3rd Division had not seen Rangers before, but Darby's group was on familiar ground when they re-attached to the 1st Division, part of Patton's Seventh Army. Said Darby, "By this time Terry Allen's 'Famous First' had come to think of my Rangers as their own special spearhead troops."

The Rangers referred to themselves as the "point" force because they were out front all the time. Intensive preparations took place in all three battalions when word of the next mission came down. Mock-ups of Sicilian targets were built and used for practice. There were a lot of new faces following Darby and they weren't like the old faces. These faces were fresh, without the scars and cares of combat. Darby, Dammer and Murray set about to put some creases in all that smooth skin.

In the early hours of July 9, 1943, a flotilla of more than 450 ships put to sea carrying a Sicilian nightmare in their holds. The 1st and 4th Battalions, beefed up by the 83rd Chemical Mortar Battalion—with new 4.2-inch rifled mortars—and an engineer battalion, were aboard the USS Dickman, HMS Albert, and HMS Charles, waiting to land as part of the 1st Division on the south-central coast of an island about the size of Vermont.

The US 3rd Division would land on the American left, with the attached 3rd Rangers at Licata. The 1st Division would land in the center at Gela with the 1st and 4th Battalions, and the 45th ID would take the American right.

At the southeastern tip of the island the British Eighth Army under Montgomery would land and move north and northwest to link up with Patton coming around the edge of the island—west, then north, then east.

Sicily is just 140 miles long and 110 miles wide, so between the American 70-mile beachfront and the British Army front to the east, more than half the southern coast of the island came under attack. Nearly half-a-million Allied soldiers were ready to do battle with about 350,000 German and Italian soldiers for control of the area.

Seven divisions were used in the assault. Only five were used during D-Day.

The idea was for the Americans to protect Montgomery's left flank while he made a run for Messina to his north after taking Syracuse in his initial landings. However, US forces were rarely static and cleared much of the rest of the island while doing so. The port of Messina on the northern coast, due north of the landing sites, was just two miles from the southernmost tip of Italy—an escape point for the enemy the Allies desperately wanted to close, especially since so many of the enemy escaped to Sicily over the 90 watery miles from Africa.

Though the Italians were in many ways subservient to Hitler, they had managed to keep overall command in their own country, which translated to Sicily. They were also to take the brunt of the damage since General Guzzoni had but three German divisions to back his 10 Italian divisions.

The Plan

General Allen put Darby at the head of Force X, composed of the 1st and 4th Ranger Battalions, a company of the 83rd Mortars, and a battalion of the 39th Engineers.

The plan was for the Rangers to attack on both sides of a 900-foot pier jutting out into the water from the small port of Gela (30,000 population), which sat atop a 150-foot hill. Behind Gela was a wide plain, perfect for tank maneuvers.

The 1st Battalion was to hit left of the pier, seize that side of Gela, and remove the threat of some coastal guns on a rise at the rear of town. The 4th would land on the right and take that side of Gela.

Twenty miles to the west, Dammer's 3rd Rangers were to hit near Licata, a small port town comparable in size to Gela. The 3rd was part of General Truscott's 3rd Infantry Division and would land on the inside left of four beachheads.

The dark hours of July 9 were no fun for the boys at sea. A good storm hit and made a lot of men seasick, but the weather cell played out before the 0300 landing time. Italian Commander Guzzoni had done what he could, pushing troops and tanks toward the southern coast. The only things Guzzoni didn't know were exactly when, exactly where or how many.

The Attack

Darby's Ranger Force X hit Sicily in the time-honored way—first, fast and furious.

Dammer's 3rd Battalion got their feet wet five minutes early, coming in companies-abreast about three miles west of Licata, at a little place called San Mollarella. Dammer took A, B, and C Companies left, and his XO, Alvah Miller, took D, E, and F to the right.

Company A went left after the enemy on the high ground while B and C fanned out to take machinegun positions and other strong points along the beach. On the right D, E, and F Companies were doing much the same. D Company got a little way inland and took out supporting enemy mortars while E and F Companies moved east about a mile to get some machineguns on a point of high ground.

Soon the 3rd Battalion had checked off every objective, enabling the 2nd Battalion, 15th Infantry to move smoothly ashore.

Unfortunately, the 3rd Rangers were "thanked" by being put in reserve—right under the enemy's bombs hitting the port of Licata. Between bombs and strafing runs, the men of the 3rd took significantly more casualties than they suffered hitting the beach.

The 1st and 4th Battalions landed on a mined beach at the same time the 3rd was assaulting 20 miles west. After coming in half lost as a result of good storm swells and an absent submarine to guide them, the Navy came to the rescue in the form of a second wave-guide and finally led the boats to shore. The confusion caused boats to land out of sequence in some spots and a lot of craft jammed the beach at once, but not before taking heavy fire from shore, much of it directed by searchlights that were subsequently shot out by Naval gunfire.

At one point, a landing craft got hung up on a sandbar and many of the occupants, men of E Company, 1st Battalion, jumped into the water, thinking it shallow. It was not, and 17 men were dragged down by their heavy loads and drowned—one-fourth of the company.

The landing was heavily contested before the first man set foot on the beach. Rangers were firing from the boats, using rockets and small arms to back-trail the incoming rounds. While passing down the length of the pier, the center section was blown by the enemy, but no one was hurt.

The beach was loaded with anti-tank and anti-personnel mines and obstacles, and criss-crossed with machinegun lanes of fire. The Rangers were taking some hits coming ashore, and D Company, 4th Battalion lost every officer and had to be led by a wounded Sergeant.

First Sergeant Randall Harris, a portion of his intestines exposed, took charge and pulled the survivors of D Company inland, despite his wounds. He received the Distinguished Service Cross (DSC) and a battlefield commission for his effort.

The 1st Battalion landed to the west of the pier, coming in with C, D, E and F Companies first, followed closely by A and B Companies.

While the 4th Battalion was fighting its way into Gela's town square, A and B of the 1st were moving through the western edge of town toward the high ground beyond to take out some coastal batteries and mortars. The two companies moved in column through the narrow streets, killing Italians as they went, one company on one side of the street, the second covering them from the other side. Reaching the gun positions, the Rangers got in among the crews and that was the end of that problem. A bonus was the capture of three 77mm guns—with sights removed—that were immediately given Ranger gun crews to learn how to bore-sight the tubes.

The mass of 1st Battalion troops took the left, or west side of Gela and moved to the center of town to link up with the men of the 4th. House to house, street-to-street, the Americans pushed through the town.

By 0800, Gela was in American hands. Defensive positions were established to defend the newly captured town, and it wasn't long before the enemy smashed against them.

Reeling and uncoordinated from the onslaught, General Guzzoni's forces had trouble bringing a decent counterattack to bear. For one thing, a lucky shell landed on Guzzoni's headquarters and severed communication. He didn't know what was going on half the time.

A gaggle of Italian tanks (Renault-type) came rumbling toward Gela from the north, supported by infantry, but fire from the sea tore into them, disrupting their advance. A group of nine tanks stopped about three miles out, left four machines under some trees, and sent five on ahead, unsupported by infantry. That was a bad mistake, because the Rangers were waiting for them.

When the tanks came into the Ranger circle they were taken under ferocious attack by men crawling on the tanks with grenades, bazooka rounds coming in, even 15-pound blocks of TNT dropped on them from rooftops.

Darby recounted an experience with one of the tanks coming up the main street of town, with Darby and his men in a jeep coming the other way. The Rangers turned into an alley with just enough of the jeep sticking out so the mounted machinegun could be fired. Darby used an entire belt of ammunition, bouncing it off the tank without injury, but the machine turned away. Darby then got a little 37mm anti-tank gun, mounted it behind his jeep, and went looking for the tank. He found it, fired three times, and blew it up. The surviving Italians, probably bleeding from the ears after the pounding, withdrew. The four tanks remaining at a distance had 4.2-inch mortar rounds fall on them at Ranger direction, leaving one wrecked.

Badly battered but being pushed forward, the tanks came back for another try, only to have the captured 77mm guns used against them. The attack was broken up.

Enemy strong points and troop masses were hit by American artillery with good effect. The four-deuce mortars were firing white phosphorus rounds with better accuracy than the eight-inch guns of offshore cruisers.

German tanks, artillery and air power were a constant threat during the landings, which continued through the night. Soldiers of both sides rested where they could, very aware that dawn would bring death to many of those who made it through the fiery night, and so it did. Gela and surrounding areas became graveyards for more Americans than anywhere else in Sicily.

Noel Dye

First we went up to Algeria from Nemours to the city of Bel Sed where the French Foreign Legion was. We had a little scuffle there because they still hadn't decided which side they were going to be on. Then we went to Tunisia. We didn't really have any trouble there, except the Germans strafed and bombed us. The Germans would hit us in the daytime, then the Italians would come over and bomb us at night. About a week before we left to go to Italy [Sicily] they moved us up to [another port] and put us on British transports. Our troop was put on the *Prince Charles*. We got bombed one night there, and got pretty well damaged. A couple of nights later we took off and went to sea.

We landed at Gela, and the 4th Battalion, F Company, our objective was to take Cathedral Square [right in the middle of town]. That was our number one priority. After that we were to go to the left up on the hills and get behind all those coastal defenses up there.

We got off the boat and went ashore, had no problems, hit no mines or anything, but E Company, on our right, got blown all to hell. They hit every mine there was planted out there. Our company went right up the street into the town and never hit a mine or anything. We got shot at a lot, of course. It was dark, pitch-black, except for a few lights of the town. It was all done at night. We were finished with our job before daylight.

Anyway, we went up about three or four blocks and then we started running into people in the street, and boy, they were shooting at us from the second story windows. We were shooting back at the flashes whenever we saw one.

At the time, Dye was the designated runner for the company. The rest of the men carried M1 rifles, but Dye was given a carbine, partly because of his position, partly because he was still sick with malaria. "Those guys really took care of me," he said. "You couldn't ask for a better bunch. That's why I went AWOL twice and went back to them." His AWOLs were from hospitals, one of which was all the way back in North Africa. He showed me the papers signed by the hospital staff saying he was leaving without consent. He went AWOL to go back to combat, rejoining the 4th Rangers in Italy, before the assault on Anzio.

I got my first Purple Heart there at Gela. We went up the street and came to a corner of Cathedral Square. Just as we turned the corner, me and Bennett [a scout]—I was a little behind him, and Altieri was right beside us. I was closest to the wall, and we went around the corner and ran into two Italian [soldiers] and they shot us both. It killed Bennett and got me right in the chest. It was pistols.

Dye said the actions of the next few moments were told to him later. He was propped up against the building wall and Bennett was lying across one of his feet. Dye does remember hearing the scout's last few breaths. "He was shot through the lung." Altieri killed both Italians.

Two of the guys [Ken Connors and Charles Grogan] grabbed me under the armpits, picked me up and started dragging me toward the beach. It was still pitch-dark and they were still shooting at us, but not as bad. They ran into litter bearers coming up from the beach and put me on a litter. My buddies went back up.

They carried me down to the beach and laid me in a line against a little wall along the road. The beach was on one side, the road on the other. They had a line of litters there. I just lay there and watched. It was easy to see [the ships firing]. It was like lightning all the time.

Dye was hit square in the middle of his sternum but the round didn't penetrate the bone.

As you know, we carried our grenades in our mess gear pouch on our chest. The bullet I got hit with went into that pouch and hit one of those fragmentation grenades, ricocheted off of it and hit me in the chest. Well, by that time it was gone—it was only a 6.25mm Berretta [about .32 caliber] or whatever they carried.

I was lying there on the stretcher and the doctor came along. And Colonel Murray came by, checking on his men. The doctor came by, and it was the doctor, Colonel Murray, and an aid man there. The Doc was working on me. After a while he turned to the aid man and said, "Well, patch him up and send him back." That woke me up. He opened my hand up and tucked this thing in there and said, "Here's you a souvenir." He had pinched that bullet against my bone and he had actually just squeezed it out.

The next day we were looking at my grenade pouch and you could see where the bullet had hit one of the little pineapples on that grenade and bounced off. We had four fragmentation grenades sitting [vertically] on each side and on top we had two concussion grenades. If it had hit one of them it would have blown me in half.

Fragmentation grenades were sometimes called "pineapples" because of their serrated surface.

It was just getting daylight when I got back to the outfit there at Cathedral Square. Altieri and the guys had already cleaned the whole Square out, except for one government building over on the left. Altieri…didn't know I'd been gone. He was up in the cathedral cleaning it out. They were shooting at us from the [top] of the cathedral over there, so they had to clean the whole thing out. There was one building left over there so he told me and Ken Connors to go up on the second floor, and he told others to go to different floors. We went up and went through it and found nothing, except one guy shot a mirror because he saw himself.

Our next job was to go up to the left and clean out the rest of the stuff up there [coastal batteries], or make sure it was cleaned out. That was the job of one of the other companies, but we went in behind them.

At that point in the interview, Dye pulled out a large old book and showed me a photograph taken of his company going "up to the left" after Cathedral Square. The book is an original volume written by James Altieri soon after WWII. Dye and Altieri are shown in a posed shot during that mission. Dye carried a carbine (a light weapon) but the photographer told him, "That's not a weapon." Dye was photographed carrying a Thompson submachinegun borrowed from his buddy, Charles Roby. Things got serious soon after that.

After we made sure everything was safe up there, we looked out and saw the Germans had lined up a whole division of tanks out there in the plains of Gela. They were coming in to try to drive us out between Licata and Gela. This was only the second day and they wanted us out of there. We could see them good. They were just out of reach of everything, even Naval shells. Seemed like the line went from horizon to horizon. Damndest line of tanks I ever saw. Ahead of them were these medium tanks; they were French Renaults with Italians in them. When we looked out across the plains the Germans were on our right and in the center, and the Italians were on our left.

Renault tanks came in first. They were little, but they were better than our light tanks, I'll tell you that. They were beautiful tanks. They came in and were running around through the town. As we got down there, one of them came out of Cathedral Square and up the road up the hill [the one the Rangers were coming down]. There were buildings on one side of the road and nothing but sand and cactus on the other side. Altieri was leading his platoon; only we were on the sandy side of the road. The 2nd Platoon was on the other side.

A tank pulled up [close to Dye's position] and spun around slow, looking for something to shoot at. Everybody hid back, and Captain Nye said bring up a bazooka. There was no ammunition for it. We had nothing to shoot at that tank with. We were lying on the ground hiding behind some little prickly-pear cactus. That's all we had.

For whatever reason, I was closest to the tank [about 60 feet], lying there behind some little cactus. He'd have wiped the whole platoon out if he'd seen us. Altieri says, "Dye, can you hit it with a grenade?" I said yeah. He said, "What do you have?"

I'd already used up all my fragmentation grenades. All I had left was one concussion grenade. He said to see if I could hit it, so I screwed the top off and threw it like a football. I ducked down immediately because the tank just took a fit. He spun the whole body of the tank around, trying to see where it came from. It must have sounded like hell inside that tank. Those things are bad.

Then he calmed down and sat real still and slowly turned that turret around, so I knew he was hunting. Altieri asked for more grenades, but see, we had been fighting for two nights and we were getting low on everything. Finally, from way back, maybe 50 feet behind me, another guy had a grenade. Those boys threw that concussion grenade from one to the other, up to me again.

I threw it and hit him again, and this time he just revved that motor up, opened the trap door in the bottom of the tank and pushed two dead bodies out of there. Then he took off, went past us. We had nothing to shoot at him with.

From talking with other WWII Rangers, I learned it is possible the two men were already dead inside the tank from other causes.

Getting Off The Beach

The morning of July 11 was not a good time to be around Gela. German tanks, moving ahead without close infantry support, hit all along the beachhead, and particularly hard in front of the 1st Division. At one point a breakthrough in the 26th Infantry section had the big tanks so close to the beach that Naval guns couldn't be used against them for fear of hitting our own men.

Much of that action was to the west of Gela, but the Rangers weren't sitting still. A battalion of Italian infantry came marching in formation down the road to Gela, aiming for the position on the northwest corner occupied by A and B Company, 1st Battalion. The rest of 1st Battalion was occupied fighting tanks. Captain Lytel, in command of the small force, rounded up everyone he could and got ready to fight 500 men with just over 100. Mortar fire was slowing the enemy, but not stopping them—indeed, they were firing back effectively.

Then, out of the blue, a Navy spotter showed up and asked if he could help. Soon the six-inch shells of the cruiser *Savannah* were pounding the Italians into so much meat. When the shelling lifted, the surviving enemy soldiers were drunk with shock and some 400 surrendered without firing another round.

About mid-day 18 German tanks hit Gela but were forced back by mortar, artillery and Naval fires called in by Rangers. The ships did awesome damage to several counterattacks during the first days around Gela, and trained Rangers directed much of that fire.

The next day, the 12th, General Patton decorated Darby with the Distinguished Service Cross and offered him command of the 180th Regiment of the 45th Infantry Division. The command carried a promotion to full Colonel, but for the second time, Darby turned down advancement if it meant leaving his Rangers.

The 1st Battalion was sent up the road from Gela toward Butera in order to take some high ground along the way. The enemy was entrenched on both sides of a pass and wouldn't be easy to move. At that time Darby's force included his control of the 1st Battalion, 41st Armored Infantry, which he sent to attack a small fort at San Nicola to the left of the pass. Ranger Companies D and F were sent to grab the area on the right. The fighting engineers were in on it, too, as well as support from the four-deuce mortars.

Striking before dawn on the 12th, the Rangers moved through enemy fire and accomplished their mission objective, but the regular infantry got lost in the dark and were caught in the open on the side of the hill at day break. The Rangers were on top of a hill opposite and could see the damage their exposed comrades were taking. They could also see a battery of five guns in the valley below them, and called for Naval fire delivered from seven miles out by the *Savannah*. The good ship obliged, nailing the fort of San Nicola with a few dozen rounds in one minute, tearing apart the defenses enough for the American ground forces to finish the job.

Butera

About eight miles north from the beach and nearly three-quarters of a mile up sat the little town of Butera. Between vertical cliffs and sharp ridges the approach to Butera was all but impossible save for one heavily defended, winding road rising into the clouds.

Butera had been by-passed by attackers before this. Figuring to starve the garrison out rather than assault straight up the road, armies of the past had let the town go. However, during the invasion of Sicily by the Allies, there were enemy engines of destruction that could rain death from great distances and be fairly accurate—if someone were upon the soil of Butera, watching the plains below for movement. Butera had to have an American flag flying over it before American men and machines could safely cross the plain or be in the open anywhere within several miles of the eagle's perch.

Of course, a handful of Rangers were given the job that ancient armies would only shrug and pass by. Darby undertook to reduce the town (fortress) by pounding it with aerial and Naval fires, but allowed just one company—E Company, under Captain Charles Shunstrom—to go up and see what was on the road.

Shunstrom was known as a fighter. He was the loader for the little anti-tank gun Darby used in Gela when working against the tanks.

The rest of the battalion stayed back, but stayed ready in case an opening was found. Darby made sure there was plenty of artillery standing by if needed by his point company.

Shunstrom and his men climbed the winding roadway as quietly as possible in the darkness and got within the Italian defensive system before they were discovered and fired upon. The first action cost the lives of one of the two platoon leaders and his RTO (radioman), but the offending weapon was quickly eliminated, as were others.

A gap in the defenses was found by flank recon and the company went forward under marching fire until close enough for bayonets. One platoon found some German officers trying to get the Italians to fight, but gave it up as a lost cause and beat a hasty retreat. The Italians surrendered.

The fortress town of Butera, a place thought to be nearly impregnable for years, had been taken by one short company of Rangers, less than 50 men.

Marching fire was a relatively new thing in those days. As opposed to fire-and-maneuver, marching fire had the men walking forward while firing their weapons at least once every three paces or so. The concentrated fire of such an action not only suppresses fire on the other side, but it keeps men moving, albeit widely separated, making them harder to hit and giving them more confidence of success. The traditional fire-and-maneuver tends to get groups and individuals pinned down once they stop moving forward.

"To halt under fire is folly. To halt under fire and not fire back is suicide. Move forward under fire."—source unknown, but wise

Porto Empedocle

Meanwhile, to the west, Patton was moving on, his sights set on Palermo, but first there were smaller towns along the way for the Seventh Army to gobble up. On July 15, the 3rd Ranger Battalion was attached to the 7th Infantry Regiment and directed to move west and take the area between Licata and Porto Empedocle.

A five hour night march with all six companies in line astern brought them to a roadblock with teeth—riflemen up high, machineguns down low—and Rangers were taking heavy fire. Of course, being Rangers, they attacked. Within about an hour the 165 Italian soldiers that still lived were taken to the "rear" under guard.

Early the next morning, the 3rd moved on toward Montaperto, the next step to Porto Empedocle. Encountering a highway, the Rangers were delighted to see a small convoy coming toward them. Everybody hid until 10 motorcycles—with sidecars—and a couple of trucks came abreast of the waiting guns. When perhaps 200 Rangers opened up at one time there was a lot of damage on the receiving end. When the dust settled 40 more prisoners were garnered. That same firepower, plus the 10 mortars the battalion carried, was used a little later to destroy some artillery batteries and take out other enemy positions, producing more prisoners, including 20 officers.

Dammer's battalion moved on beyond Montaperto to the coastal high ground that held Porto Empedocle. By mid-afternoon they were there. The town was in two parts due to a ravine down the middle. The 3rd split up, with A, B, and C Companies under Dammer going east, and D, E, and F Companies under Captain Miller going west. The mortars were set up about 600 yards to the rear, or north.

It was not an easy fight, especially for Miller's group. Heavy opposition slowed them, but didn't stop them. On either side of the ravine the sound of gunfire and explosions echoed back and forth as the Rangers rammed through the defenses.

The survivors of six companies, perhaps 350 men, took the town in less than two hours, including fighting through the streets and buildings. The total prisoner count for the day ran to 675 Italians and some 90 Germans.

The 3rd Battalion established a perimeter—using some captured weapons—began construction of a prisoner holding area, and waited. The drive forward by the 3rd Battalion had left them so far out in front they were virtually alone. Mortar rounds were scarce, and they were almost out of food. An Allied airplane appeared, dropping leaflets demanding the surrender of the port, not knowing the Rangers were there. Naval shellfire began to land close to Ranger positions.

There are a couple of accounts of this action. At issue is whether the airplane dropped leaflets or whether it was simply a spotter plane. Either way, the Rangers were in a real hurry to let someone know they were there.

The 3rd had only short-range radios and couldn't communicate at any distance, but impressive efforts were made to communicate any way they could. One account has it that oil drums were put in the water to spell out the word "Yank."

An alert pilot finally figured it out and went away, returning with a second plane that set down on the water. Major Dammer took a seat on board for the short trip to the cruiser *Philadelphia* to straighten things out and get word of the victory to Truscott.

What the Rangers had accomplished spoke well of their training and leadership, which gave more credence to the value of such a unit. The 3rd had operated more or less on its own in the operation, going forward in advance of the main party and executing reconnaissance and combat flawlessly.

A week into the invasion, July 17, the Rangers took a week or so off in preparation for the coming assault on Messina. The 1st and 4th Battalions went into rest mode just south of Palermo, in Corleone, and prepared for the next phase.

The 3rd Battalion had been resting during the push to Palermo, and was put back into action as part of the 3rd Division in a move eastward toward Messina. Darby made a statement that while Army communiqués took small notice of the many fights along the way, some of them were heavy-duty and hard on the troops. American units, often with Rangers in the van, crept forward.

Patton's drive across Sicily was undeniable, with the main body of Seventh Army troops spearing along the coast as if tracing an outline of the island, working northwest to Marsala, then making the quick turn to north and east to cover the northern coast, with Messina in the east as the main objective. The 1st and 4th Ranger Battalions acted in support of the whole, guarding the left flank of the 2nd Armored Division as it smacked Palermo.

At that time those battalions were attached to the 2nd Armored Division. The 3rd Infantry Division got to Palermo first, and the Rangers were not used heavily in that attack.

During that time Darby was again offered a promotion to Colonel and a regiment of the 45th Division, but he declined again, saying, "I felt I could do more good with my Ranger boys than I could with a regiment in a division."

Darby was a Rangers' Ranger, no doubt. Not only did he refuse personal advancement to stay with his battalions, he also wrote at least one letter to Eisenhower requesting the formation of a Ranger Regiment. He wanted permanency, but it would not happen for another 30 years.

To the southeast, Montgomery's Eighth Army was pushing north and west, forcing the Italians and Germans deeper into the mountains and towns for defense. The Americans attacked north from the port of Gela to envelop the enemy between the two forces. The Rangers were all going the other way at the time, turning the western corner of the island to come to Palermo.

At that time, Darby's X Force included two Ranger Battalions, the 39th Regimental Combat Team, and a battalion of 155mm artillery, known as "Long Toms." Unfortunately, some of those units were scattered and Darby couldn't find all of his troops in the beginning.

The night of July 20, X Force was ordered to advance along the coastal road with the eventual intent of capturing Marsala. Darby and a few men got in a jeep and went looking for the 39th, finding them some distance away about 0300. A couple of hours later the X Force finally advanced, taking the town of Castelvetrano against fairly light resistance on the 22nd. Two more days found the task force in Marsala, where two battalions of Rangers joined with the 82nd Airborne Division. Together they took Trapani, and then made for San Guiseppe, a little south of Palermo, where Americans were then in residence. The X Force and the 82nd found themselves burdened by 12,500 prisoners with their supply base 40 miles away. Darby took every opportunity to rid himself of the POWs, but it took a while. The task force then moved into Palermo, and was disbanded.

The enemy line was falling apart under the weight of the Allied advance, but the Axis forces were putting up stiff resistance as they fought to extricate their troops to the Messinian peninsula, where they had a chance of getting away to Italy. That ferocious rear-guard action slowed the Allies, who were divided by terrain into two groups. Much of the fighting was done at high altitudes in impossible terrain, allowing the Axis forces to set plenty of ambushes, forcing the Allies to conquer one ridge at a time.

The Rangers were joined by a 75mm pack artillery outfit and told to load the guns on mules for a march into the mountains. Darby, being the only one with artillery and mule experience, did his best to figure out how to do such a thing. In the dark, with much cursing and grumbling and fumbling around, Darby managed to get one gun broken down into individual weight loads and loaded on mules. There was not enough of the right kind of rope, so four-inch hawsers had to be unraveled and wrapped into smaller lines with wire. Once the demonstration was over, Darby gave the job to a junior officer, noting the job got done during the night, but no two mules were loaded the same way.

The 3rd Rangers were shuffled around from command to command while being put where they could do the most good, although by that time they were carrying supplies and equipment on 50 mules. Darby rode a mule named "Rosebud" a good bit of the time. The

3rd Division kept after the enemy, going through small towns and mountain ridges until they took a town named Patti, about 35 miles from Messina.

The enemy retreat began about August 11, with Hitler taking personal charge. No hold-or-die order this time, just get them out of there—and somehow, they did. The Army Air Force and the US Navy did not wreak havoc in the Strait of Messina, allowing four German divisions to escape, plus about 70,000 Italians.

Messina fell on August 17, 1943, 38 days after the landings. Italy sat close, brooding, waiting for the onslaught.

The Axis lost some 100,000 men as prisoners, and the dead were piled high.

US killed and wounded approached 7,000. The British lost 12,000 more.

Italy—The Bloody Boot

After a lot of high-level haggling over where to hit next and who would do the hitting, Roosevelt and Churchill, with Marshall and Stalin in the wings, decided to schedule the invasion of Europe via France for 1944. But first, the British wanted to continue gnawing at the enemy's flanks by pursuing them up the Italian mainland.

The Germans knew the Italians had about had it, anyway, and were prepared to disarm them. The Italian surrender came September 8, just one day before the American invasion, and five days after a British/Canadian force—two divisions—had landed on the extreme toe of the Italian boot.

That force came across the two miles of the Strait of Messina from Sicily the same way the enemy had fled a short time before, but the majority of the invasion units were from scattered positions around the Mediterranean. The untried 36th ID (Infantry Division) was to come across the Med from Oran to join the veteran 45th ID and the British 46th and 56th Divisions, and others. The Americans would add the 3rd and 34th Divisions and the British would put forward their 7th Armored.

In the meantime, the British were able to land some people on the heel of the boot and take a Naval installation at Taranto. The next step was to land Allied soldiers a little higher up the line and give the Germans two thrusts to contain.

Benito Mussolini was forced out of power on July 25—during the Sicily campaign—and replaced by Marshall Badoglio, a man who wouldn't mind an honorable way out of the war.

Darby knew going in he needed beefier support for his men. He had used the 83rd Chemical Warfare Battalion and their big mortars at Gela, and kept them close after that. He wanted something heavy though, and was able to find four 75mm cannons mounted on half-tracks. He put together a provisional platoon to handle the artillery, gave Captain Shunstrom the reins and set them to practicing.

Salerno—Maori

The US Fifth Army, under Lt. General Mark Clark, landed at dawn on September 9, 1943, hitting the beaches of and around Salerno on the west coast of southern Italy. The British X Corps—including the Ranger Force—came ashore on the north side of the objective, with the US VI Corps on the right, or south.

The Germans had the location of the landing figured out and were waiting behind heavy fortifications. The 16th Panzer (tank) Division hit back hard when the 36th US went ashore without air cover, trying to achieve a surprise that had already been lost. The men of the 36th, new to combat, took a fearful beating.

The Rangers were not there, having turned north at the last of the invasion run-in to hit near Maori, a few miles north and west of Salerno at the base of the Sorrento Peninsula. Maori was largely undefended and the Ranger Force walked on into town. That easy path would not continue as the Force began to pass through Maori and move north, going after the high ground of Mont di Chiunzi.

At that point, the Ranger Force consisted of three Ranger Battalions, including the cannon platoon, two British Commando units (Number 2 and Number 41), and Companies C and D of the 83rd Mortars.

The 4th Rangers, under Murray, were first on the beach. Securing a perimeter on the largely undefended beach, the 4th watched the 1st come in, followed by the 3rd. In an hour the Rangers owned the beach. Elements of the 4th moved right and left from the beach to eliminate some observation posts, gun emplacements, and cut communications. Roadblocks were established at critical places and the Rangers dug in and waited.

Part of the 1st Battalion moved north to seize high ground. The 3rd, with two companies of the 1st, moved through them and occupied Chiunzi pass, spreading the companies out north, south, and in the pass itself. From the top of the pass one could see many miles in all directions.

Rangers could see Highway 18, which the Germans used to transport supplies. Using old-fashioned muscle power the heavy four-deuce mortars were brought up and unleashed on the traffic along the road, doing much damage to the enemy line of supply. Darby got a couple of warships to join the fun, and between the mortars, cannon company fire, and Naval fire, the Germans had a tough time doing anything in that area. It wasn't long before the Germans had enough of raining death and brought troops from the big fight at Salerno to try and dislodge the Rangers.

Help was close, but General Mark Clark's Fifth Army was unable to link up with its beleaguered units. The Ranger Battalions found themselves all but cut off for nine days, fending off seven counterattacks while waiting for help.

The battle for Italy was tougher than expected, and the Rangers, along with others, paid the price in several instances for bad Intelligence and misuse of elite forces—not that it hadn't happened before. The field commanders were prone to use whomever was handy in times of great need, and the Rangers continued to be a highly valuable fighting force however they were deployed.

With no organic big guns of their own except the mortars and the cannon company—not considered "big" guns—the Rangers called on their Naval brethren to supply high explosives. Said Darby, "The Germans were denied Chiunzi Pass simply because one observer was up there with a radio and could talk to the Navy."

The heavy shelling prompted the Germans to try to get the Americans off the ridge, but repeated tries left many dead on the slopes. When they weren't attacking, they were shelling the Rangers constantly with mortars and artillery. It was cold, often wet, and the ground didn't stop shaking. Resupply for the Rangers was tenuous to non-existent.

The Rangers were given the task of subduing the enemy occupying the Sorrento Peninsula west of Salerno. The point of the exercise was to keep the route from Salerno to Naples open for the Allied advance, and to keep the enemy from using it.

To make sure things happened the way they were planned, at least in the first phase, Darby was given nearly 8,500 men; a conglomerate force of British and Americans, including Commandos, elements of the 82nd Airborne and 36th Divisions, glider-borne artillery, tank units, engineers, medics and, of course, the 83rd Chemical Mortar Battalion. Darby figured he had a pretty good bunch. "...as rugged a force as could be found among Allied forces in Europe."

He would need rugged troops because of the terrain. A tall ridge of mountain bisected the peninsula, rising to 4,000 feet and separating it into two sections. Passes dotted the ridges, and the Amalfi Drive, a long, curving highway that fairly encompassed the area, offered several routes of travel for the Germans. The Rangers and others were to shut them down. If they could gain the heights they would have excellent shooting vision for the Navy and any big guns ashore.

By September 11, 4th Battalion crept along Amalfi Drive to the town of the same name, passed it, and went further inland toward Castellamarre on the Gulf of Naples.

High ground was the key for both sides, but the Germans were dug in and moving them was difficult. The town of Castellamarre was investigated by a small unit of Rangers of the 4th and was found to hold entrenched artillery and determined defenders. Likewise the town of Gregnano, hit by Companies A and B of the 4th and a company of the 504th Parachute Infantry, was too strong for frontal assault.

The 4th moved back to Mount Pendola and dug in. On the 14th the 504th took over for the 4th Rangers, who moved into some high ground with their sister battalions near Polvico.

Patrols clashed in the mountains and the two sides jockeyed for position. Artillery fire was punishing everybody, particularly in Chiunzi Pass, where the German 88s spent the days and nights breaking rock.

Part of the 4th Battalion moved up to relieve the 3rd on September 17, and a battalion of the 325th Glider Infantry relieved the 1st Battalion. The 1st and 3rd, badly mauled by artillery and cold weather, went into reserve attached to the 82nd Airborne Division. The 4th was still at it.

On the 18th, the 4th Rangers moved out of Chiunzi pass and did some recon toward the town of Sala. The Germans took exception and a fierce fight ensued, causing casualties on both sides. There were many such small fights, and many such casualties. Still, the Germans had to go, so the 4th got squared away while the 1st and 3rd—in reserve for a whole day—filtered through them to make the attack on Sala. They found nobody home. The enemy had pulled out.

At that point, the Germans had seen the writing on the wall and were withdrawing slowly northward to protect Naples.

Not until September 29, after three weeks of fighting the enemy and the cold, were the Rangers allowed to go into bivouac near Castellamarre. It had been a tough month, with Ranger losses of 30 dead, nine missing, and 73 wounded. That is the rough equivalent of two Ranger Companies. Replacements, untrained in Ranger ways, were brought in from wherever they could be found. Training was accomplished in the field, patrolling against the enemy. If the new men survived, they learned. Nobody wore the unique Ranger Scroll insignia until they had proven themselves.

Naples fell October 1. Two days later the battalions moved again, ending up in Naples for a few days, then going into Fifth Army reserve, except for the 4th. Attached to VI Corps, it ended up in Sorrento on the 14th.

The 1st and 3rd had moved near Amalfi a few days earlier. The two battalions would each be awarded Distinguished Unit Citations for their actions in the mountain passes.

The break for the decorated units didn't last long, however, with the fight making slow going against the German Gustav Line. For the Rangers, it became rest, regroup, re-arm and return.

By early October, Italy was out of the war and the Allies held Naples against the Germans. The situation was no longer so fluid, with German General Albert Kesselring settling in behind his winter line, defending Rome at all costs. Winter in the mountains made the going tough for anyone trying to move, and it became obvious the Germans were willing to sit between Naples and Rome and slug it out.

The largely mountainous terrain was ready made for rear-guard action and the Germans made the most of it, holding tenaciously, then setting traps when they pulled out. Allied progress was slow to non-existent for about a month, even though the Fifth Army attacked hard on October 12.

As for the Rangers, time was up for their involvement around Naples. New things were about to happen, and of course, they were expected to be in the vanguard. They were pulled out of the line to spend two weeks at San Lazzaro, almost back where they started.

Each new man had to prove himself to the battle-hardened veterans. Some of the men— not many at that point—had been with the Rangers since the beginning, coming through Arzew, Gafsa, Sened Station, Dernaia Pass, El Guettar, Djebel el Ank, Djebel Berda—all North Africa—Gela, Butera, Licata, Porto Empedocle, Castelvetrano, Marsala, Trapani, Patti, Brolo, Messina—all Sicily—Sorrento Peninsula, Chiunzi Pass, and countless other small conflicts.

It would be a long winter getting across the Volturno River and fighting Von Kesselring's soldiers through the tall, snowy mountains. British General Alexander commanded the 15th Army Group, composed of Montgomery's Eighth Army, Clark's US Fifth Army, and a British Corps. This force faced 12 German divisions of various types, set into the high ground and entrenched in the small towns.

About 35 miles north of Naples, the line was drawn. The 4th Rangers would be the first to cross the Volturno on November 3, wading a ford and infiltrating 12 miles into enemy territory to seize a point of high ground labeled Hill 861 on the map. After dropping off a radio-relay team, the battalion moved into position north of the hill early on the morning of November 4. The companies split up and met roving German patrols, creating a running battle that stalled at the foot of Hill 689.

The Rangers were taking casualties, and E Company lost two men killed, seven wounded, and nine missing—presumably prisoners. The night came slowly and the Rangers tried to regroup. Murray, commanding the 4th, made ready to stage a morning attack on what was believed to be some 200 Germans on the hill. Company C was detailed to make the assault with D and F giving supporting fires. A little before noon C Company went up the hill, only to be met by devastating fire from a reinforced German position. Artillery support from the 3rd Division was not forthcoming and the Rangers had nothing heavy with which to fight back. They lost five killed, eight wounded, and six missing.

So far, in not quite two days, Companies E and C had lost a combined seven killed, 15 wounded, and 15 missing—the equivalent of more than half a Ranger Company, which was only 68 men at full strength. That meant each battle was fought with less firepower until the replacements got caught up.

The Rangers fought on with little in the way of food or ammunition, the biting cold a constant enemy, and incoming rounds a matter of course. Heavy, close encounters in the freezing mountains often found Rangers in grenade-throwing distance, with bayonets fixed for the follow-up. Though contact with the 3rd Division was made, nothing was forthcoming for the hard-pressed troops. On November 5, Murray knew they could take no more and asked for his men to be relieved.

All the action spent the Rangers, the attrition rate whittling them down, the battle-hardened, highly trained veterans disappearing fast. The 1st Battalion lost more than half its strength in a month, though the harsh conditions produced many of those casualties. The 1st is an example of what was happening to the 3rd and 4th. By the end of November, the 4th Battalion was fielding four companies—each about the size of a platoon—and the men were exhausted from the incessant pounding by German artillery and counterattacks.

The inevitable result of such heavy losses was an overall decline in experience and skill by quickly trained replacements. The heroes of North Africa and Sicily were going away fast. Over time some of those casualties healed and returned to their units.

Darby and his officers saw what was happening and renewed efforts to produce a separate Ranger Headquarters to oversee the three battalions, supplying them with material and replacements when needed. It would be a permanent position, not to be disbanded when things slowed down. Eisenhower again rejected the idea, perhaps feeling the Rangers, as elite troops, were unnecessary in the long run. As yet, the Ranger concept had been used sparingly, still not recognized as a specialized unit capable of doing big damage if used correctly. To that end, Murray appealed to Army Ground Forces for a headquarters to keep the Rangers working correctly, and especially, he wrote, "most important, to decide if the assignment is a proper one for the battalions."

In view of the reigning concept of Ranger forces by the High Command, it would seem the Rangers had a good case. Murray nominated Darby for command of a new Ranger Regiment. Darby was also writing letters, as was General Norman Cota, all asking for essentially the same thing—autonomy for the Ranger group.

The ability of the Rangers to fight well under any circumstances made it easy for line commanders to use them at the front, especially since seasoned troops were getting hard to come by. The Rangers were too good to be left idle. General George Patton had called them, "the best damned combat soldiers in Africa." High praise from a tough guy, but Patton was aware of the makeup of the Rangers; volunteers all, and philosophically independent. He also tagged them as being "the worst garrison troops I ever saw in my whole professional life."

Indeed, the Ranger's reputation for unruly behavior was sometimes deserved. Some of them perceived their special status to be a key for certain doors they weren't supposed to open, such as "ownership" of drinking establishments and immediate proof of how tough they were.

This self-concept was not helped by State-side headlines blaring things such as "Night Fighters Take Arzew on D Day, Then Smash Way to Oran." That was North Africa. By the time they got to Italy, they were certainly full of esprit de corps and held a developing public—and personal—mystique.

With attitudes about the Rangers being what they were, nobody wanted to disband them, even if the concept of such a force wasn't yet completely understood. It was just too obvious how good they were.

Venafro—One Year From Arzew

On November 8, the 1st Rangers were taken in trucks to an area near Venafro. It was a year and a day since they landed in North Africa. Their assignment was to relieve the 180th Infantry in the mountains northwest of Venafro, using their attached power from the 83rd Chemical Mortars and four 75mm cannons on half-tracks. The units settled in on top of Mount Carno and Mount Croce, around 3,000 feet, and put in about a month of what Darby termed "intense activity."

The action got rough, and Darby asked for reinforcements, adding the 509th Parachute Battalion to the ranks on the 10th, and giving them one of the peaks. What Darby called "hide and seek action" took a continuous toll from the Americans and Germans alike. At several points, the 83rd Chemical Mortars dropped 4.2-inch rounds weighing 25 pounds on the Germans in the little town of Concacasalle and the surrounding areas. The enemy sent some mail back.

On November 13, a battalion-sized attack by the Germans almost rolled over the 4th Rangers, who held with few men and little ammunition in the intense cold. By November 27, the 4th was relieved by the 180th and took a well-deserved break.

The 1st and 3rd Battalions were likewise engaged, and running short of everything.

One of the main casualties for the Americans were the communications people, down to just three of 22 men at the end of the assignment. Most of them were taken out by fire from the sky while out trying to lay new wire or repair old ones. Artillery and mortar fire killed a lot of good men on both sides during that terrible time in the icy mountains.

Meanwhile, the 3rd Battalion was still attached to the 36th Infantry Division, situated around Mount Rotondo and San Pietro, a few miles southwest of the 1st and 4th Rangers, who were having their own problems.

The heavy fighting led to a short stalemate, and the Allies were looking for a way out. Darby said, " It was heartbreaking combat."

The stalemate—or super-slow movement—brought the decision to break out with an end run to the fore. The move to the sea, up the coast, and back in to shore would change things considerably if the Allies could gain a toehold and keep it. The Germans, aware such a move would cut their supply routes and bring a large Allied force into their back door, would not permit it—at least, that's what they thought.

The 1st and 4th Battalions were pulled out December 14 to return to the Naples area for a refit and some rest, but the 3rd stayed in the battle arena another week. Once everybody had gathered in some semblance of the unit that had come ashore, they found 40 percent of their buddies gone. Replacements came straggling in, and the training began in earnest, trying to ready the new men—now a large part of the Ranger contingent—for the grinding combat still to come.

In the last days of November, the 3rd Battalion and a company of mortar men were trucked to Venafro. Company E sent patrols to satisfy recon demands for a word-picture of happenings around the village of San Pietro. Coming within about a mile, they saw no Germans and moved on to the Ceppagna area. A few days later Company F pulled a recon mission along a ridgeline of Mount Sammucro, overlooking San Pietro. One of the problems there was the presence in strength of a German unit on Hill 950.

The 3rd Battalion moved to the attack. The Rangers stopped on an ascending ridgeline about half-a-mile short of the objective when a couple of German machineguns pinned them. Fire and maneuver tactics by Companies E and F took out the weapons.

Daylight brought American occupation of the hill, but it also brought machinegun fire from Mount Sammucro. The two Ranger Companies were taking too many hits and withdrew under mortar-fired smoke. The mortar company was pinpointed by return-azimuth enemy fire enough to reduce the strength of one platoon by half.

Having taken the hill once, the Rangers were asked to do it again the next day. This time the whole battalion went, preceded by a heavy show of artillery power. Twenty-four hours after the first cresting of Hill 950, the Rangers were back in the saddle. The Germans were incensed by the loss of the observation point and pounded the hill with artillery and some counter-strokes, but the men of the 3rd held fast until relief came a day and a night later in the form of a battalion of the 504th Parachute Infantry.

In December, Darby was promoted to Colonel and given command of the 6615th Ranger Force (Provisional), which officially came on line January 16. The new unit was made up of the three Ranger Battalions, their old friends of the 83rd Chemical Warfare Battalion—4.2-inch mortars—the 509th Parachute Battalion, and a company of the 36th Combat Engineers.

Roy Murray was promoted to Lt. Colonel and kept command of the 4th Battalion, Jack Dobson took over the 1st Battalion, and Alvah Miller was given the 3rd. Darby sat at the top of the heap.

After reorganization, the Rangers took some time to ready themselves for the landing at Anzio.

The Death of a Buddy

Ranger Noel Dye told me this story after my tape recorder was shut off. It is written as well as I can remember it. This sad action occurred near Venafro.

Rangers are encouraged to have buddies to help them through the rigors of combat. It has always been so and serves to create bonds between men that can, and often do, surpass family ties. Noel Dye's buddy was Charles Roby, a young man serving as a Scout. The two were very close, and had their photo taken together in Sorrento just 32 hours before Roby's death. In the photo the outlines of rectangular objects can be clearly seen in the breast pockets of the smiling soldiers. Both men carried a waterproof pouch full of personal papers in those pockets, each vowing to retrieve it from the other should the worst happen.

Dye's Company went on a raid 12 miles behind the lines, "Just to raise some hell." Italian partisans led them the first three miles. During the action, his platoon was pinned in a defilade shallow enough that "Guys had canteens and packs shot off their backs." Things were bad enough with the small arms fire coming in, but the Germans had a little pack-mortar and began to lob rounds in on top of the ground-hugging Rangers.

Sergeant James Altieri yelled out for two men at a time to try and make some woods on the other side of an open field. Dye and Roby went together.

"I was a little lighter and only carrying a carbine. He was carrying a Thompson with extra ammunition. I ran right past him and dove over a fence into the woods. I expected any second to catch a bullet in the back."

Dye stayed down for a moment to catch his breath, and then went looking for his buddy. After asking a couple of other Rangers, he was directed back to the field.

Roby lay on his back about 50 feet out from the fence, killed by shrapnel from pursuing mortar rounds. Without thinking, Dye went out to him and sat with his back to the Germans. Roby's eyes were open, his mouth full of blood. Dye looked up at the sky, "to see what he was seeing." He saw blue sky and small, fast-moving little clouds.

Dye reached into Roby's top pocket and took his personal pack, putting it in his own pocket. He sat for "a few moments" looking at his friend.

"Years later I realized I should have been killed. There was a full battle going on and the Germans could see me. I never thought about it before that."

ANZIO—THE END OF THE BEGINNING

Mounting casualties, unrelenting cold weather, and a failure to move at more than a snail's pace meant big change had to come. As long as the Germans held the north, Rome may as well have been on the moon.

German General Kesselring was doing quite well using the troops he had available, so the idea that the enemy would have to bring troops from France and/or Russia wasn't working very well. Despite British General Alexander's 15th Army Group pushing along a protracted front, Kesselring had the high ground and plenty of artillery. The Allies were paying an unwelcome price for keeping the enemy units tied down in Italy.

The Allies needed a breakout strategy, some way to punch into the northern interior of Italy and push the Germans back. They settled on an amphibious assault on Anzio, called Operation SHINGLE. Anzio is north up the coast from Salerno and would give the Allies a toehold that would allow the occupation of necessary airfields at Foggia. What they wanted was to get to Rome—just 40 miles away—if they could move the enemy out of the Alban Hills.

No one knew that despite heavy pressure, Rome would not fall for five more months.

It would also put a large amount of Germans between the Allied forces to their north and south. The idea was to create enough of a pincher-pusher to break Kesselring's resistance along the Volturno River, and get the Allies at least as far north as the main line of German defense—the Gustav Line.

Christmas 1943 came and went, and Darby's boys had a relaxing time near Naples. All that ended when The Man put them back to work, training hard at an out-of-the-way place called Pozzuoli, with a beach that approximated that of Anzio.

The Rangers were to land in front of the town of Anzio as part of General John P. Lucas' VI Corps. The town of Nettuno, about a mile south of Anzio, was also on the hit list. The three battalions would land with their supporting units between the British 1st Division on the left and the American 3rd Infantry Division on the right.

Due to the high demand in the Pacific and the build-up for D-Day, there were not enough landing craft. The 1st and 4th went in the first wave, followed by the 3rd and the mortars. January 20, 1944, the Rangers and the rest loaded up all the extra ammo they could carry and made ready for the 0200 landing on January 22.

The heavy Naval guns in the landing armada were not used before troops went ashore in order to keep things in the surprise mode. However, a few minutes before landing craft were to touch the beach, a couple of rocket ships let go with a tremendous rush of fire. There were few Germans in the town, anyway, and the men at sea could see lights on shore.

The Ranger Force began landing exactly on time on Yellow Beach, with the 1st and 4th Battalions, each minus one company, assaulting in line abreast formation.

Things went smoothly until the Rangers were in the town, with little or no resistance from the Germans, who were expecting the blow elsewhere and were unprepared and disorganized—at first. Still, both sides were facing determined, highly trained troops with very little backup in them.

Against scattered opposition, the Rangers had time to accomplish their various missions and organize for expected counter-attacks. A main accomplishment was keeping the enemy from blowing up the harbor installations, much of which was wired for destruction. The company from the 36th Engineers spent time removing mines from the beach, and many demolition devices were dismantled around the harbor.

Three 57mm anti-tank guns were rescued from a swamped carrier and brought ashore to use against strong points. There was nobody much up front to shoot at, but artillery shells landed on Anzio with increasing regularity. Just before 0400, the 3rd Rangers came ashore in the second wave with the mission of clearing the town, which included knocking out some large-bore guns the Germans were using to good effect.

One Ranger mission was to provide linkup between the forces on either side of them. Once they met the 3rd Infantry Division they became attached to it. The linkup to both right and left was complete by early afternoon of the second day.

By the 26th, the Germans were showing some resolve, digging in, using stone farmhouses as bases of fire, and bringing in reinforcements. Rangers and other units went forward to move them out but it was slow going. Several Rangers were killed or wounded attacking strong points.

Counter-attacks were being stepped up and German patrols were clashing with Americans regularly. On the 28th the Rangers were informed they were being relieved and would be tasked for another mission elsewhere.

The Germans were dug into the mountains around Anzio, holding the Colli Laziali—the Alban Hills—the last natural barrier between the Allies and Rome. Dislodging them would be more than difficult. The owner of the hills owned the path north.

General Lucas was content to sit on his beachhead and consolidate his forces, but the Germans were steadily reinforcing while he waited, and attrition of his troops continued at a fairly high rate. He moved very slowly and with great caution at a time when a Patton-type warrior General was needed.

Fifth Army Commander Mark Clark wanted Lucas to proceed with all possible haste, so the General reluctantly made plans for a breakout, providing everything went well. One objective was to cut Highways 6 & 7, routes through the mountains necessary to any mass movement of troops to the north. Within the rough triangle formed by those two roads was a small town named Cisterna di Latina, a rail and road nexus speared by the Apian Way, a main road leading to Rome.

There are actually two Cisternas—one not far from the Volturno River, above Salerno, and the more famous one described here, located north and east of Anzio a few miles. The first Cisterna was finally broken in mid-October, but not before the 7th Infantry tried it and couldn't crack the defenses. It was by-passed on the original drive north.

General Lucas had several opportunities to get out of the hole but refused them early on. At one point Truscott wanted to take Cisterna before it was reinforced, but Lucas turned him down. In the beginning an assault toward Rome, through Cisterna, had a great chance of success—but the door closed before anything happened.

January 29 was slated for the big push, but first—and perhaps foremost—was the need to control the passes and roads. The US 7th and 15th Regiments of the 3rd Division pushed through on either side of Cisterna, got within three miles, and were stopped. Attached to the division was the 6615th Ranger Force (Provisional) under Darby, with Roy Murray at the head of the 4th Battalion, Jack Dobson taking the 1st, and Alva Miller the 3rd. Herman Dammer was Darby's Executive Officer at the time.

The mission of the Ranger Force was to take Cisterna.

The Hell of Cisterna

As the circle of Ranger history began to connect, Lucian Truscott, the man who started it all by putting the Rangers together, was in command of the US 3rd Infantry Division. It was his job to get past Cisterna and he wasn't having an easy time of it. The stone-and-cement town and the area around it were full of Germans, and they weren't budging. Somehow, there were a lot more enemy troops around than there were supposed to be.

To reach the town the Rangers had to pass through an agricultural area—flat land without cover. Though the force came from two different directions, the end result was the funneling of men into a narrowing triangle with Cisterna at its tip. In the few days before the strike the Germans had been moving men into the area with haste. Elements of the famed Hermann Goering Division were there, as well as the 26th Panzers; men with plenty of experience and plenty of ammunition.

The Hermann Goering Division was there because it escaped from Sicily.

Kesselring was preparing his own push against the beachhead and the massing of troops was part of it. Some of the German troops at Cisterna had been there just one day, which they spent digging solid positions.

The 4th Battalion was to move up a secondary road through Feminamorta toward Cisterna, with the 1st and 3rd Battalions coming through the woods to the right. In the mix were the 83rd Mortars and a few tanks and tank destroyers to go with the Rangers' own Cannon Company.

Sadly, none of the armor got as far as the 1st and 3rd Ranger battleground, but stayed near, or behind the 4th.

Riflemen stocked up, going in with crossed bandoliers over their shoulders and pocketfuls of grenades. Though they took quite a few bazookas, the heavy machineguns were left behind.

Unfortunately, there had been little recon since the attack came so soon, and the latest Intelligence said the Germans were not there in real strength. Darby wanted Ranger recon but didn't have the time. He had little idea what he was sending his men into.

The 4th Battalion should have been able to breeze through Feminamorta, but instead found stiff resistance from an enemy who wasn't supposed to be there in numbers. German troopers were all around them, dug in and ready. It was more than a hint that something wasn't right.

Some 800 yards short of Feminamorta the 4th began taking heavy fire and was stopped before dawn. American artillery was called for and used, but the enemy took it and kept firing. Allied artillery and aircraft were not used to full potential. Planes detailed to cover the armor were not used to cover the Rangers, and artillery called in to pound Cisterna was unobservable, and so cancelled.

The 1st Battalion was supposed to go right into Cisterna—without a fight, if possible. The 3rd was given orders to fight only if necessary to get the 1st into town. Cisterna was just four miles from the Allied beachhead, and much was going on around the area. The 7th and 15th Infantry were tasked with cutting the same highways, but above and below the town. There were a lot of men in a small area, and the fighting was fierce.

Nowhere was it worse than the flat killing ground in front of Cisterna di Latina.

Once through the woods the Rangers continued in drainage ditches, single-file and silent through the night. There were times when German positions were identified by the sound of orders being given to fire, but the Rangers kept moving, intent on their mission of taking Cisterna. Finally close enough, the 1st and 3rd came out of concealment and took to the road—the same one the 4th was stalled on about two miles back.

Dobson's 1st Battalion pressed forward even though communication with headquarters was lost. With no other input, the mission came first.

Daylight was coming fast and the Rangers, having been slowed constantly by too much light or too many Germans, were moving fast when they ran into a German company set in bivouac. The sentries died quietly—all but one—and the enemy sprang to life only to be cut down by a horde of Rangers using bullet and bayonet. Those Germans died, but others knew the Rangers were among them, and the outlines of the men were becoming more visible by the minute.

0700. Dawn. The 1st Battalion was caught in the open 800 yards from town, held there by German heavy guns. The 3rd was a little to the east and slightly back, but all were under fire.

The 4th Battalion was making little headway against the block at Feminamorta, two miles from the beleaguered 1st and 3rd. They would not make it in time.

Daylight brought increased pressure on the exposed Rangers, under heavy fire from fortified stone farmhouses and other strong points. Tanks, mortars, artillery, and lots of machineguns poured fire into them. German reinforcements, brought in to make a heavy counter-attack, were having a field day with the comparatively small Ranger units. The Rangers took everything thrown at them, sometimes attacking tanks with grenades in hand, sometimes paying the ultimate price doing so.

Alvah Miller, commanding the 3rd Battalion, was killed by artillery while trying to move on Cisterna. He had sent three companies forward toward the town and kept three back, but the incoming fire was too intense to do much of anything. The Rangers were attacking along Route 7 and so were the Germans, coming down the road with tanks and doing damage to soldiers with little to hide behind.

Five hours went by, grim hours full of pain and death, but in spite of heavy losses to fire and capture, the Ranger Battalions were still attacking. Later estimates of German strength that day were close to 12,000 men.

Had the Rangers known that, would they still have kept driving?

Dobson was still moving forward with the 1st Battalion, coming close to town, even getting a few elements into the area around the rail station. Those few men didn't last long in the town, either withdrawing or becoming prisoners—or dying. The 4th Battalion was taking casualties and gaining little ground. All three battalions fought without effective artillery support, but took shell after shell from accurate German guns. That fact alone could have been the deciding factor. The 7th and 15th Infantries to the right and left were also getting pounded and were making no headway.

All that morning of January 30, the 1st and 3rd fought toward Cisterna, but then the Germans hit them with a large group of tanks and self-propelled guns. The Rangers stood their ground, fighting tanks with grenades and bazookas—a valiant action that only forestalled the inevitable, as the battalions were coming down to their last bullet.

At 1430, Sergeant Major Ehalt of the 3rd Battalion called in to say he was holed up in a farmhouse with 10 men, they were about out of ammunition, tanks were outside, and he had no choice but to destroy his radio.

The 1st and 3rd together lost 12 men killed, 36 wounded, and 743 captured. Only eight men escaped.

One may wonder why the mighty Rangers gave up with only 12 dead. Many have. The reasons are probably these: a great number of Rangers were recruits, since the attrition rate through North Africa, Sicily, Salerno and Anzio took a lot of experience—and determination—out of the battalions, and in the face of overwhelming fire superiority and without fire support or hope of reinforcements, there seemed no reason to lose more men.

The question arises: What if those had been the original battalions? Would there have been a different outcome? One answer would be—probably not. Full strength, fully trained battalions may have lasted longer, but losses would have been higher. They were hopelessly outnumbered and outgunned, regardless of how good they were.

The captured men of the 1st and 3rd were taken to Rome and marched through the streets on their way to POW camps. The Germans gloated over the fall of the elite units.

The 4th Rangers—30 killed and 58 wounded—were beaten up, but still intact when it became obvious the other two battalions were gone. The next day Darby ordered another attack and the 4th went forward, taking out machineguns and farmhouses with the aid of mortar support.

Still, nothing on either side amounted to much. From Anzio south down the coast and east across the mountains and the Gustav Line, both sides were stalled, pounding each other with artillery and patrolling, patrolling, patrolling.

Cisterna did not change hands until May 25.

Noel Dye

Dye was wounded again before Anzio and sent back to North Africa—temporarily. He went AWOL back to his unit in Lake Lacrino, a training ground north of Naples.

They got all the guys who had reported in after the troops left [for Anzio], there was about nine of us. Randall Harris led us from Lake Lacrino to Anzio, and we went by boat. We got there in the daytime and we went over to the Mussolini Canal, over to the left, and we stayed that night. The next day we went farther up the canal, to where you could hear small arms fire. There were bridges over it and we stayed the next night under that bridge. We went up more the next day, and were told to look over the edge of the canal bank and see if we saw a stone farm house, but to be careful. Sure enough, sitting back there about half-a-mile there was an Italian stone farmhouse. It had two or three rooms on the bottom and one on the top. They said that's where we were going, that's where the 4th Battalion was. That was Murray's HQ. We took off two at a time, running toward that farmhouse across the open field.

At the time, the 4th Battalion was making its way toward the 1st and 3rd Battalions and Cisterna. Unfortunately, the 4th was held near Feminamorta and got chewed up trying to get through. When Dye and the others arrived, the rest of the battalion was out on the line.

We got inside and sat down. We were told we'd wait there until we got our orders. I was on a window, sitting against the wall, and Harris sat on the other side of the window. He says every now and then we gotta look out there and make sure nobody's coming up. He looked out at an angle one way, and I looked the other. We were there for maybe an hour, then zoom-bang! A shell hit the side of the building. We could hear it, firing point-blank. We could hear it coming, going by us, then we could hear the boom, hitting close to us. They zeroed in on us with 88s [German bad boy artillery piece] and took that building down around us. Murray was on the second floor. Captain Nye was, and the rest of them.

I was sitting there, and when the shelling got really intense, I had to watch [out the window] a lot, because we were afraid they were going to charge in with infantry, which is the normal way they did things. I was snugged up real tight against the wall so I could see good, but not be hit. All of a sudden I went up in the air, moved around a little bit, don't remember hitting the ground.

I woke up on a stretcher on the beach at Anzio in daylight and Colonel Murray was on a stretcher, too.

4th Battalion After Cisterna

With two battalions gone, Darby's Rangers—and the 6615th—faded away. The surviving Rangers of the 4th, however, were another matter. That much talent wasn't going to be allowed to stand by.

February 10 saw the 4th Rangers attached to the 504th Parachute Infantry and placed in what was laughingly referred to as "reserve." In that area, spread out and dug in, the Rangers were expected to hold various lines of defense and be prepared to counter-attack at any time. Artillery rounds, tank fire and mortars impacted everywhere constantly.

The 4th Battalion, about 320 strong at that point, were given more than half-a-mile to defend beside the 504th. The Rangers occupied an area on the northeast portion of the Allied lines and were hit several times by counter-attacks.

Supposed to be "in reserve" and "on the line" simultaneously, the Rangers held for 52 days against heavy attacks with a loss of just eight men. During that same time the Paratroopers were often losing a like amount—per day.

Two tanks and two tank destroyers were used in part to make a show of noise to help confuse the enemy. Ranger patrols were nearly constant during that time and many Germans were captured.

At one point, a desperate enemy drove cattle into prepared minefields to try and break the Ranger line. German patrols had a way of disappearing if they got too close to the men of the 4th.

Ranger Lester Kness was there. "Personally, I am extremely proud of this piece of action. Colonel Tucker of the 504th personally commended us."

DARBY'S RANGERS SPREAD THEIR SKILLS WITHOUT HIM

On February 17, Darby was named commander of the 179th Infantry, 45th Division. He liked it enough to again put forward the idea of a group of Rangers that size with that much hitting power. Unfortunately, Darby's time was limited. Near the end of the war he was named Assistant Commander, 10th Mountain Division, and sent to Italy. On April 30, 1945, a shell fragment found him in Torbole.

General Truscott said of him, "Never have I known a more gallant, heroic officer."

The 4th Rangers remained under command of Roy Murray, who was ill and being subbed for by Walter Nye. The two sides remained static long enough for a lot of mines to be laid and strong points to be created. There was a batch of firepower available, going both ways. The situation remained strained into March, a month of attrition that cost the Rangers six dead and 18 wounded.

While all that was going on the wheels of administration were turning elsewhere. The 4th Rangers were attached to the Canadian-American 1st Special Service Force for a short time as a whole, then on March 27, nine officers and 134 men (including Murray) were sent home to Camp Butner, North Carolina. The rest, those without sufficient time in service to get to go home, stayed with the 1st SSF.

The pioneer Ranger group, Darby's 1st, 3rd and 4th Battalions, were gone. The most experienced of the soldiers, about 150 hardy veterans, generally became instructors and administrators for new Rangers coming through the ranks. It should be noted that the majority of those battle-hardened veterans volunteered for posting with other Ranger units, but were ultimately turned down, as was the idea of rebuilding the battalions. The argument that it would take too much time to rebuild, and take too many valuable assets from combat-ready units, was enough to put such thoughts away and go with the existing 2nd and 5th Battalions in Europe.

A lot of men were absorbed into the 1st Special Service Force—the North Americans. Though the unit didn't own a Ranger designation, many Rangers filled vacant positions in the ranks, adding to the already considerable skills of the tough unit.

The 1st Special Service Force fought through Italy beginning in Anzio in February 1944, then hit the beaches in southern France, distinguishing itself along the way, with Ranger-trained men a welcome addition. In the cross-channel invasion, the Forcemen were led by Colonel Edwin Walker, and ended the campaign at the Italian border. They licked their wounds there for three months before the unit was disbanded on December 5, 1944.

For purposes of lineage of the Rangers who fought as part of the 1st Special Service Force, it should be noted that the Americans of that unit were transferred into the 474th Infantry, a new combat unit that became part of General Omar Bradley's 12th Army Group.

The 1st SSF is also regarded by some as part of the Ranger heritage—a close cousin, perhaps.

BIRTH OF THE 2ND AND 5TH BATTALIONS

A Second Round of Rangers Goes To War

The 2nd Ranger Battalion was born at Camp Forrest, Tennessee, April 1, 1943, but things were slow getting started. To get to the point of being able to replace the 29th Rangers in England and fill the slot for elite assault troops, heavy training took place.

Again, resistance from unit commanders who were asked to give up their best men was a problem and the 2nd received its share of misfits from the call on continental-based units for above-average candidates. Still, many recruits were able, and some of them had attended the Second Army Ranger School.

A series of interim commanders came and went as the 2nd Rangers trained, until Major James E. Rudder took over on June 30, 1943. Rudder was the right man for the job, garnering respect from the men by demanding high standards, improving their rations and living quarters, and treating them with respect by allowing them monthly "gripe" sessions. There is no word on whether or not he ever paid attention to what they griped about.

The 2nd Rangers trained as hard as their predecessors, with physical conditioning and toughness being paramount. There was also a good bit of night exercise, all of which led to the unit going to the Scout and Raider School at Fort Pierce, Florida in September. No vacation spot, the camp was on an island populated mostly by mosquitoes, which made the Rangers glad to get out in the water and practice amphibious tactics and the use of small boats.

Two weeks or so later the Rangers were moved to Fort Dix, New Jersey and trained some more, mostly learning tactics. On November 23, the 2nd Rangers left the U. S. from New York, bound for Great Britain and the war.

Camp Forrest wasn't empty for long, not with ETOUSA (European Theater of Operations, US Army) yelling for more Rangers to support the coming invasion of Europe. The call for volunteers went out once more, though this time it was limited to the Second Army. The strategy worked better than before, as enough volunteers (500) and a higher quality of soldier to select from gave the forming 5th Ranger Battalion a better start than the 1st through the 4th. Though activated five months behind the 2nd Battalion on September 1st, problems caused the training of the 2nd to take longer than expected, so the 5th ended up going overseas just six weeks after the 2nd. Training for the 5th was somewhat smoother since they entered a program with most of the kinks worked out by the 2nd, and the 5th didn't have to suffer through several command changes.

The 5th trained as the 2nd had, following the same line of depots and special operations readiness, and departed the States January 8, 1944, heading east. Despite the 2nd being trained first, the 5th Battalion was as ready as the 2nd when the time came. Beginning on D-Day both battalions fought through France and into eastern Europe with determination and distinction.

Training Course—2nd and 5th Ranger Infantry Battalions

The 2nd and 5th Ranger Battalions had the benefit of Instructors' combat experience as they went through training. After all, three battalions had already been trained, albeit overseas. Much more went into their training than ever before, and the pool of men to choose from was wider.

The 2nd is used here as an illustration of training for both battalions, broken into the many different places used as teaching grounds. The two battalions followed much the same path, if not always geographically, then certainly philosophically.

This section is presented in multiple stages to show how often the unit was moved, with each new training ground selected for its topography and/or its Instructors. The types of training were geared to the impending D-Day struggle even way back in April 1943, and the 5th Rangers would shortly travel the same route.

Camp Forrest

Since Rangers are defined by their intensive training, the story must begin at Camp Forrest, Tennessee, where the 2nd Battalion, and soon the 5th, were organized and took initial training.

Colonel John Sherman brainstormed the training format for the 2nd Battalion, modeling it after Marine training done at Camp Pendleton, but with modifications to fit the needs of the Rangers. The Colonel drew up the close combat course and the infiltration course, as well as other training methods.

Lt. Colonel William Saffarans, former director of the Second Army Ranger School, was the first man in charge, but it was General Benjamin Lear who pushed the project from behind.

This order started the 2nd Battalion on its way.
SUBJECT: Activation of 2nd Ranger Battalion
AG 322.171-1 (GNMBF)
3-11-43
HEADQUARTERS SECOND ARMY, Memphis, Tennessee
TO: Commanding Officer, 11th Detachment Special Troops, Second Army, Camp Forrest, Tennessee

1. For compliance with applicable provisions of basic communication as amended.
2. Unit will be housed in tents in bivouac area.
3. You are directed to:
   (a) Issue the necessary Letter orders activating the 2nd Ranger Battalion on April 1, 1943.
   (b) Observe the transfer of personnel and equipment to this battalion.
   (c) Assist the Commanding Officer, 2nd Ranger Battalion in obtaining necessary supplies through Director of Supplies, Camp Forrest, Tennessee.
   (d) Report observations and completion of activation to Headquarters Second Army.

4. Two copies activation directive as amended, Army Ground Forces, enclosed.

> By command of Lieutenant General Lear:
> Lawton Butler
> Lt. Col., A.G.D.
> Asst. Adjutant General

New Commander

The 2nd Battalion had just three months to become a combat-ready unit with an original makeup of 27 officers and 484 enlisted men. That would be broken down into a Headquarters Company with nine officers and 94 enlisted men, and six rifle companies comprised of three officers and 65 enlisted men, a small unit compared to regular Infantry companies.

The word went out for volunteers and thousands responded. For once the officers could be somewhat choosy. Word of Ranger prowess had spread through stories coming back from the forays of Darby's Rangers.

Often as not, new recruits were met and set on a five mile run. If they couldn't handle it, back home they went.

Still, with all the hype and the many applicants, the selection process was fairly slow and tedious. The men chafed to be under way. They were not well disciplined as they waited, and matters were made worse by the frequent command changes in the beginning. Some order was established when Major L. E. McDonald came aboard on April 15, but he didn't stay long, either. It wasn't until June 30, 1943 that Major—soon to be Lt. Colonel—Rudder appeared.

He did several things right away, such as changing the living conditions of the men from tent city to wooden barracks with latrines and showers. Though men had double rations, the chow wasn't too good. He changed that, too. Perhaps the best thing he did was to institute gripe sessions, allowing the men to give the officers feedback after missions and about things in general.

However, the aggressive, unruly Ranger recruits weren't so quick to change, and waited for Rudder to prove his ability to lead them. It came when a parade performance turned out badly, leaving Rudder open for reprimand from his superiors. The new commander assembled the men and offered to fight them each in turn if it took that to establish his authority.

Things changed quickly after that.

Rudder—A Short Biography

James Earl Rudder was born in Texas in 1910, the beginning of a remarkable life.

Graduating from Texas A & M with a B.S. in 1932, he was commissioned a 2nd Lieutenant in the Army Reserves. He attended Infantry School at Fort Benning, Georgia in 1941, and became the Executive Officer of an Infantry Division at Camp Atterbury, Indiana by the summer of 1942.

By June 1943, Rudder was recognized as having the capabilities to organize and train the new 2nd Ranger Battalion. He eventually held command of two battalions and led three companies of those men in the fight for Point du Hoc on D-Day.

After the breakout from the beachhead, Rudder was made Commander of the 109th Infantry Regiment in December, and fought in the Battle of the Bulge.

He left active duty as a Colonel in April 1946, continued his successful ways in private life, and became Mayor of Brady, Texas from 1946 to 1952. During that time he kept ties to the military by being active in the Reserves. In 1954, he was promoted to Brigadier General in the Reserves, and two years later, Major General.

Back in Texas he was made Commissioner of the General Land Office in 1955, the same year he took command of the 90th Infantry (Reserves). Not having enough to do, Rudder was Vice-President of Texas A & M in 1958, then President in 1959. He took over the whole Texas A & M University System in 1965.

His talents again made him a national figure when he was named Assistant Deputy Commanding General for Mobilization for the Continental Army Command. He retired in 1967 after a distinguished 35-year career.

Training Day: Part of a typical day at Camp Forrest

Training began in earnest, acquired a rhythm and escalated, following along the lines of training of Darby's Battalions. Commando training and tactics were integrated with demolitions, weapons of all types, practice at climbing anything, and lots of heavy physical conditioning.

0600 Reveille

Drill Call—Daily dozen calisthenics, plus

Then Log Drill—14-foot long, one-foot thick log, five men to a log, positioned according to command

0900 Saw Dust Pit—Two platoons, includes officers in a pit 18 feet square—go at it until one man left in the pit

1000 Obstacle Course—with explosions for effect

1030 Marching—often speed march for five miles

12 Chow

1300 Run, crawl

1530 Demolitions—there were some injuries.

Night exercises were run often, and could go all night.

At that point in their training, the Rangers were becoming most physically capable.

HHC-2nd Ranger Battalion History

A good deal of information comes from the History of HHC, 2nd Ranger Infantry Battalion, edited and published by James "Ike" Eikner. He was at Pointe du Hoc with Rudder after beginning at Camp Forrest. The information and memories contained in the compilation are fresh, having been written less than a year after the war was over. They are used by permission.

Medic Frank South and (then) Sergeant Len Lomell also give voice to the history of the 2nd.

There are tales of heroism and heavy combat for all Rangers involved in D-Day. Casualties were heavy throughout both battalions. To illustrate the depth and inclusiveness of the casualties, here are the figures for the Medical Detachment for the 2nd Battalion:

Of 30 enlisted men, 17 had Purple Hearts, and there were five Silver Stars and seven Bronze Stars among them. And that's just the Medics!

Excerpts from the history of Headquarters and Headquarters Company, 2ⁿᵈ Rangers, will appear throughout the training section. Intermixed are the author's words in italics. Clarifications of Ranger narrative are bracketed.

The Beginning

We were activated under Letter AGF, (Secret, 11-3-43) and the first of many screenings took place on the 29th of March for the first units to arrive.

Now came the shakedown: the next few days were spent marking time and taking physicals. The physicals cost us a lot of otherwise good men, for apparently minor faults were enough to drop one and a subsequent return to the parent unit. To this was added a questioning as to the individual training one had received and developed; we were all supposed to be specialists of one type or another. Later it proved we had to specialize in everything.

The following week, 11th of April, we moved into tents and were down to a third of our rated strength. Our initial compliment was to have been: in the battalion, 27 officers and 484 enlisted men, in HHQ and attached Medical [12 listed on the TO&E], 94 enlisted men and 19 officers.

Baths were a luxury at the cost of a half-mile walk to the nearest barracks and the hospitality of the occupants. Ordinarily one bathed in a tin basin setting on four pegs driven into the ground.

Major L. E. McDonald had assumed command on the 15th of April and we were on our own as a unit.

The Communications (Commo) Section was given orders for every man to be cross-trained on all systems. The Commo Section had no wire at that time, and so couldn't do quite a bit of what was called for. The answer was to "appropriate" some wire.

A considerable quantity of wire was picked up, including the line to the WAC headquarters and the MP outpost phone. Some of the men became expert at cutting out and only peeled one pole a day.

As training progressed, so did the weeding-out process. One way to find out who was game and who wasn't was to conduct a three-day, 70-mile road march over rough terrain, and on compass point.

The first night the medics were up till all hours treating bad feet and more than one left the battalion right there. Others in just as bad shape bulled it through. During the march contact was kept between air and ground through the use of panels and Piper Cubs loaned as liaison by the Air Corps. The third day, with about six miles to go, trucks picked up the remnants and that was that.

Beginning of Mountaineering

Operations found a suitable cliff for the battalion to break its collective necks on. They claimed it was nine miles out, but not on the maps we used. We found the buzzards out that way carried a day's rations and also why. By description the cliff was about 90 feet and on one side water fell from a small creek. The idea was to go down the rope and then climb the opposite slope.

Lieutenant Tovey had made the initial descent and the ropes were in place, three of them. It looked an awful long way down and was. After a lecture on the whys and wherefores, the first man started down and fell the rest of the way. It was about an hour before they were able to get him into the ambulance, badly bruised and shaken with possible fractures. The whole deal was called off for the time being and the return made. The miles back were murderous as water ran out and on the last break orders were passed down for some of the men to pick up canteens and bring water from the nearest barracks. This break lasted about a half-hour as so many men were done in. This caused a further reduction in our ranks.

The following Sunday the battalion went out and "did it up brown" without casualties except for burned hands. This time we traveled in style by vehicular transportation.

Full-Size Ranger Training Begins

The new schedule inaugurated an hour's intense PT [Physical Training] by an extremely rugged 2nd Lieutenant imported especially for the job, and another just a mite rougher to pound the rudiments of hand-to-hand combat into us. Looking the pair over we reached the conclusion the Japs would be a cinch after them. The pair took all the companies over the jumps through the course of the day and were in the pink at the close. Tired, beaten, and gasping, we hit the sack. They went to town.

To add to our miseries someone had discovered an obstacle course of such length it tired one just to walk down its outer dimension and one the camp would just as soon let be forgotten. We ran it. Jumping over board barriers with rifles slung over the shoulder, try to spear a dummy and have another drop from nowhere, supposed to stick that one with your knife. Take a pass at a rope swing, grab it and fly. The creek is a blast of sound as hidden dynamite goes off and another blast as someone flips another stick for good measure. Off goes the dynamite and so do you, off the rope into the muck. Make another pass at a silhouette as it rises from the grass and it goes off in your face. Ah! Wire—the body goes under one strand; the rifle over another; back track and your pants are in rags. Out at last to the cargo net, halfway up you hamstring yourself, as your feet are where the rope ain't. Ease over the top and some "son" steps on your aching fist. To hell with it, drop! You do with a crash and limp away to meet the jeers of those who have made it. Do you look like that? You do. Thirty-mile hikes at forced march. For every mile you made, a man fell out. That was the end unless it was a very good excuse. Every day took its toll. Every daylight hour was full and half the night.

Classes in mortars, M1, pistols, LMGs [light machineguns] signals, wire laying, mines and booby traps. Laying demolitions, fighting tanks, scouting and patrolling, sabotage. For hours on end the roar of charges filled the air as engineer officers taught us to blow a bridge, pillbox, tank or train. Hours in the water making boats from shelter halves and the construction of toggle-rope bridges.

It was spending hours in the hot sun aligning and sighting mortars. Lay on grinding gravel firing .03s and M1s till your shoulder ached or push and pull targets all day. Fire burst after burst, you and a dozen others till the targets dance. Go out and fire some weapon all day and clean it half the night.

[There were] night problems of creeping and crawling through dew-wet grass, freezing in the cold, white light of the flares. The crashing "whump" of pole and satchel charges with the attendant sick, sweet, stinging smell of TNT, and clods of flying dirt. Tracer bullets at night, infiltration, and the rounds snicking at the wire—you crawled through dust, through more showers of exploded dirt until you are gagged at the smell of it.

Rudder Takes the Rudder

Then again we had a change of command [there had been several] as Major Rudder took over the reins of the battalion. He had arrived on the 30th of June and, at first glance, was different. The first thing he did was to give one of his orientations whereby anyone could and did voice his opinions.

Frank South, 2nd Battalion Medic, remembers Rudder first heard complaints and made himself loved because he did something about them. The food was terrible when he got there, so he sent some (or all) of the cooks to Cooks and Bakers School. Another time a man told Rudder he didn't have a watch, so Rudder took his own watch off and gave it to him.

The 2nd of July marked the advent of a certain Captain Knudsen of the justly famous 1st Ranger Battalion. In the following week he was joined by Sergeants Hardin and Heacock, and later by Sergeant Shaput. All had seen action in Africa at Kasserine Pass, Faid Pass and El Guettar. The tales the doughty Captain told would cool your blood, of marching for miles in the sand till blood oozed into your boots and you could pour it out on the ground, of crotch rot so bad the blood ran and scabbed. Discipline so strict that an all night march was punishment for a company because a couple of the men took off for town. He really made it sound rough.

The ultimate was reached when the company did seven-and-a-half miles in an hour-and-12 minutes, pooped, but proud.

Knowing that some of the men would not make the grade, we were not too surprised at the action as they started weeding them out. The battalion policy changed to "If you don't want to belong, transfer out." It came just in time and found us with about 50 percent effectives. The final contingent arrived on August 7 and was composed of selected men from nearby divisions on maneuvers for the most part.

We began a series of short, fast marches of some 10 or 12 miles distance by road or compass, pull a sneak raid, bivouac and then beat our way back buddy-system to the area. The buddy system was used as an assurance of mutual protection and to instill teamwork. One could also make a point of stopping in Tullahoma for ham and eggs.

Fort Pierce

The night of September 4, 500 men stood in the rain before boarding a train bound south for Fort Pierce, Florida, a small town about 120 miles north of Miami. The men got off the train and were taken to a small island that housed the vaunted Scouts and Raiders School.

There was intensive training in amphibious assaults, infiltration techniques, and the first look at the small British LCAs (Landing Craft, Assault) that would eventually carry them onto Normandy soil. The problems continued day and night. Working in an ocean full of jellyfish and on an island full of insects, the men learned how to use colored lights to keep in touch, how to mark a beach for landings, how to take small enemy positions quickly and quietly, and dozens of other skills.

The men nodded and cracked to one another that this was quite the place and envisioned evenings of flowing liquor and fun-loving gals. The place and visions became a great disappointment as we climbed aboard trucks and didn't stop until we had rolled far across a bridge that ended on a God-forsaken island, better known as the Scouts and Raiders School. Here were several acres of nothing but sand, palm trees, and stacks of pyramidal tents.

This was the beginning of 12 grueling days that included day and night problems leaving little time for naught but sleeping. We were told that due to the delay our training would be crowded into 11 days in order that everything might be included. That was putting it mildly. Everything was scheduled, including meals, and was the type of physical endurance that took guts, but no outfit had more of the spirit and morale that carried us through.

This place was infested with gnats, mosquitoes and sand flies, which annoyed you, got into your food and drew nearly all the blood and sanity from you with their numerous bites. Misery needed company and we were elected the goats. Even the beautifully inviting water had a catch to it as it was entirely covered with dainty, pink-colored jellyfish that left a nasty sting mark.

The course was centered about rubber boats and LCAs and later one became violent if either were mentioned during free time.

A sequence of training events included landing on rock jetties, loading and unloading into LCAs from landing nets, going out off-shore and studying silhouettes in the evening; company and battalion cross-country marches which included portage of boats, making a beach head, infiltrating through beach sentries, attacking small installations, sending beach-marking teams ashore who landed prior to H-Hour, first slitting their boats in the breakers and crawling to the dune-line after which they sent signals of colored lights, made directional by means of hand-made hoods. Boat teams paddled around the island to gain coordination for the final attack of Fort Pierce itself.

The toughest night was a combined portage and paddling problem of considerable length. The rough part was in the fact that the tide was out most of the evening and the boats had to be pulled through the water and manhandled nearly all the way, and through mud you sank into knee-deep. It was as trying an exercise as we have ever had.

The final test was the attack on the city and airport that brought many a laugh and showed the fruits of our labor as it went off like clockwork. Imagine the surprise of the aged night watchman when, out of nowhere, men swarmed over the wall and Captain Lytel jammed a Tommygun in his face. All in all the school was excellent and the boys were in better shape than ever before. The Instructors gave us the highest praise for the work we had done and coming from them, that was something.

The successful men, flushed with victory, gratefully accepted passes and went directly into town and had too good a time. Restriction to base followed, but lasted only a short time. On September 17 they boarded another, nicer train.

Fort Dix

It was starting to be cold at Fort Dix, New Jersey. The pot-bellied stoves in the wooden-walled, canvas-roofed tents almost kept the men warm—when they were allowed indoors.

The 2nd Battalion was beginning to form a core of internal leaders and settle down as a group. They would need the solidarity at Fort Dix. Advanced tactics were taught there, the next stage in the Ranger profile. The men fired their weapons often, solved problems in the field, learned more about directing artillery fire, and finessed their infiltration and sabotage abilities, all while using New Jersey as practice ground.

At that point the "Sunoco" Ranger patch appeared, a blue diamond with gold borders, and the word "Ranger" also in gold. The Second Army Patch was removed from uniform shoulders, but many of the men didn't wear the new patch long because it looked too much like the oil company label. Because of this, several unauthorized patches were created.

[We went through]…the shedding of the "deuce" of the Second Army for the distinctive patch of our own, designed by Lt. Smudin, which had eye appeal, but made us seem to be advertising Blue Sunoco.

Training began with weekend passes, even though the boys had a lot of fun just a few days before in Fort Pierce. Since most of the crew was from New York, New Jersey and Pennsylvania, a lot of them were able to get home for a day.

Once everyone was back in harness, training at Fort Dix and its surrounding areas began in earnest, and no more weekend passes were issued.

This consisted mostly of firing on ranges; section, company, and battalion coordination problems; demonstrations by artillery and other units of firepower; and a two-day exercise by companies with prepared objectives to attack and destroy.

There were single-evening passes given out, and the Rangers continued in their normal vein, drinking up while they could, asserting their dominance on any given club, and having as much fun as possible to offset the difficulties of their training, let alone what they knew they would be facing overseas.

There was a lot of transferring men from one company to another throughout the history of the battalion. To meet the demands of the TO&E, when someone was promoted or demoted, according to the needs of certain sections, personnel were shifted back and forth regularly.

A company of soldiers is in many ways like an extended family—a going concern with supply and other logistical needs. At any point during the transfer of men and materials during the multiple training phases, paperwork was being created, and the needs of the men were being met.

Too early—0400—we en-trucked for a 250-mile trip to Camp Ritchie for an Intelligence problem that would determine if the outfit was ready.

From this point we proceeded into the problem that was to take high ground, held by troops in German uniforms and using Boche weapons, by infiltration. The exercise went very well, for the following morning we actually reached our objective and were declared the winners, receiving high praise from the school heads. At its completion we had a demonstration of enemy weapons, mine fields, booby traps and tactics.

What wasn't mentioned in the above report was the presence of President Roosevelt's "Shangri-La"—now Camp David—on the other side of the boundary line the Rangers were to travel. The area was heavily protected. The 2nd Battalion was the first unit to complete the exercise—others had not at all—partly because Captain Ralph Gorenson ignored a few rules and moved along the boundary at night.

Camp Shanks to the Queen

A nine-day stay at Camp Shanks, New York was next, beginning November 12. Ominously, training gas masks were exchanged for the real thing.

Our training-type gas masks were turned in for the combat-types and tested amidst the not-so-pleasant aroma of tear gas. Following the usual procedure we had to take off the mask in the chamber and get a whiff. There was the place where the strongest, hardest men broke down, and were little more than sniveling, overgrown kids.

There was also added…impregnated clothing, made gas-resistant with some tack solution. It comprised a suit of fatigues, long johns, socks, white gloves [what a target)] and headdress. We took them with mental reservations that some one would fry in hell before we would wear them—orders or no.

Added to that sobering portent was practice going up and down cargo nets. Such nets are made of heavy rope slung over the side of a ship and used to convey troops in and out of small boats, often in heavy weather with both boat and ship bounding violently up and down.

Lots of free time made the men even more restless, knowing something was up, that the time for battle was coming closer. That was verified when instruction in Last Will and Testaments was given, along with more needles in the upper arm.

On November 21, the battalion assembled and marched through New York City to Pier 594 on the Hudson River, and took ship on the Queen Elizabeth. It took two days to cram 12,000 soldiers aboard and get the mighty ship moving. There were people everywhere, waving and crying, worrying and anticipating. The ship's railing was lined with soldiers taking one last look.

Too many were seeing America for the last time.

Some brilliant officer decided to make the Rangers MPs for the trip, which took them out of the running as troublemakers. They didn't like it much, but they did it, and woe be unto him who ran afoul of them.

There were very few other soldiers aboard and our puzzled countenances were soon to change when we were informed that our job was to be MPs for the voyage, springing, no doubt, from the manner we had man-handled guys so ably across the States in bar rooms, PXs, and ladies' boudoirs. We were given badges; an outward show of authority, but the men considered this the lowest form of duty and made no bones about it.

Training in England and Scotland

It is easy to say they got on the boat and went to England. They were a part of the massive movement of men and material across a vast ocean—not an easy feat. Though it took nearly a week to get across, normal convoys took as much as 20 days. They were in a hurry.

The Lizzie, as we came to call her, was loaded to the hilt, or in Navy parlance—the Plimsol Mark, which meant 18,000 men or more, and we noted no Naval escort around so precious a cargo, and wondered why. Although the weather was good she rolled and veered most of the way over and it wasn't until we reached our destination that we found out a "wolf pack" of 30 U-boats [German submarines] had deployed in a semi-circle around us but had been detected, causing us to double back and cruise around them. Once past, our terrific speed—around 30 knots—pulled us far away from them, making the "supermen" wish they had stayed in bed. However, it delayed us somewhat so it was six and one-half days later we arrived off Greenock, Scotland, in the Firth of Clyde.

Bude, Cornwall

After disembarking in Grenach on November 30, the battalion was put on a train to Bude, Cornwall, England. Battalion Headquarters was set up at the Links Hotel, but the men found themselves farmed out to private homes, sometimes four to a house. In time this arrangement worked well, with the men and their hosts becoming quite close in some instances. It was good for the young soldiers to see the way the people had to live—with blackout curtains, shell holes in the pavements, rationing, and above all, very few young men.

The cliffs of Bude were very close to what the men would face in France, rising 75 to 100 feet in height and nearly sheer. Training began with safety ropes and everyone going slowly, but within a couple of weeks the men were scrambling up the cliffs with confidence.

This was a period of intense concentration with special emphasis on the coordination of the companies in firing and in the attack of enemy installations. Each day we became better polished and better able to accomplish our mission.

One problem was to split into small groups and "case" an airfield without detection. At a prearranged time we were to make our way to the beach, there to be picked up by assault boats awaiting our arrival. This was run to all degrees of success. As these problems sometimes ran afoul of the "Home Guard," there was always a chance of excitement and more than once we had the countryside in an uproar.

December 27 saw the battalion on its way again, this time to the southern coast of England. Saying goodbye to their host families was hard for some of the men. As with Darby's boys before them, the young soldiers and the home crowd had a lot in common—they were all targets.

In Exeter, we had an hour's break at the Red Cross Center for hot chow and it really hit the spot. We pulled into a Quartermaster area for the remainder of the night and inquiry gave us the dubious knowledge we were just outside Portsmouth. That was a long way from Bude.

Titchfield

The 2nd Rangers took shelter in Titchfield, County Dorset, once again staying with host families. There were enough soldiers to cause an overflow and some stayed in other villages such as Warsash, Park Gate, and Botley.

HQ was situated in the town of Titchfield, and it was the same as it sounds. All the men were quartered, as in Bude, in private homes and were soon on the best of terms with the folks. Since some of the men were in Warsash, it was a job keeping tabs on them. It didn't take long to find the pubs with the hard stuff. Evenings found them there.

Plans for the Commando-style raids advanced rapidly with (promoted) Lt. Colonel Rudder, Major Schneider, Captain Cook and…two enlisted men…going to London for the initial stages of planning at COHQ, Whitehall, London. They had gone there in accordance with instructions contained in Ltr. HQ-COSSAC, 14 Dec. 1943, file COSSAC/OO/136; Subject: "Use of US Rangers in Raids and Reconnaissance."

The companies having arrived—A, D, F—on the 28th of December, and billeted as follows: A Co—Titchfield, D Co—Park Gate, F Co—Botley. Working with Commando instructors began. This was our first contact with the colorful and very much publicized Commandos, veterans of many raids, and [we] found out they were as good as claimed.

Equipment was hard to get until Colonel Rudder made a special trip to London and received a blanket requisition from General Eisenhower.

In truth, Ike wasn't crazy about the Ranger concept, but once going forward, he supported them. Still, the requisition probably came from a member of his staff.

At Folkstone…Company A and selected French guides brought the group up to…94 men. Their mission was to make a raid on the coast of France in the vicinity of Calais with the purpose of securing a prisoner and such pertinent information available.

The detachment was broken down into four teams, two to an assault craft. The teams were to board LCIs [Landing Craft, Infantry] at Dover, make the run-in to the beach in LCAs, and recall the LCAs by pre-arranged light signal to again board the LCIs.

The plan of action involved capturing a prisoner first and foremost, and if that happened right away, the unit would return at once. Otherwise, Plan Two went into effect, and the force would cut the beach wire, traverse mine fields, and move inland. Going forward meant traveling through enemy strong points and there were contingency plans for detection by the Germans. The units would leapfrog each other over quite a distance, or at least until they found someone to bring home with them. They were prepared to infiltrate silently or assault, or both.

Because of the necessarily precise timing only three of the nights of the so-called "dark period" would suffice for the operation if it were to have the benefit of complete darkness. During each of these three nights in the period so allotted the Royal Navy postponed the operation due to the abnormally rough sea. On the 27th of January the raid was cancelled.

Had the raid gone forward, those Rangers would have been the first American unit to make a strike on the shores of fortified Europe—Dieppe had men from several units. The train-up was intense and thorough, and the men were heartbroken to be turned away after so much preparation. Another such raid-to-be was trained for, then cancelled for the same reason. A 16-man detachment from D Company, led by Captain Slater, was trained by Fourth Commando Instructors, and later trimmed to 12 men.

At least simulated raids were carried off successfully, as described next.

We were to make a dry landing from LCIs on a portion of the English coast thought to be an abandoned fortress. The company was to breach the wire and reconnoiter an airfield one-mile inland. Emphasis was to be placed on proper timing and stealth.

The landing went as scheduled and the recon parties made their missions while a party covered the beach. At the roll call three men were found to be missing. It wasn't until one of them was brought in by a Royal Marine Shore Patrolman that we learned the fort had been secretly reoccupied by troops, and that almost 60 men had passed through the sentries without detection. The other two missing men had scouted to the right and entered the grounds of a secret laboratory before being detected, and then only a hundred feet short of a heavily charged wire.

On January 17, D Company moved to Freshwater, Isle of Wight, for two weeks of cliff scaling on the Needles, sheer chalk cliffs reaching to heights up to 300 feet. The other companies trained in various other places, picking up specialties for who-knew-what.

Here on the Isle began an extensive course in boat work, cliff scaling, and assault work. We were fortunate in the fact we were the first of the American troops to visit the place for any reason, for it was sealed in security. The Commandoes had operated from here in their raids on the French coast and it was a sentry post for the mainland.

Rudder received orders in January 1944, from First Army HQ in London. The stage was set for the invasion, and the Rangers had a mission, as usual, to be among the first Americans on the beach. Major Schneider, then Exec of the 2nd, went with Rudder to London to add his considerable expertise in amphibious operations.

Back to Bude

Having thought for some time they were going to be sent into battle at any moment, the men of the 2nd Rangers were disappointed when they had to return to Bude in mid-February. A bright spot was seeing their friendly family hosts again, though they had already said their emotional goodbyes. In defense against any sag in the men's morale, Colonel Rudder kept them hard at it.

Cliff scaling was a main component of the curriculum. Besides ropes, ladders of four-foot long metal sections were used. A man would climb up a few sections, push away from the cliff face, and quickly add another section. Some of the ladders were built to 100 feet.

It had to be pretty shaky at the top with a rifle, backpack, section of ladder, and someone shooting at you.

A strange addition to the mix came in the form of a cannon platoon, an odd attachment to a light infantry unit. That unusual addition to the Rangers was initially led by Darby veteran Chuck Shunstrom, a gutsy man who did great damage to the enemy with his three-inch medium guns.

It was the 4th of March that we acquired, of all things, a cannon platoon, and we had assumed we would be traveling light! The cannon consisted of four antiquated half-tracks off some armored outfit's salvage depot, and mounting 75s. With half-inch armor in the shield that an AP [anti-personnel] .30 would go through, we all gave the crew our blessing. The crew was of a higher caliber than the equipment they proposed to fight.

Captain Block—Briefing

Captain Walter E. Block was chief of the medical detachment that went with the Rangers to Pointe Du Hoc. This is his eyewitness account of the thorough briefing he received about the coming mission. Captain Block was killed December 8, 1944.

It was about 5:30 p.m. on April 7, 1944 when Major Schneider called me into the operations room at the Assault Training Center near Braunton, Devon, and first showed me the "Pointe."

"That's it, Doc. That's the spot where we are going to operate. Pointe du Hoc."

On the map, it actually looks insignificant, merely a tiny protuberance jutting out from the beach-line, approximately midway between the towns of Grandcamp and Vierville-sur-Mer, on the coast of Normandy. I don't think I was particularly impressed because it looked like any number of similar protuberances on the invasion coast, and my face evidently showed this, for after looking up, the Major continued.

"Now, take a look at this," he said, slowly rolling up a thick covering hanging on the wall of the operations room.

This was a series of photographs, taken at every possible angle by airplanes, of a coastline. Closer inspection showed this to be no ordinary coastline with smooth beaches, fine-grained sand, and a gentle sloping inward. What I saw was a panorama of many air photos linked together to form one unbroken line. Carefully looking thru a lens, I saw what appeared to be an unbroken line of cliff, for the most part sheer, stretching out on either side of a sharp spear pointed outcropping. This was Pointe du Hoc. The beach was covered with boulders, broken off portions of the cliff and, in outline, was irregular.

Block understandably asked the question, "Why here when it looks so tough?" In answer Schneider took him over to another wall full of photos.

So off we went to another wall in the room and another cloth was rolled up. Here on a blow-up was an aerial photo of the Pointe and the adjacent terrain. Whereas the large overall photos had showed only the coastline, a few houses, hedgerows, paths and roads, this photo showed the Pointe itself, and the land extending about 1,500 yards to either side, and about 2000 yards inland. On the extreme tip of the Pointe at the top of the cliff was a square, whitish-gray outline. On each side of this were three round, whitish-gray masses, approximately 30-35 feet in diameter.

The major went on to explain these were six 155mm gun emplacements, two of them casemated and the others open. By casemated, he meant the guns were encased in a protective covering of concrete on the top as well as the outer walls. The square mass on the tip of the Pointe was an observation post. Each of the emplacements was linked to the others by a series of camouflaged paths and underground tunnels. Such gun emplacements were protected by coverings, varying anywhere from six to ten feet of solid concrete. Most of the concrete had been poured in the past year but some of it was at least three years old and had become harder with each succeeding month. Extending back from the cliff, and encompassing all six guns was row upon row of wire, single and double apron. Our G-2 [Intelligence] information revealed that interspersed between the protective wire, and on both sides, were mine fields.

Truly a formidable set-up! But that was not all. Extending along the cliffs, from both sides of the Pointe were open and closed machinegun positions. There were four that could readily be seen on the left flank of the Pointe, and three on the right. These were the ones that were visible and how many more there were that were well camouflaged was anyone's guess. Off to the upper left of the photo was a series of small buildings, the small town of St. Pierre du Mont.

A look at those photos plainly showed the Germans were not worried about an attack on the Pointe from the seaside. Their defenses were aimed inland for the most part, though later conflict proved many of the small arms and machineguns could be turned when necessary.

Briefing consisted of explaining every particular detail of the operation. This generally started out with a recital of the mission, the potential strength of the enemy at a given point, all the capabilities of our own and theirs, and a thorough discussion of the terrain where the mission was to be performed. A thousand-and-one other factors to be considered in a water-borne operation included the rise and fall of the tides, types of beaches, and weather conditions. The men received detailed maps of the region and adjacent territory showing enemy defenses plus all the information the Intelligence department could obtain. That included positions of mine fields, details of critical points about the guns, and so forth. To cap it all, aerial photographs of the entire territory and blow-ups showing the smaller details filled out the briefing course. Finally, each man's part in the operation was explained, and he was made thoroughly familiar with every phase of the operation.

Battalion briefing featured a set of rubber models and plaster models so everyone would have the best chance of knowing where they were and where they had to go. Unfortunately, the bombing and shelling of the Pointe left it so rough that many pertinent landmarks were obliterated [though the Germans were not].

Braunton Camp

In April the 2nd Battalion saddled up for North Devon, County Dorset, for a week of training at the British Assault Training School at Braunton Camp (Baggy Point). The British figured anyone who could get through the school would be ready for battle.

Replacements came in to bring the unit up to strength. Purging of unfit candidates was merciless and frequent, and the shuffling of men from one unit to another (including the cannon platoon) continued throughout training.

April 1 was the first birthday of the battalion, marked by a party and short skits by the men.

It was there the executive officer, Major Max Schnieder, left the Battalion and took command of the 5th Battalion. Captain Cleveland Lytel became the XO of the 2nd [Lytel made Major in June].

At Swanage, Dorset, they were initiated into the mysteries of the newest methods of cliff assault. All types of climbing were used: free hand, smooth-rope, knotted rope, toggle rope, rope ladder, and a type of steel ladder that came in four-foot sections that could be constructed to the desired length. The Commandoes had originated a method of rope anchorage by the use of a rocket-type mortar, which could launch a special grapnel 200 feet in the air.

Dorchester—Almost Done

On April 27, 1944, the unit went to Dorchester, County Dorset, England, and lived in tents while training continued. One odd endeavor was gaining experience with DUKWs (Dorchester Utility Kaiser Works), an amphibious amalgamation of parts created from a two-and-a-half-ton GM chassis with six-wheel drive, and given a hull, rudder, and propeller. The British used the DUKW successfully during the invasion of Italy, but the Rangers made some modifications of their own. A little research by a few dedicated officers brought about the addition of a 100-foot extension ladder mounted on the bow of the DUKWs, eventually equipped with a .30 cal machinegun at the top, later replaced by twin Lewis guns.

The idea of firing twin guns at other gunners on a cliff top is one thing, but to be coming at them while waving in the breeze atop a hundred-foot ladder...

FABIUS

Then came FABIUS, the dress rehearsal for D-Day.

For the first time, men of the 2nd Battalion were to work with men of the 5th Battalion. The operation combined the two Ranger Battalions with the 29th Infantry Division's 116th Infantry Regiment, and a couple of tank platoons. It was an amphibious assault geared to be as much like Normandy would be as possible. The 2nd hit the beach from LCAs, with D, E, and F Companies scaling the Dartmouth cliffs, gaining the top and advancing with D Company in the lead. Striking inland, a 12-mile march ended the day for that portion of the 2nd. Other units did their practice on different beaches. Mostly those practices were successful in terms of organization and execution, but then no one was shooting back, and the terrain hadn't been bombed into rubble. The Germans bombed the exercise, however, as it was too big to hide. Men of the 29th Division died on the beach and in the water.

One problem that surfaced was confusion over the identity of units once ashore. Rangers and men of the 116th got intermingled in places and some followed the wrong leaders. To solve that problem an orange diamond was stenciled on the backs of all Ranger helmets.

Plans went forward. Rudder was named Commander of a Provisional Ranger Group formed by the two battalions, with Major Sullivan as Executive Officer. The dreaded mission to come didn't go unnoticed by the military chiefs. General Bradley remarked of Rudder, "Never has any commander been given a more desperate mission."

THE MISSION—D-DAY

The invasion of Italy featured more US Divisions than D-Day, seven to five. The rest of the force was mostly British and Canadian. Several Civil War battles had more casualties in a few hours than in all of the assault on Normandy. There were fewer ships sunk and fewer planes shot down than at Dieppe. There are not a lot of films about Salerno or Arzew, or the battles for Tunisia or Sicily, yet one of the most-watched war movies of all time was *The Longest Day*, a film about June 6, 1944—D-Day.

So, why does D-Day grab us with such intense feelings and images, more than any other meeting of enemies any time, anywhere?

For one thing, the invasion of France was an undertaking the Allies were not certain they could pull off. For another, the area of coastline was many miles smaller than the 70-mile fronts in North Africa or Italy. Targets were crammed together in places.

The fight to gain a toehold was contested heavily, including the land to the east taken by the British. The Allies faced experienced, entrenched enemy troops with interlocking lanes of fire, troops who knew beforehand that an invasion was imminent, almost a foregone conclusion. Resistance was fierce, so bad in some places that it seemed humans could not possibly survive—yet some did. Add to that mix the vision of paratroopers floating in the sky and Rangers assaulting not only the beach defenses, but the legendary cliffs of Pointe du Hoc, and one gets the idea why D-Day sits above all others as The Battle.

Perhaps because it is so famous a fight, there is a lot of very wrong information about D-Day out there, especially on the Internet. The movie *Saving Private Ryan* contributed somewhat to the confusion by being only partially accurate when delineating landing sites and missions, particularly for C Company, 2nd Battalion.

Much cross-referencing and interviewing has been done to get an accurate picture of where and when each Ranger unit came ashore, and what happened to them afterwards, though there are still arguments about certain details. Comprehensive books on D-Day include titles by Stephen E. Ambrose, Jon Gawne, and Joe Balkoski. Robert Black has a good section in his book, Rangers of WWII.

The planning and execution of the invasion of the Normandy coast of France on June 6, 1944, was the largest undertaking of its kind ever performed. The planning had taken nearly three years, coming to a head while England groaned under the weight of the combined military forces of several nations.

Secrecy was the watchword of the day. Even though it was generally recognized the invasion was certain to come at some point, German commanders felt secure enough to go off on holiday or other business just when things were bubbling over the edge of the pot. That misunderstanding included the German commander of the beach defenses, General Erwin Rommel, also absent. He had gone to Berlin to implore Hitler to give him more strength, and to try and sneak a little time with his wife for her birthday.

Rommel, known as the Desert Fox for his victories—and final defeat — in North Africa, was one of the best-known German commanders, but was eventually, like many others, pushed aside by Hitler and ended by committing suicide.

Operation Fortitude, a complete hoax involving a fake Army Group headed—in name only—by General George Patton, had drawn German attention to the Pas de Calais, an area of France north of the actual landing sites. Sitting almost directly across the narrowest part of the English Channel, it seemed the natural site for an invasion. Much of Hitler's strength, especially in terms of armor, was centered there and unable to move without his express orders. The threat of Patton's aggressiveness kept that armor in the wrong place for the correct amount of time—after D-Day.

The weather closed in on June 5, the original target date, and Supreme Allied Commander General Dwight D. Eisenhower reluctantly postponed the assault for 24 hours. Men were already crowded aboard ships, some of which were recalled from halfway across the English Channel to wait another day. The chances of the Germans finding out what was happening increased dramatically with each passing hour, as did the tension among the waiting air, sea, and land forces.

Almost 3,000 ships and some 2,500 landing craft of all sizes were poised to sail as the wind and rain turned the Channel into a maelstrom of heaving water. About 20,000 paratroopers waited impatiently to board C-47s. Eisenhower smoked incessantly and paced the floor, also waiting. At two in the morning he was informed there might be a break in the weather for a short time—maybe time enough to go.

He said, "I'm quite positive the order must be given."

Two hours later he was told the weather would definitely clear just enough for just long enough.

He said, "Let's go."

Those simple words unleashed the greatest force ever assembled into the greatest battle ever fought. Five areas of the Normandy coastline code-named Gold, Juno and Sword for the British and Canadians, and Omaha and Utah for the Americans, were to be hit by four times more military force than was used in the invasion of Iraq during Desert Storm.

Omaha and Utah beaches were 18 kilometers apart. Omaha, about 6,000 yards long, would be hit from the north by General Gerow's V Corps, composed of the 1st and 29th Infantry Divisions, part of General Bradley's First US Army. Utah Beach, to the west, would be taken by the US 4th Infantry Division, with paratroopers of the 101st and 82nd Airborne Divisions backing them up from the inland side.

Though scheduled for Pointe du Hoc if possible, the Rangers of the 5th Battalion and A and B Companies of the 2nd would end up landing at Omaha. Company C, 2nd Battalion, was always planned for Charlie Beach at the extreme right flank of Omaha. There were no Ranger units at Utah Beach.

Pointe du Hoc, pointing north, juts like a bunion to the right of Omaha—seen from the seaside—about four miles west, and between the two US beaches. On top of a 100-foot—or so—set of nearly vertical cliffs were supposed to be six French-made 155mm howitzers. The guns could command a large area of fire, including both US landing beaches and the near sea, soon to be full of ships. The strong point/battery would be the dominion of D, E, and F Companies of the 2nd Rangers, though they expected some help.

Considering the size of the invasion, six cannon don't seem like much to worry about. Indeed, there were more than one set of guns trained on the beaches, and some were of like caliber. The significance of the guns of Pointe du Hoc lay in their placement high on the bluff right on the edge of the water with an observation post as part of the battery. Without visual guidance many of the other batteries in the area were firing blind, if they fired at all, as most of their lookouts were taken care of by Naval fire not far into the morning.

Lt. Colonel Robert Evans of 1st Division Intelligence put together a description of the target gleaned from French Underground reports and aerial photos. His research said the guns were at grid coordinates 586937, 6.1-inch cannon with a range of 22,000 yards or more—about 14 miles—and were mounted on wheel mountings with a central pivot in emplacements 40 feet in diameter. They were camouflaged with netting, but had no turrets or shields. He was mostly correct.

Range of the guns depended on the ammunition used. WWI ammo gave it 17,400 yards, but new ordnance and some adjustments to the gun carriage allowed it 25,000 yards.

There were bunkered emplacements, but not all were concealed, or finished. The fortifications were far from finished, and the shelling and bombing had done extensive damage, but the trench system still functioned. Most of the physical work done at the Pointe was by French laborers, paid a small wage.

There was a concrete bunker used as an observation post right at the headland of the Pointe. There were other OPs, but Evans didn't know just where. Underground shelters and magazines were all connected with the guns by trenches. There was still some construction going on, and there were 20mm anti-aircraft batteries placed here and there. The German unit was the 2nd Battery, 832nd Army Coastal Battalion. The inland side of the battery was wired and mined, but the seaside, the cliffs, was considered by the Germans to be impregnable. There were machineguns and anti-aircraft batteries set on the right and left flanks, aimed at the beaches. Evans estimated there were about 200 Germans defending and operating the guns.

Rudder and Schneider had been briefed on Pointe du Hoc some five months earlier, and Schneider, who had extensive amphibious experience with Darby, was still worried by the plan. He wasn't the only one. Some had termed the operation "suicide," and "impossible." Rudder said his men could handle it.

His Ranger Group was comprised of the 2nd and 5th Battalions, two Naval Fire Control parties, and an air support party, all attached to the 116th Regimental Combat Team, Reinforced, part of the 29th Infantry Division.

It is ironic that the Rangers went in with the 29th. There was a trained Ranger Battalion, the 29th Rangers, ready to go only a few months before. They had been disbanded when the 2nd and 5th came on line.

Three task forces:

A—HQ detachment, D, E and F Companies of the 2nd Battalion, and one Naval Fire Control party to land at Pointe du Hoc

B—C Company of the 2nd to land at the Charlie sector on the extreme right flank of Omaha Beach, then get through Pointe Raz de la Percee and on to Pointe du Hoc

C—commanded by Schneider. HQ detachment from the 2nd, plus A and B Companies and an air support party to go along with a Naval Fire Control party, in addition to all of the 5th Battalion to land either at the Pointe or on Omaha Beach

Company C, 2nd Battalion was to land first, followed by the rest of the 2nd and A, B and C Companies of the 5th Battalion and the rest at H+28 minutes. The second wave was to land and go down the shoreline toward the Pointe. That way Rudder had two forces moving on the Pointe from two different directions. Though not in the original plans, in addition to Ranger Infantry, the Cannon Platoon landed a little later on Easy Green to the east and joined up with F Company, 5th Battalion.

Rudder's plan was approved April 17, but was soon revised to keep the main force—Task Force C—at sea until the outcome of the first assault was known. If there was no signal of success by H+30 minutes the rest of the Ranger Force would land on Omaha and strike west as originally planned.

The first wave to hit the Pointe would be comprised of 10 LCAs (British version of American LCVP, or Higgins Boat). There would be about 20 men to each boat, and would carry D, E, and F Companies along with some Signal Corps men and some medics.

The LCAs at the Pointe only carried 20 men because they were loaded down with equipment to scale the cliffs. At Omaha Beach the little boats were packed with 34 or 35 men.

To help breach the defenses and the cliffs, each LCA carried rockets adorned with 3/4-inch rope, ropes with toggles for climbing handholds, and light rope ladders capped by grapnels. There were also some hand-held rockets, but they were difficult to use.

The boats also carried sections of steel ladders four-feet long, which could be hooked together by climbing the existing ladder with a section, pushing away from the cliff face, and adding your section. Easy.

The DUKWs would come slightly behind the first wave, boasting their tall Fire Department ladders.

Though the first wave would have four BARs and a couple of light mortars, it was determined that the Pointe would be assaulted by the first climbers carrying pistols or carbines, which are smaller and easier to handle while holding on for dear life.

In reality, if anyone carrying anything could get up the cliff, they went, and with blessings.

The plan was simple: overrun the Pointe, then go south and cut the coastal highway between the towns of Grandcamp and Vierville to prevent German reinforcements from moving freely. Once done, Rangers were to hold the road until relieved by brother Rangers and elements of the 116th Infantry Regiment when they came along the road from Vierville, scheduled to happen by noon on D-Day. At least, it was supposed to happen that way.

Pointe du Hoc was said to be the strongest defensive position on the Normandy front, and must be taken. An officer at HQ was heard to remark that "three old women with brooms" could defend the position.

The area to be invaded was occupied by the German 716th Infantry Division, under strength, said Allied Intelligence, and staffed by a large percentage of non-German soldiers, including Poles and Russians. Intelligence may or may not have known that in mid-March

Rommel inserted the crack 352nd Division in the Omaha sector. The area of the Pointe itself was defended by ethnic Germans who didn't run or surrender, as did some of the conscripts. It was decided German reserve units were so placed as to be late arriving to fend off the Ranger attack. Still, the place was littered with strong points.

Actually, Allied Intelligence did fairly well pinpointing strong points and things they or the French Underground could see, but the Germans did move some units around just prior to D-Day, including some small armor assets.

To soften things up, fire from sea and sky was to be directed at the Pointe, which for the Navy was a high-priority target. The Air Corps also pounded the daylights—and the nightlights—out of the Pointe, but nobody knew for certain if all the guns would be destroyed, so the Rangers were needed to go in there and make sure.

The Naval fire wouldn't quit until the Rangers were at the target, then go on call. Members of the 293rd Joint Assault Signal Company went in with the Rangers as a Shore Fire Control Party.

As for the Air Corps, bombers hit the Pointe many times before D-Day, but couldn't focus on it in fear of giving away the coming attack. Between shells from the sea and bombs from the air, Pointe du Hoc, just one-kilometer square, was hit by several megatons of explosives.

When all the shelling and bombing was over, what the Rangers found at the top of the cliffs was nothing like what they'd been trained to expect.

OMAHA BEACH—DOG RED—DOG WHITE—DOG GREEN—CHARLIE

Operation Overlord Becomes Reality

At last it was June 6, 1944. All the training, all the talk, came down to the big test when Rudder's boys were loaded into the boats 12 miles from shore and sent off to do battle.

The Ranger embarkation was just about the last thing to happen on schedule that day. From that point on everything changed. A swift current moving boats the wrong way and heavy smoke coming from the beaches caused some boats to land in the wrong place. On Omaha Beach things were in doubt from the beginning. Likewise, at Pointe du Hoc, Rangers were able to scale the cliffs and get some men inland, but counter-attacks were heavy and the cost was high.

Through the long day and night that followed there was no thought of quitting, even when parts of Omaha had to be closed to further landings.

Rudder had no contingency plans for failure because there weren't any. D-Day was executed without backup plans. Had it not succeeded, the situation would have been immeasurably tragic. Eisenhower counted on overwhelming force to penetrate the Atlantic Wall, and it did. Rudder's Rangers were not an overwhelming force, and received very little backup the first day, but they got the job done in their important part of breaching the line both on Omaha and at the Pointe.

Capsule Chronology and Location of Ranger Landings

Looking at the three-and-one-half miles of Omaha Beach from the sea, or north, the Ranger landings happened on the right (west) third of the eight landing areas—each different in size. From the right the first four sections of beach were named Charlie, Dog Green, Dog White and Dog Red. Rangers fought on those beach sections only. Omaha was between the British and Canadian beaches (Gold, Juno and Sword) to the east and the American Utah Beach to the west.

The 2nd and 5th Ranger Battalions were under the overall command of Colonel Rudder, but the various missions each section performed caused several different commanders to have an effect on the outcome of the landings. For instance, both Ranger Battalions were attached to the 116th Infantry of the 29th Division temporarily, but once ashore the individual Ranger commanders were in control. In turn, the 116th was attached to the 1st Division for the landings.

Then there was Schneider leading the largest portion of Rangers onto the beach. Had he not made a crucial decision while still at sea, the devastation would have been much worse.

The breakdown of the Provisional Ranger Force into Task Forces to land in three different places makes it even more confusing as to who did what, and when.

Task Force A—HQ, D, E and F Companies, 2nd Battalion, was led by Rudder at Pointe du Hoc, landing at 7:08 with the mission of destroying six 155mm artillery pieces. Task Force A was the first American unit to accomplish its mission on D-Day, although what remained of the three companies had to hold on for a day before linking up.

Task Force B—Company C, 2nd Battalion, led by Captain Ralph Gorenson at Charlie Beach, had the mission of coming to the aid of the Ranger Companies at Pointe du Hoc by traveling overland, after taking out a radar station and other defenses on Pointe Raz de Percee.

Force B landed on the extreme right flank of Omaha Beach almost at the same time as A Company, 116th Infantry, and both were hard hit. In minutes, A/116th was 96 percent ineffective. C Company was a little farther west of the Vierville draw and had some cover when what was left of the men got off the beach. They went up cliffs similar to the ones at Pointe du Hoc, though not so tall, and may have been the first American troops to reach high ground before 7:00 on Omaha that day. By getting above the beach and on a more even keel with the enemy defenses, Company C was able to cut much of the German fire hitting the beach from that area. Members of Company B, 116th, came ashore soon after the Rangers were up the cliffs, and were able to join with Company C to enlarge the foothold.

Task Force C—A and B Companies, 2nd Battalion, and all of 5th Battalion, landed separately on two different beaches at different times. An HQ detachment and A and B, 2nd Rangers, hit the shore at 7:35 at the right edge of Dog White and a little into Dog Green after being waved off the original site by landing control. The first wave of the 5th Battalion—A, E, B, and the CP—landed at 7:45 on Dog Red, about a mile from the Vierville draw, after Schneider saw A and B of the 2nd getting torn up on the beach and diverted several hundred yards to the left, or east. Five minutes later C, D, some of F, and HQ of the 5th landed between Dog Red and Dog White.

Task Force C lost almost half of the two 2nd Battalion Companies to the massed fire on Dog Green/Dog White, but 5th Battalion brought some 450 men to the seawall on Dog Red—and a few on Dog White—with only six losses. They were just far enough away from the deadly defenses at the Vierville exit—about 1,800 yards—to get inland relatively unscathed, plus the German defenses were beginning to be overwhelmed with target choices.
Missed Signal

While the three companies of 2nd Battalion assaulted the cliffs at Pointe Du Hoc, Task Force B was already ashore and Task Force C was coming in at Omaha. Maneuvering through firing warships, part of the 2nd and all of the 5th endured the same cold and seasickness, added to by the uncertainty of where they would go, at least for many of them. Those men, not knowing for sure where they would land until the last minute, had to learn both missions, and stay afloat for a longer period of time while decisions were made.

Task Force C waited offshore for the signal to come in behind Rudder at the Pointe. A successful landing there was to be signaled by two successive 60mm mortar flares—lost in the landing—or if there was a failure the code word "Tilt" would be broadcast on the radio, meaning go to Plan B. When the signal didn't come within the required half-hour there was nothing else to do.

Ike Eikner

Pointe du Hoc veteran Eikner sent this message in response to a question by fellow veteran Frank South, while editing the WWII section of this project.

If the escalade went smoothly at Pointe du Hoc, we would fire up two flares for Schneider's Task Force C to come on in. If no signal were received by 0700 hrs, Schneider would follow the alternate plan and land at Omaha Beach. If, in Colonel Rudder's view, the situation warranted it, we could transmit the code word "Tilt" at any time to authorize Schneider's Force to land on Omaha Beach. We were supposed to touch down at the Pointe at 0630 hours, but due to the British navigation error we arrived at the Pointe at 0708 hours, and then sent out the Tilt code word. At the 0630, H Hour, we were still at sea and Colonel Rudder and I were in different LCAs. Had we been together, I would have posed the question whether we should send the Tilt signal out. Major Lytle's cop-out back in Weymouth Harbor caused Colonel Rudder to lead us in at the Pointe; thus, he was not with his Ranger Group staff. This screwed things up a bit, but we resorted to expedients and wiggled through.

Due to an indiscretion by then-Executive Officer, Major Lytel, Rudder had to take command of the 2nd in the attack on the Pointe, instead of being able to command his entire force of both battalions in better fashion.

The message "Tilt" was sent and receipted for at 7:10 a.m., too late to change anything. Max Schneider had his orders and was already on the way in. At 7:30 Rudder sent "Praise The Lord," meaning elements of the 2nd Battalion were on top of the cliffs. Five minutes later the first wave of Force C was landing on Omaha Beach, coming in just behind four companies of the 116th Infantry.

John Raaen

John Carpenter Raaen was a Captain on D-Day, but he retired a Major General after nearly 40 years in the Regular Army. He wrote the After Action Report for the 5th Battalion after D-Day. General Raaen has made lengthy and valuable contributions to this section.

Raaen landed with the 5th Rangers, but his boat was a few yards inside the Dog White boundary while the rest of the 5th was on Dog Red.

The three boats of HQ/2Rangers and A/2nd Rangers landed on the embankment beyond [east of] the Vierville seawall. Beyond this embankment was the promenade, a narrow paved road, but no barbed wire. Those three boats landed fairly close together. The two boats of B/2nd landed a bit nearer Vierville, in front of the seawall. Those two boats were separated by nearly 300 yards. Beyond the seawall there was a promenade and a single apron of barbed wire. There were several beach cottages located on the far side of the promenade.

All five boats met with intense rifle, machinegun, mortar, and artillery fire, mostly from [a strong point] directly above them on the bluffs, and from the complex of resistance points at the Vierville draw.

Lt. Colonel Schneider, about 1,000 yards away, watched through his field glasses the catastrophe of his first wave's landing. He made his decision quickly and by hand signals diverted his second and third waves another 800 [or so] yards to the left where he could see the beach was quieter. The seven boats of his second wave landed at 0745 on Dog Red beach on a 150-yard front, while his third wave of six boats landed nearly on top of the second wave, but shifted about 50 yards to his right at 0750, with one or two boats landing on Dog White, the other four on Dog Red.

Beach Landing Control soon closed Green Beach—a near death sentence—shifting east.

Gathering

An LCA carrying the 2nd Platoon of B Company hit a mine, which blew off its ramp and immediately swamped it. Survivors of the blast jumped ship and did the best they could to make shore. Once in the water—the fate of many men—heavy equipment dragged struggling soldiers down. Some were able to get rid of their burdens, but many drowned before touching ground. Those who were able to make it to shore were often hit at the water's edge, causing some to remain in the water, acting dead, letting the waves take them in.

Shore wasn't such a desirable place to be. There was carnage on the beach. Heavy fire from machineguns, mortars, small arms, and pre-sited artillery chewed up the beach and the men on it. Both Rangers and men of the 116th suffered, hiding behind beach obstacles and the very few tanks of the 743rd Battalion that made it ashore. Most of those were knocked out, but the remaining machines provided much-needed support.

A rough, low seawall—some of it wooden—offered small comfort, but men made for it. The two 2nd Battalion Companies, A and B, landed at the edge of Green and White Beaches, and comprised 130 men between them as they approached the sand. Only 35 men of A and 27 of B made the dubious safety of the seawall.

That dense pocket of death wasn't widely distributed, however, and Schneider's 5th Battalion landed several hundred yards east on Dog Red, losing less than 10 men during the dash across the beach.

From the seawall men trickled in twos and threes across a small road to more hiding places in demolished houses and what remained of the brush. As they went along they used their limited tank support to hit strong points, and made good progress at first.

On the edge of Dog Green, A Company/2nd Battalion was without officers, fielding small groups led by Sergeants. Company B was down to 18 men. The surviving group didn't wait for anything, heading toward the Vierville draw on the way to Pointe du Hoc. The rest of their battalion was there, and they didn't know what the conditions were, or even if anyone was still alive.

They didn't get far before heavy fire drove them back.

The remainder of A Company assaulted a defensive position on a bluff overlooking the beach, clawing their way up, screaming, half crazy with the fever of the battle and the loss of so many men. In short order they overwhelmed the position and joined up with B Company. By 0830, A and B Companies of the 2nd were on one hill and the 5th Battalion was on another, controlling the high ground above Dog White.

John Raaen

C/116 landed close to on time [0720] on Dog White, just at, and beyond, the west end of the wooden Les Moulins seawall. The company was about 1,200 yards east, or left, of its planned landing. They did not leave the beach until well after 0730, and then probably due to General Cota's prodding [Cota didn't land until 0730]. While still on the beach, I saw

Infantrymen climbing the bluffs to my right. This was probably C/116 and the time was 0755 to 0800.

Captain Arnold knew his mission was to lead the advance and flank guards of the 5th Rangers from Vierville draw to Pointe du Hoc. He sent a patrol to find a route from his position on the beach to the draw. The patrol returned when it was unable to pass a knoll several hundred yards from the draw. Arnold tried to find a way himself, but failed and returned and tagged on to the rear of A/2nd Rangers.

This was shortly after 0800. Even tail end Charley, me, was moving up the bluffs by then.

As A and B of the 2nd slid to the left along the crest, they ran into elements of C/116 and the 5th Rangers. In the severe fighting up the bluffs, the 5th Ranger Companies had become intermingled, not only with each other, but also with C/116. Lt. Colonel Schneider put a stop to the confusion and reorganized, which included putting Captain Arnold in command of a 2nd Ranger Company, composed of the survivors of HQ, A and B Companies. He placed that company in reserve and started the war from the crest of the bluffs. Having restored order to his Force C, he had Captain Whittington's B Company, 5th Rangers lead the Force through the hedgerows to the coastal road.

Charlie Beach—Vierville Draw

The Rangers of C Company, 2nd Battalion landed as part of the first wave to the right of A Company, 116th Infantry Regiment, though separated by a little distance. The Rangers landed on Charlie Beach to the extreme right of the American line and on the west side of the Vierville Draw. Company A, 116th, landed on the other side of the draw. Both companies took fearful losses getting across the beach, though A/116 was nearly wiped out and left huddled against the seawall.

Designated as Ranger Force B, C Company left the *Prince Charles* about 4 a.m., loading into LCAs. Company Commander, Captain Ralph Goranson, rode with the 2nd Platoon. The two LCAs ran for the *Empire Javelin* and picked up A Company of the 116th, then turned toward shore, 10 miles of hell away. The idea was for A/116th to capture Vierville, and if they couldn't, C Company Rangers were to advance on Pointe et Raz de la Percee on the west side of Charlie Beach. There were gun emplacements up there, plus a radar station a little to the west, and though they had been pounded pre-H-Hour, somebody had to go up there and make sure. Once that was done the company was to make for Pointe du Hoc.

As plans go, it was a good one, but the men had to make the beach first, and that was rough going. LCA 418 carried the 1st Platoon, led by Lt. William Moody, and was hit by accurate mortar fire while still on approach. LCA 1038 held the 2nd Platoon, led by Lt. Sidney Saloman, and though the fire from shore wasn't too intense at first, the closer they got the heavier the fire became.

It was a crowded and bumpy ride in the small boats. Many men were seasick, and everybody worried about being swamped by the rough seas. Still, most of the way in was free of enemy fire—until they got close. Hitting the water and sinking up to their chests and further, some men of the 2nd Platoon died before they made the beach, weighed down by heavy packs and equipment.

Making the beach through the increasing fire was hard enough, but when the moving targets became stationary long enough to drop their ramps on or near the beach, the incoming rounds began to zero in. Heavy machinegun, mortar and artillery fire tore into the men, immediately killing or wounding nearly half of them. Every man in one boat was killed by a machinegun firing directly into it when the ramp dropped. The remaining men took off across nearly 1,000 feet of low-tide beach for the dubious safety of the cliffs. More died on the way.

The defending Germans made it rough on the invaders, taking many lives during the long run to the base of the cliffs. Much of the resistance was based in a fortified house atop the cliff, a house that repelled the first few Rangers and some men of B Company of the 116th, coming up from below.

Heavy bombing of the beaches should have left many craters for men to take shelter in, but the largest portion of pre-invasion bombs fell several miles inland, doing little damage.

B Company/116th hit the beach just below the Rangers—who had topped the bluff—and Gorenson sent a man down to guide them up. What was left of the two companies fought together for the rest of the day, silencing much of the devastating fire raining on the beaches by eliminating enemy positions one-by-one. A favorite tactic against strong points was to kick open the door of a house, throw in a white phosphorus grenade, and shoot anybody who came out.

Captain Gorenson had two plans. The first was based on the 116th clearing Vierville Draw. If they had, he could use the draw to move his men forward and get to Pointe Raz de la Percee. The second was based on the draw still being held by the Germans. There were some 30-foot cliffs there, but they could be scaled.

Since the Germans still held the draw, Gorenson went with Plan Two. Lieutenant Moody and two men went scouting west below the cliffs for the best place to get up. After about 300 yards they discovered a slight cleft in the cliff, and by using their fighting knives and/or bayonets they monkey-walked their way to the top of the cliff. Once on top they braved fire from the fortified house that was giving everyone fits and made it back to bring up the rest of the company, which was accomplished by shouting directions down to the Captain.

Official Army history recognizes elements of C Company Rangers as "probably" being the first to high ground in their area at about 7:30, but men who were there say it was more like 7:00. Either way, by the time the 5th and the rest of the 2nd had landed, men of C Company Rangers had already made the top, though in a different area. Fighting along the Vierville draw defensive line was fierce for some time before the draw was counted "open."

Trenches connected many of the strong points up there, and reinforcements were coming through them from Vierville and nearby positions. The Rangers and one boat section of B Company/116th cleaned out the enemy several times, but the positions were being re-manned via the trenches almost as fast as they could be cleared.

Lt. Saloman made it far enough to stand in an overrun German mortar emplacement and look out over the beaches, and then went back to report. The men were so entangled in the web of defenses that Allied ships couldn't separate who was who and lobbed in some shells that fell among the Rangers.

Having lost so many down below, the Rangers of C Company had just one man killed on the cliff top in the early going. Lieutenants Saloman and Moody were behind a rock when Moody risked a quick look over the top. He took a round from a sniper while trying to see what was happening. By that time the original 68 men had been devastated by the loss of 21 dead and 18 wounded. They were down to less than one platoon.

Three or four counterattacks were launched against the small American toehold atop the cliffs, all repulsed, and that and the attacks on the farmhouse left 69 German dead and a large number of wounded. The strong point wasn't taken until late afternoon, but actions against it had kept it from firing on the beach, mostly negating a main defensive position in the Vierville Draw.

At Pointe et Raz de la Percee, Captain Gorenson called for fire from the British warship *HMS Glasgow*. Shrieking shells pounded the Pointe into rubble in the early afternoon, saving many lives by eliminating the need for another assault. Gorenson followed up with a patrol to the area, and found it demolished.

Thomas Herring—5th Ranger Battalion

This interview was done by email in 2002. Tom Herring, like many others, responded to a plea for volunteers posted on a bulletin board in his unit area. A PFC at the time, he was with the 26th Infantry Division when it moved from South Carolina to Camp Gordon, Georgia, and he was ready to move on. He volunteered and was interviewed and accepted to the new 5th Ranger Battalion. He went on to train at Camp Forrest, Tennessee.

At the time I joined, I was just glad to be leaving the 26th ID. After we started training, and they began to relate to us the exploits of the 1st, 3rd and 4th in the Mediterranean, we were anxious to "get into the action."

He was asked if he was concerned about the risks associated with being a Ranger.

At 19 years of age, questions like that never entered our minds!

After we started training, and the "buddy system" was emphasized, it became apparent that depending on your buddy was necessary and most helpful. From there, the esprit de corps began generating, and such lasts to this day, as evidenced by our reunions.

Right after this interview there was a reunion of about 150 WWII Rangers from all six battalions.

Schneider took over just prior to the invasion. The former CO was, I have been told, deemed incapable of leading the battalion by several of the other officers who consulted with SHEAF [Supreme HQ, Allied Forces] and effected his removal. Schneider was apparently very capable. He had served with the 1st Ranger Battalion in Africa and Italy, and been through three sea-borne invasions. On D-Day, his unilateral change of landing location is reported to have saved many lives in the 5th Ranger Battalion.

[On the way in] many were seasick due to the rough seas. We were able to stand up until the small arms fire was getting near. I was not then nor have I ever been seasick. Guess my system is not agitated by the wave motion. In my opinion, I do not believe the seasickness hindered the Rangers from their assigned tasks, as is reported happening to other troops. Remember, we trained in numerous beach landings in all sorts of weather.

[On the beach there were] live and dead soldiers all over; several boats out of action. One LCI was hit where the side ladder connects to the deck and the ladder was blown off; then, immediately, the other side was hit with similar results. There were soldiers on the ladder at the time; shows how well the Germans had the beach zeroed in. The 5th landed away from its scheduled area due to the unilateral decision of Col. Schneider. Where we were scheduled to land was blocked up with 29th [116th Infantry] who were pinned down on the beach. When the 5th landed, the Germans still concentrated on the 29th, so we were able to get onto the beach and start up the bluff before the Germans started on us, but we were out of the zeroed in area so our casualties were fairly light. In our area, we were the first troops to reach the coast road atop the bluffs.

There is some controversy over who was first in that area to gain the bluff. Some say it was C Company, 116th. Others say Rangers led the way. Upon study, it appears there was a mix of both, since there was no concerted rush up the hill. A few men at a time went forward, and often there were mixed units operating without officers. Company C, 116th may have been the first "organized" unit up the hill, but there were evidently Rangers up there, too.

Was General Norman Cota Responsible For The Phrase, "Rangers Lead The Way?"

General Cota was the Assistant Commander of the 29th Infantry Division, a tough and resourceful man who was very influential in getting his men off the beach.

Seen at one point behind the seawall, and at another walking casually down the beach exhorting soldiers to get going, Cota was, by all accounts, a decisive factor in getting men onto higher ground.

It was very noisy and confused on that beach and most men wouldn't even notice Cota or anybody else unless they were right next to them, as Tom Herring was. The General moved from group to group, pushing, cajoling, looking for those who had the guts to go over the seawall. Very soon men realized that he was right; staying on the beach almost certainly meant death. Enough of them started out in small groups that the rest began to follow, thinking, "If they can do it, I can do it."

Captain John Raaen, CO of 5th Battalion HQ Company, saw General Cota coming down the beach. Realizing he was a high-ranking officer, Raaen ran over to him as he entered the bay made by the breakwaters. Raaen saluted and reported. Cota, a friend of Raaen's father, recognized him and asked for the situation. Raaen gave it to him saying, "Sir, the 5th Rangers have landed intact over a 200-yard front. The battalion commander has given the order to proceed to our assembly areas by platoons." Cota then asked where the battalion commander was. Raaen indicated Schneider sitting on the seawall about 75 yards away. Cota started off, then stopped and turned to the Rangers scattered around the bay and said, "You men are Rangers. I know that you won't let me down." He then moved off in Schneider's direction.

Both men stood to converse—with incoming fire all around them. Witnesses to the conversation report Cota as saying he was "counting on" or "expecting" the Rangers to lead the way.

Keith Nightingale

This was received in two different emails in 2006.

First: I heard the story from Major Schneider's RTO on several occasions and have no reason to believe it to be untrue. The first was when I was the RTB Commander in 1990 and the second this April when I met him again at Fort Benning. He hasn't changed his story.

Absent details, it was a simple unemotional statement from Cota to Schneider concluding the discussion as to how best take the cliffs. Schneider and Canham [116th CO] were in a shell hole about 300 yards west of the eastern exit causeway with Cota standing on the edge with his back to the sea. After the decision to follow a terrain feature that Cota pointed out, he turned to Schneider and said, "OK. Rangers, lead the way" in a quiet and non-emotional way. No bravado or drama.

Second: Regarding my outline of the scene where "Rangers Lead The Way" was born by General Cota, my two references are Schneider's RTO (F. Coughlin) and Lt. (JG) Ben Berger, who was the NGF LNO for 5th Rangers, and was in the shell crater when the discussion with Schneider was held. Both stories are consistent as I described. I talked to Coughlin (I think this is the spelling-his signature is hard to read) at the RTB HOF induction to re-iterate what he told me in 1989 at Fort Benning when I was the RTB Commander. Ben Berger related his version to me on the train between Carentan and Paris. I am satisfied that the general description is accurate.

Tom Herring

I was nearby. Matter of fact, we were lying at the seawall and my buddy on my right asked if I had a match. I replied they were all wet. He reached over my shoulder, poked the soldier on my left and said, "Hey, Buddy, got a light?" The soldier rolled onto his left side and produced a Zippo lighter. It was then we saw the star on his shoulder. My buddy said, "Sorry, Sir." Cota responded, "That's all right, son, we're all here for the same purpose!"

It was shortly thereafter that Cota began pacing to and fro along the beach yelling "If you don't get off the beach, you're gonna die!" over and over again. Finally he stopped at a couple of Rangers and asked their unit. They replied, "We're Rangers, Sir." Cota said, "Get me your CO." Schneider arrived in a few minutes and Cota said words like, "Colonel, we gotta get off the beach. Lead the way, Rangers!" Whereupon Schneider turned and yelled "Bangalores!"

The bangalore is an explosive device shaped like a small torpedo.

The bangalore teams jumped up, slid the bangalores under the barbed wire, and blew gaps. The 5th, led by D Company, started up the bluff to reach the coast road.

It was great to have achieved our assigned goal, even though we got there on D+2 instead of in three hours on D-Day. One thing that is not mentioned in histories I have read, is that the battleships and cruisers offshore were to start shelling the Pointe at about noon on D+2 if they did not get the signal that the Pointe was in US hands. The signal was an American flag flying from a pole atop the Pointe. The Rangers, the 29th ID, and some of the 1st ID literally rushed that morning to achieve the assigned goal and get the flag raised. The flag was raised about half an hour before shelling was to start. If the shelling started while we were still on the Pointe, we would obviously all have been killed.

The 5th went inland but did not fight again until the battle for Brest in July. They did accomplish several raids, nighttime recon, etc. I was with the 5th until it reached near the German border near Metz, France in November 1944. I was hospitalized with pneumonia and eventually returned State-side and was medically discharged in February 1945.

Possibilities

In other accounts a Ranger named Bull Dawson was given the command by Cota, or there was no actual command given at all, just a conversation in which those words were used. One account has Cota going to Schneider and another has the reverse. Either way, the famous words stuck hard.

Did his words inspire the Rangers to rise up en masse and lead everybody up the hill? No, but those words didn't hinder anybody, either. The men didn't need inspiring, anyway. They had just gotten there. The men huddling behind the seawall were mostly survivors of the first wave of 116th soldiers who had been smashed on the beach. The Rangers would have gone up the hill with or without Cota, but his presence and bearing, not to mention his words, probably helped them along.

Did some of the Rangers get bangalore torpedoes and blow gaps in the wire? Yes, the Rangers blew four gaps and C/116 blew two more. The most famous gap was blown in front of Cota and Schneider by Woody Dorman and Bill Reed of D/5th Rangers. Companies C, D, HQ, and the CP went through that gap along with men of the 116th, and probably Cota, too, traveling diagonally up the hill.

Men like Norman Cota saved more than one man's butt on that beach, and whether he said those exact words or not is irrelevant. Cota would have made an excellent Ranger, and would probably be proud to know the Rangers attribute their motto to him.

From HHC, 2nd Battalion History, After The Landing

Remnants of A, B, and C Companies plus the 5th Rangers who weren't too badly hit, pushed on as point for the 116th Regiment [coming off the beach]. Twice pushed through Vierville-sur-Mer and had to return, for the supporting units of the 29th were held up by sniper fire in the town. A series of tunnels were finally discovered by which the enemy was infiltrating the town. Blowing up the middle of the tunnel and cleaning it out solved the trouble. This job fell to the lot of B Company. Civilian snipers were encountered for the first time, both men and women, and were summarily dealt with.

A quantity of wooden bullets was found and mistakenly assumed to be for practice firing. The unusual rounds turned out to have been used by snipers who had been by-passed. The wooden rounds were very light compared to lead and had no distance. That way the snipers could fire through the Americans toward their own lines, but not hit their own men. It is said they made a nasty wound.

A detachment of tanks with Rangers [riding on them)] finally made contact on the morning of the 8th with Force A, and there was a mix-up in which we were almost involved in a firefight with our own men as the tanks fired into the woods of the Pointe, killing four men and injuring three.

It was with mixed emotions we met the survivors of the Pointe—happy to greet those still alive and mourning for those who had died, face to the enemy.

The battalion was too exhausted for further action that day and went into bivouac before Grandcamp Les Bains. Action was going on in the town itself and numerous prisoners were brought in. The men had the opportunity to gather their bedrolls and clean up. Groups split up and joined the 5th Battalion in the taking of Grandcamp. With the town cleared, we passed through to Osmansville where we stayed for two days. The outfit had started to pick up souvenirs and to laugh again.

THE ASSAULT ON POINTE DU HOC

Four miles west of Omaha Beach the other half of 2nd Battalion Rangers slowly made their way toward land. The ocean was rougher than expected, and though the LCAs were thought to be unsinkable by many, two of the first batch didn't make shore. LCA 914, a supply boat, shipped too much water and sank, leaving only one survivor. The amount of weight the Rangers were carrying precluded swimming in the cold, choppy sea.

LCA 860 was carrying Captain Duke Slater, leader of 2nd Battalion's D Company. The little boat swamped, but Slater and most of his men were rescued. Taken to a sick bay aboard a warship the men begged to be returned to the battle, but hypothermia and exhaustion led the doctors to keep them aboard. That meant Rudder was already down about 30 men. Ranger Companies were at full strength with 68 men, so the equivalent of a platoon was gone.

Slater and his men returned to the 2nd Rangers on June 19. Years later, he became the first commander of the Swamp Phase of Ranger School, in north Florida.

Throughout the small fleet of nervous Rangers—and elsewhere—seasickness was rampant. All were wet and half-frozen. Some boats had to have men use their helmets to bail, and threw out all unnecessary, and some needed gear in order to stay afloat. Vomit and salt water sloshed around their feet. The journey to shore was hellish, and more than one man was eager to get off the boats.

The run in would have taken long enough if they had been on course, but a navigational error carried Rudder's force almost to Pointe et Raz de la Percee, three miles east, and near the right flank of Omaha Beach. In the lead boat, LCA 888, Rudder figured out what was happening and made a course correction, but the time had slipped by. At that point the group was about 30 minutes behind schedule, which meant Schneider's tough decision was coming fast. The fate of some 575 Rangers hung in the balance.

Running west was no easy feat. The flotilla had to run parallel to a shore filled with people trying to kill them. It was a veritable gauntlet of fire, and damage was taken. One of the DUKWs took some 20mm rounds, making casualties out of five Rangers aboard.

Rudder's careful planning took another turn when the three companies all had to hit the Pointe from the same side because of the new angle of approach. That meant all three would land in a space picked for just two, squeezing them together. Though it seemed like a bad break, the single landing area was fortuitous because the far side of the Pointe was much harder to climb.

John Raaen

Early versions of the course change have it that an eastward tidal current carried the Rangers in the wrong direction. Not so, says John Raaen, pointing to the After Action Report of the British Officer In Charge (OIC) of HMML 304, dated 12 June 1944.

ML 304 was the guide boat for Force A. First, both his radar and Loran [navigation aid] went out. This forced him into navigating by dead reckoning. With severe tidal flow and stormy seas besetting ML 304, the OIC was forced to use visual observation. He had thought that smoke from the guns of Pointe du Hoc would reveal the location of the Pointe...[which] was covered in smoke and dust. Its silhouette had been changed markedly by bombing and Naval gunfire. He couldn't recognize it. He saw Pointe et Raz also clouded in smoke and dust. The silhouette matched that of his photos of Pointe du Hoc. He changed course and headed for Pointe et Raz! This was observed by other ships that knew where the Pointe was from their radars and Loran. But, they couldn't break radio silence to tell him!

At 4,000 yards from Pointe et Raz, the OIC launched the DUKWs, and began final deployment of his LCAs at 1,000 yards. Suddenly Rudder, among others, realized there were no gun emplacements of the point ahead. The flotilla turned and started a race to Pointe du Hoc. It was 0630 hours—H-Hour. As the flotilla headed into the tidal race—that's the RAZ in Pointe et Raz de la Percee—it could not make any real speed because of boats swamping. Enemy fire from the cliffs was mostly silenced by at least one US patrol boat which used its 3-inch gun.

Sixty years later I was standing on the top deck of the *MS Silver Cloud*. I was 90 feet above the water. The weather was clear, the seas gentle. The sun was up, though barely. With my field glasses, and knowing exactly what I was looking for, I could not locate Pointe du Hoc at a range of about two miles! Pointe et Raz was easy to spot, but Pointe du Hoc blended into the other little shadowy prominences. No wonder the OIC had problems in a storm on a plunging, rocking boat, with his eyes eight feet above the four-to-five-foot waves that drenched him constantly as he searched through early morning haze and semi-darkness.

Ike Eikner

John "Ike" Eikner was with the 2nd Battalion at Pointe du Hoc.

I joined the 2nd Ranger Battalion in early April 1943, shortly after its organization in Camp Forrest, Tennessee. I went in as First Lieutenant, Assistant S-3, but was changed over to Communications Officer when that job was vacated by the former Commo due to illness. I continued as Commo up through the D-Day operation, but on D-Day I also became acting Headquarters CO. Several of us wore different hats due to so many casualties. Later, I was promoted to Captain and continued as Headquarters Commandant until we were disbanded back in the States. I stayed in the Reserves for about seven years.

Around 4 a.m. on D-Day morning, after a breakfast of flapjacks and coffee, Colonel Rudder and I were topside on the deck of *HMS Ben My Chree*, overseeing the loading of men and equipment on the LCAs. At the last minute, we decided that it would be best to split up the Headquarters group into two LCAs rather than run the risk of losing the entire command group in one craft. The Colonel took the lead LCA, #888, an E Company boat. To this day I am not sure, but I believe I was on an E Company boat also, # 722. Yes, the record shows the Colonel and I both in LCA 888, but while loading up on D-Day morning, we decided we had too many HQ people in one craft, so some of us changed over to LCA 722.

The run in to shore provided the spectacle of the fireworks from the Naval gunfire and the bombing on Pointe du Hoc. At one point, rockets from our own "secret weapon" ships were dropping around us, and we had some choice words for the guys manning those weapons. In post-war years, I learned from a commander of one of the Rocket Ships that about two percent of the rockets would tumble out of trajectory. I told him, "Yeah, I was on the receiving end of your two percent!"

The "secret weapons" were barges loaded with hundreds of rocket launchers which released a thunderous roar when fired in quick sequence. Fearsome to observe, the rockets mostly fell short of the shore, doing little damage to the Germans.

As soon as there was enough daylight to make out the headlands, Colonel Rudder, in the lead craft, determined that we were on the wrong course and headed for Pointe et Raz de la Percee, some three miles east of our objective. It was with some difficulty that he persuaded the boatswain to flank right and take a corrective course for Pointe du Hoc with advanced throttle. The angle of our heading and the increased speed soon caused the waves to slosh over the ramp, and we were all soon bailing water with our helmets to stay afloat. We were now within small arms range of the shore and the enemy was taking us under fire. We were like ducks in a pond for them. Mixed in with the small arms were some 20mm incendiaries—big balls of fire coming right at you, but fortunately none hit our boat.

I well remember when the first bullet hit us. Ka-pop! And there was a little round hole through the rope box. I yelled, "Okay, boys, heads down! We're under fire!"

So there we were, bailing water, and some of the fellows were puking from the rough sea, and being shot at, all at the same time.

The navigational error brought us into Pointe du Hoc at 7:08 a.m., 38 minutes late. The bombing and Naval gunfire had ceased just before H-Hour [6:30 a.m.] as planned. The enemy was now up and about and taking us under fire as we came in for our landing. Since we were coming in at a different angle from that planned, all boats landed east of the Pointe.

Going Up

The lost 38 minutes meant the Naval fire lifted, giving the German defenders time to get set. One plus came when the British Destroyer Talybont and the U. S. Destroyer Satterlee hit the cliff tops with four-inch and two-pounder shells just before the Rangers landed, driving defenders back from the edge of the cliff.

The Rangers hit the beach, or least the water in front of it, at 7:08 a.m. on a front just a few

hundred yards wide. Since the Pointe pointed north, the right-most LCA was almost under it, pushed sideways by the extra company. The beach wasn't a beach at all, but a layer of "shingle," which is small rock. The area available to land was very narrow, and kept getting smaller as the tide came in.

Rommel insisted the Allies would come in at high tide when most of the beach obstacles would be covered by water, but Eisenhower fooled him and came at low tide. Farther from the objectives, but the obstacles and many bomb craters were uncovered. As the tide came in, later assault waves had great trouble with obstacles, especially those with Teller mines hung on them.

Rudder's LCA was the first to hit the beach with men of E Company. They could see the Germans on the cliff tops as they came in under building fire.

Rockets with ropes trailing were fired at the cliffs from the LCAs, trying to get purchase at the top with grapnels, but most of the ropes were too heavy, soaked on the way in. Men went in water up to their necks in many places. The struggle to go forward continued as more LCAs dropped their ramps.

The first Rangers ashore attacked the cliffs like madmen, trying to free-climb them, using bayonets to gain hold, but the earth was packed with clay, and it was too slippery.

LCA 668 fired six rockets, three of which stuck, but only one could be effectively used. Up that line went Bill Vaughn, who may have been the first of the battalion on top.

A hand-fired rocket—somewhat like a mortar—from LCA 861 found the top and Rangers quickly scrambled up the resulting line. Down below, Captain Otto Masny, Commander of F Company, wouldn't let the ramp drop on his LCA 883 until there was dry land under it. The little boat came all the way in, the only one to do so, giving Masny the best shot at getting his rockets up. Five of six stuck, and more men gained the top.

Though the defenders weren't prepared for a seaside assault, small weapons such as machineguns are easily moved, and small arms and grenades took a heavy toll in the confined area under the edge of the cliffs.

The Rangers went forward, using the rubble at the bottom of the cliff as a staging area. Pre-invasion bombardment had pockmarked the cliff face, and huge piles of dirt and rock had sheared off, leaving mounds some 40 feet high in places. On one such mound the men set a 16-foot ladder made of four-foot sections. A couple of tries and added sections let a Ranger reach the top. Though seriously wounded, he held the ladder in place so more men could climb up. Such heroics were happening all along the steep cliffs. The Rangers had a foothold at the top just minutes after landing.

Men from D Company, which was supposed to land on the west side of the Pointe, went around the promontory to see if the getting was good on that side, but found less protection and fewer mounds of rubble there. It turned out to their advantage to have landed where they did.

None of the DUKWs could get all the way in due to bomb craters in the early surf, but they did put fire on the cliff tops. A Ranger named William Stivison climbed 80 feet up a ladder and banged away with the two Lewis guns mounted on top. He was flung about 40 feet from side to side with the motion of the DUKW under him, making accuracy impossible, but he was spraying a lot of rounds each time his pendulum movement brought him to the top of the swing, which put him at the right height to fire at the top of the cliff. The Germans saw him and naturally fired back, but couldn't hit the wildly moving target.

Len Lomell introduced me to William Stivison. Asked what he was thinking when he went up that ladder, he replied, "I wasn't."

Once on top of the cliff men moved off in small groups, spreading out to meet their objectives. One such group went to the concrete observation post at the tip of the Pointe. The force was down below 200 men by the time the majority reached the top. There were about 15 casualties on the beach, more on top. The Rangers went forward.

Ike Eikner

I was the last person to leave LCA 722 and carried off a cloverleaf of 60mm mortar shells. In trotting across what seemed to be shallow water, I went down into a crater over my head. I managed to crawl out and deposited the shells under the cliff. There was a rope ahead of me and two fellows were climbing it. I was following them when the enemy began to throw down large numbers of grenades. I yelled up to them, "The enemy is throwing grenades, keep your faces in and butts out!" Then there was a very loud explosion and here comes an avalanche of rocks and dirt down toward me. I was knocked out for a while, but soon the pain in my legs roused me to discover I had been tumbled further down the cliff and was knee deep in rocks and mud. I had received no penetrating wounds when knocked off the cliffs, just lots of small cuts and bruises. I looked up to see an enemy peering down from the cliff. Seeing the butt of my Tommygun sticking up a few feet away, I pulled my gun out, took aim and -CLICK- it would not fire. It was all jammed up with mud. So here I am in the damndest fight in history with no weapon.

Why the enemy did not knock me off, I do not know. Spying someone with a radio in the little cave beneath the projection of Pointe du Hoc, I scrambled down and asked if he had sent out any messages—he had not and I transmitted the first messages at that time on the Ranger frequency using an SCR 300. The message was code for "first men up the cliff." This was receipted for with the word "roger." At 7:45 a.m. I sent the message "Praise the Lord", which meant that all essential men were up the cliff. This message was not receipted for.

Earlier on, within about five minutes after touchdown, my Communications Chief, Tech Sergeant Roach, had set up on the beach our big set, the SCR 284, complete with hand-cranked generator. We were ready for business, but could raise no one in the Force Command Net since they had not yet put down on Omaha Beach.

Among the men in the cave was one fellow seriously wounded and in great pain. I opened his first aid kit and gave him a shot of morphine. At our Ranger Reunion in San Antonio in 1985, I was telling some of the fellows about this and one of the fellows said, "Hell, Captain, that was me! You saved my life. The doctor said it was the morphine that enabled me to cope with shock."

Before leaving the cave, I helped the guys, all wounded to some degree, to pile up some rocks for protection since they were in direct line of sight from an enemy machinegun position.

Shortly thereafter I met Lt. Colonel Trevor, a British Commando who had helped us with training. He pointed to a large crater in the edge of the cliff and said that Colonel Rudder was setting up his CP [command post] there. I quickly moved all communications people up the cliff and soon we were all set up for business in the CP we were to occupy for two-and-a-half days. We immediately attempted to contact our forces on the main beach, but with no success. At that time we were not aware of the slaughter going on there, and of course a radio on the back of a dead man is of no use to anyone.

At The Top

Detailed study of the Pointe by the invaders was mostly wasted when they found the area strewn with rubble and bomb craters. Landmarks were unrecognizable. Looking like a landing zone for meteorites, the gun emplacements and the area around them were so torn that the battle zone was confined to small areas at a time. The men had plenty of places to take cover, but so did the Germans. The tumbled rubble resulted in the break-up of large groups, so the Rangers came at the defenders from many angles, causing confusion and making the Germans think there were more attackers than there really were. The bad part was the inability of the Rangers to concentrate their forces.

The Rangers knew their missions, and continued forward despite the confusion and rough going. Each company had a separate mission, with D to go after the guns on the right flank, E to destroy the #3 gun, then get the observation post (OP), then go cut the east-west road behind the Pointe, and F to take out the anti-aircraft batteries and the #1 and #2 guns.

Once the area was taken everyone was to meet on the road where part of E would already be. The other part of E Company was to stay at the Pointe and provide security for HQ when it came up.

Opposition wasn't too bad at first, except near the OP. Bomb craters made it hard to locate targets. Two groups attacked the OP, though neither one knew of the other at the time. Grenades were used to take out a machinegun, then a bazooka round was slammed through the firing slit in the front of the concrete bunker-type building. The OP held out for quite a while before being taken.

Where Were The Guns?

At the gun emplacements, Rangers found telephone poles instead of guns. The long poles looked like gun barrels from the air, and had been used to fool recon. The guns themselves were nowhere to be found, but there were still plenty of Germans in the area.

Company E and parts of F joined up and made for the road, heading west toward Grandcamp les Baines. They came to the village of Au Guay and were stopped by machinegun fire.

Other groups worked through the heavy hedgerows, overcoming various points of resistance, and headed for the east-west road.

At the battery, Rangers were still trying to find the mysteriously absent cannons. First Sergeant Leonard Lomell, wounded on the beach but still leading a dozen men from D Company on the cliff top, went after guns four, five and six. The group went from gun pit to gun pit, taking small arms fire, and found nothing. Once outside the immediate area of destruction, Lomell noticed what appeared to be tracks leading away from emplacement six. He and part of D Company followed the tracks, unsure, but certainly with an idea of what had become of the guns.

Others have said they didn't see any tracks, or what was seen were farm wagon tracks.

Lomell and his group got behind the Germans to the south of the Pointe while all around them men from all three companies began to head away from the Pointe toward the road. About 50 men, with D and E Companies in the lead and F Company at the flanks, headed out, braving machinegun fire, working toward the intersection of the main road and the narrow lane leading into the Pointe area.

It was just after 0800, and the Rangers were using a trench and hedgerows for cover—about the same as the defenders—and pushing outward. Half an hour later a short part of the road was occupied by Rangers, cutting the link between Grandcamp to the west and Vierville to the east. The men of D, E and F Companies sat tight, waiting for the rest of the Rangers and the 116th Infantry to come join them from Vierville. They would wait two days.

At that point, one of the most heroic, gutsy moves of the campaign took place. First Sergeant Lomell, along with Staff Sergeant Jack Kuhn, took off south from the intersection to follow the tracks they had seen, hoping the guns would be at the end of them. With roadblocks set and defenses digging in behind them, the two men walked away from their brothers and into history.

Not 250 yards away, Lomell and Kuhn found five of the big guns generally aimed at Utah Beach, ammo stacked nearby, and unmanned and unfired.

As for the missing sixth gun, later research turned it up as being sent to its manufacturer to be repaired. It remains somewhat of a mystery. A severe pasting of the Pointe by Allied Air on April 15, 1944, had damaged at least one gun enough to be sent to Cherbourg for repairs, but only the tube was sent. The carriage stayed on site. There were other Rangers in the area, and it is possible that single out-of-place gun was found by them.

Leonard Lomell at the Pointe

I met Len Lomell at the Ranger Round-up in Atlantic City, New Jersey, on December 3rd, 2003. Asked how he feels about his role in Pointe du Hoc, he said, "We got lucky. Anyone would have done it." For his luck he was awarded the Distinguished Service Cross and Kuhn was awarded the Silver Star.

Lomell went on to become the Battalion Sergeant Major, and eventually received the first battlefield commission in the battalion when he was made Lieutenant in Arlon, Belgium, October 7, 1944.

In addition to allowing the interview, the Hall of Fame Ranger gave me a copy of a speech he gives to various organizations and gave permission to use excerpts. West Point historians helped him out with the statistics, he said.

The eyewitness story of the guns of Pointe Du Hoc follows.

Excerpts from Leonard Lomell's speech, titled **The Guns of Pointe du Hoc, Normandy, France.**

The most dangerous ground mission of D-Day was assigned early on to the Rangers with orders to find the guns of Pointe du Hoc and render them inoperable as soon as possible, in case the mighty American firepower did not succeed as expected, and it did not.

The biggest surprise of all to the Rangers when they climbed the cliffs of Pointe du Hoc and fought back the Germans, was that there were no big guns in any of the encasements, only telephone poles or something similar.

The French Underground Resistance Units informed the Rangers right after D-Day that the big guns were never installed at Pointe du Hoc. They claimed the US Army Intelligence had been duly informed about this several times months before D-Day.

Nevertheless, the big guns were at the ready and still capable.

We still had to find [them] as quickly as we could. We had no new Army Intelligence about their new location.

There are several versions of how the Intelligence community could have been so wrong. One version has it that the French resistance gave the information to US military Intelligence before D-Day. The decision was made to send the Rangers anyway, and they were kept in the dark, though it is possible Colonel Rudder may have known. Why were they sent? Quite possibly it was because the planners feared a scenario that proved to be true. The guns were still there, just a short distance away. Had the Rangers not gone in, there was nothing to keep the guns from firing on the hundreds of ships within a 10-mile reach.

It was my first day of duty as a combat Ranger. I had never heard a shot fired in anger before. Suddenly, we new Rangers-to-be were enveloped in a world of dramatic pyrotechnics. Explosions of all descriptions, the chatter of death-dealing automatic weapons, rockets, and many Nazi soldiers, all trying kill us.

I was First Sergeant of Company D of the 2nd Ranger Battalion, acting as a Lieutenant Platoon Leader of the 2nd Platoon. We were short one officer when we landed at Pointe du Hoc.

After a stormy two-hour trip in our British Landing Craft, Assault (LCA) through cold rain and high seas and running the gauntlet of fire for three miles, 300-plus yards offshore, under fire from the German soldiers from cliff tops along the way, we Rangers finally fired our grappling hooks up with their plain-and-toggle ropes over the 100 foot cliffs of Pointe du Hoc.

The Germans were waiting for us on top of the cliffs, determined to drive us back into the sea. If we had been on time we would have caught them in their underground quarters, but we were 40 minutes late due to a British navigational error.

The Germans were waiting to cut our ropes, which they did with some success. We could not shoot back or defend ourselves very well while climbing. We were seriously outnumbered, but we prevailed even without timely and correct Army and Navy Intelligence assistance.

Shot through my right side as I led the men ashore in a wet landing, I suddenly disappeared in water over my head as I stepped off the ramp into an underwater bomb crater.

I climbed out of the water cold and wet, my right side hurting, with my arms still full of combat gear with the help of my men. We hurriedly headed for the nearest ropes and up we went as fast as we could climb.

There had been 22 of us in our LCA, and we were all up the cliff within 15 minutes, rushing through the German small-arms fire, as quickly as we could to the three gun emplacements that were our original objective on the west flank of the cliffs.

We continued to have more combat with the enemy as we moved from bomb crater to bomb crater, which had been created months before.

Unlike Omaha Beach, Allied bombers had pulverized Pointe du Hoc and the closely surrounding area for months before D-Day. The Air Force was careful not to set a pattern of bombing the Pointe, or hit it too often, but it was a good place to jettison any unused bombs when returning from a nearby mission. Consequently, a view of the Pointe from the air was much like looking at the surface of an asteroid.

This fortress [the area where the guns were supposed to be, some 40 acres in size] had underground tunnels, troop quarters [and other facilities], and the Germans popped up often, firing their weapons from where we least expected. We moved on very quickly to avoid more sniper and machinegun fire, as well as flat trajectory anti-aircraft machinegun fire, too, which was becoming more and more of a serious problem.

D Company neutralized one machinegun position on our way across the Pointe, and temporarily quieted down the anti-aircraft position in order to get by it quickly and not get pinned down or delayed as we continued our assault.

We got to our first objective in a matter of minutes after the assault, [but] the three guns in positions number four, five and six, were not there.

The forward Rangers were coming under increasing defensive fire from large-bore weapons, so they wasted no time heading inland, off the Pointe itself. There was a mission to perform, and there were other Rangers behind them to take care of the enemy in the gun emplacement. Lomell says it was considered, after seeing the destruction of the Pointe by bombs, that the Germans had moved the guns inland. Maybe they had, unless the French were right and they were never actually installed.

By the time we fought our way inland about a mile or so to the black-topped coastal road [this took about an hour], I had only a dozen men left, some of whom were lightly wounded, but able to fight on. Ten of the original 22 Rangers in my boat team had been killed or were very badly wounded.

We were behind their second line of defense. Fortunately, the Germans had no idea we were in their midst. I left all my ten surviving men except Staff Sergeant Jack Kuhn behind to set up a roadblock as ordered.

About 8 a.m. Sergeant Kuhn and I started leap-frogging down this sunken farm road heading inland, following wagon tracks between the [nine-foot] high hedgerows with trees, not knowing where it was going.

During his interview Lomell said any number of vehicles or wagons could have caused those tracks. It was a farm road, after all, he pointed out. Whether the guns traveled that way is open to question. At any rate, they followed it and found the guns.

It led to a little swale, or draw, in an apple orchard. There the big guns were covered with netting with camouflage...their barrels were over our heads. There was not a shell or a bomb crater anywhere we could see. Apparently the Army and Navy and Air Corps had not found them either. Looking over the hedgerow, I clearly saw the five big 155mm coastal artillery guns and their ammunition and powder bags neatly in place, aimed at Utah Beach.

The guns were placed back from the coast enough so hitting the beach would have been an iffy proposition simply because of elevation and depression capabilities of the weapons. Most of the damage they would have inflicted would probably have come to the shipping, bad enough at that.

The German gun crew could easily turn the guns around to fire on Omaha Beach or on the invasion fleet if they so desired. The guns were located a little over a mile from where we landed. About 100 yards away [he said 75 in the interview] a German officer was talking to about 75 of his men [some of them still getting dressed] we believed to be his gun crews, at a farm road intersection.

A few minutes earlier, Sergeant Kuhn and I had discovered another 40 to 50 Germans, a combat patrol about 200 yards in the other direction. They eventually passed within 20 feet of us across the blacktop road, behind a wall, on their way to join the German troops just referred to.

Our Rangers had totally surprised the Germans. They never expected an attack from the sea, or any human beings climbing up those steep cliffs.

The E Company Rangers were continuing to attack the German observation post or bunker on the actual Pointe edge; a mile away at the steep cliffs we climbed, so there were no firing orders coming back to the German crews where Kuhn and I were. We thought the Germans could have a roving observation post patrol out trying to relocate in another advantageous spot to send firing orders back to them as soon as possible. Still, no one was a sitting duck guarding the guns themselves that I could see, the gunners knew the Air Corp and Battleship Texas were looking for them, so I told Jack to cover me. I then went to the gun position and started to render them inoperable. It was about 8:15 a.m.

It is a matter of conjecture as to why the guns were not guarded. Possibly the Germans were afraid of an air attack, but then they were standing out in the open fairly close by. Another possibility is that they really were surprised and were just forming up in preparation to fire the guns, without the knowledge of US forces at their doorstep.

Between us we had two incendiary grenades. When the pin was pulled and the incendiary compound was exposed to air, it poured out like solder, flowing over the gears and crevices, setting and hardening up like a weld. I used them to weld and fuse fast the traversing mechanisms of two of the guns. I also silently smashed the sights of all five of the guns with my padded gun butt. I had wrapped my field jacket around my submachinegun stock [Thompson .45 cal.] to silence any sound that possibly could be heard. Then Jack and I ran back down the sunken road about 150 to 200 yards out of sight of the Germans to the D Company blacktop road block, got more grenades from our guys, and hurried back to finish the job of rendering the remaining guns inoperable. It took several minutes, at most.

Since [incendiary] grenades make no noise, we luckily managed to do our job and escaped without being discovered.

There is some controversy about the destruction of the big guns, especially about the explosion as Lomell and Kuhn were trying to leave the area. So the story goes, Sergeant Frank Rupinsky and his patrol also came upon the guns and put fragmentation grenades down the barrels and destroyed the sights—which Lomell had already destroyed—and blew up the ammo stash. Lomell says the story is pure fabrication. "Those barrels were 12 feet off the ground. You couldn't get a grenade in one of them. Even if you did they wouldn't do much damage."

Among Rangers who know, Lomell says the belief is that a man who wasn't even in that unit started the story. To make matters even muddier, Rupinsky and his men were later captured. There were two runners sent to Rudder, but it is unclear who sent them, or in what order. As for the explosion, Lomell says he still figures it was a stray artillery round from a Naval vessel that happened to ignite the powder stores for the 155s.

Sergeants Harry Pate and Gordon Luning of D Company, using different routes back to the Battalion Command Post on the Pointe, notified Colonel Rudder—mission accomplished, before 9 a.m. Our radios were not working.

Our work on the alternate gun positions successfully completed, we rejoined the other D Company men at the roadblock and began to consolidate our defensive position for the rest of D-Day and night, and to protect our D Company roadblock. In the meantime, Sergeant Koenig of our platoon destroyed all the German communications along the coast road. About this time, the remnants of our 1st Platoon joined us [about 11 men]. They had been helping to defend the Pointe where half the Platoon became casualties. We needed them now to strengthen the roadblock.

A Ranger Company consisted of 68 men. At this point in time we only had 20 men left.

The original battle plan indicated we would be relieved by noontime on D-Day by the American troops on Omaha Beach. It never happened, they were over two days late. We had gathered about 85 other Rangers during the afternoon to defend our roadblock until relieved, which we did until D+2.

Ike Eikner Backs Lomell

"While Lomell and Kuhn had gone to get more thermite grenades, another patrol led by Staff Sergeant Frank Rupinski of E Company stumbled upon the guns. Not knowing that Lomell had already damaged some of the guns, he put thermite grenades down the barrels of all five guns and also destroyed their sights. Before leaving, grenades were thrown into a large ammunition dump. Rupinski sent a runner back to the CP to inform us that the guns were destroyed."

The above is in accordance with the reporting done by the War Department's Historical Division in the book, *Small Unit Actions*. Ron Lane's book, *Rudder's Rangers* reports, and Len Lomell insists, that he and Jack Kuhn returned to the gun site with more thermite grenades and finished destroying the remainder of the guns before Sergeant Rupinski visited the area. Lomell then sent two runners, Sergeant Harry Pate and Gordon Luning, back to the CP to inform us that the guns had been put out of action. Lt. Kerchner of D Company confirms the Historical Division reporting in a taped interview with some news people in 1947. I seem to recall two different groups of runners informing us at the CP that the guns had been found and put out of action.

At the cliff side CP the Headquarters personnel were busy establishing communications, setting up an aid station in the bunker behind the CP, and bringing up supplies from the beach. Colonel Rudder and the NSFCP [Naval Fire Control] set up an OP within the casemated gun position #2 and were calling down Naval fire on any enemy concentrations seen or reported. Captain Otto Masny, CO of F Company, set up a perimeter defense around the CP area, and sent patrols against two enemy positions—a machinegun position on our east flank, and an anti-aircraft [AA] position on the west flank. Those efforts were not successful and Colonel Rudder asked for Naval fire on them. The British Destroyer *Talybont* responded with good effect on the machinegun position, but could not reach the AA position that was in defilade.

Complicating his ability to lead was a fresh wound in the thigh, taken from a sniper ensconced in one of the multiple anti-aircraft positions around the emplacements. Rudder took action, calling on the *Talybont* to rain destruction on the AA site, and killed it. Other snipers persisted in making things hot for HQ, and Rudder took his radioman and a machinegunner out to look for the snipers. They found some, called in Naval fire, and that was that, but a little later Rudder was hit again for his trouble, this time by "friendly fire."

At mid-morning D-Day, an errant shell from the British Cruiser *Glasgow* hit the side of the bunker at enemy gun No.2, where the Naval Shore Fire Control and Lt. Colonel Rudder were calling down fire on enemy targets. Fortunately, the errant shell was a smoke shell; if it had been a high explosive type, all would have been wiped out. As it was, two officers were killed, and several of the party wounded, including Colonel Rudder, who was bruised up a bit and covered with yellow powder. The Colonel called me via land phone to come up with litters to bring out the wounded.

The errant shell knocked out the radio communications we had with the *Satterlee,* and we were left with absolutely no protective fire just at a time when the enemy was redoubling his efforts to push us back into the sea. I immediately sent my Radio Chief, Sergeant

Charles Parker, down the cliff to bring up the signal lamp. I used an EE84 Signal Lamp of WWI vintage. It was tripod mounted, had a telescopic sight and a vernier screw for tracking a moving target. We used International Morse Code for communicating.

I understand Signal Supply still has a few of these in storage, but I was unable to secure one for museum display.

The lamp was first used to signal the US Destroyer *Satterlee,* which was supporting us with her 5-inch batteries. We had shipped out with two, but one was lost at sea when a supply boat went down. We quickly put the lamp into action and continued to call down the protective fire from the *Satterlee*. From my knowledge, this was the first time in military history that an infantry crew ashore had used lamp communications to call down and direct Naval gunfire on an enemy.

Eikner even had a couple of carrier pigeons. He was prepared.

I brought in two and flew them out D-Day morning stating that we had completed our mission and were in need of supplies and reinforcements—the same message that we had sent by lamp and radio via the Navy. I learned just recently that the pigeons did indeed arrive back in England.

The Fight Continues

Rudder was having trouble communicating with anybody, so he sent out messages over two types of radios and even carrier pigeons, trying to make contact. His message was, "Located Pointe du Hoc, mission accomplished, need ammo and reinforcements." He told whomever was listening he had many casualties. This message was transmitted over and over again between noon and 1300.

Not until 1500 hours did an answer come back, and the news wasn't good. Rudder was informed that all available Rangers were already on shore, and no reinforcements were available. With 50 percent casualties, Rudder and the rest of the Ranger force were on their own.

The positions at the Pointe and on the road were tenuous at best with two major counterattacks made by noon, both focused on F Company. There were Rangers spread all over the area defending the Pointe, and about 60 men a mile inland, securing the intersection of the east-west road. The Germans were unorganized during the initial attacks, but soon gathered perhaps 100 men between the road and the Pointe, cutting the forward Ranger elements loose from HQ and Rudder.

There was more to come from the Germans. Reinforcements came in from the south, giving the enemy the force necessary to counterattack, and they did several times, almost driving the Rangers off the cliffs. By that time, the Rangers were low on everything, and darkness was coming on, though it was still light quite late at night.

About then, 2100, a welcome addition of 22 men of Company A, 5th Battalion, joined the beleaguered men of the 2nd. The 1st Platoon had come from the east, an advance element, though they didn't realize it. They were surprised to find no one else there. It was discovered later that a big fight just off the beach had slowed the rest of the group down.

Despite his lack of communications—he could talk to a few elements on the road—and heavy casualties, Rudder made a gut decision to hold the road for the night.

The men dug in behind BARs, a few mortars, and some captured machineguns—about all they had for heavy weapons—and worried about the lack of ammo, mortar rounds, and grenades. The moon was nearly full and there were shadows in the trees, making it hard to discern shapes. The main Ranger force was concentrated around the intersection, with forward elements scattered on the south side of the road.

The third counter-attack came about 2330, crashing into the frail Ranger line from less than 50 yards away. It was an attack in force and quickly overran the outlying Ranger posts. The Americans made a fighting retreat to the highway, and stopped there.

The fourth wave hit an hour into June 7, and that one from rock-throwing distance. The onslaught took out a few more Ranger positions, and confusion took out a few others. The Germans were coming in from what seemed to be all sides, giving the Rangers no focus for their firepower.

Still, the Americans held on, unwilling to give up the position astride the road. Trying to locate each other in the darkness, the men were uncertain as to their own disposition, let alone that of the enemy.

It was 0300 when the final assault began. The Rangers were seriously outnumbered by then, and lost 20 men of E and D Companies to capture. Surrounded and taking a bad beating, the Rangers began to withdraw on the eastern flank while superior German forces were rolling up the western flank. There were many casualties.

Reorganization was useless in the face of the determined German line coming north. About 50 surviving Rangers filtered into the Pointe area after 0400.

Rudder definitely had his back to the wall. Even with the welcome addition of men of the 5th Battalion there were less than 100 men still able to fight, and they had little to fight with. There was still no word of relief from the rest of the 2nd and 5th Battalions, or from the 116th. They were having their own troubles, and that meant Rudder's crew was on its own for a while longer.

Not that the rest of the Rangers and the 116th weren't trying. Things just took a little longer than first thought.

Relief Heads For The Pointe

General Gerhardt, Commander of the 29th Division, had his CP set up on the beach and was busy changing plans in the face of an earlier heavy German counter-attack. He decided to reinforce his beachhead rather than make a concerted push toward the Pointe at that time.

Accordingly, the assembled relief force was smaller than initially hoped for, containing C and D Companies of the 5th Rangers, the provisional/composite company of the 2nd, and elements of the 1st Battalion, 116th Infantry. The compact group was supplemented by six or eight tanks of the 743rd and led by Lt. Colonel Metcalf, CO of 1st/116th, and Ranger Major Sullivan.

John Raaen said he thought at the time the relief of the 2nd Rangers at the Pointe was the Task Force mission, but years later realized they were really after the area around Grandcamp in preparation for seizure by the 29th Division, and if the Rangers got relieved in the process, so much the better.

By that time it was known the guns at the Pointe had been neutralized, so the immediate threat was gone. The Rangers would have to hold while other, more strategically important areas were taken out. Had the guns been firing, things may have gone differently.

The rest of the 5th Rangers—except 1st Platoon, F Company—stayed near the beach and helped work through infiltrating enemy in Vierville, gaining more ground beyond the invasion site. The 1st Platoon, all in one boat, landed near St. Laurent-sur-Mer, some distance from the rest of the battalion on Easy Green. Getting there was hard enough. The first boat the platoon boarded was sinking under them when they were picked up by a passing LCT while still four miles from shore. The large landing craft deposited the platoon in shallow water quite a way east of where they were supposed to be, but at least they made shore.

Moving up to the dunes was relatively easy and no casualties were sustained, but once there the men of the 5th had to push their way into a packed house, full of soldiers from the 29th and 1st Divisions hunkering down. Movement was not recommended, and radio contact with the rest of the 5th unobtainable, so the 1st Platoon of Company F stayed right there for six or seven hours. Patrols sent east and west returned to tell of heavy fire in both directions.

In mid-afternoon, Company Commander William Runge led his men west toward exit D-3 and got close to the Vierville draw. There were about 25 fighting men left in the unit after several were killed or wounded in the mess on the western end of Omaha Beach. Not until about 7:30 p.m. was the platoon able to travel up the bluffs and meet some other Rangers in the assault on an enemy position. The platoon spent the night there on the slope and attacked again in the morning, getting close enough to throw grenades and taking some support from men of the 29th Division. In short order the Germans surrendered, giving up 38 men to capture and leaving eight dead in an extensive dugout position.

The Germans had plenty of time to dig great emplacements, complete with hundreds of feet of connected trenches with rooms for quarters and storage built into the slopes. Our soldiers met another enemy much like that during the late '60s.

The lonely—no other Rangers—unit stayed on the beach that night, but moved forward in the early morning and worked hard until mid-afternoon when they tallied three pillboxes destroyed and several weapons emplacements taken. That mission accomplished, what happened next was completely unexpected.

Enquiries from Lt. Reville about the location of the 5th Battalion brought the platoon to the attention of Major Jack Street, then a staff member for Admiral Hall. Street had been a company commander in Darby's 1st Battalion in Sicily and was doing his best to get help to the beleaguered men on Pointe du Hoc. Accordingly, when he found Rangers with a completed first mission he sent an LCVP for them and had them brought out to a destroyer, probably the USS *Harding*. The platoon members had their needs met aboard ship and were loaded down with supplies and ammunition for the return trip. Landing at the base of the cliffs the men humped the needed supplies to their brothers up top, reporting to Rudder about 5 p.m.

The platoon was split into defensive positions and an eight-man patrol that went hunting the rest of the 5th Battalion, which they found, arriving at the CP at St. Pierre just after dawn on D+2.

John Raaen

The following is an excerpt from Raaen's story, "Intact," about D+1 and D+2, used with permission. The 5th Battalion was somewhat fragmented, but moving forward.

D+1 started with a bang. The Germans attacked from the south. With the help of the 743rd Tank Battalion parked on the main east-west road through Vierville, we held them off. The tanks had come up during the night and this fight was the first I had seen of them. The tank crews were all buttoned up and could not see or hear that we were being attacked. I jumped up on the hull of one and banged my rifle butt on the turret until a tanker opened his hatch. I then pointed out the attack and suggested they take the enemy under fire. They did just that, but only fired their caliber .50 machineguns, apparently believing the targets were too undefined for them to use their 75mm cannon.

Right after the German attack fizzled out I took two patrols out to our north and east. The second [patrol)] ended down at the beach where I found General Gerhardt had set up his 29th Infantry Division CP next to the fort guarding the exit.

Gerhardt, upon hearing the situation of the 5th Rangers, told Raaen and Pfc. Jack Sharp to find an abandoned vehicle—he found a jeep—and then had it packed with ammunition. The two men set out to locate and resupply the force moving toward Pointe du Hoc.

The town of Vierville appeared empty as we drove through and the column under Metcalf and Sullivan had long since moved out toward Pointe du Hoc. Mostly on faith, Sharp and I sped down the road after them. It was a very sporty trip. At one point the machinegun and sniper fire were so intense that Sharp and I got out of the jeep, slipped under it and pushed it over our heads past a break in the hedgerows while bullets smacked into the ammunition boxes above us. We had serious doubts when we reached a fork in the road near Le Haut Chemin. Which way, right or left? Luckily, we chose the right fork and caught up with the column, distributed the ammunition and gave some of the walking wounded a much-needed ride. When it ran out of gas, we abandoned the jeep in a farmyard north of the road, just short of St. Pierre du Mont.

Getting To Grandcamp

The makeshift column moved slowly forward through scattered resistance until a huge crater that obliterated the road stopped the tanks cold. Lateral movement was impossible due to anti-tank minefields on either side.

As usual, the Infantry went forward, but the Rangers walked into sudden heavy artillery fire, taking several casualties. The decision was made to pull the tanks and the CP back to Vierville for the night, covering St. Pierre du Mont with C and D of the 5th, men from the 2nd, and C/116th.

From St. Pierre, Sergeant Moody and Corporal McKissick were sent out after dark to try to make contact with the three companies of the 2nd Rangers at the Pointe.

Early the next morning the pair returned and handed Captain Raaen a telephone. They had somehow gotten through a thousand yards of Germans, made contact with the 2nd, and laid phone wire back. For the first time since the invasion, Rudder could talk freely to the outside world.

Both men received the DSC for that courageous action.

About 0800 on D+2 the 5th Battalion reassembled at St. Pierre after spending time in defensive positions protecting the beachhead.

A multi-pronged attack was in the offing, and six battalions were ready to go in three different directions. Companies B and E, 5th Battalion, were sent to take some high ground near Grandcamp. The mission was to help keep the Germans off the next force, consisting of the 2nd and 3rd Battalions of the 116th, and the tanks of the 743rd, pushing down the road for Grandcamp. When they were south of the Pointe, that force turned right to cut off the enemy contained in the area around the Pointe. The rest of the 5th Rangers and the provisional company of the 2nd were joined by the 1st Battalion of the 116th and made straight for Rudder.

The plan worked well and resistance was relatively light. With the aid of Naval gunfire at German positions on the cliff top, the composite force got through about mid-morning of June 8.

The happy Ranger reunion was somewhat marred when tanks of the 743rd, arriving a little late and not understanding the situation, burst out of the woods and fired on the story-swapping soldiers. A Lieutenant of the 2nd Rangers left cover and mounted one of the tanks. A pistol against the head of the tank commander ended the fire abruptly.

By noon, Pointe du Hoc was secure.

Ike Eikner

One of the first people I saw was the smiling face of Captain Ralph Goranson. We had a hearty handshake, slapped one another on the back while he laughingly pointed out all the bullet holes through his clothing. Despite all he had been through, he was still one of the most gung-ho of the Rangers. His C Company had just completed perhaps the most dangerous and most effective job of fighting on D-Day. They had shut off a deadly fire on Omaha Beach and secured the west flank of the Vierville beachhead.

Casualties—D-Day

Eikner, et al., put together these numbers for Ranger casualties for the 2nd Battalion during the assault on Pointe du Hoc and the landings on Omaha Beach. Figures, dates, and times are taken directly from the Battalion Log and History.

There has always been some question in the minds of some researchers as to the correct numbers for Task Force A at the Pointe and as to the casualty rate that they experienced. From the early days, most reports have said that Task Force A consisted of a total of 225, and that the casualty rate of that Force was about 70 percent. Upon review, I find that those figures are still just about as good now as formerly. Here's the way we arrived at the figures:

TASK FORCE A

As of the June 5, 1944 Morning Report

D Company ———————	68
E Company ———————	67
F Company ———————	70
	205
+ HQ Detach	12
+ Med Detach	8 (?)
Total	225

This does not include our supply people at sea nor the four DUKWs, nor the attached folks from 165th Signal Photo Company or the 293rd Joint Assault Signal Company.

It is reported that when the relief fought through to us around noon of D+ 2 they found about 90 effectives still armed and ready for business. Subtracting out 22 of those for the relief column that 1st Lt. Parker from the 5th Battalion brought up at 9:00 p.m. D-Day, and the eight or so we brought up from Omaha the afternoon D+1, we are left with about 60 survivors from Task Force A.

225-60 gives us a loss of 165, or 73 percent—or about the 70 percent we have been quoting over the years. Quite a few of these included those lost at sea and later recovered. We show total D-Day casualties for the 2nd Battalion at 267, which gives us a 45 percent loss for the battalion as a whole at that time.

The 5th Battalion fared somewhat better, though it still sustained 114 KIA and WIA, or 22 percent casualties. Ten per cent casualties is a big hit for any unit. Combined casualties totaled 381, or roughly one-third of the Ranger Force.

Frank South—Medic, 2nd Battalion

I met Frank South in New Jersey in December 2003. He introduced me to Len Lomell and has given me a great amount of input via emails on several occasions. This piece results from a battery of questions I asked him. It is obvious that Frank says a lot with a few words.

Training: I took basic with the Medical Detachment, 423rd Infantry, 106th Division, the initial training in military medicine. I was a freshman majoring in biology when I entered the military. While on maneuvers, following basic, we learned that the Rangers were on the base looking for volunteers. Bill Clark, who became my closest friend, and I showed up with some alacrity and applied. Our final medical Officer (Walter Block) taught us a good deal more—we became pretty well trained. Of course, additionally, we went through regular Ranger training as well.

Qualification for posting: Background and interest.

On D-Day I was a T/5 and then promoted to T/4.

Captain Block insisted on treating Rudder's wounds. I don't recall the details but I understand they were relatively light.

Including attached people, between 220 and 240 landed at the Pointe. As Rudder complained, he only had 90 or 92 men left able to bear arms. Most, by far of the casualties were by small arms. Perhaps a few by "potato masher" grenades, but these were not nearly as effective as our "pineapples."

Feelings: Overall—one of astonishment that all this was actually happening. Treating buddies—there was an overwhelming sense of mission and responsibility.

What we carried was based on the probability that we might be isolated for some time and that we had to plan for heavy casualties. The individual kits could be enlarged to twice their normal size and varied quite a bit in what was carried. Basically, they contained additional sulfathiazole powder for open wounds, several morphine syrettes, Carlisle bandages, instruments—scalpel and blades, forceps, hemostats, suturing material—sulfadiazine burn ointment, tape, etc.

In addition, I had packed and carried ashore a very large pack on a pack board on the horns of which was about 50 feet of light line to haul it in with should I get caught in surf or flip into a crater—which I did. In the AAR [after action report] it says all the medics carried one; not so, there was only one. It contained several bottles of plasma, a couple of collapsible splints, sterile saline, and more of the above. We kept morphine tablets in our usual aid station but on D-Day we relied solely on syrettes. Dissolving tablets in sterile saline before injecting would not be practical. Also, each man carried a packet that contained a syrette, sulfathiazole and a Carlisle bandage.

Captain Block packed and carried a fiber casing used for transporting shells that was packed with more medical and surgical supplies.

The supply LCA that had more medical supplies, litters and blankets, and gasoline lanterns [sank]. Those supplies became badly needed in the aid station in the AA bunker just landward of the CP. The last time I was there the bunker was still there but I suspect that erosion of the cliff will get it in the not-too-distant future.

John Raaen

While the 2nd Rangers licked their wounds at Pointe du Hoc, the 5th mounted an attack on Grandcamp Les Bains. The attack was repulsed and the 116th Infantry, supported by the 743rd Tank Battalion, punched their way through the town. The 5th was assigned mop-up duties.

The 5th didn't win at Grandcamp, but it's not as bad as it sounds. The 5th was a battalion, the 116th, a regiment supported by tanks.

Headquarters Company ended up with clearing the German snipers out of the houses along the main street. I made up four teams and led one of them. Two teams on each side of the street. I took the first house on the left side of the street; my second team took the second house. That way we leapfrogged each other. Same thing on the other side. I had teams keeping abreast of us out in the street and in the backs of the houses. It was quite a sporty course. Enter the house, make a room-by-room search. Don't miss the attic or the basement. Locked door! Bayonet in keyhole, pull trigger, kick open the door with grenade pin in one hand, grenade in the other. Most of the French were in the basements.

We slept in the hedgerows that night, D+2, somewhere just outside of Grandcamp. The next morning we attacked toward Maisy. Here was located the main artillery force of the Germans and a major headquarters. Company A said the fighting was much fiercer than even D-Day, but captured the battery and headquarters. D-Day was a German payday. Our invasion upset that routine. Four million dollars' worth of Francs were captured. We turned that over to the Finance Officer of the 29th Division.

Maisy

The 1st Battalion, 116th Regiment by-passed Maisy, and A, C, and F Companies of the 5th Rangers got the job instead, reportedly after Rudder turned it down due to the condition of the 2nd Battalion after severe Omaha Beach and Pointe du Hoc casualties. Surrounded by minefields, the battery near Maisy had been firing large-bore cannon over Pointe du Hoc onto Omaha Beach. The 5th was supported by two half-tracks carrying members of the 2nd Rangers and Company B, 81st Chemical Weapons, plus four 81mm mortars brought along by C Company of the 5th.

The 58th Field Artillery laid down a good barrage on the target before the attack, which was led by Major Richard Sullivan, the XO of the 5th. Though wounded at Omaha, Sullivan rallied his men through the minefields and took the objective, earning himself the DSC in the process. The Rangers attacked with two companies in column, taking about 15 casualties. About 90 German prisoners were taken.

Research done in France after the war produced the following figures, though the accuracy cannot be confirmed. About 600 Germans staffed the Maisy compound, which covered some 40 acres drilled with underground bunkers and more than a few weapons, including a dozen 88mm cannon, six 155mm guns, four 105mm guns, and several more weapons. A couple of allied aircraft were shot down by this position, and the enemy captured some 20 paratroopers.

Rest, Then Brest

With the horror of the invasion behind them the Ranger battalions moved a little way inland and took time to rest and refit. Replacements appeared and tried to fit in with the new veterans. By June 10 the units were in bivouac in Osmanville, but a few days later they were moved again and sat in another bivouac area being bombed all night. Between patrolling and training the new men, there was plenty to do.

During that time the battalions were part of First Army reserves, a move that unexpectedly put them in line for a new commander. Colonel Eugene Slappey was put in charge of the Ranger Force, moving Lt. Colonel Rudder down to command the 2nd Battalion.

Colonel Slappey led the 115th Regiment through the invasion, was replaced, and needed somewhere to go. The sudden removal of Rudder to a larger command opened the spot.

Through the rest of June they ate and rested and trained—and received some well-earned awards.

Both battalions were given the pleasure of guard duty for a time, and that, along with more moves and continued training, took up most of the time until August.

The 5th was supposed to be resting, but training was constant. Guarding prisoners at Foucarville, which involved securing them, taking them down to the beach for transport, and going back for another batch, took up part of the time. The battalion was also assigned duty guarding the west coast beaches since the Germans still had troops on the Channel Islands.

Ranger Major Sullivan took over command of the 5th when the "respite" was over.

In mid-August, the battalions were told of the impending move on Brest and shortly afterward became part of General Troy Middleton's VIII Corps with the 2nd, 8th and 29th Divisions.

Brest was a German stronghold—actually a series of strong points—and was by-passed on the first rush through the area, creating a large pocket of resistance fairly well cut off from escape to the south. It was also an important rail hub and a very necessary port so it was put on the docket and the VIII Corps was given the job. Enemy fortifications were complete and deadly and manned by about 50,000 soldiers and sailors with their backs to the sea.

In the beginning of the fight for Brest the Rangers were often split up into company-sized elements and used in different locations doing different things as the force moved slowly forward.

Patrols were effective and netted many enemy killed and captured. There were several short, but fierce, firefights.

From 2nd Battalion, HHC History

Bois du Molay was reached on foot on June 11 and we went into bivouac. 10-in-1s [rations] arrived and we had our first hot meal in days. Patrols were out to secure the woods and screen the armor in the area.

While "seeing a man about a horse," Malissa ran into three supermen trying to make their lines and one drew a bead on him while in that embarrassing position. By some bit of luck one of our patrols spotted them and killed the would-be sniper, wounded one, and the other surrendered.

Replacements arrived [180], and though welcome, only added to our sense of loss. It was some time before they were assimilated into the ranks. On the 16th of June we moved to Columbrieres and dug in. No rest for the weary as training began again.

Two days later another 70 replacements arrived, making a total of 250 new men. After interviews, 99 of them returned to the repple-depple, as did several other men who decided Ranger life was a little too much for them.

A daily training routine was set up until the 25th of June when we moved by motor to Valongnes. Here we took up prisoner of war escort duty.

On the 3rd of July this assignment was given up and we moved by motor convoy to Beaumont Hague where we took up a position in a chateau. The purpose was to patrol the peninsula and search it for stragglers and report mine fields and other enemy installations. The islands off this part of the coast had not surrendered at the fall of Cherbourg and an eye had to be kept on them.

This area was dangerous due to the number of uncharted minefields, and the enemy had booby-trapped some of the positions on his evacuation.

[During the middle days of July] the 2nd was ordered to check all civilians on the roads in our area and pick up all French Moroccans and North Africans. Patrols and outpost duty with attendant training of the new men continued until July 19th when we were relieved by the 15th on Group. Mines continued to take a toll on the line companies (A-F).

Most of the 2nd was in garrison duty and prisoner of war duty and hated every minute of it. Later in the month a few men got to test their abilities as snipers under combat conditions in another area, but most of the Rangers were "house-bound."

Then, as things go, a warning order came down.

The alert for movement came on the 4th of August and on the 5th we were relieved from Third Army command [attached on August 3rd] and attached to the First Army. We left Beaumont Hague on the 6th and arrived at Canissy on the 7th. Here we trained in hedgerow fighting with the 159th Light Tank battalion until the 10th when we left our station and arrived at Buais on the 11th. Here were assumed defensive positions on the high ground north of Buais with the assigned mission of securing First Army's right flank at Mortain and repelling any attempts of the enemy to withdraw south from Mortain. We were attached to VII Corps, 4th Division, with the 188th FA [Field Artillery] Battalion in direct support.

Nothing happened and the positions were maintained until the 12th when we were relieved from attachment to the Provisional Ranger Group and the 4th Division to become attached directly to VII Corps and left for a new station—Mayenne. Attached to 9th Division for administration and supply and out posted bridges across the Le Mayenne River and approaches to parts of the city.

Attached to Third Army, VIII Corps on the 17th and prepared to move to LaCondrays. On arrival there by motor convoy, a CP was set up, and this was hardly completed when a message was received to move to the vicinity of Lesneven. Here we went into bivouac and the companies began preparation for the assault on Brest.

Reading the previous few paragraphs gives one the impression the 2nd Rangers were on the move almost all the time—which they were. Between the 4th and 17th of August they were attached to two different divisions and two different corps, with several different missions in several different places.

5th Battalion—Brest Campaign

The 5th Battalion had a large part to play in the taking of strong points throughout the area, including the famous Lochrist Battery. The Rangers often faced the tough members of German Second Parachute Division during their grinding fight across enemy territory toward Brest.

On August 29, 1944, an order from VIII Corps attached Companies A and C of the 5th Battalion to the 2nd Division for operations. Company E was briefly assigned to the 9th Division at Gousneau. Easy Company kept contact between the 2nd and 8th Divisions, putting it directly in the seam between the two, which was not lost on the Germans. A heavy counterattack the next morning gave the Rangers eight casualties, and the ensuing artillery barrage cost them four more.

Able and Charlie Companies were protecting the line of advance along the Guipavas-Brest road, mostly a defensive posture for the time being.

By September 1, the rest of the 5th, including Companies B, D and F, was attached to the 29th Division for the upcoming battle for Brest. They began sending out patrols right away to find the enemy. After some patrolling of their own, Companies A, C and E rejoined the battalion on the 4th.

Before the battalion was reunited, B, D and F, were sent south to help the 116th Infantry straighten the lines. Once accomplished, the American forces were more-or-less on line to attack toward Brest. In the 5th Ranger sector there was a large draw between points of high ground that led toward the port city, but it was heavily contested by strong points. One such was named Fort Toulbrouch.

The Germans had been in the area for four years and had plenty of time to dig and build. The closer to Brest the Americans got, the heavier the fortifications and the more determined the resistance.

Company B, 2nd Platoon, commanded by Lt. Gambosi, was ordered to recon the draw, supported by 1st Platoon under Lt. Askin, which would move to a road junction near the draw and be prepared to attack south. A platoon from D Company was also involved as a supporting force.

With everyone moving into place Lt. Gambosi found himself in front of a fort—a German strong point built of concrete and bristling with weapons—but the Lieutenant saw no one and asked permission to go forward and investigate.

Working their way in through dugouts and any place giving shelter, the platoon—32 men less those already wounded or killed—moved into the interior of the fort only to find themselves vastly outnumbered. Fighting back the way they came, the Rangers had to call on the battalion reserves to help them out. Battalion Commander Major Sullivan called up every able-bodied man from Headquarters Company. HQ men were no strangers to combat, having fought through D-Day to their present situation. They were trained the same way the others were, and gave good account of themselves.

Companies B, F and D prepared to attack the fort with HQ in reserve. With B Company spearheading, the Rangers moved forward behind a heavy strafing air attack, though the first try missed by several hundred yards. A second try also missed, so smoke was laid on the target and eight P-47s plastered it with 16 direct bomb hits and machinegun fire.

The aircraft returned to strafe as the soldiers moved to the attack. Big .50 caliber rounds were hitting the Germans just a couple of dozen yards ahead of the onrushing Rangers. Six minutes after the first Americans hit the fort the Germans had enough and quit, yielding up some 247 prisoners to about 60 Rangers.

The next day, Company D and Headquarters Company took another fort and seized 300 more prisoners, while F Company fought ahead and captured another 300-plus and killed 150. The actions were not without cost, however, as some 15 Rangers became casualties.

On September 5, Companies D and F teamed up with a company of the 644th TD (Tank Destroyer) Battalion and attacked another fort. A hard counter-attack set them back somewhat, but the mission was accomplished when Fox Company fixed bayonets and routed the enemy, only to be bombed by American planes. Eighteen Ranger casualties for the day stacked up well against 100 Germans killed and some 70 taken. The next day, the battalion advanced to the ravine, killing and capturing more enemies with just one friendly loss.

The following night and next day were filled with artillery explosions, particularly around the CP. Then the battalion split up, with B and F staying put and the rest moving by foot to Loch Marie Plouzane where they got truck rides for a while, then marched some more to a preparatory area for the attack on Le Conquet. The assembly area and CP were shelled, but not yet by the big guns on the Crozon Peninsula, as they would be later.

During the dark hours the Rangers moved as far forward as possible, using as much stealth as they could. The assault on Le Conquet began the next day, with artillery shells from both sides passing each other in flight while patrols moved out under fire and conquered one enemy position after another. The list of prisoners grew daily.

Some of the emplacements were pillboxes that could hold a hundred men, others held more. The concrete structures were well-built and often fiercely defended with 88s, 20-and-40mm flak guns, and plenty of sited machineguns and mortars. Some of the "forts" were several stories tall above ground and below. To talk of taking out a pillbox is one thing, but the actual accomplishment is something else again, requiring fire-and-maneuver, fire support, air support, and raw guts.

Tank destroyers and artillery pounded the town prior to an assault by Companies E, A and C, and German occupation of Le Conquet was history two hours later. The nearby town of La Mon Blanche fell the next day. The 5th Rangers took some casualties getting it all done, continuing to lose both new and veteran soldiers from the ranks.

The town of Le Cosquer was next to fall after the battalion had come together and separated again. Baker and Charlie Companies were attached briefly to the 29th ID Recon Troop and participated in operations with them, which included more pillbox reduction and capturing more enemy soldiers. Company D led the assault on Le Cosquer, moving so fast some Germans were killed in their foxholes on the way in to town. The 5th Rangers suffered about 15 more casualties taking the town, and were shelled again by their own guns after the action was over.

German losses to wounds and death and capture far outstripped those of the Rangers. Considering the Rangers were attacking, it is surprising how few men they actually lost. Part of the reason for their success was the speed with which they attacked, which was also part of the reason they kept getting shot up by their support forces.

By September 17, the battalion was moving on fortified emplacements around Fort du Portzic. There were five heavy pillboxes a little south of Le Cosquer, and in mid-afternoon a platoon from E Company moved to contact under supporting fire from tank destroyers. One of the pillboxes proved to be stubborn. A 40-pound charge of C-2 was placed in a narrow opening in the front of the emplacement, but before it could be blown some 200 mortar rounds landed all around the area giving the platoon two KIAs and many headaches. When the charge did go off it didn't even dent the pillbox.

The Rangers weren't giving up. A couple of hours before midnight an 11-man group led by 1st Lt. Green of Easy went up to the pillbox again and placed 130 pounds of C-2 against the concrete and added 20 gallons of a gas-and-oil mix, which they poured on the structure.

It got very quiet while the patrol was prepping the box, but when it blew it burned like a torch for almost an hour. For a change, no one was lost to the Rangers.

Brest surrendered the next day, bringing a hard campaign to a close. Something less than 400 Rangers of the 5th Battalion were responsible for killing 624 of the enemy and capturing a staggering 2,114. American losses were also heavy, with the Rangers suffering 137 casualties—more than a quarter of the battalion.

From HHC, 2nd Battalion History

The battalion code name had been changed to Marauder Blue on the 13th and the battalion reattached to the Provisional Ranger Group on the 14th. The Command Post was set up at Le Folget on the 19th, with the battalion assigned tactically to VIII Corps. All companies were alerted for movement and briefed on the assault on Brest. All equipment received a final check as to serviceability and supply had the tough job of replacement over long supply routes. Every available vehicle was brought into use as well as captured vehicles. D Company drew the first assignment on a combat patrol with the 86th Cavalry Reconnaissance Battalion.

D, E and F were attached to the 29th Division and further attached to Task Force Sugar under Captain Slater.

Task Force Sugar was given heavy missions, so it was given enough punch to do the job. Both Ranger Battalions became part of it, as well as a battalion of the 116th Infantry, mortars, anti-aircraft weapons, a battalion of field artillery, and more.

Patrolling continued in the vicinity of St. Renan with desultory activity until the 25th when the battalion was assigned the mission of securing the right flank of the 175th Infantry. [Those three companies] moved to Hill 145 and were joined there by B Company. The battalion was driving south toward Le Conquet.

The main attack on Brest kicked off just after noon on August 25.

The forward CP was installed at Kerveguen on the 27th and became the hub of our activity.

Task Force Sugar moved toward the Conquet Peninsula that day, forcing its way to the guns of the Lochrist Battery. Four days later the rear CP displaced the forward CP, which moved up three or four miles. The slow leapfrogging moved the lines constantly into enemy forces, slowly pushing them back. The Cannon Platoon joined the Rangers, and every man, including cooks and bakers, took part in walking security.

Here the fact that all the men had received the same training proved its benefits for the [light machineguns] and BARs were ably manned.

The patrols kept constant touch with the enemy with resultant clashes and a small but steady stream of prisoners were brought in to the CP. At times enemy shelling and mortar fire was very severe and movement held to the barest operational minimum.

With us at this time was a force of about 700 FFIs [French Forces of the Interior] and… about 160 Russians.

The liberated Russians had been used as slave labor. They were given weapons and turned loose on their former captors. They were not nice.

Lochrist Battery

As with the guns of Pointe du Hoc, the mammoth guns of the Lochrist Battery located on Le Conquet Peninsula were a "thorn in the flesh of the battalion."

The guns were giant 280mm weapons capable of firing a 600-pound projectile. The powder cases were taller than a man and made of brass. A comparative weapon would be a 12-inch Naval gun.

Situated near the main battery were 20mm and 88mm emplacements, and many machineguns. The guns could tear up the flank of the 29th Division and so must be dealt with. The problem was, nobody knew for certain where they were in the beginning.

Elements of Task Force Sugar drove to the coast, eliminating pockets of enemy strength and helping to close in on the objective.

The 5th Rangers, under Major Richard Sullivan, were doing several different things during that time, including taking small, but lethal "forts," and cleaning up the defenses around the area. They became very good at it, using artillery and air support to soften things up before taking over. Both battalions were racking up kills and captures. The amount of prisoners became burdensome.

Meanwhile, Slater's force and others were still moving forward, that is, until they got to Hill 63, one of several in the area holding German entrenchments. Taking the hill initially was hard enough, but holding it against the ensuing artillery fire was nearly impossible. Rangers were hit often as the pounding rearranged the surface of the hill. At one point the battery at Lochrist tried to take the hill and its occupants apart with its quarter-ton shells. It would take several days to reduce the powerful German positions in the area.

Once the location of the guns was known and the heavy defenses had been breached, the attack was made on Lochrist and surrounding small towns.

From HHC, 2nd Battalion History

Working with us were four tank destroyers of the 644th TD Battalion, seven light tanks from the 741st Tank Battalion, two Recon platoons of the 86th Recon Squadron, four medium tanks of the 709th Tank Battalion, and five scout cars from the 86th. These were used in direct support but were too often out-gunned.

As with the Infantry units, tank units and others were often fragmented to make up impromptu task forces for whatever need arose. Tank Destroyers were armed to kill tanks, not to back up Infantry. They were fast, but thin skinned.

Casualties in wounded were heavy, but the battalion, after a holding action on the 5th of September during which the 116th Infantry moved in, jumped off with the 116th, with the 86th Recon as contact, and gained a thousand yards and cut the Brest-Le Coquet cable, thus isolating the batteries.

Wire and radio communication was maintained in the advance and on the 8th the Forward CP displaced forward and the battalion dug in before…the Lochrist Battery. At 1200, Colonel Rudder accepted the Battery Commander's surrender, and at 1330, Lt. Colonel Fuerst, commander of all the troops on Le Conquet Peninsula, also surrendered, this taking place at St. Mathieu.

Four men of Company A, 2nd Ranger Battalion, were the first inside the battery complex, and the story is the material of legend. What follows is the story of Lieutenant Robert Edlin, "The Fool Lieutenant," and three of his mates, who pulled off a daring, life-saving mission using Ranger initiative, Ranger discipline, and above all, Ranger guts.

Edlin's Patrol Takes The Prize

Robert "Bob" Edlin, a First Lieutenant leading a four-man patrol from A Company, 2nd Ranger Battalion, is credited with obtaining the unofficial surrender of the Batterie Graf Spee at Lochrist. Much of the information for this version of his story—and that of the other three members of his squad—is taken from the book, "The Fool Lieutenant," by Moen and Heinen.

During the Brittany Campaign of late 1944 both the 2nd and 5th Rangers were pushing hard to get through the tenacious German defenses guarding the port city of Brest and other strongly-held areas. Brest held a large submarine base and was the landing port for much of the German supplies. It was second-largest port in France and housed some 80,000 people. The Germans had been there for four years and had plenty of time to prepare their defenses to keep the Allies from using the deep-water port.

Much of the time Ranger Companies were operating either on their own or with only part of their respective battalions while reducing pillboxes and dug-in emplacements filled with men bent on turning them back.

General Ramke, a tough soldier heading such units as the vaunted 2nd Parachute Battalion, commanded German defenses. It was not an easy time for either side.

The 2nd Rangers, however, had an ace-in-the-hole in the form of Lieutenant Edlin, leader of the 1st Platoon of A Company. Small in stature but huge in heart, Edlin and his mates proved their courage over and over again during the days following D-Day, going out repeatedly with just a four-man patrol to gather information. Though that was the patrol's main mission, Edlin and his men did other things as well.

Edlin led his friends, William Dreher, Warren Burmaster "Halftrack," and William Courtney on countless patrols behind enemy lines from the Le Conquet Peninsula to Germany itself.

Between the four men there were three Distinguished Service Crosses and a few Silver Stars.

An original member of the team, William White "Whitey" was unable to continue when it was noticed by Colonel Rudder that a patrol with a Platoon Leader and a First Sergeant carried too many important people. White stepped aside and Burmaster was recruited to take his place in the patrol.

Often the 2nd Rangers—and the 5th—came up against pillboxes that contained many German soldiers, anything from a few men manning a machinegun to over 100 firing everything from 88s to small arms. In the beginning of the battle most pillboxes put up stiff resistance, but as the Americans moved forward those strong points began to give up. First, however, many of them poured fire on the advancing troops until they got close enough to take the emplacement, and then surrendered. The idea was to put on a good show first to save face, then give up before being taken or killed. That idea was not enthusiastically accepted by US soldiers on the scene, some of whom were killed while helping the enemy save face. In some cases local French civilians were able to barter surrender with holed-up and desperate troops.

In early September, the 2nd Battalion came together again for a short time. The various companies had been sending people back to Battalion HQ for supplies so it was probably good to get back and get a hot meal instead of C or K Rations or a foraged chicken or two.

It was through this maze of pillboxes and minefields that the Ranger Battalions—and many thousands of other soldiers of all kinds—worked their way across Brittany to cut off the tip of the peninsula from the rest of France. Brest happened to be on the far side of the AO.

Of particular importance in the area of Brest, 10 miles inland, was a battery of huge guns supposedly taken from the Battleship Graf Spee, monster 280mm weapons that had to be taken out.

Though the guns did not fire on the Rangers very much, the little they put toward them caused the earth to heave in torment and left craters big enough to drive a few trucks into. Other units took quite a pounding. It was said the shells "sounded like a boxcar going sideways through the air when fired."

The Graf Spee, a pocket battleship mounting 11-inch guns, was scuttled off the coast of Montevideo on December 17, 1939, when her captain mistakenly thought the British carrier Ark Royal was waiting for him to put to sea. Not wanting to lose his thousand-man crew and figuring his ship already too damaged from a previous battle to defend herself properly, Captain Langsdorff put her on the bottom. A photograph of her final moments afloat clearly shows her giant guns still in place. Source: WWII Encyclopedia, H. S. Stuttman Inc. Publishers.

About 3,000 men were set to attack the battery (fort). Elements of the 29th Infantry Division—116th and 175th—several tank units, free French, Russians, and both Ranger Battalions were part of the forces moving against the area around Brest—forces that had been hammering away at the German defenses for weeks—but first the big guns had to be stilled.

Bombers had been at the enemy also, hitting the harbor at Brest and reducing known strong points as much as possible.

Though many bombs fell on the pillboxes, damage to their interiors was relatively light. The incessant pounding was more of an incentive to quit than the actual explosions.

The attack was set for dawn of September 10, with air support beginning around midnight and artillery scheduled for right before the attack, which was to be a frontal assault.

Accordingly, the day before, Edlin and his patrol were sent in close to recon the area of the Lochrist Battery—near the town of Lochrist, it was also called the Graf Spee Battery—which was actually a series of fortifications built of solid materials—mostly concrete—and staffed with several hundred Germans. The whole area was sown with mines and a way through the minefields had to be found.

They crept within a couple of hundred yards of a large pillbox on the outer edge of the German defenses. The actual emplacement of the big guns was in the middle of the enemy compound and rose some five stories above the ground, and is said to have gone nine stories underground. The whole area was like a small town with a population of about 2,000; only they were all soldiers.

Large pillboxes anchored the corners of the compound perhaps 250 yards from the fort itself. Edlin's patrol began to work through the mined area, feeling they would be hit or blown up at any time. Suddenly, Courtney yelled out he had found a way through, following a chewed up path through the mines created by bombs. The men ran down the zigzag path and ended up in front of the pillbox. They had yet to be seen.

Flat on the cold, wet ground the four men could hear German voices inside the pillbox. The door was slightly ajar and was unguarded, but there was an enemy soldier hanging by his neck so near the door his body had to be moved aside to enter.

The enemy may have been about ready to quit, but they wouldn't tolerate deserters.

Edlin then made the daring move of entering the pillbox with Courtney and Dreher, going in fast with weapons ready, and found themselves with 20 paratrooper prisoners. Considering the odds of getting out alive, Edlin had left Burmaster outside so he could carry word back if anything went wrong. Unbelievably, nothing did.

Finding a German officer who spoke English, quick negotiations led to Edlin and Courtney being taken deeper into the compound to see the commander, Colonel Fuerst. Edlin later said he probably should have asked Colonel Rudder for permission, but he was afraid he would have said no. Instead he had Burmaster get the Germans to radio Rudder and get him to lift all fires on the fort—they were going in.

Another radio call from an observer to Company A Commander Robert Arman became somewhat famous. In essence the message was, "That fool Lieutenant of yours is up there already. You might as well go in."

But, the surrender had not yet been accomplished. Edlin, Courtney, and the German officer took a stroll through the minefield toward the middle of the compound. They were in the open but were not challenged. Entering the huge central building through a large tunnel they walked into an underground hospital full of staff and patients. The two immediately took everyone prisoner. The officer with them told his countrymen to sit down and do nothing; that surrender negotiations were about to take place.

Two Americans in the midst of several hundred German soldiers had no chance whatsoever of surviving, except it was becoming fairly obvious there was little or no fight left in the enemy. Still, there was that German pride to contend with, and Colonel Fuerst had plenty of it.

Edlin and Courtney burst through the commandant's office door and took him prisoner, but the Colonel was unruffled. Told by Edlin that Rangers surrounded him and he had better surrender the whole fort, the officer calmly picked up the telephone—with Edlin pointing a Tommygun in his face—and called one of his outposts to find there were only four Rangers in the compound. He then told Edlin that he and Courtney were now prisoners themselves.

The two Rangers weren't having any of that. Edlin pulled the pin on a grenade and stuck it "lower than his stomach." The Colonel said Edlin would die, too, but Edlin began a slow three-count. As the last number was coming out of his mouth the German surrendered. He was made to get on the compound PA and announce the surrender to his men and command them to stack their weapons and take no further action.

A Ranger patrol of four men had incredibly brought about the surrender of the huge fort and some 800 men. In a short time Colonel Rudder, flanked by Battalion Sergeant Major Len Lomell, came forward to officially accept Colonel Fuerst's surrender—the German wanted to give up to someone of equal or higher rank. Still, Rudder gave Edlin and his mates the credit.

Edlin later said that he and his men didn't do it by themselves. The fort had taken a pounding for a long time and Allied soldiers had reduced the outlying strong points one-by-one.

The rest of the Brest defenses didn't surrender until September 18, when the German garrison found itself isolated. Control of the Conquet Peninsula fell to the Free French, and the Americans moved on, though many had already gone forward.

Over the next few days the 2nd Rangers were detached from the 29th Division and attached to the 8th, giving them a little time to get their house in better order, resupply, and get ready for the next thrust. They were moved to the Crozon Peninsula where 400 Allied POWs were liberated, a member of the 2nd among them. For a short time the Rangers guarded prisoners, but there were some hard fights, too, and replacements continued to roll in—and out.

This type of fun and games went on until late September when the two battalions became part of the beginning push on the German main line of defense, sometimes called the Siegfried Line.

The 2nd and 5th Rangers began the move across France by truck and rail, headed toward Belgium. The bulk of the unit arrived in Arlon on September 28 for some well-deserved stand-down time.

From 2nd Battalion, HHC History

Arlon was and is a memory of rain and more rain. With this, our first opportunity to wash clothes, it was a matter of drying them by stages. Here Supply was able to make arrangements for salvage, of which there was plenty, and inventory equipment and shortages. The meat shortage was taken care of through a couple of well-placed shots for there was an abundance of deer and elk in the woods.

This harkens back to Robert Rogers—living off the land and making do. The Rangers of the 2nd carried M1 hunting licenses and sometimes fished with TNT, but the principle is the same.

Training commenced on the 9th of October with road marches and compass problems. These consisted of infiltration by compass point into a small town about three miles away. As this area was full of Nazi sympathizers and there were many of German descent in the country everyone had to carry a weapon. Passes were issued to Arlon on weekends and it was a relief just to get out of the area. It was possible to get a glass of beer or shot of cognac and, at times, one could get a steak dinner and ice cream.

After what the men had been through, steak, beer and ice cream must have been heaven.

Saar Campaign—5th Battalion Trains, Fights, Rests

The 5th Rangers moved inland and came to rest near a Marist Seminary near Differt, Belgium. As with almost any time they stopped, training began for the many recruits as the battalion rested and reorganized itself back into fighting shape. The local people were happy to see the Rangers and treated them well, which included feeding them.

A week into November the much-needed break was over and the 5th turned back into France. Soon they were working for General Patton, attached to the 6th Cavalry Group, which did a lot of recon work. Small actions in small towns along the way kept them until the first week of December, when heavier fighting began to make casualties in places such as L'Hopital and Aspenhubel.

In Lauterbach, a fight with a German Tiger tank pitted F Company's bazooka against the frontal armor of the big machine with less than desirable results. The armor was just too thick. More fights followed as the enemy positions were overrun one-by-one with the use of artillery and plain Ranger guts.

Called the Saar Campaign, several weeks of heavy fighting took another quarter of the battalion as casualties, 18 of whom were killed.

On Christmas Eve, the 5th Rangers were taken out of battle and moved to Metz for Christmas celebrations.

Hurtgen Forest—Hill 400

The Hurtgen Forest is roughly 50 square miles of thick woods situated atop a fairly flat plateau on the German side of the border with Belgium. Multiple small rivers and streams that divide the forested plateau into ridged areas cut the topography, with waterways running low in the middle. Each one of those sections could be defended piecemeal by well-emplaced gun positions within the trees, or pounded by heavy artillery beyond the river, or both.

In November 1944, the Americans were pushing forward toward the Rhine River, but first they had to cross the Roer—which meant taming the Hurtgen Forest and the towns within it and along its edges. The most heavily contested areas in which Rangers of the 2nd Battalion fought were roughly three to five miles apart, but the area in between was as forbidding as the dark forests of nightmares.

Close to the Roer River high ground dominates the plateau and gives anyone on top—at Schmidt and Castle Hill (Hill 400), near Bergstein—an excellent view for several miles in all directions. When the American forces began to enter the Hurtgen Forest area, Germans on those heights could see them. Those observers had a large amount of artillery on call for whatever they chose to blow up, which was everything they could see, which was almost everything.

Add freezing temperatures, rain, sleet, snow and mud to that scenario and one has a basic idea of what the 2nd Ranger Battalion and the thousands of other Americans of several divisions were up against.

The Germans put forward a very determined resistance against the encroaching American forces for several reasons. General Brandenberger's Seventh Army held the line in that area, a good place to stop the forward movement of US troops through the rough terrain—and before the river—and give German forces time to build up strength for the planned Ardennes offensive in December. Control of the Hurtgen area was necessary for the coming push, as was control of the dams on the Roer. Those dams—the Schwammenauel and the Urft—if damaged, could flood the lower plains and make it nearly impossible to cross the Roer.

To that end, German bunkers and various types of strongpoints were scattered throughout the forest and on the heights nearer the river. When US troops got inside the dim, thickly wooded fir forest, they quickly found death waiting on all sides. If they weren't being shot at from up close, then hell was continually falling on them from above.

The area of combat for the 2nd Rangers began on the western edge of the forest at a little town called Germeter, about five miles due west of Bergstein, behind which lay Hill 400. In between lay the slightly larger town of Vossenack. About three miles south of Bergstein was Schmidt, which backed up to the Roer and featured excellent high ground for observation posts. Germeter lay northwest of Schmidt about four miles.

Every square inch of that territory was accessible to German guns beyond the river, not to mention being initially filled with dug-in German troops. American movement could be seen—and replied to—from several miles away, making it difficult to build any mass of strength in Germeter or Vossenack, or even have an open-air chow line without asking for an artillery round—or a dozen rounds, or a hundred.

During the protracted campaign the 2nd Rangers were attached to four different divisions—three Infantry and one Armored—as first one, then another, took too much damage and had to withdraw. Hitler was determined to hold that area, knowing that if he lost it his left flank would be exposed when the winter offensive began, and he would be blocked from reaching Antwerp.

The Americans had their own plans for an offensive, especially since at that time Patton's Third Army had been all but stopped and the First Army was spending its time shivering in place on the way to Germany.

First Army Commander General Hodges put his V Corps, under General Gerow, in the van for the push into the Hurtgen area. Gerow, in turn, selected the 28th Division as point. On November 2 the 112th Infantry Regiment went in and was smacked repeatedly by everything the enemy had. Air support was almost non-existent due to the inclement weather. Minefields were in abundance. Still, the 112th pushed through and took Schmidt with its high ground near the river.

An odd coincidence occurred when German Field Marshall Model showed up unexpectedly and took command of the enemy defenses. A second division was added to beef up the resistance, which was already considerable.

Model ordered a counterattack on the 28th Division elements invading the forest. The attack was ferocious and the Americans were overrun, many of them fleeing in disorder. General Norman Cota commanded the 28th during the chaos that followed and had to use Engineer Battalions to plug the holes being punched by the Germans. The 110th Infantry then occupied Germeter and Vossenack with the 112th in front of them, but on November 6, the 112th had enough of Schmidt and the 110th watched in horror as desperate men ran back through their positions to escape the explosions in the forest. Casualties were very high, and mounting.

German troops reoccupied Schmidt and made good use of the heights for artillery spotting, continuing to pound the 28th until it became slightly less than effective.

WWII Ranger Battalions had about 500 men at full stretch. The 2nd was replacing an Infantry battalion with almost twice as many men.

On the 21st, the battalion moved to Esch, Luxenbourg, and actually ended up indoors for a time, ate well, and even got to play a little football in the streets. Unfortunately, nothing lasts forever. The Rangers changed attachments more often than they changed clothes. They performed necessary training for the multiple replacements and tried to gather themselves for whatever was to come. Training time was to be limited, however, and many a new Ranger would be going into battle without the full course. On November 14, the 2nd Rangers relieved elements of the 112th in and around Germeter and Vossenack

From HHC, 2nd Battalion History

The end to the fun came when we were alerted on the 2nd of November. On the 3rd we moved out by motor convoy to Neudorf, Belgium, where we were attached to the CCA/5th Armored Division. Attached also was a company of the 86th Recon and a platoon of the 628th TD Battalion. Something big appeared to be in the wind and we were briefed on a mission in the Vossenack area.

On the 14th, we were attached to the 28th Division and an advance party sent to their assembly area. Orders arrived to move to the vicinity of Vossenack as rapidly as possible. The entire battalion, less the rear echelon, moved forward by truck and then by foot to the vicinity of Germeter. The mission was to relieve the 2nd Battalion, 112th Infantry. The move was complete without incident and the CQs (Charge of Quarters) moved into position. The area was heavily wooded and there were mere fire trails upon which to move supplies. The trails themselves were bumper-deep in pea soup mud in which were buried discarded rifles, packs, bed rolls, and other undistinguishable lumps that might have been the bodies of men.

Vossenack—Germeter

By November 14, 1944, the 2nd Battalion was moving into position with Companies A and B in Germeter and the rest around Vossenack. Artillery rounds fell all over the place making movement perilous. Added to that was the constant cold sprinkled with bouts of snow and sleet, through which patrols had to be run.

One intersection on the road to Vossenack—about one mile distant—on the southeastern edge of town was obviously a plotted target for the Germans and became known as Purple Heart Corner. Ranger casualties began in Germeter. Troops took shelter in the basements of the town buildings, at least those not on perimeter duty.

Company A holed up in the basement of a house on the corner, a strong house that took many artillery hits, but kept the sub-level safe until a round or two made it through the floor. One went off with predictable results, but the second sat teetering on the steps while the men inched their way around it. Incredibly, most survived.

Patrols went back and forth between the two towns keeping tabs on each other and looking for Germans—not hard to find. Mortars and artillery and even some small arms fire was directed on the American emplacements. The Americans were firing back, to be sure, though some high ground would be better for observation. A four-man patrol was sent from A Company to recon the area around Schmidt after the Germans had kicked the 112th Infantry out. The patrol actually got to Schmidt and took a look around before reporting back through the three miles of forest and enemy. That four-man patrol was led by Lt. Robert Edlin (see the story on the Lochrist Battery) and actually got inside the town of Schmidt, or at least Edlin did, and heard American voices coming from within a building. Those voices belonged to American POWs who were being told to keep talking English. The Germans knew the Ranger patrol was there. It was a set-up. Edlin and his men worked back through the forest to give the word to Colonel Rudder.

Patrols from Baker Company kept in touch with a company from the 12th Infantry, 4th Division, on their left flank, traveling 500 yards several times a day through the rain of fire and shrapnel.

On November 20 the 28th Division—what was left of it—was relieved by the 8th Division. The 28th had suffered more than a thousand casualties and many had been captured, but the Germans still held the forest. Ranger Companies C, D, E and F were withdrawn to a "rear" area, but were still under the German artillery umbrella.

Companies A and B were to remain on line, though B was to move into the forest to protect the right flank of the 121st Infantry. The night of November 21 Company B moved into the darkness of the Hurtgen forest. Shelling had mostly stopped with nightfall and it was eerily quiet in the thick woods.

Company B got into trouble when they walked into a minefield and incurred casualties.

Try to imagine the scene. It is dark, freezing cold, the enemy is all about, and you're standing in a minefield with your buddies torn apart around you. You must act! But, where can you safely put your feet? Rangers in the company didn't hesitate to go and help.

Baker dug into a nearby clearing and hunkered down and waited for dawn. With daylight the shelling resumed and B Company got a good dose. Some shells exploded in the treetops, raining hot shrapnel down into exposed foxholes. A day and a night passed and it was Thanksgiving, though few had anything to be thankful for as casualties from the incessant shelling continued to rise. Baker Company stayed put through it all.

A patrol from A Company was sent with an aid man to help if they could, and get some recon of the area for later. Carefully moving through the terrible forest the patrol found B Company, but while attempting to evacuate the wounded another mine went off and wounded men of both companies. Eventually the patrol was able, with help, to return to Germeter.

Lieutenant Edlin again. He was on one end of a stretcher and the man on the other end was standing on a mine.

Shortly after that, A Company was sent to replace B in the forest. Going in on the 23rd, Able was to hold the ground until the 27th through plenty of shellfire. The company was then pulled back to Germeter, and then into a "nearby" reserve area with the rest of the battalion.

Companies C, D, E and F were based around Vossenack and took heavy artillery barrages for several days as each defended part of the area and ran patrols. Company F occupied about half the town and acted as guards for a couple of 5th Armored tanks, which were helping guard the town and the Vossenack ridge. As with their sister companies, Fox men didn't move around much in the daylight, but ran patrols during the night.

On the 19th, the Ranger Companies were ordered back to battalion reserve, an area out of small-arms range, but still within range of German artillery.

The 4th Infantry Division and the 5th Armored were ordered to move forward through Klienhau to Bergstein to prepare for the river crossing. Needless to say, the 4th had about the same luck as the 28th in getting anywhere. The weather was horrible and caused many cases of frostbite and trench foot, and the incredible pounding of artillery and mortars took a constant toll of casualties.

The 8th Division, operating somewhat south of the 4th, was also ordered to attack toward the Roer from their positions around Vossenack. A few days of frustrating action only served to weaken the 8th, which gained precious little ground for the price it paid.

The 121st Infantry of the 8th made it as far as Brandenberg on the approach to Bergstein, perhaps a mile distant, and were stopped. The Germans were dug in on Castle Hill on the other side of Bergstein and were laying explosives on the Americans as fast as they could.

On December 2 the order was given to hit Bergstein and the carnage continued.

Elements of the 5th Armored, being road-bound and therefore sitting ducks, were also stopped, and finally had to withdraw under the heavy bombardment. Casualties mounted and progress was slow to nonexistent in the heavy cold and rain of shrapnel.

Bergstein—Castle Hill

On December 6, General Weaver, commanding the 8th Division, asked for the 2nd Ranger Battalion to do what two divisions could not—take Castle Hill; 400 meters above sea level and full of enemy soldiers who would be able to see them coming.

The battalion loaded onto trucks and took a circuitous route through the forest to an area near the small town of Kleinhau where they put foot to ground and set out toward Bergstein.

Upon arrival, the men formed up for a march, but a makeshift patrol of five volunteers each from D and F had been sent ahead to recon for the coming mission. The patrol was briefed by a Ranger staff officer in a building in Bergstein before going up. Once they knew where they were and what was going on, they went up the hill and split up to recon as far as they could, then returned when daylight was imminent to say they had gotten close enough to hear German voices. They also found a slightly sunken road in front of the hill, a good staging area for the assault.

The rest of the battalion slogged on through the night, mindful of artillery shells coming in, also mindful that roadside ditches were filled with water. Incredibly, some of them fell asleep while walking.

Two columns of men marched along each side of the road through muck and mud and occasional shellfire, marching toward heavily defended territory in the flashing darkness. It was very cold.

Able Company went through the town, passing burned-out hulks of American armor that had previously captured, then held the town of Bergstein. Ordered to dig in, the men had to resort to old trenches because the ground was too frozen to excavate.

One platoon of A Company was sent back into Bergstein to prepare to help in the assault on Hill 400, and captured 28 Germans on the way. The platoon was never utilized in the attack.

Company B dug in along the road and prepared to face shelling and counterattacks. Throughout the next day, nearby enemy snipers made it impossible to move around. Mortar teams had duels back and forth. However, no counter-attack on Hill 400 would be made through that sector, because the Rangers had the path blocked and wouldn't move.

Charlie Company had the mission of establishing a roadblock between the town of Bergstein and a stone church at the base of Hill 400. Trying to dig into the rocky, frozen ground, Company C was taken under a heavy artillery pasting. The unit was exposed on top of a small knoll to enemy positions on the lower slopes and had little time to do much but duck.

It was Easy's mission to clear Bergstein before the assault. Easy was taking shellfire all the while, but holding the town and keeping nearby enemy units from stepping up. Right after the shelling Companies D and F moved through Company E positions in the town and made ready to charge up Castle Hill.

Dog and Fox Companies had already come under fire while holding positions around Vossenack, but what awaited them on Hill 400 was something else again.

D, E and F Companies had scaled the cliffs at Pointe Du Hoc on D-Day.

At that point it was announced to all that Lt. Colonel Rudder was leaving the battalion for an assignment as Commander, 109th Infantry Regiment, 28th Division. It was a bitter pill to swallow. Rudder was very well thought of by the men and that was not a good time for him to be leaving. The only thing that kept the men together and in decent spirits was his replacement, Major George S. Williams, a long-time staff officer and well known to the Rangers.

Using information gained by a recon patrol, plans were made for the assault by D and F. Along the front of the hill ran a sunken road in which the two companies spread out, facing the hill about one hundred yards distant.

The area around the men was dotted with burned out tanks and halftracks, making the men wonder about assaulting a position that had already repelled an infantry regiment and an armored unit. Yet, these men were Rangers and used to doing things other units could not do.

Dog Company, on the right flank of Fox, was backed by a cemetery near a church and had a minefield on its right, which protected against counterattacks before they got started.

German machinegun nests, mortar positions, and rifle pits were scattered over both slopes of the hill, but they were defending what lay on top; a second-to-none observation post that gave the enemy a miles-wide view. The OP had to go, and everybody knew it. One old veteran was heard to say, "Here we go with the old King-of-the-Hill game."

Castle Hill is recorded as 400 meters in height above sea level, but the base of the hill is already in elevated terrain. Hill 400 may be more like 400 feet in height, but it is steep and heavily wooded.

Not long before jump-off time, German mortar fire began to fall in the rear of the Ranger line, particularly on F Company. That fire was answered by American artillery on the hill, but the result was the Rangers being bracketed by explosions front and rear.

At 7:30 in the morning the two Ranger Companies made the first mad rush across snow covered open ground to the woods through enemy fire and began to climb the steep, often slippery slope. In true Ranger fashion they were yelling at the top of their voices and firing into the trees as they came. D Company's Commander and a Platoon Leader were wounded early. A red flare had been fired on the hill as soon as the Rangers were seen, a signal for death to be rained on the soldiers headed for the top.

One hundred and thirty men—two Ranger Companies—ran through a veritable hail of small arms, mortar, and artillery fire, determined to make it up that hill. They took out German positions as they went, and many on both sides said goodbye on Hill 400.

The forward momentum of the Rangers and the fierceness with which they fought stunned some of the enemy troops and sent them running for the other side of the hill. Others stood their ground and slugged it out, only to be overrun and shot down. The stunning Ranger attack had somewhat fragmented the companies. Some small elements went around the hill or in one way or another became separated. Still, they had one mission; get to the top. That they did, coming together in twos and threes and larger groups and beginning the difficult task of digging in.

In less than an hour Rangers owned the top of the hill. Prisoners captured from a concealed bunker were sent back and the bunker became very useful when the shelling started. The two depleted companies dug in on the forward crest and began the test put upon them by the Germans below. Artillery fire pounded them, counter-attacks came from several directions, but still they held. There was scant cover from the explosions. The ground was too rocky to dig any hole deep enough to actually hide in. Chunks of blasted trees provided the best cover from the singing, searing shrapnel. What trees remained were blown into toothpicks above them.

In short order nearly everyone was wounded, some more than once.

The first major counter-attack came in the D Company area about 0930 and the fighting was intense, some of it hand-to-hand. The Rangers held.

Later that morning, a head count of D Company revealed 48 of the original 65 were out of action. Just 17 men, many of them wounded, still held rifles and looked downhill.

A good-sized bunker near the top of the hill was used as an aid station for wounded Rangers—and for a few wounded Germans—but very soon the medical supplies ran out. A plea was sent to the rear for more. To make matters worse there were enemy snipers zeroed in on the entrance to the bunker, making it extremely hazardous to exit or enter. One sad loss during this time came when Captain Block, the head of the medical detachment who had been through much with the Rangers, was killed in that entrance.

The Fox Commander was telling a few men grouped around him to collect casualties and put them in the bunker when an artillery barrage slammed into the top of the hill. Everybody hit the dirt, but the CO was wounded. He tried to send a message to battalion for help, but it never went out—his radioman had been killed. The CO continued to lead his men, but frustrated by the lack of word from the Battalion CP, he determined to descend the hill himself, taking a wounded man with him. It was slow going down the hill with no roads or paths and every lead blocked by fallen trees, and the two Rangers took a wrong turn and were captured.

Some of the counter-attacks fielded more than 100 men, but the lightly armed and barely-entrenched Rangers held them off. By afternoon there were but 25 men in both companies still able to fight.

During one counter-attack in the afternoon, a D Company soldier charged a group of Germans with one of their own automatic weapons and sent them running down the hill, many of them abandoning their equipment. Rangers were quick to collect the extra weapons and ammunition because they were down to the bare essentials by that time.

Rangers of the two platoons of Fox Company didn't talk to each other much. There were only a half-dozen or so left in each platoon and they were pretty busy.

In between counter-attacks the shells fell without cease.

A further blow came when the radio was riddled with shrapnel and communication with the Battalion CP was lost. No one could be spared from the line so a few of the walking wounded volunteered to become runners, a valiant act.

Darkness and cold rain came together, making the hilltop even more miserable. Then things began to happen. Rangers from C Company and a couple of medics had made it up the hill to help remove the wounded. The last officer on the hill—from Dog Company—was evacuated and Sergeants took over command.

The litter-bearers from Charlie Company did yeoman's work that night, making several trips up and down the hill, four men to a litter with a man front and rear to guard them. The journey was made in darkness over hellacious terrain with the possibility of German patrols and artillery fire dogging every frozen, wet step. Those men undoubtedly saved Ranger lives. They didn't carry anything extra, no medical supplies, not even rifles. There was nothing available to resupply with at that time, and rifles would only slow them down.

Slim as it was, there was more help coming. A little later a platoon from E Company slid into place beside the exhausted men of Dog and Fox.

This most important battle was supported by American artillery, but not by additional troops. Considering the significance of the high ground, it would seem the Rangers would have had no trouble getting help. And yet...

The 2nd Platoon of Easy Company, minus the mortar section, fortunately arrived during a lull in the shelling and had some time to get settled and see what was going on. Easy had taken casualties earlier, during the clearing of Bergstein before the attack on Hill 400. They took more shortly after dark that night when a counter-attack followed a heavy barrage. While fighting and hunkering down, men of 2nd Platoon helped with the wounded as best they could. The 1st Platoon of Easy, down below near the church, was also taking heavy artillery fire and counter-attacks. It didn't seem to matter where one was in that area, one was liable to get blown away.

Shelling continued through the night as the men worked to get the wounded off the hill. Rest was all but impossible due to the pounding and the need to stay alert. Just before dawn a message was received that about 100 men of the 121st Infantry were protecting D Company's right flank—from the valley floor. That was all the extra manpower the Rangers would get.

Daylight brought the inevitable; heavy artillery, mortar, and self-propelled gunfire shook the hilltop for a time, then slacked off. The lull was followed by yet another unsuccessful counter-attack, though men of the 121st were made casualties, as were more Rangers.

By December 8, the only surviving officer on the hill led 2nd Platoon of Easy Company. He also had the only radio communications on the hill. That radio was used to call in artillery strikes on enemy staging areas, easily seen from the hilltop. Counter-attacks were broken up before they started—some of them.

The situation became more critical as time went by. Requests for reinforcements by battalion went unanswered. And then, by some miracle, the Germans backed off. They had been unable to regain control of either Hill 400 or Bergstein despite massive counter-attacks and artillery fire. American artillery had answered well and supported the Rangers in their efforts atop the hill, but it was Ranger courage that held Castle Hill so it could become, for the Americans, what it had been for the Germans—an Eagle's perch from which to rain destruction on the enemy.

The men of Dog and Fox Companies spent some 40 hours on that hill. Easy and the 121st endured hours there, also. The whole thing was supposed to take one day. The assaulting companies had approximately 90 percent casualties, with 22 KIA. The Germans lost hundreds. Of the 130 men who charged up Hill 400, very few made their slow and painful way back down under their own power.

Excerpt of the After-Action Report for the Battle of Hill 400

After-Action reports are great, but they sometimes leave out a lot. This summary of the fight for Hill 400 tells little of the suffering and heroism of the men involved.

A patrol from Companies D and F made a reconnaissance of Hill 400, returning at 0705 without contacting the enemy. Companies D and F jumped off at 0730 and reached objective at 0835. Company E supported the attack from vicinity of Bergstein and protected the left flank of attacking elements. In moving into position to support the attack, E Company had to clear the western outskirts of Bergstein of small groups of enemy, killing some, taking 17 prisoners.

In launching the attack, an enemy outpost on the enemy's right flank was alerted and a red flare was shot up. Soon after, mortar and artillery fire fell on E Company's position during the initial stages of the attack and on the Hill after D/F had reached its summit. As a result, the companies suffered heavy casualties from tree bursts while digging in. At 1242 a report was received that only 17 men from D Company and 15 men of E Company were in fighting condition.

Evacuation [of wounded] during daylight was impossible so the aid station was set up in troop shelter on the hillside.

A direct fire gun was laid on the shelter entrance and at times during the many enemy attacks; small arms fire was also placed on the entrance. During darkness, casualties were later carried to the Force CP and placed on litter-jeeps for the trip to the ambulance point in Brandenburg.

The Force CP and the reserve platoon, Company E, were in a church [at Bergstein] which was under direct enemy fire from both flanks. The solid masonry withstood 82 direct hits, only two penetrating and inflicting two casualties. At 1450 these men repulsed a counter-attack of undetermined strength. At 1606 a message was received that enemy counter-attacks had continued throughout the afternoon and that the garrison had been reduced to 25 men. This message was relayed to the CG of the 8th Division with request for reinforcements. At 1653 one platoon of E Company was sent to support D and F. When this platoon arrived the enemy broke and fled.

Christmas In Combat

By the 9th of December, the battalion was in bivouac, rehashing the stories of Hill 400 and the church and trying to get back in some semblance of good order. They were attached to the 28th Infantry for the brief stand-down, but were still subject to artillery fire.

Within the next few days the 2nd was joined by a company of tanks and two companies of infantry and attached to the 78th Infantry Division. The group was assembled for a move to Simmerath, where the Rangers would take up defensive positions.

The unit moved into town under artillery fire and almost lost their big radio when a salvo of four 88mm shells struck a building near the operators. The Battalion CP was set up in the basement of a hospital that took fire all day long. Communications were mostly accomplished by radio at that point, as it was all but impossible to keep commo wire intact with all the shelling.

Over the next few days, the Americans continued to build a better defensive setup under almost constant mortar fire. Patrols on both sides toured the area frequently, but Simmerath belonged wholly to the Americans. The Germans continually probed the defenses, once even running some cattle into the wire. The terrain was table-flat and neither side could move much without being seen.

Christmas found the Rangers in the line eating turkey sandwiches and looking out for counter-attacks and paratroopers. Patrols continued until the end of the month in a more-or-less static situation, though the Rangers knew German General Von Runstedt would be attacking somewhere near.

Between the 2nd and the 7th, the battalion was part of the 102nd Cavalry Group, the Ninth Army and I Corp reserve. A few replacements straggled in as the battalion was in refit, and the snow began to fall in earnest. With snow knee-deep and new men on board, training began again.

From 2nd Battalion, HHC History

It was SOP for a quarter-mile run with as many men as possible. Surprising the number of details that could be found to do. The citizens were literally shocked at the method employed in digging latrines and sump holes. An expedient consisted in the use of liberal charges of TNT.

The engineers had blasted the pill boxes in the area and it was a continual source of wonder as to how they managed to keep them from landing on the houses, for some of them almost turned turtle and lay in what might be considered the front yard.

We were literally in the Siegfried Line for we were within pistol shot of the serrated rows of "dragon teeth" [concrete anti-tank obstacles].

The end of the month brought an ordnance outfit to check all the weapons which had the appearance of the same old gesture—work the slide and if it doesn't fall apart, she'll shoot.

By late February the battalion was again attached to the 102nd Cavalry Group, and while not blowing up fish in the surrounding waters with left over German mortar shells, the men went back into training. On the way to Dedenborn, roads had to be traveled that left a good bit to be desired, pot-holed with shell craters and littered with the debris of war.

Kalterherberg was our next area, and it was a mess of battered houses, dead cattle and mazes of combat wire. Policing began at once and with the cleaning of equipment occupied all our time. It was just a couple of days and roads disappeared in a mass of ruts. Prime movers would crawl through, leaving following jeeps high and dry on their axles. The motor pool never got caught up fixing flats, for the roads were full of buried scraps of shrapnel.

Across The Roer

At that point the battalion was split up, with A, B and C Companies attached to the 38th Cavalry and D, E and F attached to the 102nd Cavalry Group. The situation became more fluid the further the Americans pushed and small towns and landmarks were cleared of the enemy. The Roer River was only three feet deep in one place. A small group tested the crossing, and a larger group quickly followed.

The Germans at first had no idea the Rangers were in the area, let alone the units with them, and small fights developed continually with few Ranger casualties but quite a few German casualties and POWs produced.

As unstable as things were, if not careful the rear units could easily have wound up on point.

Felled trees often blocked the roads with German machineguns overlooking the scene, and mines were everywhere. The men slogged on through, taking ground a little at a time without any "serious" battles.

On May 9, the Battalion CP was set up in the town of Mayschoss and two tunnels were uncovered, one containing a power plant and the other full of imported laborers from Poland, France, Russia, and other countries. These poor souls existed without food and wore rags, and were probably pretty glad to see American troops, who promptly put them all under guard.

In one day, one of the Task Forces captured four towns, took 69 POWs, and killed several of the enemy.

By mid-month 2nd Battalion was back together.

2ND AND 5TH BATTALIONS INVADE GERMANY

Crossing the Rhine

From 2nd Battalion, HHC History

With news that the Remagen Bridge had been taken intact, we knew it was a matter of hours and we would be on the road again, and so it turned out as we were alerted for the move to the vicinity of Neuweid, just east of the Rhine.

The crossing of the Rhine was epic, for this was the culmination of all our efforts of the past three months. We crossed in the vicinity of Sinzig on the longest combat pontoon bridge ever laid. It was, and is a credit to the Engineers who built it. There was scarcely a tremor in the length as the wheeled tons rolled across. In the distance, both up and down the river, other bridges could be seen, folded like jack straws, results of demolition teams not caught napping as at Remagen, not just an obstacle or scene of mass destruction, but a symbol of defeat.

The American push forward was intense and garnered more than pillboxes and landmarks overtaken. In a parallel to the Iraq wars, many Germans, or their impressed cohorts, were overwhelmed both by the force of the American presence and the hopelessness of their situation. As the Rangers went forward they were met by mentally defeated Axis troops, as seen in the next excerpt.

He identified the voices as German and cut loose with a 'halt' that scared the voices into a rousing jabber of "Kamerads!" A half-dozen Volksturmers [home guard, often old men and young boys], very homesick and tired of the war in general and Hitler in particular, foot-sore and weary under the loads of loot and the 20-some-odd miles, had been trying since before dark to surrender to anyone, anywhere, and anyhow. Things were moving so fast that outfits couldn't be bothered and kept chasing them back, each in turn nudging them along.

Indeed, there were times when prisoners were told to go surrender to somebody else, a phenomenon that also occurred in Iraq.

The Rangers moved fast, divided at the time into separate task forces, covering ground and collecting a few hundred prisoners in a short time. On the 29th of February, the battalion was reunited at Wolfenhausen and made contact with the 3rd Army on the far side of the Lahn River. There the battalion was again split with three companies to Task Force A (TFA), and three to Task Force S (TFS).

For several days the units took sporadic fire and had an occasional sharp fight, still losing men, though at a greatly reduced rate. Prisoners continued to accumulate as American units linked up. At one point a motorized 2nd Ranger patrol contacted members of the 5th Battalion, not too far distant as the American war machine homed in on the heart of Germany.

The Task Forces, along with all the other soldiers of the 2nd and 3rd Divisions, and others, were meeting light resistance. Since there wasn't a lot of fighting, the "rear" was fairly close to the action, sometimes less than three miles back, as compared to eight or nine. The American forces moved through towns quickly, picking up prisoners along the way. Rangers at a checkpoint had a car try to force its way through and opened fire, netting a fleeing German General in the process. Some Ranger units, as part of Task Forces, kept watch over V Corps as it moved up, contending with either stubborn or fleeing enemy soldiers or the often-present refugees and townsfolk, some of whom were taking their ire out on their previous German masters.

The Americans were on a mopping-up mission and encountered several varieties of the enemy—some who would fight, some who would surrender, and some who would try to hide.

From 2nd Battalion, HHC History

The enemy, so contained, made forays on supply lines, which at this time were greatly extended. Too many of them were in civilian dress and had to be questioned. The result was that it was a common sight to see apparently innocent civilians lying riddled along the roadside, or piled up in the nearest village square as a warning for any stragglers to come out of hiding. Anyone in civilian clothes and carrying a weapon was shot out of hand. Bitter, quick justice.

There were plenty of unusual situations confronting the troops as they swept through the countryside. On any given day there was no telling what they might turn up.

TFS sent a recon patrol into Mockern for a look around and found a hospital full of American and British wounded. To say they were happy to be released is to put it mildly. The biggest hunger was for a real Yankee cigarette.

The 38th Cavalry threw a cordon around the town [Bachra] and the Rangers moved in and cleared the houses of all occupants and herded them into the town square where they were questioned by a Ranger interpreter. Of 13 suspects, 11 proved to be out of uniform. Two of them made the mistake of making a break for it and were stopped permanently.

E Company [with TFS] located a former Hitler Jugend school in Schulphforte, and of 22 former instructors of several different nationalities arrested, all denied participation in the party, or of being members of the faculty.

Later, documents found in Liepsig made these men liars.

5th Battalion at Irsch-Zerf

The 5th Ranger Battalion was put on the defensive during the Battle of the Bulge, but the expected attacks on St. Avold didn't happen. By early February the 5th saw battle with the 94th Division in Wehingen, Hellendorf, and Weiten, among other places. Such fighting took a toll, and even though replacements were coming in and receiving at least rudimentary Ranger training, when the mission to interdict the Irsch-Zerf road came, the 5th was still more than a hundred men below its authorized strength of 506.

Not much has been written about the 5th Rangers at the Battle of Irsch-Zerf, yet it was a standout mission for several reasons. First, stealthy infiltration was used over many miles and hours, and then heights were occupied twice by the 5th, who used them to drop artillery on the road between Irsch and Zerf. That road was necessary to the Germans and they put out a lot of energy to remove the Rangers. They didn't make it.

The amazing story that follows can only throw words at an action—many actions—that made casualties out of almost half the battalion and cost the Germans half a regiment.

February 23, 1945, found the 5th Battalion being called for assembly from their positions strung out over six miles. There were rumors about an impending mission that had the men speculating that the job "was to be a real Ranger one."

Extra machinegun ammunition was issued, plus anti-tank mines, and one K and one D ration for each man. The mission was only supposed to last 48 hours and the men would be traveling light. At about 6 p.m., the six companies were together in the town of Rodt, which was under artillery fire. Company A took some casualties, notably two officers. Sergeants Rooney and Thomas were put in charge of the two platoons and did well.

There was but one footbridge across the Saar River near Rodt and the 5th had to wait two hours under fire for other friendly troops to cross the "jitterbugging" footbridge first. Everyone crossed the little bridge over the rushing water under fire to find themselves at the bottom of a long incline which took almost three hours to climb in the cool darkness. About an hour before midnight the battalion was at the top, breathing hard.

There it was discovered the infantry forces on their flank had not moved nearly so fast and the original plan was altered. Time was going by.

Two columns were formed with C, F and A on the left and D, E and B on the right. With C and D leading off, the battalion passed through the 302nd Infantry lines and moved north-northeast for nine hours.

Those nine hours were reported to be tough going, done in the silent mode through enemy territory with every German in the area on alert. Ranger training paid off in spades as the companies steadily infiltrated forward, up and down over wooded hills, hour after hour, cramped with the strain of movement and staying quiet.

It was soon to become very noisy. By dawn of the 24th they were well behind the lines and reconning forward with a patrol from Easy Company. The command had three companies abreast—D, E, and C from the left—with F, B, and A following in a column.

They weren't just out for a hike. Every few hundred yards there were encounters, quick firefights, and enemy prisoners. Both sides were already taking casualties, the first of many to come.

One such fight—a fair-sized one—took place at "Bloody Gulch" when Dog Company ran into about a company of Germans and engaged in a fierce small-arms battle, routing the superior force. The enemy left behind some 40 dead soldiers and gave up 18 more to capture.

If it was a full company of Germans it would have been a good bit larger than a Ranger Company of that day.

Company A had some fun when it cut a small road and captured a German staff car carrying two officers and three enlisted men. The Germans couldn't believe they were being captured. They were more than three miles inside their own lines.

The 5th Battalion continued to move forward, constantly deviating their course to confuse the enemy. Artillery still found them, however, and it was with great relief that they reached a point very near their objective—the Irsch-Zerf road. A few abandoned houses were nearby and the Battalion Commander, Colonel Sullivan, ordered a short move to take shelter there. A machinegun opened up during the move, but was quickly silenced by men from F Company, as was rifle fire from a house.

At least some of the men had shelter for the last half of the night and an opportunity to rest and eat. They would need it.

Early the next morning they were overlooking the road they had come to block by being spotters for American artillery. If the road could be cut, German reinforcements and supply vehicles couldn't use it, and advancing American Infantry would have a much easier and less time-consuming job. The battalion set up a defensive perimeter with E on the north, D and F on the east, and C on the west. Able Company plugged the southern hole after a few short fights, and Baker guarded the current 95 prisoners and acted as reserve.

Anti-tank mines quickly accounted for a half-track and bazookas were used on a tank destroyer. More prisoners were taken, walking down the road. It wasn't long before the Germans got tired of the Rangers in their midst and sent counter-attacking forces in all directions.

Able and Easy, south and north, were hit by large forces made up of 200 men and two tanks in the south, and twice that in the north. Supporting artillery laid on by the 28th FA (field artillery) helped immensely and the Germans' first try cost them more than 100 casualties and 75 more taken as prisoners.

By that time, there were some 200 prisoners—which cost manpower to guard—and the men were running out of things. Food and water were getting very low, as was ammunition. They were told some friendly tanks of the 10th Armored were coming up soon.

Meanwhile, resupply needs were becoming critical. Land travel was out, so little spotter planes tried dropping supplies. Small-arms fire kept them at 1,500 feet, resulting in the loss of many supplies that fell outside the Ranger lines or were broken up on impact.

About 0300 the next morning, about 400 Germans hit Easy Company, supported by heavy artillery and mortar fire. Ranger return fire mowed them down, but some got through Easy lines in a few places. The company was moved back about 50 yards and artillery was called on their former position—very close. Dog Company followed suit and had artillery brought around them for the rest of the night.

At daylight Fox Company attacked and regained the small amount of lost ground, finding it littered with the bodies of German dead, especially around foxholes where Rangers had held out.

Around noon some tanks did show up but they were directed to another place, not with the Rangers. The tanks were to drive on Zerf and the Rangers were to stay put and defend the area. They spent time improving their positions. They knew what was coming.

The night passed without attack, but the fog was rolling in. At dawn they came through the mist—hundreds of them—and ran into concentrated overlapping fire from three companies. Very quickly the attack was scattered and beaten down. More prisoners appeared, bringing the total near 350. Again the ground was littered with enemy dead.

Interrogation of some of the prisoners revealed the unit the Rangers were facing was the 136th Regiment of the Second Mountain Division—crack troops. The Germans had been given orders to eradicate the Rangers and were bent on doing so. The fight became somewhat personal; "Rangers against the Mountain Boys."

After three days in the gunnery spotlight the Rangers were already beyond their expected 48-hour stay. Colonel Sullivan decided to go on the offensive to take some higher ground to the south. Such a spot would be well worth having.

On February 28, more than 100 hours in, Lieutenant Harbin of Charlie Company took a strong patrol to look over some enemy-held houses in the line of attack. After 15 minutes of Ranger bombardment, including bazooka fire, 105 Germans threw up their hands.

Once the area was secured Charlie and Dog moved to secure the hill, meeting small resistance until a sudden artillery barrage plastered them flat to the ground. Intermixed with artillery shells was a type of heavy rocket the Rangers had not seen before. The two companies continued their climb within a short time and made the nose of the hill, below the top.

A lull gave everyone a respite, but soon Able came up to flank Dog and the two units advanced toward the crest under continued artillery and rocket explosions. About 200 yards from the top they were temporarily halted again by intense fire and an enemy counter-attack. In the midst of all the incoming the Rangers captured ten more Germans.

The Germans couldn't remove the Rangers from the hill, but neither was the attacking force strong enough to go forward. The companies dug in right there and on came the night full of huge explosions and little rest. By the count of some poor guy in a hole on that hill there were 400 rockets, 600 artillery rounds, and 65 "big" artillery rounds rained on the Rangers that night. There were also several probes of the area that had to be repelled.

By noon of the next day the 5th Battalion was fairly softened up.

There were five pillboxes and other positions atop the hill and A and F Companies got the call to take them down the next morning. At 5 o'clock in the morning of March 1, American artillery began a rolling barrage up the hill toward, and over, the pillboxes. The attacking Rangers followed that barrage—very closely followed—until they were on the enemy positions, much to the surprise of the defenders. In half-an-hour it was over and 115 more prisoners had been taken.

The 5th Battalion set up defenses on top of the hill and felt a little better. They had the heights and American Infantry were moving forward, as was the 10th Armored. Rest was in order but German shells and the ever-present rockets continued to fall. There were no serious enemy probes until about seven in the evening when the Germans tried to retake the hill.

Baker and Charlie were hit particularly hard by a large force and had to pull back a little to make a stand when their lines were breached. It was reported that one didn't know if German or American was in the next foxhole. Able and Dog moved up to bolster the line and heavy firing went on for almost half-an-hour, then abruptly ceased. The rest of the night found everyone awake and watching, but no other attacks developed. In the morning it became obvious the Germans had given up trying to retake their former positions.

The Rangers stayed in place for several more days even though they were wrung out. What should have been 48 hours had turned into a nightmare of nine days during which they had repulsed six major counter-attacks and captured more than 700 prisoners.

The Battle of Irsch-Zerf cost the 5th Battalion 186 killed, wounded or MIA—47 percent of their strength.

Three days later the battalion was moved to Luxembourg where it received some 190 replacements to go with the 180 survivors of Irsch-Zerf. From there the 5th became part of the Military Government in several towns and cities throughout the region.

Winding Down

With the war drawing to a close, there was less need for the elite units in the grinding conflict of attrition that pinched the Germans tighter every day. The highly trained Rangers were again given assignments to mop up die-hards, guard prisoners, and the like.

Still, there was more to find—desperate, dangerous men to deal with, and hidden horrors to be uncovered. Concentration camps were being liberated throughout Europe by encroaching Allied forces, and stories of atrocities and inhumanity began to spread.

One such discovery involved elements of the 5th Ranger Battalion and the liberation of Buchenwald. The best way to tell this story is to let a Ranger tell it.

Harry Herder

The following statements are from Harry Herder, a member of the 5th Battalion after D-Day. Some of the text is from interviews, some from a written manuscript Herder put together years ago. His is a great story, or set of stories, and we start with his unusual Ranger biography—a testament to what kind of men become Rangers.

Continuing casualties in Europe made replacements more than necessary, especially since the new guys didn't always last very long and had to be replaced themselves in the grinding combat of pushing the Germans out of France and Belgium. Into that mix was thrown the towering, bespectacled Herder.

I entered the small office-like room that contained one desk and one chair, and seated in that chair behind that desk was a Captain. He wore a blue lozenge-shaped patch, trimmed in yellow with the word "RANGERS" written across it in yellow. I entered the office in my most military manner, stood at attention in front of the desk, gave my full name and rank (PFC) and remained standing there at attention. The Captain gave me "At Ease," and I came to parade rest and let my eyes come down to his. He sat there for a moment looking at me. He mentioned that I was a "big one," for whatever that was worth, then pointed at my black armband with the Corporal stripes, and told me that I would have to lose those. I grinned, took them off right then and put them on the desk. The action seemed to satisfy him somewhat. I had no illusions that I would be allowed to keep them wherever I went.

He asked me what I knew of Ranger Battalions, and I told him I knew only what I had read, but that I liked what I had read. He asked me several other background questions, my service folder was open in front of him, and my answers to his questions did not seem to disquiet him. He must have completely overlooked the part in my file about my vision, and that was all right with me.

I had made it. I wanted it very badly, badly enough to cheat to get it, and I got it. It would be quite a while before I put my glasses back on again.

With The 5th Rangers

We were joining a group of people, the 5th Rangers, who had done a heroic job of work, no matter how you measured it. The originals in the group, and there were many, had formed up as a battalion and trained in Kentucky. Most of them had come out of the Yankee Division, which, I think, was numbered the 26th Division. I think they wore a shoulder patch with a YD on it. The men of the Division were mostly from the eastern United States, the New York area, and the Boston area.

A few of the others came as replacements after D-Day, another batch of them after Brest, and then there were the three of us. We were replacing men whom the others had known well and trusted, with whom they had sweated and gotten bloody, men with whom they had literally gone through hell. Some of the ones we were replacing had been injured and sent home, some of them were dead. The three of us were still 18 and 19 year old kids, still wet behind the ears, and we were supposed to replace these other men. We three were the new replacements in the first platoon of C Company.

The battalion took four days to train their new replacements. To train us they all had to go through the same exercises, but it was old stuff to them and not a great problem. It was an eye-opening session for the three of us new in the first platoon.

[Sergeant] Stover worked me over on the bazooka until I knew the bazooka well; he would accept nothing but complete understanding, and I agreed with him—I did want to know that tool well. Stover taught me that when firing at a tank, to aim at the seam between the body of the tank and the turret, in order to weld the turret to the body.

There was, outside of St. Wendels, a hill on which there was an older German pillbox, and they were going to train the new people by attacking the pillbox over and over again.

I reprise for myself the actions of an assistant bazooka man; #1, the assistant never gets far from the bazooka. Never! He must always be near. #2, once the bazooka is fired it is up to the assistant to load it up once again as quickly as possible. To load the bazooka I placed myself at the side of the bazooka man and faced in the opposite direction. Bazooka rounds came in cylindrical containers that were tightly closed and sealed. There was a thread one could pull to separate the two parts of the container. One threw the cap of the container away, slid the round out of the base of the container and inserted the round into the bazooka. There was a wire off the base of the round that was to be attached to a conical, helical set up of wire on the back of the bazooka. The assistant took the wire and curled it into the coil securely and then tapped strongly on the helmet of the bazooka man to let him know the instrument was once again ready to fire. Later Smokey allowed me to act as a bazooka man and to fire the weapon at the pillbox from a distance, just to acquaint me with the sights.

This training, this exercise of the attack on the pillbox with the company commander remaining in the hilltop we started by shooting tracer rounds over our shoulders. Not the shoulders of everyone, just the shoulders of the new replacements. Sitting on the hill beside him was the company demolitions man firing off buried loads of explosives as we passed near them. They seemed to need to know in a hurry how we would react to tough situations. We must have done all right. We were all retained. I remember going up the hill at the pillbox firing my Garand and reloading. I remember we called it "walking fire." We held the weapon at our hip and moved swiftly and steadily up that hill. It was here that I learned to keep the cover of the pockets for the clips for my rifle open so as to get to them easier. I don't know how many clips of eight rounds I fired, but my rifle belt was considerably lighter at the end of the day. I also found out the hard way how hot the barrel of the M1 got under those conditions.

I was one of the last volunteers allowed into the 5th Ranger Battalion, and I think the 2nd had similar activity. It was late in the war and we were not engaged in any of the bigger battles of the war but we remained a part of the battalion until the ship landed in Boston and the outfit was broken up. We did take part in a number of activities, one of them being the liberation of the concentration camp Buchenwald. We stayed on at Buchenwald for three or four days, and the things that we witnessed—lived through—remained vivid in my mind for years.

Our outfit hooked up with a tank destroyer outfit, and we did blow across the landscape of Eastern Germany with little opposition. There were only our company and the group of tankers, and we were in a hurry.

What I do remember is that we eventually drove up some gentle valley where there were trees on either side of us, when we made a sharp left turn, so sharp that those of us on the top of the vehicles were grabbing things to keep from falling off. By the time we had regained our balance, there it was: a great high barbed wire fence at least ten feet high, maybe more. Between us and the fence and running parallel to the fence was a dirt road, and beyond the fence were two more layers of barbed wire fence not quite as tall. The barbed wire in those fences was laced in a fine mesh, so finely meshed no one was going to get through it. Our tanks blew straight through the barbed wire.

I remember scouting out the area in front of us quickly with my eyes. There were no great details, but I saw that over to the left, next to and just inside of the fence and to our front, were some major buildings, and next to one of those buildings was a monster of a chimney, a monster both in diameter and in height. It might have appeared huge because the buildings next to it were only two or three stories high, but it was an extraordinary chimney. Black smoke was pouring out of it and blowing away from us, but we could still smell it—an ugly, horrible smell.

A vicious smell.

[We] were fully expecting a firefight with German troops, whose camp we had just stormed and taken. It turned out there were no German troops present.

Slowly, as we formed up, a ragged group of human beings started to creep out of, and from between the buildings in front of us. As we watched these men, the number and the different types of buildings came to my attention. From them came these human beings, timidly, slowly, deliberately showing their hands, all in a sort of uniform, or bits and pieces of a uniform, made from horribly coarse cloth, striped, the stripes running vertically. Some of those human beings wore pants made of the material, some had shirt/jackets, and some had hats. They came out of the buildings and just stood there, making me feel foolish with all of that firepower hanging on me.

The jeeps, our company commander's and a few others, rolled forward very slowly toward these people, and as they parted, drove slowly through them, to the brick building next to that tall chimney, and our officers disappeared inside. Our platoon sergeant had us form up some and relax, then signaled that horde of human beings to stand fast; he just held both hands up, palms out, and motioned them backwards slowly. Everything was very quiet. The tanks were all in slow idle. Hesitatingly we inched closer to that strange group as they also started inching closer to us. Some of them spoke English and asked, "Are you American?"

We said we were, and the reaction of the whole mass was immediate. Simultaneously on their faces were relaxation, ease, joy, and they all began chattering to us in a babble of tongues that we couldn't answer—but we could, and did point the muzzles of our weapons at the ground, making it obvious these weapons were not "at the ready."

It was then that the smell of the place started to get to me. Our noses, rebelling against the surroundings they were constantly subjected to, were not functioning anywhere near normally. But now there was a new odor, thick and hanging, and it assaulted the senses.

Before long the Rangers were being settled into buildings around the camp, still without much understanding of where they were.

Sergeant Blowers told us that some of the prisoners spoke English. Then he got even quieter, looked at the ground for as moment, raised his eyes, and looking over our heads, began very softly—we could barely hear him. He told us this is what was called a "concentration camp," and that we were about to see things we were in no way prepared for. He told us to look, to look as long as our stomachs lasted, and then to get out of there for a walk in the woods.

The lane we were walking on bent to the right as we cleared the building. We had barely made the turn, and there it was. The bodies of human beings were stacked like cordwood. All of them dead. All of them stripped. The inspection I made of the pile was not very close, but the corpses seemed to be all male. The bottom layer of the bodies had a north/south orientation, the next layer went east/west, and they continued alternating. The stack was about five feet high, maybe a little more; I could see over the top. They extended down the hill, only a slight hill, for 50 to 75 feet. Human bodies neatly stacked, naked, ready for disposal. The arms and legs were neatly arranged, but an occasional limb dangled oddly. The bodies we could see were all face up. There was an aisle, then another stack, and another aisle, and more stacks. The Lord only knows how many there were.

Just looking at these bodies made one believe they had been starved to death. They appeared to be skin covering bones and nothing more. The eyes on some were closed, on others open. Bill, Tim, and I grew very quiet. I think my only comment was, "Jesus Christ." I can't guarantee that.

We turned and walked back to the building where we found others from our company along with some of the prisoners milling around in the space between the bodies and the building. We moved gently through those people, through the doors and felt the warmth immediately. Not far from the doors there was a brick wall, solid to the top of the building. In the wall were small openings fitted with iron doors. Those doors were a little more than two feet wide and about two-and-a-half feet high. The tops of the doors had curved shapes much like the entrances to churches. Those iron doors were in sets, three high. There must have been more than 10 of those sets extending down that brick wall. Most of the doors were closed, but down near the middle a few stood open. Heavy metal trays had been pulled out of those openings, and on those trays were partially burned bodies. On one tray was a skull partially burned through, with a hole in the top; other trays held partially disintegrated arms and legs. It appeared that those trays could hold three bodies at a time. I had enough. I couldn't take it any more.

It dawned on me much later: the number of bodies which could be burned at one time, three bodies to a tray, at least 30 trays, and the Germans still couldn't keep up. The bodies on the stacks outside were growing at a faster rate than they could be burned. It was difficult to imagine what must have been going on.

Many people were involved in the aftermath of the liberation of Buchenwald. Corps of medical and mess personnel flooded the camp, along with the inevitable photographers and administrators. One visitor in particular caused quite a stir. General George Patton was not happy with what he saw there.

Herder Bio

This short biography of Herder's rambling military service is interesting for several reasons. His journey was unusual, but not unique. The kind of men who volunteer for the Rangers often showed up with other out-front units doing dangerous things. It's as though such men can't help but go forward. Included as part of his story is how he came to be a Ranger, illustrating his determination to be one of the best. There are more than a few instances of Rangers becoming Marines and vice-versa. Herder has really been around, from WWII to Korea, and as a very large Ranger-trained, jump-qualified Marine he must have been quite a handful.

I attended a college [St. Thomas in St. Paul] for one year and then re-entered the army. In spite of my glasses I was allowed into the 82ⁿᵈ Airborne. I only jumped once wearing my glasses—taped on—and the helmet banging into them was not pleasant. I should also note that at that time I was six-foot-six and 235 pounds. I served the whole hitch in E Company of the 504ᵗʰ PIR [Parachute Infantry Regiment].

After that discharge I helped my brother on the farm for several months and then ended up in San Francisco and the Korean problem got started. I went to the Army recruiter and showed him all of my discharges and asked to be assigned to a Regiment for the 11ᵗʰ that was on its way to Korea. The Army wanted no part of that so I went down the street to the Navy and showed them my background and asked how long would I be in Boot Camp. They told me three weeks. I went across the hall to the Marines and asked them and they told me 13 weeks. I went back across the hall again. That three weeks ended as soon as I got there and the football coach found out that I had played at a few places. I played for [them] in San Diego, and they promised me any school in the Navy I wanted to attend.

I chose Hospital Corpsman School. Went to the school, then up to the hospital in Bremerton for my six months of "internship." Finishing that, there was a demand for corpsmen for the Marines. I put in for that and got it and went to Pendleton for Marine Training. You could note if you wished that I have attended my original Boot Camp, Ranger Training, Jump School, Navy Boot Camp, and Marine training for corpsmen. Finishing the training we loaded up for Korea. We were about two days out of Japan when we passed Christmas. The first of the year I was assigned to B Company of the 7ᵗʰ Marines. With them out on patrol, I stood—almost—on a land mine that ended my career in the Marines and the Navy.

6TH RANGER BATTALION—PACIFIC THEATER

More than distance separated the conflicts in Europe and the Pacific. The main difference as far as getting at the enemy lay in the Japanese troop dispositions. Unlike Europe where solid ground separated the armies, the Japanese were scattered all over the Pacific islands and had to be taken out group-by-group. Often there was steaming, mountainous jungle full of dug-in enemy troops—soldiers who would rather die than surrender. That series of actions required amphibious assault, which meant lots of Intelligence gained by reconnaissance, not to mention a tough bunch of spearheaders. There was always a shoreline not far away.

To confront the Germans, one great amphibious assault onto the European continent was required. Once ashore there was lots of land and a few rivers ahead. The Allies began a slogging, push-them-back series of battles and attrition of men and materiel that characterized the France-Belgium-Germany push.

Though some engagements in Europe were in the mountains, some of it was on reasonably flat land, and often on open terrain suitable for armor. Island fighting in the Pacific was hotter, stickier, wetter, and much more bug-and-disease infested, presenting a much different set of problems as far as logistics, supply and transportation. Even the weapons needed for the campaign were different. Browning Automatic Rifles (BAR) were substituted for heavier machineguns simply because they were easier to carry through the jungle and up and down the ever present mountains.

Formation Of The 6th Ranger Battalion

Generals Douglas MacArthur and Walter Krueger (Commander, Sixth Army) knew they would need a tough raiding team to accomplish the preliminary strikes and recon. They went back to the drawing board and came up with the 6th Rangers. As a way to get around the standard misfit dumping that generally came with asking commanders for volunteers, the new Rangers were all selected from the inactive 98th Field Artillery Battalion in late December. To begin with, MacArthur wanted a provisional force for, as he put it, "employment on amphibious raids and diversionary attacks of limited duration."

Solid veteran Lt. Colonel Henry A. Mucci was named commander of the group. He was a tough guy, and needed to be, because the men of the 98th were all over six feet tall and strong, chosen as they were to deal with mule-drawn artillery.

By April 1944, the Sixth Army sanctioned the group and training began in earnest. In the hills around Port Moresby, New Guinea, officers and men trained together Ranger-style, going at it hard and long to gain the necessary conditioning. In June, it was Finschafen in the north for amphibious training, including night landings and the use of rubber boats.

Considering the Marine Raiders, who had been training in much the same way, had just been disbanded and reabsorbed into the Corps, the only unit left with such capabilities was the new Ranger Battalion. The press leapt on them. Touted as the biggest and toughest in the Sixth Army, the untried group got a little cocky, and some of the rest of the Sixth got a little touchy.

Such things were not unheard of in other Ranger Battalions.

While figuring out just how to put the group together, the Brass started them out along Marine Raider lines. Before long they realized they must change it to be more like the European Ranger Battalions, where it stayed, though equipment changes had to be made to suit the terrain and the enemy.

As with other Ranger units scattered worldwide, no central organization existed to tie them all together, and no contact was made between them.

The 6th Battalion was late getting "officially" started because the Army's table of organization provided for only five battalions, all of which were operating in the European Theater. Merrill's bunch in Burma was not considered a Ranger unit, and so didn't count in the tally. Not until the 1st, 3rd and 4th Battalions were decimated in Italy was the 6th allowed to commence operations, assuming the designation of 6th Ranger Battalion September 26, 1944, while still in Finschafen.

Henry Mucci—The Story of a Slave-Driving Man

"We knew he was selling us the blue sky, but we would have followed him anywhere."
Robert Prince

Lt. Colonel Henry Mucci was a man among men. He was all the things a good commander needs to be, and more. He was a tough human being and used his natural magnetism and drive to get things done.

His men thought very highly of him and were willing to go where he pointed. When Mucci was pointed at Cabanatuan he knew he had the right group of soldiers to do the job—and he was certainly equal to the task.

An athletic man, Mucci had boxing and judo experience and was in excellent condition, as he insisted his men be. He was also a West Point graduate who put his considerable expertise to the test in teaching much of the physical points to the men himself. He led them through the mountainous jungles of New Guinea, training them in everything and anything, bringing the men to the point of exhaustion, hating him, then pushing themselves forward for him, becoming the best they could be.

Once the training was reasonably complete, Mucci changed his attitude toward his men just a little. He softened. They knew he loved them and would take care of them. They were ready for anything, as long as he led them.

He led them well at Cabanatuan, earning himself a Distinguished Service Cross and a promotion to Colonel for a raid MacArthur called "magnificent."

Henry Mucci was tough enough to die swimming in a rough ocean at the age of 86.

Leyte Gulf Mission

The first mission plan came when a group of units originally slated for an assault were unavailable when the time came, giving the 6th a surprise coming-out party. The idea was to hit three islands flanking the entrance to Leyte Gulf three days before the invasion. One company was to hit Homonhan Island, occupy Colasi Point and clear the area. The second company would hit Suluan Island to take out radio and radar installations, and the rest of the battalion would stage at Dinagat Island, where they would destroy whatever the Japanese had at Desolation Point and the town of Loretto. Once all was completed, beacons were to be placed on Dinagat and Homonhan to guide the fleet into the harbor. It was a task perfectly suited for Ranger capabilities.

Overall there wasn't much opposition, but one battle of note came when Company B, led by Captain Arthur "Bull" Simons, had to go after some Japanese holed up in a lighthouse atop high ground. The position was guarded by cliffs on three sides with only a steep, narrow trail for access. Going up the trail wouldn't be good.

The enemy detachment was originally scheduled to be taken by Company D, which landed early on the 18th under Captain Leslie Gray. A patrol sent to destroy the lighthouse met stout resistance and lost one killed and one wounded. Uncertain of enemy capability, the company returned to the ship and then joined the other Rangers on Dinagat, opening the way for Company B's later assault on a position of undetermined strength.

Simons decided to go in at night, hitting a security detachment at the bottom of the cliffs with part of his company while the rest climbed the cliffs. The Japanese weren't expecting that method of attack and were taken quickly. However, the lighthouse wasn't taken right away. The Rangers stayed on the island for a while before Simons made his assault.

For more on this action, see the interview with Leo Strausbaugh.

After that came a couple of months of rear guard duty—not too exciting, though there was an assault by Japanese paratroopers to contend with during that time. When the US landed on Luzon in January 1945, the 6th got another worthwhile mission.

Leo Strausbaugh

Strausbaugh graduated OCS in October 1942, and got a pay raise to $125 a month. He thought he was rich. He returned to Fort Sill, Oklahoma, and was stationed with a 75mm howitzer training battery—mule pack—and ended up being transferred to the 98th FA at Fort Carson, Colorado. Within a short time Strausbaugh's unit was entrained and heading for Newport News, Virginia, to board a ship bound overseas, though no one knew where. He was a 2nd Lieutenant with B Company, 6th Rangers, when the change was made.

The following is part interview by email and part excerpts from his written statements. His memories were written down years ago in a 39-page manuscript that, after several emails in the late summer of 2004, he sent to us for use in excerpt form. His story traces the origin of the 6th Battalion back to the very beginning of his service in the 98th FA. In his words, the manuscript is "better than my old brain can remember now."

They had an open boxcar fixed up which cooked food for all thousand of us. I really was amazed when I saw two Captains, Bedke and [Bull] Simons, take big pieces of raw steak and eat it like a dog. I thought, "What kind of people am I with?"

On December 27, 1942, the 98th boarded the cruise ship "Thomas Jefferson" and set sail for Panama to get through the canal and continue from there to Australia. At one point a little liberty was given.

The next day the whole battalion got off the ship, but we were in formation only as we walked through the streets. No one in their right mind could think of turning a thousand mule-packers loose in the city.

Those mule-packers became the main force of the 6th Rangers. They were a good crew to reconstitute as Rangers—tall, muscular, and full of themselves.

After arriving in Australia the unit was told the mules would not be accepted in the country due to animal restrictions, so the next port of call for the 98th was Port Moresby, New Guinea, where they and the mules disembarked February 17. With temperatures at 100 degrees or more and mosquitoes in every breath, the 98th got introduced to the jungle fast. For food they had "buggy oatmeal, powdered eggs, powdered milk, dehydrated potatoes, canned Spam, and canned Australian rabbit—including some hair."

Captain Moss was transferred to battalion headquarters and Captain Simons replaced him. He had been battery commander of Service Battery. Simons was different. He was husky and barrel-chested. He was smart and efficient, and very difficult if anyone did not perform to his expectations. I want to note that Simons led the ill-fated prison raid on Son Tay in Vietnam as a Colonel, and also, as a civilian, led a group to Iran and broke some employees [of Ross Perot] out of jail. They made a movie about the Iran mission called *On Wings Of Eagles*, and Perot's part was played by Burt Lancaster. Hardly a match, as he was more like Telly Savalas.

An interesting tie-in with Rangers and Merrill's Marauders happened when an order came down in February 1944, to ship all the mules to Burma for Merrill to use as pack animals.

The next thing that happened to the artillery battalion was the replacement of their CO, Lt. Colonel Jim Callicut. Word came that Lt. Colonel Henry Mucci, an Infantry officer, would be arriving soon. The mule-packers began to wonder. Why an Infantry officer as CO of an artillery outfit?

In a few days I was sitting in our orderly room and in walked a short, stocky gentleman with a little mustache and silver leaves on his collar. He introduced himself as Lt. Colonel Mucci and asked to meet the officers.

Soon the five of us were ready to hear what he had to say. The group included Captain Simons and Lieutenants Shearon, Cobb, Knight and myself. Mucci proceeded to tell us that we were to become a Ranger Battalion, and none of us had ever heard of such a unit.

The unit was later designated the 6th Ranger Battalion, but it was September before the official designated name came through.

He told us we could stay and try to make it, or request a transfer, but if we did not perform to his standards, he would transfer us out. He made three statements: that we would have three missions to perform; we would be home by Christmas; and we would all be promoted to Major. None of us believed any of this, but he was so compelling that one reached a desire to give it a try.

We had 1,000 men and only needed 500, so many went out either by their choice, or someone above. Of the 35 officers, about half left and we got replacements. We had been in New Guinea for about a year when Simons came to B Battery and relieved Captain Vaughn Moss.

Most men were big because they wanted big men as muleskinners and a lot were farm boys. It was around February 1, when Mucci came in as Battalion CO. I feel most of the men were tired and fed up with the mule pack and bored and the Rangers offered a new challenge. Most of the good men stayed and a lot of eight balls wanted out. So they either got the boot or were asked to leave. We moved from Port Moresby to Finschafen, New Guinea, around June when we reorganized into six rifle companies from three. At that point Joe Shearon left B to take over E and Simons remained with B and I did, too.

We began to train and it was rough. We did a lot of long road marches, going up mountains, and through the jungles, crossing rivers and [practicing] personal combat tactics on each other. It got so rough one day that we were in a free-for-all when I was knocked to the ground and ended up in the hospital for several days.

We fixed up a rifle range where we fired all the small arms courses. The Colonel insisted we all become experts on all weapons. We did, but I admit we doctored the scores somewhat. If I had had to become an expert with a .45 pistol I would still be there.

Strausbaugh may have had trouble with the big .45, but he was doing something right. After a platoon attack demonstration for a Sixth Army Colonel, he was promoted to 1st Lieutenant, a job paying a whopping $150 a month—plus ten percent for being overseas.

As time went on with more rough training I knew our days there were growing short. Since I was an artillery officer serving in the infantry I wondered if some of the men in my platoon might feel they were being shorted since the new replacement officers were infantrymen.

Taking his platoon out away from the camp, he asked them whether they wanted him to continue to lead them, then left his platoon sergeant, Dixon, in charge and left for 30 minutes for them to discuss it.

When I returned Sergeant Dixon told me that they all wanted me to stay. To this day that has been one of the proudest days of my life.

We were ordered to move from our "home" near Port Moresby to Finschafen, New Guinea, on the eastern side of the Owen Stanley Mountains and near the coast of the Bismarck Sea. I feel every man in our unit was glad to leave but curious what they had in store for us. This move took place in August 1944.

We would now have six rifle companies of 65 men each plus a headquarters company. This was the official organization of the Ranger Battalions. I sat in on the division and Captain Simons was to remain commander of B Company and Lt. Joe Shearon was to take command of the new E Company. I sat down with Simons and Shearon and we took turns choosing the men. Simons had first pick of the officers and he selected me. So, I got to give advice on who Simons should select as I was considered second-in-command.

We continued to train by going all over the area with each platoon going it alone. General Krueger came to visit us so we knew something would happen soon and felt we were ready. It wasn't long when we got word that our battalion had been selected to be the first troops to land back in the Philippines since the Japs had taken the islands over the day after Pearl Harbor.

We were scheduled to land on October 17 and the major forces would land on the Leyete Gulf beaches on October 20. Our missions were to take the islands and destroy the enemy so they could not in any way hinder the main landings. It sounded a bit scary, but we were prepared and willing to do our part.

I was the only officer in B Company other than Captain Simons and Captain Jim Fisher, our medical officer. Tech Sergeant Roy Krueger commanded the second platoon and was very capable. They did reinforce us with some men from the motor pool, so we had a force of about 100.

A week into October the Rangers boarded several ships—for three islands—which were part of a convoy made up of minesweepers, APDs—like a small destroyer—the Rangers were aboard these—and some larger warships. On the 14th the convoy was struck by a devastating typhoon. Strausbaugh reports his ship rocked thirty-eight-degrees and no one could go topside.

Our battalion left Finschafen on October 10 for the Philippines on the following ships: A Company of the APD *Schley* for Dinagat; B Company, APD *Herbert* for Homonhon; C Company, APD *Crosby* for Dinagat; D Company, APD *Kilty* for Suluan; E and F Companies, *Ward* for Dinagat; HQ and Medical Detachment on *HMS Areadne* for Dinagat.

We were mostly all seasick and we had to hold onto the bed to keep from being thrown out. One of the minesweepers sunk, and frankly, we were scared. When the 17th came we could not possibly land in the typhoon. It was so bad our ship commanders feared the ships would turn over and sink. Frankly, it was terrible, and the men were eager to get off.

On the morning of the 18th, it was a beautiful day. Our ship got within firing range of Homonhon and blasted the beach. They lowered the boats, we climbed down the rope ladder, and the coxswain set us ashore. We hit the beach with no resistance, so I took most of my platoon and started looking for Japs while Krueger went the opposite direction. We soon ran into natives who were scared to death, but they told us all the Japs had left the island prior to our arrival, and it turned out to be true.

The battle of Leyete Gulf took place the first night we were on Homonhon Island. Our Navy and the Japanese Navy met in a large battle that practically eliminated the Japanese Navy. It looked like the biggest Fourth of July God could create, and the noise of the big guns was unbelievable.

We had some communications with us and could hear the pilots flying off aircraft carriers and the response from the ships. Some of the planes were begging the carrier radio operator to tell him where he could land. His response was, "You'll have to ditch in the ocean as we are about ready to go down as we are sinking," and shortly signed off.

Although it was a tragedy for the Americans it also saved the lives of many as it opened up the area for the landing force to make the October 20 schedule to return to the Philippines. I understand General MacArthur went ashore the next day. Had our Navy been wiped out, we would have been isolated.

While on the island the men of B Company had to forage for food since they had no extra supplies. Hand grenades were used for fishing, and some bartering with the natives brought the occasional chicken.

Suluan is a small island about five miles east of Homonhon. This is the island that D Company landed on and were supposed to destroy a Japanese-controlled lighthouse. The company returned to the ship that brought them to Suluan and it took them to Dinagat to join the rest of the battalion.

While still on Homonhon, Captain Simons called a meeting with me and about four NCOs present, along with Captain Fisher. He proceeded to tell us we were going to Suluan to take out the lighthouse and we would go by sailboats provided by the Filipinos.

One of the men questioned Simons as to this being a mission that would get a bunch of us killed. Naturally Simons got mad and Fisher chimed in with a remark something like, "You haven't seen enough blood and guts." That ended the conversation, but when evening came, I saw that some of the men were upset with the remarks made, and that I felt something terrible might happen in the company. In fact, they made some threats, so I had a talk with the NCOs and it all passed with no more negative remarks. I would always stay close to the men in the company and knew what was going on, while Simons and Fisher distanced themselves. A good idea, I'm sure.

The next morning we walked to the beach and the Filipinos had about a dozen "bonca" with sails. We loaded into them and proceeded to Suluan. The sea was rough enough that two boats capsized and we lost some equipment, but no lives. What a lousy way to travel to fight a war! After many hours we made it to the other side and sailed into a nice sandy beach in a little village. No Japs were around as they stayed up in the hills near the lighthouse. I am sure they knew we were there. We put a guard perimeter around the village for security purposes, and then we moved into the bamboo shacks with the natives. They saw no problem, as they hated the Japs.

Sergeant Copenhaver and I moved into a one-room shack with a man, wife and two young children. A hole in the floor in the corner with a curtain provided bathroom privileges. We did not eat with the family. We were running short of rations, so we got hold of rice and had the Filipinos cook it for us and we ate twice a day. I ate it because we had no choice, but for many years after the war I refused to touch it.

Captains Simon and Fisher moved in with a couple of young ladies at the edge of the village. Simons told me to run the company and not to bother him unless something serious developed. He said we would attack the lighthouse when he decided to do so.

He was not the kind you could question and you learned to keep your mouth shut.

There was only one source of water on the island…a little pool fed by a stream of fresh water for drinking, bathing, and washing clothes. When we went to the pool we had to go well armed and in groups, as we did not know just what the Japs would do, as they had to know we were coming after them. When we wanted to wash and bathe, the ladies would motion for us to undress and they would wash our clothes, as it was deep enough for us to be submerged. The Japs would come to the pool at night, but we made no effort to stop them. It would serve no purpose, as it would cause them to lie for us when we went to the pool.

The Japs were moving around to keep an eye on us and our patrols would clash and have a shoot-out. The Filipinos would get hold of a dead Japanese and drag him back to the village and down the street. They also did some surgery by cutting off ears and kicking teeth out to get the gold. I did not care for this, but I had no voice, as it was their village.

We ran patrols out and checked out the terrain. The lighthouse was a couple of miles from the village, sitting on top of a ridge. The ridge ran all the way down, and there was a trail that ran in the lowland parallel to the ridge. From the trail was a steep man-made path about six feet wide that ran up to the door of the lighthouse.

We estimated the Japs had a force of 30 to 50 who lived in, or near, the lighthouse and used it to signal ships and transmit radio messages to ships and planes.

Why Simons waited several days to attack the lighthouse is unknown.

It was around seven one evening when Fisher and Simons came to my living area and told me to get the NCOs for a meeting. In essence...he [Simons] said, "We are going to take out the lighthouse tonight. Give me twelve men [may have been 10], and I will lead them to the nearest edge of the ridge. We will scale the cliffs and move along the top until we get around a hundred yards from the lighthouse. We will then observe their activities and size up the situation. At daybreak we will assault the lighthouse and kill as many Japs as possible. Dr. Fisher will go with me. We will leave around midnight. Strausbaugh, I want you to take 35 men with you and the rest to stay in the village and be on call. I want you to be at the bottom of the trail to kill off those attempting to escape, as I do not know how else they can get away. We will shoot a flare when we attack, so watch for it so you will be abreast of the situation."

It was really dark that night. I saw Simons' group leave and I lay awake all night waiting for the four a.m. departure. Morning couldn't get there fast enough. About two a.m., I was half asleep when I heard heavy gunfire coming from the direction of the lighthouse. I was up in a hurry, and naturally we were already dressed in our fatigues as we slept that way all the time. I hollered at Sergeant Copenhaver to get the men ready to go since it was obvious something had gone wrong. Very shortly we were on the trail. I kept watching for the flare, but none appeared, and that made me feel more tense. By the time we appeared at the bottom of the lighthouse trail, it became very quiet and I observed nothing.

I spread my men out and waited for someone to appear near the door of the lighthouse since I did not have any idea who had control, or where Simons' group was. I had a bad feeling in my gut as I waited and wondered what action to take. Finally a runner came out heading down the trail, and he drew fire.

I saw it was PFC Allen. He told me they were in trouble, with two dead, some wounded, and were surrounded by Japs. Simons wanted me to come to the rescue. Some of the men around us seemed to get shook up, and I still recall what I said was, "To hell with what's happened and who's dead or wounded, we must organize to save the rest."

I told my men to spread out and move away from the lighthouse and eliminate any threat. One man did get behind a big rock and made no effort to move until I told him to get going. I knew he was really scared. I took two men and ran up the trail. We were near the top when an automatic weapon opened up on us and splattered a tree inches from us. Pure luck that it didn't kill all three of us. When he started firing, our men opened up on him, so it silenced him and all others who fired at us.

I opened the door [to the lighthouse] and Simons was standing there. The first words out of his mouth were, "Strausbaugh, you son of a bitch, I thought we were all going to be killed. What took you so long? You almost got me to believing in GOD."

More of the men came up the trail, and we escorted them out carrying the dead and wounded. The men below continued to drive the Japs back into the jungle. Steve Prokovich was dead, Buzz Couture was very critical and did not live too long, and Staff Sergeant Ray Potts had a bullet in his back and was very critical so we carried him all the way back. He was delirious and cussed me out since he was in pain and didn't know what was going on. With our men keeping a rear-guard, we came back on the trail and got back to the village. Simons radioed a Navy ship that came to the beach and picked up Potts and Couture.

Potts eventually returned to duty. Couture died on the ship. His brothers buried him near a little church on the island. "Not a good feeling."

I talked to Simons as to what had gone wrong, and he told me while they were hiding and waiting for time to attack, a Japanese came out to relieve himself. One of our guys got trigger-happy and killed him [with a Thompson submachinegun]. Our men had to start battling the Japs until they finally killed or ran off all of them, and were able to take control of the lighthouse. Some of the fighting was hand-to-hand. But, [once inside] they could not get out the door without drawing fire.

That episode ended B Company's stay on Suluan. The Japanese were finished there. Within a few days a ship appeared to take the company to Leyete to rejoin the rest of the battalion, living in tents a little ways inland. For several weeks the 6th Rangers, with other units, prepared to defend their territory against attack by sea, land, and air. They were bombed and strafed and told to expect imminent attack, but nothing serious occurred. A little boredom set in.

Lt. Colonel Mucci came to me with a reporter who wanted a story about Suluan and told me to give it to him. So I did, and later found out it made the newspapers, but they called the island Mapia rather than Suluan, due to censorship.

One day some of the men got hold of "jungle juice," and I had never seen so many drunks together. They had a free-for-all. Major Woody Garrett got into the middle of it and tried to calm them down. Someone threw a punch and hit him. I doubt if anyone hitting him realized who he was. Then Colonel Mucci got in on it and they broke it up. He gave everyone a good ass chewing, but handed out no punishment. My gut feeling is that he admired the guts these guys had.

In the latter part of December, I was called into the war room [a tent] to learn that we would load on a ship in Tacloban Bay, pull out and join a convoy to head north to Lingayen Gulf in Luzon and make a landing. I later learned we would load and pull out on January 1, 1945.

New Year's Day would be my 25th birthday, and I couldn't keep from asking myself if this wasn't a poor way to celebrate a birthday. However, the celebrating took place that night—not for me—but a bunch of guys got hold of jungle juice and loaded up. They began to celebrate by firing weapons, and someone threw a grenade into the crapper and blew it up. Mucci got a call from the Sixth Army asking if we were under attack. I have often wondered how we all survived without someone getting killed. No one would ever call the Rangers a bunch of sissies. They lived on the edge.

On New Year's Day, the 6th embarked for Luzon, joining a vast armada of other ships staging for the invasion. Nine days later, after being heavily attacked by Japanese aircraft, some of them kamikaze, the Navy opened up on the beaches and US planes bombed and strafed the assault area.

Our troops began to land January 9, but we were held in reserve, so we stayed another night on the ship. The next morning our ship pulled closer to shore and dropped the ramp. Two of our men got off and the water was over their heads. One drowned and was later found washed ashore. Whoever was in charge told the Navy they had to get into more shallow water, but the ship's captain refused so we did not get off. Some DUKWs that had already gone ashore came back out and took us to the beach. We got on shore without any resistance, so we moved in a few hundred yards and dug in for the night, expecting a counter-attack.

I later found out the Japs had mostly pulled out and moved farther north to another potential landing area because our convoy originally went further north as a decoy, then semi-circled back.

[At one point] a plane strafed the area. I dove in a foxhole on top of our company clerk, Corporal Louis Weiss, and he said something. I asked if he was okay, and he said to stay there, as it was safer. I climbed out of the hole and no one had been hit. I was amused years later when I read a book about WWII Rangers and it stated that Weiss bawled me out and told me to dig my own foxhole. Shows that you cannot always believe what you read.

From there the Sixth Army made good progress and didn't want anyone behind them. Companies B and E were sent to Santiago Island at the entrance to Lingayen Gulf to make sure there were no Japanese still there. The island was unoccupied by enemy troops, but there were a good number of civilians. When Simons found out there were no Japanese, he left the company in Strausbaugh's command and went back to the mainland.

It was late in the war and men were being rotated home on the point system. New replacements were coming in and had to be trained. Another change came with several promotions within the ranks.

Cabanatuan

During WWII the Japanese kept POW camps scattered throughout the Philippines. Such camps held men of several nations, but 72,000 Americans had been captured when the islands changed hands.

The legendary hell of the Bataan Death March left many bayoneted beside the roadway, and gave the rest an unequalled test of survival. The camps swallowed more, whittling down the numbers with disease, death from torture, starvation, and transfer to labor camps.

The forced march of the survivors of Corregidor Island and the Bataan Peninsula to the POW camp at Cabanatuan was a lethal nightmare. Many men died on the march.

One prison was believed to hold more than 500 survivors of the Death March, men from Corregidor, and a few others, mostly British. It was just 40 miles from Manila, and MacArthur and others feared the Japanese would kill the prisoners before the camp was overrun. The men left were living by a thread of time and must be taken out immediately, but getting them back over the rough terrain would be as hard as the assault to liberate them.

The camp near Cabanatuan was roughly half-a-mile by a third, but at times there were as many as 6,000 men jammed in there.

Former POW Richard Gordon told Boston public broadcasting station WGBH, "Prisoners were held in 10-man squads. If you escaped Cabanatuan, they took out nine men from your squad and shot all nine of them."

"Day by day, Cabanatuan continued to be the closest thing to hell," Army Master Sgt. Russell A. Grokett Sr., who was imprisoned there in 1942, said in an online history. "Since threats by guards were so unpredictable, the prisoners never knew what to expect from one day to the next."

It is probable that upwards of 2,600 Americans and soldiers of other nations died in that accursed camp during its existence. It is also probable that hundreds of men were removed from the camp only a few days, or weeks, before the raid, and sent to slave labor camps in Japan and China.

One thing led to another, and on January 27 Mucci was summoned by the G-3 (Operations) of Sixth Army. Orders were issued to liberate the prison camp on the Cabanatuan-Cabu road, about five miles east of the former, and one mile west of the latter.

In some accounts this was called the Cabu Prison Raid.

The road ran right in front of the prison and was well traveled and used as a supply route. In fact, the whole area was fairly well populated with small villages, making it difficult to filter through without being seen. One thing in the Rangers' favor was the hatred of the Filipinos for the Japanese. It was doubtful anyone would rat them out.

Mucci was given aerial photos of the camp and surrounding area and saw rivers and ravines between himself and the objective. It would not be easy to move undetected. He needed information and he got it from three sources. The Alamo Scouts—three teams—and Filipino guerillas filled him in as much as they knew at the time, and he promptly sent them out for more as he gathered his forces.

A third source of information came in the winged form of the new P-61 Black Widow, a twin-engine airplane outfitted for night fighting. These planes would play a welcome part in the rescue.

The 6th Rangers would field C Company, commanded by Captain Robert Prince, and 2nd Platoon of F Company, commanded by 1st Lt. Frank Murphy. Prince would be second-in-command of the 107-man Ranger force, directly under Mucci.

When it became known what was happening, a lot of men volunteered to go. At least four others were finally allowed to participate.

The Rangers boarded trucks for the first leg. Though the Sixth Army had elements as close as 35 miles to the camp, the Rangers were trucked to the town of Guimba, about 70 miles from their starting point, but that's where Mucci wanted to begin the march to the camp.

The Americans were backed by about 160-170 Filipino guerillas led by two Captains—where their rank came from is a mystery—Juan Pajota and Eduardo Joson.

Once off-loaded, the Ranger force, including the Filipinos, marched off toward the south and Captain Joson's camp. The men were traveling light, just necessities, soft caps, and a few candies and smokes for the prisoners. They made good time. At the guerilla camp they organized, made the plan of march, and at dark on the 28th they moved out.

The going was rough, not only because of the terrain, but also because there were Japanese all over the place. The pace was slower than hoped for and the group came up a little shy of the planned overnight spot. The Rangers and guerillas went to ground about five miles north of the camp and waited out the daylight under shelter-halves, or in some cases, parked vehicles.

In time, Captain Pajota showed up with his men, perhaps 70 or 80, and a few Alamo Scouts arrived with more information early the next morning. The Japanese in the camp, maybe 90 guards, were augmented by a group of about 150 soldiers bivouacking there on their way passing through. It was also known that there were several thousand troops in the town of Cabanatuan itself, and a battalion with a few tanks was camped nearby. It would be no picnic if the raid took too long and some of the Japanese forces could be assembled.

Just before dark on January 30, the three groups set off. When they could, the Rangers traveled in the center, the guerillas running the flanks.

The approach to the camp was grown up enough to give fair cover until about a mile out, and then the Rangers went into a crawl until they were within 700 yards. There they waited briefly while Captain Joson and some 80 men set up a roadblock on the Cabanatuan-Cabu road, about 800 yards southwest of the camp. Six Rangers with borrowed rocket launchers went with them to deal with any tanks that may come up the road. Pajota, with a like number of men, set up a blocking position about 300 yards northeast of the camp to prevent the battalion of Japanese camping nearby from getting involved. There was a small bridge there, and Pajota sighted it with machineguns and explosives.

On schedule, a P-61 Black Widow streaked over the camp twice in the hour before the attack, diverting the enemy's attention to the sky as the Rangers began to spread out for their various unit tactics.

Prince gives a great deal of credit for the success of the raid to others. "Any success we had was due not only to our efforts but to the Alamo scouts and Air Force. The pilots [Capt. Kenneth R. Schrieber and Lt. Bonnie B. Rucks] of the plane that flew so low over the camp were incredibly brave men."

The P-61, called "Hard to Get"—a nude blonde painted on the nose—was twin engined, which allowed Schrieber to stop one engine at about 1,500 feet over the camp, then restart it, causing a loud backfire. That action was repeated, and the Japanese watched the plane lose altitude until it cleared some low hills by only some 30 feet. The enemy soldiers watched intently, waiting for what they expected would be the fireball from a crash.

The 2nd Platoon of F Company moved in defilade to assault a bunker at the northeast corner of the camp. The signal to go was to be Lt. Murphy's first shot.

Company C, 1st Platoon, led by Lt. William O'Connell, was to hit the front gate and get it open, then race around to where the Japanese were quartered. 2nd Platoon, under Lt. Melville Schmidt, was ordered to get to the prisoners, and was split into two groups to accomplish that.

Mucci had wisely called for 50 carts pulled by carabao (oxen) to be brought to a nearby river, the Pampanga, which they had to cross to return home. The Filipinos supplied several dozen unarmed men to stand by to help the weakened prisoners get to the carts.

A few minutes after eight p.m. on the 30th, Murphy—or somebody—fired into the camp and opened the ball. A hundred well-armed Rangers let it rip, killing many Japanese at their guard posts and riddling the buildings. In short order the lock was shot off the gate and the Americans were inside blasting the surprised enemy at close range. Within 15 minutes most of the Japanese were dead or in hiding and the prisoners were beginning to be brought to the front gate. The condition of those men was a shock to the young Rangers.

There were more than 500 men in various stages of physical failure. They wore rags as filthy as their emaciated bodies. Disease ran through them like water.

To the east Captain Pajota and his men were slaying Japanese trying to get across the partly demolished bridge. The enemy, true to form, made repeated charges to move Pajota. All they accomplished was a severe reduction of their ranks, taking perhaps 250 killed to add to the estimated 200 killed at the camp.

Captain Joson, south of the camp, was also engaged, though lightly in comparison. The main problem there was a column of tanks and trucks coming down the road, but the P-61s trashed them before Joson's position was reached.

The rescue went as planned, every man knowing his job and where to find it. The POWs were carried to the gate if necessary, though some 300 of the 511 were able to walk. The rest were taken to the ox-carts, which were manhandled back over the rough and muddy ground.

Standing by the gate was Captain Fisher, who had been with Bull Simons' group on Suluan Island a few months earlier. Fisher was with a small group of men, including some Alamo Scouts, when a few mortar rounds struck nearby, wounding several.

Fisher and another man, injured as he exited the camp, were taken with the feeble prisoners to the ox-carts. Unable to make it all the way back, a small group comprised of a squad of Rangers, a POW who had been a doctor and volunteered to stay, the two wounded Americans, and some wounded Scouts pulled up short to care for the critically injured men. Sadly, Fisher and Corporal Sweezy died before help could arrive—the only two Americans killed during the raid.

When everyone was accounted for, Prince entered the camp to double-check, and finding it empty, fired a red flare. This was the signal for the Filipinos to disengage and cover the withdrawal. When he got to the river he fired a second flare to make sure.

About 300 POWs were able to walk the five miles to Balincarin, and by afternoon of the 31st, the prisoners were being cared for in a hospital.

The successful raid brought a lot of attention from the State-side press and the mystique of the Rangers grew apace. Life Magazine called the men of the 6th, "pistol-packing farm boys, hand picked for such a job." A few of the men even did "morale tours" in the states, riding a wave of escalating optimism now the Japanese were being pushed back.

General Douglas MacArthur said, "No incident in this campaign has given me such satisfaction."

The Cabanatuan Raid has become a textbook exercise for Ranger students, even today. It was one of the most famous prisoner liberation raids in military history. Lt. Colonel Mucci received the Distinguished Service Cross for his efforts and his officers were awarded Silver Stars. The enlisted men all got Bronze Stars.

Robert Prince

A Ranger Hall of Fame inductee, Prince commanded C Company and was second-in-command of the raid on Cabanatuan. This interview was taped during a long phone conversation between Georgia and Washington State just before Labor Day, 2004.

They [Juan Pajota and Eduardo Joson] were Captains, so designated maybe by themselves, I don't know, but an American guerilla [Colonel Robert Lapham] had been working with them, and vouched for them. General Krueger wouldn't let him go on the raid. He was afraid if he got captured he would not only be executed but it would be a big PR thing for the Japanese. So even though he knew Joson and Pajota and had helped to create them, he was not allowed to go. He'd been exposed for almost three years anyway. No need to do it again, I guess. A very brave man.

Without Lapham the language barrier strengthened. The Filipino leaders had some English, but not much, and conversed with each other in Tagalog. Communication between the two forces was tenuous, but it was accomplished.

I knew we had some [aerial] photos, but it must have been beforehand. We also had a big detailed map of where we were going. You should realize what the terrain was. You think of the tropics as jungle. What we walked across was more like Kansas in August, except it was rice fields instead of corn. They'd all been harvested. It was the dry season with hard mud in a ridge about three or four inches high around each paddy. No jungle. There was a lot of growth, maybe Kunai grass down by the river. It was an agricultural area, the breadbasket of the Philippines.

If it had ever been unlevel, they leveled it for agriculture. There were a couple of rivers, the Pampanga and the Cabu [which ran into the Pampanga] and they were at low ebb because it was the dry season. That was a hell of a big advantage because we could get across okay, but bringing back guys that were out of shape and hurting and all the rest would have been very, very difficult in the wet season with the rivers being about three feet deeper than they were. They were about hip-high in places from what I recall.

Prince was asked, how good were the Alamo Scouts?

Damn good. There was one officer and six men and they had been specifically trained for physical capacity, and also the ability to infiltrate behind enemy lines, which they had done a number of times in New Guinea. They'd rescued some people, I think they were Dutch, but they didn't lose a single man throughout the war [they had several wounded], but there were only about 50 of them. They were well trained, experts at what they were doing, which was infiltration and getting information.

I was with the 1st and 2nd Platoons of my company [at the onset of the assault]. F Company, 2nd Platoon had gone up this dry wash, which again, in the wet season would have been running pretty good.

It was still light and they hid right along the bank of this dry creek, which kept them out of sight of the guards until the very end. That's what started the action—a guard spotted one of them finally, and that's the last thing—he cried an alarm and was dead in a few seconds.

There are differing accounts of how the action started. It is generally agreed that Lt. Murphy fired the first round, but it is a moot point since everybody opened up immediately and Japanese began dying by the dozens under the onslaught. Prince said his impression was it had been a member of the platoon and not Murphy, but he doesn't really know.

I was right at the main gate and the two guys designated to open the gate were Tech Sergeant Richardson and Private First Class Lee Provencher. A guard or somebody fired at Richardson and knocked the gun out of his hand, and Provencher picked it up. My recollection is he's the one who shot it off.

I was standing about 15 feet away and it was all happening pretty fast. [He doesn't remember what kind of weapon was used on the gate.] All I know is he got it open and away they went. The 1st Platoon were the first ones in, that's the way it was supposed to be. They were to go through the gate, turn right, go about 60 or 70 yards, and they would be past the POWs. Then they were to turn up the center of the compound, which would put their backs to all the POWs and their fronts toward where the Japanese guards lived, and were.

The compound was about 800 yards long, but Prince said it wasn't very wide, and half of it was Japanese barracks.

They didn't go inside the barracks, they just sat outside and shot everything that showed up. They did have a garage in front of them they blew with a bazooka, knocked out a tank and a truck. Anything that showed its face, like a person, was annihilated.

I was outside. My job was to get the POWs out. The 2nd Platoon (C Company) didn't have battle orders. Their orders were to go in, get the POWs out, and get them moving. One platoon to iron out the Japs, the other to get the prisoners moving.

By the time the prisoners were coming out, Prince had moved over to where Japanese guards were being fought and didn't see them right away. He said he felt "primarily relief that we found them and they were on their way."

I was still by the gate along with some medics and some Alamo Scouts. They weren't part of the actual assault. They were just there to help if needed. That's where the mortars hit us. The only thing between us and what was going on [inside] was a wire fence. It was just a matter of feet to where the prisoners were housed. I felt I could direct what needed to be done better from where I was. I could see everything.

A mortar round landed, the same round that killed Captain Fisher [hit and wounded several, including some Alamo Scouts]. I was in the same area but other bodies in front of me protected me. They were the ones that got hit. I was right there, saw it land.

There's a story about one of the Scouts pulling a piece of shrapnel from another guy's butt. There were some more rounds, but I didn't know until later that Fisher was the only one [seriously wounded].

As to the number of prisoners able to walk versus those who needed a ride, Prince said the numbers are all estimates and he has no idea.

I wasn't down there. I was still making sure that we were finishing up what was going on.

It was my first check [not the second as some history is written]. I hadn't been in there before, but I'd been observing everything and it was fine and I was happy with the way it was going. All of a sudden there were just three of us left there, the First Sergeant, Bob Anderson, and I don't know who the third guy was. It was very quiet. The firing had stopped and people had stopped coming out. I said I've got to go in and see if I can find anybody else, and I did go into a couple of three of those Nipa huts that housed quite a few men, and yelled if anybody was there. As the book says [one of several on the subject] there was one guy in the latrine, and he was hard of hearing, but I think if he did hear me he probably figured he was in a safe place and wasn't going to come out. That's the Britisher that...we didn't know he was there. The Filipinos got him out the next morning [not guerillas, just citizens].

There weren't many foreigners in there, maybe half-a-dozen, mostly British from Singapore. But there was one Norwegian, I don't know how he got in there, but I have a picture of him. I don't know about any Dutch.

Prince related a surprising fact when he said he didn't know about the waiting ox-carts. He was, after all, second in command, but was also leading C Company and quite busy.

I wasn't aware of that. I'm sure that Mucci, with the help of Pajota and Joson had arranged for those. My understanding was that there were to be ten carts to help with those that needed it, but by the end there were 50 carts or more. The local citizenry all brought their carts down to help carry these guys out. Some of them stayed in the carts but I think some of them would walk for a while, get tired, and rest in the cart.

I was in the very rear of the column, that was my duty, rear-guard, and I took advantage of that myself, rode in the last cart off and on.

When we got there [the Pampanga] C Company and 2nd Platoon of F Company were all gone. The First Sergeant and I were the last two men across the river.

They were still fighting up to our right at the Cabu Bridge, Pajota's guerillas and the Japanese, but it had died down significantly. We walked across the river and there was one cart there with some POWs in it. I was the last man, the rear-guard. I fired a second flare [the first was when they left the compound] after we crossed the river to alert the guerillas. Pajota had just ironed out the Japanese battalion that was there. They were in enfilade position with…[machineguns]…and these guys came storming across that bridge and they just killed lots of them. They didn't lose a single man of their own.

When I got into the last cart, there was Doctor Merle Musselman, a 1st Lieutenant who had been a POW for nearly three years. We had a nice visit for about half an hour until we got to the barrio of Platero, that's where [wounded doctor] Fisher was. The commandant of the POW camp was also a doctor, and had broken his arm stumbling when he came out of the camp, and was the only true casualty among the prisoners [there is an erroneous report of a death at the camp]. He was no good to operate so he continued on back to safety.

Musselman, after three years in captivity, volunteered his services as a doctor. He made it out a day or so later. The Alamo Scouts escorted him out.

There were no Japanese in the rice fields; they were all on the roads and in the towns. We were not in the midst of Japanese. The people we met, the Filipinos, were a hundred percent anti-Japanese. If somebody they knew snitched on us, he'd be dead in no time. We were fully confident we were safe as long as we were where we were. This was not enemy territory—it was enemy-controlled territory, but certainly there were no Japs around in the rice fields.

Captain Joson had cut the commo lines running from the camp to the town of Cabanatuan where several thousand Japanese were based. Prince thinks they knew nothing of the raid while it was happening. Added to that, Joson and Pajota were between the Americans and any remaining Japanese.

The battle plan was for me to be the rear-guard, but behind me were the Alamo Scouts and the guerillas. They were the true rear-guard. We weren't worried about anybody hitting our rear. We must have been stretched out two or three miles or more. Mucci returned to our lines about eight a.m. and I got there at 10:30. An ox walks about one mile an hour [the distance was about 25 miles].

Leo Strausbaugh—Mucci Leaves

After the liberation of Cabanatuan, the 6th Rangers continued to fight the Japanese, but without their legendary Colonel.

It was reported a number of Japs were moving toward San Fernando {where the Rangers were billeted} from the east. We took off to intercept them. Captain Simons took a number of men and moved to the left flank, and I was to stay put, expecting him to drive them my way. I could hear firing of rifles so we waited patiently. Soon a Colonel from the Army Headquarters showed up. He asked me where Simons was so I told him where he should be. He then told me to do nothing immediately, but when it was over to tell Simons that he was to report to our battalion headquarters and I was to assume command of the company.

It floored me, thinking, "What's up?" In a matter of time the Japs retreated and wanted no more of us. When I next saw Simons I gave him the message. He blew his cool. He formed the opinion that he was being transferred and he did not like the idea. He left and went back, and I finished what needed to be done, and then went back to battalion. I went to HQ where I saw Major Robert "Woody" Garrett, who was our XO. He informed me that Lt. Colonel Mucci had been transferred to the 6th Division to become a regimental commander, which called for the rank of full Colonel. Woody then told me he was the new battalion commander, Simons was the new Executive Officer, and I was appointed the new commander of B Company.

Simons made Major and Strausbaugh made Captain, bringing his pay to $200 a month. At that time privates were bringing down $30. One dollar a day to go out and risk your life.

For the next jobs the Rangers were given security duty and a few short missions to run, mostly to gather Intelligence. One such mission kept B Company out for three days dodging enemy patrols.

All But Over

The life of the 6th Rangers were decidedly different than those of their brother battalions elsewhere. Since they weren't used as line troops they had fewer casualties, and they were able to perform functions more suited to their training, proving the concept of the Ranger unit not only plausible, but also efficient.

As with the other Ranger units, the 6th Battalion was deactivated at the end of the war. Their demise came December 30, 1945, while still in the Philippines.

Some amount of fame followed the raid. Captain Prince and several other Rangers were sent back to the States to speak on the war effort.

GALAHAD—5307TH COMPOSITE UNIT (PROVISIONAL)—
MERRILL'S MARAUDERS

The story of the 5307th, code named GALAHAD, focuses on the courage and stamina under constant duress exhibited by three Infantry battalions in Burma—Merrill's Marauders. It is also the story of the poster child for the overuse of military units in the eastern war.

By 1944, the Japanese were being steadily squeezed by the Allies in the Southeast Asian Theater, though even they were then planning a push into India and were fighting several nations at once. In Burma, that included the Chinese, organized and guided by Lt. General Joseph W. "Vinegar Joe" Stilwell. In his capacity as Chiang Kai Chek's Chief of Staff, he was responsible for building the Chinese Army. Unfortunately, he was only allowed to fight a small part of it. Chiang had enemies within, and was reluctant to part with his 30 divisions. They weren't the best troops in the world, but they were his, and he could hold onto power with them. He and Stilwell had a few battles of their own about that.

Stilwell was not a man to trifle with, and that, coupled with his earlier defeat and retreat (with his Chinese Army) through Burma in 1942, made him the man for the job of retaking the country. He was also Commander of U. S. Forces in that area, though he was under British Lord Louis Mountbatten, Commander of the Southeast Asian Theater.

Indeed, the concept of GALAHAD began as a brainchild of the British, and was only taken from their control at the time of the offensive of 1944. The whole thing started off with a group of British and native fighters called Chindits, under the overall command of British Major General Orde C. Wingate, another tough old soldier.

Wingate's Chindits were not a large force, but they did considerable damage to the enemy with ambushes, interruption of communications, and the destruction of supplies. They did well enough in Burma to gain notice, notably by U. S. General George C. Marshall, top man in the Joint Chiefs of Staff. Marshall was a moderate proponent of special units, and was instrumental in getting the Ranger Battalions going. As with the rest of the American hierarchy he wanted to see some Americans in the fight. The problem was who to use and how to get them there.

Marshall wasn't the only one. During the Quebec Conference in August 1943, the idea was discussed by Roosevelt, Churchill and others who wanted to see Americans on the ground in the China-Burma-India Theater.

After some negotiation, it was agreed to increase the size of the Chindits and add a U. S. Air Group for help with supply, transport and evacuation. Marshall upped the ante with a promise of a unit of jungle-tested troops to serve with the Chindits, something in the Regiment-sized range.

Operations put out a memorandum September 18, 1943, which stated that personnel for the American Long-Range Penetration Units for employment in Burma were being satisfactorily assembled at the San Francisco Port of Embarkation. Those men were not raw recruits—nearly all had spent time in one jungle or another. They included 960 men from the Caribbean Defense Command, 970 from the Army Ground Forces, a total of 674 battle-tested jungle troops from the South Pacific area, and some experienced men from MacArthur's command. The General couldn't find enough suitable volunteers with time on the line to make up the balance, so he had to choose some from trained, but untried, troops. Volunteers from the States and the Caribbean gathered in San Francisco, and those from the South Pacific were herded to Noumea, but the turnout was luke-warm at best. The necessary experience was often lacking, and malaria was too often present, but they mostly took them, anyway. That, combined with the more-than-occasional dumping of undesirables into the new unit, made it hard to garner enough worthwhile troops, especially when the word was the unit would probably suffer massive casualties. The interesting thing there is that nobody really knew where they were going at that point, except a few that weren't talking.

The result of the global gathering was a minor conglomeration of adventure-seekers, drunkards, thieves and authority-haters mated with the majority—solidly trained and experienced officers and enlisted men who had what it took to keep the rest in line. It took a while to get the naturally aggressive group under control.

To make matters worse, the unit was given the cumbersome and obviously temporary title of 5307th Composite Unit (Provisional), which few took seriously as a permanent posting for a mission that remained in the dark. Provisional meant disbandment after the mission was completed. It meant no lineage, no real insignia or banners, or anything to make them feel like a real unit.

As with the Ranger-type forces in Italy and D-Day battles, the man who could qualify as a Ranger candidate was, by definition, extraordinary in terms of aggression and fitness. The GALAHAD troops were as tough to handle as their contemporaries in the European Theater. An unflappable commander was needed, but it would be some time yet before one was found.

Even the organization of the unit was unusual. There were three "battalions" divided into two combat teams of 470 men each, a total of 2,820 men. The units were designed to be as independent as possible, with companies of scouts, demolitions, medics, mortar groups, and the inevitable riflemen. Heavy weapons were limited, at least at first, to 60mm and 81mm mortars.

Into that mix was fed Colonel Charles N. Hunter, a 1929 West Point graduate who organized and led the first group overseas from the US as interim commander. It was several months before a permanent leader was named, though many have said he was right there all the time. Hunter, lacking the desired rank to take full charge, ended up commanding the unit most of the time, anyway, until relieved at the very end. His story by itself is an example of the misuse of the entire unit.

Hunter led the Marauders a good deal of the time and has a solid place in Ranger history. Hunter Army Airfield in Savannah, Georgia—a staging area for current Rangers operations—honors his name. Many have said Hunter should have been given the reins of the 5307ᵗʰ entirely.

Once he gathered up his charges he set them on ships and sailed into history, but a few things happened between that beginning and the terrible end at Myitkyina (Mitch-na).

Arriving in Bombay, India, in late October 1943, the unit was joined by recruits from that Theater and others, and training began in earnest under the overall command of General Wingate. Colonel Francis B. Brink ramrodded the actual training, and Hunter got stuck with administration. Soon the group went to Deolali, near Bombay, for two weeks of additional training, then to Deogarh in central India for more training, which included calling in and retrieving air drops for resupply. This type of logistical support was still fairly new, and much of what was learned was by trial and error, and would be especially so under battle conditions.

In December 1943, GALAHAD joined the veteran Chindits for two weeks of maneuvers. At that point they were ready to go to war and Wingate knew it. His idea was to expand the Chindits to five brigades, add GALAHAD to the mix, and prepare for the 1944 offensive with everybody under British leadership. Too bad for Wingate, the United States, in the form of Joe Stilwell, came knocking at the door.

Stilwell went to Marshall, who went to Lord Mountbatten, with the result being a release of British control of GALAHAD into U. S. hands. To say the least, Wingate didn't like it much.

Stilwell gave command of GALAHAD to a member of his staff, Brigadier General Frank D. Merrill, but retained control of mission decisions. Within a short time, the press picked up the name of the new commander, and the unit became Merrill's Marauders. The concept of the unit was very romantic to the press, and a good bit of attention was given the group, especially at first. Stilwell liked it. He also paid a lot of attention to the 5307th at first, but Vinegar Joe had a full plate, and the Marauders were but a small portion off to one side.

Add to that the relative size of the involved forces and the Chinese come out on top in terms of needing attention. Stilwell set up his new group of hit men, complete with mule train, and let them go, letting him get back to the task of trying to get the Chinese to move forward.

February 1944 saw the Marauders in Ningbyen, in northwestern Burma, not far from Ledo, a border province between India and Burma that became the jump-off point for the offensive. The Japanese had cut the road into China by seizing Burma, and the Allied airlift to carry supplies to China was hard-pressed to meet the demand. Further, the Japanese were gearing up to go into India and were tearing up the Chinese as well. Clearly, they had to be dealt with immediately. It would not be easy.

The original plan was for Stilwell's Chinese troops to go down the Hukawng Valley toward the Japanese supply base at Myitkyina, and two British units would come in from India. In addition, a second force of Chinese would drive into the country from the east. The Chindits were to help by cutting lines of Japanese communications. The overall mission was to capture the airfield outside of the city of Myitkyina, thus depriving the Japanese of the necessary airstrip to put fighters in the battle against the Allied transport planes going "over the hump" of the Himalayas into China.

In the end, however, the British needed those forces elsewhere, and the Chinese drive from the east fizzled. Stilwell, confronted with a less than desirable situation, decided to go ahead anyway, trying to beat the summer monsoon with what he had.

There wasn't a lot of trust in the Chinese ability to fight, and Chiang did hold back his main body to fight the communists later. Stilwell knew it was coming and tried to prepare, but it seemed additional forces were not to be had. He put together a spear with the 5307th as the tip and threw it at Japanese General Tanaka's main force, about 7,000 men of the 18th Division. Those hardened veterans were by then well dug in and ready for battle, but the sheer weight of the Chinese drive—slow as it was—made them move.

There were many forces in the area, though few had the impact of Merrill's Marauders. Though relatively small—slightly less than 3,000 men—the hard-charging force cut off the Japanese time and time again during their retreat south through the mountains of northern Burma.

After preliminary training operations undertaken in great secrecy in the jungles of India, about 500 men were detached as a rear echelon HQ to remain in India to handle the soon-to-be-vital airdrop link between the six Marauder combat teams—400 men to the team—and the Air Transport Command. With each combat team color-coded Orange, Khaki, White, Red, Green, and Blue, the remaining 2,400 Marauders began their march up the Ledo Road and over outlying ranges of the Himalayan Mountains into Burma.

Those six colors are still significant today, used in the 75th Ranger Regiment patch.

The Marauders, with no tanks or heavy artillery to support them, walked more than 1,000 miles through extremely dense jungles and tall mountains and never quit. In five major and 30 minor engagements they met and defeated the veteran soldiers of the Japanese Army, the conquerors of Singapore and Malaya, who vastly outnumbered them. Always moving to the rear of the main forces of the Japanese, they disrupted enemy supply lines and communications and caused a lot of enemy casualties.

Those behind-the-lines operations accomplished the overall mission with the capture of Myitkyina Airfield, the only all-weather airfield in northern Burma.

There were also Chinese troops involved in the capture of the airfield, but Merrill got there first. Taking the town was a different thing altogether.

Compounding difficulties during maneuvers was the nagging problem of securing supplies as they moved stealthily through the jungles. The supplies they did receive were airdropped, and their wounded were picked up one at a time at predetermined rendezvous points by Piper Cub planes, and flown back to "Evac" hospitals.

Getting the wounded Marauders out of the jungles of Burma was an extraordinary feat in itself. Each of the men was borne on a bamboo stretcher by his comrades or lashed to a horse until a rendezvous point was reached. Generally an area around a small jungle village was selected because of the rice paddies that could be found nearby. The Marauders would set to work chopping an airstrip through the rice paddy, and then radio the rear echelon to send in one of the Piper Cubs. Those planes were usually stripped of all equipment except a compass and a single stretcher for one wounded passenger. Despite hazardous takeoff and landing conditions in that densest of jungles, those valiant Sergeant-pilots managed to evacuate every seriously wounded soldier to safety, though two of their own were killed in crashes.

The Marauders were the first American Infantry soldiers to fight on the Asian continent in WW II, and they did it in some of the world's worst jungles. They were only one special regiment, but they did so much damage the Japanese high command remarked later their impression was the Marauders were a force of at least division strength—15,000 men. The overall harm inflicted by the Americans was greatly out of proportion to that returned by the Japanese.

As a result of the leadership qualities of Merrill and Hunter, and the courage and determination of the well-trained volunteers of the 5307ᵗʰ, battle casualties were less than the anticipated 60-80 percent. However, a large number of Marauders unfortunately succumbed to some nasty ailments as a result of their weakened physical condition, principally Tsutsutgamushi Fever (Typhus), malaria and dysentery. The remaining ambulatory Marauders still in action at the end of the campaign were evacuated to hospitals, suffering from severe malnutrition and exhaustion.

Those men—the original Marauders and the men of the New GALAHAD—were a tough bunch and worthy to serve as a basis for today's Ranger lineage.

They weren't Rangers and never claimed to be. The words "deep penetration" were scratched off their orders. They were essentially a special unit of line troops involved in heavy combat, but like the Rangers of Europe and the Pacific, they were perhaps a little tougher, a little better, a little more determined than the average soldier. For their accomplishments in Burma the Marauders were awarded the Presidential Unit Citation and Commendation. In addition, every one of the Marauders was awarded the Bronze Star.

Frank D. Merrill Bio

Frank Dow Merrill was born December 1903. He joined the Army in 1922, and was selected to attend West Point, graduating in 1929. Other formal education includes a B. S. degree in military engineering from Massachusetts Institute of Technology.

He became the assistant military attaché at the US embassy in Tokyo in 1938. During that time he studied Chinese and Japanese. Three years later he was promoted to Major and assigned as General MacArthur's Intelligence officer in Manila. He was still there when the war began.

Transferring to General Stilwell's command as an aide, he was promoted in 1942 to Lt. Colonel. He stayed in Burma, earning a Purple Heart and building a reputation for toughness and attention to detail. In October 1943 he was tapped to lead the 5307ᵗʰ, stepping up to Brigadier General.

The campaign was brutal. Merrill suffered two heart attacks and was twice evacuated, but returned to lead his Marauders to victory over the Japanese. In September 1944 he was promoted to Major General.

His health never recovered from the rigors of the Burma campaign. He died at age 52 in December 1955.

THE NEW GALAHAD

The 2nd and 3rd Battalions came straggling in on the 19th, mostly worn out and wanting only to rest. Unfortunately, the Japanese had gained strength in a big way and tried to go on the offensive. Any advantage the Allies had was obviously lost. Since none of the battalions were effective by themselves, Merrill—there briefly—re-organized what he had left into a three-battalion "Myitkyina Task Force," and put Hunter in command. Merrill then had another heart attack and was evacuated again a day later, on May 20. What he had given Hunter was a small band of rag-tag, used-up veteran Marauders backed up by 2,600 new guys from the New GALAHAD, a couple of Engineer battalions totally unused to combat, and a bad supply situation.

The Japanese pushed hard trying to force the Allies back into the jungle where their brothers could deal with them piecemeal, but the Marauders held once they were forced back to where they started on the airstrip. It could be they could go no farther, anyway. Of the 1300 reaching the strip, as many as 100 men a day were being evacuated for a variety of ills besides combat wounds.

The New GALAHAD had been forming for some time as the second wave of Marauders, due to arrive in the following dry season. The situation being what it was, they were rushed in after only about a week in country in India. At least they were mostly experienced troops, but some had met their officers just three days before sailing and had little time to get organized. They were put in the line anyway, with predictable results. Suffice to say they weren't a lot of help at first. In time the replacement 5307th, although taking major casualties, became a good combat unit—as did the Engineers—but they had to deal with replacements for themselves, men who used to be clerks and cooks—anyone who could carry a rifle.

For more on the battle of Myitkyina see the following interview with Major General (Ret) Howard Garrison, a member of New GALAHAD, who arrived on the airfield two days after the Allies took it.

Stilwell also flew into Myitkyina airfield on May 19, the same day as some of New GALAHAD. He had come in response to repeated reports of decay within the 5307th.

What he found shocked him, but it didn't back him up any. He also had to deal with an enraged Charles Hunter, who had written a serious piece on the condition and misuse of the Marauders. Hunter was in a position to show and tell because he was in as bad shape as the rest—emaciated, sick, lacking teeth, exhausted. He laid it on the line for Stilwell, saying the 5307th was so done in it was unfit for combat. He complained bitterly on behalf of his men, but to little avail.

May 27 was the last concerted action by the original men of the 2nd Battalion. McGee passed out three times during a fight, and others were falling asleep in combat situations. In a time when a man must run 102 degrees of temperature for three days straight to be declared unfit, being tired meant nothing. It was a way of life, and had been for months, but that day the veterans of the 2nd were done.

By the end of May, only 200 of the originally deployed group of 2,400 Marauders were still in the field. Some of them were replacements themselves. The battle continued, with American presence represented by the New GALAHAD and the Engineers, along with a batch of green replacements. Hunter was still in charge, and he used the veterans to shore up the new men, having to teach some of them how to load their weapons.

Finally, Stilwell got the picture. He wrote in his diary, "GALAHAD is just shot."

Those men deemed recuperated enough to fight again were sent back to the line, provoking a storm of protest from commanders, doctors, and eventually the press back home. About 250 had already been sent back up the Mogaung Valley to fight with the Chinese against what turned out to be an imaginary enemy, but the 200 or so sent back to the lines at Myitkyina fought the real thing, and helped carry the day during the late May crisis. Many of those men had to be immediately re-evacuated. The idea to put sick men back in the line was Stilwell's, though he later expressed surprise his orders had been carried out so thoroughly. State-side publicity had put the Marauders in the public eye, much as the Rangers of Europe had been touted. When the story came out about the condition of the group, there was uproar from the public and elected officials, including the Chairman of the Senate Military Affairs Committee, calling for an official explanation.

Though banged-up and low on supplies, the Allies kept attacking, having little choice but to hang on until relieved or reinforced. Gradually, more men and supplies got in, but the airstrip had nine wrecked transports on it due to Japanese fire. The lines looked like something out of WWI, all trenches and strong points and earth raw from artillery bursts. By June 22, it was a scene from hell, made stranger by the multi-colored parachutes used for airdrops being recycled as makeshift tents. Oxcarts traveled slowly over muddy paths carrying wounded and supplies, and everywhere was disease and exhaustion.

Slowly, the Allied force grew stronger and began pushing back. The crush of firepower began to tell on the Japanese and a definite shift was seen. By mid-July, the Japanese had taken almost 2,000 casualties, 790 of them killed in action. They were weakening.

A heavy Allied force hit the town August 3 and found a tenacious rear-guard facing them. The mostly-Chinese force swept the town, though the Japanese fought to the end, many committing suicide rather than surrendering. It is estimated that about 600 of the enemy made it out, thanks to the rear-guard, but the commander, Mizukami, took his own life.

With the great battle over, every Marauder still in the field was sent to the hospital. It was readily apparent that the 2nd and 3rd Battalions were all but gone as far as veterans went, and what few individuals still capable of fighting were taken, along with the New GALAHAD and others, and reconstituted into another force.

The evacuated Marauders were sent to a rest camp, but they were not a happy bunch. No one had recognized their accomplishments, no one looked after them, and the rest camp was a "pest hole." They got a little rowdy, did some drinking, and generally acted miserable. Not even the MPs would try to police the camp, especially when the Marauders got to drinking the local Bullfight Brandy.

Hunter was relieved the day Myitkyina fell, which was two days after Stilwell got his fourth star. Hunter had protested too much trying to save his men. He would be put aboard ship and sent home, which kept him at sea for as much as a month—time enough to let the press calm down. The next day, the U. S. War Department awarded the 5307th the Distinguished Unit Citation and handed down long overdue promotions.

A week after that, August 10, the 5307th was deactivated, then reactivated the same day as part of the 475th Infantry, with the survivors being combined with 124th Cavalry Regiment (de-horsed) of the Texas National Guard, and a couple of pack howitzer units, the 612th and 613th. The whole thing became known as the MARS Task Force.

The code name for the advance on Myitkyina had been "End Run," and it certainly was for almost all concerned. All those with two years of foreign duty at the end of the battle were to be sent home, including virtually all of the 2nd and 3rd Battalions. The veterans going into MARS were mostly 1st Battalion men, plus those of all three battalions of the New GALAHAD, who were—by then—veterans themselves.

The MARS Task Force, commanded by an original Marauder, Colonel William Lloyd Osborne, went south, doing much the same as the Marauders had done—using envelopment maneuvers effectively, combining with other forces to push the Japanese back.

Those-Who-Make-The-Decisions wasted little time getting the veteran unit into action. MARS went on a very tough hike south and east through heavy mountain terrain to get around the Japanese on the Burma Road near Lashio. Contact was made by January 17.

Brigadier General John P. Willey was in command of the task force. His actions demonstrated a better grasp of unit capabilities than had previously been seen. Instead of using MARS as line troops, he put them on high ground and used artillery and constant patrolling to cut the Japanese infrastructure to shreds. The Japanese held for a while, but eventually the damage MARS and other units were inflicting proved too costly. They pulled out March 7, 1945. The Allies now had the road from Ledo, on the border with India in the north, to the Burma Road in the south, which cleared the route to China. That holding allowed a large increase in the flow of supplies to that country, plus giving the Air Force protected fields from which to fly.

Their job done, the men of the task force were supposed to be sent home, but were instead sent to China, pulling training duty until being disbanded in July 1945.

GALAHAD, known as Merrill's Marauders, became the lineage base for today's Rangers when it became the 475th, which nine years later became the 75th Infantry, transforming in 1986 to become the 75th Ranger Regiment.

Myitkyina, 475th, MARS, and China

Howard Garrison

As a member of the 2nd Battalion of the New GALAHAD, Garrison was on the ground at Myitkyina two days after the airfield was taken, and fought through the ensuing 79-day battle. At the end he was part of the remainder of the 5307th to become the 475th Infantry. He fought down through Burma from Myitkyina onward toward Rangoon, and was then sent to China to act as liaison and training officer for the Chinese.

I sent him my questions and he answered them on two videotapes. Another time we spoke on the telephone. He was 84 in 2003, still crew cut, square-jawed and sharp. Many of his responses appear in quotes.

"It was a knock-down, drag-out fight, pillbox by pillbox," says Howard Garrison, an Airborne Lieutenant who volunteered for hazardous duty and found himself in the jungles of Burma two days after Myitkyina airfield was taken by the Allies. Garrison was one of 2,600 men who answered when the army went looking for someone to replace the wasted 5307th.

"A call went out in early '44 for a jungle training assignment."

Initially trained by the 101st Airborne Division, Garrison was with a unit at the time that wasn't going anywhere "anytime soon." He volunteered and was accepted, even though he had malaria from an earlier time in the South Pacific. Things went fast after that.

"I volunteered Monday, got my orders Wednesday, and reported to my Port of Embarkation [Newport News, Virginia] on Saturday."

While he was on the pier waiting to board ship, a Western Union boy on a bicycle found him in the crowd and told him his son had been born. It was April 17, 1944, and Garrison wouldn't see his son for a year-and-a-half.

"We shipped out in early '44. We didn't know where we were going. We were on a 5,000-passenger Navy transport with no escort. There were rumors of Wolf packs [submarines]."

The ship zigzagged down the Atlantic to land at Capetown, South Africa for four days.

"Then we went on to Bombay [India]. We got some escorts for the last part of the trip." Once docked they had a visitor. "Colonel Franklin Orth came on board and welcomed us."

The men were taken to a small town named Ramgarh, which had an airfield. After about a week there, they were flown to the battle. The New GALAHAD was supposed to train through the rainy season and come in later, to take the place of the original 5307th when the dry season started again. The Japanese drive into India made everything speed up, and the men were sent in mostly unprepared. Many had not even seen their officers until three days before leaving the States.

Garrison hit the field under fire.

"The Japs were shelling the strip."

He was part of the 2nd Battalion under Colonel Charles Beach, which was barely holding together.

"They integrated us into the unit with a lot of enthusiasm. They really made us welcome. There weren't many left."

The town was occupied by about 700 Japanese the day the airfield fell, and the time was right for taking it with the troops on hand. The Marauders could still field about 1,000 fighting men at that point, and there were two regiments of Chinese with them, greatly outnumbering the enemy.

"We didn't take the town. We were waiting for the Chinese [to do it]. We figured it was some political thing."

The wait cost the Allies the opportunity, as the Japanese reinforced heavily.

Garrison was made a company commander and led the unit until the end.

"Later, I had a platoon of Kachin Rangers, but there were no Chinese [as part of the Marauder unit]."

There were Chinese there, but they and the 5307th operated independently. He said there was a line on their Allies.

"If you want to get the Chinese to move, you either have to put their rations in front of them, or their artillery bombardment behind them."

While it is true the Marauders thought the Chinese troops unreliable, they did a lot of dying during the battle, and could fight much better when motivated.

The siege of Myitkyina began, leaving both the old and new 5307th to settle into the routine of daily fighting and patrolling. "The Japs were pretty good as fighters."

They were getting their supplies by land, to boot, which made them quite strong in the beginning. The Allies had a different situation. Everything had to come by air, either landed on the strip (hazardous) or by airdrop.

"Resupply was terrible. We were at the end of the pipeline. I think we got the leftovers from Europe."

It was also hazardous for the pilots of the C-47 supply planes, attested to by nine wrecked transports on the airfield. There were wrecks in other places, too. Garrison said one day a "Dakota" went down in enemy territory and later a "line-crosser" native brought the pilot's head back in a burlap bag.

Eventually there were other planes based on the strip, P-40s of "what was left of the AVG."

The American Volunteer Group, called the Flying Tigers, flew missions in Burma and China.
"We used them to dive-bomb the pillboxes."

The planes also strafed enemy lines, usually flying parallel along the narrow divide.

"We were in contact at about 150 yards."

One day the planes came in over the American lines, firing before they crossed into enemy territory. The P-40s carried .50 caliber machineguns, and the empty shell casings were ejected into the air. Garrison said one of the heavy brass casings hit him on the head.

"I'm glad I had my helmet on."

For weeks the enemy forces slugged it out, always out looking for a way to get around, over or through each other.

"We had recon and combat patrols. We patrolled vigorously all the time and so did they, in areas neither one of us owned."

Garrison said the patrols were usually squad-size, but occasionally there would be bigger ones. To continue the patrols and replace the losses inflicted by the Japanese, replacements for men of the New GALAHAD were soon needed, especially since the original Marauders were down to practically nothing. New men were brought in from anywhere they could be found, with little or no training other than Basic.

"It was sheer murder. I had one guy who couldn't even load an M1. All he'd ever had was his '03 {Springfield} in Basic."

The New GALAHAD was taken on volunteer basis from established units. Many of them had seen combat and most knew what they were doing, but their replacements were often clerks and cooks without any experience in the field. The result of that inexperience was often fatal.

Once the fighting began taking place in the town limits, the Allies found things the Japanese left behind, sometimes in a hurry. In one case a safe was found and blown open.

"It was rough, uncut diamonds. We went a littler further into town and found another safe. We didn't have the combination, so we blew that one, too."

Garrison said there were no diamonds in that safe, but the Japanese knew they would get it open and so left a present. "It was a pile of shit."

The Japanese held out for 79 days as they grew weaker and the Allies grew stronger. Finally, on August 3, all elements of the Allied forces came crashing into town and met a tenacious rear-guard that fought to the last bullet before many of the survivors killed themselves.

"They would take a shell and hold it to their bellies, then knock it off [the fuse]. But they didn't give up."

It was apparent from the condition of the rear-guard soldiers that food may have been getting scarce. "I think they were starving."

The Japanese rear-guard managed to allow about 600 of their brethren to escape into the jungle to fight again, but the damage was done at Myitkyina. The strongly held supply base was a loss the enemy couldn't afford, and the airplanes that began to fly out of the airfield not only gave death to the Japanese for months afterward, but also helped protect Allied troops in the area.

The Allies also suffered in the process. The Chinese regiments that had originally come in with the 5307th had been decimated, and the Marauders were no more. Only the New GALAHAD and a handful of original 1st Battalion Marauders were left of the American contingent.

"My company had 264 men and eight officers. We had probably 100 replacements, but it was me and 62 others at the end. When it was over we all went to the hospital."

The math works out at 372 men total, minus 62 left, which means 310 men gone for one reason or another.

Everybody was worn out, sick and/or wounded in some way at the end.

"I hadn't taken my shoes off in 10 days. I was afraid to. When I did get them off, part of my foot came off with them. Just the bottom part."

Garrison also had his left arm bandaged from his fingertips up over his shoulder from "jungle rot," was almost crippled with amoebic dysentery, and had volunteered with malaria. Yet, he was still leading a company!

"At Myitkyina the physical set-up was probably worse than the combat."

The 5307th was deactivated on August 10, then immediately reactivated as the 475th Infantry.

"The 475th was what was left of the Marauders, plus a large contingent of replacements."

The new unit was combined with the 124th Cav (dismounted) and a couple of pack artillery units, the 612th and 613th, and called the MARS Task Force. After all the effort by the original Marauders and their Allies, the Japanese still held most of the southern part of Burma. The show went on.

MARS went south toward Rangoon and Mandalay, using much the same tactics their ancestors had—envelopment and surprise. Three months later they were finally through fighting. Some of the original men of the 1st Battalion, 5307th, made it to the end of the Burma campaign. Promised in the beginning they would fight no more than three months, they survived the three missions prior to Myitkyina, the battle for the town itself, then three more months of combat with MARS. The transplants from New GALAHAD had also been in the field several months. All of them figured it was over.

"They were supposed to send us home, but they shipped us to China. I still had my company." Garrison and his unit became liaison support for the Chinese divisions, lining up training and supplies. "We gave them '03s."

The Springfield 1903 was used by the US before the M1 came out.

The Chinese Combat Command was given other ordnance and the personnel to teach the Chinese how to use it. "We sponsored 30 Chinese divisions."

His company acted as liaison for two divisions as part of the Chinese 94th Army Headquarters. Little by little the men from MARS were sent home. Garrison was one of the last to go.

"I finally made it out in December, 1945."

Quotes From The Big Brass About WWII Rangers

General Dwight D. Eisenhower

"The Rangers were specially-trained people. They were hardy fellows and could do anything; fight anywhere, in mountains and swamps, anywhere. It took a lot of training, a lot of courage and terrific morale. In special operations they were just extraordinary. They did a beautiful job."

General Matthew B. Ridgeway

"The Rangers have a proud, enviable and enduring place in our military annals, and it was a source of abiding satisfaction to me that I was privileged to share service with them, and to come to know first hand their sterling worth and gallant performance in WWII."

General Omar N. Bradley

"Among all of the heroic activities in which the Rangers performed on many far-flung battlefields, their exploits in scaling the heights of Pointe du Hoc will always be especially memorable. It was my privilege to have these brave men under my command in Sicily and Normandy. I treasure my association with them."

KOREAN WAR HISTORY—RANGER TRAINING CENTER—1950-51

Though the Korean War lasted until 1953, Ranger involvement was through by late 1951. As this is a Ranger history, we stop when they did. It is the function of this section to show not only the terrible time our forces had in that frozen place, but also how the Ranger Training Center (Command) evolved through the dictates of need during a time of crisis. What is now called the Ranger Training Brigade still exists partly because of the outstanding job done by the Korean War Rangers.

A unified Korea had bowed to Japanese control prior to WWII, beginning in 1910. After the war, the small country, barely 500 miles long, lay divided between Soviet control in the north, and US control in the south, though America had no intention of staying there. The official US occupation lasted just six days. The United States was almost totally withdrawn from South Korea by 1949, leaving only a group of Advisors—an action partially resulting from a downsizing of the peacetime Army, and partially to give the Soviets the impression of US non-aggression.

The Soviets remained as backers to Kim Il Sung, Premier of the North Korean government/war machine. A slow build-up continued, even as Americans were limited to about 500 Military Advisors. The South Koreans, under President Syngman Rhee, had little left with which to defend themselves.

With Soviet and Chinese backing, Kim Il Sung figured to reunite Korea, or else. Rhee had no such backing. The North even called for a vote to see if the people wanted the country re-united. Nobody paid much attention. With nothing happening the way they wanted, the communists looked down the peninsula and saw a fat cow waiting to be slaughtered. That was nine million looking south at 21 million, a David and Goliath comparison. Unfortunately, David, out of ideas to attain his goal, still had a lot of big rocks and wasn't afraid to use them.

To get things rolling North Korea claimed it had been attacked, and launched its invasion. A huge force numbering 90,000 North Koreans, supported by Soviet T-34 tanks, poured across the imaginary boundary of the 38th Parallel into South Korea on Sunday, June 25, 1950, throwing the world into turmoil once more.

The narrow peninsula could boast less than 20 percent flat land, and the rest was straight-up-and-down mountains. The worst thing that could happen to that terrain was to have massive rains. It had rained all through the night of the 24th with the beginning of the monsoons, but it had tapered off about 4 a.m. when the shelling started.

In short order, the United Nations called for withdrawal of the aggressors, but was, of course, unheeded. North Korean forces were pushing southward fast, hoping to gain control before the UN could react in strength. Considering the condition of US Armed Forces at that time—down to about 120,000 in the Army—perhaps the North was hoping the US would just stay out of it.

However, the surprise attack on an ally, and the absence of Soviet or Chinese troops in the invading hordes changed things in Washington.

US analysts almost certainly pegged Joseph Stalin as the motivating force behind the communist incursion. Since America had focused on the next likely war to be with the Soviets, anyway, Korea suddenly became an arena in which to face the dreaded Russian Bear. Meanwhile, it didn't hurt to be around in force in case either the Soviets or the Chinese decided to get involved. The whole diplomatic decision-making process was very tricky during the war, from start to finish. Either way, South Korea had to be protected. The spread of communism by force would stop there.

The United States was forced to act, with President Harry S. Truman sending the Eighth Army to the war-torn region from Japan. The British and other nations also began marshalling troops, aircraft and ships.

By the beginning of July, 406 men of the 24th Infantry Division arrived in Korea, the first US troops on the ground. Called Task Force Smith and commanded by Major General William F. Dean, the first men in felt very much alone. Within days the 25th Infantry Division came ashore from Japan under Lieutenant General Walton H. Walker, who had taken command of the Eighth Army on July 13. The 1st Cavalry Division was also on hand early.

Inchon fell on July 3, and two days later US troops fought the North Koreans for the first time near Osan, and had to back up.

The North Koreans had been training. They were experienced. Momentum was in their favor and they were ready.

Unfortunately, the American boys were not ready. Post-WW II, U. S. forces were provided little heavy training and most were in too-comfortable jobs. Physical and mental toughness had declined with the need for seasoned soldiers. That is not to say there weren't still some tough career NCOs in the service with WWII combat experience, and some veteran officers, too. Those men would form the nucleus of the quick rebuilding of America's ground forces. But the lifers were few in comparison, and many perished in the first wave of violence. Still, the great American machinery started to turn, and intensive training hit the green troops with a bang.

On the other side, North Korean troops were very tough, often using unorthodox tactics that shocked U. S. troops, including coming in under a flag of truce, then opening up on unsuspecting soldiers. The enemy was accomplished at raids and infiltration, giving the Americans and their allies no time to regroup and hit back with effectiveness. North Korea was using Ranger tactics on Americans, and succeeding.

Of course, the enemy also came in screaming waves, over-running the ill-prepared South Koreans and the just getting started UN troops. Slowly but surely, the friendly forces were being pushed south, their backs to the sea.

By the end of the month the Naktong Perimeter was manned on the south by four ROK (Republic of Korea) Divisions and three US Divisions, and on the north by 11 North Korean Divisions. The situation was grim, indeed. The line from the Naktong River to Pohang on the coast was very narrow and the enemy concentrated on it, penetrating a small area and creating a bulge, which came to be called the Pohang Pocket. If that salient was broken through, the enemy would isolate Pohang, gaining a portion of the eastern flank.

War planners did some quick analysis and found the Eighth Army's style of fighting—what they had been trained for—didn't work very well in Korea. American forces were geared up to fight the Soviets in Europe, an entirely different battlefield requiring tactics suited to that terrain and an entirely different enemy. For one thing, Korea is full of mountains that fill a long, narrow peninsula—much different that the wide plains of Europe and the supposed tank battles which would be fought there. Armor had limited use during the Korean War, especially in the beginning. With Army forces staying in the valleys, on roads, in the open, North Korea had a field day chewing them up from the heights.

Since Intelligence nets had barely begun to form, knowledge of who the Army was facing, and how many, and where they were, was decidedly lacking. Something special was needed, and in a hurry. Besides the reconnaissance factor, American brass thought a lot of what the North Koreans were accomplishing against them with small hit and run attacks. They wanted to hit back before they ran out of earth to stand on.

Trying to get men and materiel into the country in a hurry and fight the onslaught at the same time was proving difficult. Supplies were scarce, and knowledge of the country and the enemy was even more so. Many maps were old Japanese versions, some of which had to be airdropped after troops got ashore.

By late July, UN forces were all the way back to the Pusan Perimeter; a rectangular area bordered by the sea on one side and the Naktong River on most of the other. The whole thing was but 100 miles long and 50 to 60 miles wide—not much considering the increasing size of the forces sheltered there.

General Walker stated there would be no further withdrawal, and no surrender. UN forces dug in and held fast while men and supplies continued arriving. US air and artillery began to take effect, stalling the North Korean drive long enough for something to happen. Several things did.

Birth of the Korean Ranger

Far East Command (FECOM), which meant General Douglas McArthur—named Supreme Commander on July 7—began receiving suggestions for elite, raider-oriented troops. The renowned leader had long been a proponent of special operations, and had ordered the creation of the 6th Ranger Battalion in WWII, using them well in the Philippines.

The concept of an elite group was tossed back and forth for a short time, and then orders came down for Lt. Colonel John McGee to put a trial unit together. McGee began his search for a TO&E (Table of Organization and Equipment) along the lines of the vaunted Alamo Scouts of WWII, but was unable to find one. The only available, and suitable TO&E was for WWII Ranger Companies.

Had the Alamo Scout organizational tables been located, there may not have been Korean War Rangers, and we might now have the 75th Alamo Scout Regiment.

McGee took his Ranger TO&E to Japan to look for recruits. Thus were the Rangers reborn.

John McGee fought in WWII, at times as a guerilla fighter in the Philippines, and was a POW.

One of the first men McGee found was a 23-year-old Lieutenant named Ralph Puckett, an Airborne officer who had volunteered for Korea. Puckett was given the job of putting the first unit together, but immediately had his hands tied by the order not to recruit veteran riflemen. There just weren't enough to go around. So, he looked at clerks, cooks, and mechanics, anybody who could, or would volunteer to fight in a Ranger unit.

By late August 1950, Puckett had it together enough to have the unit organized in Japan. There it gained the title 8213th Army Unit, which became known as the Eighth Army Ranger Company. There were several specialty units put together under slightly different TO&Es, and given designations in the 8000s, designated the Special Activities Group to throw off the enemy as to their real purpose. There was also an Eighth Army Raider Company with that type of designation.

Puckett and his new recruits crossed the water to Korea and were attached to the 25th Infantry Division, becoming the first Ranger unit in Korea.

About that time, the UN was solidifying its position—what there was left of it—and became strong enough to hold off those ground-eating attacks the North Koreans were throwing at them. Replacements arrived, and the good guys started pushing back. For their part, the communists figured the UN would soon overwhelm them if they didn't do something, so they mounted a last-push, a full effort to break the Allies and drown them in the sea. Too bad for them, they waited a little too long to slay the beast.

The North Korean Final Push began August 31 and ran through UN lines in many places. The enemy put everything into the assault, slamming into dug-in defenses for two weeks. The Eighth Army held, knowing that to surrender was to either die or wish for death. All UN forces fought to contain the rush.

MacArthur knew he was fast approaching the threshold of enough men on shore to push the North Koreans back, but looked to avoid a prolonged frontal siege with little ground gained at a time. He wanted to break out of the small defensive perimeter, so he decided to make an end-around play and land troops at Inchon, far to the north, almost to the 38th Parallel. He figured that would threaten to cut enemy forces in half, mandating their withdrawal from around Pusan in the south.

To obtain a feasibility study of the proposed situation, General J. Lawton Collins from the Army, and Admiral Forrest P. Sherman from the Navy, both from the Joint Chiefs of Staff, went on a fact-finding mission. Collins came back saying—among other things—he saw a real need for Ranger-type units. He had seen the length of enemy supply lines, ripe for cutting, along with strung-out communications in the areas around Inchon. It would be a perfect place to squeeze them. He also saw the need for a unit to counter the North Korean raiders, either directly, or with raids of their own.

Accordingly, Collins ordered what he termed a "Marauder Company" to be formed as an experiment. The men were to have an elevated training regimen that included infiltration skills and other small-unit tactics.

To gain a better idea of the needs of Theater and Field Commanders, Collins asked around for advice. One person he asked was MacArthur himself, posing the questions (in effect) of what the General thought of the idea, and had he done anything like that already?

The idea of an elite company was conceived on both sides of the world. Here again, with Collins calling for a "Marauder" unit, it is possible the official designation became Ranger largely because the Eighth Army Rangers had already been formed.

The Commander in Chief, Far East Command (CINCFE), got back to him four days later on September 26, and said (in effect) that the concept of Ranger Companies was a good one, and yes, he had indeed already started a couple of units along those lines. The Eighth Army Ranger Company was put forth as an example, though they were still in the training phase.

The push was on from several angles, and the powers that be took notice. In September, members of the Army Field Forces, the Army Staff, and the CIA met at the Pentagon for a skull session. One thing to come out of it was the decision to form one Ranger Company immediately, with three more to follow. That meant things were getting serious. Korea was turning into a nightmare, and America's Army needed help. Invitations to join the new unit were broadcast, and RSVPs began coming in.

The extra Airborne pay—well publicized —and the prestige of being in such an elite unit brought plenty of volunteers, with many of the first batch coming from the already partially qualified men of the 82nd and 11th Airborne Divisions. The next thing Collins needed was a ramrod.

The astute General knew where to look, and on September 15, he chose Colonel John Gibson Van Houten to lead the training section. The same day, Army Field Forces gave the order to the Commanding General of the Infantry School at Fort Benning to put together a suitable six-week course for the new Rangers. The Combined Arms Training Division created a tentative TO&E for the new companies, and a Table of Distribution for the new Training Section to support the new units.

Van Houten graduated from the University of Georgia, was associated with the Infantry Center, and then went through Command and General Staff College. He carried a good record in WWII as Commander of a Regiment of the 75th Infantry Division and was then Chief of Staff of the 9th Infantry Division. Ironically, he wasn't Airborne-qualified, and lacked Ranger-type experience, but he made up for it with lots of time in combat. As the Ranger candidates were often unruly and hard to deal with, Van Houten was a good choice. Known as a disciplinarian and organizer, he got things calmed down and going forward, becoming a forceful proponent of the Ranger concept.

Army Assistant Chief of Staff for Operations, Major General Charles L. Bolte, sent two messages to the Commanding General, Third Army, telling him to organize a Ranger Training Center. Accordingly, the 3340th Army Service Unit was activated at Fort Benning, Georgia, September 29. Almost immediately the 1st, 2nd, 3rd and 4th Ranger Infantry Companies were activated and training begun. The new Rangers would be given heavy-duty specialized training, and all would be Airborne-qualified.

The Eighth Army Ranger Company, activated in a hurry in the Far East, was not Airborne qualified, though its commander, Lieutenant Puckett, was. The Airborne tag applied to Ranger Companies trained in the United States.

Along with the instructions came the authorization for the new companies to wear the insignia of the WWII Ranger Battalions. The initial Ranger Training Section and Headquarters was put together by Van Houten, quickly moving to the Harmony Church area, about eight miles from the main post.

There were 20 barracks to hold 40 men each, a few outbuildings, and a rudimentary kitchen.

Harmony Church, at one far edge of Fort Benning, is still the home of the 4th Ranger Training Battalion, though the original buildings and training elements are gone. Only a sign exists in the wilderness stating the area's former status.

The search for qualified instructors began with men from the Infantry Center at Benning, but soon turned up veterans from the European Theater, former Marauders, men from the 1st Special Service Force, and the Office of Strategic Services.

Van Houten chose Colonel Edwin Walker as his Deputy, utilizing his experiences as Commander of the 1st SSF in WWII. Included as part of the staff were Major William Bond, who had been with Darby; Major James Y. Adams; Captain Arthur "Bull" Simons of WWII's 6th Ranger Battalion; Captain Wilbur "Coal Bin Willie" Wilson; and Major John K. Singlaub, formerly with the OSS.

The first recruits, mainly from the 82nd and 11th Airborne, plus a batch from the 555th Airborne "Triple Nickel"—then known as members of the 505th/82nd—showed up at Benning in early October, an amazingly fast transformation from idea to reality. The volunteers were supposed to be pre-screened by their parent unit commanders to eliminate some of the misfit problems that Darby ran into in WWII, when some highly unqualified soldiers were dumped into the pool just to get them out of trouble.

Van Houten was looking for rugged 19-year-olds with high test scores, and good at hand-to-hand combat. For a change, African-Americans could volunteer, and many did. A lot of them came from the 3rd Battalion of the 505th Airborne, and eventually made up 27 percent of the total 491-man student Rangers. They had their own unit, which began as the 4th, but became the 2nd Ranger Infantry Company, inevitably called the Black Rangers. That company went on to serve with distinction in Korea, making a parachute jump into combat at Munsan-ni.

Traditional Ranger training pervaded the studies, with emphasis on conditioning and realistic scenarios, and more than a few recruits—there was a 30 percent failure rate—didn't make it through the speed marches. As today, those men were taken away before the rest of the class returned.

About half the training was at night, which was new, and amphibious assault training, resupply by airdrop, and escape and evasion techniques were pushed. Also included were some OSS-type scenarios that involved liaison with native peoples, required some cultural knowledge of the target area, and instilled the concept of using partisans as guerilla fighters advised by Rangers.

The course ended with Hell Week, during which students made low-level jumps and blew things up over a wide area.

By October's end, the Army Field Forces had put together the first Table of Organization and Equipment for the new units. The units were to be light in composition, with a lot of firepower, but no heavy weapons. Like today, the idea was to hit fast and hard and get away. If only things had happened that way.

Company HQ had just six men, and its three platoons were composed of one officer and 32 men each. The new units were larger than WWII companies, but still smaller than a regular Infantry company. The difference was in the firepower. There were more machineguns, bazookas, submachineguns, and mortars, giving many men in the platoon something more than rifle bullets to contribute.

A problem presented by such weaponry was having to hump it all. The unit was given just two trucks and a jeep, so the men were heavy-laden.

Major Bond and others came up with a statement of Ranger purpose—as had their WWII predecessors, also to little avail—that outlined the missions of attacking command posts and observation points, artillery, and support elements, plus targets of opportunity in the rear areas. He also warned that small units were not suitable for sustained combat, partly due to size, partly due to lack of heavy weapons. Bond postulated the need for a liaison officer with the parent unit to oversee operations and usage of the new company.

Van Houten, Adams, Singlaub and others went to Korea and spoke with the Brass from the individual divisions with attached Rangers, trying to get the Ranger concept across. Since the units were so new, not many commanders knew how to use them, and had trouble sparing anyone from line duty, or using valuable time preparing suitable missions. The result was misuse of a great asset, and the paring down of the units by the attrition of line combat, a mission for which the Rangers were not suited, but still accomplished with excellence.

Once again, suggested operational doctrine was put on hold, the stated reason being that the new unit was untested in the field. The result was Ranger Companies in the Far East without a viable sheet of instructions on how to use them. At that point, who knew? It was beginning to look like only a Ranger would know how to use a Ranger Company properly, even though the unit had been formed to meet Ranger-type challenges.

Back home, the press was pushing the Ranger concept, using the image of America's toughest soldiers to gain public support—and sell papers. Besides, the public needed some encouragement after the rough beginning in Korea.

A request went out from EUSAK (Eighth US Army, Korea) to four commanding Generals for a report—due February 10—on the progress and usage of the four Ranger Companies then in-country, despite the 2nd and 4th being on the ground barely a month. Still, three of the four commanders replied in a positive way, and no one is really certain what the fourth General was thinking.

Major General Moore, Commander of IX Corps, had the 4th Rangers attached to the 1st Cavalry Division. For some reason he thought the men had been too long out of training during the trip to Korea, and needed extra physical conditioning, among other things, before they could fight. They were given guard duty for their first round. The General figured to use the highly trained, superbly conditioned Rangers as a stay-behind ambush unit, or have them go into outlying villages and set up ambushes. Then, when things were in pretty good shape, he might let them do some recon work.

On the plus side, Major General Ruffner, Commander of the 2nd Infantry Division, (1st Rangers), liked the idea of a small, compact unit able to travel good distances on foot behind enemy lines. He said in his report, "It is a ready-made force for rapid, finite operations in enemy rear areas designed to hit a particular target and destroy it and return to base rapidly by some other route."

Ruffner thought the Rangers were doing well, and should be kept from becoming just another rifle company. As did several other high-ranking officers, the General recommended a company for each division.

Major General Ferenbaugh, Commander of the 7th Infantry Division, (2nd Rangers), said it was hard to find things for the Rangers to do, but when they did have suitable missions, they did them well. He noted their high spirit, though they were only at 61 percent strength. Ferenbaugh then said Rangers should get replacements with the same frequency as conventional line units.

The 7th ID policy was to keep the 2nd Rangers—all African-American—racially separate, and set up a replacement pool just for them.

The Eighth Army Rangers, the only non-Airborne Company, were under Major General Keen's 25th Division control. He noted the Rangers were without organic support and were still dependant on other units for sustenance. He recommended the company be given enough support personnel to make the unit more self-sustaining. Like Ferenbaugh, he also noted the paucity of suitable targets. Still, General Keen wanted to keep them doing what they had been doing, and valued them as a strong fighting force.

Whatever they were doing, the Rangers were in the thick of things as the Allies began to strike back against the Chinese Communist incursion.

General Ridgeway worked fast to get things turned around in his section of the war, and by the end of January the Eighth Army was digging in its heels and leaning back the other way. By February 10, Inchon had been retaken, and a few days later the heavy battle at Chipyong-ni stopped the communists cold.

The Eighth Army Rangers and the 25th ID Recon Company were the first American units inside Inchon.

The Chinese let loose with their Fourth Phase Offensive on the night of February 13, hitting mostly against the X Corps' 2nd Infantry Division and the 8th ROK Division. A new Allied line of defense was formed with the 24th Division on the left, the 2nd Division in the middle, and the 187th ARCT (Regimental Combat Team) on the right.

The 23rd Regiment of the 2nd Division was given the defense of Chipyong-ni, a crossroads town in central South Korea. Along with that came responsibility for the left flank of the division and the resistance to any communist use of the road network in the area.

Heavy fighting stopped the 40,000 Chinese and inflicted heavy casualties on their ranks. It was the first serious loss they had taken.

In the next few weeks, Operations Killer and Ripper (March 7) were born—limited counter-offensives designed to release the Chinese hold south of the 38th. General Ridgeway set Ripper in motion, with Allied elements crossing the Han River east of Seoul.

On March 14, Seoul was back in Allied hands. The invisible border between North and South was reached once more on March 28.

By early April, UN forces were once again spread out before the 38th Parallel, just over three months since the Chinese had crossed it going the other way. A few weeks, later the Chinese tried again, mounting their very aggressive Fifth Phase Offensive on April 22, but they were stopped north of Seoul after heavy fighting and extensive losses on both sides.

While preparing for the offensive, the Chinese again used the tactic of movement only at night, hiding their forces in forests during the day.

The communists came on, but mainly hit the South Korean units and avoided American firepower—much the same as Vietnam's 1968 Tet Offensive — making small gains though those positions. The thrust was short-lived, however, and the Allies held after falling back a few thousand yards, inflicting heavy casualties on the enemy.

That communist push was to be the last major maneuver of the war. The enemy had overstepped himself, seeking gains when he should have consolidated. In many cases the Chinese had outrun their supplies—those they had, anyway—and were often hungry and low on ammo under the relentless pressure of the Allied ground and air attacks. It seemed the time for advantageous negotiations had passed.

But, the Chinese were well dug-in and fortified, and gaining ground on either side became a tough row to hoe. When the Chinese proposed peace talks be held in North Korea and the UN agreed, they tried unsuccessfully to say the UN forces had lost and had to sue for peace.

Little would be further from the truth. Eighth Army Commander General Van Fleet was very willing—and able—to dig the Chinese out of their earthen bunkers and push them back beyond the Yalu.

His boss, General Ridgeway, head of FECOM, figured Van Fleet could do it all right, but the cost would be exorbitant in both men and materials. President Truman and the Congress, taking heat from anti-war sentiment at home, agreed. Nothing else was going to happen in the way of formal aggression from America. The United Nations jumped into the non-aggression ring, and the decision was to not try and win the war in Korea. That summer peace-talks were proposed.

The opposing forces had settled into fairly stagnant warfare with a few exceptions, and Ridgeway, who had taken over from MacArthur on April 11, no longer considered the Rangers necessary.

On July 10, Army Message # 95587, containing orders to deactivate the Rangers, was in the air. By August 1, 1951, the Ranger combat companies were gone.

The Great Debate

All in all, the Rangers were given missions most line companies could have accomplished, including guard duty and anti-guerilla patrols. Too often companies were used in the front lines, either to hold or attack. Not only were field commanders largely ignorant of how to use the Rangers, the demand for manpower up front took precedent. The result was the inefficient use of a great resource, and a tall list of casualties to the small, elite units.

The attrition rate meant replacements were needed immediately and continually. The Ranger School back in the States was cranking them out, but there weren't as many veterans as in the first batch of volunteers. Lack of experienced men hampered the units in the field, and casualties among green troops ran high.

For more details about replacement strategies and the building of a core of Rangers, most of which would not see combat, see the section on Korean War Rangers Training and Actions.

Chief of Ranger Training Command Van Houten couldn't stand it, traveling to the Far East to explain to anybody who would listen that Rangers were special units, built for raids. They were not shock troops. They were not line troops. He didn't get much of an audience, especially when he said he wanted Ranger Battalions.

With few exceptions, not many Ranger-type operations were being called for, though the units were distinguishing themselves in other ways as solid, aggressive infantry with great fighting spirit. The Rangers were pretty much held in check by "conventional wisdom" and the desperate need for men on the line.

The Eighth Army was building its strength a little at a time, and Ranger units became a focal point as a source of well-trained veterans. The Army saw it as a good idea to spread Ranger training out by sending qualified individuals to different units, thereby seeding the rest of the service with what came to be known as Force Expanders.

In late December, the Ranger Training Center put out a report arguing the inefficiency of the concept of one Ranger Company per division. The idea was put forward to add more units at lower levels, or expand the whole into battalions and have operational control at Corps level. Conventional wisdom shot that idea down in a hurry. The view of Rangers as Shock Troops was too prevalent to be overcome by the proposed idea of a behind-the-lines unit. Besides, General Collins wanted one company per division and that was that.

Van Houten, ever the advocate, proposed the Army send men from other units through Ranger School, then back to their parent units. This would accomplish the same thing, but would keep existing Ranger units intact. In truth, there were only a few hundred Rangers serving in combat units and those few wouldn't go very far if spread throughout the Army. Van Houten had the right idea for boosting the overall amount of highly trained men.

At that point, General Mark Clark, former Commander of the Fifth Army in WWII Italy, was Chief of Army Field Forces. As such, when he voiced an idea, people paid attention and things got done. His idea had to do with his recollections of Darby's Battalions as excellent fighters, and the fact they would serve as good role models for increased efficiency and aptitude. In view of the meat-grinder war in Korea, Clark understandably didn't want to take men out of the field, but he went forward with his—and others'—thoughts of putting more men through Ranger training.

Clark visited Fort Benning in March 1951, and told Van Houten to submit ideas on the use of Ranger Training Command to elevate standards in the rest of the Infantry. Van Houten did just that, but like his superiors, he focused on a possible European conflict and not so much on the needs of Korea. Things were settling down into a stalemate situation over there, and the need for Ranger units was slowly being eliminated. Forward vision was necessary for the future.

The new concept was based on quality rather than quantity; the improvement of the Army as a whole became the new goal.

It would seem that the short visit to Van Houten by Clark made probable the continuance of the Ranger Training Command. The change of concept, coupled with the excellent record of Ranger Companies, later brought about the all-but inevitable formation of Ranger Battalions.

Again Van Houten proposed Ranger training for volunteers, mostly officers and non-coms, who would then return to their units to teach. Also in the works was an indoctrination program such as the Rangers have today to get men ready for what they were about to face, and weed out anyone who shouldn't be there. General Clark approved the plan in April after adding airborne training, and told Van Houten to go after it. To make things even more proper for the transition, the Ranger Training Command became the Ranger Department on April 5. Soon the Ranger students were being sent to various other camps for training in mountaineering, cold weather warfare, and tropical actions. In mid-April, the 7th, 10th and 11th Companies were sent to Camp Carson, Colorado for fun in the cold mountains.

Back in Korea the future of Ranger units was coming under the gun, just when their style of training was being recognized as the best. President Truman had a run-in with General MacArthur and replaced him with General Ridgeway, whose personality and take on the Rangers changed a few things. Ridgeway's Eighth Army Command passed to General Van Fleet.

So, with Clark and Van Houten working on the Ranger concept from one direction, and Ridgeway and Collins from another, something was bound to happen.

For one thing, Ridgeway figured the Rangers had no real mission to perform in Korea, and for another, he felt, as did others, that the elite units were taking too many leaders from the regular Army ranks. Ridgeway was not one for halfway measures, and proposed deactivation.

About that time one more player entered the debate, and more directions were given. General Maxwell Taylor, successor to General Bolte as Assistant Chief of Operations and Training, told Army Field Forces to study the need for Ranger units and Ranger training for personnel in Infantry, Armor, and Airborne (CARS) units.

The results of those studies showed Ranger Companies to be an unnecessary drain on manpower in the cold-war era—they were still thinking of Cold War Europe—but some of the Brass thought otherwise. Brigadier General Eddleman, head of the Plans Division of Army Staff, pushed the concept, saying every Field Army should have a battalion of Rangers. In answer to critics saying the best men would be taken, Eddleman replied the best men went to the Marines or paratroopers, anyway.

Eddleman's side of the debate was wasted on more conventional thinking, and plans to scatter the best units in the Army got underway.

The prevailing notion was to use Rangers as teacher/members of line infantry units rather than having their own battalions. It seemed Rangers were so popular no one wanted to do away with them entirely, though the active Ranger units were, at that point, doomed.

That the Rangers were being misused became obvious early on. Though they fulfilled their assigned tasks, they weren't fulfilling their proposed function. Too much of that great training was going to waste, considering the attrition rate among the companies. Van Houten, Collins, Ridgeway, Taylor, Clark and others saw what was happening and were concerned about the situation. The eventual decision to have the Ranger Companies stand down was the result of the Great Debate.

Orders came down July 10 to deactivate the Korean War Ranger Infantry Companies. Many of those with Airborne qualifications went to the 187th Regimental Combat Team (Airborne), and the rest went back to their parent units. By August 1, it was a reality.

Meanwhile, the Ranger Training Center made the move to the Harmony Church area on the southeastern edge of Fort Benning, an area of scrub oak and pine, lots of wilderness to get lost in, and above all, away from the rest of the Post.

There were enough barracks for 800 men, though they were fairly rough in nature. There was even a mess detachment. The Cadre settled in and waited for 197 men from the 43rd Infantry Division to show up.

On March 12, men of the 12th Rangers were formed up from the 28th Infantry Division, the 13th Rangers from the 43rd Infantry Division, and the 14th Rangers from the 4th Infantry Division to begin the third training cycle. Of course, they had to get through Airborne training first.

Once Again—Deactivation

August 1951 brought the axe to the last combat Ranger units when Major General Reuben E. Jenkins took over as Assistant Chief of Staff for Operations and Training. A product of WWI soldiery, he was decidedly anti-elitist, believing well-trained infantry could do any job the Rangers would be called upon to do. He also subscribed to the common thought that Rangers took too many top men from other units. His thoughts were familiar. Like many others, the General was interested in the idea of Ranger-style training, but wanted the seeds spread throughout the Army. He was reported to have called Rangers "prima donnas."

After much debate, he told Collins to inactivate the rest of the Ranger Infantry Companies and spread the men around.

His idea was to make all Airborne, Infantry, and Armored units capable of Ranger-type missions, focusing especially on Lieutenants, Captains, and senior NCOs. This was to be done through the "new" Ranger program at the Infantry School at Fort Benning.

There were some changes when things began to be implemented, with a new program born of Jenkin's ideas plus a few from the Army Field Forces. The thrust of the "new school" was to be focused on producing qualified small-unit leaders, as it is today. On September 27, Collins approved the change from the "special unit" concept to the much broader concept of upping the quality of the entire Combat Arms entity of the Army.

The last Ranger Companies (in Germany and at Ft. Benning) were deactivated by November, with the men going to Airborne units or back to their parent companies. Some, of course, ended up at Benning and other training facilities as the Ranger Training Command was dissolved and the Ranger Department was born.

By October 10, it had become official. The new Ranger Department of the Infantry School was open for business, with Colonel Henry G. Learnard as its first Director.

The school continued to turn out highly trained soldiers, but none of them went to Ranger units, because there were none for 17 long years.

From Center For Military History—TO&E, TDA History

As military units are recommended and formed, there must be a standardized way of handling numbers of troops and their requirements, as well as where they are allowed to go and what they are allowed to do. The terms TO&E (Table of Organization and Equipment) and TDA (Table of Distribution and Allowances) are used many times in this work, so the history of such parameters is presented here.

Prior to the 20th Century there were no Tables of Organization such as we know today. Indeed, before WWI the largest Army unit authorized was a Regiment, since nothing larger, such as a division, could be put together unless it was wartime. Still, the powers-that-be figured war would be coming sooner or later and planned for the larger units by publishing Tables of Organization in the Field Service Regulations of 1905. The first "modern" tables didn't come along until 1914.

What we now call Tables of Organization and Equipment are actually the result of the merger of Tables of Organization and Tables of Allowances, which were published apart until 1943.

Tables of Allowances also covered military schools, certain departments, and other miscellaneous installations, but since TAs had become part of TO&Es, those applications were converted to coverage by a Table of Distribution (TD) in 1936. To confuse matters further the TAs and the TDs were merged in 1943 to form the Tables of Distribution and Allowances (TDA). TDA personnel can be military or civilian. TO&E units are military only.

An authorized, approved Table of Organization and Equipment has to come before the formation of a unit, and is the actual basis for that formation. Everything about that unit is delineated in the TO&E.

TDA units are generally put together to do something there is no TO&E for, such as temporary duty. If a TO&E unit is developed for that same purpose, then the TDA unit stands down. An example would be the Eighth Army Ranger Company of Korea, a TDA unit that was retired when TO&E Ranger units came on line. TDA units are also generally non-deployable, such as training units.

Historically the number of people it takes to keep one man in the field is far greater than the number of people that actually go out into the field and fight. That means administrative, supply, mechanical, and many other units that support the line units are usually TDA.

In 1989, the Army fielded TDA units comprised of 55 percent of the officers in the service, 24 percent of the warrant officers, 22 percent of its enlisted people, and almost all of its civilian employees.

Ranger TO&E 7-87

Put in place in October 1950, the Ranger TO&E delineates the mission and capabilities of the elite unit, and lists every man and every item allowed to the companies by the Army. Though changes and augmentations were made, what follows is the gist of that allowance. Note the number of Non-Coms and the considerable firepower.

Mission: To infiltrate through enemy lines and attack command posts, artillery, tank parks, and key communications centers or facilities.

Assignment: Attached to Infantry Division.

Capabilities: Infiltrating through enemy lines and destroying hostile installations.

Repelling enemy assault by fire, close combat, or counter-attack.

Maneuvering in all types of terrain and climatic conditions, and seizing and holding terrain.

Conducting reconnaissance and Intelligence operations by penetration of hostile combat zone.

Landing by parachute, glider, or assault aircraft, the reduced-strength column adapts this TO&E to the lesser requirements for personnel and equipment during prolonged non-combat periods, and for a limited period of combat.

Without an augmentation column, the company must be attached to another unit for administration, mess, supply, and organizational maintenance.

With an augmentation column, company can operate separately for short periods of time

Augmentation was built into the TO&E to build up the companies in times of great stress or need. The reduced strength spoken of has to do with down time, something the companies had little or none of. At times, some units were way over the allotted strength, but mostly they were under.

Personnel

 1 Captain

 4 Lieutenants

 1 First Sergeant

 3 Master Sergeants

 10 Sergeants First Class

 36 Sergeants (below SFC)

 37 Corporals (E-4)

 13 Privates First Class (three of them were medics)

Weapons

 M2 Carbines—.30 cal

 M1 Rifles—.30 cal

 Browning Automatic Rifles—.30 cal (BAR)

 Thompson Sub-machinegun- .45 cal

 Grenade Launchers, used with M1

 Browning Machineguns —.30 Cal (A6)

 57mm Recoilless Rifles

 3.5-inch Rocket Launcher (bazooka)

 60mm Mortars

The Rangers were much better armed than conventional line companies.

The men often carried a variety of pistols, as well. A favorite was the old .45 caliber slide automatic Colt, but they packed 9mm handguns, and others, too. Also, assorted knives of various lengths were thrust into boot tops, strapped to legs, and occasionally thrown at the enemy.

The TO&E detailed the equipment the Rangers would have, and there is a long list containing everything from one folding chair to one barber kit to 21 five-gallon water jugs. It took a lot of mundane articles to keep a hundred men in shape and moving forward, such as 27 compasses, four sniper scopes, and nine wire cutters—but no tents.

KOREAN WAR RANGER UNITS

Table of Distribution and Allowances (TDA) Units

The "8000 Series" of designations was used for certain special units that were to carry out recon missions and support guerilla operations behind enemy lines. These units were considered temporary duty units and were activated by Far East Command. These companies were disbanded, not deactivated, therefore negating any forward lineage, though the linkage remains intact. The following is a short list, not inclusive, but pertinent.

Eighth Army Ranger Company—8213th
    August 25, 1950—March 28, 1951
    25th Infantry Division/IX Corps—Korea

Eighth Army Raider Company—8245th
    November 12, 1950—April 1, 1951
    3rd Infantry Division/8227 AU-Special Activities Group—Korea
    The Raider Company is not generally counted as a Ranger unit.

Table of Organization and Equipment (TO&E) Units

Depending on how the list is counted, the number of Ranger Companies is 15, 17, or 18. The accepted number is 17—that is, 15 Number Companies and two Letter Training Companies, A and B, formed in the latter stages of Ranger training for Korea. However, if the Eighth Army Rangers are added, it becomes 18.

Activated by the Department of the Army

1st Ranger Infantry Company (Airborne)—RICA
    October 28, 1950—August 1, 1951
    2nd Infantry Division—Korea

2nd RICA
    October 28, 1950—August 1, 1951
    7th Infantry Division/187th Regimental Combat Team (Airborne)—(ARCT)—Korea

3rd RICA
    October 28, 1950—August 1, 1951
    Ranger Training Command, Fort Benning, Georgia and 3rd Infantry Division/I Corps—Korea

4th RICA
    October 28, 1950—August 1, 1951
    1st Cavalry Division, 187th ARCT, 1st Marine Division—Korea

5th RICA
    November 20, 1950—August 1, 1951

25th Infantry Division/I Corps—Korea

The 5th replaced the Eighth Army Rangers in the 25th ID, because only one company per division was allowed, and because the Eighth was a TDA unit, and not Airborne.

6th RICA

November 20, 1950—December 1, 1951

7th Army—Kitzingen, West Germany

The 6th was the longest-running Ranger Company of the era, the only one of 17 recognized units to last more than a year.

7th RICA

November 20, 1950—November 5, 1951

Ranger Training Command at Fort Benning

8th RICA

November 20, 1950—August 1, 1951

24th Infantry Division/IX Corps/187th RCT —Korea

9th RICA

January 5, 1951—November 5, 1951

3rd Army, Fort Benning

10th RICA

January 5, 1951—October 15, 1951

45th Infantry Division, Camp Polk, Louisiana

11th RICA

January 5, 1951—September 21, 1951

40th Infantry Division, Camp Cook, California

12th RICA

February 1, 1951—October 27, 1951

5th Army, Camp Atterbury, Indiana

13th RICA

February 1, 1951—October 15, 1951

2nd Army, Camp Pickett, Virginia

14th RICA

February 1, 1951—October 27, 1951

4th Infantry Division, Camp Carson, Colorado

15th RICA

February 1, 1951—November 5, 1951

3rd Army, Fort Benning

Training Companies A and B

Eighth Army Rangers

The 8213th Army Unit was the first Ranger Company to see action in Korea, and became known as the Eighth Army Ranger Company.

The Ranger Infantry Companies (Airborne) of the Korean War, known as RICA, had two things in common—the US Army activated them all, and they were all Airborne. The

8213th did not share the title "Airborne" and was formed under a TO&E mandated by Far East Command on December 2, 1950.

The three officers of the 8213th wore wings, plus a very few of the enlisted men.

The company was considered a temporary Table of Distribution and Allowances Unit (TDA) by the Army, and was disbanded without consolidation with another Ranger unit. Because of that, there is no direct line to the 75th Ranger Regiment. No Eighth Army Ranger Company battle streamers hang from the Regimental Flag. However, having been formed under a Ranger TO&E, members of the company are entitled to wear the Ranger Tab.

They were the first to taste blood in the Korean mountains, they were on the line when the Chinese Offensive rolled over forward elements of the Eighth Army, and they are perhaps the best known of all the Korean War Ranger Companies because of the legendary Ralph Puckett.

What follows is the story of the "bastard" unit, the 8213th, the Eighth Army Ranger Company.

Ralph Puckett

Ralph Puckett, Honorary Colonel of the 75th Ranger Regiment, and other survivors of those terrible months in Korea, put together a narrative compilation of memories in 1992. Some of men who speak here are no longer with us, and it is our loss. The general history written here comes from many different sources, all noted in the Bibliography.

Colonel Puckett has been a great help with this project, and is known to all Rangers as an outstanding individual. He gave his permission to use the memories of his men as they are printed in the booklet put out by the Eighth Army Ranger Company Association while standing on the parade ground at York Field, Fort Benning, August 7, 2003.

In a quick interview with Puckett that morning, some 52 years after he was blown up on Hill 205, he said one of his toes was still draining. We were waiting for the Ranger Regiment Change of Command, in which he had to take part.

Eighth Army Rangers and 75th Ranger Regiment

Puckett sent this as clarification.

The Campaign Streamer for the first Korean War campaign is not on the 75th Ranger Regiment flag. As you know, the Eighth Army Ranger Company was in the first campaign. Many, many years ago I wrote the Deputy Chief of Staff for Personnel (who had been in the 1/101st when I was there) about this campaign credit. He said that since the Eighth Army Ranger Co was T/D (temporary) although organized under a TO&E, the streamer could not be added. I responded to the effect that if the USMA [West Point] had the opportunity to get another campaign streamer they would either change the regulation or make an exception to the regulation. The Merrill's Marauders campaigns were earned when they were a T/D unit. They were never organized under an approved Department of the Army T/O&E.

Origin and Formation

Contrary to popular belief, Ralph Puckett did not originate, recruit, train, feed and nurture the Eighth Army Rangers all by himself, and he would be the first to say that.

Among others, Brigadier General John Hugh McGee had a large hand in getting things going.

At the time, McGee was a Lt. Colonel in the Eighth Army. He reported in about the time the North Koreans were surging forward, pushing through an area that created a pocket of the enemy inside UN "lines."

The area in question was part of the Naktong perimeter, between Taegu and Pohang on the east coast of South Korea, and was labeled the Pohang Pocket.

Considering the successes of North Korean soldiers using guerilla tactics on UN forces, US planners decided to put some commandos of their own in the fight. Early on, before the Ranger Training Center formation, EUSAK (Eighth United States Army, Korea) was asking for a unit to perform such functions.

General Lawton Collins, Army Chief of Staff, was also thinking along the lines of guerilla units to counter the North Korean tactics. He ordered a feasibility study done, which led to the formation of the Ranger Infantry Companies (Airborne) to come. In the meantime, General Walker of the Eighth Army already had a plan in progress.

Lt. Colonel McGee, assigned to G-3, received orders to organize a unit for behind-the-lines action in the Pohang Pocket.

McGee, a graduate of West Point and a WWII veteran, wrote about the beginning of the Rangers in the Eighth Army Ranger Company Newsletter, published August 25, 1987.

"My initial thought of our Ranger Company was in the early days of August 1950, at Eighth Army Headquarters in Taegu. At this time the North Koreans broke through the Naktong Perimeter between Taegu and Pohang-dong, a seaport on the Sea of Japan side of the peninsula. This breakthrough extending into our lines was called the Pohang Pocket. G-3 (Operations) directed me to immediately organize a unit capable of penetrating the rear of the pocket for timely information of an enemy buildup.

Those were days of the need to do something immediately.

"My immediate thought was the Alamo Scouts, which Sixth, not Eighth Army, had organized for commando missions in WWII. This unit was named after the defenders of the Alamo, a small fort in San Antonio. The brave garrison of the Alamo, preferring death rather than surrender to the large Mexican Army force under Santa Anna, inspired Texans by their courageous stand to ultimately defeat Santa Anna; a defeat that brought independence to Texas. The Alamo became a shrine for bravery and patriotism for not only Texans, but all Americans.

"A Table of Organization and Equipment, called a TO&E, is the key for quick organization of a United States Army unit. A search for an Alamo Scout TO&E was unsuccessfully conducted by EUSAK and FECOM Headquarters. The TO&E of a WWII Ranger Company was found by FECOM. It met our organizational need. This is how close you came to being the Eighth Army Alamo Scouts and not the Eighth Army Ranger Company.

"The spirit of the Alamo must have infused itself with that of the Rangers in your great company. Your great stand on the left flank of Task Force Dolvin was a Ranger-Alamo stand against overwhelming odds; a stand that helped to hold up the Chinese offensive down the west corridor of Korea, possibly on again to the Naktong River."

McGee had already done some research into Ranger-capable soldiers when he helped in the screening process for the Eighth Army Raider Company.

McGee took his Ranger TO&E to Japan, to the Repple-Depple (replacement depot) at Camp Drake. In his search for qualified men and decent leadership, he ran across a lean young 2nd Lieutenant named Ralph Puckett. The young soldier was aggressive and smart, an accomplished boxer, and a graduate of the United State Military Academy at West Point, class of 1949.

Puckett wanted the Ranger assignment badly. He told McGee he would serve as a squad leader if nothing else was available. That was enough for McGee. He made Puckett the new company commander, though the slot called for a Captain.

The WWII Ranger Company TO&E allowed only two platoons, and Puckett ended up with two West Point classmates as his Platoon Leaders. They had already been selected and they chose him. Lt. Charles N. Bunn took the first platoon, Lt. Bernard Cummings, the second.

But first, the three men had to produce a unit out of the myriad applications they received. Some 60 were already gathered by McGee and Captain Gray Johnson and Lt. Paul Weaver, members of the new Ranger Training Staff. They began the process of going through all the paperwork, selecting only men who met their exacting criteria, then interviewing them. Puckett was not allowed to cruise the ranks of assigned combat soldiers because there were not enough of them to go around as it was. He and his fellows had to choose from among the service troops, the cooks, clerks, and mechanics, and a few replacements.

When enough men were gathered to speak to, Puckett always began the meeting with, "If you are not willing to volunteer for anything dangerous, you are free to leave the room now." That message lost a few recruits right off the bat, but Puckett didn't want them, anyway.

8 ARCO Speaks—Puckett, Walls, Summers, Cassat, Anderson, Bunn, Ross, et al.

The following narrative is intermixed with excerpts of memories of the men of the Eighth Army Ranger Company. Colonel Puckett sent this note to make sure things were formal pertaining to direct quotes from writings he sent:

"The statements immediately following the names of Eighth Army Rangers are exact quotes taken from manuscripts published in 1992 by COL (Ret) Ralph Puckett and are used by permission."

Thank you, Sir.

Jesse Anderson

I volunteered because of my discussion with Colonel McGee. I figured if I was going into combat I wanted to go with the best unit there. On entering the [Ranger HQ] building we saw Colonel McGee wearing a CQ [charge of quarters] armband and pistol. His greeting was, "Welcome. You men are the first to arrive at my new Eighth Army Ranger Company." He then addressed me with, "You are CQ until the next NCO comes in. You can make him CQ and get yourself settled in." He removed the armband and pistol and handed them to me.

Charles Bunn

[We began] interviewing men for the company the very next day after joining. The three of us [himself, Cummings, and Puckett] were responsible for picking the men and training them. I remember getting only two or three hours of sleep each night the entire time we were at Camp Drake.

Harry Cagley

[I remember] thinking, "What the hell have I got myself into now? A Ranger Company with three 2nd Lieutenants right out of school and a bunch of GIs from every organization except the Infantry."

Potential Rangers had to be the most physically fit, experienced men available, most, but not all, less than 26 years of age and single. The biggest single factor in accepting a recruit was motivation.

When enough men were selected to form two platoons of 36 men each and a headquarters element of five men, Puckett drew equipment from Camp Drake. The total of three officers and 74 enlisted men was broken down into two platoons carrying a headquarters element of one officer and three enlisted men, two assault elements of 11 men each, and a special weapons element of ten men. The Company Headquarters element consisted of Puckett and a First Sergeant, a Supply Corporal, a Company Clerk, and a messenger.

The first Ranger Company in Korea was activated August 25, 1950, per General Order 237.

At that point, Puckett, et al, proceeded to get their men in shape. Still at Camp Drake, a rigorous routine of physical conditioning began with road marches, calisthenics, and lots of running, plus the constant cadence of pushups being done.

During that time the Mohawk haircut came into being.

Richard Branham

I volunteered because the Rangers were an elite fighting force better trained and conditioned than the normal Infantry unit. [I remember] being the last to exit a building and having to do pushups. We told everyone we belonged to the submarine mess kit repair when asked about our Mohawks.

Billy Walls

My Platoon Sergeant in Basic had been a Ranger. He impressed me that the Rangers were the best. When I heard I was to be interviewed for the Rangers I wanted in. My 201 file must have impressed Lt. Puckett because I was so nervous at the interview I know I didn't. My policy in those days was to steer clear of the Brass. When he asked me why I wanted to be a Ranger my answer was that I wanted to fight with the Best. The first time I saw the whole company together I thought we needed a lot of training. I had no clue at that time how close those men would become to me through shared experiences. I do remember wondering how many of us would make it back from Korea.

One day, while drinking with two others, we saw an American boy with a Mohawk haircut. We went to the barbershop and all got Mohawks. Afterwards we went to the shower room for some serious drinking, where we were seen by one of the officers, who promptly made it mandatory for all Rangers to have Mohawks.

Ralph Puckett

I wanted to be with the best. I had wanted to be a Ranger since I first heard about them as a boy. When Lt Colonel McGee told me that he had filled the lieutenant slots, I told him that I would take a squad leader's or a rifleman's job if he would accept me. I remember the pride I had in realizing a boyhood ambition—to be a Ranger. I remember the concern I had in my own ability —was I good enough to be a Ranger and, more importantly, was I good enough to be the commander of a Ranger Company? Could I measure up to what my Rangers deserved? I remember how pleased I was the first time I saw all of my Rangers together. What a great group they were! I remember the runs we took and how quickly my Rangers began to look proud and to be proud.

I remember how busy we were. Would we ever get everything done? I was excited by everything that was happening. I couldn't believe my good fortune, and was humbled by the responsibility. I also remember the laughs—there are always funny things that happen. One was the story Barney Cummings recounted to me. He was our supply officer in addition to being Platoon Leader. Barney had been busily engaged in getting our TO&E plus a lot of special items. One of the latter was piano wire to be used for garrotes—for choking sentries. When Barney asked for some piano wire, the post supply officer, who had been badgered by Barney on numerous occasions, asked in disgust, "What key?"

I remember the Mohawks and the post sergeant who accidentally was given one. All of us had a good laugh about that.

At a later date, Puckett said he was almost certain Bill Walls made the suggestion to get Mohawks. "I immediately agreed and had a written order posted on our bulletin board."

August 28 brought forward movement as the company boarded a train bound for Camp Mower near the port of Sasebo, the jump-off point for Korea. There they took passage on the Japanese ferry "Koan Maru" on September 1. The new company arrived in Pusan the next day.

Within a few hours the men were on a wheeze-puff train, then trucks, on the way to the village of Kijang, northwest of Pusan.

McGee had already set up a rudimentary camp, which soon became known as Ranger Hill. This would become the training site for the next few weeks, though it was immediately set up with a defensive perimeter because there were North Korean guerillas around.

The next step was to set up a training regimen, which McGee based on his own experiences in the Phillipines, and notes from his brother, George, a battalion commander with Merrill's Marauders in WWII. Of course, current Infantry doctrine was included. Since the Rangers were supposed to be an irregular unit, such training had to hit home, and so included both recon and combat patrols (often the same thing), raids, and trail blocks, among other things. Conditioning continued to be a priority.

Puckett took McGee's recommendations and formulated four goals:

Each Ranger will achieve the best physical condition of his life.

Each Ranger will become highly competent and thoroughly trained in his weapon and the skills of the individual soldier.

Each squad, section, platoon, and the company will become a highly competent fighting team, thoroughly proficient in small unit tactics.

Each Ranger will develop the spirit and confidence that his squad, section, platoon, and the company are the best in the Army.

Though they were Rangers, and therefore considered forthright, elite and specialized, the company program was still based on the Infantry ethic of move, shoot, and communicate. Live fire exercises were common. In addition to toughening their minds and bodies, the men learned how to use compass and map, demolitions, camouflage, communications, and a myriad of other things. Through it all, the men were made to hump heavy loads for long distances, a situation made for griping as well as building endurance.

Puckett also pulled inspections and kept the men marching, either parade-style, or forced marches with full gear up and down the Korea hillsides. He and his fellow lieutenants also had to learn how to plan and conduct infiltrations, raids, ambushes, and patrols, and to get help from indirect fires. They weren't given the benefit of any organized schooling; they simply studied Field Manuals. Since they were all "green" everybody had a lot to learn.

Sleep was a thing of the past, and though it took a toll on both enlisted men and officers, combat conditions dictated the necessity of surviving under otherwise intolerable conditions.

What those Rangers were going through was basically no different than what current Rangers go through on the way to becoming the best of the best. The main differences were in terms of technology, but the principles were the same.

As in Ranger classes today small-unit tactics were used beginning at squad level and progressing to company-sized employment both day and night. Also as today, Rangers were expected to work at night as well or better than the enemy.

After each exercise, Puckett did something nearly unheard of at that time; he asked his men for their comments and observations. When the men talked things over and any problems were uncovered and discussed, they were made to do the exercise again to make certain they all got it right. Two things came of this—one was more grumbling, the other was sure-footed actions in combat.

Jess Anderson

The [training] goals were accomplished very well. The training phase molded individuals into a close-knit team. First it was a group of men who became a squad, which became a part of an assault team, which was part of a platoon that was part of the company. It was a pleasure to see all of these men working together, more so each day, to make our company the best in Korea.

Rick Branham

Map reading, vehicle patrolling, weapons firing, night patrolling, hand-to-hand, bayonet drill, and hill assault were all accomplished very well, as were squad and platoon tactics. I remember all of the above, and many times thinking Lt. Puckett was half mountain goat. Water was scarce. No bathing.

Snits Fazenbaker

I think we were over-trained. Better to be over than under. The thing I marvel the most about my training, how could three West Point officers take over my life to the extent that I would wade in rice paddies full of human waste, and sometimes "face down" and get up and do it again, get up and report, "I am proud to be a Ranger, Sir, even if I don't smell like one." If this doesn't tell you something about the leadership qualities that come out of West Point, then I give up.

Gray Johnson

Weapons training was performed on rangers laid out not exactly according to the book. Rice paddies, hills and valleys and mountainsides dictated where and how far target would be placed. Our targets were makeshift. For rifles and automatic weapons we fired across the rice paddy. Mortar firing was a little more difficult. First makeshift targets were placed [painted] up the side of the mountain across the short valley. The mortars, base plates and ammo were lugged up a mountain on the near side of the valley. Distances were unknown so it was necessary for Rangers to sense distances across the uneven terrain. Results were far better than expected.

Harry Winters

What I remember most about Ranger training is the number 20. If you are last in formation, Puckett says, "Give me 20." Got your hands in your pockets, "Give me 20." *Put your hands on your hips*, "Give me 20." Any kind of goof up, "Give me 20." But every 20 was done with the spirit of a Ranger. Because when Puckett asked for 20, he gave 20 with you.

Ralph Puckett

They gave me everything I asked and more. I'm sure that many of them must have hated my guts each time I would say, "Okay, let's do it again." We would attack the same hill time and time again, each time correcting previous errors and moving with a little more sureness and competence. I was determined that no Ranger would die because he wasn't physically fit or could not shoot, or did not know what to do, or did not have the discipline to carry out his orders no matter how difficult. We were going to use every minute of the day and night to hone our skills.

We were a small company—there were only 67 of us when we finished training, so there was no room for slack. Every Ranger had to know his job and be able to do it well. And he did. That training paid off in combat. Whoever said, "The battle is the payoff" knew of what he spoke.

Of greatest importance was that Ranger Spirit—that knowledge that together with your Ranger buddies your unit can complete any assigned mission. That spirit comes as a result of hard, effective, training in tactics. You and your buddies become a team. Working together, there is nothing that is impossible.

It was during this time Generals Collins and MacArthur were discussing the whys and wherefores of Ranger Companies. It was agreed the actions of the Eighth Army Rangers would be watched and the results made known to the Ranger Training Command at Benning, both to gain from their experiences, and to further explore the feasibility of special units.

MacArthur speeded things up for everybody when he forced the Marine landings at Inchon, beginning September 15, 1950. All of a sudden the proposed purpose for the Eighth Army Rangers disappeared along with the Pohang Pocket when the North Koreans fled homeward.

Eighth Army G-3 (Operations) Colonel John A. Dabney and McGee got together to figure out what to do with the Rangers. Though the company had used up only five of the granted seven weeks of training, McGee thought they were ready to go. All they needed was a parent to feed them and give them something to do.

McGee wrote the following training report on the Eighth Army Ranger Company and submitted it to Eighth Army Commander, General Walker, on October 1, 1950.

HEADQUARTERS
EIGHTH ARMY RANGER TRAINING CENTER

Subject: Training Report of Eighth Army Ranger Company

To: The Commanding General

Eighth United States Army Korea

In accordance with TWX dated 28 September 1950, GX 25155 I, report is submitted on the status of training of the Eighth Army Ranger Company and recommendations are made for the Company's future employment.

The Company has completed four of the seven weeks authorized for training. It has received intensive infantry training with special emphasis on the subjects of physical conditioning and patrolling.

Unity to include a chain of command and the development of a sense of duty responsibility in the Non-Commissioned Officers has been achieved.

The Company is prepared to undertake the following type missions:

Raids

Reconnaissance patrolling

Combat patrolling

Motorized detachment

Trail blocks

The following are factors to be considered in the assignment of tactical missions to this company.

Present strength:

American Officers—3

American Enlisted Men—63

Korean Enlisted Men—10

Total—76

Administration: Mess and supply facilities are at the battalion level. The Eighth Army Ranger Company does not have a unit mess or any unit transportation.

Missions: The Company possesses great firepower and a high degree of mobility over difficult terrain. Successful employment in combat will largely depend on the achievement of surprise. To achieve the element of surprise, adequate time must be provided the Company Commander for reconnaissance and detailed planning.

Recommendations: That effective 11 October 1950 [5 ½ weeks of training], the Company be assigned to combat duty.

That dependent on tactical employment the present camp mess and transportation facilities initially accompany the Company. Transportation to be augmented in event employment demands it.

That the combat value of this Company immediately be studied with the view of either expanding it into a Ranger Battalion or deactivating the Company.

On October 8, 2nd Lieutenants Puckett, Cummings and Bunn became 1st Lieutenants. Soon after, the company joined the war in earnest. The Eighth Army Rangers were assigned to IX Corps, and thence to the 25th Infantry Division (Tropic Lightning). The agreed-upon purpose of the employment was for anti-guerilla operations.

The company moved to 25th Division Headquarters near the town of Taejon on October 12 and was linked up with the division Recon Company. There they received further orders and a load of ammunition and other supplies. Taejon was also where some South Koreans were added to the mix, and spread out through the company. The first job they were given was actually an anti-guerilla operation in the area of a village named Poun.

Charles Pitts

During the movement from Ranger Hill to Taejon, I was impressed with the poor roads and many destroyed bridges necessitating fording. The saturation of artillery and air strikes on the hills outside Taegu caught my attention; that is the almost total devastation resulting from such which had been a part of the defense of the Pusan Perimeter. Taegu itself lay in ruins and I was rather amused when Lt. Cummings insisted that the unit police its C-ration cans after eating in a destroyed railroad yard. In Taejon we spent a couple of days getting lined up with the 25th Division and provisioning ourselves with ammo.

The Rangers found the 25th Division Recon Company about 30 miles from Taejon, at Poun, and went to work immediately. Lt. Cummings and the 2nd Platoon based themselves in a nearby hamlet while the other two sections stayed at Poun, that is, while they weren't out with the Recon Platoon gathering up left-behind and/or fleeing North Koreans going north away from the advancing allies coming out of Pusan. Some of the enemy soldiers were quick to give up, and some tried to fight their way past.

Puckett stayed on the move, spending time with each platoon in turn. He continued to implement discussions of platoon movements, insuring a kind of quality control. Fortunately, the company was doing better in the field than they were with simple logistics.

The Rangers' TO&E, such as it was, didn't provide for mess or transportation personnel or equipment, so the company was dependant on the 25th Division Recon Company for sustenance and other supplies, and mobility. The Recon Company was up to the task, though there was never enough to go around. As in all wars and troop deployments, a certain amount of scrounging went on.

The first Ranger casualty occurred October 17, when a South Korean Police unit that mistakenly identified the Rangers as North Koreans lightly wounded Japanese-American Corporal Haritoku Kimura. He was back in the saddle in a short time.

The 25th ID soon had things in hand in that area, and the Rangers ran out of work. Good timing there, because the division was reassigned to the area including Musan-ni and Ui Jong-bu.

November 3 brought new orders to the Eighth Army Rangers, and the word spread to get ready to move out to Kaesong, just shy of the 38th Parallel. The next day the company moved some 176 miles by foot, rail, and truck to reach their new "home" about midnight.

Again, their mission was to help mop up left over North Koreans and deal with any guerillas still operating. U.N. forces were driving northward so fast they were outrunning their supply lines in places.

Home looked closer than ever.

Charles Pitts

Now, a bit about Kaesong. There had developed a general idea that the war was about over by the time we reached there. Indeed, I broke out the company on a number of occasions to practice a review, which we assumed we would be involved in at the termination of hostilities. The I and IX Corps on the west were advancing about as fast as their vehicles would carry them and the X Corps, which had been established as a separate command, was practically on the banks of the Yalu in the east.

Near Kaesong we participated in Task Force Johnson for a few days near Musan-ni, and I believe, Panmunjon. I recall that our men found a bathhouse with a large reservoir, some wood, and a local man to heat the water. Of course the whole platoon took advantage of this. Meantime, some of the Wolfhounds [27th Infantry] found the place. There was some heated discussion about who should retain possession and it seems remarkable that part of one of our platoons would be ready to take on a large part of the 27th RCT over this facility.

Though the Rangers had been "blooded" in small contacts, they still had not been in a major fight. They were certainly capable, and when the chances came to exchange fire, they did well. They moved out at dawn on November 12 and made a routine patrol to the village of Tongduchon-ni without any trouble.

Continuing on toward Ui Jong-bu with the mission of setting up a roadblock, the 2nd Platoon walked up on 14 North Koreans arrayed along a trail.

The sudden showdown produced a quick firefight during which the Koreans had two men fall. One of them turned out to be a Captain. There were no Ranger casualties.

The company moved on to complete their mission of standing roadblock duty, where they stopped and searched civilians. In Korea, as in Vietnam, the enemy had but to change clothes to blend right in with everybody else.

Bill Judy

Quite a bit of our time was spent on patrols trying to ferret out guerillas and remnants of the North Korean Army who had been bypassed by U.N. troops on their drive north out of the Pusan Perimeter.

My first real contact with the enemy happened one afternoon when we came down out of the mountains and fell out for a break. A buddy and I were relieving ourselves in a sort of ditch when we heard someone in the rear of our column sound off with "Enemy in the rear!" We jumped up, grabbing our weapons, and immediately spotted three North Korean troops to our right flank and rearward running away from us. I said to whoever it was, "There they are! Get 'em!"

I threw my rifle up, sighted, and fired. To my surprise, one fell on the stone fence about three feet high around this Korean house. My buddy didn't get a shot off, and the other two got behind the fence and under cover. In a matter of a few minutes, it was all over and things began to quiet down. Quite a few of our guys on this patrol had fired their weapons to our rear and we had shot five or six North Koreans, with the remainder of them getting away by running back into the same mountains we had just come through.

My buddy and I went over to this guy I had shot and we discovered he was a North Korean Captain by his uniform and he had an older .32 caliber Harrington Richardson pistol in a shoulder holster and a bandanna full of ammo (about 100 rounds) still clutched in his hand, which I immediately confiscated and kept the remainder of my time in Korea on my person at all times. I remember different guys commenting how they would've hated to go into combat with a weapon, such as it was, against us who were pretty well equipped. Some of them (N.Ks) had only grenades and others had nothing, as we found out later.

On another of these patrols we set up an ambush and stationed ourselves on each side of a fairly deep depression in the hillside. About two hours later, our scout ahead of us informed us on a walkie-talkie that a party of guerillas was coming our way, so we got ready. Safeties could be heard clicking off and every one knew what was about to happen. Approximately nine enemy soldiers in a single file a few yards apart came in view on their way down the trail into our midst. You could have heard a pin drop it was so quiet.

As the enemy approached a predetermined spot, an interpreter, a South Korean soldier who spoke the North Korean dialect, called to them to halt, throw down their weapons, and surrender. But they decided instantaneously to fight and went for their rifles. Needless to say, that was foolhardy on their parts because in less than a minute eight of them were dead and one, a younger fellow we estimated was about 16, had crawled into a hole in the rocks. Somebody had observed his actions and through the interpreter's urging, he was convinced to surrender.

I was designated to escort the prisoner to battalion for questioning. We were about seven miles inside what could be considered enemy territory and I was afraid of being ambushed in much the same way his patrol had been. I kept trying to get him to cooperate, but apparently he couldn't or wouldn't. Finally he became convinced and we arrived at battalion. I turned him over to an officer and returned to my unit, which was about ready to curtail its activities.

As far as I can remember, we had not suffered any casualties, and everyone was in high spirits and felt we were living up to the Ranger tradition.

By mid-November, Task Force Johnson was moving farther north. The Rangers and the 25th ID Recon Company took the lead, clearing mines when necessary, and providing security for the armor. A few days later TF Johnson took a break. The Rangers separated from them and returned to Kaesong via a night march in falling temperatures.

The Eighth Army was on the verge of finishing the trek north when the Chinese got involved. All along the line the Chinese were putting on pressure, especially against I Corps. They had come across the Yalu in force, combining with North Koreans to meet the U.N. forces coming north—some of them camped on the banks of the border-river.

Task Force Dolvin
    Morning Report Extract
    22 Nov 50
    Pres for Dy 3 Off 60 EM
    22 Nov 50 Co arrived Kunuri North Korea 0100 hrs & made preparation to join
    Task Force Dolvin. Co departed Kunuri North Korea 1000 hrs 22 Nov 50 & jd
    Task Force Dolvin at Yong-po-dong North Korea. 1600 hrs 22 Nov 50.
    ROK enlisted 9

John Summers
    At Kaesong, we got a resupply of ammo and all our weapons were fired getting ready
for the move north. When we did get the word, it was about 8 o'clock. We moved out of the
building we were occupying. I remember Morrissey jumping up on a tank. I rode in the bed
of a 2-½ ton truck. Whatever had wheels or tracks is what the Rangers went north in. It was
long, cold ride for every one. You couldn't stay warm as we wore the short jackets, pile cap,
and shoepacks. By that time it was below zero

    The Rangers were attached to, and under control of, Lt. Colonel Welborn Dolvin, leader
of the 89th Medium Tank Battalion. A new task force was forming under Dolvin, and would
bear his name. The 25th Division was sent forward as a counter-offensive effort to blunt the
veteran communist forces and Task Force Dolvin was selected to be the tip of the spear.
    The components of TF Dolvin were:
    Company B, 89th Medium Tank Battalion with Eighth Army Ranger Company's 1st
Platoon attached; Company E, 27th Infantry Regiment with the Assault Gun Platoon of the
89th attached;
    Company B, 35th Infantry Regiment with the 1st Platoon of B/89th attached; 25th ID
Recon Company; Company C, 65th Engineer Combat Battalion; and Recon Platoon, 89th
Tanks.
    The Rangers stopped briefly on the banks of the Chong-Chon River while the Task
Force was forming. The cold was an increasing factor in all operations, in the field or in the
foxhole.
    Thanksgiving day was November 23, the day the Americans were to move forward to
the Yalu. Though the Chinese were coming across the river in places, they had not made their
move in front of the 25th ID. It would not be long in coming.

Ted Jewel
    I remember the cold Thanksgiving Day we spent not too far from the Yalu River, when
we began to hear rumors of Chinese soldiers in Korea.
Bill Judy
    As I understood it in November, every one was saying we would be home for Christmas.
Someone had heard that the North Korean Army had been annihilated. We were ordered to
join TF Dolvin for the final push to the Yalu. We were given orders not to fire across the Yalu
even if fired up, as this would have been considered an act of war on our part. To this day I

wonder about that order and have always figured I would've returned the fire, but we never reached the Yalu.

A concerted attack on the enemy was planned for 10 a.m. the next morning. Accordingly, Ranger patrols were sent out as far as five kilometers to see what was in front of the massed 25th. When the attack went forward the Rangers and a platoon of the 89th Medium Tanks charged up Hill 222 (224) and overran the enemy. There was the first major cost to the Rangers in the form of three men killed—two by friendly fire—and three wounded, plus a South Korean soldier wounded. The 89th Tanks had mistakenly fired on the Rangers. Puckett ran down the hill to the tanks and got them to cease fire.

The Rangers and the rest continued the attack, and took the hill, despite the problems with recognition. Nothing much happened during the night while the Task Force dug in.

As TF Dolvin moved forward with the 24th and 35th RCTs, the enemy backed up a little, but not far. The Chinese did release some 30 US prisoners that first day, who were picked up by the 89th MTB (Medium Tank Battalion).

Morale was high—for the time being.

The cold was beginning to tell on the unit, and all other units in the vicinity. As if the fighting weren't bad enough, the men had to contend with weapons—and themselves—freezing up.

Billy Walls

I was a machinegunner with the 1st Platoon. We were with the tanks from the 89th Tank Battalion. We came under small arms fire from Hill 224. We left the tanks to form for the attack with the 2nd Platoon leading the assault. I watched them go up the hill where they drew small arms fire from the Chinese. At this time, our tanks opened up on the Rangers from the rear. I saw the shells hit into the Rangers. Lt. Puckett ran screaming to the tanks and stopped the shelling.

John Summers

Early on the morning of the 24th of November we moved out riding on the tanks. Most of my assault section was on the third tank. We moved up the MSR [main supply route] and went through a Cav [1st Cavalry Division] roadblock.

About another mile, we came under machinegun fire from our right flank. The tanks moved up into a line and we jumped off and started across a large rice paddy. We were running for a small rise to our front. Cagley was to my right and Lt. Cummings was to my left. Cagley was hit in the face and Lt. Cummings overtook me and hollered, "You are now the Platoon Sergeant! Get the Rangers over the rise and hold up!"

Coming up the rise to my front, I looked back over my shoulder just as one of our tanks fired at us with the tank's gun. They also were firing machineguns at us. Our platoon cleared the rise. This is where I came upon Joe Romero. He had been shot through the chest. We regrouped and waited for the 1st Platoon to move up on our left flank.

PFC Morrisey was right flank man for the 1st Platoon. We again got the word to move out across another large rice paddy. We reached the base of 224, went right into the assault.

After a rough climb, we reached the top. Any Chinese that had been there were gone. We tried to dig in for night attacks.

Though fires were burning on parts of the hill, we froze. I dug in with West-By-God Judy and he made a good foxhole buddy. I know he kept me from getting frostbite on my feet. He would rub my feet and stick them under his arms. When my feet were warm, Judy took off one boot at a time and I would warm up his the same way. As cold as it was it helped to prevent frozen feet.

Nothing much happened that night, though about 2300 hours I heard a shot and found Ranger Stewart had accidentally shot himself in the top part of his leg. He was in the same hole with Harry Winters. We had Stewart taken back to the aid station. Before he left he gave me his German pistol, which I carried for the remainder of my time in Korea.

Merle Simpson

The previous night (24-25 November) had been one of the coldest nights I had ever endured. Like all US service men, we were not equipped for such cold weather. The plain combat boots and two pair of socks had little effect on the cold. Our light winter coat was of little value in such extreme temperatures. Little did we know what effect this weather would have on our weapons until the following night on Hill 205.

Our sleeping bags did not arrive for us to use on Hill 224. After the cold became almost unbearable I decided to build a fire. I immediately was told to extinguish it but replied, "I would just as soon be shot as freeze to death." Many other fires sprang up on the hill. Little did we know the strength of the enemy at this time or I am sure more caution would have been used.

Sleep was out of the question and to see the sun finally rise the next morning was as if we had been given a second chance.

The temperature continued to drop. Five more men were taken to the aid station for cold-related injuries. Between the fight for Hill 224 and the cold, the Eighth Army Rangers were reduced to 51 men able to fight.

Still, the Task Force continued forward with the 35th and 27th RCTs taking a beating but not stopping. The Rangers were in the middle of the action. Coming upon Hill 205, Rangers riding tanks came under fire and dismounted.

Ralph Puckett

I jumped on the back of a tank, knocked on the turret, got the commander to open up, berated him for not firing a single shot after which he began to fire. I jumped off the tank and yelled, "Let's go!" to the 1st Platoon where I was located.

With the tanks firing on the observations of Puckett and his men, and air strikes on Chinese positions called in by Dolvin, the Eighth Army Rangers took the hill with heavy Chinese small arms fire coming down on them.

When the Rangers reached the top of the hill, the Chinese had pulled out. The cost to find that out was six Ranger, and three ROK casualties.

Hill 205
Merle Simpson

Our battle for Hill 205 was fought up this small valley of rice paddies, which at the time seemed very lengthy. Lt. Cummings asked me where my men were. I was then instructed to return and find my squad. They had somehow remained at one of the dikes near the start of action, so my return meant three trips through the rice paddies. I was receiving sniper fire and was unable to pinpoint the location. Somehow, William Judy saw the sniper firing from a big crock or jar used to make kempshe or something, and kill him.

We proceeded up Hill 205 without resistance and Lt. Cummings told me how to deploy my men and to dig in for the night. With my rifle leaning against a tree and my ammunition belt hanging from a branch, I proceeded to dig my foxhole. I heard someone shout and looked up just in time to see this soldier in an odd looking uniform running down the hill. By the time we realized that a Chinese soldier had stumbled into our area he had slipped back into the trees without being hit by any Ranger fire. Everyone began digging as fast as possible, for I think we all knew what was coming.

Ted Jewell

During the early hours [on the hill] I recall hearing voices from a distance. Our Korean soldiers told us they were not speaking Korean, and it was later confirmed they were speaking Chinese.

When the Rangers were atop the hill and had no one else left to fight, Lt. Puckett set up a circular defense with his machineguns looking down the likely routes of enemy approach. He had his men dig in for the night—they were in an old cemetery—but he wasn't done getting everyone aligned for a decent defense.

Puckett had to go down the same hill his company had just ascended to set things right with artillery and command. During that visit he had a chance to look at the S-3 maps and found the Rangers were exposed on their right flank by several kilometers. The right side of his perimeter was hanging out in space, inviting envelopment. Puckett went back up the hill and strengthened his defenses as best he could. The temperature continued to drop, making any movement more difficult as the men dug in and waited.

About 9:00 p.m. the angry sounds of a firefight came to the Rangers from their left flank, held by Company E of the 27th Infantry Regiment. The noise swelled quickly as a platoon was overrun.

Charles Pitts

On November 25, real disaster struck. I was at the base of Hill 205 with a couple of vehicles and trying to have some hot chili carried to the top. Not long after that, I began to hear considerable firing to the right of our company [he was facing the hill] and then the tempo increased along the TF front. That must have been about 10:00 p.m.

I asked what was happening and was told the Chinese had attacked repeatedly in force and that massive casualties were mounting.

It was very cold and an icy wind was blowing. The moon was up as the Chinese masses moved along the Chongchon River. The battle was gradually joined by more and more soldiers as they came in contact with American and Allied units along the front.

To dislodge the Rangers, a large Chinese force formed not far from the perimeter defenses and attacked suddenly, blowing bugles and whistles and beating on drums. They came in a rush and caught some Rangers reaching for their weapons, but the alert perimeter guards put up enough of an initial outpouring of fire that the defenders were able to coalesce and keep the Chinese back.

Puckett used artillery along with heavy Ranger small arms and grenades to dispel the first attack.

An hour after the first attack had begun, the second battalion-sized wave washed in. Heavy attacks were being made all along the front around the Ranger position.

That charge was also beaten back by the Rangers and skillful use of artillery, as was a later third try by the Chinese. Each attack was beefed up over the previous one, and it was getting progressively harder to stop the Chinese momentum.

By the end of the fifth communist onslaught the Rangers were piling up enemy bodies so fast they needed more ammunition. Some of the enemy had breached the perimeter, and in places Rangers were fighting with bayonets and knives.

Merle Simpson

At approximately 2200 hours the first attack came. I, like all the other Rangers, felt there was no outfit or unit in better condition than we; so let them come on and let's see who would weaken.

Each attack was beaten back and eventually the call went out for more ammunition. Since I had the heavy weapons squad, which was limited in this type of fighting, I sent them back to get ammunition, as I tried to defend our position. Since my squad was deployed around the rear of our position I was receiving less fire than the frontal squads.

As each attack seemed to increase in fighting and time, our weapons became hotter and hotter. In between attacks, our weapons cooled down and started jamming up. My M1 finally failed to eject by itself so I took my trench shovel and beat it open to replace new ammunition.

During the night, PFC Judy came by and got into my foxhole. He was carrying only a bayonet. He watched to the right and I watched to the left. Eventually the thumb catch sheared off my weapon and we were left with nothing but bayonets and hand grenades.

Ted Jewell

Because of the previous napalm bombing of the hill, small fires were still burning. Later in the evening we heard trumpet calls and loudspeaker voices telling us, "Tonight you die, Yankees!" Some of us yelled back obscenities.

Sometime later, mortars started crashing down on us, shattering trees and generally scaring the hell out of us. Then the mortars stopped, and soon we were engaged in a firefight with our unseen enemies.

Then there was silence for a while, until the shelling resumed again. After the shelling stopped, we again repulsed an attack on the hill by the Chinese infantry.

Some time later, we were hit again with mortars, only this time it was the heaviest barrage of all. Shortly after it stopped, the infantry assault started. I remember firing my carbine continuously at figures coming over the hill in between the flashes of gunfire and exploding grenades.

Bill Judy

My squad was on the northeast side of the hill. Ranger Bob Sarama and I dug a foxhole on a little ridge beside a ditch line. Rangers Bourque and Nowlin, a machinegun team, were on our right. A light skift of snow was on the ground, but our artillery had set some fires in different places.

We could see enemy activity in the valley below us and it was obvious they were making preparations to engage us later that night. Ranger Sarama and I had M1s, ammo and grenades, and felt we were ready for most anything they chose to throw our way. It was getting considerably colder, and as darkness closed in a feeling of apprehension was prevalent. Keep in mind, at this point, I still felt we were engaging remnants of the North Korean Army and this would probably be a last-ditch effort. I thought that very shortly it would be all over and we'd be headed back to the States.

About 2200, quite a few mortar rounds came in. Very shortly after the barrage, they came up the hill directly to our front, firing as they came. Being dark, I couldn't estimate how many, but it was obvious to me that we were outnumbered. Sarama and I started returning the fire, hitting a few of them, causing them to stop and take cover about 75-100 yards down. Then they tried to crawl up the ditch line. I started tolling hand grenades down the ditch at about five-minute intervals. We could hear them talking. It seemed every time one of our grenades would go off, some of them would yell, so we knew we were doing damage.

All of a sudden, three of them charged our position from different angles close in. I got the guy in the middle with one shot. Sarama got the one on the left and the last one was coming from my right firing his burp gun. At that inopportune moment, my rifle jammed, so I yelled to Sarama, "Get this guy!" He swung his rifle over my head and fired, striking him in the upper torso because it actually turned him flip-flop and silenced him. Miraculously, neither one of us had been scratched. I cleaned my rifle and cleared the jam.

There was another guy behind a tree in front of us. Every once in a while he would squeeze off a round and we kept trying to pick him off.

They started mortars again and came at us again in frontal assault. Firing was coming from our positions along the north part of our perimeter and our artillery was falling amongst them. We held them off again and everything began to quiet down. A mortar round struck to the right and just behind our position and I was blown out of the hole and down the hill a few feet. When I got my bearing, I realized I was going down the hill, so I turned and jumped into the same hole with Sarama again.

About that time, Ranger Puckett crawled around the hill and inquired how we were doing, to which we replied, "Okay, I guess. At least we're still here!" He reached out and gave me a pat on the back and after a moment asked if I was sure, and showed me his hand. It was covered with blood so I asked, "What happened? You get hit in the hand?" He just shook his head and I realized it was my blood. I hadn't even felt any pain.

We informed him about the guy to our left front and between the three of us we finally eliminated him. Lt. Puckett left us shortly thereafter. I remember him saying we were surrounded. I thought he had been wounded but I didn't know where.

Puckett was carrying shrapnel in his thigh at that point, and was to become a victim of mortar fire shortly. As the story goes, Puckett was on the radio, calling for artillery and being told there wasn't any available, when a couple of mortar rounds landed nearly on top of him and Lt. Cummings, tearing up Puckett's feet and both cheeks of his buttocks with shrapnel. The bottoms of his feet were so torn the young Lieutenant almost lost one foot, and ended up losing a big toe. There was no way he could have walked off Hill 205.

He said his wounds were: Shrapnel from mortar rounds in both feet and both cheeks of his buttocks, a thigh wound from a grenade fragment, and a wound in one arm.

"Nobody's got it right except Lock." (J. D. LOCK—author of "To Fight With Intrepidity")

With respect, Sir, we hope we got it right, too.

Although several books say Cummings was killed immediately in the blast, Puckett said the fact is nobody knows what happened to him. "Before Walls picked me up I asked him to check my foxhole that was only a few feet from where I lay, to see about Barney Cummings and Jim Beatty. Neither were there. I later asked about anyone being left behind. Both times Walls assured me that we were the last off the hill. I am positive that he believed that. He was probably correct."

Bill Judy

We repelled another attack with the last of our ammo. I saw enemy coming up the hill again. I had an empty M1, so I hid behind a rock and got ready. I was going to use my M1 as a club on the first guy who came around the rock. I hit the guy around the eyes and he flew over the hill sideways. However, my rifle came in contact with the rock and broke apart.

I took off for the Platoon CP and stumbled onto Lt. Puckett, who was lying on the ground wounded. Rangers Walls and Pollock came from somewhere and I asked them to help me get him off the hill. He still has his .45 and three or four rounds of ammo. Walls got his left arm and I got his right with his face down. Pollock carried Walls' rifle and we started dragging Puckett. As we went over the hill and started down we ran into an enemy machinegun emplacement and before we knew it we dragged him over their position, knocking the gun off its mounting, and I fired what was left of the .45 ammo at them in the hole. Ranger Pollock took over for me.

I continued down the hill to find the tanks and started back to get Puckett. By this time, Chinese were all over the place, but we met Walls and Pollock still dragging Puckett. We got him to the tanks and put him on the back of one of them.

Merle Simpson

Somewhere between 0300 and 0400 hours, their last attack came. I heard Judy say, "Look out, Merle!" and I turned to see the Chinese over-running our positions. We immediately jumped out of our foxholes and by that time they were streaming by us in a crazy frenzy, shooting Rangers in their foxholes. I remember bumping into them while running toward Sgt. Morrissey's section. Since they were firing at Rangers in their foxholes we eventually outran them and joined Morrissey's squad.

I screamed at him to watch out and he said, "Fix bayonets!" I said, "Fix bayonets, hell! There are hundreds of them!"

By that time he could see their outlines on the ridgeline and he said, "Okay, let's go," at which time we started off the hill. Someone immediately got hit in the arm and I grabbed him and we all started over the hill. It was so steep that they could hear us running and falling, but they kept shooting over our heads.

Merrill Casner

Soon, the enemy overran us, passing over us and going on, but soon more came and checked us out. They began to shoot and bayonet us that were lying there wounded. The Hawaiian Ranger was shot in the face. I was shot in the back of the head but I survived, and with the help of the Lord I escaped, crawling through enemy lines and reaching the tanks.

The last Ranger I saw fighting on the early morning of November 26 at about 2:30 a.m., was Wilbert Clanton. I will swear at least six Chinese were on him. How many he killed or wounded will never be known by us, but I bet the North Koreans and Chinese know how many that Ranger took with him.

Billy Walls

We were hit hard again and again and we were low on ammo. About this time I heard someone yelling to fix bayonets and something about a counter-attack. Shortly after that, everything got calm and quiet. The full moon made it almost seem like daylight. It was at that time we saw someone coming around the hill. We covered him until we realized it was Ranger Judy, who had been wounded. He told us we'd been overrun on the right and Lt. Puckett had been hit. He told us where to find Lt. Puckett and we told him to find Morrissey and send help.

Walls' memories and those of Bill Judy are in conflict here. The reader can decide which one is correct, and whether or not details of 40-year-old memories matter so much as the overall view. Puckett said, "Judy was instrumental in my being saved. He was the first to see me as I was on my hands and knees by my foxhole. I told him to leave me behind. He went to get help. Ran into Pollock and Walls and told them where I lay. They came to get me."

Pollock and I started around the crest of the hill where we ran into three Chinese. We shot them. I don't think they returned a shot. We continued around the hill until we saw Lt. Puckett crouched on his hands and knees. I asked him if he was all right. He answered, "I'm hurt bad." I gave Pollock my weapon, picked Puckett up, threw him over my shoulder and started running. The Chinese were close, but Pollock held them off until we got in a small draw. By then I was so tired I couldn't carry Puckett any longer. Pollock caught up to us and asked if Puckett was still with us. Puckett said, "I'm still with you. I'm not going to leave you." Pollock answered, "We're not going to leave you, either, Sir."

At one point, Puckett ordered us to leave him. It was an order we didn't hear. Puckett was worried that we might be leaving someone behind, but we assured him we were the last ones on the hill. The draw we were in was full of brush and trees. Meanwhile, we were trying different ways to carry Puckett—all too slow—he finally told us to lay him down and drag him, which we did.

At one point, I asked him if he was all right. He said, "Yes, I'm all right. I'm a Ranger."

J. P. Vann Takes Command

Captain John Paul Vann took the reigns of the reconstituting Eighth Army Rangers on December 5, 1950, and promptly began to reorganize the company.

Vann had been a navigator in B-29 bombers during WWII, but had gone Airborne in 1946. The 25th ID brought him to Korea in July of 1950.

A character of the first order, Vann would go on to become a hero several times over during his military career, both in Korea and in Vietnam.

A small man, Vann had a huge heart and capacity for work. He took to the task of building and reorganizing the company like he was made for it, recruiting from within the 25th Division ranks, and using those from the replacement pool who fit his exacting profile. There wasn't a lot of time to properly train the new men, but the veterans did their best.

The company was allowed a third platoon.

Morning Report Extract

December 10, 1950

Eff 10 Dec 8 A Ranger Co 8213 A Unit reorganized per GO 188 Hq EUSAK dtd 17 Oct 50. Auth strength: 5 Officers 100 enlisted men.

The new TO&E for the company not only increased its size, it also eliminated the special weapons squad, and made the three squads in each platoon into 10-man groups. The Eighth Army Rangers really got some kind of parity with the new Ranger Infantry Companies, (Airborne), that were coming over when they were authorized a couple of jeeps and a deuce-and-a-half. They even got some cooks and a couple of communications men.

The company was also authorized to receive replacements from the newly formed Ranger Replacement Pool. There was at least a modicum of screening before new men went to the experienced company.

Charles Pitts

On a bright cold morning I was out at one of the squads' holes and somebody told me there was a Captain that would like to talk to me. I went to see this Captain, who was some 100 yards distant. Vann proved be a suitable replacement for Ralph Puckett. Not exactly a man a First Sergeant could fall in love with, but a man of courage, mental ability and high moral values.

A First Sergeant occupies a rather strange position if he knows his job. On the one hand, he must have loyalty to the unit commander and be able to execute his will, and at the same time make that will agreeable to the enlisted members of the unit so they will perform willingly. This takes a lot of diplomacy, and sheer gall on occasion, especially if from your own experience and personality you do not exactly agree with the man on top. While there were several occasions during which I did not personally agree with Puckett or Vann, I thought highly enough of them both. I have a son named Ralph and a grandson named Paul.

John Summers

After what seemed like forever we finally arrived at Kaesong. The long cold march was over, and though the Ranger Company had suffered many casualties and left many brave men dead on 205, the company stayed together as a fighting unit. At Kaesong we got our new company commander, Captain John Vann, and the company was once again brought up to strength. They added another platoon. Captain Vann was no stranger to the Korean War, as he had come over to Korea with the 25th Infantry Division, and he told us that he had always wanted to command a Ranger Company.

At Kaesong they sent us some more replacements, and each time a truckload showed up Captain Vann asked them if they wanted to fight with a Ranger Company. One truckload I remember, after they were asked that, every last one of them jumped back on the truck, saying they wanted no part of a Ranger Company.

Lieutenant Bunn remained in command of the 1st Platoon, Lt. Glenn Metcalf took the 2nd, and Lt. Richard Stiles took the 3rd. Though the new TO&E allowed more than 100 men, at that point the company fielded about 70.

Charles Pitts

In any case, we received orders to proceed to Kangwa-do, an island west of Seoul at the mouth of the Han River, to preclude the Chinese occupying that place, which would have placed them on the flank of the US Eighth Army.

Our close association with the Turkish Brigade began here, since they occupied the mainland adjacent to the island. Some DUKWs (a six-by-six truck with a boat hull for a body) were attached to us at this time and we used them to transport the unit and its impedimentia to the island. In order to transport our wheeled vehicles we bound two of the DUKWs together and made a ramp on top of them, then floated the whole contraption across the narrow expanse of water to the island.

John Summers

Our mission was to take over and control the entire island, which had around 300,000 civilians on it. The Chinese were using this island to hop from the mainland, move south on the island, then move back over to the mainland. This would put them south of the Eighth Army's front line.

We out-posted the island, and had our CP in the town of Kangsha-do. We sunk all boats we could find and destroyed all boats that tried to land on the island. For what it's worth, I found this type mission ideal for our company. We were also sending out recon patrols up the coast of the main land, using the Navy DUKWs. On one patrol we got into a good firefight, and at the time we were 10 or 12 miles north of the island.

Another part of the Ranger task was to help in the evacuation of the civilians. Vann reported moving almost 4,500 civilians to the mainland in a two-day period.

Christmas found the Rangers still on the island. As the story goes, a couple of fishing vessels were confiscated, lashed together, and made into a pontoon raft for a three-quarter-ton truck to be floated across to the mainland. This accomplished, the truck was filled with turkey and trimmings, and floated back across to the island. A delicious meal was prepared and the company was rotated through so all could have a share.

Three days later, orders for relief of the Rangers came through.

When Eighth Army Commander Walton Walker was killed in a jeep accident, the force was in temporary disarray. It was enough to force further withdrawal, which brought the Rangers off the island.

New Eighth Army Commander Matthew Ridgeway wasted no time getting things turned around and began a counter-offensive late in January. The Rangers were put to work "out front" of both the 25th and 1st Cavalry Divisions.

John Summers

When the Chinese made their big push on the mainland we got orders to pull off and join the 25th Division. We did this during the hours of darkness. At one point they were thinking of taking us off of the island by navy boats, and possibly using a submarine. We all thought that this would be a good idea. Anyway, we loaded up on the Navy DUKWs and went over to the mainland and marched toward Seoul, on Ranger in front of another. Though it was cold and the moon was bright, we made it back into friendly lines without incident.

We were soon patrolling north of the 38th Parallel. We were in front of the 25th Division, and also the 1st Cav.

On one night we moved into the positions of the 24th Regiment of the 25th Division, and they had just left, leaving a lot of their equipment and weapons behind. We found some weapons half-buried in the foxholes. This was just another reason why I was glad to be a Ranger.

Charles Ross To The End

In a few weeks, Captain Charles Ross came aboard as XO. Two weeks later, on the march, he became the commander.

Ross was a WWII veteran of the South Pacific Campaign, a proven leader with extensive patrolling qualifications, and Airborne. He was not Ranger-qualified.

By February 10, the Rangers exited Suwon and traveled to Inchon in the early hours, patrolling along the way, and arriving about 5:00 p.m. During the day the Rangers were joined by members of the 25th ID Recon Company, experienced old friends who walked with the Rangers toward Inchon, stopping frequently to deal with booby traps and mines left by the retreating enemy.

Frequent stops to deal with planted explosives kept the pace down, but the two companies eventually made it into Inchon. Given the security mission again, the Rangers patrolled the southwestern section of the city until running upon a small North Korean unit occupying some necessary high ground near an outlying railway station.

The 25th Recon Company provided mortar support while the Ranger 2nd Platoon routed the enemy, killing two.

J. P. Vann never got the chance to show what his Rangers could do. He accomplished the rebuilding of the company after its devastation on Hill 205—a fine act in itself—but no large battle or heavy contact was made during his short tenure. Captain Ross took over February 13, when Vann was called away to be with his sick child.

After 164 days of near-continuous front line combat duty, including four major campaigns, and a Presidential Unit Citation from South Korea, the first Ranger Company in Korea stood down. General Order 172 was read aloud to the assembled Eighth Army Ranger Company by Captain Charles Ross on March 28, 1951—the day they were disbanded.

Some of the men went to Airborne units, including Rangers, and others were scattered throughout the 25th ID.

Captain Ross, the last commander of the Eighth Army Rangers, went on to become the last commander of the 1st Ranger Infantry Company (Airborne) in August of 1951.

The position of responsibility of the Eighth Army Rangers passed to the 5th Ranger Infantry Company (Airborne) on March 31.

KOREAN WAR AIRBORNE RANGERS TRAINING AND ACTION

The Eighth Army Rangers were the first Rangers in Korea, but certainly not the last. In the States, Ranger Infantry Companies were formed as fast as they could be taught, an average of about four months from start to finish.

Of the 15 "number" Ranger Infantry Companies (Airborne) formed during the Korean War, only six saw combat. Of course, all of the new units received the same type of training, which inevitably got better as things went along. With that view, the last companies trained should have been the best trained simply because of the experience of the instructors and adjustments to the course. However, the first half of the companies through the new Ranger Training Center were the ones to go to war, with the exception of the 6th, which went to Germany, and the 7th, which stayed at Benning. The 1st through 5th, and 8th Companies went to Korea.

The rest were held in check in case the Soviets started something in Europe, and to act as replacements and instructors. Whether going to Korea or not, those were some tough boys coming out of Ranger training.

When General Lawton Collins came home from a tour of Korea—what he could see—he brought with him an idea that played itself out over the next year or so, beginning with a memorandum from Collins containing the concept of a "Marauder" Company. Collins wanted one company per division to perform behind-the-lines raids on static elements such as headquarters sites and artillery batteries. Even then, the thinking was to give the new units nothing extra in the way of mess and administration, requiring them to "feed" off another nearby unit.

The companies were to be limited to 100 men divided into three platoons, which were to be further divided into three squads of ten men each. For armament they were to have light automatic weapons with machineguns mounted on jeeps.

The General's proposal was studied by G-3 (Operations) and though accepted in theory, the concept was radically changed. The machineguns on the jeeps were gone, every man had to be Airborne-qualified, the name was changed to "Ranger," and the size of the units was increased.

Each new company was descended from a WWII Ranger Company, beginning with the four A Companies of each Ranger Battalion, all the way through to the 15th RICA.

WWII Battalions carried six companies, so there were plenty of lineages available.

Under Colonel John Van Houten, training commenced at the Infantry School at Fort Benning, commanded by General Burress. That single site didn't last long, and soon Ranger students were in the mountains and the swamps as well.

Cadre for the new school were recruited from men with WWII Ranger experience, including men from the First Special Service Force and Merrill's Marauders. Such men made a solid corps of tough, knowledgeable instructors. As for Airborne soldiers serving at the time, the call went out for volunteers from the 11th Airborne at Fort Campbell, but that unit had given much to punch up the 187th Regimental Combat Team (RCT), so most of the men came from the 82nd Airborne. Some 5,000 men volunteered, from all different MOSs (Military Occupation Specialty), so there was a ton of wide experience brought to bear.

Five days after Van Houten got his orders to get started on September 20, the first group of volunteers arrived at Fort Benning. The Director of Training was Lt. Colonel Henry Koepcke. The initial workload for training was set at six-48 hour weeks, but almost immediately lengthened to 60. Before long, the six weeks became eight very full weeks of very heavy work. The days were full of instruction and intense physical conditioning. Subjects included land navigation; how to bring direct and indirect fire from artillery, air support, and naval support to bear; weapons training with domestic and foreign pieces; and much more.

The heavy conditioning was for an intended purpose other than just having tough fighting men. Such men had to be able to move good distances in a hurry. Van Houten stated it flatly, saying his idea was, "To prepare a company to move from 40 to 50 miles cross-country in 12 to 18 hours depending on the terrain."

The men walked day in and day out, and when they got where they were going, like as not there was a raid or ambush to carry out. The companies were expected to move long distances and still be able to fight when they arrived.

One reason the US Army had such trouble capturing Apache Indians during the late 1800s was their ability to move 50 miles a day on foot through harsh terrain. Try to imagine hiking 50 miles through rough country in a driving cold rain with 80 pounds of equipment hanging all over you. Then add in the need for silence, constant watchfulness, and the possibility of sniper fire or an artillery barrage. Sound like fun?

October 2, 1950, 19 officers and 314 enlisted men organized into three companies and started training. On October 9, a company-sized unit containing five officers and 135 EM began training. They were originally designated the 4th RICA, but that was changed to the 2nd. These men were all African-American, and became known as the "Black Rangers."

TO&E number 787, dated October 17, set the mark at five officers and 107 men per company. At the time, conventional line companies sported six officers and 212 EM. Each company was separated into a Headquarters platoon and three rifle platoons of 33 men each; further division made a platoon HQ and three squads of 10 men each.

Squad armament was pretty hefty with two BARs, four M1s, and four M2 carbines, but even that could be augmented by .45 caliber Tommyguns, mortars and rocket launchers.

The companies were authorized 36 Thompson submachineguns as well as nine 3.5-inch rocket launchers, nine 60mm mortars, three .30 caliber air-cooled machineguns, and three 57mm recoilless rifles. Crew-served weapons were kept at company level and issued as needed. Either way, between the normal squad weapons and those kept ready for heavy need, the Ranger Companies humped a lot more weight in arms and ammunition than regular line units.

The Rangers cared for those weapons and other equipment, with strict guidelines enforced by the watchful eyes of instructors. Continued inefficiency in such matters got a man booted from the unit, and competition to be the best of the fledgling companies was fierce.

The first four Ranger Infantry Companies (Airborne) were graduated November 13, 1950. The new Rangers received the Ranger shoulder insignia and unit guidons.

Two days later the first group left for San Francisco, the point of embarkation to Korea. The very next day trainees for the 5th, 6th, 7th, and 8th Companies began to arrive at Benning. The full cycle began November 22.

By January 20, the 3rd, 5th, and 8th Companies were ready to be sent to Camp Carson, Colorado for some mountain training in some cold weather for a month before leaving for Korea.

Running up and down the Rockies in weather cold enough to freeze anything got the Rangers used to operating in the thin air and numbing temperatures. Cold-weather gear was issued, including trigger-finger mittens, and regular training in the arts of war continued, though geared to winter war.

They were frozen and wet most of the time. No place was flat. They sometimes had to tie their sleeping bags to trees to keep them from falling downhill while they slept. As if that wasn't enough, they even had to train with mules, though they would never use them in Korea.

Ranger training was hard and hazardous. As part of the graduation exercises (Hell Week) for the 3rd (second time through), 5th, 6th, 7th, and 8th Companies, a low-level night parachute jump was laid on over Lee Field at Benning. The men were dropped in a static-line jump from too low an altitude for their chutes to deploy and work effectively, causing some 22 casualties, one of them fatal.

Airborne training was mandatory and most men had it prior to coming aboard, but the later companies from the National Guard did not, and were made to go through the four-week course before going to Ranger School.

Before long the attrition rate weighing on the combat companies brought the call for replacements. This was a problem because the incoming recruits were to be returned as Ranger units to National Guard Divisions and not used in combat.

The decision was made to use the 7th and 9th Companies at Benning as replacement pools. Some of those men had already gone and the ranks were depleted, so nearly 200 men of the 82nd Airborne volunteered to fill them. Unfortunately that resource couldn't be used continually, as it was a Strategic Reserve unit and had to stay at full strength.

The move to add more Ranger Companies brought G-1 and G-3 representatives together on February 20, under the direction of the Department of the Army, to decide how to put more Rangers in the overall American forces while still providing replacements for the existing 11 companies.

At that time, the Ranger Companies were arranged thusly: 1st, 2nd, 4th in Korea, 3rd, 5th, 8th about to go to Korea, 6th in Germany, and 7th, 9th, 10th and 11th either at, or coming to, Fort Benning.

While the situation in Korea was still in flux and the amount of Rangers ultimately needed there was still unknown, certain Army brass wanted that style of training to be spread all over, and nine more companies were in the works. There were plans to put Rangers with the 28th, 31st, 43rd, and 47th Divisions, three non-divisional companies for the Caribbean, and one for Alaska, plus one for replacements only for FECOM (Far East Command). Since about one-third of those beginning Ranger training didn't make it, and another fifth were required as replacements, it took two recruits to produce one qualified man for a new Ranger Company. So, in order to produce the proposed nine companies—some thought 11 would be better—it would take more than 2,000 volunteers to fill the bill.

On March 5, the 3rd, 5th and 8th RICA boarded the *General William F. Hase* with many other troops of the Air Force and Marines, headed overseas.

The three war-bound companies reached Pusan on March 24, after a tumultuous shore leave in Kobe, Japan. By the 31st, they were coming into Inchon by sea. After a long seasick voyage the three companies parted, with the 3rd going to the 3rd Infantry Division, the 5th to the 25th Infantry Division, and the 8th to the 24th Infantry Division. In less than a month they would all be in the thick of some very heavy combat.

The Ranger Training Command became the Ranger Department April 5, 1951, and was gearing into full swing.

Still, nobody knew for certain what would happen in Korea, so Ranger Companies were still being formed. The Fourth Cycle was in the beginning phase as the Third Cycle closed out.

The second wave of Ranger Infantry Companies arrived just in time for the Chinese Fifth Phase Offensive. The communist forces made a last-gasp attempt to stop the Allied advance beginning April 22 with a massive effort, but stopping short of significant gains north of Seoul.

The newly arrived Ranger Companies were thrust into the fire almost immediately, becoming involved in several serious fights as the Chinese pushed against the Allied lines.

Back in the states, volunteers completed airborne training and reported for Ranger training, while others were just coming in for the beginning courses that may get them as far as the real thing. The new men were to assigned to the 12th and 14th Companies, and two Trainee Companies labeled A and B. The Fourth Cycle got under way April 30.

Not long after the Chinese April Offensive, there was enough progress in peace talks and stalemate on the battlefield to produce a stagnant theater of war in which men died while negotiators carefully plied their trade in far-away cites. The days of the Ranger Companies were counting down, though it was not generally known at the time.

Van Houten was promoted to Brigadier General and left the Ranger Training Command on August 7, 1951. His successor, Colonel Wilbur Wilson, saw the addition of the word "Airborne" to the Command, which was soon renamed the Ranger Department.

The last training cycle for Ranger Infantry Companies (Airborne) ended September 1, 1951.

RANGER INFANTRY COMPANIES (AIRBORNE)

RICA Battle High Points

A list put out by the RICA Association highlights the major combat operations of the Korean War Rangers.

RAIDS

    Changmal

    Hwachon Dam

    Hill 383

    Topyong-ni

BATTLES

    CQ45954 (map coordinates)

    Chipyong-ni

    299 Turkey Shoot

    Bloody Nose Ridge

    Majori-ri

    Hill 628

    Objective Sugar

    May Massacre

    Sangwiryang

Ranger Awards

Individual awards were commonplace among the Ranger ranks. Of the seven companies to fight in Korea, there were four Distinguished Service Crosses, 33 Silver Stars, and 43 Bronze Star Medals. There were many other awards, and the number of Purple Hearts was huge.

Individual units also collected hard-earned awards, including two Presidential Unit Citations awarded to the 1st Ranger Infantry Company (Airborne).

History—1st—15th RICA

1st RICA

Commanded by Captain John Striegel

Directly descended from WWII Rangers, as were they all, the 1st RICA came from Company A, 1st Battalion. Most officers for this company were volunteers, but not all. Some came from the 82nd Airborne, some from the replacement depot.

November 25—the day the Chinese came across the Yalu River in Korea—the company boarded the troop ship *C. G. Morton*, leaving harbor at 1:00 p.m. An announcement was made that the North Koreans were on the run and the war was about to be over, which gladdened the hearts of everyone on board except the Rangers, who were spoiling for a fight. A subsequent message was aired reversing everything said in the first announcement, since news of the Chinese invasion was just coming across the wires. The Rangers were actually happy.

Captain Striegel contracted hepatitis and was temporarily replaced by Lieutenant Alfred Herman on December 6.

Training continued aboard ship until disembarkation in Japan. The company entrained for the short trip to Camp Zama, leaving shortly thereafter by ferry for the 150 mile journey to Pusan.

Landing in Korea December 17, 1950, the company was attached to 2nd ID, which had the 38th, 23rd and the 9th Regiments, as well as attached Netherlands and French Volunteer Battalions.

On arrival, the 1st Company found the 2nd ID refitting near Chjungju. By the end of December the Division was back in harness near Wonju, a rail and road nexus that was the center of the American line. The 1st Rangers were immediately placed out front of the 23rd and 38th Regiments and commenced patrolling duties.

The communists captured a four-man patrol on December 31. Not one made it back.

When the Chinese thrust slowed, the Eighth Army began Operation Thunderbolt and the 1st Rangers were alerted for a possible recon mission deep behind enemy lines, but General Ridgeway thought otherwise. If the Rangers were caught back there, he surmised, they wouldn't get out alive. The mission was scrubbed before actual orders could be given. If such a move were to be made, a larger body of men, such as a Regimental Combat Team, would have to go.

A couple of patrols on January 2 brought some action about six miles west of Yong Dong rail station when they established an outpost near a bridge. A man was lost there on a patrol, killed by his own men trying to get back into the lines.

The 2nd Division was hit hard by three North Korean Divisions near Wonju on January 7, pushing them back a little. The Rangers were in the thick of the delaying action. A couple of days later, in the frozen, snow-bound morning, a patrol ran into an estimated 200 enemy near Chungchon and a firefight developed. The crippling cold was hard on both men and weapons as both 2nd and 3rd Platoons were sent in to back up the patrol. The fight escalated for a time, going on into the afternoon, but both sides decided to break it off and things died down.

The company was on patrol, setting up an ambush about four miles out front of the 38th Regiment on January 16 when they received word to move forward toward Wonju until they made contact. Support was set up for a deep scout and the 1st moved into the town of Kirichi. There were supposed to be about 30 North Korean soldiers there, but when the company arrived, they found 31 women. They stayed the night.

They were subsequently attached to the 9th Regiment to be "used to the fullest" in patrols to the north. Between the 20th and 31st of the month they patrolled heavily in the vicinity of Sillim-ni.

A couple of jeeps mysteriously appeared in the Ranger unit, and the men mounted machineguns on them and went on vehicular patrol. This resulted in locating what was perhaps half a company of the enemy that the Rangers attacked and drove into a pre-set blocking position where the fleeing unit was destroyed.

The last of January found the 1st Rangers on patrol near Chipyong-ni, in a hot area known as the Twin Tunnels. The dark tunnels were spooky, but Rangers patrolled right through them.

The beginning of February again found the Rangers out in front of the 38th Regiment. Oddly enough, they couldn't find much in the way of opposition, so they set up an ambush. One platoon sat around fires, acting as decoys, while the rest of the company hid out and waited. Before long, the bait was taken and the Rangers had their fight. The enemy didn't hang out very long, withdrawing before the massed firepower of the 1st RICA.

Changmal Raid

A day later, the company moved to Hoengsong to prepare for one of the most famous Ranger raids of the war. The Headquarters of the 12th North Korean Division was located nine miles behind the lines at a town called Changmal.

Here was a mission the Rangers had been trained for. Planning was detailed and thorough. The terrain was rough, the cold mountains full of the enemy. The 1st was to travel outside regular communications range, so a light plane was to over-fly them at certain times on February 6 and act as radio-relay. No circling would be allowed so as not to give away the company's position.

It was a good idea that didn't work. The small fixed-wing couldn't find the Rangers, so they were out of touch almost the whole trip.

Using compass headings and landmarks, the company set out through the moonscape topography, heavy-laden with tracer ammunition and confidence.

Near the small town of Songbau, two squads were placed on a ridged overlook while the rest moved down in the valley, supposedly covered by the men up high. Unfortunately, that small element came under fire, and time was taken to outflank the attackers and eliminate them.

The 1st closed on Changmal in a wet deep-freeze to see lights and hear voices in the houses of the town. One platoon was sent forward to check things out. A guard challenged them and the fight was on.

The Rangers were close, some within 10 yards, and they threw bullets and grenades as fast as they could as the enemy poured out the buildings. The ammunition was all tracers to better direct fire. The night was lit up by the streaking death. The North Koreans were overwhelmed in short order, the town on fire. Their job done, the Rangers turned for home.

A prisoner captured on the way back told them the town they'd just hit was actually what they'd been told by 2nd Division G-2, the HQ of the 12th NK Division.

The route home was longer than the way in, and the Rangers were carrying three wounded men over the rugged terrain. The decision was made to leave the wounded with a small stay-behind force while the rest of the Company continued on to friendly lines. The idea was to send a helicopter out for the group in the field.

The decision to leave his men behind, even temporarily, must have been a difficult one for Company Commander Herman. One man was seriously wounded and may not have survived the arduous trip back, and transporting stretchers over such terrain would be slow going, indeed.

The lead group returned to the 38th Regiment lines in the late afternoon of February 7, and told their story of men still out there. A helicopter was called for, but it developed engine trouble and couldn't fly.

Time passed.

About dawn the following morning a Ranger patrol was sent out to bring the men back. On the way they were surrendered to by seven North Koreans who told them the North Koreans had withdrawn, suspecting the Rangers were part of a larger attack. Good news, but it left the patrol with prisoners that had to be taken back to American lines. More time passed.

Seven men of the 1st Squad, 1st Platoon, had been left with the three wounded men. They sheltered in an abandoned hut, no doubt wondering what was happening while they shivered in the violent cold.

At that point, heroic action was performed by First Sergeant Romeo Castonguay, who didn't like the way things were going and went out on his own to get his men. In time, he found them and got them organized, building a litter out of ponchos for a man shot in the legs. The small group traveled about six crow-flight miles, but added many more going up and down the mountains.

First Sergeant Castonguay would die a few days later in an assault near Chipyong-ni.

For this action, the 1st Ranger Infantry Company (Airborne) received the Distinguished Unit Citation. In the words of Major General Clark Ruffner, "Their devotion to duty and desire to get the job done is a splendid example of our American soldiers with an aggressive spirit and the will to win."

Al Bukaty

Al Bukaty was cornered in the back of the NCO club at CFM during the 2004 Open House. Our conversation about how well Rangers do in the business world brought these comments.

Well, when you went into the Rangers, you had that something ingrained in you, and you'd probably be successful no matter what. It took a certain type of individual to want to volunteer for the Rangers. If I'm going to be in combat, I would want to be with the Rangers.

Bukaty originally signed up for three years in 1947.

Once the war got started, we all got extended for another year. That was when I joined the Rangers. I think it was August 1951, when we all got sent to the 187th [Regimental Combat Team, Airborne]. We were a little bit afraid the war would be over before we got there.

Bukaty went over as a Private and came back as a Sergeant First Class.

I spent a lot of time as a PFC in the 82nd, but once I got in the Rangers...

What follows was tape-recorded.

I have a story about the battle of Chipyong-ni. That was a very famous fight. I was there from beginning to the end of that.

Just before the battle of Chipyong-ni we were sent out to capture some prisoners. A French reporter went with us, and he got killed. I was right there when he got killed. The first and last time we ever took a reporter with us.

Our company commander was Lieutenant Hermann, from St. Louis, Missouri. He got crossways with the Colonel there at Chipyong-ni about taking a hill. The Commander asked for supporting fire before we sent our troops across to go up the hill, and they refused to give it to us. He got crossways because of it. I think the Company Commander might have been relieved of his position because of it.

We had a fella who joined us at Chipyong-ni. His name was Sergeant Rinard, and he was only with us a couple of days and he got killed. I don't know what possessed me, but I wrote his widow a letter back in 1951. The reason I wrote the letter, he was only there two days and he got killed, and she probably wondered what the hell happened. He's there and he's dead. He didn't really know anybody. He wasn't there long enough. So, I told her how he passed away...how brave he was...that she should be proud of the exploits that he had.

I didn't think anything about it, but now this 2004, and five or six months ago I got a phone call.

Turns out it was Sergeant Rinard's son, Steve. He had the letter. They met in Iowa after speaking on the phone several times. Bukaty found out that Rinard had been a Ranger in WWII, was captured twice, and escaped twice.

I was really amazed that after 50 years that letter showed up.

Chipyong-ni

In the early evening of February 11, the 1st Rangers left Chipyong-ni and went on a patrol to the small town of Miryang-ni, which featured a little high ground they hoped to use as an observation point—the hills around Chipyong-ni were not very tall. After dark the patrol found some enemy dug in on a ridge and got a sample of Chinese heavy machinegun fire interspersed with mortar rounds. The Rangers were undeterred, going forward until they were able to take a prisoner and inflict damage. One man was lost in this action.

For a short time after that the Rangers and B Company of the 23rd Regiment were placed in Regimental reserve, where they endured frequent mortar fire. Another man was lost there.

Allied elements around Chipyong-ni—including a French Battalion—were arranged like a wagon train circle, knowing an attack was imminent, but not knowing the direction. The night of February 13, the sky fell in.

The night turned eerie when bugles and cymbals produced a cacophony of discordant noise designed to instill fear in the waiting Allied soldiers. A heavy artillery barrage lit up the area just before midnight, followed by the Chinese storming forward into massed Allied fire. The fight raged all night, with the communists withdrawing just before dawn to escape the coming aircraft.

The next night they were back at it, throwing away the lives of their soldiers so fast the Allies began to run low on ammunition. In places, the Chinese were able to push through temporarily. A run into G Company, 23rd Infantry, busted a hole through a hilltop position about 3 a.m. and caused the Americans to withdraw. The hole just sat there, waiting to be plugged or infiltrated, with a contingent of Chinese setting up defenses at the top of the hill.

A combat team was hurriedly put together out of units who had never seen each other before, including about 33 Rangers under Lt. Mayo Heath, 28 men of F Company, 23rd Infantry, and the remaining G Company men of the 23rd—there weren't many left.

The small hill had to be taken, and the Ranger commander made it known he thought the hill should be prepared by artillery fire first and the Rangers should be given the mission as a Company. He was overruled mainly because there wasn't any heavy ordnance to spare.

The Ranger platoon would take the right side of the hill with F and G Company, 23rd, on the left. French troops and Allied tanks were also in support, but it was not they who went up the hill. The attack up the hill began about 6:30 in the morning with the men racing forward into dug-in mortar and machinegun fire. The "heavy" weapons carried by the Americans, amounting to a few machineguns and 60mm mortars, were soon mostly out of action due to incoming fire.

The attack was so confused by the irregular make-up of the combat team that several errors occurred. Among them was the firing of French machineguns into the Rangers, as well as a few .50 caliber rounds from a tank. The platoon of Rangers was taking it from all sides. In all, 12 men of the platoon were hit—more than a third. In spite of that, the only Americans to reach the top of the hill were Rangers. The few who made it were joined by wounded Rangers still moving forward, and together they defended the hilltop against overwhelming odds, the sharp battle coming down to hand-to-hand fighting. The last surviving Rangers had to withdraw when no help was forthcoming. Platoon Leader Heath was one of the dead.

Early the next morning, 2nd and 3rd Platoons of the 1st Rangers and B Company of the 23rd were sent in to try again. The idea of prepping the hill was belatedly considered, and 155mm artillery and quad-.50 caliber machinegun fire was directed at the Chinese, who could not hold in the face of all that incoming steel.

The 1st Rangers were all but done in from the fight, losing 11 killed and 31 wounded. Between those losses and the injuries that had come before, the Company was down to about a platoon of effectives.

May Massacre

By May 1, UN forces had been pushed back south of the Kansas line—an imaginary line set as a geographical goal—several thousand yards below the Hwachon Dam. The new line was called "No Name Line" for obvious reasons.

The Eighth Army, reorganizing hourly, began to push back. The 1st Rangers, previously attached to the 38th Infantry of the 2nd Division, were transferred into a new Task Force, called Zebra. Joining the Rangers were B Company, 9th Infantry, and F Company, 38th Infantry, all backed up by a battalion of the 72nd Tanks.

The Rangers had taken replacements and returned wounded and were over a hundred men strong as they spread out on ridgelines north of Chuchon-ni. Nothing much happened there—a good thing—since the French were on the Ranger left and the ROK were on their right. The 1st Rangers took a prisoner, and then went into reserve with the 72nd Tanks until Zebra was attached to the 2nd Battalion of the 23rd Infantry on May 14.

A couple of days later, the Chinese thumped the 5th ROK out of position and exposed the east flank of the 2nd Division. Task Force Zebra was on the right side of the 2nd Division line and faced 12 Chinese Divisions trying to swing through the hole left by the fleeing South Koreans.

The enemy hit all along the 2nd Division line, which was constantly shifting itself to accommodate the attacks. The Rangers were moved more to the center of the line with the 38th Infantry, arriving just in time to be involved in heavy attacks on its command post.

The Chinese were coming down from the north in long lines and attacking boldly, coming on through heavy US artillery fire. Their bodies began to stack up.

At one point the hard-pressed line of the 38th began to crumble. The 2nd Battalion was overrun and another hole developed. The 1st Battalion was not operating as a full unit, and the whole Regiment was in danger of being overwhelmed.

The 1st Rangers were sent in to plug the hole after a Dutch Battalion tried it and was repulsed from Hill 710. As the Rangers were going up the Dutch were coming down, and they didn't paint a very good picture as they told the Rangers not to go up there. Of course, being Rangers, they went, anyway. They took the hill, holding it long enough for the division to get its legs back under it.

The Chinese didn't want the Rangers there and tried hard to dislodge them, showering fire down from higher ground. Masses of enemy troops were on the move, but more than 30,000 artillery shells smacked into them, killing an estimated 5,000 or more. They were attempting to envelop the 38th Infantry before it got reorganized, but the Rangers stopped large portions of them from moving forward.

Eventually, enough of the enemy did get through. The 38th, along with the Rangers, was ordered to withdraw. It was not easy to get away, as the Chinese almost had the units surrounded. The US took many casualties trying to break free, and a lot of them were Rangers. There were also more than a few men taken prisoner, including Captain Carrier of the 1st Rangers, who would later be killed in captivity.

By May 19, only 62 men of 107 were able to do their duty. The 2nd Division has lost about 900 men. But, as bad as it was, the Chinese had lost an estimated 35,000 men in that portion of their failed Fifth Phase Offensive, leading to the action around the Rangers and the 38th becoming known as the "May Massacre."

For their actions the 1st Rangers were awarded a second Distinguished Unit Citation.

Captain Charles Ross took over the reins of the 1st RICA on June 8. He had been the last commander of Eighth Army Ranger Company, and he would be the last commander of 1st RICA.

Al Bukaty

We were in trouble and calling for air support. The first plane that came in bombed our hill, strafed it. Some of the guys got killed. The second plane that came in right behind him—he had napalm. Thank God someone had the presence of mind to put a panel up [identifying marker panel]. The second guy saw the panel and hit the proper hill. The way he dropped it, I said a prayer, but it went above us and went forward and hit the Chinese.

We were leaving. I was doing delaying fire and I was probably one of the last guys out. The Chinese were behind us and on the side of us. When I got down there [rally point], the Chinese were in front of us, and most of the Rangers were gone.

There were Chinese up the hill [where he had just come from]. I got hit [through the arm]. I figured if somebody's shooting at me, they got me in their line of fire, so I lay down. I did a flip at the time—the bullet didn't knock me over—probably just a reaction, it happened so fast. So I lay there, and I knew they were watching me and if I moved, I'm going to get shot again. The Chinese were walking right past me. I was on my face...and I could see their tennis shoes. Nobody bothered me. Probably lay there for two hours without moving. It started getting dark. I started looking around and I heard a voice. "I thought you were dead!"

There was a guy lying right next to me, doing the same thing. I didn't know it. He was a little behind me. He was wounded real bad. I had some morphine syrettes and I gave him a couple of shots.

The two men began to move slowly, but every time the wounded soldier moved, he moaned.

I said, "You gotta be quiet, or they're going to hear you." It was quiet out there. There was nobody else. It was the two of us and the Chinese.

They did hear him. I looked up and I could see some silhouettes. I could see the Chinese come down, five or six of them.

Bukaty said the idea was to get to a short drop-off and try to crawl as far away from the enemy as they could.

But, he panicked. He got up and started running, and he got chewed up. I didn't know where to go. There was a hay pile there and I crawled right into the center of that thing. The Chinese came by, and they were standing around the hay pile, laughing. I thought they knew I was in there. Finally, they went back up the hill and back down the hill.

There was a gully right there, and I thought, I'm going to get in the gully, because there was a large stream there, and I wanted to get in that stream. I got down to the bottom of it, and now it's raining. There's a path there. I got close to it, and there comes a Chinese patrol. I wasn't three feet off that trail, and I pushed my face into [the ground]. They had raincoats on. They walked right by me and didn't see me. I got into the water and got centered, and kind-of crawled away.

Bukaty stayed in the stream for some time, through the night, encountering another Chinese patrol along the way. Sometimes he could almost stand up in the water; sometimes he had to lie down. Finally the stream "petered out," and he started walking, until an American sentry challenged him.

2nd Rangers

Commanded by First Lieutenant (later Captain) Warren E. Allen

From Company A, 2nd Ranger Battalion, WWII.

The 2nd Company left the States with the 4th on December 9, and got to Japan on Christmas Eve. The flight to Korea the last of December with five officers and 116 EM ended with attachment to the 7th Infantry Division, made up of the 31st, 32nd, and 17th Regiments.

Segregation was the order of the day for the division—via Corps HQ—and the men of the 2nd were kept separate. Every one was an African-American and as such they were known as the "Black Rangers."

The Rangers went forward with the 7th ID to Wonju to get in the way of the enemy coming down from the northeast. Arriving in Changnim-ni January 5, they found it full of guerilla activity. A roadblock was established a couple of days later and about 20 of the enemy tried to pass through early in the morning of the seventh. The Rangers fired them up and they scattered. A few hours later an enemy force of about 150 attacked the 2nd Rangers' HQ and a nearby medical facility. The move was broken apart by the Rangers, with the loss of a man and three wounded.

The 7th Division reacted to the frequent guerilla attacks by imposing a strictly enforced curfew in the Tanyang area. The policy was: if you were Korean, you better not be out after dark or your life may be forfeit. This policy was tested a few times with bloody results.

January 9 found the 3rd Platoon of the 2nd on patrol near Changnim-ni in the morning. As with their brothers in the 1st Company, a firefight ensued and they waded in the snow until mid-afternoon.

A couple of days later, the company was given the mission of being part of a counter-attack force made up of American and ROK troops. The mission of these forces was to hold the passes around the Tanyang area.

The cold was bone crunching. Weapons froze along with the men.

The company came upon a village and cleared it, taking up positions there. A man was lost to a non-combatant female on entering the village when she pulled a pistol and murdered him with his weapon slung. She joined him immediately.

At dawn on the 12th, the company sent a recon element out which took fire and was pinned down. Reinforcements were sent and heroics were performed by two Rangers who repeatedly showed themselves to the enemy until fired upon, which diverted the enemy's attention long enough for the patrol to extract itself.

Try to imagine yourself deep in snow with bullets coming in so hard no one could get away. Then figure you expose yourself to that fire, over and over, drawing the metal death to you so your mates can get free.

Majori-ri to Chechon

The village of Majori was supposed to be full of enemy soldiers as American forces, including the 2nd Rangers, looked down upon it from the heights. The Chinese had withdrawn, however, and taken up high positions of their own on the other side of town. The Americans had to go down into the town and secure it, then fight their way up the opposite slope—all while being fired upon from above.

Eight men of the 2nd died there, along with many others.

There was not a lot of open ground, but there was some, and the US soldiers had to cross it. Many died in a half-frozen creek running beside the town.

With very little time to regroup after the battle, the company moved about 12 miles to Tanyang and went into patrol mode, looking for guerillas until near the end of January, when they were attached on the 29th to the 17th RCT.

During the first part of February the company was attached to different regiments as needed, moving around to plug whatever hole was open at the time. Eventually, they came to Chuchon-ni, and were attached to the 32nd RCT. The target was Chechon—captured on the 20th when the Rangers went through in a whirlwind.

Musan-ni—First Ranger Combat Jump

The 2nd was taken 200 miles to Taegu after that, and attached to the 187th ARCT. Training continued for a proposed airborne mission as the company—with the 4th Rangers and the 187th—practiced jumping from aircraft and becoming—if possible—more proficient with their weapons.

Then came Operation Tomahawk, an offshoot of Operation Ripper. The plan called for an airborne assault at Musan-ni, just 24 miles northwest of Seoul. The idea was for the 2nd and 4th Rangers and the 187th to jump in, and then link up with Task Force Growden, coming up from Seoul with some tanks.

As each company would require four C-46 aircraft—and the 187th was three battalions strong—the jumps would be made in serial fashion with the Rangers in the second wave behind the 3rd Battalion of the 187th.

Also used were C-47s and C-119s, most of which went to the 187th.

At 7:30 a.m. on March 23 some 90 C-119s and 50 C-46s and C-47s began lifting off the runway at Taegu with H-Hour standing at 9:00 a.m. The 187th alone would require almost an hour to drop. In all, close to 3,500 men would make the jump.

At 9:15 a.m., the 2nd and 4th made the first combat jump in Ranger history. Overall, of 3,500 jumpers, there were slightly more than 100 casualties upon landing. They were cared for by Indian medics.

The first few men of the 2nd Rangers to reach their assembly area reacted to some Chinese machinegun positions prepped to shower fire on the rest of the company, and took them out. Those men were to turn in the first prisoners.

The 2nd were under control of the 2nd Battalion, which sent them to take Hill 151. First, however, the Rangers went through the village of Sangdokso-ri, killing six of the enemy and capturing 20.

The attack on Hill 151 garnered some air and mortar support as the 2nd charged forward. The hill was taken with the loss of one man and the wounding of two others. Later that evening the link-up with TF Growden was made.

The 3rd Infantry relieved the Rangers and others, and the 2nd made it back to Taegu on March 31.

Four days later, they were on the move again, assigned as a training unit for black replacements coming into the 7th Division. Fifty-two men initially reported for duty, the first of many, and the ranks of the company swelled. There was talk of forming a provisional Ranger Company. Before long, there was a full complement—per TO&E—of Rangers in the company, and nearly 300 more "attached." The men of the 2nd were tasked with training men carrying an MOS of "driver."

Still, there was a war on, and the 2nd Rangers were walking patrols and filling holes along with their training duties, which gave the new men ample opportunity to learn the rigors of war first hand.

The Chinese Fifth Phase Offensive of April 22 put everybody to work. Some ROK units were broken up by heavy assaults and the 35th Regiment, ROK 6th Division, was in disarray. The 2nd Rangers were beefed up and the company took over the slot previously held by the re-organizing 35th.

The 2nd Rangers were, like all the Ranger Companies, in the thick of the fighting against the communist offensive. The Chinese were probing along the contact points of the various UN units, looking for weak spots. The 2nd Rangers were sent out to deter them.

The Chinese had taken Hill 581, but the 2nd took it back, leaving the enemy with nearly 150 casualties. Not to be outdone, the Chinese—estimated at Regiment strength—countered with a strong attack after midnight, an assault that degenerated into hand-to-hand combat. Company XO James Queen saw no alternative but to call artillery fire down almost on top of the tenuous Ranger position.

Though the war was "winding down" for the Rangers, the various units had work until the end. In June, the 2nd Company spent a few days attacking the enemy beginning with Hill 772 and continuing beyond. The attacks were routine for the tough Rangers, yet the attrition took one more killed and 15 wounded from their ranks.

2nd RICA—Queen, Payne, Allen, Lyles

This interview was taped in Atlantic City, New Jersey, during a two-hour meeting in December 2003, with four veterans of the 2nd Ranger Infantry Company (Airborne)—the vaunted "Black Rangers" of the Korean War. These four men, James Queen, Sam Payne, Don Allen, and Paul Lyles, all gave input to the history of the unit beginning with how they came to be Rangers.

Queen was the Executive Officer of the 2nd RICA and was the chief speaker. The subject matter on the tapes tends to jump around some, but in order to present it in context it appears here in unabridged form. What you read is what I heard.

Queen: There were five black units, but the dominant black battalion in the 82nd Division was the 3rd Battalion of the 505th Airborne. After that was the 80th Anti-Aircraft Battalion, and then the 758th Tank Battalion. Airborne units had a tank battalion at that time. Most of the recruits came from the 3rd Battalion. The 3rd Battalion was the "triple nickel" renamed (555th).

The service integrated the 555th into the 82nd. They just changed us over. We just changed guidons—the same people. Instead of being the 3rd of the 555th, we were the 3rd of the 505th.

Payne: All of the guys that went into the 2nd Ranger Company, all of them came out of the 505 and the 555th and they were all black units from the get-go.

We were the only black Rangers. [There were none in the other Ranger Companies to begin with] Until later on, when they started integrating. All the blacks went to 2nd Company. In fact, we couldn't pick up any replacement jumpers because of the segregation policy.

The question was asked about how the men got to be Rangers.

Queen: It was a universal call, but remember now, black soldiers were in a separate cantonment area of the post. We were not next to the white units. We were like about three miles from the post area where the main division was. We were in what was called Spring Lake area, where all the blacks were—758th Tank Battalion, 80th Anti-Aircraft Battalion, 666th Truck Company, 587th and 585th Ambulance Companies—all the black units were in this one area.

If you go to Bragg now where the main PX is, that was our area.

The notice was sent down verbally [Regimental First Sergeant's Call], then they set up a recruiting team. They visited the 80th and the 3rd Battalion. They were up the hill from us about half-a-mile. That's how I found out, next morning at Reveille.

Allen: Most of us got it by word of mouth. Somebody came in and told us there was a Ranger outfit forming up. We didn't even know what that meant. But, it was an opportunity to advance ourselves. I was doing good and I didn't want to go anywhere. But they said, you go with the Rangers, you get to see some fighting, going to get some rank—they make everybody a Sergeant in the Rangers. So that's the way we went.

Payne: They really asked for volunteers. Most of these guys…were volunteers, first for the Airborne and then the Rangers, consequently everybody there wanted to be where they were going.

The questioning turned toward war, but the chronology is somewhat skewed.

To begin, they were asked about being a "replacement company" in Korea for a time.

Queen said the company roster got as high as 300 at one point, when it should have been about 107.

Queen: It was politics that ended it. That Sunday when Parks cooked that cobbler and put salt in it instead of sugar—we were always in the process of scrounging—we were attached and detached in the flick of an eye. We had no organic mess. We would order rations with one unit and be with another when the rations came in. The question is, do you go all the way back there, or do you scrounge up what you got? We tried to carry as much as we could. That's why we did some "moonlight requisitioning" of vehicles and things like that.

What happened was, we were training and the word came down there was a breakthrough up there. The division was alerted to move within 24 hours, so we moved from X Corps to IX Corps. Under the IX Corps we were no longer under Almond [General Almond commanded X Corps] and the segregation rule didn't apply, so the men went to where they were [previously] assigned. We had men who were assigned to the Band, Quartermasters, Tankers, MPs, but they were on special duty, detached service to us.

We left one officer with them to [help them disperse], and we went immediately on an overnight trip, and changed from X to IX Corps overnight.

The entire 7th Division made the change.

Queen: Well, what happened, we thought we were going to go to the 25th Infantry, but they changed it and sent us to the 7th Division. They were short of manpower and they were picking up every replacement they could. The battalion we joined, there were only 25 original men left from the Hungnam Evacuation. The rest of them were casualties or [missing].

The whole division was in bad shape. So as far as having an advance party to meet us…

Queen: They were in bad shape. Food and ammo were scarce. You know how we got our first load of ammunition? We shared our ammo with the Band. We got one case of hand grenades, that's all. It was just what we brought on our backs was what we had. We didn't bring any ammunition [besides personal small-arms ammo]. There was a ship blown up [the ammo ship].

Allen: Well, there was no welcoming committee. People say, well, what did you want, a band? No, we didn't want a band, but there's a unit up there we're going into, half of them wiped out. Even if you got to send a Private back to say, oh, man, we're glad to see you guys. Nobody ever said that—until after we went into a couple of battles—then everybody wanted those black Rangers. We earned that right. When we went up the hill, nobody was there. Everybody was running. But we had said we're not going to run.

You know how the bayonets are, they're blued. We took all the bluing off our weapons. I remember taking my bayonet and sticking it down in the sand, scrubbing it until it got shiny. When you start up that hill you demonstrate it. Wave that bayonet so the sun can shine off of it. And most times when we got up the hill, there wasn't anybody, because they were gone.

The second night we got into a firefight.

Queen: The first of January, the X Corps started moving back up. The 2nd Division was in the lead; behind them was, I think, the 3rd Division, then the Marines, then the 7th, then the 187th. Everybody had to go up this one road. There was only one MSR [main supply route] for the Corps. So, we moved out on the first. It took us two days to get up to the line, around Tanyang and Chunchon.

The "line" was about 40 km below the 38th Parallel. The situation was extremely fluid at the time. The UN forces had taken a huge blow from the Chinese and were in the middle of reorganizing, trying to fight back, and plugging holes at the same time. Into this mix were thrust the untried 2nd Rangers.

To the right of us were the ROKs [South Korean Capitol Division], all the way over to the water's edge.

Payne: A lot of times you wouldn't have a main line of resistance [MLR]. When we started pushing back up north, that's when they starting establishing…

Queen: The guerillas were coming down the mountains. The mountain range was between the sea and X Corps. That's what was happening. They were coming down, going behind the big units and attacking the auxiliary units. The Americans were sticking to the roads.

Payne: Before we really knew you were supposed to take the high ground first, then the main road. You got to stop going up the main road.

Queen and Payne both stated here that the main reason for the Rangers being there in the first place was to counter the guerillas. They ended up going way past that job description.

Allen: The front lines were quiet. Wasn't anybody getting killed up there. It was the guerillas, back where we were.

The men said they were a line infantry unit at that point, and didn't initially have an anti-guerilla role.

Queen: We were assigned to the 17th Regiment. The Regimental Commander gave us the job of holding open the Tanyang Pass. The Pass was like the Khyber Pass like you read about in India. It was a vital pass. It would only hold one-way traffic through it. MPs were on guard up there.

We'd let one line go down, then hold them up and let the other line go down [the other way], then at night, we'd hear them say, button up. So, we'd hold the north end of the pass, we were guarding the Regimental Aid Station, we were patrolling around there to keep the area clear.

This was January 4th to about the 15th or 16th. The whole Division moved up on the 14th, around Chunchon.

Payne: Any time one of those Regiments like the 17th or 32nd, any time they have a 10-day engagement, 2nd Company would be spearheading that operation.

The talk turned toward the move on Majori.

Queen: I went as guide for A Company of the 32nd. We were attached to the 17th, but overnight we were attached to the 32nd because they were getting ready to make a big push against a guerilla battalion up in the hills.

Allen: This wasn't anywhere near the front lines. We never did get up to the front lines. The first or second day we were there we got in a firefight and lost a man. Our job was to get [a school and aid station] on the side of a hill.

To show the kind of situation we were in, the enemy at night would come directly into your foxhole. As soon as we got there, it was dig in, dig in. The "old" airborne was like that. When you stop, dig in. Well, the ground was hard, so we got some of these "friendly" South Koreans, come for cigarettes, and they'd dig you a hole. We were wondering why they could see so well at night. We see flashes, we shoot up into the hills, but they're coming right into the holes.

So the next morning some of the same guys come along, and then some GIs on their way up to the front, and we'd ask how those guys could shoot so good at night. They'd answer, hell, they ought to be able to hit you, you had them dig your hole!

We learned a lot then. Anyway, there was this road, a valley to the left, through the hollow.

Men of the 2nd occupied the schoolhouse.

A train used to come down that track [winding down the mountain] and fire on the [17th Regiment] aid station in the schoolhouse. The mess hall was set up in the building, and I was in the chow line when the word came out—here comes that damn train again! The bullets came through the ceiling of the schoolhouse, and I'm standing there with my mess kit and the bullets hit the stewpot near me.

I said, I'll be damned, and I threw my mess kit and grabbed my rifle and we ran out. Somebody said, go up on that track and get that train. Well, Glenn Jenkins had the bazooka. We ran up there, but by that time the train had [gone into a tunnel]. Somebody said, go get 'em! So, I'm running behind the guy with the bazooka and I got a BAR. We ran halfway up but we never saw that train. But, from then on whenever that train came we always had it covered.

A day or so later we got the word to mount a patrol. We were running patrols all around in there, because the guerillas operate at night, and we told them [command] no problem because we did most of our training at night. Good.

That day…we went up into this pass, and the village [Majori] was down below us. You could see them going in and out of that village. My buddy said, how many you think are down in there? I said, I don't know, but there's a lot of them. We estimated 500. I'm telling you, from a peon's standpoint, now—Jim [Queen] was back at the office, running things—we had no officers with us, we came back. We told them, you've got 500 guerillas up there.

The recon of Majori was done by a squad of about 10 men.

We didn't go down into the village. We were up on the high ground. The road up there is like ice where the water is coming downhill. We had several guys injured just trying to get up the trail.

We told them about [the guerillas] and they said, ya'll are damn liars, there aren't any 500 guerillas up there. The next morning, we get the word the whole platoon is going back up there. So here we go, we went back up, scattered out, looking down with binoculars. There were [still] 500.

Allen recounted a story about stopping to clean weapons beside the trail up the mountain and when all the weapons were apart and dripping diesel fuel, soldiers of the 32nd began coming through, heading for the top. A passing officer, a Colonel, Allen thinks, yelled out for the Rangers to take the rear position. So, Allen went up for the third time. On the way, a man carrying mortar ammunition in cans had his hand freeze to a container and had to go back.

We get up to where we had observed two days down into the village. We looked down and saw the first part of the battalion had started going into the village.

You could see the other side of the village, in the snow, the trail going up into the mountains.

About that time we had three prisoners [taken in the village by Battalion Recon] and they were brought out into the open. They're not with us anymore, that's all I say about that. We were watching and we said, wait a minute! We don't do things like that!

The Rangers left their high spot of observation and followed the rest into the village. The terrain was only open in a few places; there were heavy woods on the other side of the village and more as the hill climbed behind it. The enemy was in the woods above the village and the Americans were tasked with climbing up after them.

The enemy had cleared the village and gone up to the hills there, and they saw this. And they said, what the devil's going on? They went up and around us and when the firing started it was just like shooting fish in a barrel. Two or three of these guys [Rangers] I was looking right at when they died. One kid had the mortar. He got hit, another kid came over, pushed him over the hill, grabbed that mortar tube. He got off one round. Now, we didn't have base plates, I don't know what happened to them. He fired that one round and turned around to look at me and I saw a hole right in the middle of his ear. He put his head down and that was the last of him.

That's when Boatright said, nobody else go out there, and then he said, oh, they got me, they got me! A little while later he said, they got me twice!

I said I've got to be dreaming. This ain't real. There was blood everywhere, people were dying. I pinched myself.

There was a kid, I didn't know his name until I went to his memorial service, he was right beside me. I heard him go 'oh!' and I looked down and a bullet had hit right in the center of his foot. I was going to tell him something, but he started jumping. He didn't make any noise, but he was jumping. I could tell machinegun bullets were hitting him.

This man may have been named King, and Allen was holding him when he was hit and killed.

Then Holley [a tough guy, boxer] got hit. We went up to him; he was down on the ground, sitting. We tried to lift him up but he was big, heavy. We couldn't lift him. He told us to drag him over to a tree, and then said, ya'll go ahead and save yourselves, but get out of here. Just give me some ammo. He had his rifle, but he was out of ammunition. We went around to a couple of dead guys and got him some bandoliers.

They told us when they found him the next day when they went back up in there; they had bayoneted him to the tree. All his ammunition was gone.

A little while later we started back and Lt. Pryor, I don't know how he got so far up front with the lead element. He came back across the hill, and he was lying down. He had a hole right dead center of his helmet and blood was coming all down there. He had…turned green. It split his head open. I hollered, stretcher! We got Lt. Pryor on a stretcher, I don't know where it came from, and took him back to the rear. A little later Captain Allen, Company Commander, got hit.

Some way or another Pryor got up off the stretcher. He's still hit. That's the respect he had for the Company Commander.

About that time [somebody] said, let's go on back up there and see what we can do. We went back up into the fighting. People dropping like flies. Got behind this same rock! Still see my buddy lying there on the ground. So I said, I ain't going out like this. I had a BAR, and you know a BAR fires from an open bolt. You cock it and when the bolt goes forward, it's fired.

I could see the guys [Chinese] all up there firing down. So I took aim at one guy just as clear, had him in my sights, and click! I thought, you bastard! I can't believe it. Come all this way, all this training, and this thing won't even work. So I pulled it back again, it did the same thing.

The cold was so intense the bolt on his BAR wouldn't slide forward fast enough to fire.

I started to throw it down and then thought, well, let me try something. I unzipped my pants and I wet all over it. I tried it again and it went boom! Just one shot. Cocked it again and it went two shots. Then the third time it started working. I said, I'm all right now. I'm ready to go.

Shortly after that the order came to pull back. Too many men were being hit and no ground was being gained. Allen and his mates were angry and wanted to go forward, not backward. "If we didn't go forward," he said, "they'd get us right there."

It was a small village. Fifty people at the most. Beside the village was a stream, maybe a foot deep. A lot of the fighting was done right in that stream. I walked a long ways in that stream. In fact, a pistol I've had for years, a dead Lieutenant was sitting [slumped over] on a rock. His face [was gone]. But he had a pistol. Now, my pistol, [.45 cal] the hammer was broken…

There were a lot of bodies in that water.

Two companies of the 17th, B and C, had gone up the hill before the Rangers and had taken terrific losses both in the village, where there was little cover, and in the brief open area before getting to the woods. Some platoons were down to five or six men. Caught in heavy fire from the heights, there was little choice but to pull back.

That's where a lot of those bodies came from. Some of them were floating [there was much ice].

Two platoons of the 2nd had come out of the fighting, but the 3rd Platoon got in trouble.

We got the word—Buffalo [the word was used as an identifier for the 2nd and sometimes the 4th Companies]. We had just come back from that patrol up there. We got to go out there and get 3rd Platoon. One platoon was on the right, one on the left. So we started up the valley and we could see them up there shooting. Somebody said to take the high ground. So we broke off and walked the ridge line on down (until the shooting stopped—apparently the Rangers scared off the enemy who had the 3rd Platoon pinned down.) So we came on down the hill.

We were only in that schoolhouse a week; it wasn't long. You didn't sleep at night. At night they would send us out on patrol.

There was a small village about a mile up the road from which enemy sharpshooters would come and fire on the Americans in Majori. A patrol was sent to discourage such things.

Hills were all around that schoolhouse. On a hill up to the left some snipers were firing all day long. This section...up the road come a section of quad .50s and twin .40s. We said, can you give us a hand? They said, sure, what do you want? We said, they're shooting at us from that hill over there. The .40s went on up the road a ways. The .50s said, tell me where you want it. So, the .50s threw a lot of rounds on the side of that hill and we weren't bothered no more. They said, think that got them? We said, yeah, thank you, and they went on.

Down a road a little way and a little time later the 2nd Rangers were facing the town of Chuchon. There are varying accounts of this battle, but the men of the 2nd were quite clear in their memories about February 20.

Queen: We came to the main town where the headquarters were. We crossed this little stream and the town was on the other side. We had support, some quad .50s."

Allen: I'm telling you they never fired. They were put in position—we had two machineguns on the flank and they started firing. We went over [a brick wall] and got in the water and started on across. Somebody hollered, tell them damn fools to quit firing, they're hitting close to us. When we came out of the water that's when we started getting fire back [from the enemy] coming from every which way. That's when they said, come up out of there and let's go. And we were going through there. Everybody was in the village. I never will forget. They said, kill everybody and you won't have to worry about them. Then two little girls came out of a house. I don't know if their parents had gotten killed or what, there were a lot of dead bodies up there. They came out and they [were saying a lot of words in a hurry]. Then [one of the men] turned his weapon on them and said, there's two of them. I said, oh, no, no, no, we ain't killing no kids here. He said, all right, but you watch. We'll have to come back.

At that point I told the men that some history was written a little differently than what I was hearing. They laughed and said most historians got the story from morning reports and after-action reports, and they were frequently wrong, and/or misleading.

Queen: This village of Chuchon was also called Tanyang-ni, it was right on the outskirts of Tanyang.

Allen: There weren't too many roads going north and south. This village controlled that road.

They spoke then of the Japanese maps they had with American names superimposed on them. They said there might be three or four villages or hamlets in close proximity to each other, and all were known by a common name on the maps.

We talked to some of the guys coming off the line, and they would say, we hear you guys are kicking ass back here. We haven't fired our rifles in I don't know when. It was quiet on the front lines.

Allen recounted a tale of going into a village where all were asleep, including the enemy. There were machinegun positions and the Rangers sneaked up on them and grabbed the barrels, pulling the weapons out of position. The 2nd Rangers opened fire then, and all hell broke loose.

We went through there. We had the officers running out the doors in their underwear.

We walked for a long time to get there; it was way behind the lines. I have no idea what the name of the village was. We didn't know where we were. Nobody told us. The only information I got that night was "Lock and load." They told us, if you have to do somebody, do it with a bayonet. Don't anybody shoot until you get the word.

Payne: We went out on patrol; we ran into some Chinese, they were riding horses. We were on a combat patrol; the whole company was on it. The Chinese were up in the hills, and they spotted us and we spotted them, and they hauled ass. Later, somebody called artillery fire.

The following part is unclear as to name or designation of the area or the hill. It is possible it was Hill 581, as the Rangers were there on May 20.

Allen: We were up on a hill. They said ya'll guys gotta come out of there. We said, no, we can't come out of here in the dark. Give us some support. The next morning there were bodies everywhere when they came up and they were saying, damn, these are some hell of a soldiers.

Queen: Our philosophy was: if you give this hill up, you're going to have to come back up here. Just as well pay the same price to stay up here as to come back. I said we're not going to retreat. We're going to call artillery in, and keep on calling and calling. If anything, we'll be beat back, but we're not going to leave this goddamn hill.

Payne: In the evening, we saw the Chinese and the North Koreans crossing the river. We had to hold that position. We were digging in. They brought more ammo for us because we expected a fight. We saw the Chinese coming in—but they didn't hit us until about three or four in the morning. This is where we were almost overrun—the 3rd Platoon [got separated].

Allen: This is one of those things where the lines are pulling back but you don't get the word. You get back and you say, hey, what are you doing up there?

Queen: We called artillery in close enough to where splinters and things were hitting in the tree line above us. They were firing 105s. We seldom had 155s.

We had been on Hill 581 for about a week. We had a nighttime withdrawal. Two-thirds of the company set up on the river-line, and I brought a third of the company back. We had more ammunition than we could carry [an unusual occurrence]. When I got back to the Battalion CP, nobody knew what the hell was going on. So I told them, we're going to lay down right here and when you find out where the rest of the company is, you tell us.

They hit us the next day. We could see them coming. That's when I started calling artillery in.

Lyles: Right on our position.

Queen: Later on that afternoon they attacked us and tried to take the hill from us. We fought all afternoon.

Queen was astounded to find there was another American unit on the hill with them. When the wounded were taken down, a platoon—probably from the 32nd Regiment—was about 60 yards behind the Rangers.

We left the combat outpost line, past the Battalion CP, and a guy gave me a verbal order, go back up that damn hill, and that's all I got. I didn't know where the CP was; last time I saw Battalion CP it was way back toward the rear. I didn't know where anybody else was or what the attack plan was at all.

We had tables that told us when first light was and when sunrise was. I wanted to attack at first light, so I spread the company out and told them to fix bayonets. I gave my rifle to somebody; all I had was my pistol.

The conversation drifted and questions hit on Musan-ni, the first Ranger combat jump. The 4th Rangers were also involved.

Queen: We got word that we were going to be sent back to report to Eighth Army. I took the advance party. On the way back we ran into 8th [RICA] Company.

Fourth Company got back there before we did. We [all] went down and joined up with the 187th. We knew some of the people in the 187th. But the 187th was also not taking any black privates. Any blacks that came through were assigned to us or were sent back. We spent about a week there training. We got some men from 7th Company [used as a replacement company from Benning] at that time. We split them up, putting new men with old men and formed a mortar section. The idea of putting a tube with a regular platoon wasn't working out too well. Since we had no forward observer we had to make do with our own firepower. I was the recoilless rifle platoon leader, and I had a machinegun platoon leader also. We had some of the best mortar men in the Regiment.

We were attached to the 2nd Battalion, and the 4th was attached to the 3rd Battalion. They called an alert a couple of times, but the front line was moving so fast…

Our mission was to take Hill 151. I think 4th Company was to take Hill 205. They were adjacent hills to each other, connected by a ridgeline. I was the last man to jump. We were the first ones to capture our objective, the first ones to capture some enemy, and the first to take weapons.

There was no lost love between the 187th and the Rangers. For example, the Rangers had too much rank [lots of Sergeants].

We jumped from a C-46; it had two doors [one on either side]. We had about 15-man sticks. It was one of the first times we saw integration—in the Air Force. Our crew chief was a black man, and there were others.

I saw Ridgeway [General Matthew Ridgeway] on the DZ [drop zone]. He came in his little Hellfire [airplane]. He gave the commander of the 187th hell because the 1st Battalion dropped on the wrong DZ.

We saw the 4th Company fighting up Hill 205. The battalion commander warned us, wanted us to go help them take the hill, because they hadn't taken it yet. We would have crossed a little ridgeline and hit them [the enemy] on the flank, but we were told no, they wanted the tanks to go up there.

We had taken Hill 151 and were getting ready to attack northeast to try and link up with the 3rd Division. We saw them [4th RICA] in a firefight on the last day [on a different hill]. To me it was almost comical. The Chinese were throwing grenades and the Rangers were throwing them back, everybody popping up and shooting

Queen was asked how he figured such a fight was comical.

Allen: You had to see it. We were looking through tank binoculars. It was a show for us.

Queen: They looked like puppets. They were at about 150-200 yards.

Allen: We were just laughing, watching them throw grenades at each other. We said, what the hell is going on over there? They're too slow! Somebody said, come on, saddle up. Fix bayonets. Let's show them how to do it. Nobody was scared. Everybody was laughing. Come on, we want to show them how to do this thing. But I think they had taken the hill by then.

The enemy took many more casualties than the Americans, but there were a number of wounded among the US troops, including the Rangers. The 2nd Rangers lost only one man killed, and there was a certain amount of bravado among the wounded.

Allen: Nobody ever said, oh, man, I'm hit bad. [One man] got hit in the stomach, stood up and said, ah, State-side! Lot of guys get shot in the arm—hot dang! I'm going to the hospital and be with the women-folk. Nobody cried.

3rd Rangers

Commanded by Captain Jesse M. Tidwell

Descended from Company A, 3rd Rangers, WWII.

Upon completion of training at Fort Benning the total number of "survivors" was too few to make four full companies. The 3rd Rangers were used as a source of men to bring the 1st, 2nd, and 4th Companies up to fighting strength. New men were added to the remaining members of the 3rd and the company was made to go through the cycle again with the 5th, 6th, 7th, and 8th Companies.

They went into battle yelling, "Die, Bastard, Die!"

In the beginning of April, the 3rd Division was moving north near the Imjin River, slowly forcing the enemy back. For a time the Rangers went forward with everybody else, crossing the river and moving forward to Chorwon with the 65th Regiment—attacking.

Bloody Nose Ridge

The morning of April 11th, men of the 3rd climbed up on the broad backs of the tanks of the 64th Heavy Tank Battalion and joined F Company of the 65th. The units created a small task force with the mission of penetrating the line and causing problems for the enemy.

The force was certainly armed well, considering the heavy tanks were carrying an armed-to-the-teeth Ranger Company supplied with some 57mm recoilless rifles. But, as they moved out, they were unaware some of them would soon be in an historic fight, or that many wouldn't be coming back.

At the village of Kantongyon the task force began to take fire. The 1st and 2nd Platoons went in to see who was shooting and make them stop. The tanks were directed to targets and shattered them point-blank. In short order the village was cleared and the Rangers moved up a hill beyond it to find themselves looking into a valley with ridgelines all around. That exposed valley was their intended route of march.

Mortar rounds began to peg them as they moved down the hill. The communists on the heights around the valley were waiting for them.

At that point the task force was accidentally split, with each of two parts taking a different way, leaving the 1st and 2nd Platoons with just two tanks going in the wrong direction. The needed mass firepower of the main tank element was putting distance between them with every minute gone and nobody realized they were separated right away. Another mistake, far from trivial, occurred when the two tanks with the Rangers got separated from the platoons they were supposed to be supporting. The men of the 1st and 2nd Platoons couldn't see the tanks at all. Though in the end the tanks didn't get too far away, this act left the two platoons of Rangers on the ground alone, and under increasing attack from above.

They were caught in the open, unable to go forward or backward without being under fire. The only option for the Rangers was to advance. As they went, an order was sent by radio for the platoons to withdraw under fire from the tanks. The tanks apparently didn't get the message, or the Rangers didn't, because they kept advancing through flying shrapnel, taking casualties as they went.

Eventually, some tanks did come up behind the Rangers and were directed by the Ranger Commander to support his men by blowing up some of the lower enemy positions. That, and the 2nd Platoon wiping out another strongpoint eased some of the direct fire coming in, but the mortars were still working hard.

Things got hot and heavy before the men got past the main line of defense. Rangers of the 1st Platoon went after the enemy positions with bayonets fixed and no intent of stopping.

Only eight men of the 32-man 1st Platoon gained the top of the ridge. The rest had been killed or wounded on the trip across the valley and up the hill. A total of three men survived without wounds in the attack across 700 yards of open ground. This action became known as Bloody Nose Ridge, a well-known part of the Ranger Legend.

While the costly assault of the 1st and 2nd Platoons was taking place, the 3rd Platoon, in the center of the valley with the rest of the tanks, were also under fire. It took some time, but eventually the task force was reunited. After such a blow to personnel, the depleted Rangers were given a guard mission, protecting a vital bridge over the Han Tan River.

On April 14, the 3rd Rangers and the 3rd Division Recon Company, with support, formed Task Force Rodgers and moved north without heavy resistance.

When news of the 3rd Company's fight at Bloody Nose Ridge came over the wires at home, it sounded like an adventure novel to young boys all over the country. Rangers might have worn Mohawks, carried switchblades, and swaggered a bit, but they were necessary heroes to a nation starved for good news.

The two companies came together again April 20, linked up with some tank retrievers sporting 40mm guns and .50 caliber machineguns, and some engineers. The group went after five tanks, out of commission behind the lines in front of the 3rd Division. Before covering more than a few miles the combined unit ran into ditches dug across the road to act as tank traps. Prepared enemy positions peppered the Rangers as they crossed the ditch and moved to clean out the opposition. One of the tank retrievers mounting a quad-50 began to lay fire on what was supposed to be enemy positions, but got some rounds into the Ranger 2nd Platoon, as well.

The tank traps were filled in so the rest of the unit could cross them, but again a quad .50 fired into the Rangers, this time the 3rd Platoon. It was unfortunate, but not enough to stop the Rangers from securing the area and allowing the machinery through.

A couple of days later, the 3rd Rangers and the 3rd Recon were at it again, assaulting a fixed position and overrunning it with grenade attacks—they also received the same. An order to bring back a prisoner was all but ignored as the men of the 3rd smashed the enemy, leaving few alive.

Heavy combat was also taking a toll on the Rangers, and by the 23rd only enough men for two platoons remained effective. They moved to the Han Tan River—a branch of the Imjin—and hooked up with the battered British 29th Brigade, which had been severely cut up when the 1st ROK Division abruptly pulled out and left them exposed to attack. One British battalion had suffered severe losses, with the survivors becoming separated from the main group. The Rangers went looking for them.

N The 3rd ran into dug-in enemy positions situated on the high ground and wisely withdrew a short distance. During the night, a high point observation point was established, but forward motion was still in doubt. Other elements of the 3rd Division tried to get through, but repeated pushes were stopped. The British were close by, but the Chinese managed to keep the two Allied forces apart, smashing an assault by a tank/infantry team and making heavy counter thrusts.

The Allies couldn't hold against one particularly determined assault, and the 3rd Division began to withdraw. The 3rd Rangers were taking a hard hit on the line when they were alerted to withdraw behind an artillery screen.

The 3rd Rangers joined Task Force Ferret on June 17, making inroads six miles deep into enemy territory and conducting sweeps to remove any pockets of Chinese trying to dig in.

4th Rangers

Commanded by Captain Dorsey Anderson

Descended from Company A, 4th Ranger Battalion, WWII.

The 4th Rangers got to Korea with four officers and 118 EM shortly after Christmas. They flew in from Tachikawa Air Force Base. Attached to the 1st Cavalry Division, they headquartered in Seoul. No immediate missions were available, so the 4th walked security in the rear while the Cav was in reserve near Seoul. Later they guarded the 82nd Field Artillery Battalion.

Soon the Division HQ was moving south ahead of the Chinese, but the Rangers were ordered to stay put until transport was available. With no food, the company had to scavenge for supplies. Finally, trucks showed up to take them out, just when a possible opportunity to fight with the last unit in the line came open. Too late in the offing, the 4th had to pull out.

After all the guard duty the men traveled to Taegu, where the company was attached— along with the 2nd Rangers—to the 187th RCT in late February. Planning and training up for an airborne mission went forward, but it was cancelled as they were boarding the aircraft. There was great disappointment as the men really wanted to fight as they were trained to do.

During this time four volunteers from the 4th Rangers went on detached service with the Eighth Army for a secret mission designed to blow up railroad tunnels far behind enemy lines. The men were paired with 19 South Koreans and dropped over snow-covered, mountainous terrain. The drop did not go well, the force was widely scattered, and the Chinese were alerted to their presence. Over a period of some 20 days the group—once all together—evaded the enemy and moved toward their goal. They never made it, and though three Americans were rescued by helicopter, that event cost one bird, damaged two more, and left a Navy pilot and the fourth Ranger on the ground where they were eventually captured.

For more on this incredible story of survival see Ranger Robert Black's excellent volume, "Rangers In Korea", published by Ballentine.

Musan-ni

For overall details up to the point of assault, see 2nd Rangers.

The first-ever Ranger combat jump was performed at Musan-ni on March 23. The 4th was under operational control of the 3rd Battalion, 187th ARCT. The first Ranger mission was to capture Hill 205. The hill was heavily defended and the first two assaults did not carry. Air support pounded the enemy for a while, and then a third try by the Rangers got them to the top on March 24. One man was killed and nine wounded—a low figure for three assaults on a fortified hill.

The next few days were spent chasing the fleeing enemy and rooting out left-behind troops. On the 28th two platoons of the 4th took Hill 279, thus securing the left flank of the 187th. It was a good thing, too, because the enemy came that way later in the day, only to be repulsed by the tough Rangers.

The 4th Ranger Company had a total of 22 casualties during the Musan-ni operation.

The 187th and the Rangers were relieved by the 3rd Infantry and sent back to Taegu, arriving there on March 30.

Ed McDonough

This interview was taped in Atlantic City, New Jersey in December 2003.

Ed McDonough was with the 4th Rangers as they fell into Musan-ni. He joined the Rangers from the 82nd Airborne. He said he thought the war would be over by Christmas and he wanted to get in there. The Rangers were his ticket to carrying the vaunted BAR in combat. Years later, he said he has no regrets.

We jumped C-46s. The 187th took all the C-119s [there were also some C-47s].

We had 119 [men] maybe, but 111 jumped, five officers. Joseph Anderson was the company commander. It was about nine in the morning when we jumped—we took off about 7 o'clock from Taegu.

He was asked what he saw when he exited the airplane.

Rice paddies, and the Air Force was there, bombing them around the hills. By the time we hit the ground, I think it was some guys from the 2nd Ranger Company, they put out these machineguns—there were Chinese there.

Another thing was green smoke. We were supposed to jump on the green smoke, but I guess everybody was using it, because there was green smoke all over the place.

The 2nd Rangers jumped first with the 2/187th, hitting close to their target area. The 4th wasn't so lucky—they were dropped in the wrong place—in an area the 187th had already secured. The amount of green smoke around the various DZs probably contributed to the miscue.

We were dropped in the wrong DZ. It was close to our objective, but it was the wrong one.

By the time we got to our objective along the road, there were some Chinese, but somebody had killed them, probably guys from the 2/187.

There were about 100 casualties from the jump itself—out of more than 3,000 men—but almost a fifth were the result of another bad drop. One plane carrying men of the 187th went off course.

One stick didn't make it. The airplane must have veered off the DZ and went into the mountains. The guys jumped and they all landed on the mountain, 19 of them, and they all got killed. We could see their chutes just barely open [before they hit].

We were to take a hill—205—1st Platoon was the lead platoon, and they took a lot of casualties, maybe a dozen or more [WIA]. Only one man was KIA on the jump, my assistant BAR man, Fred Manship. I was in the 2nd Platoon.

After they cleared it out we went up on the top and just spread out, watching the mountain maybe a thousand yards ahead of us, a big mountain. The Air Force was bombing it with napalm.

The higher elevations were snow-covered, though the overall weather wasn't too bad. At one point, McDonough said, he and his Ranger buddies watched, fascinated and frustrated, as about 600 Chinese wended their way down the side of a distant mountain. He wonders to this day why no artillery was put on the exposed enemy.

The 4th Rangers stayed atop the hill for a while, then attacked another hill and dug in. During this time McDonough rose up enough to take his pack off and was hit in the back by a sniper. The round exited his chest, making him one of 22 casualties of the 4th for the operation.

That was it for me. It just missed my heart. I was lucky. They put me on a hospital ship and operated on me, and then I was sent to Japan. I was going to go back to Korea but I came down with hepatitis [he thinks from a blood transfusion] and that was two more months in the hospital.

By the time I could go back, they'd been deactivated.

Hwachon Dam

For the 4th Rangers and the 7th Cavalry Regiment the battle for Hwachon Dam was a logistical nightmare as well as a surprise. The logistics involved boats and equipment—the surprise involved a lot more Chinese troops than were expected.

The plan to disable the gates of the dam was quickly conceived and implemented—so quickly that few of the components had a chance to assemble and equip properly. What follows is a look at a heroic stand by the 4th Ranger Infantry Company (Airborne) during what proved to be a frustrating and unfinished mission.

There were several dams in Korea located in strategic places, some under the control of the South, some held by the North. One such was the 275-foot tall dam across the Pukhan River, outside the town of Hwachon, which formed a 13-mile long reservoir about a mile wide.

The dam was deep in very rugged mountains, way up there, and held by what was thought to be a light Chinese garrison. This particular dam became a threat when someone noticed the flood plain, should the dam gates be opened, would probably cut IX Corp in two, as well as knocking out several downstream bridges and supply points.

The Eighth Army was pushing north, with elements of IX Corp moving toward the area of the dam. Major General William Hoge was IX Corps Commander. The bulk of any damage by flooding would come to his troops. It was apparent the Chinese were holding the gates of the dam shut in order to build up the water behind it. The huge gates were six-by-10 yards and weighed several tons. Eighteen of them spread across the face of the dam.

Hoge reasoned that a small team of men could get in there quickly and blow a portion of the gate mechanism so the gates couldn't be raised. He went to Eighth Army Commander General Ridgeway with the idea.

Ridgeway had already looked at Hwachon Dam and the flood menace. With the gates open the downstream levels would quickly rise 10 to 12 feet, wreaking havoc over a large area. The idea of air strikes was discarded because a broken dam was the same as opening the gates.

Aircraft eventually destroyed Hwachon Dam.

The 7th Cavalry Regiment of the 1st Cavalry Division—including the 4th Rangers—sat right in front of the dam. Naturally, they were given the job of eliminating the threat. It should have been a fairly simple operation, but Intelligence missed a few hundred Chinese troops.

Ranger Company Commander Dorsey B. Anderson brought his men forward to the map point "Kansas Line" to join the 7th Cav, and began his own recon of the situation. So far, the orders were tentative. The action would begin only if the Chinese made a move to open the gates, but Anderson made his men ready. He was of the opinion that a quick strike made across the river by the Rangers at night would surprise the enemy and allow his men to penetrate the dam and get the job done.

Anderson figured to move the Rangers across by boat. He had no idea how hard it would be to produce the boats, or the impact that logistics problem would have. The fact the Rangers would be in full view of any remaining Chinese on the return trip in daylight did not deter him.

Refresher training with explosives was initiated, and Anderson visited a similar dam to view the gate mechanisms and figure the best way to damage them. The Captain next went aloft to take a look at the dam and the terrain around it. He couldn't see any Chinese fortifications, but the mountainous path his men must take extended nearly a mile from the water overland to the dam.

Unfortunately for Anderson's 4th Rangers, it was decided elsewhere that a major sweep by the 7th Cav would be a better idea. Once the area was secured, the Rangers would be able to just waltz in and blow the place up. This was only the first try, but nobody knew that yet.

In the pre-dawn hours of April 9 the gates began to slowly edge open. Within a few hours 10 of the 18 gates were in various stages of allowing the Pukhan to cascade forth. Downstream the levels rose more than seven feet over the next several hours.

General Hoge had all the reason he needed to order the dam taken immediately. Complications began with the imminent pullout of the 1st Cav, although the 7th Cav was to leave last in order to be on the scene long enough to complete the mission. Orders to the 7th took the form of "if you can pull it off soon, and don't get hurt too badly."

About noon the day the gates opened, three rifle companies of the 7th made to cross the Kansas Line and move on the dam. The Rangers were close behind, ready to get inside and do the deed. Progress was slowed immediately when Chinese strong points were discovered hidden in the slopes. The attack was halted right there, and before long the night closed everything down.

When the overland attack had been stymied, the idea of Rangers-over-water came back into play. Though the land operation was still on the table, General Hoge believed the Rangers might have a better shot if they acted in concert with the 7th assault. This concept was pushed forward when the second attack by the regiment failed, with heavy casualties.

The necessity of bringing boats and associated equipment to the river would take time, it was argued. The regiment was ready to be relieved. The argument stopped there when Hoge pulled rank, making it very clear the dam was to be taken by the 7th, by whatever means, and it better happen soon.

Meanwhile, the Chinese closed six of the 10 open gates. Nobody knows why, but they did, and water levels began dropping. The immediate need for an assault on the dam went away with the extra water. General Hoge acted accordingly, placing the whole operation on the shelf so the Marines could take over for the 7th Cav during the night of April 10.

By five o'clock that afternoon, Hoge changed his mind again. The reasoning behind the change was simple. The Chinese could continually open and close the gates to harass troops downstream if they were allowed to stay where they were. That, and the pause necessary to replace the Cav would give the enemy a chance to strengthen already formidable defenses. Time was of the essence.

The 7th Cav and the 4th Rangers were to stay and solve the dam problem.

Since two attempts at overland frontal attack had failed, the Rangers became the last best hope of getting the job done. Plans were made for the 4th to get across the river on boats and work their way about a mile through very rough terrain to the dam. Two Cav battalions would come in from two other sides as a diversionary tactic, while the 3rd Battalion would remain on the other side of the river as reserve and backup for the Rangers.

Anderson knew well that such a gathering of material would take too long, and the remaining hours of darkness would be few. It didn't matter. The company would go.

But first, the Rangers were beefed up some 20 machinegunners and mortarmen of the 7th Cav, and weapons were sighted in for support fires from across the river. There were about 30 artillery pieces dedicated to support of the Rangers, but they were eight and 10 miles away, reducing their effectiveness. Still, it was probably nice to have them.

Everything necessary for the assault had to be brought in manually because of the lack of roads, and the Rangers waited long and left with little. There were supposed to be 20 boats to ferry the Rangers, but only 10 showed up on time.

The second group of 10 boats did eventually show up.

There were not enough motors for all the boats, which didn't matter because the Rangers were going to paddle across to maintain silence. The motors they had didn't work, anyway.

Pre-dawn of April 11, it was discovered one of the 10 boats had a hole in the bottom, leaving only nine. With only 10 men to a boat, that meant 90 men could cross at one time, leaving a large portion of the Rangers and attached Cav troops to wait for the second round. Volunteers from the 7th Cav were to pilot the Rangers over and bring the boats back.

First to go was a heavily armed platoon commanded by Lt. Michael D. Healy, charged with "taking" the landing area. Part of the platoon carried demolitions for the dam. The men occupied three boats and were just disappearing into the mist when the rest of the first wave pushed the other six craft forward. The second platoon of Rangers, commanded by Lt. Joseph W. Waterbury, also held Captain Anderson and some attached troops.

The trip across the river took 45 minutes, and the second platoon didn't land until just before dawn. Whatever happened next would be done in daylight.

The two groups soon linked up on the way uphill, and Anderson took overall command. With Healy's platoon on point, the Rangers aimed for the dam. Not long after, some troops up ahead were heard shouting, and then seen to be waving at the advancing Rangers. It quickly became apparent the men were Chinese and probably thought the Americans were their comrades.

When the mistake was discovered, two men of the Ranger force became casualties, one of them dying. Any hope for surprise was gone.

The dead soldier had been the radioman for the artillery forward observer, who called in his own requests. Presently, artillery and mortar rounds began to land ahead of the Rangers.

Lt. Healy and five men were out in front during the fight to gain the crest. With supporting fire they made it, then continued forward after an enemy machinegun. Overwhelming the gun crew with grenades, the few Rangers atop the hill opened the way for the rest who came screaming up the slope, scattering a small surviving contingent of enemy troops.

Once they owned the hill, the Rangers had to stop for the time being and wait for the rest of the company to come across the river. The men dug in and stared into the mist that mostly obscured the dam. They were isolated in their high spot, with water on three sides and the dam in front, and no telling how many enemy soldiers waiting for them to move. To add to the problems, the weather was not allowing any air support.

Two boats had returned to the opposite shore by then. Just after 6 a.m., they loaded up two of the three remaining squads of Rangers that formed the third platoon, commanded by Lt. James L. Johnson.

From the time the first boats left the shore in the quiet darkness to the link-up on the hilltop, less than four hours had elapsed. Some 90-odd were present after paddling their way across the river and making it up the hill, some of them fighting all the way. At least the company was mostly together, and could form either a strong offense or defense, as necessary.

They would need the firepower.

The boats returned once more and were boarded by the remaining squad, the Company Exec, and six Korean bearers on hand to carry needed ammunition. For once, the motors worked. Since firing had broken out no one figured on a need for further stealth, so the two boats lit out across the river. Quickly they ran through the fog, only to run out of it and be suddenly exposed in full daylight with nowhere to hide. Enemy rounds began searching the water for them and the two craft changed course several times without finding a way in. Reluctantly, they returned to shore.

Up on the hill, Anderson was facing a decision. To go forward toward the dam would leave him exposed in the rear, since reinforcements had been turned back. He feared being cut off. He decided to extend his line to the left and secure another small hill located closer to the shore. That would give him a back door.

Lt. Johnson's platoon got the first crack at it, but was quickly pinned down by machineguns and mortars. The men looked up to find some 50 Chinese bearing down on them, and grenade explosions punctuated the sharp fight that followed. With the Rangers occupied with the first attack, a second, much larger attack hit and almost swept the Americans off the hill.

The Chinese came in like a tidal wave—blowing their bugles, running straight at the Rangers, not stopping, not taking cover, just coming on. Though supported by 4.2-inch mortars and artillery fire, every weapon the Rangers could bring to bear was necessary to even slow the Chinese surge. The action was intense and confusing, and men's memories are admittedly hazy about the details of how many grenades they threw, or how tightly packed were the enemy it was almost impossible to miss. However it went, if it is possible to track such chaos, one thing was clear—the Rangers still held the hill, or at least they still had a few hundred yards of dangerous ground.

Captain Anderson made what was probably a very wise decision and requested the 7th Cav come get his men out of there while they still had somebody to come get. Word came back to stay put. Another rifle company was on the way to reinforce and resupply. They would have to hurry, Anderson knew, because the men were down to nearly nothing. He gave the order to fix bayonets. It was only noon.

Meanwhile, the 7th Cav was having its own problems. Two diversionary attacks were planned, but the 2nd Battalion again ran into very strong fortifications and heavy fire while trying to force the way open to the dam and draw some attention away from the Rangers on the other side of the dam. The 3rd Battalion sent a company to cross the river via footbridges, but when the Chinese had opened the gates, the bridges were washed out. In lieu of direct support, the Cavalrymen threw artillery fire to try and hold down the Chinese.

The situation was becoming more desperate by the moment. The huge firepower the Americans hoped to bring to bear was stolen by the weather and the terrain. Without air support the opposing forces were very nearly equal, with one exception—the Chinese were dug in.

As time went by, the weight of the US Army began to tell, as the Americans were able to solidify their positions and bring in reinforcements. It was obvious by then that frontal attacks by the 7th Cav were useless, which left the Rangers hanging out in the wind. Orders went out to get somebody over there to help them. Fortunately the other 10 boats the Rangers were supposed to have had arrived, and there was a way to get more of the 3rd Battalion across the water.

The loaded boats didn't get going until early afternoon, and they took some fire getting across. It wasn't enough to stop them. Before long, a full company of the 3rd and the remaining Rangers and ammunition bearers were moving up toward the hilltop.

At that point, there were some 300 soldiers well supplied with ammunition atop that ridge, which made things much more difficult for the Chinese to remove them. Pressure could be applied toward the dam and perhaps the mission could finally be completed.

General Hoge was having second thoughts. The dam was a tougher nut than he was told to expect. He knew it would take a division to secure the area around the dam. He didn't have a division.

Hoge decided to cut his losses and get everybody out of there. Word filtered down to the 7th Cav that they could quit whenever they were ready. Colonel Harris, Commander of the 7th, saw no reason to hang around. Night was coming and the Chinese would hit hard after dark. The bulk of the 3rd was still on the wrong side of the river, and it was sleeting when it wasn't raining.

Harris sent a radio message across the Pukhan for his men to withdraw, beginning with the Rangers—the forward-most unit—filtering back through men of the 3rd.

Frustrated at being recalled when the chances of success were increasing, yet glad to get off that hill before dark, the Rangers were able to withdraw peacefully, as were the men of the 3rd.

5th Rangers

Commanded by Captain John C. Scagnelli

Replaced Eighth Army Rangers in 25th ID in March 1951.

On April 3, the company got a mission to recon a town near the Yong- Pyong River, and moved across the water. Infiltrating about a half-mile inland behind enemy lines made them the first unit on the right side of the Allied lines to cross the 38th parallel. They met the Chinese at dawn of that day, pushing them back, and were waiting patiently when the forward elements of the division caught up with them later.

Hill 383

A week passed and the 5th was back in action. They crossed the Han Tan River in a night march, and penetrated miles into hostile territory with orders to take and hold Hill 383. They were to stay until the 24th Infantry could attack on a wide front and relieve them. Set up on high ground, a Ranger observation post would be an invaluable asset during the assault, plus it would keep the Chinese from using the hill for the same thing.

On the morning of April 11, the 5th attacked uphill into heavy fire and were repulsed. Air support was called in to pound the enemy positions, and the company charged up again. The Chinese were not budging. A terrific fight for the summit raged for several hours, with the two sides close enough to hurl grenades at each other. It was past four in the afternoon before the Rangers were able to dislodge the stubborn enemy.

Setting up defenses atop the hill, the Rangers were expecting the 24th Infantry to be coming along any moment, which probably seemed like a good idea, since the Chinese were not happy about losing the high ground—and to a mere company, at that.

When it got good and dark, the Chinese began lobbing a lot of mortar rounds into the Ranger perimeter, then blew their eerie bugle discords and followed the barrage with a heavy ground attack. The 5th Rangers knocked the oncoming enemy soldiers down as fast as they could load and fire, but the Americans were behind communist lines and the Chinese were reinforcing. The attack spread to three sides of the hill, and the Rangers had no choice but to withdraw.

Two wounded Rangers volunteered to stay behind to provide covering fire, not wanting to burden the others under such heavy attack, and knowing their sacrifice would give their brothers a chance to get clear. Sergeant William Kirshfield and Corporal Walter J. Maziarz, Jr. gave their lives that night in the finest Ranger tradition of courage and brotherhood.

There was only one way out for the withdrawing Rangers—the fourth side of the hill—a nearly vertical drop. The men either jumped or tried to claw their way down and several were injured in the process. Withering fire during the get-away wounded eight other Rangers.

The company was occupying a slot between the 24th and 27th Regiments on April 18. The next day the 5th was attached to the 27th for OPCON (Operational Control).

The Chinese Fifth-Phase Offensive was pushing the Allies hard. By April 27, the 25th Division was making a strategic withdrawal and the 5th Rangers were in the fight. Working with the 27th Infantry, the Rangers counter-attacked when the regiment line was hit hard and breached in the area covered by 2nd Battalion. The fighting was so intense that many front line officers were hit and Ranger NCOs were leading line companies for a time.

In mid-May, the 5th RICA became part of Task Force Hamilton. A diverse grouping of special units made for a large, but well-rounded, force. A company of tanks and a platoon of assault guns from the 89th Tank Battalion provided the punch, supported by a recon platoon of the 89th, artillery forward observers, tactical air control people—even a medical detachment—and, of course, the Rangers. Added to the mix was a detachment from the 65th Engineers to help with mine detection.

The powerful task force went forward about three miles and ran into determined resistance. Mines were killing tanks and enemy fire was picking up. The 5th Rangers moved forward, climbing, as usual, into fortified enemy positions dug into the hillside. The fight took almost all day before the Rangers made the top of the hill and Chinese fire ceased.

The ordered mission of locating the Chinese line and bringing back a prisoner was accomplished at the cost of four dead Rangers, and 15 wounded.

By May 23, the 5th was waiting for the new US thrust, Operation DETONATE, to commence. The 25th Infantry Division wanted a heavy raid behind enemy lines to disrupt Chinese communication and supply, so a new conglomeration of units was put together and designated Task Force Dolvin. Colonel Welborn G. Dolvin, Commander of the 89th Tanks, was also the namesake of the first TF Dolvin, which worked with the Eighth Army Rangers.

Tanks and men went forward near daybreak of May 24, and encountered a lot of nothing. Seeing no Chinese attack being imminent, Dolvin was reinforced with a battalion of infantry, more tanks, and some engineers.

That meant heaving fighting was probably in the offing, and it was, commencing within 24 hours. The Chinese hit the armored column hard, dispersing the foot soldiers, but only temporarily. Task Force Dolvin rolled on, chewing up enemy resistance as it drove north, creating a hole large enough to push Allied troops through to the 38th Parallel and beyond.

There were Turkish and Canadian among them.

The 5th Rangers happened to capture 26 prisoners on the way.

Objective Sugar

The 5th Rangers were attached to the 27th Infantry in early June and were given the mission of assaulting Hill 722, a fortified piece of rough terrain loaded with Chinese. The

Rangers figured a flank attack was better than head-on, but discovered the enemy was strong everywhere.

Chinese soldiers hidden in "spider-holes"- a la Vietnam—would pop up and shoot from any direction, and fortified bunkers supplied the rest of the incoming rounds. Under heavy fire, including mortars, the Rangers withdrew, regrouped at the bottom, and charged up again.

There were large rocks littering the top of the hill, and among those the fighting was fierce. Grenades flew from both sides, and both sides took mounting casualties.

Once ensconced at the top, the badly hurt Rangers asked for reinforcements to help hold the position. There were none to be had.

The 5th Rangers, with five men killed and 26 wounded while taking Hill 722, had to withdraw

6th Rangers

Commanded by Captain James S. Cain

This company had very experienced commanders. Captain "Sugar" Cain had been with the 1st Special Service Force in WWII, and his Executive Officer, Captain Elred E. Weber, was with that unit also, plus the 1st Ranger Battalion. The Company First Sergeant, Joseph Dye, was with the 1st Battalion, too, having landed with the British and Canadians at Dieppe, and survived the North Africa campaign. Such leadership produced a battle-ready company that was shipped not to battle, but to Germany, in case things heated up in Europe.

When the men of the 6th found out they weren't going to Korea, there was much hollering and gnashing of teeth. Morale suffered.

They made extra jumps at the end of the cycle to prepare for possible European-style combat.

The US ship *George Goethals* took the 6th Rangers to Germany, departing the Brooklyn Navy Yard February 7. Ten days later the ship took berth at Bremerhaven, where the 6th boarded a train for Kitzingen and went to work for the 1st Infantry Division.

The Rangers had been warned their move was very much under wraps, and were somewhat disconcerted when the town was flying banners welcoming them.

Morale was still a problem as the men wanted to be in the fight in Korea, so the officers did what officers do—they put the men to work training to be all they could be.

Heard that before?

Indeed, the 6th became a top-notch unit and a focal point of excellence for other troops in the region. For a time, the unit actually acted as Opposition Forces to help train the other American troops in the theater.

Not a good thing, having trained Rangers with the mission of ambushing and infiltrating you. There are stories about returning Vietnam vets acting as OPFOR in Stateside Ranger camps and raising havoc with the students.

If they couldn't be in actual combat, the 6th Rangers certainly practiced their craft as if they would be called any moment. It became common practice for 6th Rangers to test the security of other US units in the area, stealing through sentries and suddenly appearing in command posts and other off-limits places.

Commanders throughout the area yelled and cursed—and tightened their security procedures.

7th Rangers

Commanded by Captain Robert W. Eikenberry

The 7th RICA was kept at Benning as RI Cadre, and as a replacement pool. The company often received men from the 82nd Airborne to fill the ranks.

In late January 1951, five officers and 69 enlisted men of the 7th Rangers found themselves in Korea as replacements.

On March 28, the official word came down, officially placing the 7th and the 9th as Replacement and Cadre Companies.

8th Rangers

Commanded by Captain James A. Herbert

This company has a short, but distinguished history of battle. At one point they were put in an untenable situation, and were almost wiped out by the Chinese on Hill 628.

Known as the Devils, the unit reportedly went into battle yelling, "We'll all be killed!"

299 Turkey Shoot

On April 15, 1951, the 8th Rangers separated into three platoons and went into battle with the 24th Infantry Division, attacking north. Early in the morning the Rangers passed through the 19th Infantry and went behind the lines on patrol. The 1st and 2nd Platoons found nothing and returned to friendly lines. The 3rd Platoon also came up empty, until they turned for home. The sounds of light small-arms fire alerted them to something happening nearby.

An Intelligence and Recon Patrol from the 19th was moving away from the firing, and the Rangers watched from a short distance as Chinese troops moved in behind them. When the enemy was sufficiently within the Ranger kill zone, the torrent was unleashed.

Lieutenant Berk Strong led several assaults, pushing the Chinese back and inflicting considerable casualties, but soon the more distant enemy units began to throw ordnance at the Rangers, including accurate mortar fire. The Chinese—estimated at two companies—counter-attacked and the Rangers were taking casualties. Since they were only a patrol to begin with and not there to take ground, the unit withdrew back to US lines. Ranger losses were two killed and three wounded, against more than 50 enemy dead.

Hill 628

During the Chinese Fifth Phase Offensive that began April 22, 1951, a multitude of changes took place all along the Allied lines as the giant forces pushed against one another. In places, huge holes opened up and weaker units were broken by the flood of enemy troops. One such was the 6th ROK Regiment.

Located on the right flank of the 24th Infantry Division, the 6th broke under the onslaught and retreated—a kind word—several miles. This left the division flank wide open, and the enemy was pouring through the gap.

They were gratified to discover the ROK gift of 18 howitzers and nearly 100 machineguns.

The 8th Rangers were sent into the void to see what was happening. On April 23, 90 Rangers went out in front of the 21st Regiment and moved uphill. There were three separate hills before them—628, 1010, and 1168—and nobody really knew what was on them.

Loaded for bear, the Rangers of the 8th climbed all night. By dawn, they were spread out along the ridge at the top of Hill 628 where they were joined by a few stragglers from the southbound ROK Regiment.

Around the middle of the morning the men moved uphill again, this time toward the summit of Hill1010, a good four-hour climb.

Chinese were coming in from all sides. US artillery was seen to be hitting in front—and behind— the Rangers' position on 628. Definitely not a good place to be. The Rangers went forward.

The top of 1010 was occupied by the Rangers, who had yet to find any enemy close by. A patrol was sent up the last hill—1168—and finally found a few Chinese who refused to fight and ran away. The patrol returned to 1010 without incident.

The view afforded to the Rangers on 1010 allowed them see large numbers of Chinese moving to the east. The gap between the 24th Infantry Division and the 1st Marines was continuing to grow.

Early in the day of April 24, Allied lines were beginning to reset themselves, albeit in more southerly positions about four kilometers back. The 8th Rangers were now farther out front and they hadn't moved.

The Rangers were reporting enemy movement from their perch on 1010, and pretty soon the Chinese figured out they were there and began probing to find them. It is probable that Ranger and Chinese patrols passed each other in the darkness of the mountain night. In any event, the Chinese chose to settle in on 628 and a few other spots.

A few hours after midnight, rear areas of the 24th and 25th Division were taking hits from infiltrating Chinese. The gap between the US lines was allowing the enemy easy access to flanks and rear areas.

Sunrise of April 25 brought orders for the Rangers to withdraw, keeping to the ridgeline of 628. It wouldn't be easy. They ran into the Chinese on 628 right away, and had to fight their way through them, doing as much damage as possible to delay Chinese incursion on the 5th Regiment as it tried to settle itself.

The enemy had dug in well on 628, and was putting down a heavy wall of fire from entrenched machineguns and mortars. Rangers were taking hits, but kept coming, moving along narrow ridges where often only one man at a time could go forward.

One after another the 8th took out machineguns, only to have the weapon re-manned in moments. The noise must have been incredible as BARs hammered at full throttle and grenades went off everywhere. The broken terrain caused the main battle to be fragmented in small, vicious, fights in scattered locations.

Somehow, by sheer grit and determination, the surviving men of the 8th Rangers were on the top of Hill 628 before 9 a.m. Unfortunately, they were surrounded, running low on ammo, and shot up pretty badly.

They did have radio contact with the 2nd Battalion, 21st Infantry, and through that link tried to get the 5th Infantry to help them out. It took a while, but eventually a couple of platoons from the 5th tried to get through to the Rangers. They couldn't get in, and the Rangers couldn't get out.

The situation was getting worse by the minute. Captain Herbert went down, and Lt. Strong was hit. Everybody was firing, even the medics. Things looked grim.

Help came at last in the form of artillery fire blowing advancing Chinese into pieces. Guns of the 52nd Field Artillery kept the enemy off the Rangers long enough for the 2nd and 3rd Platoons to try to get out of there. Withdrawing off the ridge, they were still under intense fire, and artillery was being called in on the top of 628.

The Rangers received a message to get out any way they could.

Individual heroics were widespread on the way down, as in many places it was every man for himself. Some hope of help came when contact was made with elements of the 6th Medium Tank Battalion. Word came back that the 3rd Platoon, Company C, 6th Tanks, would wait for the Rangers to get down off the hill and take them back to US lines.

Getting off the hill took great effort. Lt. Giacherine, who reportedly did a solid job, led much of the withdrawal. Chinese attacks over the top of the hill were met by direct fire from Rangers pulling reverse-slope rearguard. Added to the misery of the enemy were Corsairs from the Navy dropping napalm on them.

Wounded Rangers made their way down as best they could, some of them holding themselves together for just that one more step. At the bottom, four tanks had mercifully waited, also out front and on their own several thousand yards into enemy territory.

By noon, the 8th Rangers were "home", after paying the price of that terrible fight. Of 90 men who began the mission, 25 were wounded and several were killed.

Task Force Byorum was formed May 18, and included two tank companies supported by the 8th Rangers and a company of the King's Shropshire Light Infantry—about 100 British soldiers. In addition to the firepower of the tanks, there were a total of eight half-tracks in the task force, each sporting a quad .50 system. That made 32 .50 caliber machineguns, an awesome amount of concentrated firepower. To round things out, Task Force Byorum even had an ambulance.

The combined unit crossed the line into the badlands and burrowed deep. Enemy shooters found the Allies right away, and kept peppering the task force with harassing fire.

The second day out the column was hit by a guerilla-type ambush involving Chinese soldiers dropping out of trees and crawling close along defiles and ditches to try and disable the armor with grenades, bangalore torpedoes, and attachable explosives. The Rangers fought hard to protect the tanks and half-tracks, and at one point tanks were hosing each other down with machinegun fire to keep the Chinese off.

This quick, but vicious fight didn't hurt the Allies much, but the enemy incurred some 350 casualties.

A few days later, the 8th Rangers moved forward with a task force whose mission was taking the town of Chonggang-ni. The going was tough getting to the town, since the Chinese were fighting a well-prepared withdrawal backed up by 120mm mortars. These big mortars did a lot of damage to Allied troops, as American 4.2-inch mortars did to theirs.

After slugging it out with die-hard enemy last-ditchers, the task force arrived at Chonggang-ni in a mood unfavorable to the Chinese. The combined firepower of the force was directed on the small town, with artillery fire thrown in for good measure. The target was devastated under the incredible destructive power, leaving more than 400 Chinese casualties in the suddenly empty town.

Topyong-ni

The advancing 24th Division had Intelligence that a small group of houses in a hamlet named Topyong-ni were being used to feed enemy troops. The 8th Rangers were sent three miles across the lines to clean the place out.

Artillery was used as a holding device rather than as an attack support, the shells landing outside the hamlet in a ring of fire designed to keep any help from arriving while the Rangers did their job. Unfortunately, things started off with some rounds landing among the Rangers, stunning them, but not enough to stop them.

The 2nd Platoon attacked while the 1st and 3rd Platoons acted as a blocking force to keep anyone from getting out, or in. The enemy was caught in the heavy Ranger fire and badly cut up as they tried to flee out of doors and windows.

9th Rangers

Commanded by Captain Theodore C. Thomas

The 9th RICA was kept at Benning as a replacement pool for Korea, its ranks partly filled by men from the 82nd Airborne.

This company, like the 7th, was used as a replacement and cadre company. Also like its counterpart, the 9th was full of veterans who were highly "upset" by this decision.

On May 29, the 9th Rangers were activated for the second time, this go-round with the 31st Infantry Division. Captain Billie Mitts was in command. The new Ranger Company began Airborne training with the new 15th RICA.

10th Rangers

Commanded by Captain Charles Spragins

Staffed by volunteers from the 45th Infantry Division, Oklahoma National Guard, on July 1 the company was sent to Japan in case it was needed in Korea.

The 10th Rangers made the first parachute jump ever accomplished by US forces in Japan.

11th Rangers

From the 40th ID, California National Guard, the 11th was also sent to Japan just in case. The 11th Rangers also jumped in Japan, at least once landing on beaches.

12th Rangers

Commanded by Captain Harold Kays

Activated February 1, 1951 from 500 volunteers from the 28th Infantry Division of the Pennsylvania National Guard, it was March 18 before 197 acceptable applicants appeared at Fort Benning to begin training.

Trainees graduated June 26, and were then sent to Camp Carson, Colorado for mountain training.

13th Rangers

Commanded by Captain Victor K. Harwood

Built with volunteers from the 43rd Division, New England National Guard, the unit formed up March 13th at Fort Benning to begin training.

They graduated June 26, and were then sent to Colorado for mountain training.

14th Rangers

Commanded by Captain Samuel L. Amato

The 14th was activated February 27 to begin training. Staffed with volunteers of the 4th Infantry Division at Camp Carson, it returned for mountain training after graduating Ranger School June 26.

15th Rangers

Commanded by Captain Paul W. Kopitzke

The 15th was activated February 27 to begin training. Volunteers were from the 47th Infantry Division (Viking), Minnesota/North Dakota National Guard. Airborne training began May 29, 1951.

The 12th-14th Companies, plus TDA Companies A and B, stood formation for graduation decked out in black berets.

Who Fought In Korea?

Below is a listing of Allied forces, though only the American units are delineated.

South Korea

17 Infantry Divisions

6 Independent Infantry Regiments

2 Marine Regiments

8 Tank Companies

The South Koreans were notoriously bad soldiers, especially in the beginning, but the Americans who were there mostly agree the ROKs got a lot better over time. Still, as in Vietnam years later, the enemy elected to direct the most force at the national troops and not at the powerful Americans.

Other United Nations Combat Forces

These nations contributed troops and material in various amounts and were generally attached to a larger unit, often of another nation. For example, a battalion of Turkish soldiers in one US Division, or a company of Ethiopians assigned to a US or British Regiment. The general consensus among American soldiers was the Allies sent some good men to the fight.

Belgium

Great Britain

Colombia

Ethiopia

France

Greece

Luxembourg

Netherlands

Philippines

Thailand

Turkey

United States

The US contributed nine Army Divisions, a Marine Division, and a couple of regiment-sized units over the total time of the war. These units experienced very different actions depending on when, and how long, they were on the line. Air assets are separate.

1st Cavalry Division
2nd Infantry Division
187th Regimental Combat Team
3rd Infantry Division
7th Infantry Division
24th Infantry Division
25th Infantry Division
40th Infantry Division
45th Infantry Division
1st Marine Division
1st Provisional Marine Brigade

India, Italy, Norway, and Sweden all contributed in non-military ways, such as medical personnel and other support troops.

LRP FOUNDATION—COLD WAR EUROPE

The great wars were over. Everyone hoped there would never be another global conflict, or even anything as bloody as the short Korean War. However, within a few years there was again a need for stalwart, highly trained men to plug the holes made by politicians. Rangers were called upon to help, as they have been since the beginning.

The term "Long Range Patrol" has been around since WWII, and probably was used before that. Patrolling at a distance is not exclusive to Rangers, nor is the function of reconnaissance, yet, by adding the word "unit," that term and its cousin, "Long Range Reconnaissance Patrol," have become almost exclusively applied to Ranger units. During the Vietnam War era, Ranger unit predecessors were the only ones given that designation at their formation.

The first LRRP units, small and provisional, were not in Vietnam, but in Germany, pushing the envelope against their own troops in order to stay poised for a possible Soviet strike.

Such units were formed at battalion and brigade level—elite groups bent on perfecting and inventing new techniques, gaining knowledge that would find its way to Vietnam and beyond.

The year was 1958. Platoon-sized units were paving the way for company-sized units to come.

The catch-all term "Lurp" is used often in the following text to signify either LRRP or LRP, except when delineation between the two is necessary. Both are pronounced the same.

Mike Martin

More than a few Rangers involved in this project suggested Mike Martin as a valuable addition. Martin spent time in Germany as one of the first LRRP members, and had two tours in Vietnam before going to Korea in 1972. He also spent time at the Mountain Phase of Ranger School in Lumpkin County, Georgia, and has trained soldiers in many other ways.

He attended 18 military schools, serving as an Instructor in several. He was the first American to graduate from a school in Norway run by British Commandos. He was the First Sergeant of seven companies, and Sergeant Major of five battalions, an Engineer Group, a Combined Field Army, and several other organizations. He retired in Korea in 1986.

His two interviews were recorded over the telephone in June 2006. Other parts of his story can be found in the Vietnam section.

I came into the service in 1956. I went to Basic Training at Fort Jackson [South Carolina]. That was a little unique because they still carried the designation as an Airborne unit, because the 101ˢᵗ had been there.

We went to Fort Bragg for the second eight [weeks]. They formed up a Cadre out of the 82nd Airborne and they put us down in the old barracks down by the airfield, and each unit had so many Cadre, like the 504th, 503rd, whatever. They called it the Airborne second eight, and they stopped that after my class.

Germany

I was assigned to Charlie Company, 504th. Then we went to Jump School. We made the last night jump at Fort Bragg at Jump School. I stayed about a year there at Bragg. The 504th was going to gyro to Germany, so I volunteered. We had to re-up if you had less than three years in the company to go with them. So we went to Germany [in 1958] and I was in the advance party. We went to Mice Kaserne. The 504th was the first over, and then the 505th came over. The 505th had one end of the barracks and the 504th had the other end. It became an Airborne Brigade later. We had some pretty famous people in the thing. General Mataxis, who was later one of the commanders of the 505th, and Tony Herbert. Herbert was put out of the Army, but he was the highest decorated individual of the Korean War, and he started a Ranger Platoon in the 505th. We didn't have one in the 504th; we had a Recon Platoon. All the units there were Battle Groups, not regiments.

2/501 and Ranger School

Then I returned to the 82nd and was assigned to the 501st. That's when I went to Ranger School, from the 501st. I went as an E-4.

The 501st is now a 101st unit, but Martin says in those days it was both 82nd and 101st. "There were a couple of units like that."

I went to Ranger School in December 1960 and graduated in 1961.

When I started the class they were mixing the officers and NCOs together in a billet in Fort Benning. That only lasted about four or five nights. Then they changed back. On patrol we were all Rangers and there was no rank. They told us that was the first time that had been tried, but Walt Sanders—he's a Colonel now—told me they had done that in their class, but I don't know because they told us we were the only ones.

After Ranger School, Martin went back to the 2/501st. He said that battalion was the first to use helicopters for roping and rappelling up in the mountains of Virginia. "That's all we did." That was 1961.

V Corps LRRP

There were other Long Range Patrols and Recon Platoons begun even earlier than the V Corps LRRP, but the V and VII Corps units are considered the first "recognized" LRRP units. Having said that, they are not "officially" recognized as a foundation for lineage, but they are definitely related by linkage to the present day Rangers.

I made E-5 [after Ranger School] and came back and they had Operation *Swift Strike* [1961] one year and they were getting ready to do it again and they asked division-wide for volunteers for a new unit that was forming in Germany called Long Range Patrol. I said, well, I'll volunteer, but it was a whole division and they said they were only going to take a few guys. All the guys who had served in Germany, really, volunteered, but you had to have a certain score on your Army testing in the field of communications and so forth. They picked 13 of us out of the division. I went over and they had formed up the Long Range Patrol. It was V and VII Corps. That was 1961.

When we volunteered it was only for V Corps. There is a misconception that they both formed at the same time [Lurps of V and VII Corps]. The V was formed first, and a couple of months or so later the VII Corp [Lurps] formed up.

We [V Corps Lurps] were forming up at Wildflecken, Germany. Major Reese Jones was company commander and Major Edward Porter was the XO. We had Lt. Murphy in the unit, who later got the DSC and was put in for the Medal of Honor. Sergeant Major Martinez was the First Sergeant—a unique guy, fought in WWII and Korea, and later, Vietnam. Most of the Platoon Sergeants and so forth had combat experience.

We had two platoons. We had a patrolling platoon and a training platoon, and a commo section. The training platoon did the same things as the patrolling platoon, but the patrolling platoon was [would be] the first to deploy. We were divided up into five-man teams.

For communications, when I got there, we had the old PRC-10s, and later we got the PRC-25s, the first ones. They were unbelievable. We ran a training operation with them, and I got commo of 70 kilometers off a PRC-25, which is unheard of. For our main radio we had CW high speed. All those guys had to go to radio school to take code CW [eight weeks]. We had a radio, I forget the specification, but we called it a Trac-77. We had a commo chief, a Sergeant Wiggins, he could communicate on those things back to the States. We sent everything in code when we were out in the field.

The VII Corps [Lurps] was formed at Stuttgart at Nelligan compound. Prior to those there had been two other—starting around 1957, Seventh Army started experimenting with Long Range Patrols. The 505th used a Ranger Platoon to run long-range patrols, and some of the other units. The 3rd Infantry Division formed up a Long Range Patrol Platoon. When we formed up the V Corps, several of the patrol leaders came out of the 3rd Division. I think they formed up in about 1959.

The unit was called, he thinks, the 3rd ID Lurps, with no separate numerical designation.

The first one I became familiar with [while] in Germany, the Southern European Task Force [SETAF] formed a reconnaissance platoon in Italy in late 1957. They operated in Italian Alps and [other places in Italy]. It was a very professional unit.

A Korean War (non-Ranger) veteran named Stamper first commanded that unit.

I pointed out time and time again in staff studies, they had helicopters organic to their unit. I always said the pilots had to be familiar with your type of ops in order to have success. They worked well with that. It was the 110th Aviation Company. They [recon unit] got outstanding training because they went to Mountain School with the Italian soldiers and their Lurp units.

Were they the earliest LRRPs? The answer is no, considering long range patrols were used in WWII by both sides, and in Korea. However, the "modern" concept of American long range patrolling may have started there, or in the 11th Airborne about the same time. Martin said there was a LRRP school in the 11th Airborne during 1957. The guidelines for training were very similar to those laid out for the European LRRP units, but he said, "They didn't have the sophisticated radios such as the CW."

The V and VII Corps LRRPs in Germany were the first identified or recognized as Army [TDA/temporary] units.

I designed the unit insignia [crest]—now called Distinguished Unit Insignia—for V Corps LRRP Company.

Abrams and the Beret concept

At that point in time, the US Army was hesitant to accept anything that reeked of special troops or Special Forces or Rangers.

We were in Wildflecken at that time, and Lt. Murphy flew to England and purchased some British Commando Berets [maroon] out of his own pocket and brought them back. We started wearing those, and VII Corps started wearing berets, but Abrams took them away.

However supportive of special troops Abrams was, he was also "Army regulation" all the way.

90 Days

General Abrams—I think this is where his concept of the 1st Ranger Battalion came from—he came in there and took over V Corps. A Major had taken over the [LRRP] company, and General Abrams told him he had 90 days to show him something or he would disband the unit.

It just so happened there was a major field operation they did every year in Germany at that time. That thing kicked off and within minutes—and I mean minutes—the V Corps LRRPs had pinpointed every major unit, every artillery site, anything of that nature we had pinpointed and had it back to V Corps G-2, and that made a believer out of Abrams. That's the only reason we survived. That was the latter part of 1963 or '64 for sure.

Honor Guard and More

Then, and this happened to VII Corps, too, because we were Airborne troops, and appearance-wise we were so much sharper than other units, they wanted to use both of us as Honor Guards. For example, the V Corps [LRRP] was picked to go down to the 20th anniversary of the D-Day invasion, and we were the major unit down there. I was in the Color Team and the whole company was in the Color Guard. We paraded at Normandy Beach and other places. We were the only American unit sent down there. There were British, French, Dutch—you name it.

When Abrams got orders to leave the unit we were his Honor Guard. We lined up at the I. G. Farben building. We lined up on both sides of the road all the way down to the main street. As he came by we would present arms.

He did a turn around on special ops and Airborne troops and I think the V Corps LRRPs were the ones that did that.

Jack Daniel

Jack Daniel was in Germany when the Lurp concept was being tested. His words here are excerpts from several conversations, all taped. Some of the information came from a dialogue we had about Mike Martin, a well-known Ranger who has authored several books about Vietnamese Rangers, their Airborne, and their Marines.

Mike Martin is a great Ranger. He was with the Vietnamese Airborne as well as the Vietnamese Rangers. He was fortunate enough to be in the first recognized group of LRRPs [in Germany]. Not to say he didn't deserve it, because he did. There is no better soldier that ever put on jump boots than Sergeant Major Mike Martin, and I have that respect for him. But he wasn't the first Lurp.

I was in a Lurp organization [LRRP] that was not official. It was unofficial—that is, we did not have a TO&E, or for that matter, an approved TDA.

I did a lot of very interesting stuff, and it was from the ground up. We'd never had Lurps in the organization.

We had a very great V Corps Commander, Paul D. Adams. He had been one of the deputy commanders of the 1st Special Service Force [of WWII]. General Adams had this test unit. We already had Lurps. We had them formed, and we had them training, doing Ranger training. The General got this idea of an "economy of force" unit to use against the Russians, to call in air strikes and artillery. Nukes. They were called Long Range Reconnaissance Patrols, except they didn't want them to move much.

They were provisional then. They were an ad hoc unit. They were the first LRRPs.

You see, the Russians outnumbered us terribly, and by that time we had gone to the Pentomic Division, which had five Battle Groups instead of having regiments. A Battle Group was close to five thousand people. Not as big as a regiment, but bigger than a battalion. Eisenhower is the one that directed the Army to do it. Because we had such huge frontages against the Russians, we had deployment plans where we had to move forward and move into contact. What they did with the LRRPs, they did infiltration, or stay behind, parachute entry, or helicopter entry. There was only one Airborne unit in Europe at that time—the 11th Airborne. Instead of being in reserve, where it should have been, it was up on the line, on the Austrian border.

We were before them [the V Corp]. They took us ad hoc. They would just take us and test us. We would form a temporary arrangement in these big field exercises. And finally they formed in each Battle Group; it was called a Long Range Patrol Platoon.

General Adams and Colonel Gallaghar, Assistant G-2, coined the term LRRP. It was a provisional unit quartered south of Frankfurt.

Training for V Corps LRRPs included putting together "economy of force" six-to-ten man teams to adjust artillery and air strikes on the Soviets.

Steve Melnyk

I met Steve in New Jersey, but this interview was done by email in early 2004.

My service in our Long Range Patrol Platoon, Headquarters Company, 1st Battle Group, 28th Infantry, 8th Infantry Division, was from March 1958 to March 1959. [We were] located in Baumholder, Germany. The post billeted approximately 18,000 American troops, 5,000 German troops and 2,000 French troops. These were the days of the Cold War and the threat of Soviet communists. Our LRP Platoon was an independent and separate organization that was organized and assigned under the administrative control of the Headquarters Company. The unit was under the direct supervision of Division G-2, who was Lt. Colonel Martinan. None of these units were ever a part of the organic TO&E Recon Platoons of the respective Battle Group. Our LRPs were used for deep penetration and stay behind force multipliers against these Soviet threats. I remember our orders coming from Division G-2.

Our platoon was made up of two Long Range Patrols, and a third one was never manned. Each patrol was usually made up of six members. All were interviewed and selected by Lt. John Daniel, who served as a Lane Grader/Instructor in the Florida Ranger Camp. He was Airborne and Ranger qualified. He had been trained in demolitions and communications, as well as being a Jumpmaster at the Infantry School at Fort Benning, Georgia. He was a strong and intelligent leader, a perfect match for this outstanding group. His leadership excelled.

I still remember my interview with Lt. Daniel over 46 years ago on the third floor of those German barracks at Co. C. I told him about growing up in the tough coalmines of western Pennsylvania, where my dad was a coal miner. The company store owned us. As a young boy I hunted and trapped weasel, muskrat, fox, coon for their furs for money. I worked on a farm during harvest. [It was a legal excuse not to go to school then.] I told him about my parents leaving Ukraine to get away from the communists without any contact for 18 years. Communists would read letters and never permitted them to get through.

I could speak and understand Ukrainian, with knowledge of Polish and Russian. I had the highest qualification score with the M1 in Basic Training and stood on the reviewing stand at graduation at Fort Riley. I also had qualified for OCS. I was fortunate to be selected for this LRP.

All members selected by Lt. Daniel were required to speak at least some German and to be fluent in one other language. They were extremely talented, and brought languages of Italian, Swedish, Norwegian, German, Polish, Ukrainian, Hungarian, French, Spanish, Russian and Czech to the group. With these languages we were well represented in Europe. We were all required to have high SAT scores and were required to be qualified with .30 cal machinegun, the BAR, carbine, the M1 Garand rifle. I also qualified or fired the rocket launcher, Thompson submachinegun and .45 caliber hand weapon. While with Special Forces, I carried a long-barrel 9mm in a holster that could be used as a rifle or hand weapon.

Three members were already Airborne-qualified. All others volunteered for Airborne training, but unfortunately, were not permitted to go to Jump School at Furst and Felberde. We also had four members who had seen active combat duty in Korea, South America, and Hungary.

Our LRP had three demolition graduates and two Morse code graduates, while others trained with 10th Special Forces Group in Bad Tolz, Germany. I received a certificate from Colonel Mike Paulick, Commanding Officer for my training in the Alps at Bad Tolz.

My group leader from the British SAS was a Major who led us in the mountain and guerilla training. The SAS trained with us there in the 10th Special Forces Group. The British SAS jumped in at night in the mountains of the Alps where we grouped together.

1st Lt. Daniel and Master Sergeant Mastrovito [Korean War Airborne Combat Veteran] provided an intensive training program with constant field training. They were highly trained, and passed on their skills to us. We all became great map-readers and compass users. I remember one escape and evasion mission where I was being chased for about 10 miles while others got captured. I used my compass and traveled alone at night and survived.

We also had a broad variety of classroom studies that included the geography and terrain of Europe with other subjects. This would be important in our troop movement and enemy movement, since we were always behind lines.

All patrol members were required to be in outstanding physical condition and were constantly tested in the individual skills of hand-to-hand combat, bayonet and knife fighting, cover and camouflage, individual movement, adjustment of mortar and artillery fire, demolitions and bridging mine fields and use of tactical air transportation. I remember getting in the ring with Lt. Daniel many times for hand-to-hand combat.

While rucksacks seemed to be part of our every day uniform, with 12-mile forced marches and five-mile runs, we even used skis on some snow events. My job was to carry a small generator in front of my chest with my rucksack on my back. This was used for the Morse Code communications.

Clearances, such as top secret and secret, were given yet some had difficulty with family ties in communist countries. All members trained with the Air Force Escape and Evasion program, some of which involved interrogation.

The mission of the LRP Platoon was to acquire enemy targets at a sufficient depth to interdict enemy supply lines and disrupt communication. This was to be done by use of air strikes, artillery, and on occasion, selected ambushes. Our Long Range Patrol constantly tested other units in the field with us, working behind their lines, being injected by helicopter or infiltration of their lines, sending out signals by Morse code through out Germany. It became almost standard procedure for our Long Range Patrols, led by Lt. Daniel and Master Sergeant Mastrovito, to infiltrate lines when units were in the field.

Our skills were outstanding in infiltration. One mission I remember, we infiltrated and stood over a commanding officer while he was asleep. He was not a happy camper when we woke him up and destroyed his helicopter.

They began to offer rewards for the capture of us in the field. This included cash and even beer.

While serving in the LRP, I was selected as Soldier of the Month, 28th Brigade twice, and Soldier of the Month for Baumholder Post. I was preparing for Western Europe Command competition when I left the service. I also received a Certificate of Achievement from General L. R. Moses at Bad Kreuznach, Germany for duty while serving as a member of The Long Range Patrol.

Bob McMahon

McMahon left the Mountain Camp in Georgia in 1964 as an E-6 with orders for Germany where he served with the 24th ID as a Platoon Sergeant, then later with the LRRPs. His interview was recorded and also involved his service in Vietnam, available in the Vietnam section.

I was with the 24th ID Battle Group with a mechanized platoon. I was with Easy Company. They had a company commander who wanted an E-6 "blood stripe" to give one of his cronies and they figured they'd get mine. The First Sergeant warned me that if I knew any place to go [in the division] it would be a good idea because they were looking for an excuse to bust me and promote this other guy.

There can only be a certain number of Sergeants of various ranks in each unit.

I went over and saw a friend of mine who was in the Division LRRP platoon. I was accepted and stayed with the LRRPs for about two years over there.

We did a big operation and we were attached to one of the Corps at Nelligan, and I believe that was V Corps. We were opconned to them and they had Operation REFORGER, where they brought a division over from the States. We operated and aggressed against them with the LRRP unit. One of the guys in [that unit] was Bob Schroeder. He was at the Ranger Camp when I went back there.

He said his unit was designated Division LRRPs, and then he had a surprise. Although there were no Ranger combat units listed for that time period, McMahon said they were there.

We had two platoons. We had a Ranger Platoon, which was [the] strike force, then we had the Long Range Recon Platoon. Mainly what we did was surveillance, and we operated with AN-GRC 9 radios and Morse code. We operated for the division. Whatever they wanted done, that's about what we did. Even as far as having to form a division honor guard, which I was part of at one time.

We were the aggressors against other units, and tested their knowledge. It was interesting and very good. A lot of fun. Cowboys and Indians stuff.

Bill Spies—157H

The first TO& E that I am aware of for LRRPs was in 1962. I believe it was 7-157H—maybe just TO& E 157H. First Sergeant Romo could tell you plenty about those companies. Some were TDA unit, and some may have been provisional before coming under 157H. There are records of them in both of the Army Museums in Carlisle, Pennsylvania, and in DC. Those 157H companies all had three recon platoons of four six-man patrols, plus Platoon Headquarters, and a very large commo section of maybe 75 to 100 signal personnel.

The commo section was split into three teams, and when a patrol, or several patrols, was out on a mission 75 to 100Ks out front, they had to erect three separate antennas [stations] placed a specific distance apart, in line, on a specific azimuth. They provided 24-hour per day contact with the patrol(s). Three stations were required as they operated on UHF and the beam bounced off of the troposphere and then back down to earth. Because the troposphere is egg-shaped, the angel of the bounce varied at different times of the day and required three base stations to ensure 24 hour contact.

Criteria

There is a very specific criterion to establish if a unit is whatever it is designated as, be it armor, cavalry, Armored Cav, recon platoon, Ranger, LRP, etc. You analyze these:

Combat mission

Organization—numbers of troops in the various levels and in its basic unit—is it a team, a fire team, a squad, a patrol, etc.?

Specific skill(s) required of members—language, weapons and vehicle identification, physical strength of a high level, IQ of a certain level, special commo skills, etc.

Training, is it special—HALO, SCUBA, SERE, etc.?

Equipment

Those that are similar are classified as others of the same kind.

V Corps LRRPs to Company A, 75th Infantry (Ranger)

There had to be a core group of trained men to form the first Lurp units, and to give training to those just coming aboard. Many of those men were trained in Germany and/or helped train the men who would eventually become members of Company A, 75th Rangers.

The following chronicles the movements and evolution of the primary Ranger unit, Company A, a company of highly-trained and motivated men that was never deployed to Vietnam as a unit, though quite a few individuals ended up over there.

Before the jungle-creepers of Vietnam came the watchers of the mighty Soviets.

On July 15, 1961, the V Corps (Abn) LRRP Company was activated as part of the Seventh Army at Wildflecken, Germany, with Major Reese Jones as the original commanding officer.

By September 1962, the unit was named the 3779th Provisional LRRP Company (Airborne). However, Special Order 188, HQ 82nd Airborne Division, Fort Bragg, NC, dated August 15, 1962, listed the unit as a Recon Patrol Company.

Mike Martin said, "You know how that works, some clerk got it wrong."

Indeed, Special Order 207, dated September 25, 1962, got it right, listing the unit as a US Army LRRP Company (Abn) when referring to "ration separately" administration by the 14th Armored Cav. A further mislabeling came in 1965, when a clerk simply called them a US LRRP Company when the unit went to the rifle range.

That company eventually became Company D, Long Range Patrol (Abn), 17th Infantry, on May 15, 1965, and then became Company A (Airborne Ranger), 75th Infantry, in 1969. That makes it the longest serving DA authorized LRRP/Ranger Company in the US Army.

Originally placed with the 14th Armored Cavalry Regiment for administration, the company wore the Seventh Army shoulder patch with Airborne Tab, but it was first and foremost a V Corp asset. It was the only unit near the East German border on jump status. They were a new breed of soldier and they were proud of it, training relentlessly to go the extra mile.

In late 1962, Lt. Robert C. Murphy flew to England, and splurged on maroon berets for the company with his own money. Somehow the Lurps got them authorized by the Commanding General of Seventh Army for both V and VII Corps LRRP Companies.

General Creighton Abrams assumed command of V Corps in 1963, and revoked the company's maroon berets when he found out they had not been authorized by Department of the Army.

Though banned in Germany, the maroon beret lived on as a cover for Vietnamese Rangers and their American Advisors.

T he company crest was designed by Mike Martin and the motto "Cum Animus Et Successus" (Through Courage, Success) was added by Lt. Murphy.

Esprit de Corps was running high, and Vietnam Lurps were still three years away.

At the time, V Corps was spread all across West Germany to block the threat from four of the top six avenues of Soviet ground aggression. The new Lurp Company patrolled during field training exercises, and ran simulated missions against air installations and Army posts, including deep penetration exercises. Much of the patrolling was done in certain corridors, including Fulda-Hanau, Coburg-Bamburg, Bad Heisfeld-Giessen, and Bad Kissingen-Wurzburg.

Ominously, the company was also trained to infiltrate an area and place atomic munitions, as well as locating targets for tactical nuke strikes.

The company moved to Edwards Kaserne outside Frankfurt, with Captain William Guinn assuming command from Major Edward Porter in January 1963. The shoulder patch was changed from Seventh Army to V Corps with Airborne tab.

The company moved yet again May 9 of that year to Gibbs Kaserne in Frankfurt and became part of the V Corps Special Troops (Provisional) working for V Corps G-2 (Intelligence).

1964 saw the issue of AN/PRC-25s FM voice radios to replace the AN/PRC-10s. That was a big improvement over previous lack of communication with the various other armed forces.

The company also traded in its M14 rifles for the new XM16E1 5.56mm rifle in the autumn of 1964.

Yes, they had a high malfunction rate even when new in Europe, as well as in the Republic of Vietnam (RVN).

The changes of equipment and a dedication to professionalism brought about an end of provisional status with the first Table of Organization and Equipment, 7-157E, and the first Long Range Recon Company Field Manuel, FM 31-16.

The TO&E also boosted the strength of the company to 208 men, fielding 24 five-man patrols, where the previous small units were four men. The company leaders were all Ranger-qualified and every man was Airborne.

The mission didn't change much, though, and the Soviets continued to be the target as the company honed its considerable skills in camouflage, communications, infiltration, and just plain firefights. FTXs were run in all possible scenarios relating to possible Soviet aggression.

The TO&E also formalized the trend towards Ranger status with a requirement for 24 Patrol Leaders, three "Killer" Platoon Leaders, the Ops Officer, Executive Officer, C.O. and First Sergeant to be Ranger qualified. All 208 LRRPs had to be parachute qualified.

There was another unit as part of the VII Corps, with its own story, and no less important than the V Corps Lurps. This particular history follows only the V Corps Lurps.

When the unit became Company D in 1965 it maintained the same mission and the same position right in front of the expected main thrust routes of the Soviet army. The company patrolled extensively and used everybody as targets, including their own people. Deep penetration, infiltration, and locating enemy battlefield targets were all on the agenda.
Bringing The Expertise Home

American forces began to leave Germany in 1968, cloaked under the title REFORGER (Redeployment of Forces, Germany). Company D found itself at Fort Benning, Georgia, with Captain Harry Nieubar in command.

The Fort Benning barracks was on Kelly Hill, and the company was the only active duty Airborne unit on the post. Having no other current designation, the men still wore the V Corps patch and were used as Aggressors at all three Ranger training sites. They were pretty good at it too, because about half of the company consisted of Vietnam combat veterans at that time, most of them from the 101st and the 173rd.

The company also ran the RVN Orientation at Fort Benning. Instructors were very much into ambushing students at any time, and reportedly used a lot of det cord and artillery simulators to get the young men used to sudden big bangs.

When Company D, 151st Infantry, Indiana National Guard was alerted for service overseas, V Corps Lurps helped get them ready to go.

By that time, D/17 (became A/75) was training for both European and RVN operations. Then, the Army added Riot Training. The latter caused some spectacular events that made the Army re-think LRRP participation in crowd control.

Perhaps they were a little too enthusiastic.

Vietnam was going full blast in 1969 when the company began sending trained LRPs overseas almost weekly to serve in Lurp units. By that time, the company was fielding the standard six-man teams—the same as those in Vietnam.

Then things changed again. General Abrams decreed all Lurps would become Rangers as of February 1, 1969, so D/17 LRP became A/75 Infantry (Ranger), with Captain Thomas P. Meyer commanding. Oddly enough, there were not many Tabbed Rangers in the unit at that time. They were Lurps.

Although the men were given the Ranger unit crests, they were made to wear the shoulder patch of the 197th Infantry Brigade, and were still effectively opconned to V Corp as a recon unit. That affiliation was the main reason the company was never deployed to Vietnam.

Fort Hood, Texas, welcomed A/75 in early 1970, where they were assigned to the 1st Armored Division, commanded by Captain Johnathan Henkel.

Since the new technology relating to various sensor systems had been brought forward in Vietnam, someone was needed to carry the program into the future. The Rangers' top mission until mid-1972 was to support MASSTAR (Mobile Army Sensor Systems Test, Evaluation, and Review). The job wasn't as dull as it sounds, because the company was mostly used in an aggressor capacity against troops using the test devices.

Stealth and information gathering became the first focus, and lessons learned were used to good effect 20 years later in the first Gulf War.

The mission changed again in July 1972, to provide Long Range Reconnaissance capability for the 1st Cavalry Division, but the secondary mission was still to stay in a high state of training for the original mission of V Corps LRRP. A/75 did, in fact, deploy to Germany on an annual REFORGER exercise in 1973 to do exactly the same work as their predecessors did in the early and mid-60s. By that time more than 80 percent of A/75 personnel were Vietnam veterans.

1974 was the beginning of the end for A/75, with the new Ranger battalions forming around a nucleus of key people, many of them former A/75 members. The new 1st Ranger Battalion sent former A/75 CO Captain Clark and First Sergeant Bonofacio Romo to the company. They recruited a lot of personnel who left the company in mid-1974.

Second Battalion CO Lt. Colonel A.J. Baker also came to Fort Hood with his CSM and recruited another two-or-three-dozen men.

The change occurred at Fort Stewart, Georgia in October 1974, but though the men of the old Company A were used to fill the ranks of the new Company A, the lineage for the new unit was taken from Company C, Vietnam Field Force Rangers.

The company was deactivated and its guidons cased for the last time at a fixed-bayonet parade in December 1974. The last A/75 Commanding Officer was Captain James P. Fitter. The last First Sergeant was Gary Carpenter, who would later become the first Regimental Sergeant-Major of the 75th Ranger Regiment.

VIETNAM

Sacrifice and Success—A New Day for Rangers

There is no simple way to tell the story of the Vietnam War. From the beginning, the reasons for American involvement in that far-off place were unclear to most people, including a lot of administration officials in Washington. Over time this cloudy issue became a full-fledged thunderstorm, and rained all over America's parade to stop communism in its tracks.

To understand how we got there, why we fought the way we did, and why we could not hope to win the political war, one must look at the overall picture of Vietnamese history, starting at the end of WWII. The Geneva Convention of 1954, the French defeat at Dien Bien Phu, the huge exodus above and below the 17th Parallel, President Kennedy's unwillingness to commit and President Johnson's plunge into the 1965 build-up—all had significant effects on the progress of the Vietnam disaster.

Interspersed throughout this narrative are interviews with men who were there. Not all Rangers in Vietnam actually served in Ranger units. Ranger-trained individuals were scattered throughout the forces then, as they are now, because from 1951 until 1969 there were no Ranger units outside of training facilities. Their stories are here because they are Rangers by virtue of the Tab, if not by membership in a designated unit.

The dedication of these highly trained men bolstered the ranks of the Army units, including the 1st Cav, 82nd Airborne, 101st Airborne, and 173rd Airborne Brigade. Then there were the Advisors, some of whom were in-country from the late 1950s—men who pushed, cajoled, fought beside, and sometimes died with the Vietnamese Rangers and ARVN (Army of the Republic of Vietnam) troops.

Special Forces and Ranger personnel at in-country schools did much of the training of Viet soldiers. Such training of the Vietnamese dates back to the 1950s, done many different places in many different ways. Much of the new Lurp/Ranger training was also done in-country, at Recondo schools and by individual units. Before a man could go out on a mission with a Lurp/Ranger unit he went through two-to-three weeks of heavy training, so he didn't go out there and get himself or somebody else killed. Recondo School was generally attended by a few men from one company at a time.

But that was later. In the beginning the US wasn't there in force, and the onus of victory was on the South Vietnamese.

From the start, the idea was to get Vietnam to stand up for itself and reject the communists. It became evident very quickly this would not happen on its own.

The US backed France in a big way in its re-colonization efforts after WWII. They were allies, after all, having just vanquished the Germans—though it was the Japanese in

Vietnam. The US was paying a large part of France's rebuilding costs, plus supporting its war effort in Vietnam, Laos, and Cambodia, and adding heavier aid directly to Saigon in the early 1960s. The alliance with France didn't do much for pro-US sentiment in Vietnam.

Though it was costing US taxpayers a chunk of money to do all that, neither Eisenhower nor John Kennedy wanted to commit troops beyond Advisors—yet. Unfortunately, the South Vietnamese government seemed quite unable to stem the Red Tide on its own, let alone create a functioning socio/economic situation.

A few years later things were still going downhill in Vietnam. A new American President, Lyndon Johnson, took over when JFK was assassinated. Johnson wasn't so sure how to proceed, either, and took the more cautious route in the beginning. It was obvious to him something had to be done, and his Secretary of Defense, Robert McNamara, agreed. The American people knew little of what was going on in SE Asia, so there was no ready support for a buildup of troops. The trigger had to be found before the weapon could be fired.

Then the Gulf of Tonkin incident occurred, and LBJ had what he needed to go forward.

Most conflicts have a "trigger event" that set aside political caution.

In late 1963, a clandestine war against the North began, with mercenaries from several nations hitting the enemy from the sea and air and blowing up railheads and whatever else they could reach. It was from this action the Tonkin Gulf incident stemmed.

August 2, 1964, in the Gulf of Tonkin—bordering the east coast of North Vietnam—the US Destroyers Maddox and C. Turner Joy were on a recon patrol when they were fired on by enemy PT boats. The US insisted the ships were on a "routine" patrol when they were hit, but North Vietnam had complained the day before about attacks by South Vietnamese Navy boats and Laotian Royal Air Force planes.

There were more than a few attacks and insertions of agents against the North prior to that time.

Maddox and air assets from the carrier Ticonderoga hit back, damaging three vessels. LBJ wasn't sure what was happening, but he beefed up the Naval forces in the area. August 4, McNamara and LBJ exchanged several phone calls discussing the situation. The Maddox command thought a second attack was imminent. McNamara recommended retaliation after the second attack, which he was being told was happening via torpedo assault from enemy ships in the area. Ticonderoga launched eight aircraft to take a look at the other vessels, but found nothing amiss. Nobody got blown up. Somehow, communications and assessment didn't get the message to Washington. Johnson went on television to brief the nation on the Gulf of Tonkin Crisis. He said because of the second attack the US had flown retaliatory strikes against North Vietnam, destroying 25 or so PT boats, and smashing their bases with the loss of two US aircraft. While announcing the bombing of the North, a major step toward heavier escalation, he also said those famous words, "We seek no wider war."

Though McNamara said, years later, that a second attack never happened, but the North was bombed heavily on PT bases and shipping facilities in retaliation. If we had known, said McNamara, we wouldn't have sought retribution. In 1965, Johnson is said to have commented, "For all I know, our Navy was shooting at whales out there."

So, even though there was heavy evidence that no second attack took place—there is more than what is listed here—the administration, and by extension, the media, told the world that North Vietnam was the aggressor in unprovoked attacks on US forces.

On August 2, the Congress passed the Gulf of Tonkin Resolution, which, among other things, stated the US would protect its interests in SE Asia.

The door stood open.

Tonkin Gulf Resolution

Joint Resolution of Congress H.J. RES 1145 August 7, 1964

Resolved by the Senate and House of Representatives of the United States of America in Congress assembled, that the Congress approves and supports the determination of the President, as Commander in Chief, to take all necessary measures to repel any armed attack against the forces of the United States and to prevent further aggression.

The United States regards as vital to its national interest and to world peace the maintenance of international peace and security in Southeast Asia. Consonant with the Constitution of the United States and the Charter of the United Nations and in accordance with its obligations under the Southeast Asia Collective Defense Treaty, the United States is, therefore, prepared, as the President determines, to take all necessary steps, including the use of armed force, to assist any member or protocol state of the Southeast Asia Collective Defense Treaty requesting assistance in defense of its freedom.

This resolution shall expire when the President shall determine that the peace and security of the area is reasonably assured by international conditions created by action of the United Nations or otherwise, except that it may be terminated earlier by concurrent resolution of Congress.

Nine years later, in 1973, Congress used the last clause to cut off funding for the war.
White Star—1959-62

For more on this subject, see the interview with Colonel (ret) Sydnor in the Son Tay section.

Operation White Star, or whatever it was called at the time, is important because it employed more than a few Ranger legends, and because it was the real beginning of Special Operations-type missions of the Vietnam era. It was also America's first attempt at physically opposing communism in Southeast Asia.

Things were bad in Laos and getting worse. To counter the communist threat there, the US brass decided to try and train the locals to fight the good fight. To that end, the CIA was given the mission of making that happen, so they naturally went to the military. Over a long three-year period, US Special Operations soldiers spent time among the Laotian ethnic groups, mainly the Hmoung. The idea was to support the main force, the Armee Clandestine.

Training commenced under the code name "Ambidextrous" for the Special Forces soldiers chosen to go. The men were trained in various ways, including new radio communications and at least two languages, plus being mandated to read certain books, such as *The Ugly American*.

In July 1959, a "unit" in civilian clothes—Group I—was inserted into Laos under the command of WWII Ranger legend Lt. Colonel Arthur "Bull" Simons, and given the code name "Hotfoot." Simons remained through the second group until June 1960, when Lt. Colonel Magnus Smith took over. By 1960, it was Group IV, commanded by Lt. Colonel John "Shark" Little. That was the whole deal, except for a 12-man psy-war team added at the end of "Hot Foot."

In April 1961, Group V came aboard and took the new code name "White Star." By October, it was once again being run by Lt. Colonel Simons.

Simons was responsible for the organization, logistics, and training of the first group.

There were about 100 men in the first group, and even at its peak White Star fielded just over 400. It was not a huge undertaking, and although there was fighting, only five men in three years were killed. It was a training mission that ultimately fell short of its goal of stopping the communists in Laos when a Declaration of Neutrality was signed in July 1962.

Perhaps the best thing about White Star was the training the Americans got while training Laotians.

LRRP, LRP, RANGER

Americans were in Vietnam beginning in the 1950s, and the war lasted until 1975, but this project deals with Rangers and their predecessors—gone by 1972. There are several reasons why the section on Vietnam is so large. The length of time in-country, we'll say six years, 1965-1971, is the longest combat service in over 300 years of Ranger units. That amount of time allowed the opportunity for many Ranger-qualified individuals to gain experience—and for others to gain the title.

The number of men serving in Ranger roles and Lurp/Ranger units, and the number of surviving veterans all have importance, but none so primary as the evolving role of the far-walking hunters. Rangers of today exist largely because of the results the men of Vietnam produced—the proven worth of well-trained individuals with more than an average dose of intelligence, physical capabilities, and above all, guts.

The wars in Afghanistan and Iraq may produce more combat-experienced Rangers over time—now five years in Afghanistan and nearly four in Iraq—but Vietnam-era soldiers defined small unit tactics. Many leaders of Ranger training served in Vietnam. The information and techniques they gathered and taught has been modified to fit current needs, but the concept—the philosophy—remains the same.

The Beginning

It wasn't long after US forces were in South Vietnam that the need for eyes and ears became very apparent. Accordingly, each commander from division down to brigade organized their own versions of a recon unit, tailored to their Tactical Area of Operational Responsibility (TAOR) and the needs to be met at the time.

Remember, they were learning as they went. At that point the only Lurps were in Germany and had not seen combat, though they were very organized and well trained. Unfortunately, there are few jungles in Europe, so the new style of combat found in Vietnam had no predecessors except for Merrill's Marauders in Burma in WWII and the Pacific campaign of the same war.

Since there were variations in the needs of different divisions and brigades, there were variations in the organization and make-up of each LRRP unit. For one thing, they were small. Most began as platoons with a provisional designation. There was no central command structure for these units. They worked for whoever organized them.

Volunteers all, many had no formal Ranger-type training going in. The ones that did have that training became the leaders and teachers. A Recondo School—for training to fight against a new enemy in a new place—was begun in Nha Trang and originally staffed by Special Forces men of Project Delta. By 1966, regular Infantry was included in the training sessions, and so began the LRRPs.

The first Long Range Reconnaissance Patrols were composed mostly of men who had graduated the Stateside Ranger School, or had attended a Recondo school of the 82nd Airborne or the 101st Airborne in the States, or had gone through the Jungle Operations Center in Panama. The leaders were as qualified as anyone could be at the time, considering there was little or no combat experience among them. On-the-job training was the order of the day for most new men—after being quick-trained by their unit mates and/or taking a Recondo class.

Indeed, replacements coming through the 101st Airborne's Screaming Eagle Replacement Training School (SERTS) were often so green they were put on security duty in a bunker at Camp Eagle (101st main base in Vietnam) and didn't even know how to use all the weapons they were given.

However they were deployed, the first units did it without an Army Table of Organization and Equipment (TO&E). They were supposed to be temporary, but as they began to prove their worth, their position and mission evolved with knowledge gained.

Some of the first recon units were mechanized, as with the Recon team of the 173rd Airborne Brigade, though that didn't last long. Unit capability was fitted to the task and the terrain. Mountainous jungle was hard on the mechanized units. They took the title "Recon," but they weren't Lurps.

Smaller, quieter patrols were undertaken, and helicopter insertions were used more frequently.

The LRRPs began to do what the Ranger concept dictates. They began to get behind or among the enemy and use stealth and a fast-increasing knowledge of terrain and tactics. They began to understand their enemy and the way he fought—and must be fought.

LRRPs started the show for all to follow, plying their changing trade from 1965 with the formation of a LRRP unit of the 1st Brigade, 101st Airborne. The Army decided to make the provisional units formally a part of the whole in December 1967, with their own TO&E for company-sized units.

The new units were called Long Range Patrols (LRP), dropping the word "reconnaissance" because of the—slightly—changed mission. LRPs were often staffed by LRRPs of the predecessor units, among recruits from other units and replacement depots, and the war went on. These stronger units still did some recon, and also mounted ambushes, raids and the occasional prisoner snatch, plus calling in death from above on the enemy.

Lurp units, and later Rangers, became expert at directing attacks from the air by fixed-wing aircraft, helos, or artillery. Many enemy soldiers perished because a Lurp/Ranger was on the heights with a radio.

Each LRP Company had its own training and indoctrination classes, as would the Ranger units to come. The men learned early on that one poorly trained fool could get everybody killed. Training evolved as new knowledge became available. Medical training was stepped up so that any man on the team knew how to deal with a sucking chest wound, insert an IV or treat shock. That training saved a lot of lives until medevac birds could take a man out.

The evolution of the patrol continued, along with a more aggressive role played by the helicopter. Mobility made a huge difference, and the LRPs could get in and out quickly, doing the increasingly dangerous and important job of gathering Intelligence and harassing the enemy.

The Army, with a gentle push by Creighton Abrams, COMUSMACV, decreed that February 1, 1969, was the last day for the LRPs and the first day for the new Rangers.

The LRP units became Ranger units, and the war went on. Veterans say not much changed operationally, but the new designation boosted morale. The work of those courageous men was finally being recognized.

It was a big step, creating new Rangers. They were the first operational Ranger combat units since WWII. Pentagon Action Officer Lt. Colonel Bryan Sutton, sent to find military legitimacy for the new unit, was told at the Center for Military History that the lineage of the WWII Battalions already belonged to the Special Forces, given to them at a time when there were no Ranger units, so he had to look elsewhere for suitable ancestors. As it happened, President John F. Kennedy had a liking for the SF and was a big booster, but that's another story.

Sutton tried to find a TO&E for the Alamo Scouts of WWII, but could not because they had been a provisional unit. That's how Ranger lineage came from Merrill's Marauders of the Burma campaign, who in no way saw themselves as Rangers. They were simply closer than anybody else.

In 1974, when the 1ˢᵗ Ranger Battalion was being formed, Colonel Kenneth Leuer somehow got the colors back from the Special Forces, but the lineage still traces to the Marauders.

From there the Marauders were absorbed into the 475ᵗʰ Infantry, thence to the 75ᵗʰ Infantry, which added the designation (Ranger) to each company. For example, Company F, 58ᵗʰ Infantry (LRP), became Company L, 75ᵗʰ Infantry (Ranger). The one exception was Company D, which kept its designation with the 151ˢᵗ Infantry, but added the Ranger tag and fought in Vietnam.

A total of 13 Ranger Companies fought in Vietnam, spanning a gap between February 1, 1969 and August 15, 1972. That number, of course, doesn't include the Lurps before them.

The 5307ᵗʰ Composite Provisional—Merrill's Marauders—was used as a line unit, three battalions of hardy souls who marched down through Burma hitting the Japanese at every opportunity. However, the show in Burma was primarily a British and Chinese affair and the Marauders were hundreds among thousands.

The Marauders—3,000 of them—mostly performed envelopment maneuvers that were but a small part of the total effort in Burma. Still, the professionalism of the small units did not go unnoticed. The Secretary of the Army, Stanley Resor, bestowed the title Neo-Marauders on the 75ᵗʰ Infantry for having lived up to the reputation of the original Marauders.

Though the lineage has taken on an honorable tone, the gulf between the Marauders of WWII and the Rangers of Vietnam was enormous. For more on this subject see the section on Lineage.

The Ranger Companies were made up of volunteers from all parts of the Army and were mostly trained in-country where they were formed, though the kernel of most units were its LRP predecessors. This on-the-job type of training was second to none for giving the men a fighting chance in the enemy's jungle. By that time, there were plenty of hardened veterans to train new men—though the rate of attrition from rotation, wounds, death, and short-timers, not to mention various schools and R&R, often kept the units below standard in terms of manpower.

By 1969, there were "shake-and-bake" NCOs leading six-man teams in the field. The percentage of two-tour experienced LRP/Rangers was shrinking.

A new man had to prove himself to his new unit members in order to be accepted as a peer, doing well on patrol and being an integral part of the group. Only when the other members of a unit were satisfied was the new man allowed to wear the red, white, and black scroll shoulder insignia with unit designation. Indeed, most units wouldn't let a man out on patrol until he had satisfied them in training.

One of the many things a new man had to master was noise discipline. This was partially accomplished by packing a rucksack in the correct manner, both for easy access to necessary items, and for comfort on a long walk—such as packing your poncho liner next to your back. Once a ruck was completely packed the men jumped up and down to see if anything clinked. If anything made noise it was repacked or taped with camouflage tape.

Once in the field, all communication was made by hand signals, expressions and body language, or whispers that couldn't be heard 10 feet away. Most team leaders didn't allow smoking in the field—of tobacco or anything else—though the line companies usually did. Smelly stuff like smoke, deodorant, even soap, was taboo in the field. Likewise, a Lurp/Ranger team was careful to leave no trails and no litter, even burying physical waste, where scavengers who knew there would be bounty to collect often followed a line company.

The Vietnamese civilian, let alone the military, was adept at using nearly everything the Americans left behind, from explosive material to beer cans.

The discipline and professionalism of the Lurp/Ranger prevented discovery, and therefore promoted longevity. Sometimes teams would be discovered in an AO, but were not able to be precisely located because they left no trail, and when they went to ground they were invisible.

The Rangers continued to evolve their tactics and techniques, relying heavily on the helicopter as a means of insertion and extraction, protection and resupply.

When a warning order came down the line a day or two ahead of an insertion, the Team Leader (TL) was briefed by the company commander and the two made an over-flight of the intended area of operations (AO) to identify any practical landing or pickup zones, water supplies, terrain features around known enemy positions and the like. Though it wasn't always possible to over-fly an AO beforehand, it was generally accomplished. When possible, the helicopter was flown by the pilot who would be doing the insertion. The flight line would be over the AO without stopping, continuing on for a while, then returning the same way for another look without giving away the insertion site.

Often there were a few false insertions before and after the real thing to throw off LZ watchers.

Artillery and air support was brought up to date to protect the team—and not fire on them by mistake. Radio support and relay were set up, reaction forces were alerted, weapons checked and test-fired, and the all-important water stored in canteens.

The importance of water cannot be understated. Though teams were often in jungle with many running streams, getting to them wasn't always easy, and halazone tablets would have to be used to purify the water they did get. More than once a unit in the boonies would have to come out because they were out of water. Food was secondary.

Ammunition was the "other" consideration. Though teams often carried more than a basic load, ammo ran short quickly if a firefight was sustained for any length of time.

Bring food if you can, but we've got to have water and bullets.

A six-man team fit into one Huey, but heavy teams needed two or three. Either way, there would be a Command and Control bird (C&C) orbiting above with a couple of Huey or Cobra gunships and maybe a Little Bird observation helicopter closer down. Once the team was in and had moved off the LZ into cover without contact, the TL would release the birds.

Sometimes an LZ would be hot, but usually it was the PZ (pickup zone) where the action against aircraft was the worst. If a team was being tracked or chased, things could be rough during extraction.

On insertion a team might get to cover, "lay dog" for a while, then begin to move, only to find an enemy unit is coming toward them, alerted by an LZ watcher. Resulting contact meant calling for an immediate extraction using helicopters that were already at, or almost at, home base.

If things went well, meaning an undetected insertion, the team would lead off with a point man, slack (second man), Team Leader (TL) third, then senior radio operator, junior radio operator, and the rear guard. There was also an Assistant Team Leader (ATL) who usually took the slack (second) or rear (sixth) position. The point man kept direction and the slack man kept the pace—actually counting paces to keep clear how far the team had advanced. Each man had an area of responsibility, both visually and tactically. If anything happened, practiced drills known as Immediate Action Drills (IADs) were used to fire up the enemy and get away.

Different teams used different IADs, but most were about the same. The idea was to fire and cover, fire and fall back, with one man covering the squad, then another, until contact was broken. If the enemy wasn't a large unit, the team may stop a little way off and set an ambush with a booby-trapped claymore or grenade as a "present" for the enemy.

When not in contact the teams would walk through the day and take a night defensive position where—depending on security alert status—one to three men would take time to scarf some freeze-dried LRRP rations, or grab some shut-eye. Teams were often set for the darkness on 50-to-100 percent alert. Staying awake all night and being ready to fight or fly in the morning was something that had to be done. The usual shift was two hours, though some preferred an hour-and-a-half.

Any man that fell asleep on guard duty didn't walk many more missions, nor did anyone who snored. At times, the enemy would be out looking for them in the night and could be very close. Any small sound that didn't fit the natural noise of the jungle—or wherever they were—could bring death.

Delving deeply into enemy territory, small teams located enemy bases and supply lines, practiced stunning ambushes, did wire-taps and disrupted communications, occasionally snatched prisoners, occasionally did Bomb Damage Assessments (BDA) after B-52 strikes, and even went into recently defoliated areas to see what was uncovered.

Teams inserted into such areas walked through recently dead foliage, an area saturated with poison. Seldom did they find much, a few uncovered bunkers, but the enemy had departed. The BDAs were much the same as far as results. Any enemy KIA were usually removed before US teams went into an area, looking much like the surface of the moon with acres of huge craters.

Throughout the tenure of these units, whether LRRP, LRP, or Ranger, US forces benefited greatly from the accumulation of Intelligence and the disruption of enemy functions, plus the elimination of many enemy soldiers.

In the final evolution, the Rangers of Vietnam became much more than just eyes and ears. Their adaptability and professionalism became so necessary to the success of the larger units that the Army couldn't help but continue the line. When the last of the Vietnam Ranger Companies stood down in 1972, less than two years passed before the concept came alive again in the form of the 1st Battalion, 75th Infantry (Ranger).

VIETNAM RANGER EVOLUTION

The Long Range Patrol units of Vietnam were known by three separate designations during the years 1965-1972, though the overall mission remained much the same. The actual origin of the LRRP unit occurred in Germany in the late 1950s. There is more on the European Lurps in a separate section because, even though they were the first, they were not one of the 13 TO&E-Lurp descendants—the Vietnam Ranger units.

Those 13 companies of Rangers did not just fall from the sky already trained and in place. What eventually became the basis of the Ranger Regiment was the final form of an evolution that began as an adaptation to a great need in 1965. The European Lurps proved certain techniques to be valid within the overall concept of long range patrolling. Their experience was not wasted when training began in earnest for Vietnam.

The story of the Lurp/Rangers of Vietnam can probably never be fully told, but even a good job of it would entail several volumes. Accordingly, this project features only one line of descent—or ascent—as an illustration for the rest. The use of this line does not in any way mean these units were better than the others.

Picking out one Ranger Company and its predecessors to showcase as an example was difficult. The choice of one line came down to the simple fact that several men from these units were easily accessible as interview subjects, and the three units involved were all part of the 101st Airborne Division.

In addition, the longevity of this particular line of far-walking hunters is noteworthy because it stems from the first such unit in Vietnam. Beginning with the formation of the Long Range Recon Patrol (Platoon) in 1965, the LRRPs of the 1st Brigade, 101st Airborne were later reorganized into the next phase—F Company, 58th Infantry, Long Range Patrol. The LRRPs of the 1st Brigade helped fill the ranks of the LRPs of F/58 in the beginning of 1968.

That unit, in turn, was phased out in early 1969 and replaced by—again, reorganized into—L Company, 75th Infantry (Ranger), and attached to the 2/17th Air Cavalry of the 101st. The three units are totally separate—on paper. The connection between them is by linkage, not lineage.

Changes on paper were reflected in the field as well, particularly in terms of assault and insertion capability. Added responsibilities of ambush and prisoner snatch made recon only a part of the function of the LRP units, though it remained their bread-and-butter mission.

That is not to say the LRRPs of the 1st Brigade didn't do ambushes. They did, and well.

The size of the LRP unit was beefed up to company strength. Heavier patrols were sometimes made, using 10-to-18 men instead of the standard small unit of six.

February 1, 1969, LRPs became Rangers by decree of the Department of the Army. The move was pushed by General Creighton Abrams in order to raise morale, and perhaps maintain a higher degree of professionalism, which had been seen to be falling off as many of the original cast and crew were rotated State-side. The character of the war was changing and everybody knew it, but the need for elite professionals remained.

Associated changes in designation didn't alter the fact that most of the units stayed right where they were, doing what they did best. Over the years the small units had become so effective the enemy put bounties on some of them, a sure sign of respect for their capabilities.

Such bounties were not restricted to the 101ˢᵗ.

Information gathered plus damage done to the enemy made the Rangers and their predecessors indispensable to the success of larger units. From the original concept of "eyes and ears," the Lurp/Ranger units had evolved into a highly effective, fearsome, and deeply committed recon fighting force.

To give an idea of the flow of Ranger evolution through Vietnam, the following is a capsule history of the three Lurp/Ranger units related by linkage through the 101ˢᵗ Division. These units are also bound through comparable character and courage, each adapting to its own time period and particular needs.

The First of the First—1st Brigade, (LRRP), 101ˢᵗ Airborne Division

Organized in August 1965, the LRRPs of the 1ˢᵗ Brigade were the beginning of a line of units dedicated to excellence in the pursuit of military Intelligence and harassment of the enemy.

It should be noted that the original platoons were not TO&E units, instead being labeled "provisional," and therefore having no unit lineage or history.

Training began in September, primarily done by Ranger-qualified individuals and graduates of a Recondo School. The platoon-sized group was tactically employed in October with one officer and 34 enlisted men, broken down into a headquarters section and four recon teams.

Headquarters was composed of a Platoon Leader, Platoon Sergeant, Operations Sergeant, Communications Chief and assistant, and a light truck driver—though they usually had no vehicles.

The Recon teams were made up of a Team Leader, two recon scouts, two scouts doubling as communications men, and two scouts doubling as medics.

Given the mission of infiltration into enemy territory—Indian Country—to see what was out there, and sometimes to lead a larger unit in, the small new unit wasn't sure exactly how to go about it. The men learned on the job—the best and most dangerous kind of training.

Teams tended to stay out three-to-six days, keeping in touch with other teams and base camp with two PRC-25 radios and usually an AN/GRC 46 radio. Communication was key to the team's success from the very start. Often, a relay station was set up between the field and base to make sure the signal reached home.

They were mostly qualified Airborne, but generally insertion was done by helicopter or foot march—even by boat. Helicopters were just coming on line as a viable means of transport, and there weren't so many as later in the war. Logistics and tactics were still being worked out as knowledge of the enemy and terrain accumulated.

The men of the 1st Brigade LRRPs learned fast and fought hard. In 1966, platoon members were awarded a Silver Star, 29 Bronze Medals with V device, four Army Commendations for Valor, 10 Purple Hearts, and 25 Air Medals.

They were busy. They proved their worth.

They took on the nickname "Old Foul Dudes," though most of them were 20 years old.

The concept went forward. The next year things changed. A plan was made to increase the size of the unit to two officers and 59 enlisted men, adding two snipers and two radio operators to each team. The teams would grow from six members to heavy teams of 10 or 12. The idea was to patrol farther afield and maybe do some light engagements.

The unit continued to provide Intelligence for the brigade throughout 1967, until the Army realized the need for larger, more permanent units.

The mission was broadened, platoon became company, designation changed, and the term "reconnaissance" was dropped. Late 1967 was to be the end of the LRRP teams, and the beginning of the Long Range Patrol. By early 1968, the transfer was complete.

Company F (LRP), 58th Infantry, 101st Airborne Division

Company F, 58th Infantry, has a long and distinguished history dating back to its organization in Pennsylvania in June 1917, as part of the 4th Infantry Division.

The company was in and out of service as needed for 50 years, fighting in both World Wars, and used for everything from service in an armored unit to being a headquarters company.

When Vietnam came around, Company F was again called upon, reactivated in-country on January 10, 1968 with the designation of Long Range Patrol, or LRP. The 101st Airborne Division was still the parent unit, but the "new" unit now had a TO&E designation, and therefore unit history and lineage.

Original personnel came mostly from Cadre (Instructors) at Fort Campbell's Recondo School and the LRRPs of the 1st Brigade. They were some tough, motivated men with lots of skill.

The Old Foul Dudes were used to provide immediate experience to F Company, and there were some tense times putting the old guys and the new guys together.

It had to be tough for a man with six months in the bush to have a man with six weeks in-country try to tell him how to do his job. Somehow they eventually sided up and got along. Within a few months, most of the originals were rotated out, anyway.

Darol Walker, Division LRP Company First Sergeant

In 1967, after returning from my first tour in Vietnam, I was assigned to the 101st Airborne Division Recondo School as the School Sergeant Major (NCO in charge). Some time mid-year the Assistant Division Commander, Brigadier General Clay, and the G-2, Colonel Charles Beckwith {later to command Delta} came to the school and told us General

Westmoreland wanted a Long Range Patrol (LRP) Company in every Infantry Division in Vietnam. We knew the division was going to deploy in December 1967.

The 1ˢᵗ Brigade was already there and had a Long Range Recon Platoon (LRRP). Since all Cadre of the Recondo School were Ranger School graduates, we were selected to form this new company. We started recruiting personnel and trained at Fort Campbell and the Army's Florida Ranger Camp. We deployed to Bien Hoa (Vietnam) 4 December 1967 with Captain Peter Fitts commanding. After arriving in-country, the 1ˢᵗ Brigade LRRP Platoon was reassigned to our company.

We were activated as F Company, 58ᵗʰ Infantry, and remained that way until February 1969, when the company was re-designated L Company, 75ᵗʰ Rangers.

As to the original fill-in and training of F Co. at Campbell, we did not completely fill the company, and we continued to recruit even when we got in-country. If my memory is correct, about 95 percent of the Cadre at Recondo School volunteered for the company. Many of them had already served a tour in Vietnam. We started our training at Campbell and used some of the training schedules we used at the school to train, especially patrolling techniques. We added, or I should say Colonel Beckwith added, a very extensive live-fire course. Colonel Beckwith had also commanded the Florida Ranger Camp at Eglin Air force Base, so we took the company down there for a couple of weeks training on advanced Long Range Patrolling.

There was a little animosity between the LRRP Platoon, who called themselves "Old Foul Dudes," and the new company. This was bound to happen, since they had already been there and had many missions under their belts and we were all FNGs [Fucking New Guys] to them. All of that went away as we trained [some with the Australian SAS] and integrated everyone into the new company. I don't believe, due to the type of mission we had and the small size of our patrols, that you would find a tighter organization anywhere in the Army. They were so dependant on each other to accomplish the mission and for survival that a very strong brotherhood developed.

Getting Started

As the unit got settled and organized, its parent, the 101ˢᵗ Airborne, was just fully in-country. There was a lot to do, and the LRPs did everything but long range patrolling for a while. Two teams were sent north from the first base at Bien Hoa to help find a new spot for the 101ˢᵗ, but the Tet Offensive of 1968 set all plans aside for a few weeks.

The company had been sent from Bien Hoa to Song Be to assist in securing the city, and only half the men got back to Bien Hoa before fighting broke out. Both parts of the company saw plenty of action during Tet. It was January 28 before they were reunited.

A new location was found for the division near Hue in the northeastern part of RVN, and F/58ᵗʰ was one of the first units sent to secure it, meeting up with its two six-man teams already there. The new base was called Camp Eagle, and there was a lot to do to get it up and running. For a couple of months the company pulled security, a necessary thing because Hue had been partially occupied by the communists for 27 days during Tet and the area was still very hot.

The LRPs kept the road open between Camp Eagle and Highway 1, a main artery, and did some close-in ambushes to keep the enemy on his toes. The monsoon arrived, teaching everybody how to build a dry bunker. The troops found out that nights in the tropical jungle could be cold, especially when everything was wet. At times the temperature could drop into the 50s. Considering the high humidity, that's cold when you're wet and wearing light jungle gear.

When the weather finally cleared, helicopters were made available to the unit.

It was May 4 before the first long range patrol was made. The unit was combat-ready.

A seven-man team—including the Team Leader—was inserted into mountainous jungle northwest of Fire Support Base [FSB] Birmingham. They made contact right away, killed at least one enemy soldier, and were extracted two hours later.

The second mission followed the next day, when two teams went in. Both made contact and were extracted within two days. It was just a taste of what was lurking out there.

The usual mission was still reconnaissance out where the enemy was. There were no actual "lines" as in previous wars. The "front" was where you were shooting.

At any time, the LRPs might be surrounded after insertion. The enemy could come from any direction. The mission of the LRPs was to catch them at their own game, laying down ambushes and melting away. The teams also called in artillery and air support to defend themselves or to knock out bunkers or concentrations of troops. Often, such tactical support was called in very close to the LRP perimeter to keep from being overrun. Such times were almost as dangerous for the LRPs as for the enemy.

The enemy would figure out where the bombs and artillery were hitting and get inside the fan, between the LRPs and the explosions. That meant they weren't getting hit as hard, and that the explosions would drive maybe a platoon of them into the LRPs—a six man team. The gunships up above couldn't use rockets or fleshette weapons too close to friendly troops because of the inherent scatter of the projectiles.

Over the duration of the year, the men of F Company made 124 LRP missions to gather valuable Intelligence for the division. They also claimed 62 enemies KIA, while losing five of their own, with 14 wounded.

It is unknown how many more NVA were killed by TAC air and artillery called down on them by hidden teams, but the count was a lot higher than the eyes-on body counts.

Success of the mission, and comparatively low casualties, was in large part due to the pilots and crews of the various helicopters assigned to the missions. Generally, five "birds" were used to insert one or two teams. A lift ship made the troop carry, and a chase ship gave close cover and was ready to do an immediate extract if things went very wrong. There were also two gun ships—usually Hueys, later Cobras—and a Command and Control (C&C) bird. The company commander often flew in the C&C bird, circling above the LRP AO on insertion and extraction. The gunships also flew a high orbit until needed, when they could scream in with cannons and rockets, devastating anyone below.

Over time the gunships evolved from UH-1B Hueys to Cobras and were used in several different combinations with Scout Birds (H-13, then OH-6).

The pilots and crews were from the 160th Aviation Group, and stayed with the LRPs in base camp. They were a courageous bunch, held in high esteem by the men on the ground.

Teams worked west of Hue (Camp Eagle) as far out as the A Shau Valley, south to the 85 east-west grid, and north to the 30 east-west grid. Information on enemy troop movements, positions, and trails was continuously reported.

Darol Walker

As a senior NCO, Walker often took the position of "belly man" on extractions.

First of all why a "belly man" anyway? With a four-man chopper crew: Pilot, co-Pilot, crew chief and door gunner, each with an area of responsibility to watch. Most importantly, clearance for the main and tail rotors—someone has to have the responsibility to guide the pilot down to the patrol on the ground. The best way to observe the area was to lie down on the floor of the chopper on your belly and look out the door on either side straight down— hence, "belly man." This man was always from the LRP Company and most times one of the senior NCOs. When an extraction was called, the first question always was is it "hot" or not?

A hot LZ meant people on the ground were shooting at you.

In a cold extraction things are a little more relaxed, but going down in a bomb crater or other small opening is always hazardous. Hot extractions are another thing! I recall when it was my turn to go on a hot extraction I would immediately have to pee (nerves). We used "piss tubes," which were artillery shell containers buried in the ground with a couple of feet exposed above ground and you would piss in these tubes. Sometimes my legs would be shaking to the point I couldn't hit the tube.

Once airborne, every thing was OK and you sort of put everything on autopilot. My practice was to carry my CAR15 and a 40mm grenade launcher with an ammo can for both. I would put one weapon in each door and go from side to side firing if necessary. The deal was to get in and out as quickly as possible but it never worked out that way. Typically in a rope ladder or McGuire rig extraction. Nylon climbing ropes were used on the McGuire rigs; they are 120 feet long so the chopper would hover above the extraction site low enough for the ropes to reach the ground. There you are in a dead hover, and not able to move until the team has gotten into the harness on the end of the ropes. That s when Charlie would try his best to shoot you down. We had gun ships flying 360 {degrees} around us putting down suppressive fire, and the door gunners and belly man firing all we could. The hardest thing was to control the pilots. Their natural instinct was to pull pitch and di-di [leave in a hurry] out of there. We had to constantly persuade them to hold what they had.

Another dangerous point for the teams was once they were in the rigs. You had to make sure the pilot went straight up high enough to clear the trees before he moved forward. There were instances of pilots flying teams into trees in their haste to get out of the area. We also had a round hit one of the ropes on an extraction and drop a team member back to the ground. We were able to recover him OK. For me, and I'm sure with most people, when things are real hot everything seems to be going on in slow motion, you don t really notice any hits you are taking unless one hits you. There is lots of gunpowder in the air and that seems to stimulate your adrenalin. Most times we weren t aware of hits to the aircraft until we got back and saw the bullet holes.

There were plenty of times in Lurp/Ranger missions that helicopters went in—and stayed. There were also times when desperate men pulled weapons on pilots to keep them in place long enough to get everybody out. A hovering helicopter is an easy target, and the NVA/VC had .51 caliber machineguns with a long reach and a heavy punch.

Try to imagine—or remember—being in a Huey, soaked in noise and blood, with enemy rounds popping through the body of the aircraft, people being hit, screaming; you're pouring fire out the door and you can't even see anybody, everything inside you is pushing you to get the hell out of there—and yet you stay. You have to stay. Your buddies are still out there.

In June, the company trained a platoon from the 1ˢᵗ ARVN Division Recon Company, taking the students out on patrol as part of their training. The Viets learned quickly.

From talking with men who were there, the author has learned this was not always the case. There were complaints the Viets wouldn't fight, had no noise discipline, and were lazy. But, maybe that was just that one time, or just that one unit.

The company was attached to the 2/17ᵗʰ Air Cavalry in October, giving them a huge leap in mobility. Suddenly, helicopters were everywhere, and LRP missions increased in size and scope. Five to eight teams would go out at once, covering a much larger area, and in turn being covered by the birds and reaction forces of the Cav.

There were plenty of firefights, but a bad one came in November. A 12-man team pulled an ambush on ten enemy soldiers, killing nine, but one got away, though carrying a bullet. The team searched the bodies, collecting weapons and documents, then prepared for extraction a short distance away. While moving toward the LZ, the point man was hit several times by automatic weapons fire. The team got him inside a quick perimeter, firing back all the while. The firefight escalated, with the LRPs not knowing how many they faced.

Try to imagine yourself in that position. There is incoming fire from all directions; bullets whining overhead, into your position, you never know when one will find you. Your buddies are down, bleeding, maybe dying, and your rifle is so hot you don't dare touch the barrel. Your fortifications consist of a slight rise in the ground and a bunch of foliage. There is so much noise you can't hear the radio. You can only pray someone on the other end is listening and will send HELP.

A sudden explosion from an unknown source killed three of the team—a fourth died later—and wounded seven of the 12-man team—with one already down. Though wounded, some critically, the surviving LRPs continued to fight and try to care for the worst wounded, expecting to be overrun at any moment. A medevac bird lowered a Jungle Penetrator twice, though it had trouble getting it in the right spot at first, and got a few wounded out, but help on the ground was needed to go with the Cobra fire from the air.

Then, at the last moment, when death seemed inevitable, the LRPs heard their brothers coming through the trees, clearing a path through the enemy to reach them. Instead of a reaction force of infantry, the first to reach them were their own mates from F Company, some of them in whatever clothing they were wearing when the call came their brothers were in deep trouble.

The men of F Company reinforced the perimeter, steadied the wounded, and got the banged-up team out of there.

A quick-reaction force of "Blues" from the 2/17 Cav was also inserted, giving the US forces enough firepower to disengage. Before extraction was complete, some of the reaction force and more LRPs were wounded.

Different teams had different colors for recognition. A "red" team was Cobra gunships, a "white" team was light observation helicopters, a "pink" team was a Cobra and a light bird, and the "blues" were Infantry back- up.

F Company continued to distinguish itself with professional performance in an ever-widening role, making such special operations indispensable to the success of the whole.

The Army, seeing the importance of top-grade performance from its LRP Companies, decided to upgrade morale and give credit where credit was due by re-designating the LRP companies and giving them their own lineage and history.

All well and good in the long run, but at the time a lot of the men didn't even know it was happening until it was done, and noticed few changes even then. The importance of the move to Ranger history is proven by the continued existence of Ranger units.

Company L, 75th Infantry (Ranger), 101st Airborne (Airmobile)

Attached to the 2/17 Air Cavalry

"Every member of L Company, as a minimum, was Airborne-qualified. Even though we did not use a parachute to infiltrate enemy territory, the Airborne Spirit was alive in each of us. We had each been measured when we 'stood in the door' to face our fears. We passed that test to become a member of the Airborne brotherhood. Volunteering to be a Ranger in Vietnam, in the 101st Airborne Division (Airmobile) was yet another measure of courage and commitment."

Robert Suchke

On December 5, 1968, General Creighton Abrams approved the reactivation of the 75th Infantry as the parent regiment of all Army Long Range Patrol units. As of January 1, 1969, F/58th was deactivated, then reactivated as Company L, 75th Infantry (Ranger), along with all the other LRP companies. Lineage thus originated with Merrill's Marauders of WWII fame.

The lineage is expanded on in the Lineage Section, and the LRRP, LRP, Ranger Section.

Though some of the same people made up the unit, and they stayed with the 2/17 Cav, the mission changed just a little. The elite group was given more time in the field to observe and report and interdict supply lines and troop movements, and less time pulling security for downed birds and Camp Eagle. The designation of Ranger finally gave them the status they had earned for several years, and curbed excessive or abusive use of these Special Operations units.

In 1969, Company L ran 310 patrols, almost twice the number of previous years. Counted kills topped 20, with many more accounted for by called-in fire from artillery and air support. Approximately every third patrol made contact with, or had observation of, the enemy.

In addition, the teams gathered Intelligence on water sources, terrain features, and possible LZ locations, plus giving training in rappelling and McGuire-Rig extraction to Screaming Eagle (101st) Division troops.

Occasionally, the outer firebases would be shut down due to bad weather and the Rangers had to be supported by artillery from Camp Eagle's 175mm howitzers firing at maximum range. The teams would sometimes get out a long way from Eagle, and run out from under the canopy of the big guns, relying on air support for safety. They tried hard to keep that from happening, however, and the teams were almost always covered by artillery from somewhere. Almost always. When they got way out there, communication was slim to poor to none, so relay radios were often set up on high points to direct commo.

In March, three teams combined to alert Fire Support Base Jack of a large group of the enemy moving toward the base. Rangers harried the enemy with small arms, grenades and claymores, and brought artillery and gunship fire on them, smashing them even as they tried to withdraw. The Rangers' pre-emptive strikes saved the base from attack.

The teams were put out in strength in July, with five and six small units going out at once to achieve saturation patrolling.

In December, extreme weather caused a patrol to stay in the field for 10 days before extraction was possible. A company record was set, but there probably wasn't much joy in it. Rations were carried for maybe a day more than the mission called for, and finding water could mean being seen by the enemy.

The first day of 1970 found a heavy team surrounded and fighting for its life to get to an LZ for extraction. Infantry support from D Troop, 2/17 Cav was inserted to help get four US wounded out.

Once the enemy had located a team, time became very important. Enemy soldiers would scour the countryside if they thought Rangers were watching them. False helicopter insertions and extractions helped hide the location of the teams, but if fire was called in on the enemy, it became obvious someone was controlling it. Contact often brought enemy from nearby locations, hoping to destroy the hated Rangers.

Missions were usually run in four-kilometer-square grids. Even given the nature of the terrain in the mountains, and the slowness of movement by the teams, it was not a huge area. If the enemy got wise to the team's presence it didn't take them long to narrow down their location.

There were 33 missions in March—a busy month—including a raid into the A Shau Valley. Two heavy teams of 18 Rangers and five Engineers combat-assaulted the location and found signs of serious activity, including tracks of large earthmovers. One team blew a bridge and a bunker while the other team secured a downed 2/17 Cav aircraft and checked out a road for interdiction fire points.

During that time the teams began using sensor monitoring, such as "sniffers" to pick up the smell of urine. There were several different devices available to detect the enemy, and the Rangers put them to good use. The sensors had been around for a while, and most of the men didn't think they were worth much. For example, the urine sniffer also picked up buffalo urine, and the seismic sensors picked up walking buffalo, which sometimes got bombed.

When nothing else was going on, Ranger did more training for ARVN Recon teams, running joint operations in the field.

More heavy teams went out, using 50 percent security during NDPs (night defensive positions).

One such team (Grasshopper) in the Khe Sanh Plains got into a fight with an unknown number of the enemy, taking casualties and running out of ammunition. LOHs (light observation helicopter) flew over and dropped grenades to the men to keep them going. Those "little birds" also had teeth, and did a lot of damage strafing enemy positions. The team fought through the night until making an emergency extraction by a rope ladder dangling from a helicopter, under heavy fire, at three o'clock in the morning.

Such acts were not uncommon.

Tragedy struck in May.

A six-man team (Kansas) in the Ruong Ruong Valley was acting as radio relay for another team, plus doing some recon, and reported only a small amount of enemy movement. Four days into the mission the team was in a night defensive position (NDP) and sent a negative situation report at 0430, meaning all was well. That was the last communication from the team. About four hours later helicopters from the Cav hovered over the team's location and counted six bodies. When Cav ground forces recovered the dead, their weapons and one radio were gone. No expended US brass was found.

Regular sit-reps were monitored around the clock. If one was missed, the company commander was notified. If the second one was missed, people were up in the air.

The loss was terrible, but the Rangers of L Company sucked it up and went forward, running 31 missions in July. The NVA was infiltrating heavily into the Khe Sanh area, so that's where most of the missions were run. Recon was again a priority.

Sometimes they were introduced into the middle of things. At one point, heavy team Ferrari took fire immediately after landing that developed into a serious firefight. Helicopters played a big role, spying more than 40 bunkers and a big generator, all the while laying down fire and directing the Rangers from above. The team was extracted with six wounded.

In the "rear," the Rangers were teaching when they weren't fighting. Three classes of elite infantry—the Hoc Bao from the 1st ARVN Division—had undergone training with the Rangers and were ready to graduate. The final class was a 36-hour patrol in enemy territory with four Rangers as Advisors.

Through the summer, Intelligence on the enemy's whereabouts continued to come from the small unit. In August, the teams brought information confirming the infiltration of the 5th NVA Regiment from Laos, and a missing Sapper Battalion was found.

In November, Team Bills ran into an NVA Regiment and shadowed it unseen until the fourth day when contact was made and Bills had one wounded man. Things heated up fast, with NVA soldiers firing into the Ranger position from very close range, wounding a second man. Artillery closed around the unit until gunships could arrive and tip the balance of firepower. A helicopter tried to extract one of the wounded via McGuire Rig but the bird was hit several times, wounding troops inside. The wounded Ranger fell from the McGuire Rig and hit the trees. An aero-rifle unit from the 2/17 Cav arrived and joined in, eventually locating the body of the fallen Ranger. It still wasn't over until extraction, and the team lost another man before then.

L Company was presented with the Valorous Unit Citation for extraordinary heroism during the period December 7, 1969 to February 16, 1970, in a ceremony at Camp Eagle.

Operations changed a little in 1971, when Rangers took part in Operation Lam Son 719. The company was deployed in six-man teams, platoons, and even full-strength for certain missions. Lam Son was an incursion into Laos by South Vietnamese troops, supported by Americans only on their side of the border. With strict orders not to penetrate Laos, the US teams were used to provide Intelligence for larger elements about the enemy build-up around the border area.

Lam Son turned out to be a disaster for the South. There were huge casualties among the ARVN, and the supporting US fliers suffered greatly, also. Some 700 aircraft were shot down or damaged beyond repair.

For more on Lam Son 719, see the interview with Steve Pullen (2/17) and Bob Suchke (L/75).

Teams operated in and around Bach Ma, Spear Valley and the Ruong Ruong Valley, with some moving around abandoned Firebase Ripcord. Rangers were looking for the enemy as usual, tracking roads and trails and figuring who, and how many, had been on them recently. They made several contacts.

In March, 21 teams went out, some still around Ripcord, some along sections of Route 547 between Firebases Rendezvous and Blaze. Teams also worked Route 548 in the A Shau Valley. There was a lot of contact, and two POWs were taken.

The first 10 days of April, teams went into the Spear Valley and did recon, but after that there were some company-sized raids and stay-behind ambushes of platoon size in the A Shau.

L Company and D/2/17 raided along Route 548 and disrupted NVA communications. A stay-behind ambush was set, catching a six-man commo team. Americans fired on the enemy and brought in gunships, killing the first element and engaging a larger force they didn't originally know was in the area. The Rangers lost two dead and had four wounded in the action.

Another raid followed, another ambush set. The radio-relay team for the ambush team ran into dug-in NVA and the fight was on. For three days and two nights the battle raged, the team whittled down by three dead and one wounded. Finally, reinforcements got close, but the Blues of B/2/17 were stopped by heavy fire. D Troop 2/17 was inserted, but it, too, was pinned and pounded. Two days of heavy air strikes and artillery fire failed to dislodge the enemy, even when another company was brought into the fight.

At the end, a small Ranger team of volunteers combat-assaulted the area and was able to pressure the enemy out of their holes. The fierce fight cost the enemy heavily, and produced excellent Intelligence about the 5th NVA Regiment.

Through early summer, the company spent time training and advising Hoc Bao and other ARVN troops, and training new personnel.

By mid-summer, the 1st, 2nd, and 3rd Brigades of the 101st were all requesting Ranger assistance.

L Company, 75th Rangers, was organic to the 1st Brigade, 101st, which operated independently. The 2nd and 3rd Brigades had their own recon units, sometimes referred to as Long Range Patrols, but they did not become Rangers of the 75th.

Between recon and raids, 23 missions were run in June, including a company-sized raid. Some of them produced firefights and more than a few casualties.

In July, a further change had the unit back to six-man operations again, with a shift in area of responsibility.

Missions began in the Ba Long Valley area and a forward base was manned at Dong Ha and later, Quang Tri. The 3/5 Cav deployed some teams that month with several contacts and a lot of Intelligence. One team went with the Hoc Bao into the A Shau as Advisors and interpreters. There was contact, with more NVA casualties than ARVN.

As summer wore on, the Rangers stayed with the 3/5 Cav quite a bit, also spending time with the 1st and 2nd Brigades of the 101st. Much of the recon was done around Fire Support Bases (Veghel, Normandy, Rifle) where evidence of enemy activity was noted. Three teams working with 2nd Brigade around FSB Rifle made contact with an NVA unit all on the same day. All three teams (Cora, Ann, Stella) linked up after contact. First Lieutenant David Grange kept the teams together and repulsed an NVA probe of Ranger positions using small arms fire and grenades.

The Annual David E. Grange, Jr. Best Ranger Competition is usually conducted in April at Fort Benning, Georgia. Father and son were both in Vietnam, but Best Ranger is named after the father. Then-Colonel Grange was in command of 3rd Brigade, 101st.

The combined units were beefed up by C Company, 1/501, and death from above was called on the enemy. As night approached, the Rangers led the US force to an LZ for extraction. Elements of the 2nd Brigade exploited the contacts with the located enemy forces.

Other inserted teams also had contact in nearby areas, using artillery and air support to suppress enemy movement.

Such actions by the Rangers continued until October 15, when the company was detached from the 2/17 Cav and attached to the 3rd Brigade/101st, moving from Camp Eagle to Camp Evans. Ten teams worked with the 3rd Brigade during the last two weeks of the month around FSBs Gladiator, Helen, and Firestone. At one point a nine-day mission was undertaken on a walk into the mountains, where much sign of the enemy was noted.

November was the last operational month for L Co Rangers in Vietnam. A total of 18 teams worked in support of the 2nd and 3rd Brigades. Seven teams gathered recon Intelligence for the 2/506th Infantry, calling in artillery on sighted enemy and suspected base camps. Six teams worked with the 1/506 in the region southwest of FSB Jack. Two teams were used along the Song Bo River, finding several indications of enemy movement there.

They worked right up until the end. November 24, 1971, Company L (Ranger) was ordered to stand down. December 5, the unit was inactivated.

All over RVN Ranger units (and others) were being taken off line. Pressure on the enemy was drastically reduced as the eyes and ears became blind and deaf.

Steve Pullen and Robert Suchke

This interview was recorded May 28, 2003 in Pullen's home in Dahlonega, Georgia.

Steve Pullen and Robert Suchke fought together in Vietnam in 1970-71, both being Ranger-qualified beforehand. Pullen ran a platoon of Aero-Rifles (Blues) of B Troop, 2/17 Cavalry, 101st Airborne Division. He later flew OH-6 Cayuse "Little Bird" helicopters in the Lam Son incursion into Laos, sometimes in support of L Company (Ranger) teams.

Suchke fought with Delta Troop of the 2/17, and later walked trail with L Company (Ranger), 75th Infantry, still working for the 101st.

They saved each other several times in Vietnam, becoming brothers in the hellfire of combat.

They had not seen each other in 20 years when this recording was made. Between memories, they taught me.

Suchke: The 101st Division had a battalion-sized organization called a squadron, and its main mission was reconnaissance and quick reaction. There were five Troops, which were company-sized organizations in the 2/17. There was a Headquarters Troop, then there were four "letter" Troops: A, B, C, and D.

A, B, and C were Air Cav Troops. They had "Guns" [Cobras], "Little Birds" [OH-6 scout birds], and they had Slicks [UH-1H Hueys], which carried infantry, like the Blues. They had a real good mix of Scouts, Guns, and Slicks.

Other divisions had much the same arrangement of air cavalry. The Hueys gradually went from UH-1B to the UH-1H. Before the Cobras came on line, the Hueys did the gunship role, and continued doing the job in places afterward.

We really went from just north of Da Nang all the way to just below the DMZ, all the way [west] to the Khe Sanh area. That was the Division Recon Zone, and guys like Steve flew either first-light or last-light missions on a routine basis, looking for stuff out there.

The other part of what I was telling you, other than the air units, was they had Delta Ground, which is what I was in. It was like three platoons of Blues. Each Air Cav Troop had a platoon of Blues, but Delta Ground was like a company of Blues. And then we had L Company Rangers, which I was in later. They inserted six-man teams that operated out of Division Recon. And they would go out there and move maybe a couple of hundred meters a day, real quietly. Sometimes they'd stumble into something …need help. Guys like Steve would come along with a Pink Team …Cobras, maybe a Little Bird, and get the Ranger team out of it.

There was a kind of a color code. A White Bird was a Little Bird. A Red Bird was a Cobra and a Blue Bird was a Slick. It carried the Blues.

Pullen: Whenever you put red and white together you get pink.

Suchke: Not many people know that.

The Cav used a color-identification code for air units. White was for observation helicopters, like the Little Birds; Red was for gunships; Blues were the quick reaction force to help Rangers disengage or continue the fight and to gather Intel after a fight; and a Pink Team was a "Gun" and a Little Bird.

Pullen: Now, the guys in the south flew two OH-6s. They flew cover and guns and scout. They used them differently.

Suchke: They didn't have [UH-1B gunships] in our area that I recall.

Pullen: We were up in the high mountains. When those Hueys came up to fight in Lam Son 719 in February, they found they couldn't operate. The Huey didn't have the same power as the Cobras.

The Hueys and the Cobras originally had the same engine and transmission and both sounded the same when flying in, but the Cobras weighed a lot less, especially considering they didn't carry all the men and equipment the Hueys were burdened with. A good illustration would be putting a 289 cubic inch engine in a bug-eyed Sprite.

Suchke: I was still in D Troop until mid-February, 1971, and then I went to L Company. We were a reaction force. If an aircraft got shot down, or if a Ranger Team got in a bad firefight …basically the same as the Blues. In fact, it was almost exactly the same thing, only we were just a larger unit.

Pullen: My rifle platoon [Blues], on my best day, I could field 18 guys. Now, that doesn't mean 18 guys going into the wood line, it means 18 guys. That's on the books. Some on R-and R, some on convalescent leave, some in the stockade.

Sometimes he did it with 15 or less, though a platoon should have been 30-40 men.

Suchke: My platoon, I could probably field 24 guys. Generally I'd get four aircraft, I'd get ACL-6s [Acceptable Cargo Load-six men]. [On each bird] …I'd put a leader—an NCO—I'd put a machinegun for firepower, I'd put a radio for communications, and I'd put a couple of other guys, a couple of riflemen, a scout, and a thumper [M79 grenade launcher].

So I'd have leadership, firepower, and communications, no matter what got on the ground. Because sometimes we got shot at. You get one bird in, two birds in—if they got in there and didn't have enough to protect themselves, communicate, get some more help, you'd be in a fix. So you learn to cross-load.

Lot of times the NVA around an LZ, they'd let the first bird get in without firing, and just fire at the second bird.

Pullen: D Troop to me, in my perspective, was the fist the Cav had. Whenever you had an airplane down…they'd put the Blues in, but if it was a hot area, they'd put the Blues and Delta in. The Blues were trained to "rig" aircraft. I don't think that was a mission of Delta's.

Suchke: Only rarely.

Downed helicopters were routinely lifted out of the bush by CH-47s, slung underneath like cargo. Sometimes they were so badly damaged they were just blown in place.

Pullen: Delta Troop really provided security. They bring a lot of firepower to the table.

Pullen told a quick story about being under heavy fire and having 50-plus men of Delta come roaring in. Suchke noted that three platoons plus a headquarters section could produce about 75 men to add to a fight.

Suchke: We weren't the typical infantry, with one or two machineguns. I had a machinegun [M60] for every six guys. We had four M60s.

Pullen: And I'd have two squads with two M60s.

Suchke: Plus, what was really great, this was one of the most beautiful organizations in combat you can imagine—we were on the ground, and guys like Steve Pullen were in the air. If you [Pullen] got shot down, you knew who we were. We weren't strangers. We'd go drinking on Cav night or whatever. [Pullen agreed] The next day he may be out there in the thick of it, on the ground, got shot down or whatever. We'd get permission to go in and get him out. Or, we'd be out there getting hammered, mortared, or something. We'd get the Cav—the Air Cav guys—the Little Birds and the Snakes to come in, and they'd put steel on target, you know, 25 or 30 feet in front of our position.

Pullen: I think I told you why we were fighting. It wasn't for red, white, and blue. It wasn't for mom and dad, and it wasn't for Chevrolet. We were fighting for each other.

People don't understand that. I was fighting for him and he was fighting for me. I knew that if anything happened to me, he would die trying to save me.

Suchke: I feel the same way. He'd take blade strikes and fire up the ground trying to return fire on the enemy.

Blade strikes occurred when a helicopter came down too close to the trees and began chopping the branches to splinters, or when a bird was at too much of an angle and dug into the ground with the main rotor, such as when coming into a steep incline. Dig in a little too much, and the results are catastrophic.

Pullen, in response to a question, talked about how he got a Blue platoon first, then was finally able to fly after seven months, and only Little Birds, at that.

Pullen: I came in and it's just, everybody in the Cav Troop was Armor. I came in as an Infantry officer. So, they looked at me and said …[a platoon leader was needed]. "You're going to get your ground time."

I said, wait a minute, they just sent me to Cobra school, and the guy said, yeah, everybody here is Cobra-rated. You got the rifle platoon. The Blues. [The fact he was a Ranger didn't help him get off the ground]. So, the agreement was I'd have it for 30 days, while they found another Lieutenant.

Pullen said that too many Lieutenants were getting killed or wounded, and that his commanders didn't want to make personnel changes then. He had to wait until later, when the Army was downsizing during the gradual withdrawal from Vietnam.

Pullen: It wasn't until we got to go into Lam Son, as the 101st started to get smaller, there were Lieutenants available. That's how I got into the cockpit. At the end of seven months [as a Blue], I only had four hours of flight time. I had a hundred and something air assaults, but only four hours of flight time. I was riding in the back.

That was nothing. Every time a Cobra engaged a target and they could confirm a body, they put us in. I've been on sometimes four, five, six insertions a day. Not too often, because they were looking at two Cobras and a scout. The only time things got bad was when we made a couple of tactical mistakes—didn't really have a good idea of what was there when we put the Blues in. Our squadron commander was very aggressive. Aggressive to the point where sometimes …he saw the picture differently than we did, you can't find fault with that. As a Lieutenant, I saw things a lot differently than he did.

A few things were said between Pullen and Suchke about their old commander, Robert Molinelli, ending with Suchke: "God bless him. He's passed on. He was a great guy."

Pullen: He was very brave. He used say, like that old Patton thing, blood and guts. Well, it's his guts and our blood. But you couldn't fault his mission. If we were out there beating those jungles, finding those NVA guys, those three Troops, Alpha Troop to the north, Charlie to the west, Bravo to the northwest, we were finding guys, we were finding them all the time. So as a Blue guy, I was kind-of sitting on strip alert back here at the pad, and as soon as the scouts would say, "Hey, we got people running through the jungle." Captain Rosenthal, who was our company commander, would say, "Lieutenant Pullen, saddle up!"

Suchke: Get it on!

Pullen: Yeah. So, we'd go in. Our mission was to pick up the dead. See if there was anything we could find on them.

When the call came for backup, it wasn't for tea parties in the boonies. A call for the Blues was often a call for help. Sometimes, if a Lurp/Ranger team was in trouble, members of that company would precede or accompany the Blues in to help out.

At that point, Pullen talked about the various identification marks, even laundry marks on the enemy uniforms, and how the equipment they carried had various significances. He also talked about what they would and would not turn in.

Pullen: I saw a Chinese belt; you think I was going to turn that in? [Suchke laughed] Because when I was a brand-new Lieutenant, I used to tell the guys, tag it, I guarantee you'll get it back. They'd say, L.T., it's not coming back, and I'd say I'll make sure it comes back. But that stuff didn't come back. So, we used to give them maps and diaries and stuff like that, but personal gear, like a helmet with a star on it …

Suchke: That stuff had minimal Intelligence value, anyway. What they wanted were maps, frequencies, call signs—anything written.

Pullen: So that's how I got on the ground. After seven months and only four hours of flight time, I was starting to panic. I wanted to fly Guns.

Suchke: You never did fly Cobras, did you? [Pullen: no] Well, you were the best Little Bird pilot I recall.

Pullen: That's my friend talking.

Suchke: Well, that's true.

To make his point, Suchke had me verify to Pullen that he had given me this story before he knew Pullen lived in the area.

Suchke: 16th November 1970, when that Ranger team got into contact, and we went in, you were doing, like lawnmower passes at treetop level.

Pullen: Yeah, you couldn't see where anyone was.

Suchke: Somewhere out near Maureen. Not too far from Ripcord. Veghel wasn't too far away. [Those are Firebases not far from the A Shau Valley, all of which had seen too much action.]

A question was asked about his time with L Company Rangers involving an area around the abandoned Firebase Ripcord, which had been evacuated under fire and was still frequented by NVA patrols. Ripcord had been a bad experience for a few battalions the 101st Division, torn apart by incoming mortars and rockets. Patrols and excursions met with stiff resistance from the NVA until finally, with men dying every hour, the base was abandoned. Ranger patrols were run near Ripcord and the other nearby bases after the area was pounded by US artillery and air strikes when American troops were taken out.

During the battle for Ripcord, the immediate command structure of the 101st from Brigade to Battalion was nearly all Ranger-qualified.

Suchke: We inserted teams near Ripcord. We'd give a six-man Ranger Team an operational area that would be a box of about four grid squares [four kilometers square]. They'd be inserted in the corner of one, and over a period of five or six days, maybe seven days, they'd move through that area, then at a pre-planned pickup zone [PZ], they'd be extracted. While they were in there, there would be contacts. They'd report everything they observed. Signs of enemy activity, movement, any enemy litter, anything that would be significant to Intel.

There were several assigned missions on any given outing. Sometimes teams were inserted to ambush the enemy and/or try to snatch a prisoner (some of whom were survivors of ambushes), and sometimes they were to verify use of a trail, locate an enemy unit, or just wander through an area and see what was there. A typical mission might be six men out for five or six days.

Differences

Suchke: We can give you a feel for what it was like when we were there. But you got to realize that Vietnam was probably four different wars, because you had four different Corps areas. You had all the way from [above] the Central Highlands to the rice paddies, and each guy had a different experience.

There followed a general discussion of the differences between the Corps areas, the troop demographics over the years, and the areas of NVA/VC influence. From south to north, Vietnam changes radically in topographical makeup. The mountains of the Central Highlands rise to the peaks along the DMZ, while east toward the coast there is farmland and pasture. In the south the delta is water in the wet season, dust in the dry, and flat. Much of the country is either forest or jungle.

Pullen: We didn't come up against VC. Not like in IV Corps or III Corps. They used to have VC Main Force Battalions. Those were some bad dudes. But then, they fought guys with single shot rifles. Not everybody had automatic weapons.

We had some guys that came in from down south. When the 1st Cav stood down, their aviators came in to the 101st. Remember—divisions were starting to stand down. Well, those aviators had a hard time transitioning, based on what they faced down south. We're talking about 37mm, radar controlled, integrated air-defense system [NVA anti-aircraft weapon]. It wasn't like a guy shooting at you.

Pullen: I've actually been at 5,000 feet, I'm flying behind the Cobra, and I'm looking at puffs. These are two or three miles ahead of me. At 5,000 feet, I'm doing 60-70 knots, and there over where the main fight is—I'm going to the fight, I'm not in the fight—I'm looking at white, black, and I remember my observer, who sat in the back, saying, "Hey, Sir, what is that? Are those like marking rounds?"

They were flying through WWII-style flak. Helicopters from all aviation units involved took a serious beating, with many losses, in support of ARVN forces during Lam Son 719. Eventually the order came down to ground the Little Birds because of losses. Alpha Troop had lost 10 of 10, and Bravo—Pullen's unit—was down to about half.

Guys down south didn't have that. Some guys made the transition, some guys didn't. The losses we sustained were because guys were used to flying slow, and kind-of blowing the trees aside and looking down. The NVA liked it when they did that. It made their day when they just slowed up over them.

Suchke: They had triple-A [anti-aircraft artillery]; they had main NVA units. And they fought; they didn't just scatter to the winds [as the guerilla VC often did].

Lam Son 719

One of the largest operations of the war, Lam Son used ARVN troops to cross the Laotian border to sack NVA supply caches and set back a suspected offensive. Americans were not allowed on the ground in Laos, but they flew air cover, did medevacs and brought supplies, all under horrific anti-aircraft fire. In addition, there were several big fights and lots of small ones on the Vietnamese side of the border involving US troops trying to keep supply routes open to the ARVN. There were huge losses in men and equipment on both sides. The story of the fight, and all its ramifications, is heartbreaking.

Pullen: If you'll recall, I guess it was in March of 1970; Nixon made the decision to go into Cambodia. They did that, and then in early 1971, he made the decision to go into Laos. The major push was to go into Laos and deny the NVA sanctuaries, bases, and supplies.

Both men then identified the village of Tchepone as the furthest penetration to be made by the ARVN. Tchepone wasn't very far into Laos. ARVN armor made a foray some miles in, but they were stopped dead and had problems getting out.

Suchke: We staged out of Khe Sanh. We reopened Khe Sanh Firebase. [The Marines abandoned it a few years earlier after a huge battle during Tet, 1968]. We combat-assaulted [CA] into the base. It was reopened in January 1971.

US Air supported the Vietnamese ground units. There were no US units to be there (Laos) on the ground, although [laughs] a couple of us did go over there. We had to get aircraft back.

Pullen: Alpha Troop was carrying the load at Lam Son. Bravo kept the actual valley clear, and Charlie kept further to the south clear.

Suchke: Alpha Troop was based out of Quang Tri, just east of Khe Sanh.

Pullen was shot down or crashed several times during his career. He was asked what it was like.

Pullen: [It took him a minute.] Terrifying. Really terrifying. Suddenly you see this light. [flak burst] You can tell when your aircraft is hit. It's kind-of like throwing rocks on a tin roof. That's what it sounds like. When your doors are open and your observer isn't firing, you can hear it.

He was also in the back of bigger birds as a Blue platoon leader.

Pullen: I'll be honest with you, most of the time I had a headset on. I was trying to listen. Trying to get the last instructions I could, because a lot of times we'd abort. We'd be on short final and the scout would see something and a decision would be made to pull us out. Until we got that coordination down, I had a couple of times where we would step out with my RTO and two guys and hear the radio say "Abort." [Suchke laughed]

Well, now it's six of us on the ground. So I always kept the headset on until the last minute, asking, "Are we green?" They'd say, "Yeah, you're green." Then I'd put the set down. I wasn't going to be left on the LZ.

But, to answer your question about what it's like to be shot down, I've had it where they've hit the engine, and they'd take the engine out, and auto rotated to the ground, and been picked up in a second. I've had where I've gone into the trees, and that's when the blades snap off, and the plane will tumble and roll, and comes to a stop, and you take off the harness and look around, and you always think you're going to grab your M16 and your bandoliers of ammunition, but you never do that. You scramble out to a clearing and somebody drops a McGuire Rig or some kind of a ladder or something. I've had it where I've actually had a skid shot off. That's an interesting experience in itself, because you have to have two skids to land. So, when I came back to base they had to build up these sandbags, and I had to sit there and hover this thing until they could build them up.

I'd be so tired I've had blade strikes. I hate to admit that. Sometimes we'd fly 10 or 12 hours a day, and I'd find myself just [exhausted] ...especially during Lam Son. I looked at my flight records, and during January, February and March, you're looking at 100, 110 hours flying time. But at 80 hours you were supposed to get a waiver from the flight surgeon. I remember the first time I went to see him. I said, well, Sir, I got 80 hours. I guess you'll be grounding me. [He was given 20 more.]

So I went to him and said, well, Sir, I got my 100 hours, and he said, "Well, the Troop commander said to give you 15 more." So there was no end. At least in our Troop there was no magic number. Eighty was the number you shot for. But it could be 100 or 120. That's a lot of exposure time as a scout.

Little Birds—22 feet long—would fly low, just over the tree tops sometimes, looking for the enemy, actually trying to draw fire, while a Cobra floated above, waiting for a target. The scout birds, basically a glass bubble with skids and a rotor, took a lot of fire. However, they were incredibly maneuverable and had teeth of their own. The pilots and gunner/observers of those aircraft exhibited a high degree of courage. There are stories of flying under the canopy, down a trail, low enough to read footprints.

I kept trying to be in a Gun [Cobra] platoon, because there's something about being low.

We're fast, but low. I really like those guys up there, because you take fire, you drop smoke, you mark your target, this guy's coming in. That's the guy you want to be.

Suchke: He's blowing the elephant grass apart [blade wash], trying to draw fire, or see the enemy, and then throwing a smoke grenade at them, and then roll right or roll left, and then the Snakes up there behind him put some nails on top of the smoke.

It didn't take long, on average, to respond to a call for help.

Pullen: Oh, 30 or 40 minutes. [Suchke agreed] Because we always had a team on standby. I mean, all you had to do was blow the battery, hit the gas, the starter was already cocked. I can remember, even on Cav Nights [Friday night], which is not good because ...we were young guys, and we consumed ...[Suchke: Ample quantities] ...Yes. And the last thing you want to do is get a team in contact on Friday night.

The following is an excerpt from a story Pullen and Suchke told about a rescue. Suchke's D Troop, all three platoons, were deep in the jungle. It was raining and there was serious fog. No aircraft could get to them for resupply or extraction, so they were trapped there with enemy all around. In a later interview, Suchke said they had one C-Ration each for five days. "We dined sparingly."

Suchke: [They came] hovering up through the fog. It was the neatest thing in the world to see those aircraft. We could hear them [at first] and we were ...Hey! We're over here! Go this way!

Pullen: There were three of us who volunteered. We dropped our mini-guns off, dropped the observers off, and took water and rations, because that's what they needed. So, the Squadron Commander [Lt. Colonel Molinelli] said, well, I'd take it up there, but my Huey is too big to get in through the trees, and the Cobra is my most valuable bird and I can't lose it, and they can't carry anything, anyway. So he says, you guys, can you do it? So, Mike Goff, and another guy by the name of John Hendricks and I, stripped everything off of our OH-6s. John Hendricks was an Instructor Pilot, and Mike and I were going to be number two and number three behind him. He had an instrument rating. He had to turn all his lights off. You can't imagine, when he [Suchke] tells you the weather came in, it was right down on top of the trees.

I had so much water. When I went to the rear detachment guys, they said, yeah, yeah, we just want you to carry [a little] of this stuff. Well, Jiminy Crickets, we had enough food and water to supply a battalion. But, they needed it.

Pullen humbly leaves out the 15-mile run down the "blue line," a watercourse running a meandering path toward Delta Troop. They flew nose-to-tail because of the fog, down on the deck, between overhanging trees. When they got there, they still weren't sure they were in the right place.

We hovered until somebody came on and told us, we hear you, steer left or steer right. The only problem I had was, you're me and I'm the ground guy and I say steer left …

Suchke: We'd say, we hear you southeast of us, and they'd take a reverse of that and come northwest. [Pullen laughed] Well, they got into us, kicked out some chow. [Pullen: Got this injured guy out.] Yep, loaded him up and got him out. [They had a man suffering from "body immersion," what is now called hypothermia, from constant exposure to chill rains].

And then somebody had the bright idea, hey, we got him out, why not get everybody out?

We were okay. We had some chow and stuff. So they started shuttling us out two or three at a time. Somebody, I think, brought a Huey in.

Pullen: They did, later in the afternoon.

Suchke: I was one of the last guys out.

Pullen: See, we weren't qualified to fly in that kind of weather, but we would have died trying to help them.

Suchke: They'd come get us. They'd come get us.

After Vietnam, Suchke went to the Mountain Ranger Camp in Lumpkin County, Georgia where he served as a Captain Instructor from 1971-74. Steve Pullen recovered from injuries and surgeries and returned to duty in 1972. In 1973, he was made to go through the Mountain Phase of Ranger School again—he'd passed it in 1969—to prove he could carry a rucksack and be an active member of a combat unit. Banged up by 11 crashes, shrapnel wounds, and surgery, Pullen passed. "I'd have quit if I failed." He said he would have ended up in the supply corps, or something like it—a position he was loath to accept.

Suchke didn't know Pullen had already qualified, and thought him a first-timer. He found out the truth during this interview.

Pullen retired as a Colonel and Suchke retired as a Lt. Colonel after distinguished careers in different fields.

These two tough, resourceful men exemplify the Ranger traditions of brotherhood and courage.

Training and Preparation Influence Mission Outcome
By Robert Suchke, L Company, 75th Infantry (Ranger)
Used with permission.

In L Company, 75th Infantry Rangers, as in all military units, training was the most important activity we did besides actually going to the field on a live mission. Some commanders have said, "Training is everything, and everything is training."

In order to be on a Ranger Team, each individual had to be highly trained in his particular skills and responsibilities, and the whole team of six men had to train together to know Company and Team Standard Operating Procedures as well as how each other functioned under stress. The best individual training course available for Recon units was MACV RECONDO School at Nha Trang.

Still, any new Ranger candidate had to qualify with the men who mattered.

Training was geared to make each Ranger skilled and prepared to accomplish the missions assigned to L Company. All individuals who volunteered to become a member of L Company Rangers were screened and tested.

The training/testing phase lasted about two weeks. Training consisted of Physical Conditioning, NVA Weapons, NVA Tactics, mines and booby traps, Call for Close Air Support, Call for Indirect Fire, First Aid, Marksmanship, Combat Firing Techniques, Helicopter Rappelling and STABO Extraction, Use of Explosives, Use of Terrain, Movement Techniques, Map Reading, Use of Compass, Camouflage, Hand-and-Arm Signals, Survival, and more.

Practical and written tests were given to each candidate to test his knowledge. Those who passed were taken on a training patrol to make sure they were ready for the real thing. Even after a soldier was assigned to a Team, he was on probation until the team accepted him. Only after successfully participating in a live mission with a Team was a candidate considered a Ranger.

However, if the Team Leader was not pleased with a candidate, he would not be accepted, and was sent back to his original unit.

Rangers also trained other US units, such as the Recon Platoons of several Infantry battalions, plus the Hoc Bao [elite Viet troops], and the 1st ARVN Division Recon Company.

In many line units …training was considered a luxury …for replacements. In L Company Rangers, training made the difference. We knew that what you practiced in training, you would instinctively do in combat.

In order to properly train, one needs to understand the mission. L Company Rangers operated "Out Front" [unit motto] in the Division Recon Zone in small teams of four-to-six men. The Recon Zone extended all the way to the Laotian border and included areas like the Roung Roung and Ashau Valleys, and the Khe Sanh Plains.

Usually, Ranger Teams operated well outside the fire fan of artillery and had to rely on close air support if enemy contact was made.

Reconnaissance was the primary mission of all teams, however, there were some radio relay, wiretap, POW snatch, and larger combat patrol missions. Occasionally, there were short fuse, "thrown together" missions that we got tasked to do, but they were not the norm. Recon was the "bread and butter" mission.

Plan the mission, rehearse, infiltrate the AO, locate and observe the enemy without being detected, report that information, exfiltrate safely and debrief was the ideal way it was done.

Missions were planned at company, squadron, and division levels. If division needed information on a particular forward area, Rangers got the mission.

Planning was conducted in detail in the company TOC. The mission box [four to six grid squares] was assigned to the appropriate team and the team members started their preparations. The team was assigned a code name.

Over-flight or aerial recon of the box was usually attempted, although not always carried out due to bad weather or other considerations.

Rucksacks, load bearing equipment [LBE] and weapons were prepared. Weapons were test fired and muzzles taped to keep out mud and rain. Loads were checked for noise and security. Radios were waterproofed, tested, and call signs and code words issued. Each man had a code name to not give away his real name over the radio. Movement techniques, hand and arm signals, enemy contact drill, RON [remain over night] procedures, map information and other mission-critical tasks were rehearsed over and over until the team leader was satisfied.

Just before infiltration, each Team member camouflaged his face and hands and checked his equipment one last time. Then the Team was taken by truck to the waiting Huey.

Infiltration was by helicopter. We trained in loading the aircraft, getting out quickly and moving off the LZ. Infiltration was also done by helicopter, rappelling into areas not suitable for landing.

Rappelling took practice and required confidence, so a nearby rappelling tower was much in use, as well as a 2/17th Air Cav UH-1H Huey, when available.

Once on the ground, the team needed to get to a concealed area in the jungle as fast as possible. Many LZs had watchers or ambushes set for landing helicopters. A crucial period was the moment of insertion into the enemy's back yard.

Training previously conducted in movement techniques, observation, land navigation, map reading, noise and light discipline and stealth all paid off once the team was clear of the infiltration LZ.

Teams usually did not move great distances, and 500 to 1000 meters a day was about average. Carrying 80 to 100 pounds of gear, you did not "bust ass through the woods."

Each Ranger Team member moved slowly and deliberately to not make a sound. Listening halts were conducted frequently to detect possible NVA presence. Regular situation reports [Sitreps] were called in to the Ranger Company TOC, but the spoken voice of the Ranger radio operator [RTO] was just a whisper.

If an NVA element was observed, it was reported ASAP. When possible, a Pink Team consisting of a Cobra gunship helicopter and a "Loach" [light observation helicopter] armed scout bird, would be launched to attack the enemy.

Sometimes, a Ranger Team had to watch silently from their concealed position as a hundred or more NVA soldiers would pass by, never knowing they had been observed.

The Ranger Team would necessarily have to avoid contact to insure its own survival. If conditions permitted, a team could call in an air strike on a much larger unit, and later be safely extracted without being compromised. If detected by the enemy, the team would initiate an immediate action drill that had been previously rehearsed.

Immediate action drills (IAD) are designed to get a team out of an area of incoming fire in the quickest, safest, way. The idea is to immediately put out a wall of fire while hop-scotching each other away from the enemy.

Training here meant the difference in life or death. Proper training became instinctive reaction when faced with a life-threatening situation. Everyone on a Team had to do his job exactly right to survive an enemy contact.

The overnight halt was another key activity that included night security procedures, radio watch, chow and maintenance on equipment and individuals. Each team had its own SOP for RON procedures; like no person stands after dark, heads to the inside in a circle [to pass the radio handset], and others.

Teams would often use a buttonhook maneuver to move in a RON site to watch their back trail in the event they were followed. One or more claymore mines on a shortened wire were usually employed for added security.

On the planned day of exfiltration the Team tried to arrive at the PZ [pickup zone] early to observe for enemy activity. Extractions were often conducted at first light while infiltrations were done at first light, last light, and even in the middle of the day so to not set a pattern. Exfiltrations could be as simple as climbing aboard a Huey, or a ladder extraction, or STABO extraction using the special harness each Ranger carried as LBE.

Once back at [Camp] Eagle, the mission was not over until each team member had been debriefed and a record made of all observations, routes, water sources, trails and signs of enemy activities. This report was put in a folder to be filed in the TOC. The next time a Team was assigned a box near this AO, it would be studied thoroughly.

Bob McMahon

By the time McMahon got to Vietnam he had already served as a LRRP in Germany (1962-66) and had several tours at the Mountain Ranger Camp in Georgia. It was there he got his orders in 1966, which first sent him to Jungle Warfare and Survival School in Panama, then to the 1st ID in Vietnam. Because of his background, he was wanted in several places.

When I got over there [RVN] at 90th Repple [replacement depot], I was held back and interviewed by a Captain from Special Forces. They wanted me to go and be an Instructor in their LRRP School. They had a LRRP School where they taught the Division LRRPs. The LRRPs were provisional; they had no certain number designation. Each division had a platoon of LRRPs and they were all volunteers. But, I more-or-less got shanghaied into the 1st Division. A buddy of mine, Hoyt Phillips, came down there and I told him they had already cut orders on me and I was going to the 5th SF. He said he could get those orders changed, but I didn't believe him. Well, he did.

Next thing I know, I'm in the back of a deuce-and-a-half going to Di An to the 1st Infantry Division [headquartered near Saigon in III Corps], and from there to Phu Loi and the LRRPs. After I got there, I said, hey, this isn't bad. I like it.

The 1st Division was pretty well spread out.

Battalions were being moved around at that time, reorganizing, as was the Lurp structure.

I left before they went to company size. Just before I left, they started drafting a bunch of people in from different divisions over there—mainly those who were Ranger-qualified. One of the guys I got was Redden Brinkley. He was Cadre up there at the Mountain Camp for a period and then he wound up over there with a battalion of the 82nd. He came down to my outfit [for some training] and the first training mission we operated out of Phouc Vinh, he got blown away. Point man tripped a booby trap. They evacuated him and I didn't see him again until I got back to the States in 1968.

When McMahon was with the 1st ID he served as a member of D Troop, 1st Squadron, 4th Air Cav, LRRP. Unit orders came from Division G-2.

We had our own aircraft in D Troop (Air). We used our own B-model and C-model Hueys. The scouts were the old bubble, H-13.

The H-13 preceded the OH-6 "Little Bird" and looked like a glass bubble with a miniature oil derrick sticking out the back. You could literally see right through most of it.

We did mainly recon missions. General Depuy used to tell us, if we got out there and got in a firefight, which did happen at times, he said we couldn't really accomplish our mission. He wanted us to go out and find them, report them, and then he would send troops in to take care of them.

We worked in five or six man teams [and] stayed out two or three days.

Whatever area we were operating in, they would move an operations element close to where we were being inserted. If we needed assistance, they were within 15 minutes. D Troop had another platoon of aero-rifles [to send]. I don't remember what we called them, but we got along good. We worked together a lot.

Within 15 minutes of the time we called they would be on station. They would be [waiting] at a Special Forces camp or an ARVN base or somewhere they could set up, put a tent up, get the antennae up for the radios. Any time we had a team on the ground we had 24 hours over-flight. During the daytime, we used the O1-E [two-place Cessna] and at night we used the Otter. We had radios in there. We only had to refuel one time in a 12-hour period. You get up there, cut your power way back and just sort-of coast around up there in the general area where we had continuous commo with the team on the ground.

We did good. We kept the General happy. Other divisions would send people up to us and we'd take them out on missions with us. I know 9th Division [based in the delta] sent up a Lieutenant and a Sergeant. They went out on a mission.

We operated around Phouc Vinh, Quan Loi, over towards the western border. We didn't cross it [the Cambodian border] that we know of, but we kept a team over there a time or two. We staged out of Tay Ninh one time I remember, up there by Nui Ba Den [Black Virgin Mountain]. We used it as a forward operating base a time or two.

All the people I had I felt were professional. Everybody I had in the platoon were good people.

McMahon went on to say that if sometimes a few guys would party a little too hard at the base, they were straight and conscientious when they were in the field.

LRRP/LRP/RANGER UNITS OF THE VIETNAM ERA

LRRP

At the start of the Vietnam War there were only two Long Range Recon Patrols operating, and both were in Germany, under TO&E 157H.

Co. D, 17th Infantry, (LRRP), V Corps
Co. C, 58th Infantry (LRRP), VII Corps

The rest were organized and trained either in the States, in Vietnam, or both. Some of the original LRRP Platoons of Vietnam folded and disappeared, but the majority became LRP Companies. As far as any comprehensive list goes, the closest we can come is the presentation of a list of LRRP units accepted by the 75th Ranger Regiment Association, formed in July 1988.

V Corp—based in Germany
VII Corp—based in Germany
(All others were in Vietnam)
9th Infantry Division
25th Infantry Division
196th Brigade
1st Cavalry (Airmobile) Division
1st Infantry Division
4th Infantry Division
1st Brigade, 101st Airborne Division
3rd/506th Parachute Infantry Regiment
199th Brigade
173rd Brigade
3rd Division

LRP

Co. E, 20th Infantry, (LRP), I Field Force Vietnam
Co. F, 51st Infantry, (LRP), II Field Force Vietnam
Co. D, 151st Infantry (LRP), II Field Force Vietnam
Co. E, 50th Infantry (LRP), 9th Infantry Division
Co. F, 50th Infantry (LRP), 25th Infantry Division
Co. E, 51st Infantry (LRP), 23rd Infantry Division
Co. E, 52nd Infantry (LRP), 1st Cavalry Division
Co. F, 52nd Infantry (LRP), 1st Infantry Division
Co. E, 58th Infantry (LRP), 4th Infantry Division

Co. F, 58th Infantry (LRP), 101st Airborne Division

71st Infantry Detachment (LRP), 196th Infantry Brigade

74th Infantry Detachment (LRP), 173rd Airborne Brigade

78th Infantry Detachment (LRP), 3rd Brigade, 82nd Airborne Division

79th Infantry Detachment (LRP), 1st Brigade, 5th Mechanized Division

Ranger

On February 1, 1969, Long Range Patrol Companies evolved into Ranger Companies of the 75th Infantry.

Two companies, A and B of the 75th, stayed in the US, and Company D kept its designation as part of the 151st Infantry, though it took on the Ranger identity.

That left 13 Ranger companies organized and deployed in Vietnam.

Co. C (Ranger), 75th Infantry, I Field Force Vietnam, Feb. 1, 1969 to October 25, 1971

Co. D (Ranger), 75th Infantry, II Field Force Vietnam, Nov. 20, 1969 to April 10, 1970

Co. E (Ranger), 75th Infantry, 9th Infantry Division, Feb. 1, 1969 to Oct. 12, 1970

Co. F (Ranger), 75th Infantry, 25th Infantry Division, Feb. 1, 1969 to March 15, 1971

Co. G (Ranger), 75th Infantry, 23rd Infantry Division, Feb. 1, 1969 to Oct. 1, 1971

Co. H (Ranger), 75th Infantry, 1st Cavalry Division, Feb. 1, 1969 to Aug. 15, 1972

Co. I (Ranger), 75th Infantry, 1st Infantry Division, Feb. 1, 1969 to April 7, 1970

Co. K (Ranger), 75th Infantry, 4th Infantry Division, Feb. 1, 1969 to Dec. 10, 1970

Co. L (Ranger), 75th Infantry, 101st Airmobile Division, Feb. 1, 1969 to Dec. 25, 1971

Co. M (Ranger), 75th Infantry, 199th Infantry Brigade, Feb. 1, 1969 to Oct. 12, 1970

Co. N (Ranger), 75th Infantry, 173rd Airborne Brigade, Feb. 1, 1969 to Aug. 25, 1971

Co. O (Ranger), 75th Infantry, 3rd Brigade, 82nd Airborne Division, Feb.1, 1969 to Nov. 20, 1969

Co. P (Ranger), 75th Infantry, 1st Brigade, 5th Mechanized Division, Feb.1, 1969 to Aug. 31, 1971

LINEAGE, LINKAGE, AND ACCEPTANCE

Now comes the hard part. Since there is no hard-and-fast list of all the LRRP units of the pre-1968 era, it is difficult to figure who belongs to what in terms of Ranger ancestry.

For one thing, such units were provisional, smaller than companies, and had no Table of Organization and Equipment of their own. Without a TO&E, there is no recognition by the Army of any lineage outside the parent unit.

Another problem with lineage and acceptance of legitimate LRRP status comes with the various unit associations, such as the 75th Ranger Regiment Association. The Army and the associations vary somewhat in historical acceptance.

Further complications arise from the word "lineage." In many cases. "lineage" is more accurately termed "linkage," because though one unit followed another within the same overall parent organization, the immediate lineage is not reflected in the unit designation. An example would be F Company (LRP), 58th Infantry, which was subordinate to the 101st Airborne Division, but followed the lineage of the 58th. Therefore, the unit was "linked" to the earlier 1st Brigade, 101st Division LRRPs, and "linked" to the following unit, L Company, 75th Infantry (Ranger), but has no actual designated unit lineage.

Though some large units fielded what were termed LRRP components in the early days of Vietnam, most were absorbed when the job was no longer necessary, and/or worked well inside the range and duration of actual LRRP missions.

When LRRP platoons were needed they were formed, and several stayed long enough to become part of the next step—the TO&E Long Range Patrol Companies. Parent units such as the 1st Brigade of the 101st, the 173rd Brigade, the 1st Cavalry Division, the 1st Division, the 196th Brigade and others fielded LRRP units whose line was continued, linked by purpose, and therefore accepted as genuine.

The whole concept of LRRP function was based on small units (six men) a long way from home, often at the far edge of, or outside of, artillery range. They would stay out for five-to-seven days at a time. Members of such units seem to have trouble giving LRRP status to any unit not following those parameters. It is a touchy subject, and there are several versions of how it should go.

On the other hand, there are units claiming LRRP status because they were given that name by a commander, gave themselves that name at the time of inception or took the name post-war, but are not accepted by the 75th RRA or by members of "legitimate" LRRP units.

It is easy to go through historical records and pigeonhole recon units, saying this one is a "legitimate" LRRP, this one is Hatchet Force, this one just took the name after the war, this unit went to Recondo in the States but didn't fight as LRRPs in Vietnam, these guys only went out two klicks and stayed overnight…..

But, considering what the men on the ground went through, what their memories are, I'd hate to be the one with the final say about who is, and who is not, a genuine, pre-1968 LRRP.

Of course, there are those who couldn't hide from the job, and so found it necessary to come up with guidelines for eligibility for membership in the associations.

The 75th Ranger Regiment had these guidelines as of summer, 2003:

Any active unit with a direct link to a Vietnam-era unit and currently has an LRSD (U) unit of its own, AND/OR any unit recognized by the separate division LRRP/Ranger Associations, is recognized by the 75th RRA.

An example of the former would be the 1/101st Division LRRPs of Vietnam and the link to the current 101st LRSD.

An example of the latter would be the 3/506 Parachute Infantry Regiment, an outfit with a lot of history. The 3/506 acted as a separate brigade for three years in Vietnam, though they were technically part of the 101st. A LRRP platoon was formed within the brigade and is recognized by the 101st LRRP/Ranger Association because they acted independently of divisional control, which means automatic acceptance by the 75th RRA. That one comes by linkage.

There is another rule-of-thumb regarding brigade-level LRRPs. Only separate brigade units are considered as "legitimate" brigade-level LRRPs, as all others were under divisional or Field Force control and are therefore considered divisional units. This has led to some controversy over LRRP status for some brigade-level units.

An example would a platoon of the 3rd Brigade of the 101st Division, which trained at Fort Campbell, Kentucky, graduated Recondo School there, and thought of themselves as LRRPs.

Then there were the Hatchet Forces. Larger than LRRP units, these heavily-armed reaction teams had a rough job in Vietnam, and had great names such as Phantom Force, Tigers, Hawks, and Recondos. But they are not given LRRP identity and the attached lineage/linkage to the Rangers because they didn't run the same kind of six-man/seven day missions the LRRPs did.

There were also plenty of Recon Platoons at battalion-level, but Recon doesn't necessarily qualify as LRRP.

Willie Snow, a Ranger, was part of two Hatchet Force units. "We killed more than the Rangers every day. We were not Lurps."

The specialized formula for LRRP/LRP/Ranger unit missions is specific enough to stand alone as criteria. When there is any doubt of legitimacy, or a status claim is made, the formula is cited.

Lurps/Rangers from accepted units are quick to say they would never take anything away from Recon or Hatchet units that did their jobs amazingly well under terrible conditions, but criterion must be met.

The issue will probably never be resolved, much like the issue of who may wear the Ranger Tab. Again, criterion must be met. In order to wear the coveted Tab, a man must either graduate Ranger School, or be in combat with a Ranger unit. That's pretty straightforward, but the controversy reverts back to acquired Ranger lineage. A unit calling themselves LRRPs, but not recognized as such, has no lineage/linkage to back up the right to wear the Tab.

The term "LRRP" was used as a buzz-word by the press and the public information section of the Army in those days, given erroneously to many small-unit endeavors, though a team doing LRRP duty once or twice doesn't make them LRRPs if they don't fit the total criteria. There were other long-range patrols, namely MACV-SOG, but they weren't LRRPs, either.

RANGERS IN NON-RANGER UNITS AND AS ADVISORS
(CO VAN)

There were Rangers in Vietnam several years before the formation of the first Lurp units in 1965. The Ranger Department had been turning out classes every year since 1951, and there were some WWII and Korean War Rangers still active when the US got involved in Vietnam in the mid-1950s. Still, classes in those days were relatively small, and combat arms officers were not "required" to attend as they are today. Those with combat experience were highly valued as Advisors in the beginning of the war. Unfortunately, the war lasted so long that most of those veterans were gone long before the end of things. Some of them survived two wars to die in Vietnam.

The gap left by those departing veterans had to be filled, and training was stepped up. Ranger-qualified men without combat experience, but with plenty of savvy, also stepped up to fill the necessary role of Advisor to ill-trained and often ineptly led troops of South Vietnam.

One of the first things the US did was send Advisors of all types, both civilian and military, to aid the South Vietnamese in their fight against the communists. Those Advisors were largely Special Forces soldiers at first, some of whom were Ranger-trained, but there were no American Ranger units at that time to use as a basis for operations.

In the beginning, Advisors were at corps and division level, but a pressing need to get the ARVN going spread them out as far as battalion level and eventually into the villages with Mobile Army Training Teams (MATT) in an effort to build local militia. More than one Ranger coming over from the States found himself teaching civilians how to shoot rifles.

American officers and non-coms were living with—and sometimes dying with—Vietnamese soldiers. Relationships varied between the counterparts, but many former Advisors report they were treated well. However, as in any army, there are different types and calibers of units. The best of those were the Biet Dong Quan—the Vietnamese Rangers—battalion-sized units spread throughout the country. As time went on, more and more American Ranger-qualified soldiers were sent to the BDQ as Advisors.

There is a rather large group of former BDQ soldiers living in America, and they have their own associations. However, some of them have joined American Ranger Associations, as well.

Another special unit was the Hoc Bao. American Special Forces and Rangers trained them, and they became excellent fighters, feared by the enemy.

Advisors often lived in the field with their adopted units for weeks at a time, doing damage and taking damage, but always going forward. Most of the time their advice was taken, sometimes not. In some cases the Advisors could do just that—advise—then stand back and watch. Vietnamese commanders were sometimes unwilling to take advice that would cause an act of aggression, or put them out on a limb.

Giving advice and guidance was only part of the job. Advisors also worked the radios and took care of liaison with overhead aircraft and artillery batteries on firebases.

But that's another story, and best told by men who were there.

There were also Rangers scattered throughout Army units in various parts of the country. Units large and small were led by men with the Tab, from division command to platoon sergeant and down into the squad level. It was not until later, during the mid-to-late 1960s, that Ranger-qualified individuals began to migrate toward the long-range patrol.

Wherever they were, Rangers got the job done, or in too many cases died trying. Whether with designated Ranger units after February 1969, eating rice in the boonies with Vietnamese soldiers, or members of the original far-walking hunters, Ranger-trained men continued to be Force Multipliers, teaching and bolstering morale and efficiency everywhere they went.

Edison Scholes

Major General (Retired) Edison Scholes was a Senior Advisor to the Vietnamese Rangers. Before taking that assignment he was a rifle company commander of Delta Company, 2nd of the 8th Cavalry—a 1st Cav man. His second tour was somewhat different. See the rest of his biography under his interview about Panama.

I went back over to be part of SOG—most of my Special Forces Detachment (10th SF) were going to SOG.

SOG—Studies and Observation Group—was a special unit of top-notch SF soldiers.

Most of [those guys] were highly trained in unconventional warfare. I went over with orders to go there, but when I got to Saigon they came on the airplane and got me. General Abrams had told the 5th [SF] Group to get out of the country, and they were turning over all Special Forces Groups to the Rangers. I said, you can't take me because I'm going to SOG. I called SOG up and they said, we've got top priority, we'll call you back. They called back and said there is one program we don't have priority over, and they've got you for the Ranger program, we'll come and get you in six months.

So I ended up as a Major [1970] in I Corps hoping for a battalion of Vietnamese Rangers, but I got up there and they had decided to leave the Senior Advisor of the Ranger Command. They had formed a Ranger Command. In our Corps we had the mobile group, which was three battalions, and we had nine Special Forces Battalions along the borders. A Ranger Group was three battalions. Things were falling apart then and the NVA were everywhere. People [SOG] couldn't stay on the ground hardly any time. The NVA were all over them whether they HALOed in or helicoptered in.

Everybody had the same problem [including US Rangers]. The American units had pulled back. They used the 101st helicopters on the Lam Son 719 operation, the largest operation of the war.

Lam Son 719 entailed a foray into Laos west of Khe Sanh, but US troops weren't allowed to cross the border, only back up the Viets with artillery and aircraft.

Our group [Viet Rangers] went the farthest west. The Viet Airborne division and the Viet Marine Division got cold feet and backed out of that in the middle of it [and didn't tell anybody] and left the 1st ARVN Division and our Ranger Group, which almost got annihilated, together with the 101st choppers that were shot down like crazy.

The other nine battalions [Viet SF] were strung out all across I Corps, and some of them were better than American battalions. One of the battalions, people kept telling us, that the 23rd Division [US] was going to lose LZ Maryanne. We kept passing that Intel on to them that the NVA was preparing to attack Maryanne together with the VC, but they wouldn't believe us. Then they got overrun. We had to put a Ranger Battalion down there. We lost 50 of them when a Chinook went down carrying them in there. It was mechanical [not shot down]. It was certainly no mission for a light Ranger Battalion.

Daniel—Bio

Jack Daniel is one of those Rangers who has been there, done that. It would be no mean task to write a complete book about his experiences. What are listed here are the bare bones of the distinguished career of a Hall of Fame Ranger.

Graduating VMI in 1954, he went through Ranger School in the winter of 1954-55, followed by Airborne and Jumpmaster Schools. Rather than go to a regular unit, Daniel was assigned to the Florida Ranger Camp before relocating to Germany where he, among other things, presented Ranger training to elements of the 28th Infantry. While in Germany, Daniel took part in what was probably the first unofficial Lurp unit trained specifically for that type of action in the US Army.

Along the same lines, Daniel served as Test Director for the Long Range Reconnaissance Patrol Platoon, organized and developed for division and corps as well as Battle Group usage.

Before long he ended up in Vietnam as a MACV Advisor to I Corps. From there he became the first Senior Advisor to the 1st Ranger Group (Vietnamese) and went on combat operations with the 11th, 37th, and 39th Ranger Battalions. On August 12, 1966, he was wounded in the leg by shrapnel and took a year to recover before being shipped back to Vietnam. After spending time as Senior Advisor to the 42nd (Viet) Infantry near Dak To—where he again saw a good bit of combat—he was given the job of Senior Advisor to the 2nd Ranger Group. He believes he is the only man to be Senior Advisor to two different Ranger Groups.

In all, Jack Daniel fought his way through much of the war after refining techniques in Germany that would later be used in Vietnam. He held most of the command positions available at one time or another, and taught many a man how to do it right. His words are listed in several places in this work, but this part is about his time in Vietnam with the Vietnamese Rangers.

John (Jack) Daniel

In the first place, I have a very, very high opinion of the Vietnamese Rangers. Like anybody else, they get scared, and they have their crazies, and they have people that are just unbelievably brave. They have some that are perhaps a little timid on occasion and need a little urging, but I think they are just as fine a soldier as anybody every produced.

I want to say from my heart that I do love the Vietnamese. I admired their soldiers. We've got a lot of great guys—some you know, and some you should—Snake Collier and people like that, and they were Advisors with units, some of them with the Vietnamese Airborne. I know one or two guys who served with the Vietnamese Marines—they were the cream of the crop, so to speak.

They might get scared—tell you they're scared; but they'll never leave you.

Daniel was in his first tour as a Group Senior Advisor and was with the 37th Viet Ranger Battalion in a particularly heavy contact.

It was my policy to go down to each battalion. I wanted eventually to go into combat with each company in order to better assess their capability.

I think it was probably some time in February 1966. It was down in Quang Nai Province, which is the southern-most province in I Corps [east of Highway One in the vicinity of Nui Dau].

We were making a sweep east of the highway and the South China Sea comes in right there, so we were moving north. The whole battalion was making the sweep, and we were behind the lead company.

We were seeing sort-of heavy contact. When I say that, I mean there were no mortar rounds fired at us. I don't recall any rocket-propelled weapons. But, very heavy, intense automatic fire. The company point was driven back. I was with the company commander and the battalion commander. The CP was driven back on top of us, so myself and Bill Meyers, the Battalion Advisor, were right there. We decided we were going to lead—I wouldn't call it a counter-attack—but certainly a display of force in order to make sure these guys were not being driven back too far by the local VC. Back in those days, you really didn't know who was VC. In fact we called them PAVN—People's Army of Vietnam—which was an organization made up with North Vietnamese officers and NCOs and some few VC officers. Primarily Viet Cong troops.

We immediately returned fire ourselves and urged the Vietnamese Rangers—the ones who had retreated—and continued to move forward in a skirmish line and eventually drove the VC back. We captured several and killed several. I don't know if they knew they were firing on a whole battalion, which was a mistake on their part.

The 37th has three United States Presidential Unit Citations. One was at Khe Sanh years later.

A question was asked about a comparison between the BDQ and other Viet soldiers.

It depends on what division they were in. The 1st Vietnamese Division was probably as good as almost any other Viet unit. I'd say it was as good as the Airborne and as good as the Rangers. That's the division that was in northern I Corps. The 2nd Division wasn't anywhere near as good.

What happened with the 2nd Division was that the way they used the 37th Rangers nearly killed them all off. That was one of the reasons we wanted to form the Ranger Groups. They were totally misused.

They gave a terrific account of themselves during Tet, '68. They were up there above the Perfume River.

The 37th Ranger Battalion was attached to the 2nd Division at one point.

Daniel went on to say perhaps the 2nd Division Recon Company and one Regiment were okay, but the rest weren't up to par. Of the 1st Division, he said he didn't serve with them, but he knows their reputation and knows men who served with them.

I was wounded before that time and medevaced. I was in the Great Lakes Naval Hospital undergoing plastic surgery [leg] getting ready to go back to Vietnam. I got back in July of '68.

Daniel was hit by mortars and recoilless rifle fire during a mission and his tibia was shattered. A subsequent bone infection in his leg left him with a permanent limp.

I was bowlegged in my right leg and knock-kneed in my left. That's tough for a guy from Tennessee, got one leg shorter than the other, anyway.

A little humor, then he got serious.

The Vietnamese Airborne and the Marines, many of them were evacuated when we pulled out of Vietnam. Probably a fairly large number of the Viet Marines [and their families]. Nobody saved the Rangers. They fought to the very bitter end. I have two counterparts [Vietnamese Colonels] who died in North Vietnamese prisons. I stay in contact with my interpreter, who was fortunate enough after being in prison for six or seven years to get out. He lives in Fort Worth, Texas. I'll call him at least once every two months just to see how he is.

We called them the cross-eyed panthers. They had a [black] panther with 13 teeth painted on their helmets. The eyes were such they were looking directly at the enemy, and therefore cross-eyed.

Spies—Bio

Major (Retired) William Spies has had a long and distinguished career as a Ranger. He joined up in 1955 and retired in 1978, and held every command position in a rifle company from Fire Team Leader to Commander, except First Sergeant.

Among other postings, he commanded a Counter-Guerilla Warfare School in Korea, fought in Vietnam—where he lost a leg—and was Deputy Director of the Ranger Department as well as the Commander of the 4th Ranger Training Battalion at Fort Benning. He was also largely responsible for the drafting of the 1st Ranger Battalion TO&E in 1973-74. These accomplishments are but a part of Spies' resume.

This tough Ranger made 25-mile marches and 100 parachute jumps on an artificial leg.

As of spring, 2007, he was the Executive Secretary of the World-Wide Army Rangers Association.

Acting as an Advisor to the Vietnamese, he didn't work with the Army at all, but with the Marines, though he was an Army Ranger. Spies worked through and with the III Marine Amphibious Assault Force (MAAF) under Major General Fields, acting as Advisor to elements of the 2nd ARVN Division. The two-company group was called Dai Cong, or Com—as close as Spies could get to the spelling—which means "explosive." They were an elite group, and very tough. The Marines called them Strike Force and Recon.

William Spies

All the men in the unit had to have lost a blood relative to the communists in the last three years. They were fiercely loyal. There were two companies, so we could get up around 300 people, but we never went on a 300-man operation, because I couldn't speak Vietnamese for one thing. If we were screening for the Marines or the Vietnamese, I'd take a company to do that, but most times, for the first four or five weeks I was there, I broke them down into small teams, and I'd take the Sergeants out and show them how to patrol.

I had a great interpreter named Bai. He had a Master's Degree and he could speak pretty good English. He hated a damn green tracer [enemy tracer]. I mean, one round broke over your head and he would say, "Dai Uy [leader], I'm so feared, I'm so feared." I'd say, "Bai, you got to get up and walk," but he was so afraid he'd be trembling. But he never refused to go out on patrol with me. He was a professor, taught in Da Nang. He had a lot of nerve, but he didn't like any firefight.

When we went on operations with the Marines, they [the company] were OPCON (operational control) to me, but when we went with the Vietnamese, I was an Advisor to them.

Spies was attached to the 1st Force Recon Battalion, III MAAF (Marine Amphibious Assault Force), as operational control and logistics. He had one American Sergeant with him, but that was it. "The Marines got on me, boy."

When Spies got orders, it was from the Marines, and he took his Sergeant Major, Phi, and his interpreter, Bai, with him. When the Vietnamese got orders, they came through the senior officer present, and Spies didn't know exactly where those orders came from. Generally speaking, the Army didn't work with the Marines as Spies was doing.

I've got a copy of the secret orders where I was with them. At first, a four-star general came down and said, "No, we don't want any Army working with us," but they got down how many buffalo we killed, and how many elephants, and I think, how many POWs we brought them. I was on Manhattan with them, Missouri, Kansas, and that's the only one I have a copy of, about three weeks I worked with them on Kansas. [State names were used as operation code names.]

What happened on my first operation, when I got involved with them, we had Vietnamese radios. We went out into the A Shau Valley where we were working in March of '66, the latter part of March. The first "Puff the Magic Dragon," that was a C-47 with a gatling gun in it, I'd never seen one. We were watching from up on a little ridge, and we knew the NVA were going to try and take that place. I was reporting about two-and-a-half battalions there. We were walking around in the jungle, and we had a pretty good head count. Sure enough, one of those nights the NVA attacked the A Shau camp and they overran it. In the process of them attacking it, here came this damned old airplane in the dark…rrrrrupp…rrrrupp…and just lit up the side of that hill. I don't think he killed a hell of a lot, but they knocked a lot of rocks out, set off some land mines. But the North Vietnamese took that hill, and they shot that airplane down.

I saw it going down. But, you know how the jungle is, it was a valley and a big old hill, so I couldn't tell exactly which crease it was in. What happened to us, right after we saw the plane go down, we lost radio contact and couldn't make a report.

So, I thought, well, we'll just walk on back to Da Nang [east, all the way across the top of South Vietnam]. I'll just go across topography. There's one big river between Da Nang and where I was—I knew that. So, we headed for Da Nang. The first night I was off the map. We kept walking every night. Took me nine nights before I recognized anything. That next morning, I looked down, and I could see I was on the coastal lowland. You could see the rice paddies.

I looked down to my left and saw a camp down there, which I recognized as Tra Bong Special Forces Camp, on the Tra Bong River. I said, well, it's daylight, and I'm going to move in daylight—today. So we went on down.

Over to my left I was pretty sure I saw a white mountain that I called Marble Mountain, but Jack Daniel says, no, Marble Mountain is out on the coast. It's just above Tam Ky, which sits below Da Nang. I saw this little mountain, but I couldn't see Da Nang, because I had missed Da Nang by about 40 klicks! I had intentionally gone a little bit southeast, because that's where I thought Da Nang was [no map!]. I should have gone due east.

There were five Vietnamese and myself. I was point man, compass man, and patrol leader. Now, Phi would be on the end, sometimes a little corporal named Hep, but usually Sergeant Major Phi. Every time I went out on patrol SMG Phi would insist he go with me, or Corporal Hep. Both of them killed people with their fingers and their feet. Phi could hit a man right there, and he's dead. I don't care who it is, if Phi puts it on them, they're dead. He could kick a man and kill him, too.

Bill Spies is somewhat vertically challenged, about the same height as a Vietnamese, and at that time, about the same weight. He said he and Phi never "tussled," though Spies used to box, but he's not sure he could have beaten him. Don't get me wrong, he says, "We loved each other. Phi was like a brother."

Ken Bonnell

Information about Ken Bonnell and his three Ranger sons can be found in the section "Family of Rangers." This interview is part of a longer one conducted by email.

I served two tours in Vietnam. I was a Captain during both tours. My first tour was November 1968 to October 1969. My second tour was January to December of 1971.

During my first tour, I was the Senior Advisor to the 34th Vietnamese Ranger Battalion [commanded by Captain Chu]. Shortly after working with the 1st Infantry Division in the Tu Duc area and securing the water treatment plant there in August 1969, the Ranger Battalion was deployed rapidly to Fire Support Base Jon, near Loc Ninh [in eastern III Corps, near Cambodia]. We landed in an assortment of fixed-wing aircraft under heavy small arms and mortar fire to reinforce the 1/11th Armored Cavalry Regiment, commanded by then-Major Bonson [later Brigadier General Bonson]. We became part of Task Force Wright [commanded by Lt. Colonel Lawrence Wright, later Brigadier General Wright], which was part of the 1st Cavalry Division's Task Force Casey [Major General Casey, commanding]. We were under fierce attack from the elements of two NVA divisions and two VC [units] that wanted to take over Loc Ninh and make it the new VC capitol.

After three days and nights of wave attacks, we broke their attack and they started to withdraw back towards Cambodia. Hundreds of NVA and VC were killed along and inside our wire [perimeter wire around the firebase]. We immediately began a pursuit. I believe that this pursuit began on August 12, 1969. As we pursued them, they set up a large L-shaped ambush. I felt suspicion that an ambush was likely and I warned the 11th ACR that we were being sucked in. We all agreed that the Vietnamese Rangers should move along the Cav's flank, while they went straight ahead into the "L."

Quickly, we discovered their ambush positions in well-developed trenches as the Cav took heavy fire; they had wire communications laid to all of their positions. Once we discovered that we were at the end of the long part of their "L position," I advised the Vietnamese

Ranger Commander that we should fix bayonets and charge immediately down their trench line. My Senior NCO, Staff Sergeant Eads, went with the lead Ranger Company and the battalion commander and I followed them with three more companies. Before long, we all were engaged in hand-to-hand combat. However, the Rangers fought extremely well, and with the Armored Cav at our left flank we turned the ambush into our victory. I believe there were around 100 NVA/VC killed and numerous weapons captured, to include Chinese communications equipment. We had very few casualties.

Later Major General Casey, Commander of the 1st Cavalry Division, flew in and gave the Ranger Battalion Commander and Staff Sergeant Eads Silver Star Medals. As a result of my combat experience at Loc Ninh from August through September, I received the Bronze Star with V, Air Medal with V, and the ARCOM with V. I believe that it was my Ranger training that gave me the sense to make the right judgment call to fix bayonets and charge the ambush.

Bonnell was sent north after that.

I [then] commanded Fire Base Rakasson, which was close to Fire Base Ripcord in the mountains overlooking the A Shau valley [I Corps]. We were above the clouds most of the time. I had a lot of heavy artillery on the base to protect …because it could reach into the A Shau and Laos. Even though I saw a lot of action during this tour, and had a lot of close calls, I did not receive a scratch.

Still a Captain, Bonnell took part in the largest operation in the Vietnam War—one that featured Vietnamese troops carrying most, but not all, of the burden.

In March 1971, I was the Commander of Echo Company, 2/506th Infantry, 101st Airborne Division. As part of Lam Son 719, we moved out of Camp Evans on March 20 and were sent up north to occupy positions along Highway QL9. We had units at Camps Carroll and FSB [Fire Support Base] Vandergrift, while the Battalion HQ and my company occupied FSB Khe Gio.

Later on, headquarters was moved to another location. I was ordered to protect a key bridge just below the firebase along the main route below the DMZ that ran into Laos during Operation Lam Son …the South Vietnamese/US attack into Laos. The American Corps Commander made the importance of this bridge very clear to me; however, I do not recall his name. This was the only time I ever met the man and his stay was brief. I only remember he wore three stars and was very direct with me on the importance of my mission at Khe Gio. He walked me out onto the bridge and told me, "Captain, this bridge must be held at all costs, and if this bridge falls you had better be in the middle of it."

This bridge was vital because it could not be spanned quickly if it was destroyed. The NVA knew this. and they hit us constantly with mortars and artillery, then they tried sapper attacks with explosives. When all these failed they tried wave attacks across the Song Cam Lo River at the northern base of our positions. The positions consisted of my company [which held a sniper platoon, a recon platoon, and a mortar platoon of six 81mm mortars], and at the time some units that needed to lay in with us for the night. I had put up a lot of mines, and wire under and around the bridge. I also put up several searchlights to cover the bridge with snipers on duty covering the approaches to the bridge at all times. As some ARVN mech units were withdrawing after being chewed up, we asked them to give us two .50 cal machineguns. After some trading, we got two guns and some ammo. I purposely did not have them test-fired so the enemy would not know that I had them.

Also about this time, a Duster Platoon of four tracks [40mm automatic grenade launchers] came from the north at dusk and asked to logger in with us for the night. I put them on the perimeter of the hilltop defenses. Early the next morning, the NVA came at us in strength from the north bank of the river along with artillery fire. With the firepower from the .50s and the Dusters combined with my mortars and small arms, the river ran red with blood of the enemy.   The enemy bodies were numerous and we had none killed. Not one enemy soldier penetrated our defenses.

Mike Martin

Martin did two tours in Vietnam after having been a member of the first recognized LRRP unit in Germany in 1961-62. During his tours, he ran the gamut between Advisor to the Vietnamese Rangers (Biet Dong Quan) to PRU (Provincial Recon Unit) to running MATTs (Mobile Army Training Teams). He went to Vietnam from Germany.

In 1965, I volunteered to go to Vietnam, but the company commander [LRRP] wouldn't release me. So I wrote General Westmoreland a letter and he sent me a letter with orders assigning me to Vietnam. I'll always remember having to have a passport to go to Vietnam [from Germany].

I had told Westmoreland I wanted a Ranger unit, and they assigned me to the 32nd Ranger Battalion at My Tho, in the delta. That was the 7th ARVN Division headquarters. Another unique commander there was Colonel Sid Berry, the 7th Division Senior Advisor.

Berry later became the commander of the 101st Airborne Division, and Superintendent of West Point.

I was there two or three months. The 44th Battalion was on down south. They were working out of Can Tho. They ran into a major regimental-size ambush and they had 70 Rangers killed that night, and many wounded. All the Advisors were either wounded or killed. Jerry Devlin was the Senior Advisor at that time. Captain McNamara was our Senior Advisor. The other NCO on our team was Sergeant McDonald, a very professional NCO. I've never seen an NCO know more about map reading and weapons and so forth. He was a great big guy, on his third tour by then. Captain McNamara told him he was sending him down to the 44th, and I said why can't I go. McDonald just extended again and this is where he wants to be. He outranked me [E-7 to E-6] and he said I could go.

Later, Martin saw a Major who said he had heard of the transfer.

He said, buddy, that's a Co Van [Viet for Advisor] getter. There's never been an American left that unit alive [or at least unscathed]. I was the first one.

I went down there and they had moved from Can Tho to Soc Trang. We lived out with the Vietnamese.

Second Tour—PRU, MATT

On my second tour in Vietnam I asked for the Rangers again. They sent me out to Tan Son Nhut [MACV] airbase. That was 1968.

I was there the first day getting the briefings [can do, cannot do]. They're going to send you out to a Vietnamese unit, but they tell you not to eat the food and don't drink the water.

Martin went back to his quarters and found a message that he would be picked up in an hour. As promised, "a black sedan" with a man in plainclothes came to get him.

I had been assigned to the Combined Studies Division. They took me to town and put me in a hotel. Next morning we went out to this place and the commander was a Marine Colonel. He told me I was being assigned as a PRU Commander [Provincial Recon Unit], which worked under the Phoenix Program [run by the CIA]. There were several of us. They sent us up to Vung Tau and we went through the Vietnamese PRU Course there for two days. We went back and received briefings from all the different CIA people in Saigon.

I was assigned to III Corps. I got up there and the guy said, "I've already got a PRU commander. I don't need anyone." I turned around and went back. Then I was assigned to Chou Duc [Chou Phu Province], down on the Cambodian border.

The Phoenix [people] didn't stay with the CIA. They stayed in a [different] compound. They had a little Captain there, and a Sergeant, and they wore civilian clothes. The concept was that the Phoenix would identify these VCI—Viet Cong Infrastructure, the leaders—and the PRUs were the action arm. They'd give them the list and they'd go after them. Those shitbirds never did anything. I read several books where guys that worked in the Phoenix program said they did this, and they did that, but I talked to PRU operators in [all the Corp areas], and with the exception of about two, the Phoenix never did dip for them. They'd give you names like Ho Chi Minh or General Giap or something like that.

So, we created our own Intel. So, you didn't take a PRU that was out of a different province or corps area, because you wanted them to be very familiar with the people and the land where you were working. I went out to see one of my people one day, and he was plowing with a water buffalo. We all wore black pajamas and you couldn't tell him from the locals. We'd have them sit around and watch the monasteries and things like that. They could come and go at night; they knew every trail.

Most of the PRUs I had [about 80], maybe half of them were ex-VC. They'd come over or we'd captured them, and they'd work for you.

Martin said some units were down to 40 men, but he tried to operate in the field with about 60, broken down into teams of 18 men (or so).

You could form it up any way you wanted to. You were definitely in charge. I had a very colorful PRU Chief. He'd been wounded 18 times. He looked like a Mohawk Indian, and he had all gold teeth. He wore a little derby hat, and he smoked a water pipe with opium stuff all the time. But when he went into combat he didn't fear anything.

One night, we were in a truck riding down to the Cambodian border to set up an ambush and I heard him telling my [Chinese] translator that, "This is where I got wounded twice last year. This is a bad area." I'm looking around, and we're riding down there in a flatbed truck and he's got a little derby on—not quite your military operation. But, he was very effective. They were terrified of him in that province.

After about eight months, Martin and the CIA operatives were not seeing eye-to-eye. "They were completely worthless."

I left and went to a MAT Team up in II Corps. I think I spent four months with them. I formed up a MAT Team. I think that was the nature of my career. They relieved two officers and two NCOs that tried to form a new team because they refused to live out with the Vietnamese. I went in there and formed up another team, and stayed the rest of my tour with that team.

The MAT Teams were really unsung heroes. They would stick you out in the middle of nowhere with very little support. It was up to you. You'd have a platoon or a company. I was lucky and had a company, and mine was a Regional Force [RF], but sometimes they'd stick you with a Popular Force [PF], which was even lower down.

The RF/PF units were known collectively as "Ruff Puffs." They were not the finest troops in the field, so the MATT staff had a lot to take on, especially without a lot of outside support. Martin related a story about finding five men out in a rice paddy, protected by one single barrier of concertina wire, and armed with nothing more than M16s. The little group had been dropped off by helicopter and spent the night out there all alone, and "they were scared to death." Evidently Charlie didn't know they were there, and Martin told them flat out they wouldn't survive another night. They were supposed to form a MAT Team. Martin got on the radio and got them some help.

He said some MAT Teams got help from MACV, but many didn't get enough.

I left there in December 1969, and was assigned to the 2nd Ranger Company in Dahlonega, Georgia [Mountain Phase of Ranger School].

Doug Perry

Perry is retired (First Sergeant) from the military now, and living in Dahlonega, Georgia, home of the Mountain Phase. After his retirement he was placed in command of security for Camp Merrill and eventually elevated to GS Captain grade. He seems a quiet, unassuming man, quick with a smile, quick to help out. He is also one of the Ranger Legends I have run into in the course of researching this book, both in combat and as a Ranger Instructor at Camp Frank D. Merrill.

Beginning in December 1965, he acted as an Advisor to ARVN regulars, and to the Biet Dong Quan "Black Tigers"—the South Vietnamese version of the Rangers. He spent a lot of time in the field with the 42nd and 44th Battalions.

This piece is the result of several interviews and conversations over four years, though the main content was recorded sitting in his truck back in Penn Cove, behind CFM.

I went in the Army March 26, 1958, and went through Ranger Class 6-62—January, February, March.

I left here [CFM] December 1965, and went to Vi Thanh, Vietnam, in Choung Tien Province. That's in the Delta. I left the Mountain Camp with orders for MACV. Their HQ was in the Kophler Hotel in downtown Saigon. We were taken there on buses with PSP [pierced steel planking] on the sides.

PSP eventually was made of aluminium, but still called PSP.

Perry began his tour with the 21st ARVN Infantry Division as an Advisor. The 21st was headquartered in Bac Lieu, but Perry stayed mostly around Vi Thanh a few miles north.

We operated all over, all the way to Ca Mau at the tip of the peninsula. We [often] went on Riverines [boats]. They carried us in, and Birds, too. The first time [1966], the Riverine force was not that far south. They were just coming down from Saigon on the Mekong [they called it the Nile]. It just splits off everywhere.

The Riverine force was Navy boats, Swift boats; they had a 40mm [grenade launcher] on the bow, .50 calibers on the sides. They were little boats, but you could get about a platoon on one of them.

I stayed six months with the 21st ID as an E6, a heavy-weapons Advisor, then went to Bac Lieu with the 42nd [Vietnamese] Rangers—BDQ. With the 21st I went on a couple of operations with them [42nd]. One of the Advisors, Harbell, got killed up there, so I filled in. Later on I kept working with them, and then I went and joined the 42nd.

We staged our operations [21st ARVN] out of an airfield—Bac Lieu, Soc Trang, Bien Tuy at Can To…that's the only place you could refuel the choppers, so you staged out of those airfields.

The battalion commander used to be a company commander in the 42nd. Captain Sanford Cochran was my Senior Advisor with the 21st ID and he was Ranger-qualified, and he didn't want to go to no damn Ranger Battalion, but I did more than anything else. Him working with me and some other things is how I got transferred to the Rangers.

It was a Ranger's job. I didn't feel like I was doing my job with the 21st. I needed to be with a Ranger Battalion. I was like Sergeant Major Gilbert—I wanted to be out there doing my job instead of some non-Ranger job.

I worked for him. He's the one that said, hey, I'm going to start getting Ranger-qualified NCOs in these Ranger Battalions. When he first got there they didn't even have a position for him, so he went out with the APCs [armored personnel carriers] just to get some combat time, get to know the terrain.

Bob Gilbert became First Sergeant of L Company Rangers later in the war.

I guess it was May or June 1966, I went to the 42nd. They were out of Bac Lieu. They stayed in the delta, in the Corps area where you were assigned. The Ranger Battalions were assigned to [IV Corps]. The I, II and III Corps had their own Ranger Battalions.

There were several BDQ units in the delta, though they seldom saw one another except for certain large operations. It is worth noting that recruits for the BDQ did not always volunteer, as did American Rangers. They could be assigned right out of Basic.

They actually pulled men from the Infantry and the PRUs. They go on these recruiting drives in the villages and get these people and put them into a small training course right there. We've had replacements come into Soc Trang and they'd go right to the Ranger compound and they'd start training them. A lot of times, we'd go out with people and they'd tell me, new guy, just out of training. Before you could work with the BDQ you had to go to a training center, before you could be known as a Biet Dong Quan. They did it in Nha Trang or the Seven Mountains area, but it was all live fire.

There were rappelling towers, CA (combat assault) practice, work with choppers, weapons training, and much more.

You go as a unit to the training center. The whole battalion. There were Advisors at the training centers, and their counterparts. They would take the men out on training exercises, live fire on actual combat missions. There were Special Forces at Nha Trang and along the border, but in the Seven Mountains area we had Vietnamese and American Advisors doing the training. There were hardly any Special Forces BDQ Advisors. I don't know of any. There was a small percentage of US Rangers [at first], but in '69, when Knuckols and me were there, we could see the difference.

We started getting more Ranger-qualified people in there. If you had that Ranger Tab on, the Vietnamese knew that. A lot of Vietnamese officers in '69 were Ranger-qualified from America.

Perry was questioned about the makeup and actions of the BDQ Battalions.

A BDQ Battalion was usually about 250. Between 200 and 250. At one time we were down to 175 after a few major battles. They pulled you back then, to Bac Lieu or wherever you were assigned, and they fill you back up again and get you re-equipped and put you back out on operations. We took a lot of casualties.

When we went on a heli-borne assault, a CA, a lot of them got killed when they first got on the ground. That's where we took most of our casualties.

We had UH-1B gunships. They were so slow they could be shot with crossbows. The first time I saw a "snake" [AH-1G Cobra] I thought it was VC.

A question was asked about changing tactics to avoid extra casualties when doing a combat assault.

Really, that went across later. When I went back in '69, I could see different tactics being used. They used false insertions and actually had empty ships go in and check it out first. If it was okay they'd put us in.

On the Ranger teams, you had usually a Captain or a Major—if it was a Captain it was a senior Captain—and usually a Lieutenant, two NCOs, and an RTO with a battalion.

The heavy team, usually the command group, went with them into the field—what we called the Soft Element, which was another NCO and the other officer, which was Lt. McKnight with us. *Danny McKnight became well known because of his actions in Somalia in 1993. He was also the XO of the Mountain Ranger Camp as a 1st Lieutenant, under Brian Cunningham.*

We went with the reserve company—the rear company—and that way if the command group or lead company got into it, we could maneuver and come through and give them support in case they got into something they couldn't handle.

The Command Group [Senior Advisors and counterparts] would usually go in the center. If you had A Company going in first, the lead company, then the Command Group would be behind it with Bravo Company or Charlie and they'd be intermingled in there.

You couldn't actually call headquarters a company; it was just a group. You had three line companies and a Command Group. We had 70-75 in a company, but usually it was no more than 65 [about the size of a WWII Ranger Company].

We always went out as a battalion. Ranger Battalions were never split. We stayed in the field four-to-six weeks before. We'd set up in a village and operate out of there. We'd set up night ambushes and go out to strategic points during the day.

Later on, they had that "win the hearts and minds of the people," and the Rangers did a lot of that because Vietnamese civilians really respected the Black Tigers. The other [units] like the PRU [Provincial Recon Units] and the RFPF [regional and local militia], they'd steal like everything because they were part-time civilians, part-time military. They recruited them to serve around the villages and man some outposts. They were always stealing off the civilians, but we wouldn't let the Rangers do that too much. Some of them you couldn't control, but…geese, chickens, pigs, rice, everything.

At times various units of either side were liable to go through a village and steal anything that wasn't hidden well enough. Imagine an armed group coming to your house and cleaning out your pantry—on a regular basis. Such things have happened since the first conflicts.

We tried to get them not to do it, but sometimes the lead company would kill a pig, then the next company coming by would start to clean it, and by the time we got there with the Soft Group the pig would be cut up and gone. When we stopped, they'd start preparing their evening meal. That was the best meal of the day. For breakfast they'd have soup or something, then a light lunch [whatever they had], and immediately after that they'd have to have a siesta.

When they were out winning the hearts and minds of the people they'd stop in a village and the people would turn out [1969]. We stayed in the field most of the time.

MACV had a compound in Bac Lieu, where the 21st ARVN ID was headquartered. Both the 42nd and 44th Rangers were attached to the 21st.

The Rangers had a compound on the other side of Bac Lieu and we'd go out there during the day when we weren't out in the field. They'd get their stuff together and start training, and they'd have classes, just like American soldiers. The Vietnamese NCOs and officers taught the classes. I was heavy-weapons—11 Charlie—and we'd show them how to set up the 81mm mortar, and at that time they had the 57mm recoilless rifle, which was a useless piece of shit because the ammo weighed so much we couldn't carry much in the field.

The 60mm mortars usually went with the lead company. They usually didn't even take the base plates; they'd just use their helmets to set them in. It was more of a hand-held job.

Perry was asked how the BDQ operated.

We'd go out on an operation and if we got good contact, normally we'd pull back to Vi Thanh or where ever and go in again the next morning on another combat assault. If we didn't have too much contact we'd probably stay out in the field overnight. The next day they'd throw some more units in there and we'd get our Intel reports up and they'd say, well, a VC Battalion is located here...they'd get their Intel from going through these villages.

If we had heavy contact we'd try to get out of there for the night. We'd try to end the battle. They'd put C&C [command and control] ships up. We had counterparts in the helicopters all the time, Vietnamese and Americans. Everybody had a counterpart.

Ranger units were used primarily as shock troops. Usually they went in first, and if they got good contact then they'd throw the Infantry battalions in there, they'd start the armor—APCs—then they'd start the RFPF going out from their different villages and try to end the battle there. Sometimes they didn't. Lots of times we'd get light contact and it never developed into anything.

That's one thing about the VC—the NVA were ready to fight any time, but the VC weren't. We'd hit a small group of VC and the battle was over. They would group up, like the Ta Do VC Battalion, one of the worst in the delta. If you ever hit them, you were in for a fight because they usually stayed together [400-500 men].

It wasn't always easy to find the VC. Perry was asked about combat in the delta.

It all depended on the Intelligence. The Air Force spotter planes flew everyday, and the Shotgun L-19s [fixed-wing] were the Army's spotters. They'd fly and see who was in position along the canal lines. In the delta you only had canal lines and that's where the VC stayed. They didn't stay out in the rice paddies. You could see where they had gone from one canal to another and dragged their sampans with their weapons on them through the rice paddies at night.

When you'd come in a Huey on a CA [combat assault] you'd have to land out in the paddies. We tried to land at least 500 meters from the canal line if we were expecting contact. That would give everybody a chance to get on the ground and start maneuvering before we got into small arms fire. We were losing choppers like everything back then, so we changed tactics.

If you hit the canal line, everything was booby-trapped; they were ready for you. They dug trenches—everything filled up with water during the rainy season—and they'd have these huge urns made out of clay. They'd dig those in and jump inside them so they wouldn't be standing in water. They were some big clay pots. Usually the major canals were a hundred meters across, houses on both sides, then rice paddies, then maybe a klick away was another canal line. The delta was just one giant canal interlaced with other canals. There were major canals, and then there were crossing canals, so they could flow water into their paddies.

[After landing in the paddies] we'd walk in until we got close enough to fire, and we would start shooting. If there was anybody there they would answer us. Some times we'd fire and not get anything. As soon as the helicopters started going in, the civilians would make a wild break. All the huts had bunkers in them and they would crawl in there or they would try to get the hell out of there in their sampans because we peppered that area with air support, gunships, and artillery.

Unlike other Corps areas, in the delta we didn't have the luxury of being able to move our artillery with us. There were only certain places it could go because it was towed. If we couldn't airlift them in—sling-lift them with a Chinook—we'd have to tow them.

There were certain places, villages mostly, where batteries could be placed and cover an area out to 10 or 12 klicks with 105mm. As for the VC, it was mostly small stuff.

They would use small arms, RPGs, mortars, everything they had. They had mortars just like we had, plenty of 81mms. They used ours, captured stuff. They'd overrun these outposts, the RFPF outposts, and they'd get everything they had. They'd get it from Laos and Cambodia.

If they were in battalion size we'd have a major battle. If they were just platoon or company-size VC we'd overrun them, they'd get the hell out of the AO. We'd regroup and try to get our Intel reports up and go in the next day. If not, we'd stay in the field. I have stayed out there and worked gunships all night long.

The Advisors on the ground talked directly to the helicopters. That's one reason we were there. We controlled the gunships, the Viking gunships, that's the ones I remember most. They were out of Soc Trang. The old B-model Hueys. We'd work them, we'd talk to a Vietnamese counter-part and we'd say, we're receiving small arms fire from this point on the map and we'd pop smoke and we'd say, okay, 250 meters on an azimuth to such-and-such, and they're reporting major contact up there, heavy small arms fire, mortar fire.

The gunships would come in there and we'd talk to them. We could tell as we progressed if there was going to be a major contact. We worked them all night. They'd bring gunships in with the lightships, they had Shadow and Superspook, and we'd use them at night and in the day.

The men on the ground—American or Vietnamese—could talk to the gunships, but not the close air support, the A1E Sky Raiders or the fast-movers. For that, they had to talk to the C&C ships orbiting high above. They could see more of the battlefield and called in most of the heavy air support.

An interesting note—Perry said the Vietnamese had no word for helicopter. An aircraft was a "pico" (phonetics, here), and a helicopter was a "pico wop-wop."

Sometimes we used the *New Jersey* [battleship]. They loved to come down in the delta. Sixteen-inch fire, 20 klicks into the delta they could put a round in your hip pocket. In a rice paddy, they'd blow the mud out and make a big crater. But, if it was a big battle, they'd bring the B52s in.

If we were using close air support in the night, they'd [VC] would use the darkness to cover their withdrawal, and they'd get the heck out of there. But, sometimes they would stay and fight.

If they were equipped to fight, they'd stay, but if not, they would go back and put their rice paddy clothes on and go to hoeing rice the next day. You couldn't tell who they were.

There were Chinese and Russian Advisors down there. The whole time I was there I never did see a real live Russian Advisor. I saw some they said were Chinese, but we had Chinese Nungs working for us, too. But, if you look at a dead Oriental, who can say whether he's Chinese, or Vietnamese, or Cambodian or Laotian. A Vietnamese could probably tell, but we couldn't.

The question was, who had the last word on the ground, the Vietnamese or the Advisors?

The Advisors did. In 1968-69, they got to where they didn't want to pull back from the canal lines 500 meters to be picked up. We simply said our choppers are not coming in until we get 500 meters away from this wood line. They'd say, there's no VC here, no VC, they can land right here. No. The minute we'd bring the birds in they'd slip in along the canal lines and shoot our choppers, because everybody was getting on the choppers.

The question was what did the battalion do if they were out overnight?

The Vietnamese would get us a hut to stay in. They would disperse into the village; some of them would dig in. But the Command Group stayed in the huts. They would just commandeer the Vietnamese huts. We slept in their beds, which were nothing more than just boards on sawhorses with a mosquito bar around them. No padding, usually just a clean board, they just put a pillow on it, no mattress. Boards were laid out, and they had been used so much it was real shiny, like mahogany. A mosquito bar and a pillow or two and that was it. They slept in their pajamas [the ones they wore all day].

For a bathroom, they'd run out to the canal lines and shit in there. They had latrines built out over the fish ponds and they raised what we called shit fish. That's what you ate for supper that night. They weren't bad if they were cooked enough.

When we went into a village they'd commandeer whatever. They made sure their Co Vans [Advisors] were well taken care of.

Often the soldiers were given money (piasters) to buy supplies from the villages, but sometimes the money got pocketed and the supplies were simply commandeered, a thing the VC always did. American Advisors did what they could to keep that sort of thing down, but they were there to advise on tactics, not personal behavior of the troops, which was supposed to be looked after by the Vietnamese commander.

They [BDQ] liked us because we kept them alive. We had everything, and they didn't have anything. It all depended on us to get stuff in there and get them evacuated, and make sure they had air support [and artillery, technology, experience, etc.]

Sometimes they would argue tactics, but they would never, never argue if we wanted them to do something. They'd say, well, we don't believe this is right, but we'll do it. Then later on, when they found out we were going to pull out—I talked to several Advisors after that and they said they [Viets] didn't want to do anything. But they took care of us, and when I left there, there were Vietnamese pilots flying the gunships and the slicks.

Working with a counterpart could be difficult. "Sometimes we could hear the VC down the road at night doing psyops in a vil {using a loudspeaker}. We couldn't fire on them because they might be standing on the steps of a shrine." In that case the counterparts would sometimes refuse the Advisor's advice.

After a tour as an Instructor at the Mountain Ranger Camp, Perry returned to Vietnam in early 1969 and was made a member of a MATT, or Mobile Army Training Team. Not to his liking, his membership ended barely a month later when he got back to the BDQ, this time the 44th Battalion. Much had changed.

When you went back, if you were with the Rangers before, they'd try to get you back. When I went back they had the Groups set up, the 4th Ranger Group. They didn't have that before. The Advisors were with the Groups, and the Groups controlled all the Ranger Battalions in IV Corps. There were a bunch of Ranger Battalions down there [in the delta].

Art Hill, from down at Benning, he was with the one up at My To. I saw him a couple of times on operations when they'd call us all in. Don Stafford and…others were with the 5th Group out of Can To, and we'd see them. They went in the C&C ships later on. The first time it was usually just somebody from the 21st ID, maybe their commander or the G-3 or S-3, and they tried to control things.

Later on, people from the Group would get up there and it would be a Ranger war. All the Ranger Battalions would go in. They'd have different objectives.

For the first time we had pre-planned artillery fire. We could get it a lot quicker. They'd move it in as close as they could, wherever they could get it.

Our artillery support was mostly ARVN. They were located at District and Provincial Headquarters. They could drop one in your pocket.

Featured were 105mm howitzers, 4.2-inch (107mm) mortars (aka four-deuce), and 81mm mortars. The next question was were you ambushed much as a battalion-sized force?

If you ran into a major force they'd let you come in, especially if we only put one battalion on the ground. They could tell if you were putting a major force in there, helicopter after helicopter going in.

We'd be staged out of Vi Thanh or Bac Lieu or somewhere, and we'd ask the chopper pilots before we got on, do we have contact? Is it a hot LZ? If they said it was hot then we'd get ready for a good firefight, but a lot of times, believe me, it was nothing. The VC picked their time to fight. If they were well organized and they were in force, you bet your sweet bippy you were in for a fight.

They'd wait, try to trick you, start sniping at you 400-500 yards out. Once you got out of the chopper you'd hear rounds going over you. If you were taking casualties you could see the wounded being brought back. The Soft Team, the light team, would help them get back and work the medevac.

Those major canals were close together. There was one area down there where two canals, there was nowhere to pull back to because the VC would be on both canal lines and we had to stay in the middle. They might be a klick apart [not much for a mortar], but you had these cross canals and interweaving canals and it was just a mess some times.

The major canals didn't have the monkey bridges over them, but the cross canals did and that's the way the VC [and everybody else] got across them. It was nothing but a log and a handrail, just coconut logs and you'd go up, level out, and go down the other side.

During my research I heard about this: In 1966 an order was supposedly given that the BDQ shouldn't wear their Black Tiger insignia during assaults because the enemy would see the patches and run away. I asked Perry about it.

I learned this from the 44th mainly. If they knew there was going to be a big battle they would not [most of them, anyway] wear that Black Tiger insignia. They didn't want the VC to know who they were. If it was a small battle they did want them to know they were the Black Tigers.

They went into battle hollering Biet Dong Quan Sat Cong! [BDQs Kill Communists!].

The Biet Dong Quan were somewhat eccentric about their headgear and unit patch. This was evidently picked up by some of the Advisors. The BDQs called themselves the Black Tigers, though the patch worn on sleeve and maroon beret features what Americans would call a black panther.

The Vietnamese don't have a word for panther. It's either a tiger or...so they were the Black Tigers. I wore the maroon beret in the field. We carried our steel pots, but most of the time we didn't wear them. Most of the Command Group wore the berets. The BDQs were real good about wearing their steel pots. They were good in the rice paddies. You can scoop out a hole in a minute with a steel pot.

Singletary—Bio

In 2002, Earl Singletary was voted a Distinguished Member of the Ranger Training Brigade for his long service—almost seven years—in two tours as a Ranger Instructor at Camp Frank D. Merrill, the Mountain Phase. He has also been an Airborne Instructor, a Drill Sergeant at AIT at Fort Benning, and served two tours in Vietnam, first with the 502nd of the 101st Airborne Division, then as an Advisor to the Vietnamese 5th Ranger Group Recon Company. At various times he was also an Advisor to the 30th, 33rd, and 38th Ranger Battalions.

After his first tour in Vietnam, he was rotated Stateside to be an Instructor at the 101st Recondo School at Fort Campbell, Kentucky. From there he went to the Mountain Phase, then back to Vietnam, assigned to MACV. By 1970, he was back in the mountains for his second tour.

Among his awards and decorations are three Bronze Stars, one of them for valor, and an Army Commendation Medal (ARCOM) for valor, not to mention a Purple Heart. He also garnered the Ranger Tab, Vietnamese Ranger Badge, Drill Sergeant Badge, Master Parachutist Badge, and Pathfinder Badge.

Singletary retired from the military as a First Sergeant in 1980 and went on to have a second distinguished career in law enforcement. This interview was taped at his home in Dahlonega, Georgia, in November 2004.

Earl Singletary

When I was a young troop, the things that impressed me were the people with the badges and the Tab and all the stuff you had to wear on the uniform. I set a goal. I said I shouldn't have to look up to anybody. I should have all those things on my uniform. I could achieve all those things. More than anything else, it was be the best you can be.

I was an Airborne Instructor when I went through Ranger School in 1965. There was a guy in the Airborne Department, a Corporal Walters, he went through Jump School, a good soldier, went through Ranger School, came back an Honor Graduate. So, I wanted to go.

I had a Platoon Sergeant, Voss, who was in the 1st Ranger Company in the Korean War. I put in for Ranger School, but I was disapproved. I told him I wanted to go and he said, "Are you sure? Let me tell you what will happen. One of these days you'll wind up in some place like Dahlonega as an Instructor." I said, no, that won't happen. I just want to go. Whatever influence he had, two days later I went to Ranger School.

However his Platoon Sergeant did it, not everybody was aware of his assignment. When he got to Ranger School there were no orders for him to attend. He attended Class 8-65 anyway.

When he had been an Airborne Instructor, several Ranger Instructors came through his course and he "paid them special attention." When he got to Ranger School, those Instructors were waiting for him. "They wore me out."

When I got out of Ranger School, I volunteered to go to Vietnam and I was assigned to A Company, 2nd Battalion, 502nd [101st Airborne]. When I arrived, we had 12 enlisted Rangers in the company. I got there in December 1965.

When I was assigned to the company, I was considered excess [as an E-5 Buck Sergeant]. They didn't have job for me. They put me in charge of a machinegun, which is usually a job for an E-4. In three or four weeks we went on our first operation up to Tuy Hoa and made our first major contact for the battalion with the NVA [January 1966 in II Corps].

Long story short, by the end of February, of the 12 Rangers originally in the company there were only two left. All the rest had been killed or wounded. The reason was Rangers ran all the patrols. Colonel Anderson, Battalion CO, had Hatchet Forces. He would send out these six and seven man squads and Rangers were the leaders.

That's why everybody was killed or wounded in such a short time, including myself. I was wounded February 4 in action around Tuy Hoa. I was shot in the back about noon, and then about five in the afternoon I got shot again in the leg. Medevaced by helicopter about six o'clock.

We were out in a squad, about eight of us. We went down to check out a village. We found some eggs and we were picking them up to supplement our C-rations, and we got ambushed by about 35 NVA.

It wasn't supposed to be a combat patrol. It was really just to go down and check the village out. It wasn't occupied, we didn't think. We were walking along a rice-paddy dike. The village was [essentially] in two parts. There was a church [pagoda-type] on one side, in a little complex we were going to. They were behind the church and along side it. They opened fire on us and we returned it.

Me and another Sergeant moved around and got on their flank and started firing them up pretty good, so they fell back. That's when we got a call from a FAC [Forward Air Controller] up above and he said, "You've got 30-something of those guys running away from you."

So we pursued them, got them out in the open and killed 17 of them. They fell back into a bunker complex, but by then we were calling artillery fire on them.

We got stopped because the artillery fire was so close to us we had to get down. Once we got down they gained fire superiority. We never could get back up to make an assault. Lieutenant Wallace was killed, I was wounded and another Sergeant was wounded.

The artillery had stopped [but the NVA hadn't—they were in a bunker and the arty didn't hurt them much]. I got up and turned to a Private and said, let's go. He was getting up and I turned and that's when I got hit in the back. It was kind of a glancing blow. The bullet went in, hit a rib, and came back out. The guy that hit me was firing a Browning Automatic Rifle. They killed him later and captured the weapon, and from his position they could tell [who hit him]. Later in the day I was lying there and was hit again.

I was still firing. We had problems—ran out of ammunition. We stopped firing. I was down to one magazine. I said, well, save this for whatever comes last. I told the Private that was right with me; just stop firing. At the time we didn't know what they had, how many were over there, if they were going to charge or what.

Then we were caught in between the NVA and [our] company that was coming up behind us. Caught in a crossfire.

That was the worst feeling I've ever had. Out in a rice paddy behind a dike about [a foot] high.

Between the two groups there were about a hundred men pouring lead in both directions just over the heads of Singletary and the survivors of his squad. To make matters worse the only "heavy" weapon they had was one M79 grenade launcher, and the M16s were proving unreliable. The perils of the M16 are discussed in more detail in the weapons section.

It's a terrible weapon. That day my weapon jammed three times, and several others jammed, too. The only thing we had with us, out of all eight of us, because we dropped our rucks to go down to the village, was one section of cleaning rod. We put that cleaning rod down the barrel to knock the round out. Failed to extract. We kept passing this thing around as the weapons would jam.

As the fight progressed air strikes started coming in—A1E Sky Raiders [propeller]. It was something to lie there and look up in the sky and see those things coming down, smoke coming out of the wings [machinegun fire], dropping those bombs. All this was going on within 200 yards.

In time, the rest of A Company came all the way in and overran the bad guys. Initially, the company had been on higher elevation and was able to see the fight going on below, perhaps a thousand meters distant. It was they who were calling in the artillery. Singletary said if they hadn't done that his squad would have "been right in amongst them" and been overwhelmed.

"It was as close as I ever came."

Tour Number Two—1970

Being non-deployable as a Ranger Instructor, Singletary had to either volunteer for Vietnam— didn't always work—or seek a transfer to another unit outside the Rangers, or both.

The Department of the Army came up with this deal, if you would volunteer you could pick your unit of choice [in Vietnam]. I picked MACV, which would put me as an Advisor to the Vietnamese Rangers.

Singletary then voiced feelings that have been heard several times in the course of researching this book. Asked why he chose Vietnamese Rangers rather than go back to the 101st, he answered thusly.

At that time the rumors were flying about discipline problems they were having in American units—fraggings of commanders, discipline gone to hell. In 1966, I can talk for my brigade [1st/101st], they were probably the best Airborne troops in the world. You didn't have to encourage them to fight.

They were gung-ho and they would get it done. But the erosion of discipline starting somewhere around 1968-69…we had two people in our company that refused to go on an operation. We went on the operation and came back and they had been court-martialed. They had been sentenced to five years apiece in Fort Leavenworth.

Later on, refusing to go on an operation was accepted. That's why you'd have a 120-man company, but you might only have 60 of them in the field. The rest didn't want to go. They used all sorts of excuses. Commanders didn't want to rock the boat, the media was down on everybody, and so they got by with it.

While there are undeniable reports of such behavior, it was not as widespread as the media would have us think. Most of the doping and fraggings and refusing of orders was done in the rear. Still, Singletary has a good point when he says overall discipline was eroding. The soldiers of 1966 were volunteers. The soldiers of 1970 were largely draftees and had grown up in an anti-war environment. The atmosphere of the war had changed. That is not to say there weren't some good men out there—because there were.

One island of sanity was found in American Ranger units, filled (mostly) with volunteers who had undergone rigorous training. The Ranger units, both US and Viet, were solid for a reason.

Singletary was assigned to the 5th Ranger Group, made up of the 30th, 33rd, and 38th Battalions, plus a Recon Company.

Bounced Around

At that time it was kind of assumed you'd go to a Viet Ranger unit because you were Ranger-qualified. It was headquarters, when I joined them, at the racetrack in Saigon. The rest were south and west of Saigon.

I was originally assigned as an S-5 Advisor. I was a utility man. Any time one of the battalions went on an operation and they needed another Advisor, I went to that battalion. When you're the new guy on the block you're assigned temporarily to a battalion, guess where you go? You go to the lead company, and guess who gets in all the firefights? Well, after about a month of that—and everybody was saying I had a cushy job—well, that cushy job was going to get me killed. They assigned me to the Recon Company as their Advisor. The position called for a Captain, and there were a lot of young Captains that wanted it. It was kind of a prestigious position. I stayed there a couple of months and finally the senior Army Advisor got so tired of hearing the Captains moan and groan he said, look, I'm just not going to put anybody with the Recon Company and he assigned me down to the 33rd Battalion.

They had some problems in the 30th Battalion where the Advisor got in trouble with the battalion commander, who threatened to kill him, so they moved him out and sent me over there to smooth things over. Here I go in, and he already hates Americans. They usually take pretty good care of their Advisors, but they treated me like dirt for a few days. Gradually, they warmed up.

What stopped it, I was sitting there one day and a Vietnamese came over to me with a recoilless 90[mm] and said, "Can you fix this for us?" I said sure, and tore it apart. They had the cable misguided and I fixed it, and it would fire. Just like that, I was a good guy. I was invited to sit with the battalion commander and eat supper. I guess they were waiting to see if I was going to smoke pot or get knuckle-headed, I don't know. I stayed there for a couple of months.

I went to Zuc My Training Center, the Ranger training center, to be re-trained, then I went to the 38th Battalion. I was the only Advisor that kept getting bounced around, and I don't know if it was because I was good or bad. About the time I'd get rapport going I'd get transferred.

I won't say I saw a lot of combat, but I saw enough. We were running missions out around Tay Ninh and an area called the Pineapple. We were mostly south and west of Saigon, [near] the 9th Infantry Division. They were right on the edge of III and IV Corps.

He was asked about the quality of the Vietnamese Rangers.

They were good soldiers, very aggressive. In fact, they were sometimes too aggressive, I thought. They called us Advisors—I only had one company commander I had to advise. The rest of the time I was calling medevacs and air strikes and artillery.

One company commander had 12 years experience in combat. They all averaged years.

We worked as companies most of the time, and occasionally as a platoon. When we would get in a firefight the Rangers were just hi-diddle-diddle straight-up-the-middle. No problem fighting. They fought. Sometimes at night they might hunker down a little bit, but generally the company commanders were very aggressive.

I saw a commander shoot at his own people with a .45 because they wouldn't assault at night. When they got to the wood line, they hesitated because the Viet Cong were there, and he started bam—bam—bam, screaming at them. They figured it was better to go in the woods with the bad guys than stay out there with their company commander.

Their discipline was a lot different than American discipline. They would beat a soldier. They believed in hands-on discipline. But the soldiers, when you ask them how they felt about the commander beating on them, they'd say, well, I deserved it. They loved their commanders.

The problem with the Vietnamese, if the commander got killed, the unit started to deteriorate.

Singletary earned a Bronze Star (with V) for actions he took with the 5th Ranger Group Recon Company in 1969. Of the citation for his medal he said, "They make it sound really great, but all you're doing is doing your job." The citation said Singletary moved "without regard to his personal safety" to get his company going.

They came and got me, I was in downtown Saigon, they said, we've got problems. So I went out to the company. We went down Highway One in a deuce-and-a-half, which concerned me because it was at night and the rest of the company was spread out along the highway. I thought, man, if they're sucking us down here for an ambush, it's my fault. Fortunately, it didn't happen.

They [enemy] had tried to overrun one platoon we had down there. We got off the trucks and got on line. They were dropping flares from a gunship. It was the first time I'd ever witnessed a full company on the attack at night. It is an awesome sight—under flares—where you could see them. It was all flat country where you could see a hundred people on the line in the attack. That's where the commander started shooting at his people to get them to go into the wood line. Well, we busted on into the woods and started taking fire.

We got pinned down when we got into the woods. When we moved on out and broke through, overran the VC, then we linked up with our platoon. They really didn't want us to break through to that platoon [they were using RPGs]. Naturally, they wanted to finish wiping them out. We had to get to them. When we got them out, they [enemy] made one assault on us, but they realized it was a lost cause.

By then I had a gunship, a Super Spooky with a 20mm Gatling gun. It was the first time I'd ever used Gatlings that close. It was sort of funny. I asked the company commander, how far? He said 200 meters [for the rounds to impact beyond the perimeter].

I dropped a strobe down the barrel of an M79 [grenade launcher] and put a blue cellophane wrap on it and pointed it at the airplane. I started flashing, and nobody could see it except the guy in the air. He pinpointed my position and identified it. I told him, 200 meters, 360 degrees.

He shook everybody up. I mean, shook me up. The ground would shake and jump up in the air and fall back down. They were putting one of those [explosive] 20mm rounds in every square foot. The company commander said, no more. For about 10 minutes after he stopped firing it was the quietest place in the world. Couldn't even hear crickets chirping.

Then way, way off, the ones that had survived were still running. One of them turned around a fired his AK back at us. They were getting back to their sampans.

I told the gunship, just from here to three miles down the river, just shoot the whole river up.

What was it like in the south?

We were in III Corps, which was under the tidal influence. The tide would come in and we might be knee-deep or waist-deep in areas, and then the tide would go out and we'd have mud. Terrible area to operate in.

The line between III and IV Corps was serpentine in fashion, but just because the delta was on one side doesn't mean parts of it didn't creep into III Corps. Nipa palms, canals, paddies, and dikes—all could be found in southern III Corps just like in IV Corps.

Booby traps were really a major challenge. We had people blown up all the time on booby traps. They used some American mines, but generally we found the Chinese equivalent to the [German] Bouncing Betty. They'd go up about waist high and go off. [They used] improvised hand grenades, improvised unexploded artillery shells—most of it trip-wired. Very little of it was hand-detonated. We took more casualties from that than anything else.

Still, he said it was a good tour, "If there can be such a thing."

You had a lot more chances to go into Saigon and get cleaned up, get a fresh uniform. The first tour [with the 101st] we used to be in the field 30, 45 days. We got back and slept on the ground in a tent. There [III Corps] you went on an operation, came back, and you went to a hotel and took a shower. Mamasan would have your fatigues ready for you. In 15 minutes you could be on the street in spit-shined boots and a starched uniform. You could drink a cold beer in a bar.

The next day you get out in the mud again, but you didn't have to worry about getting the mud out of your uniform because you had somebody to do it for you.

The showers and starched uniforms were not a daily affair.

The longest I stayed out on an operation was eight days. You would usually go out and stay with a company for seven days and then another Advisor would come in and you'd come out. The companies might be out on a firebase, what used to be an American firebase. They would run operations every day and at night out of that base and you'd stay with them.

When you got back you got a two-or-three day stand down, and then you'd go to another company.

A three-day stretch in Saigon meant the Advisor who had taken his place was still in the middle of his seven-day run with the company, so Singletary (and others) often began their run with a different company. At that point in the war, Vietnamization was well under way and the resulting downsizing of American forces left fewer qualified people to fill the vacant spots. A soldier could no longer be sure of his assignment, whether already in-country or just arriving.

I'd gotten word there were five or six Ranger Instructors coming from the Ranger Camp to Vietnam. I met them at Ton Son Nhut, the airport. It was Doug Perry, [Roger] McDonald, Tom Boggs; several guys I knew. This was in 1969. [Most were on their second tour.] I carried them out to the Ranger High Command and said these guys want to get assigned as Advisors to Ranger units. They said, sure, we want you. We'll pull some strings and get you guys assigned.

The next day [at Personnel] a big, fat Master Sergeant, a Leg, got up there and said, "Your Ranger shit didn't work this time. You're all going to Mobile Training Teams (MATT). That's where they went, but I think they all eventually got to a Ranger unit.

[At that time] we started getting in non-Airborne, non-Ranger people as Advisors, and the Vietnamese hated them. The last two we got in, well, the guy from the 30th I had to replace was a non-Ranger, and we had another guy near Tay Ninh, we got surrounded out there [with the 33rd Battalion] and they told us, get to an LZ and we'll lift you out. Two companies on the ground, I was with one, and he was with the other.

We found an LZ with water about knee-deep on it, but the trees were about as high as this house. I had one company there and the other company moving to it, but it was all thick vegetation. This guy started crying on the radio, wanting me to take a platoon and come over and get him and bring him to the LZ so he could get out when I got out. I said, hey, pal, you move with your company over here.

We knew the situation. They were trying to get us out of there so they could bring in a B-52 strike on those guys. They knew we were surrounded, but we hadn't made contact yet. That was almost into Cambodia.

A few more comments on the lack of enough proper personnel, and then the subject changed.

The biggest "find" we made over there was due to a screw-up. We made a helicopter assault and they put us into the wrong area. We went into the edge of the US 1st Division over by Tay Ninh by about a klick. They put us right in on top of an [enemy] hospital. Fortunately, most of the people there were not fighters. There were very few security people. Mostly it was nurses and doctors and wounded. It was a huge medical complex and we landed right on top of it. It was all underground and in bunkers. The 1st Division didn't know it was there.

A hell of a firefight broke out. We [one company] killed all the bad guys around there and took all the prisoners. Then, when they realized we were into something big, they brought more companies in and secured the area, destroyed the complex and all the medical supplies.

Suchke—My First Mission

Lt. Colonel (Ret) Robert Suchke gave permission to use this cherry-busting story.

They say the only difference in War stories and Fairy Tales, is Fairy Tales begin, "Once upon a time" and War stories start with, "This is no shit!" So, here is the story about my first mission in-country. This is no shit!

It was July 1970. I arrived in Vietnam when the big fight at Firebase Ripcord was going on, so the assignment folks in Long Bien handed me orders for the 101st Airborne Division. I felt pretty good about that, as the "Screaming Eagles" had a great combat history and were known as a good unit. I was recently with the 82nd Airborne Division, so even though I was not going to a paratrooper assignment, there was still a lot of the Airborne tradition in the Division. After SERTS [Screaming Eagle Replacement Training School], a week long orientation for "FNGs" at Camp Evans just north of Hue, I was assigned to D Troop 2/17th Cav. The first guy that I met from my new unit was Staff Sergeant Martin O. Tomlin, who introduced himself as my Platoon Sergeant. I took a look at this soldier and immediately liked what I saw. He had an air of confidence about him and was sporting a black and gold Ranger Tab on his left shoulder. I knew we had covered some common ground. He got me squared away with all the necessary gear and I met my platoon, "the 3rd herd."

So, here I was in Vietnam as a brand new 1st Lieutenant Platoon Leader and had not yet seen combat. Almost everyone in the platoon was talking about the 8 July combat mission that had bloodied the unit and taken the lives of some fine soldiers. I heard many stories from brave men who had experienced intense combat out there in the Khe Sanh plains. I heard the sadness and respect in their voices when names like Sergeant Cruse, Sergeant Frank and Sergeant Walker and others were mentioned.

Over the next few days, I started to get to know the men a little better. Dan Terry was a tall soldier with several months of experience in the bush and was my RTO and driver. I learned that I had an M151 quarter-ton truck (jeep) and a whole slew of other vehicles that I was responsible for. There was a Scout Section with machinegun jeeps (like rat patrol); an Anti-tank section with 106mm recoilless rifles also mounted on jeeps; a mortar section with one 81mm mortar with a three-quarter-ton truck and finally an Infantry Section with another three-quarter-ton truck. All these vehicles were for the ground Cavalry role for base defense of Camp Eagle as a reactionary force (if needed) and also for convoy escort to provide security and firepower as necessary to take care of any enemy foolish enough to engage us. I remember we practiced rolling out to some sector of Camp Eagle on several occasions to see how long it took for us to respond in case of an attack.

The month of July 1970 was nearing its last days when the whole troop was alerted for a mission with the Hoc Bao, a South Vietnamese unit that was known for its fierce fighters. The Hoc Bao was a battalion-size element based at the old imperial capital city of Hue. The Hoc Bao unit lived in and around the Citadel of Hue when not in the field. The Hoc Bao were similar to the Vietnamese Ranger Battalions, just not in name. I remember that their symbol was a black panther on a triangular shaped patch. After I was summoned to the TOC (tactical operations center) for a quick briefing, I learned that the Hoc Bao had located an NVA weapons cache out in the Khe Sanh plains area near the Laotian border.

It was late in the day and I was told that my platoon would have four UH-1H helicopters to carry us out to the LZ, near where the Hoc Bao were located. We moved to Scabbard Pad, near the 2/17th Cav Headquarters. The ACL (allowable cargo load) was six pax (personnel), so Staff Sergeant Tomlin and myself organized the lifts. That gave us field strength of 24 men. The Cav being different than a regular Infantry unit, we had more gear and weapons and used that to our advantage. We put an M60 machinegun, a PRC-77 Radio and a Sergeant on each aircraft with an assortment of other weapons, such as M79 40mm grenade launcher, M16s, hand grenades, LAWs and claymore mines. The gear was broken down, so each soldier carried his fair share plus water, rations, extra radio batteries, first aid kit and personal comfort gear like poncho and poncho liner. No matter if one or all aircraft made it in to the LZ, in every helicopter there were six soldiers with leadership, firepower and communications.

We loaded on the helicopters and shortly took off following what seemed like a long line of other helicopters. Someone handed me a headset that let me both talk on the helicopter's internal commo system and also transmit and receive radio messages while in route to the LZ. In the background was the Armed Forces Radio Network—AFVN—playing music. I was thinking to myself, this is a hell of a great way to fight a war, music and all.

Flying out over the very beautiful country, I was amazed at the scenery. We flew fairly high, around 6,000 feet, and it was cool. The treetops looked like broccoli bunches in various shades of green.

The flight was fairly long from Camp Eagle and I remember thinking to myself on the way, "this is real." I glanced at my weapon. The bullets we have in our rifles are not blanks, but live ammunition with pointy ends. This is not training like I had been on so many times before. The aggressor out in the field was likewise not using blanks. Our enemy was the North Vietnamese regulars and they were good. I wondered how I'd do.

I distinctly remember Charlie Pride singing in my headset "All I have to offer you is me" as we started going down. We landed finally just before dark. There were members of the Hoc Bao unit as well as soldiers from the other platoons and Troop Headquarters already on the ground. The LZ we landed in was a cornfield. The NVA had garden plots scattered here and there in the jungle to feed its troops.

After a quick commo check with Captain Craig, D Troop Commander, we moved out in single file. It was now dark and I'll admit my pucker factor was going up. Here we were, deep in enemy territory, moving in a file at night and not really knowing where we were headed. I imagined enemy soldiers behind every tree. After close to an hour of humping through the jungle on some dim trail, we finally linked up with the main element of the Hoc Bao and established a perimeter. Sergeant Tomlin positioned the men and Dan Terry and I established a platoon command post near an old bomb crater.

The Hoc Bao had several ambush patrols out covering the trail network in the area. After we had been in position for a few hours, there was a sudden but intense burst of automatic weapons fire outside our perimeter. It was later learned that one of the Hoc Bao ambush patrols had been successful and had killed a NVA soldier believed to be a message carrier. Around midnight, we heard the reports of mortar fire. Enemy mortars were shooting at us! I was out of my CP area and as soon as I heard the first mortar, I ran and jumped in the bomb crater hole. I landed squarely on Dan Terry, my RTO, and apologized immediately. I know I landed hard on him, but he never complained. I was impressed that he made it to the hole ahead of me. The enemy mortar rounds landed near our position, but luckily no one was wounded. The mortar fire stopped as quickly as it had begun, but the rest of the night was without much rest.

The next day, we learned that the Hoc Bao had indeed discovered a large cache of over 100 NVA 122mm rockets, numerous B-40 rockets and other ammunition and equipment. The B-40 was the rocket that RPGs utilized. The find was so massive that the 2/17th Cav Commander, Lieutenant Colonel Molinelli, and some photographers landed in a hastily cleared LZ to investigate and take pictures of the find. Several of the rockets and fuses were evacuated for further analysis in the rear. The large 122mm rockets were over six feet long and each weighed around 100 pounds. They had a range of about 11,000 meters (11 klicks) and packed a serious high explosive charge. If the rockets were moved closer to U.S. firebases in the area, they would present a significant danger. The NVA most likely had plans for this huge cache in future operations. The cache also contained 60 sets of NVA uniforms, over a ton of rice and 14 cases of medical instruments. Most of this gear was evacuated by helicopters.

While Colonel Molinelli was on the ground, he asked the assembled soldiers within earshot, " Who here knows how to blow all this up?" I looked around and since no one else had volunteered, I said, "I do Sir!" I figured with Ranger and Jungle Expert training under my belt, I could handle a few explosive charges, and then we could all get back to Camp Eagle. Colonel Molinelli asked me what I needed, so I told him and within a half hour everything I had asked for was brought in by helicopter. I now had a case of C-4 plastic explosive, a box of non-electric blasting caps, a roll of time fuse, a roll of det cord and a pack of M-60 fuse lighters. I was all set to blow up those rockets.

Sergeant Tomlin, Dan Terry, a couple more soldiers and myself soon started off to the cache site with all the explosives and a radio. While the others provided security, Tomlin and I rigged the bunker with explosives. We stacked at least a dozen of the 122mm warheads in a pile and used the entire case of plastic explosives to make sure each warhead was covered. We laced the det cord between charges to connect the other blocks of C-4 and insure good detonation of everything in the bunker. This bunker, partially underground, had rockets piled floor to ceiling with rocket motors, fuses and B-40 rockets all over. There were also stacked metal cans that had small arms (AK47) ammunition in them. We made sure that they each got a block of C-4, too.

After we had the explosives in place, there was some discussion about how long to make the time fuse. In Vietnam, time fuse and caps were not totally reliable due to the high humidity. We had fresh caps from a sealed box and new time fuse, but just to be sure we set four independent sets of caps, fuse and fuse lighters. This charge was quadruple primed! After one more check of everything, I called on the radio that we were ready to set it off. We used about 10 feet of time fuse for each cap so we had time to move out of the danger zone. When I got the green light, we popped red smoke and gave the cry, "fire in the hole" over the radio and also out loud. Then we ignited the fuse lighters, made sure the fuses were burning and moved out quickly back to the main body. We were about 10 minutes away and had covered several hundred meters of ground when we were rocked by a tremendous explosion. A huge fireball and black cloud was now where the bunker had been. Pieces of wood, dirt and other debris were raining down on us. The bunker where we placed the explosives we later found out was just the top layer. The bunker had several levels below that one. When we blew the rocket cache, the whole mountain seemed to go with it because there was so much more under the first layer.

That was a successful mission, my first. We destroyed a large quantity of enemy rockets that would have been used against American forces, so we felt pretty good. As a FNG, I felt I had done ok, too. The only down side was that from that time on, anytime there was something that needed to be destroyed by explosives or a helicopter LZ that needed to be blown, 3rd Platoon got the job. It became a regular thing and we called them "firecracker" missions. That name stuck, and later over in L Co Rangers when I had to have a code name, I chose "firecracker." All you 3rd Platoon guys who remember this mission, I thank you for putting up with the FNG Lieutenant and helping me learn as time went by.

We had a great team and I'll never forget you guys!
Robert K. Suchke

Roger McDonald
Considering the convoluted and lengthy nature of the war in Vietnam, some people found themselves back and forth several times as part of different organizations on both sides of the ocean. Roger McDonald has a long history as a Ranger, though he was never in a Ranger combat unit. He went from school to battle to school to battle and changed units many times. His story is too complex to break up, so what is presented here represents his whole career—187th, 173rd, 101st, 1st Cavalry Lurp, Recon, Recondo School, Ranger School and MACV Advisor.

McDonald contributed to this project several times, but most of this interview was conducted at his home and in the back of the NCO club at Camp Frank Merrill. Sadly, only some of it got on tape. He made me turn it off several times to tell me the really juicy stuff, then made me promise not to print any of it.

In service in 1953, Roger McDonald (Mac) stayed with the 187th Airborne through 1956, and then transferred to the 101st Airborne at Fort Campbell, Kentucky where he was based for eight years. Ranger School came in 1962, after a tour through Recondo School at Fort

Campbell. In 1964, Mac joined up with the 173rd Airborne Brigade and went to Vietnam a year later, where he reenlisted and became a member of a recon platoon with the 1/327.

The 173rd was the first American Army combat unit in-country in March 1965, with the 2nd Battalion laying the foundation for the new military base at Bien Hoa, and the 1st (Mac's unit) staying in Vung Tau for a while. That area later became a big R & R center because of its beaches.

Mac then spent six more months in-country with the 101st before being rotated stateside to the Recondo School at Fort Campbell as an Instructor. By 1966, he was back in Vietnam, this time with the 1st Cavalry Division as a member of a recon platoon, then as a member of a LRRP.

His second tour completed, Mac returned to the States and became an RI at Camp Frank D. Merrill in Georgia. For 18 months, he served as NCOIC (non-commissioned officer in charge) of the Patrol Committee. He wasn't through overseas just yet, as he and others were sent back as Advisors and Instructors to the South Vietnamese in 1969, working for MACV.

1970 brought him back to CFM, where he was again NCOIC. Mac retired as a First Sergeant at the end of that tour.

Mac in RVN

In 1965, with the 1/173rd, Mac found a few brother Rangers. "Most officers were Rangers, but there were only two or three enlisted men per company. Most Infantry officers go to Ranger School and Jump School. Still do."

The Recon unit of the 173rd was mechanized, being comprised, said Mac, of "six jeeps with M60s mounted on them, plus an HQ jeep and the Old Man's jeep. We also had four 3/4-ton trucks with .50 caliber machineguns mounted on them. The unit became known as [Captain] Sammy Tucker's Task Force."

Being motorized meant the unit couldn't sneak up on anybody, and eventually the long range, stealthy type of patrol evolved. In the beginning, though, "We were the eyes and ears of the battalion. Without recon, there's no telling what they might find out there."

Tucker's Task Force was often used as a spearhead for larger movements, a much different job than that of Lurp teams to come.

"I spent six months with the Herd [173rd] after I got to Vietnam. Eventually, we were having too much fun at Vung Tau, and they moved us up to Bien Hoa [where the 2nd Battalion already was working]. After about six months the 101st came fully in-country. The 1/327 [part of the 1st Brigade] came in at Phang Rang. They asked if senior NCOs and officers from the Herd would exchange places with some of theirs so the experience wouldn't leave Vietnam on rotation dates. They'd have experience in both units. So they asked for volunteers and I said, yeah, I'll go. I hitchhiked up to Phan Rang [he doesn't know how the rest of the men got there]."

The Colonel in charge asked him where he wanted to be assigned.

"I said Delta Company is fine. They had the 106s and the 81s. I was a good heavy-weapons man. I spent six months with them, and then rotated back to Fort Campbell to Recondo School. After five months there, I got orders for the 1st Cav [1st Cavalry Airmobile].

"I remember when they went into the Ia Drang [he was with the 173rd then] everybody said they better be careful. They got their shit kicked. They did good, but …they were looking for a firefight and they got one.

The movie "When We Were Soldiers" is about that legendary fight.

"Then I got rotated back to Recondo School and got orders again, and went back to the Cav. When I got back, they needed a Recon Platoon Sergeant for Delta Company, 1/8, so I got that. I stayed with the Recon Platoon and we ran some good patrols. That's where I met Joe Musial [later awarded three Silver Stars]. I had to build my platoon up, we didn't have enough people, they said, go hire and fire, but be careful, don't step on any company commander's toes. We didn't have a platoon leader yet [that's why Mac did the searching], so I went straight to the mess hall and got Joe Musial."

Musial was cousin to Stan Musial, the famous baseball player. Mac thinks he was Ranger-qualified, but had been busted several times for fighting, and was working as a cook in a rear area as a Spec-4. Musial went on to greatness as a leader.

"The best leader I ever had." Mac said Musial was big and mean, but could do things on patrol that others just talked about. "He was one of those guys, you couldn't have him in peace time. You put him behind glass, and in case of war, break the glass.

"So, I ran that for a year. They said, if you'll extend we'll make you an E-8 [First Sergeant], put you down in a bunker as the S-2 [Intel]. I said I'd do it. So, I went home on a 30-day leave. I got back, and before I could get back in the field, Sergeant Kelly [a red-headed Irishman, he was Mac's First Sergeant in Recondo School] found me. He said, Mac, I need a suitable replacement or they won't let me rotate."

It turned out that Mac owed Kelly and so felt bound to accommodate him.

"His company commander was General Reuben Tucker's son. So I reported to that Captain. I asked him what his requirements were. He said, 'I don't want to be in this man's army. My daddy went to West Point, so I went. I want to stay right here in An Khe, play with the nurses and sign the papers. You run the company.' I said, you got a First Sergeant, sir.

"I did that for the next six months. We had a good unit. It was the Long Range Recon Patrol Company for Division [1st Cav]."

1st Cavalry LRRP

"The operation starts with the planning phase." That phase included over-flying the intended area of insertion, picking out an LZ, and coordinating plans with practically everybody. Radio relay stations were set up, helicopters laid on, usually one insertion Huey "slick," a couple of gunships, and a Command and Control (C&C) aircraft.

Mac's Lurp team was generally comprised of six men.

"We'd send one to three teams in to find out what's in that AO." The choppers often made several false insertions to throw off the enemy before dropping the team, then a few more after. Mac mostly rode a C&C bird, and looked out for his men. His CO was happy to stay in An Khe and let him take the runs. Patrols could last anywhere from a few minutes to seven days, depending on what the teams ran into on the ground.

"If the Patrol Leader calls for an extraction, then you go get his ass."

The patrols did recon, watched set positions, monitored traffic on small trails up to and including parts of the Ho Chi Minh trail, and could call in the veritable wrath of God on the enemy via fixed-wing aircraft, artillery, or helicopter gunships. There were instances where a small team stayed in place on high ground and caused the destruction of hundreds of NVA or VC without being caught. There were also times when they did get caught. Eventually, the enemy would figure out where they were and come after them.

"When they get artillery, they know you're there."

Extraction came quickly after that, if at all possible. Sometimes it was not, and the team had to "lay dog" and wait it out, or be taken under fire.

With or without contact, the teams tried not to move at night. "That was SOP." After dark, the team would go into an NDP (night defensive position, also called a RON, or remain overnight) in "the most secluded spot we could find" and the six men (or four, or two), would sit back-to-back in a circle, or lay prone in a wagon-wheel configuration—after setting out trip flares and/or claymore mines.

If they felt safe, some would get a little sleep, but there was always at least "one man awake with a handset." The radio was the only link to safety, and regular sitreps (situation reports) were called in. In times of extreme danger, no words were said, with communication made by way of squeezing the handset button to cause a squelch noise at the other end. At least they knew the team was still alive if they got two clicks.

When possible, a sitrep would be made in the SALUTE form. An encompassing report, it stood for Size (of enemy unit), Activity, Location, Uniform (to tell if they were VC or NVA), Time (often "right now"), and Equipment. Sometimes the report on enemy equipment had to wait until the enemy was using it on the LRRP team. Very likely the next radio contact would be to holler for an extraction.

If they had time, the team would eat once a day, a Lurp ration. "I'd eat half, you eat half." The trash went back in the rucksack, the NDP or wherever they stopped would be sanitized, and only an expert tracker would know the team was ever there.

The success of the LRRP teams prompted the enemy to act. "Charlie started anti-LRRP teams." The small units had rewards posted for them. "A Ranger Tab brought a price on your head." Accordingly, no one wore insignia on patrol.

The teams had a trick or two learned from experience. When four men went on patrol, they often took two indigenous personnel ("Indig") with them, either Vietnamese or Montagnards, called Yards.

Yards and Vietnamese didn't get along too well, Mac said. "You want to punish a Vietnamese, throw him in a tent with a bunch of Yards." The Yards were much better in the jungle and in battle, so whenever possible Mac would trade a Vietnamese for a Yard.

The small, but robust tribesmen had their own camp at An Khe, needing no help to keep the enemy at bay. An elder woman ran the camp. "She looked like Mammy Yokum, smoking a big corn cob pipe." The matriarchal society had a reason for being—the men kept getting killed.

"We'd dress them up like Charlie [VC]. They looked like him, talked like him, and carried an AK47." The two men, dressed in black pajamas, would be placed at point and at drag. "That way, if they bumped into us front or rear, the VC might think they're one of theirs. You get the first shot; yell an azimuth [compass heading] in English, run, set up an ambush, then extract. You get the hell out after being compromised."

Contact wasn't a good thing, Mac said, because, "We wanted to stay and call in artillery."

Taped Interview at Camp Merrill

Mac spoke of an officer taking over the company, a man who didn't believe the Lurp reports all the time, and sometimes left teams in the field under fire, without extraction. Men died because of his refusal to get them out. Mac said if he had that man with us then, he'd take him out in the woods. The officer's name will not be shown here, as it is not the function of this book to second-guess anybody. But, those who were there will know who he was.

He was an S-2 [Intelligence] Captain, and it was [normally] good for an S-2 Captain to take over, because we were working with him. But, he just wasn't...you know.

I was up in Ban Me Thuot going to a funeral. One of my Montagnards got killed and I went to his funeral. If you don't, they won't work for you. When I got back, he [the officer] was sitting behind the Old Man's desk. I looked at him and said, where's my company commander, and he said he got killed. I said, the hell he did! He never left An Khe!

He had flown down to Phan Rang to recruit some people from the 101st to work for us, because we were getting short handed. Coming back in his little bubble chopper (H-13) he got shot down and killed.

Mac and the new commander didn't get along for various reasons, so Mac decided to go back to the 1/8.

He said, "You can't leave me; you're my First Sergeant." I said, "I'll get you a replacement, sir." So, I went down where they come in, and the first Airborne E-8 I found, his name was McDermott. His eyes got kind-of big when he saw my Tigers [tiger-striped uniform worn by the Lurps]. I said, "This is your lucky day. You can take over as the First Sergeant of the Long Range Patrol Company." Boy, his eyes lit up, and he said, "Where'd you get those Tigers?" I said, "I'll tell you about that. Don't go to Pleiku and get them. Send for them."

So I took him back, introduced him to the Old Man, packed my stuff, and went back to the 1/8. I had about two months to go. About three days later McDermott got killed, traveling in a jeep up to Pleiku to get those damn Tigers. The Old Man called me and told me to come back, and I said forget it, I'm out in the field. So I ran that company for two months.

At the time, the 1st Cav was moving up around Khe Sanh in the north to help the Marines there. Mac was asked to stay until that was done.

They asked me for one more month to get the company moved, and I said okay. We got them up there to Hue and Phu Bai and got established. I was 19 months in-country and they said, one more month, and I said, no, not on your life, I'm going home to see my family. So I left the 1st Cav and rotated back to the Ranger Camp [mountain camp].

Coming off patrol five months later [Doug] Perry yells, "Hey, Mac, you got orders!" I said, "That's bullshit. This is my third tour. I don't have any orders." I thought he was just joking, wanting me to go into the orderly room and they'd laugh at me.

Mobile Army Training Teams

I'll be damned if we didn't have deployment orders. Doug Perry, myself, and T. Boggs from here, and three more Rangers joining us from Benning, had to go to Fort Bragg and go through Special Warfare Training and some language. Then we went to Fort Bliss for 12 weeks of language course [Vietnamese], and then back to Vietnam.

This, after three tours in Vietnam. See the interview with Earl Singletary for more on this.

The Army works in strange ways. The reason we went back I didn't find out until two or three years ago. Creighton Abrams asked for us. At that point in the war [1969], they thought they could still salvage it. They took all the experienced people that had been over there two or three times and they brought us all to Vietnam and put us on Mobile Army [Advisory] Training Teams. That was J. P. Vann's idea.

John Paul Vann was an American hero who ran the gamut from Hawk to social reconstruction. There is more about him elsewhere in this book. He was killed in a helicopter accident.

He had two Corps as a retired Colonel. He was an amazing little man. He wasn't real big, but he flew his own chopper, and he'd fly into an outpost you were just setting up under fire, and he'd jump out with his cowboy boots, and stick out his hand and say, "I'm J. P. Vann, how you doing? How's everything going?"

We'd [MAT Teams] go to a little village, and we'd try to outfit them enough so they could thin Charlie out [civilians, known as Regional-Popular Forces, or Ruff-Puffs]. We had a unit right down the road with a post, a Vietnamese Army Post, and we'd supply them with weapons and we'd take them out and we'd fight. But, what we'd do, on a MAT Team, we'd go out and live with them.

MAT Teams were usually four men: a senior NCO, an RTO, and maybe a Spec 4 and a Lieutenant or a Captain.

We'd set up a tent right near the village, and then we would train them to fend off Charlie. We'd give them everything, but we couldn't give them M60s because Charlie would take them away [Ruff-Puffs were often overrun].

Our asses were hanging out. In fact, all three of us, Perry, Knuckles from Florida, and myself walked off MAT teams. We got up one morning and said, to hell with this, and went to a Ranger Battalion [Vietnamese Biet Dong Quan].

Mac also ended up with the BDQs of the 44th Battalion, yet another posting for a travel-weary Ranger.

The MAT teams would go from one village to another. They'd build up a village until they thought, okay, they're good enough, then they'd go to another one and do the same thing. Most of the teams took over old Special Forces compounds. The SF at that time went from commanding to advising. That command that they had, the Vietnamese hated them [for commanding]. They shot a lot of them. They fragged their team houses and stuff. So they just took the SF soldiers and moved them out, and we took over. Nice team houses. When they went to advising the Viets that was a different thing.

On my last tour I was down in the delta. Working with little people, living with them. Not too good. Been with American units all this time. Can't trust the little people. They'll run off and leave you in a firefight. Rangers [Vietnamese] did pretty good. They tried.

Mac talked about a parachute drop in the delta with the BDQ. There weren't too many of those.

We jumped on top of Charlie one time. Did good. It was a successful jump. We surprised them, killed the shit out of them, had a good time. Went back and this little SOB wanted to do it again the next day. I said, "No, no, you don't do that." He said, "Oh, yeah, we go back, we get good body count." I said, "I'm not going with you." They went, and had a bunch of casualties. You can surprise Charlie once; you aren't going to surprise him again. Charlie was a good unit. The NVA were better, much better.

The NVA came south in more force after Tet 1968 had decimated the VC ranks, but they had problems with the locals because they were, in effect, foreigners.

They had problems joining up. I'll give you an example. We [MATT in the delta] went out one day on patrol. We were supposed to ambush a certain area. We get out four or five klicks, and I'm the counterpart of this Dai-uy [Captain]. He sent somebody forward and there was a hell of a firefight. I mean, a big battle up there and we weren't even in it. People were coming back and he says, "Okay, we go back to the team house now. We've got plenty of kills."

I said, "What are you talking about?" What happened was an NVA unit was moving down to join up with the VC, and a big VC unit was moving up to join up with them. They met, and the two leaders got in an argument over who was going to be in charge, and they got into a firefight and killed the shit out of each other.

Our job was done that night. We went back to the team house.

A question was asked about recoilless weapons such as LAWs, 57mm rifles, and others. Mac told this old war story.

When the recoilless first came out an enemy got hold of one, but didn't understand about the back blast. The officer stood right behind the gunner with a pair of binoculars and yelled, Fire!

Everybody thinks Charlie was just a little guy in black pajamas running around; didn't have anything. China was supplying them, Russia was supplying them, they had more tanks and stuff up in the DMZ area. Not down south. You can't run a tank in a rice paddy.

Mac was asked about his time with the LRP unit of the 1/8 of the 1st Cavalry Division in II Corps.

First of all, our home base was in An Khe, but we had outposts, different little LZs. We would send units out, and we'd coordinate with the battalion commander. He was going to go into that area next week to sweep and destroy [the term began as search and destroy]. He'd send us in there first to find out what's in there. I was running the patrol. Had four Americans and two indigenous people on this patrol. We'd send them out a maximum of seven days at a time to monitor the Ho Chi Minh Trail or find enemy complexes.

It took two gunships and three slicks to put one patrol in. We'd do it right. We had our own SOP. When a helicopter is flying low level you can hear it, but you don't know where it is. We'd put a team on one of those choppers, and we'd go in and hit two or three false LZs, then drop them out and keep on going, and nobody knew where we dropped them. We kept two gunships overhead in case it got hot.

You drop a team in, the team goes and lays and listens and doesn't do a thing. They'll call and say, okay, good insertion. Then they'll go on with their mission. If they get compromised, you pull them out.

One of the birds covering the mission insertions and extractions was the Command & Control helicopter, which usually had the company commander riding above the LZ/PZ and controlling the situation. In Mac's case, his CO preferred to remain in An Khe, so Mac, as First Sergeant, took his place in the C & C. Otherwise, he would have been a "belly man" in the extraction bird, as was Darol Walker (see F/58th Lurps).

My Long Range Patrol Company had the best record in Vietnam for not getting people killed until I left and [a new company commander] took over, and then he started hurting people.

If you do it right, keep your SOPs right …the only person I lost when I was First Sergeant was my front scout. He got up out of an RON to take a piss, he was a Montagnard, dressed like Charlie, AK47, he was walking back into the perimeter, hadn't told anybody he left, and this guy woke up, saw Charlie, and shot him.

If my people did get compromised, or bumped into a superior force, they had an SOP to get away from them. They would fire them up, holler an azimuth and a distance and take off. Stop, set up a hasty ambush for whoever might follow, and fire them up, then go another direction. Bam! Fire them up, and pretty soon they'd quit chasing your ass and you could go to the LZ and get extracted.

Known as an Immediate Action Drill, each unit had its own version. For the first 30 seconds, a lot of firepower went out as a cover for quick withdrawal.

It's SOP. You train these people up to the hilt before you put them out there. My unit was well trained by Sergeant Kelly before I got there. I didn't have to put in any SOPs. I had to *learn* the SOPs. Then I made sure they did them, and it's a good thing I did.

The talk turned to Intelligence needs, and what would or would not be turned in. If a unit found documents they would turn them in, but often weapons and other relics were kept, if possible. Mac told a story about catching a VC paymaster and his staff. After disposing of 17 of them in a cave, they confiscated their money, and kept it. Mac said it was used for R & R, to send home to families, all sorts of things for the unit. "We put it to good use."

We were out in the bush one time, this is when I was with the Recon Platoon of the 1/8, before I took over, and I had maybe eight or nine men with me. We were going to look for a sniper who'd been shooting at troops of this other company. And he'd been killing people. They said go find him.

Well, that company left about the time we went in, but they forgot a man out there. There was a man on the ground when we got there. I just attached him to my patrol.

We were supposed to find this sniper, so I played Robin Hood. We built a big fire, we got some ponchos and stuff and made some false figures around that fire, and then we just waited. I walked up the trail to check my people. Two of them, this kid I'd just picked up and another guy were both facing down toward the fire, eating! I got on their ass and turned them around and said, you watch out that way.

I walked back past the fire and got hidden again and I heard pop, pop, pop! I ran up there, and this sniper and his buddy had come down that trail. That kid from the other company, I had just turned him around, saw them and fired them up. He killed the guy who had [a weapon Mac took to be an Uzi], but the other guy got away, jumped off the trail and was gone. He must have had the sniper rifle. Well, we put our fire out and took off. We took the Uzi with us, called in and told them what happened, and they sent a chopper out for the Uzi! We said, look, this kid killed him; this is his Uzi. We tagged it with his name, but when we got back to the rear, it was gone.

Captured!

I was down in Kim Phong Province [in the delta] with a MAT team. This was the base of little people. Somebody told the commander [of the Vietnamese, a Major, Mac thought] the first successful ambush on any NVA, who were infiltrating down, would get a bunch of money. So they came to me and said, "Mohk"—they can't say Mac—you go out with us. We have Intel!

About 10 klicks out, in all-VC territory. The NVA was supposed to have a meeting with the VC leaders, coming on that canal that night, in this little village. Well, his Intel was pretty good, so we armed up and went out. When we got to the village, we laid a claymore ambush on that canal coming down, and got them all ambush-ready, and here they came. Talking. We ambushed them successfully, killed the shit out of some NVA and VC leaders.

So, I said okay, lets go. I mean, when you ambush somebody, you leave the area. Not this little big-headed son-of-a-bitch [Vietnamese Lieutenant]. He wants to get everybody up in the village. It's two o'clock in the morning. Pitch dark. You couldn't see your hand in front of your face. He wanted to get everybody up in the village and chew their asses out for having NVA/VC there. Waking everybody up, trying to get them into the middle of the village, and I heard "thump, thump, thump"—damn mortars coming in.

There was a big, long ditch there, and I grabbed my RTO [a Vietnamese] and we jumped into the ditch. Just as we got in, the mortars hit. It wounded a couple of our people and everybody started running, getting out of the village.

Well, I was stuck down there in that damn ditch, and a machinegun opened up right down the ditch. I couldn't move. I was on my back, my M16 was in the mud; it was muddy as hell down there. My RTO was on the other end of the handset, and he wanted to run. I said, no, don't move! Hell, that machinegun had us right there. [Mac leaned his head back and passed his hand close to his face, miming tracer fire right above his nose].

The RTO, panic-stricken, jumped up out of the ditch and was immediately hit by small-arms fire. Mac said he could hear the rounds strike the man.

So, he fell back in the ditch [still alive]. I waited until the machinegun quit firing and I started to get up to grab my RTO, and flashlights hit me in the face. I said, oh, shit! My M16 was gone; it was under the mud. They grabbed me, grabbed my RTO—he was screaming and hollering because he was hurt. Pulled us out of the ditch, frisked us real quick, took all my web gear, even took my patrol cap, stripped me of everything and stuck me in a little hooch. A little mounded-thing, I think it was a pigpen. God, it stunk!

They stuck me in there because, by that time, this American Lieutenant who was with me had rallied some of the troops to come back looking for me. Got them in the firefight. He's hollering, "Sergeant McDonald!" and I can't answer. But, they didn't find me.

I had a Browning Hi-Power short barrel [9 mm] stuck down in my crotch [from behind]. I knew I had six rounds in that thing. It was still with me. They didn't take it. They didn't find it, because they were still in a firefight, and didn't have time for a good search. Black as hell that night.

So, they stuck me in this thing and I thought, well, I'll shoot myself. I had a subdued Ranger Tab on and I knew they were going to hurt me. Then I'm thinking, why should I kill myself, they're going to kill me anyway. I might as well try. So, I stuck my head out. There was a guard on the left and one on the right. In Vietnamese, I asked them for a cigarette. They just laughed and pushed me back, but I knew where they were then.

I got my gun out, reached out, shot that one, [he turns, finger pointed] shot that one and took off. I mean, I bet I broke the hundred-yard dash record in that rice paddy. Don't ask me how I dropped my gun. I think it hit my pants leg while I was running, and I wasn't about to go back for it. I ran until I was sucking ice. I was expecting to get shot, but it was so dark I don't think they even saw me.

Meantime, the Lieutenant and everybody else took off. They were gone. I ran until I could not run another step, and I lay down in that rice paddy. I thought, oh, shit, they're going to hear me because my heart was beating so hard. My adrenaline was way up there. I laid there for about an hour, catching my breath and wondering what in the hell am I going to do now? I'm out in the middle of a rice paddy with nothing. No map, no compass, no weapon. I was 10 klicks from a friendly unit. A pretty good ways. I thought, which way do I go? I remembered coming into the village, and I had a star that I always watched when I leave an outpost, and I thought, I've got to take a left.

So, I took a left, and I was just dogtrotting, I was so tired. I hit a road, but I didn't know where I was, so I thought, I took a left the first time; I'll try another left. I turned and didn't go 500 meters and I bumped into my own outfit. I hollered coming in. They were waiting on me.

There is nothing lonelier than an American out in the middle of a rice paddy in the dark with nothing but his clothes and his boots.

Mac said the only thing that saved him was his Lieutenant coming back after him, because the enemy was in a firefight and didn't have time even to bind him. He thinks his captors were NVA because "If they'd have been VC, they'd have probably just killed my ass."

When I got back, a Major asked me where all my stuff was. I'd gone out in full battle gear. I said, "Sir, it's right out there, if you want to go get it. Go 10 klicks and take a right."

We sent a recovery party in there the next day and they found my RTO tied to a tree [mutilated and dead].

THE NEAR MISS AT SON TAY

*C*olonel (Ret) Elliot "Bud" Sydnor was interviewed for this story, but he also sent a long transcript *of a previous interview done by Lt. Colonel Bob Morris. Excerpts of Sydnor's remarks from that piece appear in the following narrative. His interview and biography come after.*

There were many attempts to rescue American POWs during the war, but only a few succeeded in bringing a US soldier home. Most of those attempts were made in South Vietnam or in Laos, but there was one carefully planned raid/rescue made in the Dragon's Den, deep inside North Vietnam at a little compound known to the POWs as Camp Hope.

Just before Thanksgiving 1970, veteran Special Forces troops—all NCOs led by Ranger-qualified commanders—suddenly appeared in the sky over the small prison compound near Son Tay, just 23 miles west of Hanoi, and lay waste to the garrison there and in another nearby place—but the prisoners were gone.

That controversial raid has been debated ever since, mostly over the question of success. Was it a failure because the prisoners weren't there? Certainly that part of it was, but the propaganda value of having American commando-types 23 miles from the North Vietnamese capitol was immense, especially since the force got in and out without any serious casualties. The raid on Son Tay has been highlighted as a template for a successful mission.

It all started when a few POWs had an idea. Over time recon photos began to show odd formations of laundry and piles of dirt in the Son Tay compound. The prisoners had been using a tap code for years to communicate with each other, and somehow they were able to transfer that code to various objects strung together to be seen from above. They were not missed.

Throughout the war, various US Intelligence agencies had been gathering bits of information wherever they could concerning missing personnel, particularly fliers shot down over the North. Their concerns were not misplaced, considering pilots and other airmen were falling out of the sky at the rate of one or two a day in 1970, and had been doing so in increasing numbers since 1964. Those who made it to the ground alive were often broken up from smashing into their aircraft while trying to eject at 400 miles per hour, sometimes in a tailspin. Once back on earth the locals were liable to kill or maim any round-eyes over five-foot-six. If an airman was "lucky" enough to reach a POW camp he could look forward to unbearable torture, starvation, seclusion, and disease.

North Vietnam had signed the Geneva Convention accords in 1957, but took little notice of the part about humane treatment of prisoners. Only a few men were released before the end of the war, but they had been treated a good bit better than most.

The problem with rescue was obvious; most of the camps were either in Hanoi or close to it. Infiltration by Americans was out of the question—too easy to spot them. Inserting a team of native agents was considered, but they usually went in by parachute during a regular flight, and by 1970 the bombing of the North had been over for two years. Agents placed earlier had been captured, killed or had defected.

The mission was cleared through the Joint Chiefs of Staff, notably Chairmen General Earl Wheeler and his successor, General Moorer. The task of overseeing the planning of a raid to recover the estimated 70 POWs from Son Tay was given to an essentially unknown but important component of the Pentagon. In the "E-Ring" underneath the Joint Chief's portion of the Pentagon was a small office headed by Brigadier General Donald Blackburn, the Special Assistant for Counterinsurgency and Special Activities—known as SACSA.

Blackburn was no stranger to Special Operations, having commanded SOG, the Special Forces secretive Studies and Observation Group. He knew the appropriate players necessary for success in such a mission and went about gathering them. Blackburn needed the right man to lead the raid and he found him in Colonel Arthur "Bull" Simons, a legendary Ranger who had served in the 6th Ranger Battalion in WWII, and had tours in Laos and Vietnam. At the time he was G-4 of the XVIII Corps.

Simons chose his own team leaders; Lt. Colonel Elliot P. "Bud" Sydnor and Master Sergeant Richard "Dick" Meadows, both well-known Ranger combat leaders. The raiders were all NCOs from Special Forces—several wore Ranger Tabs, as did all three leaders—and were considered to be some of the best available. Of 500 original volunteers, some 100 were trained, but when the final choice came down only 56 were chosen. The rest did some loud grumbling.

No insignia was worn during the raid, and very little during training. When the ground force members did have occasion to wear their berets, they wore the flash of the 6th SF.

Bud Sydnor

Very late in August, I arrived at Eglin Air Force Base to discover that the only people I knew personally were Simons and Meadows. Colonel Simons had recruited volunteers from SF units at Fort Bragg. I know now that my initial acceptance was begun by Meadows vouching for me as the stranger who was to be the Ground Force Commander. It was the beginning of the longest and loneliest three months of my military career. I was determined to do my best to prove I was worthy.

Meadows told me years later that when asked, "Who the Hell is this new guy?" he answered, "A Pro!" And that may be the best compliment I've ever had.

To be sure, nothing was done in the open. As clandestine missions go, Son Tay was one of the most secret of the war, a fact that gave rise to several problems with people who wanted to know before they would cooperate. A few well-placed phone calls usually solved that.

President Richard Nixon and his Secretary of State, Melvin Laird, were in on it almost from the beginning, and Nixon had the final word on the go-ahead. The operation was tricky for many reasons, one of them being that the Paris Peace Talks were in full swing, and nothing would be allowed to tamper with them. Of course, should the rescue succeed, it would have given American negotiators a trump card to play if they could say US forces pulled off such a raid so close to the NVN capital, and have rescued prisoners tell their stories of ill treatment to the world.

Accordingly, Blackburn and his staff had to work with a lot of agencies and branches of the Armed Services, but only a very few got to know what they were working on. The CIA, DIA (Defense Intelligence), NSA and several other agencies gathered information in various ways, although since there were no assets on the ground in North Vietnam, much of what they had came from photo analysis from SR-71 flights some 80,000 feet up. There were also "Buffalo Hunter" drones used at low level, but mechanical and programming failures and NVA gunners limited Intel from that source. The high-level birds were better, but a wisp of cloud over the camp could block direct sight.

An Air Force Brigadier, Leroy Manor, was placed in overall charge of the raid, though he would sit it out at Monkey Mountain in Vietnam, cursing the inadequacy of the most up-to-date communications available. Manor was the right man for the job, having command of USAF Special Operations Forces, and as such was familiar with inter-service coordination.

Training for the assault teams took place at Eglin Air Force Base—primarily Duke Field and nearby areas—in Florida (hence the Air Force General) under such secrecy that mock-ups of the prison compound were made of materials that could be taken down quickly whenever Soviet spy satellites were overhead. Wooden 4x4 posts formed the shape of the compound and buildings with walls made of cloth that were taken down whenever not in use. A river that ran past the compound was etched in the ground by a bulldozer, and at least one tree was planted.

The pattern and frequency of those satellites was well documented.

The operation was incredibly intricate. The Army, Navy, and Air Force were involved in everything from staging bases in Laos and Thailand to the largest night operation Navy pilots had ever flown.

All the while Blackburn and his deputy, Colonel E. E. Mayer, were putting the complex rescue operation together. His sources were figuring out how many POWs might be in the camp, and by the time they were ready to go they even knew the names of most of them. The more SACSA discovered the more people were willing to go, even when it was felt—maybe—that the camp was empty. Through new photos and a surprise source in the Northern hierarchy, word came down the prisoners had been moved because the Song Con River next to the camp had flooded.

It is possible the flood was a result of another US endeavor to the west—cloud seeding.

Then, later photos showed it was possible someone was back in the camp, but it was unknown just who it was. All they had to go on was a few new tire tracks and some laundry hanging up. The decision to go was made anyway, for the simple reason that if the POWs had indeed been moved back in to Son Tay and the rescue was called off, it would have been inexcusable, especially in light of new press releases from the North listing POW deaths in the camps. The possibility of an empty camp was not related to the raiders, though Manor and Simons may have known.

Interviews have shown that if they did know, they didn't tell anybody else.

The different elements trained relentlessly for months, including pilots of the several C-130s and helicopters (H-53 and H-3) who had to fly a perfect winding route through North Vietnam, staying too low and banking away precisely at the right time to avoid enemy radar systems. Mission leaders Simons, Sydnor and Meadows, in conjunction with Blackburn and Manor, tried hard to plan for every eventuality, including equipment failure, compromise, and the possible need to rescue the rescuers.

Bud Sydnor

The initial training for Army was PT and the normal SF refresher subjects one might expect. The AF units were doing their own types of training. Colonel Simons decreed the eight-hour training day start at 0400 and end at noon. Later, we started at noon to have time for three daylight rehearsals, breaking for supper, then reassembling for three night rehearsals.

The three-and-three rehearsals went on to the end of September, but all the "what if" questions were put on hold until the Alternate Plans were revealed.

[In early October] the Alternate Plans were briefed to the Assault, Command [Security], and Support Groups. Basically the plans were four in number; Black Plan, if the assault bird could not physically land within the compound walls, it was to land outside the walls near the SW corner tower, disembark and negotiate the wall with explosive charges or with a ladder, or both. The other Alternate Plans were based on the premise that if only one of the three birds carrying groups of the Ground Force was missing, the mission would continue on the color-coded Alt plan related to the missing force. Blue was for Assault, Red for Security and Green for Support. Led by Blueboy [Meadows], Redwine [Dan Turner] and Greenleaf [Udo Walther]. I was Wildroot.

When the October weather window was cancelled [unknown to any but those who knew the target and dates] the Force continued to rehearse all plans into November. These additional rehearsals relate directly to the ease with which the Force activated Plan Green at the objective on 21 November.

To give the raiders a better chance of getting in and out undetected, or at least unchallenged, the Navy would launch a large diversionary raid [59 sorties] over Haiphong Harbor and other places. However, they wouldn't drop bombs; they would drop flares—while SAMs flew all over the place. The Air Force would supply some F-105 Thunderchiefs for Wild Weasel duty to deal with the SAMs, and some F-4s in case any MIGs showed up. There were also five A1-E prop planes to cover strafing missions if necessary. The actual assault/rescue force was small compared to the air show above North Vietnam that night.

Two helicopters carrying the assault force would land outside the compound while a third waited a short distance away to pick up any rescued prisoners. Two more HH-53s also waited not far away. A smaller bird, an H-3, carrying Meadows and a squad of soldiers, would crash-land inside the compound, purposely grinding the rotor blades into a tree that was just in the way. Mattresses covered the floor of that bird so the men could lay out spread-eagled to absorb the shock of falling the last several feet.

Those men were responsible for the POWs and any enemy they found inside. Outside, Turner [Redwine] and his team would clear a barracks building of enemy guards, blow a hole in the compound wall, and take care of any extra targets. A third force was to act as security on the ground.

Finally, all was ready. Although the weather had been forecast based on years of occurrences during that particular time of year to be just right between November 21-25, a stray typhoon came out of nowhere and headed for North Vietnam. General Manor had no choice but to move the mission forward by 24 hours.

There were three helicopters labeled Apples One, Two and Three, and they carried the assault force for the inside of the compound, the assault force for outside the compound, and the security team. Simons was in One, Sydnor in two, and Meadows in the smaller H-3. Apple Two was transporting Sydnor and his three-man element plus the 20-man Security Force [Redwine].

Bud Sydnor

In accordance with the preliminary plan for the before-touch down plan, we loaded weapons, turned on radio sets, etc. I was seated just behind the pilot compartment on the aircraft port side and right beside the receiver of the portside mini-gun. I was to fire only if Plan Green was activated. The approach to the insertion point for Apple Two was planned to be directly West to East, but prior to touch down a sharp "S" turn was made. I later learned it was an adjustment from a heading for a compound 400 meters south of the objective.

Apple Two was following Apple One, which carried Simons and landed in the wrong place.

Just before touch down the starboard mini-gun was fired, which was in accordance with the basic plan. But then, the port mini-gun right by my head was fired. Then the pilot announced into the intercom that Apple One was missing.

My command group moved toward the drainage ditch enroute to a small building near the south wall of the compound. An armed soldier in shorts appeared. I had two hands full of radio mikes and asked RTO Paul Poole to shoot him. When fired at, the soldier disappeared into the heavy brush around the ditch. I could hear Blueboy [Meadows] calling to the POWs on the bullhorn announcing who we were and what action to take as we came into the cells. We could hear weapons firing in the compound and from the Redwine elements clearing outside buildings.

Shortly after that Blueboy transmitted the first of three reports; 'Negative Items (no POWs), search continues.

Simons and the group in Apple One got through trashing the other compound and made the short flight to join the rest of the Force. The original plan was immediately put back in effect. When Meadows made his last statement that no POWs were in the compound, the Force began to withdraw.

Since there were no extra people the third helicopter was not needed and the entire force loaded aboard Apples One and Two. In the sky they were about to inhabit, SAMs were seeking overhead aircraft, finding an F-105 and flaming it. The raiders eventually picked up the crew on the way home.

The only hitch on the way back was the sudden possibility that one of the raiders had been left behind. Since the whole Force was aboard two birds instead of three, the practiced count was off by one and it took several adrenaline-minutes to recount and satisfy the numbers.

Once back at Udorn Air Base, the raiders went their separate ways. Brigadier General Manor and Colonel Simons went to the Pentagon to tell their story and the rest went back to Eglin to clean their weapons and put away the various tools of war. It was over after just 29 minutes on the ground.

Yet, the treatment of the POWs remaining in North Vietnam somehow got better after that. There were less beatings, better food, and most importantly the prisoners were allowed to be together. If that was the total benefit of the raid, then it wasn't wasted on the men who inhabited the tiny, solitary cells in Hell.

Sydnor—Ground Forces Commander—Son Tay Raid

This interview was conducted by telephone and tape-recorded in October 2005, after several calls and snail-mails took place. Operation White Star and other postings of Sydnor's are included to show the ties between Simons, Meadows, and Sydnor—three legendary Rangers.

Sydnor was with the SAS on an exchange program in 60-61.

Dick Meadows and I were the Captain and Master Sergeant that were chosen as the initial ones on the program. There had been some talk between General Blackburn [head of SOG and later, SACSA] and Colonel Tony Drummond of the SAS about having an exchange between the 77th SF [later the 7th] and the 22nd SAS. I stayed about 15 months and he stayed maybe a couple of months more.

When did you first get involved with Special Forces?

When I finished the Advanced Officer's Course down at Benning in June of 1959, I was still looking for something to do, because I'd already had a company over in Korea. I had all those things behind me so I was ready to look for new ground. I volunteered for Special Forces and that's where I was assigned. I got there [77th SF at Fort Bragg, North Carolina] in June.

I met [Meadows] there, but I didn't get to know him well. When I first joined they were up at Pisgah [National Forest], so we finished up the training the 77th was doing and walked out on the Appalachian Trail. When I got back sometime in August, a guy named Captain Lynch was escorting me around and showing me what Smoke Bomb Hill had to offer, and off in the distance there was a guy he recognized, Master Sergeant Dick Meadows. He said, "There goes Dick Meadows. He's the best we've got. Any time anything good comes up and he's available, he gets it."

Then, much to my surprise, they paired me up with him about six months later to go to England to the SAS.

Do you know when Meadows got his Ranger Tab?

It had to be early. He became a Master Sergeant in an artillery unit [in Korea] because he took over the battery when a whole bunch of other people got killed. That was back when you had the job, you got the stripes. When he got back to the States, knowing he had never had any garrison time as a Master Sergeant, he applied for Special Forces. We talked about it [later].

That was in '51, possibly '52, when SF got on the roles of the Army. It was probably '52 because I went to Jump School in '53 and a guy had on this red patch with a parachute and a glider in white. Nobody had ever seen that patch before. He told us it was a Special Forces patch and that was about all he would say about it.

That was January 1953, the same year Sydnor got his Tab.

On the Son Tay mission, did you know Meadows would be part of the team before you got there?

No. When I got to Fort Benning in June of 1970 from the War College, they assigned me to run a Tactics Committee and I knew that Meadows was on the post. But I didn't see him, and somebody told me he was TDY [temp duty] to Washington.

Well, to hear Dick Meadow's story, he said when Colonel Simons was looking for someone to be the Ground Force Commander, he put my name in the pot. That was, of course, after we'd served...with the SAS. He had been off doing SOG and stuff like that. Simons said, "Well, I don't know where Sydnor is." Dick said, "Well, he just arrived at Fort Benning." So I got a call directly from Colonel Simons, who had Meadows up in the JCS starting to make the plan for Son Tay. Colonel Simons came down to Benning and interviewed me and he said, "There's something going on that's good for the United States, good for the Army and good for Special Forces. Do you want to be part of it?"

That question was asked in a parking lot.

I trusted him because I had worked for him on White Star over in Laos. I knew that Meadows was up there with him. That was probably the most trust-worthy two I'd ever known. So I said yes, in the blind. He asked me if I could meet him there [parking lot] because he was going to turn around and get the next plane out.

White Star 1961-62 Laos

Operation White Star was a Special Forces training mission in Laos. It is where Sydnor and Simons met.

He practically set up White Star in '59. Blackburn chose him to be the one. They didn't really know what they were going to do. They knew they were going to advise [the Laotians] and he started to put it all together.

When I got back from England [with the 22nd SAS] it was kind-of my turn to go to White Star. That was the third group to go. The first two were in civilian clothes. My first introduction to him was when I got on a plane—I was down in [an area] which was over next to the Cambodian border. I went in because they were fixing to pay my interpreters in Laotian money instead of Thai money, so I was going up there to protest. When I got [up there] I told them I wanted to see Colonel Simons because I was greatly concerned about losing my two interpreters. They said, he wants to see you, too. They sent me up on the plateau.

Down in the foot of Laos, which is shaped like a keyhole, there's a plateau about the size of the big island in Hawaii. It's somewhere between 3,000 and 4,000 feet up right out of the jungle. The people I'd been advising were, well, I couldn't brag about them at all. When I got up there to take over, a group called the Old Maquis who had been armed by the French some time before, they had promised us they would recruit us a hundred people if we would train them and arm them. Then we would re-train and re-arm them. That's what Colonel Simons wanted me to do on the plateau. I got my CIB in Laos. We had several combat contacts there.

The hundred were a unit sort-of like a home guard of the Laotian Army. They had a reputation of not welcoming visitors, meaning the Pathet Lao [communist group]. We had an asset, Mister Caudeau, who was violently against the Pathet Lao because they had killed his college-age son. He was a cattle and tea-plantation owner. He was a great patriot, half-French and half-Vietnamese. He lived and worked in Laos.

Mr. Caudeau was a door opener.

When I first got to Laos on White Star they assigned me to Attapeu. They had a regular battalion and sort-of a National Guard battalion there. Each one had about 400 men in them.

Asked if they were any good at all, Sydnor responded, "No."

We went over there for six months, and at the end of that Colonel Simons was ready to go home and I was ready to go home. That would have been March of '62. This is where I got to know him. He came down to our little camp, which was right in the middle of the jungle with an airstrip made out of an old dry rice field. He ran things from there. He extended myself and a Master Sergeant Gray, who was his Sergeant Major. So the three of us got extended for three months and I got to know him as well as anybody ever did. He was a loner.

Right after Sydnor retired in 1981, he was contacted by Ross Perot's people about a book being written about Simons. They endeavored to make a list of Simon's close friends, but soon discovered there were none. Later, when Simons was working for Perot rescuing hostages in Iran, he said his wife was the best friend he ever had. She had just died.

Simons died in 1979. I was running the Ranger Department when he died and they called up and wanted us to provide the pallbearers for him. We did, out of the Florida Ranger Camp.

Between White Star and Vietnam, Sydnor assigned Captains to Infantry units overseas. He said it was one of the hardest jobs he ever had due to the long hours. "They all wanted the top men, but the top men weren't always available."

I got to Vietnam in October 1967. I took command of the 1/327 [101st Abn] about two weeks before the Tet Offensive in '68 [January]. I took it over and all of a sudden there started being reports of people coming through the zone. We were at Song Be. They said, hey, come on out here with your people, you're going up to be attached to the Marines until the division can close on you. So, the 1/327 went up to Phu Bai in I Corps. We worked for them for about six weeks as the division was closing in to Camp Eagle.

Sydnor said his only contact with the 1st Brigade LRRP Platoon was as a support unit when they got in trouble, and when he worked as the S-3 before taking command. "We knew where they were, and we made plans for where we wanted them to go."

It was a great command. I really enjoyed it, and we never lost a man on my watch. When I say lost, we never had one missing. We had lots of combat and got lots of people hurt and killed, but we never left anybody behind.

[Between 1968 and 1970] I went to school. They let me finish my Master's Degree I had started when I was working for the Infantry Branch. While I was in school they picked me for the War College, so I had two years of school back-to-back.

He got out of the War College and went to Fort Benning where people tried to talk him out of the mission Simons proposed.

That's where I got recruited by Colonel Simons. I couldn't tell them [nay-sayers] why TDY orders were coming, but I had to tell them that they were. I had no idea where I was going. All I knew was orders were coming down assigning me TDY to the JCS [Joint Chiefs of Staff]. I had to tell them [at Benning] because they had just given me the best job a Lt. Colonel could have in the Tactics Department.

Why was he picked to be Ground Forces Commander? Other than the fact he was a superb planner and administrator, he was also a proven combat leader and known to be a man who got things done, whatever it took.

According to Meadows, he [Simons] had already asked one guy who was running the Florida Ranger Camp. I forget his name, but he was married and had a whole bunch of kids, some of them young, and he said no. Anyway, he was talking to Meadows about it and Meadows threw my name in. Simons had extended me in Laos to help keep things the way they were. He was going out, too. He had already been replaced. We worked well together. Frankly I think he came down to Fort Benning, instead of just talking to me [on the phone] to see if I was fat and lazy. I don't know that, but that's the way he worked. He was very positive. You always knew what he wanted. Always.

Sydnor got to the Son Tay mission after the initial plans had been made.

It was complete without any alternate plans. It took me about 30 minutes looking at the model to go over the plan. That was the first thing Colonel Simons said to me. "I want you to go in there where the model is and take this—seven or eight pages—and it was how we were going to land and how we were going to attack the place and how we were going to exfiltrate with the prisoners. Simons, myself, and Meadows were the only ones that were going to go in on the ground that knew [the destination].

How hard was coordinating the inter-service cooperation?

They turned it over to us, of course, it all had to do with picking the place [to train], which also, if it had been at Bragg it would have been an Army General, but at Eglin it would be an Air Force General [as overall commander, Brigadier General Leroy Manor]. They picked Eglin because the Search and Rescue School was there. All of their best pilots were collected at that location. They lived a double life. They flew their training missions, and then in the afternoon and night they came and flew for us.

I've had this question: When did everything really chill and people quit talking among each other, finding fault with the training and how much we were doing? It was when we started firing behind each other's feet at night, live fire, in CONUS [at Eglin]. We said, man, we're taking risks you just don't do. That happened some time during the first month of training.

Were you in the loop for Intelligence coming through SACSA (and other agencies)?

We took what they gave us. A couple of times it was real interesting. They said there was anti-aircraft warning in the [guard] towers. We said, wait a minute! What exactly was that? They said, AW. We said, that's Automatic Weapon!

They also said, we think one of the POWs has died, because right outside of the compound—because of the high water table, they bury them almost right on top of the ground and dig a trench around them and pile the dirt up over the body and the casket. We said, hey, that's an anti-aircraft position.

They wanted to put a bird inside the compound, but we had a lot of static from the Air Force. They don't want to put a ship in jeopardy unless they have to. So, right up until the last of our training, this lead guy, Air Force Colonel [Walter] Britton, would bring that up again and say, "Why can't we just land that outside?" I said, "You've read the same stories I have about WWII. If they have a plan, that will give them a couple of extra minutes to do that [kill the prisoners]."

We held to that right to the last minute to prove we could do it, while we were training. We proved by moving the fence back 15 or 20 feet that we actually could land a chopper in there without sticking the blades in the tree we planted.

Word has it that the tree in the actual compound was somewhat taller than anticipated.

I debriefed all those people, and I think it was Meadows that said we didn't know what the composition of the tree was, but when he shoved the blades into that tree and dropped the eight or nine feet to the ground, we exited the aircraft, and the air was full of firewood. We were taking a risk because we didn't know the composition of the tree, whether it was bushy or had some big limbs in it. If it was [wrong] it could have turned the chopper over. One of the reasons we picked that [type of] chopper was that its design had a rotor-head brake. Most of the other choppers do not have.

Some of the Navy birds had such brakes so the rotors could be slowed and stopped quickly "And get it out of the way for the next guy." Meanwhile, the brake is to slow it down after power is cut—it doesn't work in the air.

Whether or not they activated the thing, I don't know. The whole thing was to hover over a seven-foot wall with the tail of the chopper. The only way to clear it was to push the blades into the tree and cut the power at the same time.

Were there buildings outside the compound wall, and were there people in them?

Well, that was a very, very small compound. It was 185 feet long and about 130 feet east to west. All those buildings on the outside were very small. On the south side there were three buildings. One was a washhouse and one was a chicken coop. Then, there was the largest building. It was a barracks. We dropped everybody that came out of them. If they didn't, we went in and got them.

How many were killed?

We can only go by what we saw drop, and that was 27. That was several different places. Some of them got taken out from inside the compound—some of them got taken out at the gate on the east side. It was a total of 43 after I debriefed them at Eglin. They gave me a count of 16 at the Secondary School [where Simons landed by accident].

Were they all NVA?

We don't know. We didn't take any bodies or anything. The assumption was there was at least a platoon. Everybody had a rifle and there were some automatic weapons there. They would have been guarding the compound. We had 30 minutes before any of the known reserves could come from the citadel across that bridge into our area. We did not know there was anybody down at the Secondary School. We were told [later] that [the school] was a command and control center for surface-to-air missiles in the area. That was never any part of this thing.

It has been surmised that the school held Chinese or Russian advisors, but Sydnor said, "If they do {know} they had more information than we had."

Did you know beforehand that Simons was going to land at the Secondary School?

Of course not. I was the most surprised person. He didn't tell me where he was, and he didn't tell me he was going over there after we had gone into the plan. He didn't tell me to go into the plan [the Green Plan, plan B, executed when Simons was noted missing].

The key was, when Colonel Allison, the commander of my bird [Apple Two], said Apple One is not here, I grabbed hold of Redwine [Team Leader] who was sitting by me, and holding on to his harness, we got off the plane. I told him, when you open your net, say Plan Green is in effect.

That did not affect Meadows and the Blue Team at all. I could hear him inside on the bullhorn, but I was busy. I said before, I trusted him with my life. Neither Simons nor myself ever went into the compound to see that he had done it right and was reporting the facts.

Where was Simons after he got back from the mis-landing?

He wasn't close to me. He was short of the south wall of the compound. We stayed separated by design all the way through the training. In training what he would do when his bird would touch down—unless it was live-fire—he would go around looking to see what people were doing and how they were doing it. He was kind-of supervising my operation. He told me at the beginning, the first night we were at JCS, I'm the Task Force Commander, I'm to be in an aircraft over the objective, but I'm telling you now I am not going to put people on the ground without being there myself. Then he said, work it out. What we did was add one radio operator, spread all the radios between him and his two and me and my two. We rode on different birds.

So, he was the Task Force Commander but he was letting me run the show because he directed me to.

Did you have any idea the POWs may be gone before you went in?

That was the greatest surprise of all. All of us, we had no idea [including Simons]. Nor did we have a plan. Nor did we know where they went. General Blackburn, the SACSA, made a big pitch on that. He said, tell me positively that they're gone, and they [the spooks] couldn't do that. That was in the National Command Center the night before we went.

The After-Action Report was the product of several different people's input and collective debriefing, taking almost three weeks to write.

Do you consider the raid a success even though no prisoners were rescued?

Yes. Because the result of our failed mission scared the North Vietnamese so badly they concentrated all the outlying camps in Hanoi. As a result, there was less torture, they were able to organize the 4th POW Allied Wing, they got to talk to each other. There was very little isolation, except for Admiral Stockdale and some of the leaders. That's why they were reasonably healthy three years later when they got released. That is in large part because of the unsuccessful raid. We did not accomplish the mission, but the results were favorable.

There was a White Paper written after the Iran debacle, and a lot of those things we proved you should do, they simply didn't do.

Sydnor went on to say the two missions, though related in terms of logistics to an extent, were really apples and oranges when comparing size of the target and number of people and cross-service involvement.

Sydnor Biography

Elliot P. "Bud" Sydnor began his military career in submarines, serving on the USS Raton from 1945 to 1948. Once out of the boats, he graduated from Western Kentucky University with a Bachelor's Degree, and was the Distinguished Military Graduate in August 1952.

In 1953, he was a Platoon Leader with the 11th Airborne and a year later he was a company commander for the 2nd Infantry Division in Korea. In 1955-56 he was the S-3 for a battalion of the 25th Infantry Division. Three more years of Airborne assignments in the States led him to a posting with the 22nd SAS in England. He returned to Special Forces at Fort Bragg in 1962. In 1964, he graduated from the Command and General Staff College and in 1967, he put the Armed Forces Staff College behind him.

He ended up in Washington serving in the Infantry Branch for three years before going to Vietnam as the Battalion Commander, 1st Battalion, 327th Infantry, 101st Airborne. He stayed with the 327th until 1968. In 1969 he earned a Master's Degree from George Washington University.

In 1970, after graduation from the War College, he returned to Fort Benning only to be recruited by Colonel Arthur "Bull" Simons for the Son Tay raid. He subsequently helped in the planning, liaison and execution of that famous raid into North Vietnam.

After that he returned to Benning and served on the Staff and Faculty of the Army Infantry School. He took command of the 1st Special Forces Group in Okinawa in 1973, and a year or so later he was Chief of the Infantry Branch. He became Chief of the Company Grade Combat Arms Division not long after. He was the Director of the Ranger Department from June 1977 to May 1980.

Sydnor finished his distinguished career as Director of Plans and Training for the Infantry Center at Fort Benning.

He earned a lot of brass and ribbons for his exploits in the field, plus becoming extremely well educated. He was awarded the Distinguished Service Cross, the Silver Star, the Legion of Merit with two oak leaf clusters, the Distinguished Flying Cross, the Bronze Star with V device, the Air Medal *with nine oak leaf clusters*, the Vietnamese Cross of Gallantry with Silver Star, the Combat Infantryman's Badge, the Master Parachutist's Badge, the coveted Ranger Tab, and the Special Forces Tab. He is a member of the Ranger Hall of Fame.

He retired in August 1981.

Simons Biography

Arthur D. "Bull" Simons began his military career as an ROTC Cadet at the University of Missouri, receiving his commission in 1941. His first posting was in artillery, a position he carried through command of a battery in the Pacific war between 1942-44. At the end of that period, the whole battalion was trained-up and re-designated as the 6th Ranger Battalion. Simons became a company commander and battalion XO. He participated in several hazardous landings with the Ranger Battalion in the Philippines.

After World War II, Major Simons left the Army for five years before returning to active duty in 1951. He served as an Infantry Instructor at Fort Benning, Georgia and a Ranger trainer in the Amphibious and Jungle Training camp. Other assignments included tours with the Military Assistance Advisory Group—Turkey, and the XVIII Airborne Corps before joining the 77th Special Forces Group (Airborne) in 1958.

In 1960, he served as Deputy Commander/Chief of Staff of the US Army Special Warfare Center. He commanded the White Star Mobile Training Team in Laos from 1961 to 1962 and the 8th Special Forces Group (Airborne) in the Canal Zone from 1962 to 1964. From Panama, he was assigned to the Military Assistance Command, Vietnam, Studies and Observation Group (MACV-SOG), which conducted numerous behind-the-lines missions in Southeast Asia.

Colonel Simons is best known for his role as Deputy Commander of Operation Ivory Coast, more famously known as the Son Tay Raid. Ably assisted by his ground forces commander, Lieutenant Colonel Elliot Sydnor, and his assault force leader, Captain Richard Meadows, Colonel Simons and his 56 raiders penetrated deep into North Vietnam on 21 (night of 20th) November 1970 in a daring raid to rescue US POWs. Unfortunately, the camp had been evacuated before the attempt. After returning Stateside, Colonel Simons served with the XVIII Airborne Corps.

The Son Tay Raid would not be Colonel Simons' last attempt to free prisoners in a foreign country. In early 1979, after his retirement, Colonel Simons was asked by H. Ross Perot, then Chairman of Electronic Data Systems, to plan and conduct a rescue operation to free two EDS employees who were taken hostage by the Iranian government. In February 1979, Colonel Simons' planning efforts proved successful as he organized a mob in Tehran, which stormed Gazre prison where the EDS employees were being held hostage. The two Americans, along with 11,000 Iranian prisoners, were freed. Simons and his party fled 450 miles to Turkey, and were later returned to the United States. Noted author, Ken Follet, wrote a best selling novel, *On Wings of Eagles*, (Morrow & Company, 1983) about the rescue. The book was later made into an NBC TV mini-series starring Burt Lancaster, though it is said he looked more like Telly Savalas.

Bull Simons died May 21, 1979.

His decorations include the Distinguished Service Cross, the Legion of Merit (with four Oak Leaf Clusters), the Silver Star, the Bronze Star, a Purple Heart, the Armed Forces Reserve Medal, the WWII Service Medal (Pacific Theater), the Philippine Independence Ribbon, the Viet Nam Service Medal, the Combat Infantry Badge- 2d Award, and the Master Airborne Qualification Badge.

Simons and Meadows are both buried at Barrancas National Cemetery near Pensacola, Florida.

Meadows Biography

Richard J. "Dick" Meadows was born in 1931 and left us July 29, 1995. He compiled an outstanding legacy of daring, audacity and brilliance that earned him a slot in the Ranger Hall of Fame.

During the course of this research, nothing but good things have been said of Meadows. More than a few men held him in high regard.

Meadows lied about his age to join the Army in 1947 at age 15. He began his military career with the 82nd Airborne Division as an artilleryman, and then transferred to the 187th Regimental Combat Team for a tour in Korea with the 674th Field Artillery Battalion. His actions in Korea earned him Master Sergeant stripes, making him the youngest man to hold that rank during the war.

Beginning in 1953, when Meadows volunteered for Special Forces—his Ranger Tab came very close to that time—he spent the rest of his career with one Special Ops unit or another. He was instrumental in the formation of many programs and organizations that still exist, including Special Forces, Military Free Fall Parachuting, and the formation of SFOD-Delta.

He was selected to be the first NCO—joining Colonel Sydnor—to participate in an exchange program between the 77th SF and the British Special Air Service (SAS), where he acted as Troop Commander. He went on several exercises and one actual mission in Oman.

During Vietnam, he spent time under Colonel Simons in Operation White Star in Laos, then later became part of MACV-SOG under General Blackburn.

His exploits during two tours are legendary in the SF/Ranger community. At least a dozen times Meadows went across the border into Laos and North Vietnam, gathering information and occasionally, a prisoner. He also called in plenty of fire from above on the Ho Chi Minh Trail.

In an unusual move Meadows was promoted from Master Sergeant directly to Captain. He was just that good.

In November 1970, he was chosen by Colonel Simons to help plan and organize the Son Tay prison raid into North Vietnam. Named as the ground assault commander, Meadows and his team crash-landed a helicopter inside the compound and searched for prisoners—of which there were none. Still, the heroic mission is a case study of excellence in planning and execution.

His last posting before retiring in 1977 was Deputy Commander and Training Officer at the Swamp/Jungle Phase of Ranger School at Camp Rudder at Eglin Air Force Base. After his retirement, he continued working in the Special Operations field with both military and civilian groups.

One famous excursion involved the Iran hostage attempted rescue. The Iran situation and much of his work with Delta was done after his retirement. When the Iran rescue attempt went sour in the desert before reaching Tehran, Meadows—inside the city and making ready—was left abandoned and had to work his way out of the country.

Meadows seemed at times in his career to be almost super-human. He was the go-to guy.

He earned the DSC, the Silver Star (w/oak leaf cluster), Legion of Merit, Bronze Star (w/v device), Air Medal, Meritorious Service Medal, Joint Commendation Medal, Army Commendation Medal (w/two oak leaf clusters), CIB (many times over), Master Parachutist Badge, Glider Badge, Ranger and Special Forces Tabs, and SCUBA badge.

He was posthumously inducted into the Ranger Hall of Fame. The induction took place at his funeral.

IN-COUNTRY TRAINING

The American military seems to love schools. From Basic forward, soldiers are required—or volunteer—to attend schools relating to their present job. The Vietnam War presented special problems for the military. Jungle/mountain fighting against a seasoned, determined enemy was not something the Army was particularly good at. Infiltration, stealth, booby-traps, tunnels—all were new to the majority of America's forces.

Accordingly, the Army began schools to handle the orientation of the new soldiers to the perils awaiting them. Some of those schools were already in existence; some were formed for the occasion. Jungle Warfare and Survival School in Panama stepped up its course load, and some divisions began schools of their own, such as the 82nd Airborne and 25th ID. The school at Fort Campbell was on 101st Airborne ground. There was also a school for the XVIII Airborne Corps at Fort Bragg.

There were two major Recondo Schools during the war, one in the US at Fort Campbell, Kentucky, and one in Vietnam. Both schools were staffed by Special Forces and Ranger personnel—often the Instructors were both—and were considered an important, if not essential, step in jungle training and recon techniques.

There was a pre-Recondo course, much like the pre-Ranger course today, that found out which men were ready and able to take on the challenge. Although many types of soldiers attended the course, the emphasis was on Lurp/Ranger small unit tactics and techniques. Many of the graduates of Recondo were either going to or coming from a Lurp unit.

MACV Recondo

In Vietnam, the Recondo was located in Nha Trang and backed by MACV. General Westmoreland ordered the school opened in 1966, and from then until its closure in December 1970, the three-week course produced more than 3,000 graduates—and that with a 40 percent failure rate. When things went right, 60 men began the course every two weeks.

It was closed briefly during the Tet 1968 Communist offensive.

Recondo was founded by Colonel Lewis Millet (MOH winner), and Colonel Francis Kelley, Commander of 5th Special Forces. The course began with five enlisted men and four officers as Instructors. Each was on his third or fourth tour.

MACV Recondo was originally formed through Project Delta and staffed by Special Forces soldiers who weren't on a mission at the time. Word of the small school spread, and Allied troops began to apply from all over the country. Soon the burden was too much for the 5th SF project to handle, and control passed to MACV.

It is said that General Westmoreland decided on the term "Recondo" for the school, using an established contraction of the words "reconnaissance" and "commando," although he changed the second word to "doughboy" to fit American terminology. Either way, some also felt the "do" at the end was more of an acknowledgement of the Japanese word for "the way," as in the martial arts and the code of Bushido.

The motto was: Smart, Skillful, Tough, Courageous, Confident (SSTCC).

Week One: Classroom work, maps, weapons maintenance, rappelling, ocean swim test, learning foreign weapons, live fire with all weapons, and physical conditioning (including a seven-mile run with full equipment, and the Recondo Sand Bag Runs).

They were also heavy on stealth: no smoking, no bug juice, no soap, never remove equipment even while sleeping, don't move during the VC two-hour lunch break, and practice listening to natural sounds in the bush.

Week Two: Helicopters, selection of LZ, PZ, use of Maguire Rigs and STABO Rigs and others for extraction, improvisation. This section was done on Hontour Island, five miles offshore.

Week Three: Field exercises, real combat patrols—often a trial by fire, called "You bet your life." This was done with six-man teams with an Instructor or two, where the students did everything, including radio operations, land navigation, and taking point.

Honor graduates received a Bowie knife with an inscription, and a better chance of staying alive.

Steve Pullen

Pullen is excerpted in other places in this book.

"I learned how to operate in the jungle there. Sergeant Chapel taught me how to read trails, and signs along the trails."

Such signs, arrows or piles of stones indicated direction to the VC. Pullen said he learned many life-saving things, such as silent communication. "Everything was hand signals. There was no talking in the bush."

One thing setting the in-country school apart from its Stateside counterpart was the use of live ammunition. Another was the lack of Aggressor Forces—friendlies that act the part of the enemy in simulated combat. The MACV students did their Practicals in the bush.

"There was always a possibility of contact," Pullen said.

The school lasted three intense weeks, and often came on the heels of Ranger School. The two training periods together produced a much more qualified jungle fighter than either by itself. The results spoke for themselves, and other soldiers knew the difference.

"The Recondo badge sets you apart. You needed a badge or a Tab, but either one would do." In that situation, he said, the badge was probably more important. If a man wore the badge and a Ranger Tab, others knew he could be depended upon, that he had lots of training and above all, had passed. The training often made the difference in battle.

"Ranger School gave me great confidence in myself and made me a better small-unit leader. Recondo School gave me confidence I could operate in Vietnam. We had great Instructors at both schools, but the big differences were in Ranger School we were in the United States, we used blanks and simulators and the OPFOR were soldiers from Fort Benning. At Recondo School we were in Vietnam, we used live ammunition and the OPFOR were NVA/VC. I remember when we received our welcome at Recondo School, the officer told us that a patrol in the last class had been involved in a brief firefight with at least one NVA/VC. It teaches discipline. It taught me before you eat or sleep, you clean your weapon and you set out security." Pullen pointed out that after a couple days in the bush it is too easy to find a hide site and just fall out without taking care of those things that keep you alive. The discipline was driven home hard, so it would stay there when the chips were down. The thinking was if you can't make it through school, what are you going to do when you're six days in the bush, exhausted, perhaps wounded and/or being chased? To give up was to die, and maybe your buddies, too.

Only the best survived the schools.

"Recondo School was the most professional school I ever attended. It was all business and it was designed solely for long range patrolling. The days were long and the three weeks went by quickly. In those three weeks we were taught a variety of subjects. The first week was in the classroom. The second week was on a small island and the third week was the exercise in enemy country. What became very obvious to me soon after arriving was that I had acquired several bad habits while operating the Aero-rifle platoon (reaction force used by the Air Cav units). The SF Instructors were very experienced and they quickly zeroed in if any of the students used bad judgment or bad technique. They were great mentors. One told me several times to "forget what you learned at Ft. Benning and at SERTS (Screaming Eagle Replacement School) because if you don't you will die, or worse, get someone else killed in Vietnam."

Stateside Recondo

The idea of Recondo Schools was not new when America became heavily embroiled in Vietnam. The first was formed in late 1958 at Fort Campbell, Kentucky. The 82nd and 101st Divisions had schools, as did a few others.

Roger McDonald

"Major Lew Millett was in charge. He wore a big old handlebar mustache, but nobody else could have anything." The school was a three-week condensed Ranger course. "We called it the 'Rangers' Revenge'"

When five students were killed in one year, "They damn near closed it." Adjustments were made, and the school remained open.

"I went to Recondo School, then Ranger School, and had a breeze."

Still, one doesn't want to say too much about previous training while in Ranger School. "I wore my Recondo badge to school. Not a good thing."

McDonald was with the 101st, which had the practice of sending Recondo grads to Ranger School.

"It was a hell of good school. A good, hard little course. It was a good way to get quick training for replacements."

All Instructors at the Fort Campbell school were Rangers, and McDonald took his turn there, staying seven months. "I had a good time as Cadre, but not as a student."

The main difference between Ranger School and Recondo was the length, which gives greater time to learn more things—that, and the prolonged conditioning, which never lets up. McDonald illustrated that point with this story from his time as an RI at Camp Frank Merrill, the Mountain Phase of Ranger School.

"I had a SEAL in the class, and I asked him which was harder, SEAL School or the Ranger School. He said in SEAL School they have one Hell Week, but Ranger School has nine weeks of it."

Earl Singletary

I went to Recondo School [Fort Campbell, 101ˢᵗ], and they added a week when I got there. I taught techniques of formal instruction. The school was three weeks long. The commanders were saying, you're sending us back good trained troops, but we want troops that can train other troops. They don't know how to teach classes. So, my job was to teach them how to teach.

They had to actually teach classes and be graded. That was why the extra week came in, so it was four weeks long.

It was a mini-Ranger School. In a lot of ways it was tougher than Ranger School. Nobody tried to get you to stay there as a student. Really they tried to get you to leave. They tested your endurance and your fortitude.

For example, in the barracks they had a sign up over the door that said, "If you can't take it, make it—dial 6101 Base Cab. If a guy said he quit, nobody tried to talk him out of it like they would in Ranger School. They'd say, "We'll help you pack."

Singletary said there were no Ranger-qualified personnel coming through Recondo while he was there. However, the Instructors were all Rangers.

In Recondo School at Fort Campbell we had trained [recon people attached to 101ˢᵗ]. The last two or three months I was there they would send us a group of individuals and we'd take them out on patrol. Say I'd go out with 10 men and the mission was to select people who would become [Lurps]. We'd spend a week with them in the field. We'd come back and I'd say out of the 10, for example, five of these guys would make it. The other five went back to their unit. Then another group would take them to the Florida Ranger Camp for swamp training. They kept weeding them out.

Colonel Beckwith was the G-2 at Division [101ˢᵗ], and he was the one who formed this company. He selected all the NCOs, took the Recondo Instructors. He said he wanted all the Recondo Instructors to go back as Team Leaders and Platoon Sergeants.

If his timing is correct, the unit he refers to must have been F/58 LRP.

He developed, supervised, the Recon Company in 1967, when the division was getting ready to go over with the 2ⁿᵈ and 3ʳᵈ Brigade.

The Cadre of F/58 was largely made up of Recondo Instructors, so the school shut down. Singletary declined to accompany the unit because of a flap over promotion, and went to the Mountain Camp as an Instructor. Others from his circle to go over included Roger Brown and Darol Walker (see his interview in the Lurp section.)

Howard Denton—82ⁿᵈ Recondo

The 82ⁿᵈ Recondo School was probably very similar to the ones at Campbell. I used to know the DA Reg or whatever that authorized it as a TO&E unit within the division. It was basically a "mini-Ranger course" designed to teach patrolling techniques and Ranger-type operations to selected personnel, usually E-4s or E-5s. It was a two-week course, and it was very tough. Not all made it. During my time, we put through not only 82nd personnel, but also a platoon of USMC force Recon from Lejune, a platoon from Canada's "Princess Patricia's Canadian Light Infantry" from Vancouver, ROTC groups, and for military demolitions and tactics, some US Marshals.

The Recondo School was on the north edge of Fort Bragg [North Carolina] on the Little River, about 13 miles west-northwest of the 82nd area in the middle of the woods, and north of Salerno drop zone. We had a log cabin (really!) HQ, a shack Mess Hall, a classroom building, two barracks, a helluvan obstacle course, slide for life, 40-foot rope drop, 50-foot rappel tower, and a fine survival trail. Only the rappel tower remained as of 1998. The rest have been replaced, and it is now a different school, but with a similar mission.

Our NCOIC then was an E-8 named MacDonald, the TAC NCO was SFC Lajos (No-Slack) Noszak, others were mostly E-6s and E-7s. All had earned the Ranger Tab and many the CIB. Some of their names were Dennis Leinick, Gary Tenehill, Doc Langworthy, Jerry Champion, Howard Schedtromph, SSGs McGuire, Ed Donovan, Law, our reliable Supply Sergeant Joshua Holmes, and my Ranger schoolmates, Fred Weekley, O'Dell McGee and Bill Acebes. There were others whose names I don't recall, I'm sorry to say, but they were all Rangers. The best there is.

The curriculum included classes on patrol organization, combat and recon patrols, warning orders, frag orders, operations orders, immediate action drills, actions at danger areas, silent hand-and-arm signals, poncho rafts, rappelling, survival, radiotelephone operations such as encoding and decoding and call for artillery and medevac, combat first aid, map reading, including terrain orientation, intersection, resection, and orienteering, basic military motivation, and other stuff.

Classes never finished before 10 p.m. Then they had a tough five-day graded patrol much like Ranger School. Some quit, some got lost. Many excelled.

During Denton's time at the 82nd Recondo, the 1st Ranger Battalion was being formed (1974).

We, and the rest of the 82nd lost some outstanding NCOs to the Ranger Battalion. We even lost some Recondo Instructors, either to the battalion or to replace NCOs who went to the battalion. We really lost the cream of the crop.

State-Side Ranger Training During Vietnam

Rangers were being trained throughout the Vietnam War by Cadre of the Ranger Department at Fort Benning and at the Mountain Camp, both in Georgia, at the Swamp Phase in north Florida, and several other places.

These men were used mainly as Force-Expanders and Advisors, and to populate the ranks of LRRPs, LRPs, and Ranger units.

Especially in the beginning, only a small portion of Lurps went to Ranger School. Most were trained either at a Recondo School or by their fellows. Even when all Lurp units became Rangers in 1969, there was still a minority of Ranger School-qualified individuals in the ranks, although that changed as the war progressed.

Bill Spies

I walked Lanes as a First Lieutenant and as a Captain in 1963-64. I was assigned to the Patrolling Committee and I walked Lanes in all three Ranger Camps, plus walking Lanes for

Officer Candidate School (OCS) and Infantry Officer Basic Course (IOBC) classes at Benning. I also taught Battlefield Techniques (patrol organization, entering and leaving friendly front lines, setting the compass, and navigating using the stars—all in bleachers or classroom), SERE, and Code of Conduct to OCS, IOBC, and IOAC.

Later, when we were scaling down toward the end of the war, we were losing Cadre. But, the school year was set up and we were still doing 16 Ranger classes a year. We were still doing the basic officer's classes (OCS) down in Stewart and Quitman Counties [Georgia].

At one time, the Patrolling Committee within the Ranger Department at Benning had more Infantry Captains assigned to it than Germany had assigned to them [two Corps]. We had 120 Captains in the Patrolling Committee alone. That was during the Vietnam War when they were coming back over here for a year, then rotating back overseas.

During wartime, promotions come quickly due to attrition of existing officers and the need for new units. One could be a 1st Lieutenant in 13 months, and possibly a Captain in two or three years.

So, here we are working. I worked 90-to-105 hours a week. We had to put in time reports. About the third time they called me about my damn time report, I said, "Let me tell you all something. Whoever you got out there that's a *man*, I want him to come out here and stay with me just one day. Doesn't have to stay a whole week. Just stay with me one day, buddy." Finally General Latham told them to get off my back.

I had NCOs, that when we went out of cycle, I just turned them loose for a few days and said, "I don't want to see you guys." Then we could work eight-hour days, when we were out of cycle.

I started out in Operations over there [Mountain Phase] in 1973. Snake and I, Sergeant Major Jim Collier, we spent all of the Christmas holidays from daylight to dark, and later, writing the TO&E for the 1st Battalion. Snake and I were doing that.

James "Snake" Collier later became Sergeant Major of the Ranger Department.
He served in Vietnam as an Advisor.

THE BIG JUMP—WAR AND PEACE—AND WAR

Alpha, Bravo and Charlie Companies—Pre-Battalion Days

By 1972, all Vietnam Ranger Companies were inactive. There were still long-established training units working, but they were not deployable. The only "combat" units left were three companies located in the United States, and their duties varied widely.

In 1971-73, Alpha Company was at Fort Hood, near Abilene, Texas; Bravo was based at Fort Carson, Colorado; and Charlie Company worked out of Fort Benning, Georgia. The three companies trained under their own command and were constantly on the go.

David Cress

Ranger David Cress was a member of Charlie Company Rangers, 75ᵗʰ Infantry.

I remember we were attached to the 1ˢᵗ/29ᵗʰ Infantry Brigade somehow. There were two other Ranger Companies, Alpha and Bravo. The Ranger Battalions were just forming in 1974. Some of our guys went there after they re-upped.

When I came out of Ranger School and went into C Company, it was not yet full. The idea was to fill it up with graduating Rangers who were not committed somewhere else. Vietnam was tailing down and they were not sending Rangers over any more. We picked up some Vietnam Rangers as they came back, maybe 10 or so.

There was a training group of Rangers who trained the Ranger students at Camp Darby, Camp Merrill and what we called the Florida Ranger Camp. We would interact with them all the time. Our company was divided between those Ranger camps almost continuously. We would train under our own leadership at those camps, as well we would serve a purpose for the Ranger School Cadre and act as "aggressors or foreign enemies" that the Ranger students could sneak up on and gather Intelligence on, etc. These duties were quite boring and often our group became energetic and creative in making it real and difficult for the students. Our commanders tried to interact with our role as aggressors, and make it more realistic for us by incorporating some level of mission practice where we would chopper in, or parachute, or patrol in, to try and make it training-effective for us, but all in all it was a drag and we felt it was beneath us.

The majority of Rangers in C Company were cross-trained in different schools as the opportunities arose. I went to Navy S.E.R.E. in Maine, as well as Scout Dog School, Tracking School, and of course, almost all of us were Airborne.

It's hard to envision a Ranger not being Airborne, but there are a few "Legs" out there.

All the schools were utilized by at least someone in our company, and then they would come back and teach the rest of us as much as they could. We were a very close bunch, as the company was originally formed from our core group and we stayed together the whole time.

We did a lot of parachuting. We practiced jumping from all types of helicopters; as well we practiced jumping at night with no light. Even jumping with dogs (not a good idea). We jumped everything and every way imaginable, I guess.

We were in a lot of field parades. Any time a senior officer retired, some of us had to parade.

We were separate from the base at Fort Benning in that we had our own area away from the rest of the base and did our own thing when we weren't moving around. We would be some place between those three camps for about a month at a time, then get four to six days off, comp time.

They would use us for showy-type things. We did a half-time show for the Houston Oilers. It seems like our company was constantly out in the woods or swamps away from Fort Benning, and split up between the three Ranger Schools, but when they needed something pretty they would call some of us back to put on a show of some kind.

At the very end of my time—out in August 1975—they started to bring non-Ranger personnel into our company and this pissed everybody off. Our company was definitely turning into something else.

The future was probably known concerning the battalions, so the majority of our time we were out in the boonies. When we came across other guys in our company, we would always find out some new adventure, someone went to some school, some small group got assigned to some war game, some guys were doing a traveling Ranger history show to attract new [recruits]. It's like we'd link up as a complete company only rarely. There were about 50 original guys in this company that stayed together the whole way, and we were originally in as Vietnam was still going and ended up doing just whatever.

Don't get me wrong, we had a ball, and certainly tested everything in every way, and pissed off almost everyone at some point in time, but Vietnam was at an end and we were a collection point, and maybe a place to pause while they figured out whatever.

We were used in whatever ways they could figure to utilize our talents. We were very energetic with few places to go, so they did the best they could to keep us busy. Our ongoing training was intense. We had a few fatalities and the normal amount of broken bones and things. It made for great stories and life-long friendships.

We were all brothers. I loved them all, even the ones I didn't like.

There were decisions being made at that time about putting together a Ranger Battalion, and the three companies were certainly being looked at for a core group. Other than that, there wasn't much for them to do. They couldn't go to Vietnam, they weren't needed in Germany, and so they ended up training most of the time. Eventually some of that talent made it to the Ranger Battalions—some of that talent, and some of that Brotherhood.

FORMATION OF THE 1ST RANGER BATTALION—1974

Keith Nightingale—Standing Up A Ranger Battalion

Colonel (Retired) Nightingale went through the Ranger Course between January and March 1966. He was the original commander of Headquarters/Headquarters Company (HHC) of the 1ˢᵗ Ranger Battalion in 1974, and became commander of the Ranger Training Brigade. He worked through two tours in Vietnam as a company commander for the 101ˢᵗ Abn (D/1/502), April 1971- February 1972, and as Division G-2 for the 101ˢᵗ. He also spent time from March 1967 to May 1968 as a Senior Advisor to the 52ⁿᵈ Battalion, Vietnamese Rangers (BDQ). From there he became the Assault Force Commander during the invasion of Grenada in 1983, and was then Deputy Operations Officer during the failed Iran hostage rescue attempt. Later, back in the southern hemisphere, he became Director of counter-drug operations for SOUTHCOM.

This interview is the result of several email exchanges in the summer of 2004, although Nightingale has given much help in other areas since that time.

Putting together something like a Ranger Battalion from scratch is a monumental task. Ways and means had to be decided on first, and there were no manuals.

Design and Construction

We had several issues at the larger level, and they reflected on my tasks (this is a book in itself), but here are the key pieces as I saw them in summary:

What is a Ranger Battalion? How should it be constructed? How should it be organized and trained, and by what principles/methods? How should it be employed in the overall structure? What are its support requirements? What should be the internal standards, and how should they be promulgated/achieved?

How will it be manned/recruited? Finding officers, senior NCOs and junior EM was pretty easy. Finding mid-grade NCOs was very hard. The other obstacle was the intransigent, but covert, opposition of the Institutional General Officers commanding the bases/posts we were assigned to recruit at. Naturally, they didn't want to allow their best troops to join the Rangers, and covertly frustrated recruiting by a variety of means.

In several cases, Ken (Leuer) had to backdoor them with [General] Abrams to gain access. In most cases, our senior NCOs worked the post clubs and we established clandestine recruiting stations. Ironically, the 101ˢᵗ (Sid Berry) was the most difficult to access/work but ultimately gave up the most recruits due to NCO efforts. It was uncomfortable for me personally, as I had just come from the 101ˢᵗ and was on tap to be Berry's aide when I opted to go to the new Ranger unit. Ken, in a usual burst of insight, made me the senior team leader. The Special Forces recruiting was our worst, as they (the NCOs) simply were not prepared to pay the price.

My biggest internal issue was in trying to organize the 50-plus HHC into a viable field organization, as well as compete on an equal footing with the rifle companies on Banner Day.

The question was, "How did you figure out who to call to accomplish all the advance planning and coordination to get the Rangers functional on a global scale?"

This was an iterative process. We worked with XVIII Abn Corps and Joint Exercises Branch of JCS as well as FORSCOM and TRADOC. We all learned together. People needed to know what we could and could not do. We needed virtually 100 percent support, as we had no organic vehicles or liaison teams, as did other MTOE [military table of organization and equipment] elements.

The question was, "How hard was it to get all those organizations to work with you?"

Mixed bag. No one—logically—understood what a Ranger Battalion was, or how to use it and what it required. The shock for them was the amount of logistics they had to provide if they wanted to use us. Within the Joint HQs, there was a concept we were just super light infantry and should be employed accordingly—on the line, rather than in specialized or quick strike roles. Concurrently, the other Joint support structure we now enjoy—SOF airlift, comms, etc—did not exist, so the support techniques had to be invented.

The first Ranger Joint Exercise was at Fort Bliss under [Colonel] Art Stang—not to be confused with the Ranger School course that fluctuated between Fort Bliss and Dugway. *Solid Shield* was an annual Joint exercise that brought XVIII Abn Corps, USN, and USAF/USMC elements together in a variety of scenarios, usually to rescue some helpless mythical country that asked for help.

Finding The Right People

KCL [Colonel Ken Leuer] created recruiting teams to visit each FORSCOM/TRADOC post. The team usually consisted of a couple of the First Sergeants and a company commander. We were to spend a week there recruiting all grades. One of our shortfalls was the E-6/7 grade in addition to junior enlisted men. Per CSA (Chief of Staff, Army—Abrams) guidance, we were to be "fully supported and encouraged" by the Post CG [Commanding General] and staff.

The basic concept was that we would arrive on Post and meet with either the Chief of Staff or the G-1 and brief him on the plan. We would then have a briefing for all interested troops the next day—after publicity and notification within the Post. At the briefing, the lead (a company commander) would brief on the Ranger Battalion concept, what the training plan was and how we would do business. We made it very clear through a discussion of Ranger standards, the PT, road march, POT (Performance Oriented Training), etc, issues and the challenges imposed on all grades. We also made it very clear that the NCOs were the heart of the program and that they would make it happen. The First Sergeants would then address NCO management and issues. Our bottom line was that we were offering the audience—if they could make it—an opportunity to be part of the "finest light Infantry battalion in the world."

We then established signup interviews with every volunteer talking to one of the team and asking questions, and then signing a volunteer statement. We would take those volunteer statements and provide them to the G-1.

The CSA message required the Post to provide those soldiers without interference.

Reality was the following: The Post leadership usually worked hard behind the scenes to discourage access to us and to minimize the availability of troops to attend. On more than one occasion, I was told by a senior officer (usually a brigade commander or 06 staffer) that I would never get access to the soldiers, that he would strongly discourage any soldier attempting to volunteer, and that this initiative would undermine the ability of the Army to recover from Vietnam. In one instance, I was told bluntly by a CG that this initiative was going to be strongly opposed by him personally and that I was jeopardizing my career by disrupting the institution. He went so far as to put a letter out to all commanders, carefully skirting the line, but making it clear that he would look on any loss of soldiers as a reflection on that unit's leadership.

The ability to access the troop base was severely restricted/limited so publicity was minimized. The NCOs resolved this by making rounds to all the NCO clubs and barracks, spreading the word and using their local friends within the units to disseminate. Concurrently, the officers (myself/other company commanders) worked the Officer Clubs and personal friends.

The volunteer statements were usually copied and shipped to the line organization with a strong encouragement to interview the volunteer and discourage his direction. In some cases it worked, but not with the majority.

Regarding the recruited NCO issue, here are my recollections: We went through what I estimate to be about 300 percent of NCO (E-5/7) fill until we finally settled on the achievable situation that was "home grown," taking a grade structure hit to get an NCO who could do the job. We would get a functioning E-6 or E-7 from the outside in some cases, but it was an exception.

Most of the NCOs we recruited were simply not prepared to pay the physical price or bear the leadership burden. They were mesmerized by the "glory" and the opportunity for a black beret, but couldn't cut the standards. In many cases, the junior enlisted men ran the Squad Leaders and Platoon Sergeants into the ground and they quit out of embarrassment. Concurrently, the Performance Oriented Training approach put the direct burden on the Squad Leader/Platoon Sergeant and many were not prepared to be in the spotlight. They had to be equal or better than their men, and in many cases the junior EM were quicker/smarter. This is probably a reflection of the Army at that time where we (the Army) didn't really know how to train, the officers were afraid to assert themselves, there was no clear distinction between officer and NCO roles, and the Army lacked a coherent philosophy regarding either training or leadership—which is exactly why Abrams created the Ranger Battalion concept— not bad for a tanker.

I would make an addendum comment based on a reflective review of your question. A number of NCOs chose not to volunteer, as it was clear to them that the demands on their time were more than they cared to dedicate. I had several prospective candidates tell me that either their family situation would not permit a Ranger-type environment or that they had a pretty good situation at present and didn't want to jeopardize their career path by risking transfer to the Rangers. This was particularly true of Special Forces NCOs.

That is not to say some of the Special Forces soldiers weren't willing and able. The Green Berets were doing some of those types of training within their own framework. Mike Martin commented during his interview that the 10ᵗʰ Special Forces Group also tried a LRRP concept in training. "Later, in the late '70s, they had a Ranger Company in the 10th that I had never known about. They taught LRRP operations. Mike Smith was the First Sergeant of that unit."

For whatever reason, our interviews usually went along the line where the NCO would quiz me on exactly what sort of "good deal" the Rangers had to offer him and how we could fit in his personal educational goals into the training year. Not being in the used car business I made a note not to offer the guy a job.

A contributing factor was the Cadre of very good First Sergeants and core Platoon Sergeants we had. They had been through everything from Day One and were extremely hard and judgmental on NCOs that couldn't hack it. There was very little slack for "teaching and coaching." The new NCO either got it right quickly or moved on. Many simply were defeated psychologically after a short time.

Ultimately, what happened was the junior EM took over through attrition, eg: a Spec 4 or E-5 became the "acting Squad Leader" and de facto—the real Squad Leader. We had enough E-6 Squad Leaders to insure that one or two were in each platoon and usually had an E-7 Platoon Sergeant in each company. However, "growing our own" soon became the only rational way to proceed. POT permitted that, as sleeve rank was less important than training knowledge.

Army Training Evaluation Program (ARTEP)

The ARTEP and POT is inter-related and key to understanding the core of a Ranger Battalion. In the beginning, KCL had established that the Rangers (working with FORSCOM and TRADOC) would write a Light Infantry ARTEP using Performance Oriented Training standards. This was a totally new approach to the traditional Army training program. Captain Jim Montano was given the staff task to put this together.

KCL brought in the Cadre (officer and NCO) to write the basics of a light Infantry battalion from individual to battalion/unit level. We dissected each level, wrote specific POT Task, Condition, and Standard on 3 x 5 cards, murder-boarded them and distributed them. The troops—or initially Cadre—then worked them and revised them as appropriate. Once accomplished/acceptable, they were passed to Montano to consolidate. This evolved into a completed Light Infantry ARTEP (Ranger) and was provided to FORSCOM/TRADOC to exercise.

The ARTEP concept was a TRADOC initiative that KCL both proposed to develop and to exercise using the Rangers as the guinea pigs. This was an outgrowth of the overall analysis of the Army training base/philosophy and its inherent weaknesses, eg: too ambiguous, not specific enough at all levels, too open to gaming, insufficiently taxing or clear, insufficiently reflective of Joint assets available and integration of internal/external support assets, too hard to develop specific training tasks, and focused on the wrong things.

As we built the ARTEP document for each level, we went to the woods and exercised the draft, eg: Squad/Plt/Co/Bn. For example, HHC went to the field during company ARTEP training and did Ranger Battalion HHC sort of stuff including movement, communications, reports, logistics operations, NDP [night defensive positions], etc.

Ultimately, we had a graduation draft ARTEP conducted at Fort Stewart by a team of outside evaluators (Ft Stewart and Ft Bragg). We then migrated to Fort Bragg, where we had our first real ARTEP conducted by the 82nd. The results and adjustments from this exercise were then forwarded to TRADOC as the final draft Light Infantry ARTEP. Supplements were developed for Rangers, Airborne and Air Assault. Hence, the Army had an ARTEP for all light Infantry units (recall that was the rage at the time due to transportability issues) with supplements for specific type units.

Kenneth Leuer—First Commander of the 1st Ranger Battalion—Biography

There are a lot of Lieutenant Colonels in the Army, but when a search was conducted for the right officer to stand up a new Ranger Battalion, only a selected few had the qualifications and gumption to get the job done.

When General Creighton Abrams decided he wanted a Ranger unit after Vietnam, he put in motion the logistics train that would lead to the formation of the 1st Battalion, 75th Infantry (Ranger). An important part of that train was picking the first commander. In 1974, then Lt. Colonel Kenneth Leuer was chosen to organize, train, and make ready for combat the first battalion of Rangers since WWII.

Major General (retired) Leuer has had a long and distinguished career by any standards. He is an inaugural member of the Ranger Hall of Fame, and has received the Order of Saint Maurice, Primicerius Level.

Leuer began his standards of high achievement early, becoming two-time state wrestling champion in Wayzata, Minnesota. He also earned All-State honors in football. At the University of Iowa he won the 1956 NCAA Wrestling Championship at 191 pounds, and took a Big Ten title as well.

His military service includes tours with the 82nd Airborne Division; 8th Division; 2nd Division; Special Forces; 173rd Airborne Brigade (Vietnam); Pentagon; 101st Airborne Division (battalion commander in Vietnam); Commander, 1st Battalion, 75th Infantry (Ranger); Commander, 1st Brigade, 24th Division; Chief of Staff and Assistant Division Commander, 4th Mechanized Division; Commanding General, 193rd Brigade; Assistant Commandant, United States Army Infantry Center; DCSOPS; J-3, G-3 (operations), Korea; Commanding General, 5th Mechanized Division; and Commanding General/Chief of Infantry, United States Infantry Center.

His many awards include the Combat Infantry Badge, Ranger Tab, Master Parachutist Badge, Special Forces Tab, two Bronze Stars and 13 Air Medals. There are many more.

Upon his retirement from active duty in 1988, Leuer became the President/CEO of Goodwill Industries until his second retirement in 1999.

As of 2006, he was still very active as President of the Executive Committee for the Ranger Hall of Fame and Chairs the Ranger Memorial Foundation. A brief version of his biography doesn't show the force and determination of the man who gave 32 years to the Army, serving 26 of those years as a Ranger.

What kind of a man was chosen to head the first Ranger Battalion since WWII? His record shows him to be a man of courage and determination, dedication and discipline—a man who would not quit until the job was done, and done right.

Kenneth Leuer

"Rangers are my number one love. Anything I can do for Rangers, I'd be happy to do that."

My first interview with the General was tape-recorded at his home in Midland, Georgia, in May 2004. He gave me much after that via email and further conversation. Although various topics are covered, his interview—with a few exceptions—remains intact in this section.

On Airborne in Germany

I was commissioned in 1956, and I came to Fort Benning for the Basic Officer's Course. At that time I was only signed up for two years, and I'd already taken a job at Minnesota Mining. I was going to do my two years and that's it. All my family served during WWI and WWII, and I was going to serve. While I was here I played football for the Basic Officer's Team, and we had some pretty good football players.

At the time of this interview he looked like he could still play.

I wound up being assigned to the 82nd Airborne Division. I did my Jump School at Fort Bragg [home of the 82nd]. At that time they were loading up the 11th Airborne Division in Europe, the 101st Airborne Division was back on the rolls, and of course, the 82nd. Both at Campbell and at Bragg they were running basic Airborne training.

I was in the 325th [of the 82nd]. Then the call went out that the 504th and the 505th were going to gyroscope to Europe. The 504th going in December of 1958, and the 505th in January 1959. We went to Germany. Two units of the 11th Abn came back to Fort Bragg to replace us. We went to the 8th Division in Mice [Germany]. So, basically, the 11th was deactivated.

Elements of the 11th became elements of the 1st Cavalry Division.

There was no Airborne left down there. They pulled out the 11th Division. The only Airborne left in Germany were the 504th and the 505th. We were part of V Corps.

We had an infamous individual in the Battle Group name of Tony Herbert. He was in the Korean War. Tony wrote a book, *Conquest To Nowhere*. Pretty bright guy. He convinced the Battle Group Commander, Colonel Mataxis, to activate a Ranger Platoon. Tony had taught in Ranger School, and he had some of the guys, the NCOs, in the Battle Group. So, he put together a "Ranger" platoon. Now, it was totally TDA [temporary], not authorized, non-supported. That came about in '60 and '61.

On Vietnam and How He Became 1st Battalion Commander

My first time in Vietnam was '67-'68. We put the 3/503 together at Fort Bragg and deployed to the 173rd in October 1967.

The 173rd (The Herd) was an independent brigade that came ashore at Vung Tau in 1965. The Herd ended up having some big-time fights.

At the same time we went, and on the same activation orders, the 1st Brigade of the 101st received its fourth battalion, which was the 3/506. The three-battalion brigades went to four battalions to give them greater maneuver capability. I was a Major, and I'd been in SF, and I was at Bragg, and this opening came available and I called Branch and said I want to get there. So, I got the job as the Battalion XO.

I went by ship [with 3/503, from San Francisco]. We got over there in late October 1967, and I came home in October of '68. That tour, I was XO of 3/503 for about six months and I was Aide to General Rossen for five months and he came back. I stayed as the Deputy Operations Officer in XXIV Corps for a month. They gave me the job of writing the Corps SOP. It was tough, but I got it done in a month.

When 1st Cav moved north right before Tet [January 1968], I left the 173rd and went north with General Rossen as his Aide, and we put together a new Corps up there. When the Cav got ready to go into Khe Sahn, we were with them almost daily in the coordination and preparation for the assault into Khe Sahn.

General William B. Rossen had been in command of the First Field Force in II Corps, and became Commander of the new XXIV Corps in the north.

The 101st was headquartered at [Camp] Eagle, outside of Hue/Phu Bai, and it was XXIV Corps. I was there when it [XXIV Corps] came on board. In 1968 when all hell broke loose with Tet, I had just moved down near Cam Rahn to be General Rossen's Aide. At that time he had FFI, which was really II Corps area, which was five Provinces.

Tet hit. The Marines had the responsibility for I Corps area. Things aren't going well. We're reeling, trying to figure out what the hell happened. We've still got cities that are occupied by the Viet Cong [Hue, for one].

The General gave a description of the situation and it boiled down to this: the Navy flew for the Marines and the Army was covered by the Air Force, but neither covered the other. There were big gaps and something had to be done. Force integration was necessary, and the XXIV Corps was created for that purpose

We put together a provisional corps to take over the upper two provinces. We had the 3rd MARDIV [Marines], the 1st Cav, 101st moved up. We had a couple of brigades. We had a brigade out of the American Division [23rd ID], another separate Marine Regiment moved up, and then we had the 1st and 2nd ARVN Divisions, plus some of the ARVN Rangers.

Westmoreland and the SecDef and the President said we need another Command and Control Headquarters up there. That was too many elements to be under that Marine commander.

So, they moved DEPCOMUSMACV [General Creighton Abrams] up, and he became the Commander of PCV—Provisional Corps, Vietnam. Abrams needed a Deputy and he chose Rossen, and I was his Aide, so up we go. I had just come out of the field and thought, my, there's a lot of stuff happening. I didn't know what was going on. It was Tet.

We moved in behind the III MAAF [Marines] and they moved further north. The PCV took over that headquarters complex at Hue/Phu Bai. We were provisional, so we got a Signal Unit from over there, and a Chemical Unit from over there, and other divisions were tasked with providing staff officers. It was a put-it-all-together kind of thing. Things like coordination of Air were worked out.

Leuer said before this was accomplished an Army unit could be in trouble and Navy/Marine aircraft, though closer, could not help. This did not bode well for soldiers in the field who depended on close air support. "You could have Army guys wrapped around the axle down there and the Marine pilots couldn't do anything to help."

Some of the supply problems were getting worked out. It was a major effort. But, here you've got this Army Provisional Corps subordinate to the Marine Command, but in many ways pretty much operating under COMUSMACV. Along about midsummer [1968], they named the Provisional Corps, Vietnam—the XXIV Corps.

Abrams had become COMUSMACV [when Westmoreland left]. Rossen went down and became the III MAAF commander for a month.

There were several instances of Army/Marine overlap during Vietnam.

Rossen and Abrams and Westmoreland and the officer who replaced Rossen [in the XXIV Corps], they'd all been classmates along the way. General Abrams and General Rossen were particularly close. It was a very neat time for Zeb Bradford and myself. He was Abrams' Aide and I was Rossen's Aide. At night, five, six, seven o'clock, whenever they'd rap it out at the headquarters, we'd go to the hooch where Abrams and Rossen were living and have a cocktail. They would talk.

Zeb and I got to listen [as Majors] to this interface about this commander and that commander, and it wasn't all talk behind the back, I can assure you. We also got to hear about what they thought was going to happen as a result of the President's announcement [LBJ—that he wouldn't run again], and Bobby Kennedy got assassinated. We were privy to all these discussions, and then we went to eat and sat at the same table, so the conversations continued.

The question was raised as to whether that exposure to Abrams was the beginning of the line Leuer followed to command of the 1st Ranger Battalion about six years later.

I don't know. That was 1968, and I was named to the 1st Batt in 1974, and I had not seen him in between. He was a very personable man. He was very hard, direct, and manly in appearance, but he was very personable. When we would be sitting around, having a beer or whatever and relaxing a bit, he would talk to me or talk to Zeb, and he wanted to know about me, about my background; my family.

He and General Rossen were talking about athletics. General Rossen said, "Did you know Ken was a national wrestling champion?" Abe says, well, no, tell me about that. I said, well, I won it in 1956 at the University of Iowa. I thought that was it but he pressed on. We must have spent the next 45 minutes talking about wrestling and what it did for me, what I thought it did, and what he thought athletics does for a person.

It is likely that Leuer's athletic prowess and fitness were added considerations in Abrams later decision to put him command of a unit that put fitness high on the list.

I said I didn't see him another time, but now that you bring it up…there but for the Grace of God go I. Let me tell you something here that was a defining moment in my life. 1972, I take command of 2/501 and immediately moved the battalion onto Firebase Tomahawk, south of Hue/Phu Bai. This firebase had been overrun the previous two years in April. And now it's April. So I moved in and the firebase was terrible. It deserved to be overrun every April.

We went to work on it, replaced the Foo Gas [like napalm in a drum], replaced the claymores. Most of them had the C-4 out of them.

Sometimes the soldiers would take the C-4 from a claymore and break it up into small pieces for cooking. It burns very hot and only a small amount will heat up your beenie-weenies.

Cleaned up the weeds and we're working our ass off. Then, here comes the division commander, and I get a call he's got Abrams. They land, and I showed them around the firebase. I've got guys out there working their butts off, putting in Tanglefoot, which are the wires close to the ground.

We had to stop firing [artillery] because the chopper came in, but I had them continue fire. We were firing in night defensive fires and close protective fires, and doing all the right things. So, we walked around where some of the troops were putting in Tanglefoot, and he says, Leuer, that Tanglefoot isn't tight enough. I said, I understand, Sir, but they're spinning it up. Okay Sir, Yes Sir, so I have to make sure that Tanglefoot is tight. We talked a little bit, he didn't say much else, and off he went. Well, the next week, here comes Corps Commander General Dolvin and the division commander.

At that time there were still 90 US fighting battalions in country, and why was I getting all this attention? Well, the division commander got off [the bird], and Dolvin, and I said, what can I show you? You were just here a week ago. They said, take us to that place where Abe said the Tanglefoot wasn't tight enough. I said okay and we walked up there. They looked at it, reached out, pulled on it, and Dolvin said, "Looks tight to me, Tom." Then he tried it and said, "Sure is." Well, that's it. Turned around, got back on their chopper and flew away. I thought, what the hell is that all about?

I'd been in command now six weeks, and things are starting to come together, and that firebase is in pretty good shape. The big anniversary date [for the attack] comes and nothing happens. Nothing.

Later, he found out why the Tanglefoot scenario.

Tom Tarpley, the division commander, had gone south, and he was down at IV Corps doing some work down there. He came up to say goodbye to me. Tarpley looked around, talked to the troops, and then he said he wanted to talk to me. We went in. We didn't have much. I'd already pulled everything into the perimeter at Hue/Phu Bai, and we'd already turned Camp Eagle over to the ARVN. Well, he sat down and popped a coke, and we talked about a few things. Then he said, when you go back to Campbell you're going to be working under a division commander and he's kind of a hothead, so don't let him bother you. Then he said, one final thing. Remember the Tanglefoot situation? I said, yes Sir, that's often bothered me. He said let me tell you what really happened. Firebase Maryanne had gone down about three months earlier. That was in the Americal Division. It had been attacked, run over, and nothing was left. There had been a brigade commander on that firebase, an assistant division commander, and a division commander on that firebase. None of them took corrective action. So, Tarpley says, Abe got back to Saigon and he felt so concerned because the senior man is always responsible—and he was the senior man on that firebase—and he left without making sure something was corrected. So, he got back and called the corps commander, Dolvin, and he called Tarpley. That's why Dolvin and Tarpley came a week later.

Abe said, give Leuer one week and go out, and if that Tanglefoot isn't tight, relieve him. So, you say, there but for the Grace of God. I don't know if that stuck in his head. I think General Bernie [Bernard] Rogers was the DISPER [head of Army personnel], and my file was sent to the DISPER who chopped [8-10 files] to the final three [candidates for command of the 1st Ranger Battalion]. Bernie Rogers told me later that when he walked in, Abe said, "Who should it be?" Rogers said, "My number one choice is Lt. Colonel Leuer."

Leuer said he believes Rogers' nomination was the main reason he was chosen. Rogers later gained four-star rank and became Army Chief of Staff.

I was the last one on the aircraft from Hue/Phu Bai. That would have been around the end of March 1972.

The 2/501 closed out the remaining 101st elements when they left Vietnam. Leuer went on to command both the 1st and 2nd of the 501st.

I came back in early April of '71, and came home in '72. Took command right after I got there [Vietnam] of 2/501. I was to be the first battalion commander designated to command for a year instead of six months. I commanded 2/501 for a year in Vietnam, and my Battalion Task Force brought the 101st colors back to [Ft. Campbell]. After we got back to Campbell, the 101st had absorbed the 173rd, so some of the units had to go. The 2/501 Colors were deactivated and we took over 1/501 Colors.

On Ranger Training and 1st Battalion Train-up

I went to Ranger School in 1962. I was back here [Benning] for the Advanced Course, and during the course I signed up for Ranger School. As you can see, this is my guidon [which he showed us]. I was Honor Graduate of my class [as a Captain].

Class 9-62 was the last course of the fiscal year. We probably had about 50 Captains in it because there were two Advanced Courses that graduated about the same time. I graduated the Advanced Class in the morning, and that afternoon I reported in to Ranger School. There were probably 20 or 30 Lieutenants and 40 or 50 Non-Coms.

Our TAC Officer's name was Hal Jordan. He was a fine man.

There was not an RTB [Ranger Training Brigade] at that time. It was a Ranger Department, just as the Airborne was an Airborne Department. It wasn't until I came back as the Assistant Commandant, and then the Commandant [of Benning] that we changed it to a training brigade, and the Airborne Department to a numbered battalion. I really wanted to make the Ranger Training Brigade the second regiment of the 75th, and have the 4th, 5th, and 6th Battalions, which we have lineage on, and I didn't get it.

At the time of this interview he was trying again to bring the second regiment into reality.

The questioning turned to the status of incoming recruits for the battalion.

One of the requirements for selection of the officers and NCOs is that they have the Tab before I would even look at them. The arrangements I made with MILPERCEN [Military Personnel Center] were that they would nominate. I could interview. They'd send them in. Accept or not. They would send me files and I would say, send these guys in for an interview. If they sent someone in and a couple of weeks later [they didn't make it]...no paperwork, no hard feelings, send them back and get on with their business. That arrangement lasted for about eight months.

We gathered most of our Cadre here at Benning—officers and NCOs, and we had some enlisted. At that time there was an enlistment option for Ranger School. A lot of these young men coming in were very fine soldiers, but they weren't ready for Ranger School. So they would fail Ranger School, and the Sergeant Major would take a look at them. We picked up probably 40 or 50 of those young individuals and kept them in the battalion. Six months or a year later, we'd send them back to Ranger School and they were outstanding students.

We had a two-pronged attack. We had officers coming in, NCOs coming in for interviews, and if we kept them they stayed, the family to follow. They didn't follow here; they went directly to Fort Stewart [eventual home of the 1st Battalion in southeastern Georgia, near Savannah].

I made probably eight trips, went to installations. Fort Campbell, Fort Hood, places like that. Not very successful, I might add. I went to the 101ˢᵗ first, because that was my combat unit. General Berry was the CG. He was a favorite of mine. He was the ADC of the 101ˢᵗ, and he and I got along very well when I was a battalion Colonel, so I thought that was the place to go.

We got there and he said, "What are you looking for?" I said, "Top-notch soldiers." He said, "That's what I've got, and that's what I'm keeping."

As a Brigadier General, Sidney Berry ran the fight for Firebase Ripcord in 1970. He was Acting Division Commander of the 101ˢᵗ while Major General Hennessey was away.

I can understand that. What I can't understand is, we had an Army of 1.4 million men at that time—troops—mostly men. I was going to get 600, and I was hearing stories and people were telling me, you're getting the cream of the Army. You take the best 600 people out of it and we've got nothing left out of 1.4 million soldiers?

Our next stop was at XVIII Airborne Corps. Having been in the 82ⁿᵈ a couple of times, I thought, well, this is good home ground. Out of those two trips, the 82ⁿᵈ and 101ˢᵗ, Fort Bragg, Fort Campbell, I think we got five people.

So the Sergeant Major and I loaded up and we went back to DISPER and said, it ain't working. Folks aren't letting anybody out to interview, so we can't get a line on anyone. That's why we started this program where they [DISPER] nominate and we interview. But, we still kept sending teams out to other installations.

Once I went back to the Pentagon and told them what my problems were, there were some very serious back channels run out. Cooperation in the field improved tremendously. I think it came from the Chief of Staff's office [Abrams].

So, everybody is coming in here and we're training very hard. We're running, we're shooting, and I'm implementing this Performance Oriented Training, so I've got people doing task analysis, tearing a mission apart for its critical elements. [They were] developing the training for each of those elements and the standard that you have to meet in order to be successful at the top. I'm training Cadre to do this, I'm learning to do it, and we're all working together. We're looking at it and asking, will it work? Will it win with that? Because Silver Medals in combat don't do much for you. That's second place.

We were developing critical tests for some critical missions. As we developed this we hired some people to type and print this stuff on 3x5 cards and 5x8 cards so every leader trainer, down to and including Fire team Leaders, had a set of the task, condition, and standards that they're responsible for training. Everybody is training to the same standards.

We were doing all that here while we were filling with Cadre and with other troops. Most of the troops other than Cadre, the lower troops [Privates, Specialists], were being sent directly to Fort Stewart and given a reporting date just a couple of days before we're due to jump in.

On 1 July 1974, we loaded three C-130s here and jumped into Fort Stewart. We jumped about 180 men. That was the official welcome of the 1ˢᵗ of the 75ᵗʰ to Fort Stewart.

On the 13ᵗʰ of July I moved the battalion to Tac X, a big training area deep in the swamp. It had been used during the Vietnam era as a helicopter training area. They had some barracks-type buildings out there.

We went full-strength by 1 August. They let me go 10 percent over. We trained very hard. Everything was live fire. Everything was live. If they set a claymore, it'd damn well better be a claymore going off. If it said Foo Gas, it'd better be Foo Gas. If it said C-4, it'd better be C-4.

Foo Gas is a petroleum product

I don't think we fired 50 blanks in six months. That's the way it had to be. And nobody hurt. You don't train to hurt people. If you *don't* train, you're going to hurt people!

Once a month we would pull in, clean everything up, have a day of athletics. We called it Banner Day. We had a banner that was made up of the six colors of Merrill's six combat teams. Whoever won Banner Day got to carry that on their guidon for a month. It was a big thing. We had everything from flag football to softball to sprints, boxing, judo—we did the whole thing. Boxing was usually the feature event that would finish out the day. We had a big picnic lunch and then gave them three or four days off. Get out of there. Go.

We always had a parade each month. Big, full-blown pass-in-review parade. So, we were doing the whole thing. We were doing rough, tough training, military courtesy parades, athletics, and families involved. It became a very close group.

We had two qualifying road marches, although we did a lot of marching. The first one was before we left Benning to go to Fort Stewart. It was a 20-mile road march to be accomplished in six hours with a 90-pound ruck on your back, and be in formation. Those that did not make that did not accompany the battalion any longer. Later on, after we were at Stewart and had trained-up, our final FTX [field training exercise] before being declared mission-ready was another 20-mile road march—after we'd been in the field for 12 days. Again, in six hours or less, in formation, with 90 pounds on your back. Those who didn't make it [were gone].

On History, Uniforms, and Insignia

I had a free reign to do anything I wanted to do, and the money to do it with. After we decided we were going to be Rangers and not anything else, we got into the Ranger heritage pretty deeply. Did a lot of work with the Department of Heraldry—the little old ladies in tennis shoes up there—but they're wonderful. I charged the Sergeant Major in maintaining the lineage and history of the battalion, and that every Ranger in that battalion had to know the fundamentals of the history of that battalion of the Rangers. If I found one that didn't, he and I would do the road run, and I set the distance. He [SMAJ] didn't like to run. He did a marvelous job. New troops would come in, within 24 hours I would see him some place—indoctrination time.

The only resistance I had was from Jim Bowers, the head of the Ranger Department. Phil Piazza [of Merrill's Marauders] had given their Colors and lineage to the Ranger Department [after the Special Forces gave them back]. I wrote a letter to Colonel Bowers asking if he would turn the Colors over, and he would not. I then asked the Marauders, Phil Piazza and another man…to get the Colors. Well, Bowers balked on it. So, finally, General Tarpley [CG of Benning] came to visit. When Bowers balked again, I went to the CG and 24 hours later Bowers flew in and we had a little ceremony.

The first thing we had to decide was what are we going to wear on our heads? Well, you can't be a Ranger without a beret. So, what color should it be? Well, we'll wear what we're authorized to wear. I said, "What are the Rangers authorized to wear, Sergeant Major?" He said, "The black beret." I said, "Find me the document."

Turns out they wore the black beret in Korea, in Vietnam; the Ranger Department was wearing the black beret—no authorization, ever.

For more information on the black beret, see the section with that title.

The first authorization in the history of the United States Army for the wearing of the black beret was in 1974, and it's printed in the 1975 change to the regulations. You got to buy this stuff. You can't have the troops buying it. You can't get DA money if it's not authorized.

The following are excerpts from a tape recording Leuer made at the Ranger Memorial.

Another item of interest in the history of the 1st of the 75th involved establishment of the uniform and other items of dress. We, in the 1st Battalion, had the opportunity to put the footprint down. In doing so, we went to Darby's Rangers of WWII and chose the shoulder patch you wear today, the scroll, which they established. As we moved along in developing the flash that we wear on our beret, we went to Merrill's Marauders. Merrill had identified his units as combat teams by colors. Those colors are found in the flash today. The green, the red, the khaki, the orange, the white, and the blue.

The uniform we chose was a camouflage uniform. In 1974 the BDU uniform as we know it today did not exist. The "cammies"...were worn in Vietnam by the Long Range Reconnaissance Patrol units. That's basically where the modern day Ranger uniform came from.

On The Abrams Charter and Its Implementation

There are several examples of "parts" of the Abrams Charter to be found on the Internet, claiming to be excerpts of the written document. Here General Leuer dispels all such notions.

There is no such thing as a written Abrams Charter. I'll tell you exactly how it happened. At the time I was selected, I was assigned here at Fort Benning. I had finished Senior Service College in July 1973, and I came to Benning and immediately went to Florida State [University] to study a new approach to training called "Performance Oriented Training." At Florida State they had a Department of Educational Technology, and some of the gurus of Performance Oriented Training convened there. There were several of us there to learn.

I came back and I was to implement Performance Oriented Training and train the faculty here at Fort Benning. They gave me the resources to put together the program and the Instructors and all the rest of it. We started the training and it was tough, tough, tough. It's hard work defending the standards and meeting the standards.

So, I'm working on all of that and the word comes that my name is up for Commander of the Ranger Battalion. That would be my fourth battalion to command. I said I really hope I get it. That's a real challenge, because the Army is on its ass at this time, and we need to do something. Right after it was announced, the Commander of TRADOC, General William Depuy, [came down]. He had a division in Vietnam and was just a splendid man. He was also DISOPS [Division Support Operations].

I never got to see him until late afternoon. I was told; General DePuy wants to talk to you in private. Meet him at the airfield at 4 o'clock or whatever. So, I'm down there at 3:30 and I'm pacing back and forth, and he's running late when he comes in.

The two men went inside—alone. From that point on, Leuer said no one heard their conversation. Words in quotation marks are direct quotes as Leuer remembers them.

He says, "Well, what do you think is expected of you?" I said, "Well, I've heard we're supposed to be the best-trained Infantry in the world, and that's all I heard." We were supposed to set the example of what the Army should be as we pulled out of the doldrums of Vietnam.

He said, "That's about right. You have a challenge, Ken." I thought, "Hey, that's not bad. He's calling me Ken." If he was pissed I might be Leuer.

[DePuy said] "Our Army is in the worst shape it's been in a century. What Abe expects..."

Now, there was no tape recorder, there was nobody taking notes, I've got a little 3x5 card, but I'm listening, I'm not writing. Everything that exists that you see as the Abrams Charter came out of that room in my head.

People have added to it, taken from it, whatever. The things I remember; it'll be the Gold Medal Infantry of the world; they'll be able to do more with their hands and weapons than any other Infantry unit in the world. Wherever they go they'll be recognized for their superior excellence. There will be no hooligans or bums in that organization. If there are it will be disbanded immediately. If, in any way, you disgrace the United States Army or the US as a nation, the commander alone will bear the consequences. There will be a Creed that they will develop, that they will live by, train by, and fight by.

Later in the interview the General remembered another part of the Charter, a significant part involving NCOs.

Because of my background and experience, I was absolutely positive that if this was going to be successful...because another part of the Abrams Charter was that members of this organization will go throughout the Army and be the example of professionalism in how to train, how to live and how to fight. And a lot of them have. We've had Sergeant Majors of the Army. We've had all of that.

The NCOs bought in right from the start. It wasn't, well, let's see if he can prove that he means what he says. They got in and got their hands dirty and made things happen. The success of the Rangers today, the success they have spread throughout the Army, is a direct result of the professionalism of the NCOs in that first battalion.

They stuck to the standards, they supported the standards, and they trained their troops to reach those standards. We had no hooligans or drunks. I had the battalion about a year, and I think the tally showed about 120 people that came, signed in, didn't make it, and left. Some were good people—they just couldn't handle the physical end of it. This was Olympic-level training.

The NCOs played such a key part in this whole thing and they still do. If it weren't for them, it wouldn't have worked. That's not to belittle the officers. They did a great job. But the officers could do officer work, too. But certainly they were directly involved.

First Sergeant Bonifacio Romo, A Company, was one of Leuer's favorites. "He was a model," he said. "Ask him if he had a hand in how the troops were trained and worked. He did. He did a great job."

On Ranger Hall of Fame and Ranger Memorial

I'm always very careful to make sure they're separate. We don't mix one into the other.

They came on line together. I was not the President [EC, RHOF] until 1996. They both came into being around 1990 [first induction was 1992], and we really got moving around 1992, and of course we dedicated the Memorial in 1994.

I think there are about 50,000 living, walking, talking people who could be called Ranger out there who could get a stone in the Memorial and say they are a part of this great brotherhood.

Project research shows more like 80,000 Rangers out there. See the section, "Just How Many Rangers Are There?"

Lt. General (ret) William "Buck" Kernan took the reins of the RHOF in early 2007.

Ron Rokosz

Brigadier General Rokosz was a Captain in 1974 when he took the position of original commander of B Company, 1st Ranger Battalion. He is also probably the first, and maybe the only, man to command all three Ranger Battalions and be a part of Regimental HQ as Deputy Commander under Wayne Downing. This interview was conducted via a series of emails in June 2004.

I was a Captain and had completed the Advanced Course at Ft. Benning, then was assigned as an Instructor on a tactics committee there when the Army announced the formation of 1/75th. I recall that I was out at one of the ranges and someone had a copy of the Army Times. The headline read, "Army forms Ranger Battalion." I commented, "Wow, how would you like to get a chance to be in that?" Went back to the offices and there was a call from the Infantry Branch asking me if I was interested. At the time, Lt. Colonel Leuer was in some staff position there at Fort Benning, so I was able to interview directly with him. I was selected as B Company Commander.

I went to Ranger School right after IOBC in 1969. At the time, Vietnam was raging and only those scheduled for Airborne units got a jump slot. I did not go to Jump School until I went to Benning for IOAC. So, when I was selected for 1/75, I had a total of five jumps! Made life interesting as all the NCOs were Master Parachutists, and most of my Lieutenants were Senior Parachutists.

My recollection is that the initial selection was made of battalion staff officers, company commanders, CSMs and some senior NCOs—First Sergeants and some E-7s. Not sure of the number, but it was a relatively small group initially brought on board.

We had a headquarters building out in the Ranger training area. I remember being shown the briefing papers from General Abrams (then Chief of Staff), explaining the rationale for the formation of the battalion. In short, they wanted the Army to showcase an elite unit. Believe a lot of this was in response to the malaise that fell over the Army at the end of the Vietnam War. We began a training program there at Benning—lots of tough PT and, especially for the officers, classroom work on Performance Oriented Training. Believe we were the vanguards of that in the Army at the time.

Task-Conditions-Standards. Later, at Stewart, we took the battalion's missions and broke them down into sub-missions, all the way down to the squad level, with task, condition and standards for all. There was an entire wall in the Battalion S-3 office covered with 3x5 cards displaying

all these tasks and sub-tasks.

I recall that Leuer gave the company commanders a stack of officer files for Lieutenants that had been selected, and the four of us (company commanders) sat down together and decided who would go to which company. The most unusual thing I recall is that we advertised Army-wide for volunteers at the lower ranks. Each company commander headed a recruiting team that went to different installations, made presentations to those interested, then personally interviewed each volunteer—anyone who had any disciplinary problem at all was discarded. So, the initial personnel who manned 1/75 were all quality people, all with prior experience in some unit—down to the lowest PFC. I headed the team that went out to Fort Lewis.

I recall the move to Fort Stewart. It was the sleepiest, quietest post in the Army. I am sure Stewart was selected because Bo Callaway was the Secretary of the Army at the time, and he was from Georgia. We jumped into Fort Stewart, and then made a road march into the main post on our arrival. The period at Stewart was when we received all the troops for the battalion and went through an incredible training program, lots of field time, road marching, tough PT, etc.

It was at Stewart that the Ranger Creed came about and it became engrained in the battalion.

Ken Leuer set the tone in terms of professional conduct and I think that was one of the hallmark distinctions about the battalion during that period. The one thing that Leuer did that set the tone for 1/75 for years to come was to reinforce what today is referred to as "quiet professionalism." That term is so overused, but Leuer meant it. We were never allowed to use

the word "leg"—absolutely forbidden, as we were to show respect for all Army units, regardless of branch, etc. So, no one was allowed to use any "leg" cadences when we did PT. We were constantly reminded that our personal behavior was absolutely important, and that no ill discipline would be permitted. As a result, wherever we went, people would comment on how well behaved Rangers were. For example: Right after we moved to Fort Stewart, two young soldiers threw some firecrackers out of a car in Hinesville over the 4th of July weekend. The sheriff called Leuer, said it was no big deal, but asked him to remind soldiers this could be dangerous. The two soldiers were immediately thrown out of the battalion and reassigned.

This level of personal responsibility was so ingrained that we let the entire battalion go for a day in Juarez, (or Tijuana—not sure) and there were zero incidents.

We went to Norfolk for amphibious training sometime in the first year. We were to occupy barracks that were being vacated by Marines who had trained ahead of us. We dismounted convoy vehicles and formed up in battalion formation in front of the barracks. The battalion was "at attention," while there were Marines above us, pouring beer on us out of open windows. Not a soldier moved in the formation. Lt. Colonel Stang came up, saw what was happening, and went and dealt with the Marine Commander.

Arthur (Art) Stang ...later dropped dead from a heart attack on a parade field at Fort Bragg when he was Chief of Staff. This prompted the Army to take a close look at annual physicals, especially cholesterol levels for senior officers.

Bill Spies—Abrams and the Creation of 1ˢᵗ Ranger Battalion TO&E

The TO&E (Table of Organization and Equipment), which is the blueprint for the organization, was largely put together by the Action Officer, Major William Spies. In an email answer to questions about that time, Spies outlined the specifics of creating the Ranger TO&E.

An Action Officer—in staff parlance—is the officer tasked to draft and staff a project or a study, etc—such as construct a TO&E.

I was assigned to the Ranger Department in 1973. The Deputy Director assigned that duty to me. I had a close associate from the Combat Developments Department, USAIS, Sergeant Major Jim "Snake" Collier, who assisted me in drafting the TO&E.

SMJ Collier had been an advisor to the ARVN 81ˢᵗ Airborne Ranger Battalion (the only Airborne Rangers in the ARVN, all others were either just Airborne or Rangers.) He was an experienced Ranger-qualified paratrooper. He later became the CSM of the Ranger Department while I was wearing the two hats of Chief of the Benning Phase and the Assistant Director, Ranger Department. Jim was inducted into the Ranger Hall of Fame just this year [2003].

Our guidance was to form the organization for a Ranger Battalion consisting of 650 men, including approximately 30 officers (this was over strength). There was an outline of both conventional and classified missions that the battalion must be able to accomplish.

We started in late November or early December of 1973, and had a deadline of January 1, 1974.

I then was tasked to draft and staff the first Field Manual—Ranger Battalion Training. In that the USAIS came under TRADOC (training and doctrine), they had to sign off on our efforts first. Then we went to FORSCOM for their agreement, and FORSCOM took it to the Air Force, Navy, and Marines.

Much of the following information was obtained in a taped interview with Spies.

He [Abrams] said, and I can't quote it exactly, but I'm pretty damn close to it, he said, the reason I'm going to have a Ranger Battalion and not a Special Forces Battalion, not a Special Operations Battalion, is because every time I saw something outstanding happen down there in Vietnam, a Ranger was doing it. This might have been the first week in December 1973, at TRADOC HQ in Fort Monroe.

It was an information briefing hosted by General Bill Depuy, CG of TRADOC. General Abrams, Army Chief of Staff, and General Kerwin, CG of FORSCOM and a few others were there. Colonel Hatch of USAIS Combat Developments and Major General Tarpley were there representing Fort Benning. I was only a listener in the audience, not a player in that meeting. I was tasked to go, as I was told that I would be appointed the Action Officer to draft the TO&E. In the later meetings I was a player.

What came into my mind at the time was, "Good God, what if those Ranger Instructors had done less than they did? What if they put out mediocre Rangers?"

Abrams came to Fort Benning to see Spies during the formulation of the TO&E.

That was the only time I ever got any briefing from him directly. At that time, it had not been decided…we still thought this battalion might be formed at [Fort] Bragg and become what eventually turned into the Delta Force.

General Abrams wanted a Ranger unit as an alternative to Special Forces. He was (reportedly) not overly fond of SF at that time. The Green Berets were in a low spot just then, having lost most of the core group (pre-1970) to injury, death, or rotation in Vietnam. Abrams and others apparently felt SF wasn't up to the tasks designed for the Ranger concept, but were rather considered more a long-deep-cover organization.

Steve Hawk

Hawk was an original member of the 1st Ranger Battalion in 1974, an Honor Graduate of Ranger School class 6-75. He later became an RI at several training spots across the country, most notably at the Mountain Ranger Camp. As of late 2006, he was Chairman of the US Mountain Ranger Association. The following is the result of our second interview, conducted in his home in Lumpkin County, Georgia in the late summer of 2004. Hawk detailed the train-up of the 1st, and several other things.

Recruited by First Sergeant Neal Gentry in 1974 right out of Airborne School, Hawk and 13 others were given the option to immediately attend Ranger School or go to the Ranger Battalion for a while, then go to school. The rationale was the young men were not ready for such a hard school yet, and had a good chance of failing. Hawk was the only one to choose the battalion—and some much-needed experience—and the other 12 failed Ranger School.

When the battalion got there [Fort Stewart] in July '74, we ended up the first two weeks just collecting people. It seemed like there was a flood of people. I was a Private, so I got assigned the duty of making sure everybody got to their bunks and they got to see the Sergeant Major or the Colonel. I was the highest-ranking E-2 there. Two weeks later I got promoted to PFC. We got all our jungle fatigues; we got our black berets.

Every morning it was PT. I mean we PT'd our butts off. Mike Martin was our First Sergeant [B Company]. By August we were semi-full. We started doing actual training. Basically it was a Ranger School.

Performance-Oriented Training was just coming into use, changing much about the way Rangers learned, and were subsequently graded. For more on this, see interviews with Ken Leuer and Keith Nightingale.

There were these long wooden boxes, in fact they were 90mm recoilless rifle ammo crates, and in these crates were cards. They would pull a card out and you would train on that. It had everything and anything you were supposed to be able to do as a Ranger.

Pull a card out, okay, Task, Condition, and Standard, and this is it. From July 20, while we were filling, we were going over these [cards], but what we're doing is not training on them, but testing them to see if there's anything that has to be re-written. So, when you're the only Private in the company, you get to do all these things while the NCOs stand around and watch and make decisions.

Hawk hated Individual Movement to Contact, known on the card as Individual Movement Technique (IMT). "I'm up—he sees me—I'm down. I IMT'd up and down that field I'll bet a hundred times while they told me things like, "Roll left instead of right".

In the beginning everybody had to know everything about Ranger history. We were more concerned—because we drew our lineage from Merrill's Marauders—that we know mostly that. We knew about the WWII Battalions, the Korean War Companies, the Vietnam Companies, but our history was the Marauders. GALAHAD.

The Coat of Arms [75th Infantry, Ranger] you didn't describe as blue and green. The 75th crest was described as a shield, quartered, vert and azure, with the sun of China in the left hand quadrant, upper, and the star of Burma in the lower right. The star represented the working relationship in that theater of operations. The star of China has 13 points, which represents the 13 colonies of China. The lightning bolt, which goes from upper right to lower left, represents the quick-strike characteristics of the Rangers.

The lightning bolt is also used to signify a bastard unit—one with no parent unit.

You had to know that, on January 30, 1974 that General Order, I believe it was 131, was the order that started the Ranger Battalion. You had to know that General Creighton Abrams was the father of the original Ranger Battalion. These are things you had to learn in the first area.

The first actual training exercise when we left the main cantonment area was at Tac X, which is the northern part of Fort Stewart. That was when we had kind of weeded through the wannabees and the ones who really wanted to be there. We went out there and trained. We trained in everything. We had PFCs calling in artillery. We had Privates calling in airdrops. It wasn't the NCOs, the E-6 and E-7, who were calling in aerial resupply. It was the Privates and PFCs standing on the ground, saying, "With one bundle, stand by. With one bundle, execute, execute, execute."

They wanted to train everybody to take the leadership position, so that if somebody got knocked down or was killed, the next guy could step up. Everybody had to know everybody else's job.

I knew how to use the Prick (PRC)-77. I knew how to use the 74-Bravo. These were the radios that were TO&E to the Ranger Battalion. We also had the PRT-6, and the PRR-4, which were the little squad radios. The receiver clipped on the side of your helmet and the transmitter clipped onto your web gear, and it was a piece of crap. If you couldn't see the guy, you couldn't talk to him—it was a line-of-sight radio. The best thing to do with it, because it was so scratchy, was to write a note on it and throw it at him. That was the only way you could talk to him. He'd throw it back, hopefully.

We had numbers on our helmets and little scopes on our M16s and we had play war. We trained in radios, we trained in rappelling, Australian [out of helicopters], we learned how to tie knots. We learned how to do medical evacuation. We learned first aid that you would not believe. I took first aid in Basic, in Infantry training, but I'm talking a whole new type of first aid. First aid where you learn to do sutures, where you knew how to handle a gunshot wound or major burns. We had to go through from the point where the injury happened to the medevac. In several cases we actually had to do real live medevacs. There was a guy there had his knife on his web belt the wrong way and ended up stabbing himself in the femoral artery. So, here we go, we've got first aid training—stop the bleeding, protect the wound, treat for shock, then medevac.

Now, your cooks, your clerks, all went to the field. Nobody stayed back. The First Sergeant's rucksack was just as heavy as the Private's. Colonel Leuer's rucksack was just as heavy. Everywhere we went we road-marched, or we ran. We did a lot of running. We never slacked off on PT. PT was just an every day thing—you got up and you ran your five miles—and it was five miles, it wasn't four-and-a-half. Five miles was the minimum.

With Colonel Leuer you could pretty much tell how far you were going to run on Mondays when you had battalion PT. The whole battalion ended up on the parade field and you could tell how far you were going to run by the attitude of his dog [an Irish Setter]. If the dog came out and sat next to the PT stand you were going to do your daily dozen [calisthenics], and then you were going to run five miles. But, if that dog came out and ran up and down the ranks and was just…spirited, then the Colonel was going to come out spirited, and you might run 10 miles, or 12 miles.

We actually killed the dog. Not with knives or anything, it died on a run. We ran the dog to death. It was so foggy in Fort Stewart one morning we ran, we got lost on a tank trail, and I know we ran at least 20 miles because I went out and drove the damn thing.

That was battalion PT and Lt. Colonel Leuer was right there with them. "He was hard core."

When reviewing this section General Leuer replied to Hawk's description of events with this:
Ken Leuer

The dog story—not exactly correct, but a good story. The correct version—the dog was a golden retriever. Ran every Monday, my day to lead PT with the Rangers. Other days I would join a company, but only follow the unit. The dog—Dazee—loved being with the Rangers. The day in question, weather was terrible with fog. I always measured the route and ran it on Sunday, the day before PT. Folks got wise after a time and would watch all day Sunday to see where I was going, but for the day in question we missed a turn and were into the second hour of running. I was not sure where we were, as we could not see over 20 feet. The dog stopped at one of the ditches—filled with water from the night before—and she fell partially in. About a platoon of soldiers, I was told, broke formation to rescue her. I did not see the incident because of the fog. Dazee died and was buried on the farm I grew up on in Minnesota.
Back to Hawk.

We were getting people in, but we were losing them just as fast, NCOs and enlisted. Because of PT, because of "we gotta do what? I gotta get my hair cut every week, my boots gotta be shined?"

A lot of those guys just came back from Vietnam and they weren't going to spit-shine a pair of jungle boots. It just wasn't in their nature. There was an inspection on something just about every day.

Tac X finished up the end of August, and we all went back to the cantonment area. Now we're into September of '74, and we're continually training. We did small boat movements [on local rivers]. We hadn't been out of Georgia yet. From July to December we never left Georgia. We trained. We had very little time off. Saturdays we worked. Usually half-day and it was a full-dress inspection [or some kind of inspection].

Sundays you actually got off, and that was the time you spent in front of the TV that picked up one TV station, and you shined boots, or you played with your uniforms, or you cleaned your weapons. If your weapon wasn't clean on Saturday, then you spent Sunday cleaning it.

Being an M60 gunner, my weapon was hard to clean. I've thrown a lot of rounds. We shot continuously. When the Army was cutting back on all the training the Ranger Battalion was training more. We live-fired constantly. They would give you a .45 [semi-auto pistol]. As a gunner I carried a .45. In the Regular Army, with a .45, you might shoot a hundred rounds a year. They would take us out there with a case of .45 ammo per person. That's a lot of rounds. When your thumb wasn't tired loading that magazine, your arm was tired from holding that .45 up. You'd shoot your target and qualify, then you'd shoot someone else's target, or you'd try to cut a pine tree down. You were just shooting, all the time.

Hand grenades—we got so many hand grenades to throw that after a while you just sat on your ass on the berm, pulled the pins, and throw them over your shoulder, over the berm, just to get rid of the damn things because you didn't want to turn anything in.

M72A2 LAWS, M203 grenade launchers—everybody had to shoot every weapon. I knew how to fire the 90 [recoilless rifle]. I knew how to set up the mortars and fire them [60mm]. I knew how to fire the sniper rifles. They trained us on the M79 [grenade launcher], but they transferred over to the 203 [grenade launcher slung under an M16, and now under an M4].

The 81mm mortar of WWII days was considered way too heavy to jump. In those days everything had to go out the door [of the airplane]. The 90mm was the only thing we bundled out of the door. We had to learn how to do that—how to set up a door bundle for a 90 and for things we needed.

We jumped all the time. We jumped every conceivable time an aircraft was available to us. I got more jumps in that first six months than most guys get in a 10-year span. We jumped C-130s the most, but we also jumped C-7 Caribous out of Dobbins Air Force Base. The bad part about the Caribou is that the floor, the ramp, is plywood, and it travels at such a steep angle that when you step onto the ramp you're gone. You'll slip if you're not careful. The best thing to do is when you get to the hinge on a Caribou, just run out, because you're going to go out anyway.

I can remember one time we were jumping, and the aircraft were landing, and we were also doing air traffic control. You were learning how to set up an airfield. To have a PFC talking to an aircraft commander about how to land…

December comes around and it's ORTT [Operational Readiness Training Test]. We went through that and it was cold, it was nasty, and we completed that test with no problem.

Except that it was cold and nasty and the future of the Rangers depended on the outcome.

Rokosz [Ron Rokosz was B Company commander] was bad about gassing people. Every chance he got, Rokosz would throw a CS [tear gas] grenade at you. I don't care where…if you were…in the slit trench, Rokosz would throw a grenade at you. You better have your gas mask with you. You'd be eating lunch; he'd gas you. You'd be walking through a wooded area and he'd have it already powdered. He'd come through in a helicopter and spread the crystals. So you'd be walking through the bush and all of sudden your eyes would start watering.

It had rained three days before, just straight, and my gas mask filters had gotten wet, so you can't breathe through them. So we were walking through this area that had crystals everywhere and everybody put on their masks. I put mine on, flared it, tried it, I couldn't breathe. I yanked it off and just walked through the crystals.

Hawk tried to tell me that he got to the point where CS was "just a strange cologne." Okay.

After we passed the ORTT, everybody started going to training [outside]. People were being sent to schools left and right—specialty schools—Pathfinder, NCO Academy. They were being sent to Ranger School.

The 1ˢᵗ Battalion, as today's battalions, was not comprised of 100 percent Ranger-qualified soldiers. Also, after ORTT, everybody went on block leave and came back in January.

We had a lot of dignitaries come through. General Abrams would come down. I remember when DePuy came down. When he came, Hog [Roger] Brown was my Platoon Leader, and we set up claymores to do a live-fire demonstration for him. Well, Hog didn't like the idea of the claymores being that far out, because the gooks would turn them around on you.

The claymore mine is actually a recoilless-type weapon, detonating frontally with 700 steel balls, which creates a back blast that can be lethal. The protective range behind the weapon should be about 50 feet. During the Vietnam War enemy fighters would sometime sneak up to an American position and turn the claymores around toward their owners, then make noise so the soldiers would set them off—in their own faces.

So, he wanted the claymores just barely out in front of your berm. [How far?] Uh, barely. You're in the back blast zone. We're talking 15 feet in front of your berm. I can remember setting off a claymore and having it blow the whole damn berm back in my hole with me. That Georgia sand, you know?

DePuy came down, and Hog went around and collected up all the spaghetti and beef chunks C-rations he could find. So when DePuy came down to have dinner with us, to talk to the troops, Hog gave him spaghetti and beef chunks. That was the nastiest…it was the only meal of C-rations that you'd want to eat at night [so you couldn't see it].

So we were sitting there and Hog was chewing. He constantly had a chaw of Red Man or Beechnut or something in his jaw. He was heating up his C-rations over a heat-tab, stirring it up, and he spits. Well, when he spits this big old brown glob of stuff lands in his spaghetti and beef chunks. Hog just stirs this slop up in his food and then he goes to eating.

Hawk related several stories of his early time with the 1ˢᵗ Battalion, but most of them can't be printed here. The stories included gross-out contests, women of questionable morals, and a bar called the 82ⁿᵈ Club out on the highway. Remember, the men were very young and very aggressive.

All that time we were constantly changing over people. There were always new people coming in and people leaving. We lost a lot of people. You would go to the field one day and come back and somebody would be gone. One of your friends is gone. You could ask, and sometimes you could find out where they went.

It was a hardship unit, so a lot of people would just go down to a unit there at Fort Stewart. They were just starting the 24ᵗʰ Infantry Division in January of '75. A lot of them left voluntarily. It was just that hard.

In 1975, I went off to Ranger School so I really don't know what was happening in that time period…just that the battalion was training in the area. I do know they sent a composite company in January to Alaska, to the North American Warfare Training Center. They went to Fort Greely.

I came back from Ranger School and went with a composite company to the Canal Zone to the Jungle Operations Training Center [Panama] for three weeks.

Members of several branches of the military attended "Jungle School." The school was heavily attended during the Vietnam War and afterward. Graduates were awarded a patch signifying Jungle Expert. A composite company is one made of members of different companies.

I came back...maybe a week, and then we reported to Fort Bliss. That was kind of a quick thing. Go out there, live fire, do some desert survival training.

It was one of those things where we did C-141s [jet transport], low-level flight, nap-of-the-earth flight [lots of up and down].

They invented these Air Force lunches that consisted of green salami. By the time we got to where we were doing in-flight rigging [chutes] everybody was puking. I'm looking at my buddy right across from me, his name was Nels Nelson, and I'm saying, okay, just look at me, buddy, don't look at anybody else. I can smell the puke, I can hear the puke, but as long as I don't see it, I'm not going to puke. So, Nels and I sat there, just staring at each other, and finally they opened the door of the aircraft and we stood up. When we stood up Nels puked, and when he puked it went right down the back of my neck. Of course, that caused me to puke. When they opened the door this rush of puke just slid out the door.

I got out of the airplane. I had multiple twists because I slipped when I hit the platform, on the puke. I went out in a horrible position. About the time I got untwisted, I hit. I stood up to get my parachute, which had draped over a big mesquite bush, I stepped in a prairie-dog hole and like to broke my ankle, looked up and there's a cameraman from CBS. I waved at him [with one finger], so I knew Mom wasn't going to see me on national TV that night.

Then we had to march from the drop zone to Camp Donna-Anna. Part of the major training area is in New Mexico. Camp Donna-Anna and another camp are in New Mexico, but they're part of Fort Bliss, Texas.

Bliss was where they tested all the missiles and anti-aircraft, so they had this huge open desert area. We trained in desert survival, and we did live-fire exercises. That's where I almost burned up some barrels on my M60. Had a guy named Bernie Ricketts, who was brand-new, shoot an M72A2 LAW into the ground about 15 feet in front of our position [it didn't have time to arm], and it skipped up and went way up on Rattlesnake Ridge and exploded. He was aiming at an old '57 Chevy that was down below us.

We had a live-fire withdrawal; there was a gully that was right at six feet deep. We're all running down this gully and they've got M60s live-firing over our heads, criss-crossing [Hawk is over six feet tall]. You couldn't drive a 10-penny nail up my butt with a sledgehammer. After seeing Bernie Ricketts shoot that LAW I'm wondering if anybody else had their eyes closed.

After Bliss, I went with a composite company to West Point, New York. That was for three months. I drove to New York in my pickup with three other guys. A guy named Mike Etheridge, just retired—he was Sergeant Major of SOCOM—Ed Knowles and Jack Waddel.

We trained Cadets all summer. This was a Recondo School. This was unique because in 1975 they were determining whether or not they would allow women to go to West Point. This was the first time that a group of female staff officers came and observed summer training to see if the females could go through.

Here we were training all these people and these female staff officers are coming around all this bunch of Rangers. We weren't the best guys to be around.

Everybody had to be Tabbed. We didn't send anybody up there that wasn't Tabbed. My particular courses I taught were Water Survival and Small Boat Movements. There's a lake up there we called Lake Nasty. My job was to teach them how to use an RD-7 [and another small boat], how to embark, debark, give way together, steer left—rubber baby buggy boats.

When they started the initial formal instruction I dressed up like a Cadet. I would fall in line and get in the back of the class. Sergeant Tony [and another Sergeant] would give this big long speech about not falling asleep in the class and what would happen to you. Well, I'd fall asleep. They'd [come charging] through the class and grab me and I'd be screaming, you can't do this, I'm an officer and a gentleman! Well, they'd throw me in the lake.

We had this all pre-planned, of course. I actually had to jump about 10 feet to clear the rocks, but they would throw me as hard as they could, and I would jump, and I'd clear the rocks. I'd dive down to the bottom of the lake where we had a tank [Scuba]. I never would surface. I sat under the lily pads, and then slowly moved my way around, dragging the tank along the bottom, until I was out of sight. Well, the Cadets never saw me surface, and they'd think, "These sons-of-bitches are crazy! They'll kill you!"

He was asked twice and he swears the above is true.

We were the first enlisted people to ever eat in Corcoran Hall, which is where the Cadets eat. Prior to that, enlisted men, unless you were working there, were not allowed inside. We were the first enlisted people allowed inside there, and probably the last for a while.

1975 was the first time we were given marching orders for an actual mission [to rescue the crew of the Mayaguez].

The Mayaguez was a container ship sailing about 60 miles off the Cambodian coast, when it was corralled by Swift boats (American made) manned by Cambodian Khmer Rouge. The 39-man crew was sequestered, then removed from the ship after it was anchored at a small island about 30 miles off the coast. The Marines came in from several directions on a rescue mission and finally managed to retrieve the crew, but in so doing, lost 13 dead, 44 wounded, and three missing. The Air Force lost two killed and six wounded, plus 23 more killed in a helicopter crash. Most of the Marine casualties came when they landed in Cambodia and met heavy machinegun fire. However, the crew of the ship was back in American hands in a short time.

It was between the time we came back from the Canal Zone and when we went to West Point. The mission was the USS Mayaguez was captured. The Ranger Battalion was alerted.

All this time, through '74 and '75, we're constantly getting these alerts, called Alpha alerts. That was to see how fast you could get the battalion together. We had to do it; I think it was under 12 hours we had to be ready. Things had to be palletized [for pushing out of airplanes], your C bags, your D bags, your A bags. We had everything set up in bags. If you were going to Alaska, you had all your cold weather gear in your A bag. If you were going to a desert environment, that was your D bag. Then you had your C bag, which was European.

So you'd run in there and grab whatever bag you needed and then go get palletized. We had to be able to pack all of our personal belongings, inventory it in a box, seal the box, and have that over to another area that could be sent home to your family. All the time we used to practice these deployments. Well, one day in '75 we got an Alpha alert, and everybody said, well, okay, here's another training exercise. We were put on trucks; they pulled all the flaps down so we couldn't see, and left out in the middle of the night. We were not given any briefing, we were just told to go to sleep.

They got us up about two o'clock in the morning and started issuing ammo and we looked at it as a live-fire alert. But, when they started issuing live frags [fragmentation grenades] and atropine injectors [for gas attack] and live .45 ammo, we knew something was up. So, then we knew we were going in hot. Then we went to a mission briefing. Luckily, the Marines managed to get their own people out, so we were called back. We were actually in the air. We were in route.

In September of '75 we went to the Republic of Germany for REFORGER.

Essentially this was rearranging (Reorganizing) the Forces in Germany after the Vietnam War to meet the continuing Cold War threat.

Our part of it was called FLINTLOCK, which is where all the Special Operations groups got together and trained. That was the first time I jumped with the Germans and earned my German jump wings.

About October time frame, I was back in Fort Stewart for about two weeks and got orders to go to Primary Non-Commissioned Officer's Course (PNOC). I left in November to go to PNOC at Fort Benning. Prior to that they just had the NCO Academy, but now they were starting training...as far as primary, basic, advanced, First Sergeant, career-path type of training. I was one of the first ones to go through PNOC.

Hawk made it through PNOC and BNOC (basic) but left the Army before ANOC (advanced). By the time he got to Alaska he was a Spec 4, had been promoted to Sergeant, but had not received the paperwork yet.

Generally speaking, graduating Ranger School automatically upgrades rank to Sergeant, or at least one rank higher, but Hawk says the Rangers didn't always honor that. They only had so many slot, so if you wanted to stay in the battalion you had to take the slot that was open.

In a way this reflects the WWII scenario of many of the incoming Sergeants and Corporals having to relinquish their stripes to get into the Ranger Battalions of the day. It is also the reason there are so many non-Ranger qualified soldiers in today's battalions. They are Privates and Specialists who, if a Ranger School graduate, would have to be promoted and would lose their place in the battalion due to TO&E restrictions. Chiefs and Indians must be kept in balance.

Prior to going to Alaska I went before the E-5 Board. Wayne Downing was Chairman of the Board. When we came back from Alaska, Downing pinned my Sergeant's stripes on me. Then he left and tried to take me to 2ⁿᵈ Battalion [just forming, Sept. 1975] with him. I wouldn't go. He became commander later on in '76. I told him I'd helped start one [battalion] and I wasn't going to start another one.

In January of '76, the battalion again is deploying around the world. This time we deployed as a battalion to Fort Wainwright, Alaska to train. We did our ski training. We had an [Eskimo name] that is supposed to be a 300-pound sled that you carry your squad equipment on. It was man-pulled, so 300 they felt was maximum weight. Our sleds weighed anywhere from 700 to 900 pounds.

After Alaska, the whole battalion went to Panama, and while they were there I was in HALO School [High-Altitude, Low-Opening parachute jump].

[When that was over] I was a Buck Sergeant and I was given a squad. I was 20 years old. All this time we were still training. We never stopped training. They'd find new ways to train us.

That summer of '76, I decided to train my squad in survival, and I carried my entire squad down the river with nothing but a knife and a canteen. We stayed five days. They had to find stuff to eat, to catch. We had the chaplain with us and he was a pain in the butt because he always wanted to know where we were. At one point we went under I-95.

There is a Stuckey's not far from there and Hawk wouldn't show anyone the map.

So they wouldn't slip off and go to Stuckey's. We sat up overnight probably less than a mile from the Stuckey's, but I wouldn't tell them.

During the summer of '76, they sent me up to Fort Eustis to learn how to drive Soviet vehicles and [not Soviet] locomotives. I was a licensed diesel locomotive driver. One of the missions we planned was to steal a train traveling across Georgia with a nuclear warhead, hijack the train, move into an area and disarm the device.

In 1976, everybody was training everywhere. People were gone constantly. You're having to fill spots, get your people trained. The goal of the Squad Leader was to get your people as much training as they could possibly handle. At one point in time in '76, I had everyone in my squad Ranger-qualified. Everybody in my squad had been to at least one Hooah School—Pathfinder, HALO, SCUBA, whatever. I had the best squad in the battalion, and I'll be damned if somebody didn't realize that. Then they started pulling people. I started with a whole new group of people.

We went back to Germany [REFORGER again]. That's where the battalion was part of REFORGER, but our part was FLINTLOCK, and we were going against the 101st. That was the time I led the entire B Company. We broke up into squads to recon into sectors to try and find the 101st. We didn't know where they were.

My squad was reconning one night and I ran into the barrel of a towed Vulcan [a type of gatling gun]. It was that dark. I was able to back away before anyone realized I'd hit it. We reconned it, and come to find out we were in the dead center of the 101st Division HQ. Somehow we had infiltrated in and didn't know it. They didn't know it, either. So, I backed my squad out to an overlook position, left one of my Fire Team Leaders with three people to just watch. I backed off two or three klicks and got on the radio and started calling—got hold of the company commander and we assembled the company.

Then we went back in. A guy named Ron Fallon, also a Squad Leader, was right behind me, and I was leading the company on this route I took the first time. We got to the same Vulcan and a guy says, "Halt." I didn't say anything. He said, "Continental," which was the challenge. I didn't say anything. I took another step. He said, "Halt." I said "continental," and he said "Cadillac."

Now, we had the challenge and the password. Ron and I took out that gun crew and tied them up the way we were trained to do—tie them with their own bootlaces and gag them with their socks.

The 101st Brass knew the Rangers were out there somewhere, looking for them.

After we got past them we went down to the next one and the guy was a little smarter. Of course, Ron was right behind me, and he said, "You son-of-a-bitch, did you forget the password again?" The guy says, "Do you know him, Sarge?" "Hell, yeah, I know him, he's the worst troop I got." "Well, if you know him, you guys come on in." So, we took out the second gun.

So, then we're moving through, we took out a couple more security positions, and as I lead the company down to the TOC [tactical operations center], which we had identified, we're dropping off Rangers, two-man teams. At a pre-designated time we all burst into the TOC, and others burst into the tents.

The Commanding General [of the 101st, John A. Wickham, later to become Chief of Staff] was sitting in a tent with his Major who's in charge of security in the TOC, and a Sergeant Major, and we burst into the tent. John Jay Owens is the B Company Commander, and John Jay says, "Good evening, gentlemen, we're the 1st of the 75th Rangers, you're all our prisoners."

We went over and wrote down all the coordinates for all the 101st units off this big display map they had. I took their Operations Orders and stuck them in my shirt. We erased their board. We used their radios to start calling artillery on every unit they had, and then slipped out, we didn't fire one shot.

I've got an award downstairs hanging on the wall from that. It's called a Tiger Certificate.

After we ex-filtrated and broke back up into our squads, they stopped me about five or six miles out and asked me on the radio if I had the Operations Orders for the 101st, which I did. "Well [they said], you gotta take it back." I got an order to take them back, so we didn't bother with stealth or anything, it was daylight, we just walked in. Weapons slung over our shoulders. I took my entire squad back in.

Wickham fed us. I gave him his Operation Orders back. We sat and talked to him for a long time. We chowed down like big dogs.

We had 30 days, and we accomplished our mission in seven days. So, for the rest of the time they were looking for something for us to do. We started going out looking for British SAS [Special Air Service]. Found them asleep in a little hamlet.

Hawk was showing us photographs, and we came upon one of a skinny version of the big man we know and a soldier named Tom Carter, his roommate. They later had an apartment together. Carter was killed in Baghdad in 2004, victim of a roadside bomb. He was not in the military at the time.

David Hill

David Hill was part of the 1st Ranger Battalion in 1977-78 as a member of Bravo Company. He left as an E-4. Captains Roberts and Guthrie ran the company during that time.

This interview was recorded via telephone in late December 2004.

My time with the Rangers, in some ways I have to consider that the high point of my life in terms of learning about myself and being dedicated to the greater cause.

I turned 18 the last year of the draft in 1972 and said, well, if my number comes up, I'll go...and four years later I'm joining the Ranger Battalion. I was working in a gun shop in Atlanta and a Colonel Valentine, a Reserve Colonel, a BDQ guy, talked a lot about the Rangers and got me interested. I started doing some reading on it and decided if I was going to try anything, I wanted something challenging.

My First Sergeant was named Carpenter [Gary Carpenter—Ranger Hall of Fame]. He was one of the people that impressed me the most in battalion. He was sharp as could be, as straight forward as could be.

When I first got there I was stuck in the weapons squad, 2nd Platoon, as an ammo bearer for an M60 gunner. That lasted about two weeks, and then they made me a grenadier. Nobody else wanted to have to carry the weight (M203). I don't remember how long I did that, but then they needed a Platoon RTO, so I ended up doing that most of the rest of the time I was in battalion.

I went to Ranger School in 1978. I think I started in March, got recycled out of Camp Darby at Benning. Made it through the City Phase, and we were out patrolling and I got sick and got stuck in the hospital and missed some days of training and got recycled. Started with the next class and graduated in June.

He joined the battalion as his first posting, so he is a Batt-boy, "born" in the battalion. In those days there was no Ranger Indoctrination Program (RIP) that all Batt-boys go through now. RIP came on line a little later.

I don't know the attrition rate of my [Ranger School] class. I do know when I was in the battalion, what was typical is you would be in the battalion during all the normal training for about six months. You were selected to go to Ranger School, and that was sort of an extended RIP. I know the attrition rate in the battalion at the time was close to 90 percent. There was a huge dropout rate.

Other Rangers have confirmed this. Even without a vessel such as RIP to perform the weeding-out process, six months in the battalion in full training pretty much culls those who don't want to, or cannot, continue the hardships. Hill was asked about the tough training methods and his reasons for staying.

What hit me the most, what I remember of that time is that this was the kind of job that during the week I really hated it, but during the weekend it was really cool. It was pretty tough being in the field and doing stuff, but when you were off duty you were proud of being able to deal with it.

When I got to Ranger School, what we went through there was essentially what I had been doing with the battalion for a year. The level of intensity in the battalion in training was pretty high.

We got up at 0500 and were in formation by 0600 and ready to start the day. First formation was PT. We wore white shirts and shorts and jungle boots. We'd do our PT and go for a run, at least two miles. Once a week it would be farther. On occasion we'd have a 10 or 20 mile run, but mostly it was [shorter].

We did have what we called inclement weather PT, which was in the basement of the barracks. There was an open area down there. If it was particularly wet or cold we'd go there.

The rest of the day we'd either have classes or be out doing some kind of training.

I had 15 jumps while I was there over an 18-month period. I didn't jump much, but I was there during the era that I call "Carter's Rangers." I think one of the most telling examples we had to deal with in terms of restrictions on money and [other things], I remember we had to do a training mission where we were jumping into Taylor Creek, getting going and doing some kind of patrol. We couldn't get airplanes from the Air Force. Didn't have enough money to get the planes down there for us. We did a simulated drop where we're driving down the middle of the drop zone in deuce-and-a-halfs, and every 50 meters two guys would jump out. I remember thinking; this is the elite of the Army?

Military downsizing after Vietnam left many (most) units in all branches without the wherewithal to continue the heavy training the war brought about. President Jimmy Carter was at the helm at the time. Later President Regan brought things back up to snuff, or near.

I don't recall any night classes while we were in garrison. They [stood us down] about five or six at night. One of our favorite places to go was Camp Oliver [northwest part of Fort Stewart]. If we were on a patrol or an exercise, the training would go all night sometimes. I remember we were doing weapons cross-training [live-fire]. We were getting to shoot the mortars and the 90mm recoilless. At night we were doing infiltration exercises. One of our Sergeants would set up a booby-trap lane that set of trip flares and stuff. The exercise was to go through there at night without tripping anything.

Training close to home was the order of the day due to fiscal limitations, but there were some deployments for training purposes.

The only place I went was Panama for jungle training. There was a composite company put together to do an exercise in the desert [probably Fort Bliss, Texas]. I didn't go on it.

We did jump into Eglin [AFB] in Florida, and we jumped into [a Fort in] Wisconsin.

Hill remarked the battalion was somewhat segregated by platoon—that is, the platoon and the squad became the main focus of its members. Asked if he knew Steve Hawk, who was also in the 1st Battalion at the time, and in Bravo Company to boot, Hill answered thusly:

There was some overlap [between platoons], but we never actually met. He was in 1st Platoon; I was in 2nd. [As far as] between companies, I very rarely met anybody from another company, and I didn't really get to know people from another platoon very well.

With the Vietnam War just over by a few years, Hill was asked how many veterans were there.

Most of the NCOs there were Vietnam vets. In fact, my Platoon Sergeant when I got there was Sergeant Lour, and he was definitely a role model. He said when he first got to Vietnam he was a PFC and about six weeks later he was a Sergeant First Class or something like that. It was from attrition. He was two days in-country and his company got ambushed and lost like 90 percent of the people.

He had a lot to teach. That's what impressed me the most about Sergeant Lour. We in the Ranger Battalion were Infantry, light Infantry just like everybody else in the Army, except our viewpoint was that we were supposed to be better than anybody else. That meant doing it by the book, and sometimes doing it by the book doesn't always make sense. That was one of the things Sergeant Lour dealt with when we were out training one time. He was being very diplomatic about it, saying the book is a great place to start if you don't know anything. And, it's good to know how to do things by the book, but sometimes you need to know a little bit different, you know, and then he'd go into the real stuff. He had us out there teaching us how to move, how to be quiet and be sneaky, and the things that weren't covered by the book.

We were doing some recon, and he had a lot of tips and techniques and things from real life that sure kept a lot of people alive.

Hill decided to leave the battalion, "To see what the other side of the Army was like." He ended up in the 25th Infantry Division.

My motivation for leaving the battalion was they had made B Company the Scout/ Swimming Company. There was a point in time where they had activated the Delta Detachment [which changed, or added to, Ranger missions] and they were still going through about a two-year ramp-up period. They told us we were the fill-in, or stopgap people. They were looking for somebody to fill that role immediately while they were waiting for Delta Group to be [on line].

One of our companies was supposed to specialize in nuclear device recovery—they were mainly thinking about backpack nukes at the time. The other company was specializing in combat in built-up areas—urban warfare stuff. We were the Scout/Swimming Company, and they were basically trying to make SEALs out of us. Frankly, I am not a good swimmer. They were doing helocast, jumping in the water two or three miles off-coast, coming in while it was dark, doing recon, then swimming back out and being picked up.

The men wore wet suits, fins and mask, and they carried M16s strapped to their bodies. Hill said the barrels were plugged, usually by a condom, but the weapons were otherwise open to the water.

I only did that once. I had a Platoon Leader who convinced me to become the acting Company Supply Sergeant.

The company commander needed a warm body to fill the role of Supply Sergeant, so even though just an E-4, Hill took the job after completing Ranger School. This was the time when the battalion was about to move the short distance to Hunter Army Airfield from Fort Stewart.

Everybody but me knew that when we moved a lot of stuff was going to come up missing and nobody wanted to be responsible for it. I also missed a lot of training. I was attached to the 1st Platoon for training. When we went to Panama I didn't get to jump in. As Supply Sergeant I had to stay on the plane and make sure everything got where it was supposed to go.

Here Hill tells a story involving a mistake made by another Ranger—in command of a Platoon— and per the policy of this project we omit his name.

There was a Lieutenant…who was our Platoon Leader, and during the battalion FTX [in Panama] he was given an instruction to move his platoon while we were waiting for resupply. He took one of the squads, running through the jungle, and parked us on top of a hill, and went running back. When I say running, this was about a two-hour movement. He told us to sit still and he would go back and get the rest of the platoon, and then he promptly went out and got lost. He was lost for a day, and then when he was found, he couldn't bring them back to where he had left us. Then he told the company commander that we must have moved.

We had no radio. He had one radio for the platoon and he detached us without a radio. He was one of those people that didn't think the rules applied to him. One of the things we always did was tie everything to us with dummy cord, and he didn't do that. Panama is hilly and slick and muddy and you're going to fall down sometime. On the way back he tripped and fell down a hill and lost his compass, which is how he became lost. I know he got in some kind of trouble because the company commander had him running individual PT when we got back to battalion.

It was an interesting experience because I was attached to the squad but I wasn't really part of its chain of command. I outranked the squad leader, a PFC. We stayed out two days. Sort of a standard thing you learned after being in battalion for a while, you never took all the food into the field they issued you because it was too much, you didn't need three meals a day. The other thing was you never ate all your food either, because you didn't know if you'd get resupplied.

The Platoon Sergeant left us out there and said he'd be back before dark, but I, and Sacknit [his friend], having been there a while, knew he couldn't make it back before dark. We were prepared to be out there all night, at least. The next day, we're tactical still, in our patrol base on top of this hill, seven hours after dawn the platoon still hasn't shown up, and we hear a voice, wandering north of us, yelling help! Help!

We didn't know who it was [probably the Platoon Leader]. What we did know is that the evaluators down there, the Opposing Force, would use Psyops, anything to trick us into giving away our position. We certainly were not going to be yelling back at somebody yelling help. The Squad Leader and I went out to see if we could learn anything, try and spot the person. We did find a trail, and it was three people, but we'd only heard one voice. We thought maybe this one person was lost and the other two were tracking him, or it was just a trick. We didn't try to catch up with him. We just went back to our position.

Toward the afternoon the Squad Leader was freaking out. He wanted to get us up and moving through the jungle. I said, look, if they've lost us, then we'd have two groups running around at the same time and we'd never find each other. We knew the next day was when the extraction was scheduled, but we didn't know where.

I basically pulled rank on the Squad Leader and said, look, we're not going running through the jungle. Just get comfortable. Obviously, we're not part of the exercise anymore. We'll just stay here the night and in the morning we'll figure out what to do.

We knew where there was a low clearing on a ridge where they had inserted us and I figured if all else failed, we could go back there and they could see us. As it turned out that was the extraction point. As we went in they were hollering at us and we were hollering at them.

Steve Bishop
This interview was recorded on the back deck of the Overhang Bar at Camp Frank D. Merrill..

My name is Steven Douglas Bishop and I went through Ranger School class 11-72. My TAC Officer was Captain Boltz; my TAC NCO was Sergeant First Class Gary Littrell [Medal of Honor winner]. He is the reason I wound up in the 1st Ranger Battalion.

I came into the Army and went through Basic and AIT at Fort Polk, Louisiana. I had enlisted with an option of going to the NCO Academy—called the NCOC back then, and you would graduate a Buck Sergeant. It was commonly called the Shake and Bake course. I graduated in October 1970, and I went through Jump School from there.

I went to the 173rd in Vietnam, came back and we became the 101st.

The 173rd was an independent Airborne Brigade before that, and the first combat Army unit to land in Vietnam in 1965. There are several men in this book with experience in the Herd. Bishop had been in Vietnam "five or six months," so when the Herd rotated stateside, absorbed by the 101st, he had no choice but to go with them. Some time in 1972 the 101st took on parts of the 173rd and 187th Brigades. Bishop was then with 3/503 after Ranger School.

One of the first people I met when I got off the bus, after we went through Jungle School [basic in-country orientation] when we first got there, or whatever they called the damn thing, was Tom Brock, who is retired from up here [north Georgia]. He had been wounded on one of the hills, and he was the first person to meet the bus. In fact, I wound up in his platoon.

By the time 1972 got there, I guess I was still in the 173rd when I went to Ranger School. The way I got selected was our Brigade Commander, his name was Colonel Hemphill, got transferred to become the School Brigade Commander at Fort Benning. He somehow pulled 30 slots for the 101st for Ranger School, which was almost unheard of.

We did a thing, PT test and like that, like a qualification program, but it wasn't exactly RIP, but almost. I don't know how many people we started out with, but 30 of us wound up going, and I think 17 of us graduated.

My vision of Ranger School, and this is the way it was when I went through, you take the knowledge you get from Ranger School, and you take it back to your unit and you train your troops. That was what I was most proud of.

I got word at Fort Campbell [3rd Brigade, 101st], all of a sudden they were going to go out in the field, this was maybe March 1974. My Sergeant Major was Scully McCullough. His son-in-law was in my platoon, and he was Ranger-qualified. Somebody came up to me and said, "Hey, you got a phone call down in the orderly room, it's the Brigade Sergeant Major."

I was the oldest member of my company, and at that time they [101st] were going off jump status and going to the Bullwinkle Badge, the Air Assault School. Sergeant Major McCullough said, "Look, I know you've been trying to leave. They're forming a new unit and it's going to be the 1st Ranger Battalion. They're going to be recruiting on post today and if you want to go, tell your commander." That's why they were moving everybody out in the field. Because they were trying to keep everybody there that was Ranger-qualified.

I went and told my commander and he let me go. I went home and put on my spit-shines and my starched fatigues, drove over there and parked. When I got out I saw a guy walking around with a black beret. I walked up to him and he was a Lt. Colonel. It was Colonel Leuer. I went up and saluted him and said, "Sir, I understand you're having interviews for the 1st Ranger Battalion and I'd like to come up and see if I can get selected." I fell in on his right side as we were walking down the sidewalk. He stopped, looked me in the eye and said, "Sergeant, first thing, we do things right in the 1st Ranger Battalion," and he grabbed me by my arm and moved me over to his left side.

He took me in and introduced me to Sergeant Major Gentry. It is my understanding that Sergeant Major McCullough and Neal Gentry were good friends. I got selected, and at that time Gary Littrell had gotten assigned, I think he was the G-3 Sergeant Major for the 101st. I was having trouble getting my orders.

Everybody else was reporting to Fort Benning. My friend Mike Cheney was gone. It wound up I cleared Fort Campbell, Kentucky, on a DA [Dept Army] message, which I guess was like a fax back then, but I didn't have clearance papers. Somehow Littrell got the things for me. I didn't actually see a set of orders until I reported in to Fort Benning. He had contacted the S-1 NCO of the 1st Battalion and the guy was busy, I mean they pulled people from all over the Army to go there. I was one of about 65 to report in.

We did all kinds of stuff, rope bridges, road marches, one morning we got up and made a tape of cadences, land-nav courses…Don Clark was my company commander in the 1st Battalion. He was a hell of a soldier, he was a good officer; I don't know why he didn't have a Ranger Tab. He could have passed Ranger School.

They were going to have a cookout. There were some officers that had a .22 rifle and they were going to kill this steer. They kept shooting it in the head and the bullets kept bouncing off. We had an NCO, Sergeant First Class Haynes, and he finally said, "You're just making that cow mad." He went over and got a ball-peen hammer and hit that cow in the head and it dropped dead right there. That's how the cadence got started. "Cow-killer, cow-killer, feed me please."

I was with the battalion probably a month before they went to Fort Stewart. A lot of people came and went. You could hold up your hand and leave when you wanted to. There was a whole lot of pride involved there, though. It's like when I went through Ranger School. I wasn't going to quit, that's just the way it was.

We were writing lesson outlines and stuff like that at Benning. That's when they came up with new lesson outlines of tasks, conditions, and standards. My Platoon Sergeant was in Ranger School. Joe Alderman was his name. He graduated while I was down there and came back to the battalion.

We spent a lot of time in Building Four [a huge edifice in the middle of Fort Benning] going through classes. We did a lot of PT and we did a lot of road marches.

Bishop then told a story about a Sergeant Gibson. After a long day training most men took a shower and went to town. One night a bunch of Rangers were trying to get into a Denny's restaurant for some chow around midnight, but there was a long line. Gibson made his way inside to the bar—still wearing his jungle fatigues—and ordered a bowl of hot water and coffee. He pulled a LRRP ration out of his pocket, mixed it up in the bowl of hot water, and ate while everybody else was still standing in line.

Hawk [Steve] was there. He was a PFC at the time, and there weren't very many of them.

Anyway, we left Benning and went down to Stewart and things started to settle down. We started doing our thing. My old buddy Mike Cheney came up to me, probably in July, and he said there were six spots to go to Navy SERE [Survival, Evasion, Resistance, and Escape] School, two from each company, and he wanted to go, and why didn't I put my name in, too? So, I put my name in and got it. There were six of us from the battalion that were first to go to Navy SERE School. I came back with two black eyes, got the shit kicked out of me for a week. That was the only school I went through in the two years I was there with the Ranger Battalion.

I went to Jungle Expert School in Panama, but we went as a unit, which was different than if you went there on your own. You got the Jungle Expert patch, but it wasn't the same.

That is unusual, as battalion members were going off to school frequently.

With the 1st Ranger Battalion, God, we sat on the airstrip so many times…it's a funny feeling, you get calls one or two o'clock in the morning and they start issuing brand-new

90mm recoilless rifles. You know something's happening. They can come back the next day and say, hey, it's just a post alert, but they're not going to bust those babies out of their cases for that.

EAGLE CLAW—DESERT ONE

November 4, 1979, Iranian militants took over the US Embassy in Tehran, taking a total of 60 hostages. Though some few of the hostages were released over time, there were still 53 Americans being held when Operation Eagle Claw—the attempted rescue mission—went forward.

Major General John Vaught, who wore the Ranger Tab, assembled a joint task force of Army, Navy, and Air Force personnel under the auspices of the Chairman of the Joint Chiefs of Staff, General Jones. Several other General Officers and a host of other high-ranking officers were involved, along with many staff and line personnel. Plans were presented and discarded as options were either accepted or ruled out.

There would be a rescue only if the right people were able to be in the right place at the right time and be trained the right way to perform the mission. It took hundreds of people working thousands of hours planning, training, and perfecting the rescue operation—just in case they were called upon to go.

Though the rescue never fully took place, Eagle Claw marks the first time Rangers were considered for a Special Operations mission such as an airfield seizure. When the planners looked around for a mobile, airborne, quick-strike force they found a limited inventory. They needed muscle, but they also needed brains and training. The Rangers were the logical conclusion to secure whatever bases were required.

The plan called for Delta operators to take the Embassy, locate the hostages, and get them out. Ranger units were to support Delta by acting as security at the forward bases before and after the rescue. At first about 100 Rangers were in training for a possible airfield seizure, but in the end just a dozen were used as a road block team at Desert One on the first night. There were, however, several other Rangers involved in planning and operations.

A good percentage of Delta troops are Ranger-qualified. The significance of Eagle Claw to Ranger evolution is large, not only because of the presence of many Rangers in various positions, but because this was the first time a Ranger unit had supported Delta, thus becoming part of the relatively small Special Ops community.

Months passed while diplomatic pressures were applied, but finally President Jimmy Carter felt he had no further options and turned the Joint Task Force loose.

The distances involved made it difficult to move the men and material necessary for such a mission. The Air Force was the largest contributor, putting six C-130s on the ground in a remote area of Iran, landing and taking off in the desert at night using night-vision goggles.

Navy H-53 Sea Stallion helicopters were flown in and arrayed behind the C-130s, which had been fitted with fuel bladders for the occasion.

KC-135 tankers flew orbits to refuel the C-130s going into and out of Iran. C-141 jet transports outfitted as hospital ships were on call.

To prepare for the mission, Air Force crews flew practice runs all over the globe, getting together only a few times to prove they could perform as required. It was not an easy task. The helicopter crews were replaced at one point because of an inability to fly at night in desert conditions.

Colonel Charlie Beckwith, who had a big voice in the planning, was running Delta. His insistence on the number of men going in never wavered, right down to the last minute. Delta would put in some 120 men, or they wouldn't go.

Delta and the Rangers practiced incessantly for whatever scenarios they could think up. What actually happened was beyond anyone's state of preparedness.

On the night of April 24, 1980 the big C-130s landed in the desert on two makeshift strips on either side of a road. The place had been pre-marked by some brave men. The 12-man Ranger roadblock team and Delta troopers fanned out and posted security while the planes were maneuvered into place to refuel the expected helicopters.

There were immediately problems. Communications were hampered in several ways, leaving commanders out of touch with the appropriate people.

A fuel truck came down the road the C-130s were landing astride and was stopped by the roadblock team. A burst into the engine didn't stop the truck, so a shoulder-fired rocket was turned on it. The projectile went under the cab of the truck and exploded in the fuel tank behind, creating a large fire that severely hampered anyone wearing night goggles, such as the landing C-130 pilots.

Next came a bus carrying 44 passengers, blundering into the area and giving the roadblock team a mass of people to deal with.

The main problem, one that could not be overcome, was with the helicopters.

One helicopter turned back to the carrier Nimitz (point of origin) and another set down in the desert short of the objective, both with mechanical problems. The birds were flying at 100-to-200 feet above the deck, and ran into what the Iranians call a "haboob"—a cloud of suspended dust—making it next to impossible to maintain eye contact with the ground and therefore, stability in a helicopter. The crews barely made it through.

Of the eight helicopters sent to Iran, only six were necessary to transport Delta. There had been some maintenance problems with the birds aboard the Nimitz, so it was hoped that at least six of the eight would make the trip. Six made it to Desert One through the dust, and despite commo problems and a large number of detainees, the mission was still a go.

Then, a leaking hydraulic pump caused millions of dollars and thousands of man-hours to flow freely down the drain. One of the helicopters taking fuel behind the C-130s was reported out of commission, making only five aircraft fit to fly.

Beckwith refused to go if he had to leave part of his force behind. The mission had been carefully rehearsed with the number of men he had, and would be compromised with any less.

The helicopter pilots refused to carry any extra weight, considering the altitude, air density, and several other reasons. The brass was contacted and a reluctant decision was made to abort the mission.

Trying to turn the aircraft around to leave brought sudden catastrophe when a helicopter tried to move a short distance away from a C-130 to allow it to turn round. The chopper lifted off to "ground taxi," but blew up a storm of dust, blinding the pilot. Thinking he was moving left, the aircraft moved right instead, plowing into the forward area of the C-130 and exploding.

The burning aircraft lit up the desert and stunned everyone, leaving eight men dead and five injured, some with serious burns.

It was bad, no doubt. However, as with other military missions that don't go quite right, lessons were learned. The horror in the desert ended up saving lives years later in other missions. There are men involved in this project who were there—but they can't talk about it yet.

GRENADA

In 1983, the United States and the Organization of Eastern Caribbean States fielded some 7,300 troops to enforce the second change of government in six days on the tiny island nation of Grenada. An operation code-named Urgent Fury was put together in a very short period—aimed at what President Reagan and others thought of as a Marxist stronghold.

Grenada is just off the northeast coast of South America, one of a long chain of islands in the Caribbean. Some 90,000 people live on 133 square-miles of tropical paradise under the nominal protection of Great Britain.

The southwestern portion of the island houses the Grand Anse Medical School, where about 600 American students studied on two campuses, one of which was the True Blue Campus.

In 1979, Maurice Bishop and his New Jewel Movement—decidedly Marxist—overthrew the elected government. Bishop, a charismatic crusader for the poor, was popular even though his opponents often found themselves in prison. He allied himself with communist Cuba, shutting down local media opinion.

On October 19, 1983, just six days before the invasion, a group of people from the Grenadian Army, controlled by former Deputy Prime Minister Bernard Coard, moved to overthrow Bishop's government. This group, called the People's Revolutionary Army (PRA), was also Marxist, perhaps more hard-line than Bishop. He was tracked down and summarily executed with about 16 others at 18th-century Fort George, then a military barracks. This action came to be called "Bloody Wednesday" and has produced several accounts, most of which are fantasy. The people of the island—most of them—were very upset by Bishop's death. The result was a welcome mat for American troops.

Although the main force on Grenada was its own "army" of about 1200, there were nearly 800 Cubans, though the Cuban government said they were mostly construction workers. Those "construction workers" were well armed and put up a pretty stiff defense.

In addition to the Cubans, Grenada also hosted about 50 Soviets of one type or another, and lesser numbers of North Koreans, East Germans, Bulgarians, and even a few Libyans. This was, after all, the Cold War under Reagan, and he was pushing hard against communism, which was pushing hard against democracy.

The significance of the invasion of Grenada has several points. Besides the disaster in Iran in 1980, it was the first time the Ranger Battalions had a serious deployment since their inception in the mid-70s. It was their first test. It was also the first real test for SEALs and for Delta as surgical strike forces. Moreover, it was the first time they had all been used at one time, along with 160th SOAR and all the other special operations units.

Although the invasion was an obvious success, there were so many blunders and shortfalls of equipment and communication that improvement was mandated. The creation of the 1st

Special Operations Command (SOCOM) was one outstanding result of the mishaps that occurred. Other improvements were made in equipment, communications, and techniques that allowed a much more balanced and coordinated movement against Panama in 1989.

There was another significant point, but this one was purely political, and up for grabs as far as correctness goes. President Ronald Reagan was upset with the idea of another country, even so small a one as Grenada, going communist and hooking up with the dreaded Cubans. He was aware of the new airfield half-a-year before the invasion and saw it as a threat. It could have been used to support strategic or tactical aircraft, or to import equipment and materials to insurgents or other units hostile to the United States. The Grenadians said the airfield was installed to handle tourist jets, but nobody believed them, probably since the Cubans were building it.

Ground and Air Forces

    1st and 2nd Battalions, 75th Infantry (Ranger)

    2nd Brigade, 82nd Airborne

    SEALs—Teams Four and Six

    SFOD-Delta

    Marine force

    Air Force Special Tactics Combat Control Teams (CCT)

    Squadrons of AC-130 Spectre and MC-130 Combat Talons

    160th SOAR (Black Hawks and Little Birds)

The island was divided between the Army in the south and the Marines in the north. SEAL teams operated in both areas. The majority of the fighting was done in the south. Over time the forces built up to about 5,000 people, but the two Ranger Battalions, about 400 Marines, a large handful of Delta and a small handful of SEALs made the original assault. The 82nd Airborne landed some 800 men later.

Two days before the invasion, the SEALs were tasked to gain Intelligence on Point Salines and the landing beaches there, and to place landing beacons on the runway for the Rangers to home in on. The idea was to drop the men in the water far out to sea and have them power into shore using Zodiac inflatables. Though several tries were made, this was never accomplished due to heavy seas, overburdened soldiers, swamped motors in their Zodiacs and a vigilant coastal patrol. Sadly, four SEALs drowned before even starting for shore.

The most potent force the US delivered to Grenada came in the form of Airborne Rangers. Their tasks were the seizure and security of Salines Airfield and True Blue Campus of the Grand Anse Medical School, both in the southwestern tip of the island. Other Ranger missions involved taking Richmond Hill prison and a supposed stronghold, Calvigny Barracks.

From coup to invasion took just six days, so there was little time for anyone to prepare. The Rangers began moving almost immediately upon receipt of their first warning order.

The initial plan—the one that never comes off—was to land three C-130s full of Rangers on the airstrip and assault inland from there. Once the immediate area was secure the 82nd Airborne would land and expand the perimeter. Released from airfield duty, one company of Rangers would move to the True Blue Campus and look after the students.

After that it was to be Calvigny Barracks, which was supposed to be an army camp of sorts.

That was the plan—this is what happened.

The First Assault

First, the SEAL team could not get ashore, so no homing beacons were on the runway and no accurate Intelligence was forthcoming. On-the-spot air recon saw many obstacles on the runway, so the decision was made to drop the Rangers instead of landing them. The lead aircraft then had navigation equipment failure and dropped back, allowing other aircraft to go ahead.

The first jump was conducted at 500 feet or less without reserve parachutes. There was a 12-15 second fall and the first batch of Rangers was on the ground. Unfortunately, it was almost daylight. The problems with everything from logistics to egos had slowed things down enough to put the previously planned night invasion off until right about dawn.

Some of the planes were given opposing orders at different times which resulted in Rangers taking jump gear off, then having to quickly put the essentials back on for a jump they were told they wouldn't make.

When it was obvious a full-scale jump was desirable, the request was reportedly made and denied. The Rangers would jump piece-meal, and the attached Engineers of the 82nd wouldn't be first on the field to clear obstructions.

Still, the mass of power drove through the lightening sky and began to disgorge Rangers about 5:30 in the morning. Only a few made it down first—a platoon of B Company, 1st Battalion and the Battalion Tactical Operations Center were lonely on the ground. It was almost half-an-hour later before part of A Company came floating down, and another half hour before the rest of that company landed. Not until after 7:00 were the rest of the two companies of the 1st Battalion on the ground.

Company C was elsewhere, having been separated to accompany Delta on a mission to take Richmond Hill Prison.

The men of 1st Battalion dropped into fire. There were anti-aircraft batteries (23mm) and .51 caliber heavy machineguns trained on the incoming flight of C-130s. The AA guns were situated above the airfield along a rise and were unable to depress their barrels enough to hit the big planes coming in at 500 feet. Eyewitness accounts state the blazing rounds went right over the tops of the aircraft. Unfortunately, the machineguns were putting bullets through the airspace the Rangers occupied during the short drop. Later examination showed more than 100 holes and "burns" where rounds had punched through or skimmed off the canopies. Undoubtedly, hot lead was passing through the risers and on both sides and below the dangling soldiers. By some miracle of odds, no one was hit coming down.

Once fully on the ground, 1/75 organized itself on the east end of the runway.

A few minutes after 0700 the sky was filled with the 2nd Battalion that made the drop with much more speed, though they were also taking fire. The battalion was down in 10 minutes. Some of the AA had been eliminated by then, but there was still fire in the sky.

Automatic fire that had been aimed at the planes then focused on the men on the ground. Pinned down and taking rounds, the Rangers wouldn't stay long. One or two of them jumped up and went at the enemy, prompting the whole unit to go forward yelling their battle cries. Very soon the incoming rounds from near the airstrip were all but silenced.

Vehicles parked on the runway had to be removed, some by hotwire, some by pushing. Some even had the keys in them. A hot-wired bulldozer flattened stakes driven into the ground with wire strung between them. One vehicle hot-wired was a sleek Jaguar, which ended up with a trunk full of ammunition.

The commander of A/1/75 was John Abizaid, now a four-star General at the helm of all forces in the Middle East Theater in 2006. Abizaid reportedly rode one of the bulldozers up a hill to take down one of the quad-.51 caliber machineguns that were shooting at the parachuting Rangers. Another bulldozer was hot-wired by Ranger Shoma.

By mid-morning, a platoon of Rangers from 1st Battalion was at the True Blue campus while others were moving north, holding the runway and advancing onto high ground. The 2nd Battalion had secured its area on the west side of the runway and gone north to Canoe Bay.

C-130s, refueled at Barbados while the runway was being secured and cleared, began to land and disgorge vehicles and other equipment including dirt bikes, gun jeeps and Little Bird helicopters.

About mid-afternoon, somebody noticed two men of B/2/75 were not there. The commander went looking for them, guessing their location to be near the Cuban lines. A captured Cuban construction worker was sent forward under a white flag—with about a dozen Rangers—to see what was what. The man went alone into a building full of Cubans and asked them to give up the Rangers or be smashed. The two Rangers and 17 Cuban wounded were taken out, and about 90 Cubans surrendered while they had a chance.

Also in the afternoon, three armored vehicles—BTRs with air-filled tires—counter-attacked, moving toward the runway. They chose a bad time to do so. The majority of the Rangers were at the eastern end of the runway preparing for a major movement east, and a lot of 1/75 men were dug into blocking positions along the approach of the BTRs. The vehicles had scant chance of making the runway. Members of A/2/75 moved through the medical school campus and set up another blocking position. Elements of 1/75 hit the enemy first, unleashing a torrent of fire that pounded the vehicles with 90mm fire multiple times, some at maximum range (400 meters). There was infantry inside the BTRs, and those who survived the 90mm and LAW hits tried to get outside—and they died there, many with M60 rounds in them.

They were not the only ones to feel the power of the Ranger push. Positions on the ridgeline above the runway were overrun one after the other.

A major loss that day came when an RPG and machinegun fire suddenly hit a gun jeep with five Rangers aboard. The Rangers were thrown around and shot up badly in the first volley, but the survivors fought back. One of them climbed back up on the vehicle to get a machinegun and ammunition. Eventually the small group was whittled down to death. Only one man escaped, with five holes in him and an AK47 taken from a dead enemy soldier.
Brendan "Duke" Durkan

This interview was taped at Camp Frank D. Merrill, home of the 5th RTB, where Sergeant Major Durkan was top NCO in the S-3 shop in October, 2005. He graduated Ranger School in May 1984 (Class 7-84), but was in Grenada as a 20-year-old PFC in the 1st Ranger Battalion.

I was with [3rd Platoon] B Company, 1st Battalion, based out of Hunter Army Airfield in Savannah.

[I wasn't aware of what was going on with the other units] until later, afterwards, being a PFC. At that time you're focused mostly on your fire team, probably no higher than your platoon or company. All of our senior leadership were combat veterans from Vietnam.

Were you with the part of B Company that came down first?

No, that was 1st Platoon. B Company and A Company hit first.

Specialist John Reich (1/B/1) was reportedly the first man down.

That was because of the cross up with the aircraft. Also because we de-rigged. That was very interesting. I still remember it very well. I remember trying to sleep in between the wheel well and a jeep. They woke everybody up way before the 20-minute [mark] and said the runway on the island was clear—de-rig. Probably about 30 minutes out. It was daylight. We de-rigged and we passed everything to the front of the aircraft, started out-rigging our rucksacks, and prepping everything to get ready to go in for an air-land mission.

Somewhere before coming into the island, whether there were shots or the first planes coming over realized [something wasn't right], so the first four or five didn't de-rig and the others did. So all the trailing [planes] had to go back around and re-rig. Everything was stuffed into kit bags and thrown to the front of the aircraft to get it out of the way. So the same chute you had, and reserves—there were no 1950s jumped in at that time except machineguns and mortars. Everything was still loose-rigged on the side, tied in with your belt. We tried to rig all that back in. Of course, all the rucksacks were de-rigged, so the majority of the ammunition, claymores, and LAWs were strapped or thrown back on, whether it was a claymore as a reserve parachute, LAWs stuffed on the side, M60 ammunition stuffed in your pockets or down your shirt as your shirt was tucked in. Any way for getting it in was the way for having it.

Each man still carried the maximum load of his personal ammunition as part of his regular gear.

We were lucky not to have to deal with NODs or NVDs [night vision] at the time because they were still one to a squad or one to a platoon.

So, it was organized chaos to say the least, and no JMPI (Jumpmaster Personnel Inspection) afterwards. We were JMPIing each other, whether you were Jumpmaster-qualified or not. It was a quick rig. It was probably 20 minutes at the most by the time of re-issuing the chutes back.

How many men on that C-130?

It was not a full rig because there were no seats. It was slick, had the gun jeeps on there; had the bikes [250cc dirt bikes]. We did not have any Little Birds on that aircraft. The jeeps had M60s and they were the old standard CJ-7.

We were just [getting each other ready] the best we could. How we ever got all our equipment back, our rucksacks and all that other stuff, I'll never know. The rucksacks were left on the plane. Unless you were really good about…but I personally didn't see anybody do it, but there were people that were able to rig their rucksacks and jump them back in again. Me, being a young PFC with the amount of jumps I had…I was just stuffing ammunition.

Did that make it lighter going down?

I don't know if it was lighter [ammo is heavy]. I remember my Platoon Sergeant [Rogers]—we dumped everything out of our rucksacks but the two-quart canteen, one pair of socks, a poncho, and an entrenching tool. No shaving kit. It was all ammunition, claymores, LAWs...

The Jump

The jump was at 500 feet with no reserves?

Some people did [have reserves] from the initial aircraft, but they were already on the ground. We didn't have reserves. Only a few people had them on.

There was sporadic fire. In our perspective it seemed [close], but when you look at the results afterwards, nobody was killed in the air. Probably a lot of holes in the chutes. I don't recall seeing any holes in my chute, but I remember seeing a lot of tracers.

The odds of the jump were extremely successful. We had one hung jumper [still attached to the aircraft, but hanging outside] in 1st Platoon, B Company. Maybe one or two broke their ankles on the runway, which was significantly filled with the amount of stuff that was around.

Alpha was down before us, because they had the lead in the drop zone where the hangers and the houses were up on the northern side of the runway, or to the left as our approach was coming up.

What happened when you hit the ground?

Hit the ground, saw, like normal, some people rolling their parachutes like we did in training, saw some that were just cutting their parachutes away, hopping and popping, canopies blowing everywhere with the wind. Lots of people lying down. A lot of people running.

There were no real maps—they were tourist maps, and no real imagery or photographs for us. I'm sure there were for higher leaders. [But, for us] it was just where your platoon was supposed to go on the runway, the assembly areas where your company mission was supposed to go.

[We] were supposed to get off the airfield and move north into the high ground into a support position, because I was part of a machinegun team. The [overall] objective was to push out and overtake the airhead so that additional landing forces could come in with the bikes and the jeeps, etc.

Second Battalion came in later on, but 1st Battalion had the airfield mostly. Only a small percentage of 2nd Battalion came in [at first]. Alpha Company [1st Battalion] had the west half of the runway. Second Battalion was supposed to pick up most of the follow-on missions to the Cuban barracks and so on.

The 1st Battalion elements got bumped from going after the students when 2nd Battalion birds got into trouble at Calvigny. It wasn't the same mission.

We were supposed to go in there with the Black Hawks for the follow-up missions off the airfield, and we had to get off when the two aircraft collided. Our platoon was loaded up on the birds and had to come off after the accident [at Calvigny barracks].

Were you there when the armored cars came onto the runway?

I still remember that pretty well. It was almost comical in a way, because it was like Daffy Duck during hunting season. By that time we had a real good foothold. Some of the Grenadians were telling us where the Cubans were; we already had the high ground support-by-fire positions. A lot of it was long distance, farther away than our capabilities of reaching with our weapons systems. We still maintained great posture. Mostly the snipers could reach out further than our '60s.

Some of the snipers [Sergeants O'Leary and Magnus], some of B Company's best snipers were reaching out and touching a lot of them.

Who were they shooting at?

The Cuban forces that were out there, and also the same ones who ambushed Alpha Company's gun jeep. We were looking out, watching the valleys [between the high ground occupied by Rangers] and observing fields of fire. No real gunfights were going on at that time. It was mostly hold position and wait for the forces you could hear on the airplanes still coming in. The follow-on forces. They landed right behind us.

The 82nd was coming in after our fights and our gun jeeps were starting to push out the perimeter. It was sometime later when the armored vehicles came down from the east side, coming from the campus heading down toward Point Salinas.

It was like a turkey shoot. Everybody wanted to take a shot. The LAWs were coming out. The 40 mike-mikes were coming out, the 7.62s. Everything was bouncing off. The 90s[mm] were not employed at that time. Later on, they went down by the airfield and engaged, and the 90s smoked them. It was a matter of minutes. The 90s stopped them, but I know we brought in the Corsairs and the Cobra gunships, and Spectre was up above.

Spectre, with its miniguns and other ordnance, was firing in several places on the island.

It seems like there was some fire from the initial one [BTR], but nothing effective. They were shooting down the airfield. We were on a piece of higher ground and could see it coming down the airfield as they made the turn coming in. The only thing you know is true is from your perspective, and on this one hill it didn't look anywhere effective, but if somebody was down on the airfield or further down where A Company [was] it might have been effective.

A Company was downfield by the hangers. Fire from the armored cars was essentially directed toward that point. The 90mm recoilless rifles were employed from airfield level, not from the hill where Durkan was, due to the range.

The FOs used them [the Spectres] and other great assets. It was a real good feeling seeing the Marine helicopters flying around out there, seeing the Cobra gunships flying, the Corsairs flying over you. When it got dark you could look up and see Spectre—see it sitting up there—and it was a real good feeling. There was a lot of support in the area.

Did you have an idea of how many enemy soldiers you were facing?

I think it was agreed it was about 600, so about a battalion. That's why we went in with a battalion-plus. It's hard to say [how many]. I remember sitting in the perimeter with prisoners coming through and not being able to tell which one was Cuban and which was Grenadian, because there were mixed uniforms. We'd have an ambush set and a couple of guys would come walking thru with flex cuffs on and we'd think, "That's interesting." Not something you see everyday.

They were processed out, God knows what they did to interrogate them, but they did a good job segregating them and pushing them out quickly. Hard to say how many people were out there. The ones we were fighting were definitely Cubans. We saw some Grenadians, but [they and] even the Cubans, I would have to say the majority of them we saw, except for the real hard-liners, only a few, would do their duty. They would fire their one magazine of their AK47, then surrender. [Then they could say] I did my job, I was overwhelmed by the Americans, but I fired my gun at them.

The notion of doing one's duty, then surrendering, has been seen in all wars, particularly in WWII. When the Germans and Italians knew they were losing, they would sometimes fire off a few rounds—and maybe kill some Americans—and then surrender. US troops under that watch often had a hard time restraining themselves when prisoners were taken after getting in a couple of last licks. In truth, some didn't make it back to the rear.

Richmond Hill Prison

The first day left the Rangers with five dead and six wounded out of the original landing force. Those figures excluded C/1/75, which had a different experience all together.

Delta had some objectives of its own, and those Rangers provided the muscle. The two groups were flown in by Task Force 160 (160th SOAR) to take down Richmond Hill Prison.

The Night Stalkers of the 160th flew MH-60 Black Hawks to Barbados in preparation, but put their AH/MH-6 "Little Bird" helicopters on C-5 cargo planes. They also flew in support of Delta's probe into Fort Rupert, reportedly an HQ for Grenadian General Austin.

Richmond Hill prison, supposedly loaded with illegally held political prisoners, lay at the bottom of a valley with nearby high ground, on which sat Fort Frederick and some anti-aircraft weapons.

The operation was weighed down by several factors. Primary among those was the late-notice switch made from SEAL Team Six (the original assault group) to Delta, which meant no time to gain adequate Intelligence. They had no idea what they were flying into, and so did not know about the guns above the prison, or the fact they couldn't land outside the prison as planned.

The helicopters were a little late arriving, so the mission had to be carried out in daylight instead of planned-for darkness, sealing the fate of the helicopters and the men in them.

The terrain around the prison is up-and-down and there is no room to land several birds at once for a frontal assault. A quick decision was made to hover over the prison and fast-rope down into the courtyard.

The AA at Fort Frederick was a couple of hundred feet higher and was firing level and below at the sitting-duck helicopters as they attempted to hold steady over the prison, from which came heavy small arms and machinegun fire. Delta and the Rangers were caught in that maelstrom and took grave damage. At least two attempts were made to insert Delta and the Rangers but the cost was too high. Men and machines were getting shot up badly. There was no available air support.

The prison walls were some 20 feet tall and loaded with guard towers, barbed wire, and firing positions. The ground it sat on fell away nearly vertically on three sides. Down one of those sides fell one of the Black Hawks, mortally wounded. The rest of the birds landed a ways down the hill and were immediately pounded by enemy fire from above.

They were trapped and had to wait for reinforcements from Point Salines.

Gary Curtis

Curtis was with Delta under Colonel Charles Beckwith during Grenada operations. He graduated Ranger School in 1964 and served a stint as an RI at Camp Frank D. Merrill's Mountain Phase. He rose to the rank of Major. The reason Delta's operation is included is because, as Curtis said, "Half the house is Ranger, half is Special Forces." In other words, the Ranger Tab is no stranger to a Delta resume. "That's the way it turns out," he said. "They're about the only ones that make it."

We had to disassemble our Black Hawks, put them on C-5As, and fly them to the Bahamas. It was like Grand Central Station, watching us unload the Black Hawks and reassemble them.

Unfortunately, the Air Force couldn't get us there on time, like we were supposed to hit the island in the middle of the night, but we ended up arriving in Grenada in broad daylight. The more we got in-country, the closer we got to our objectives, the volume of fire picked up, picked up, picked up.

The objective was to liberate the prison.

I'm just sitting there in the door shooting down at the guards, who are shooting back at us [hovering above]. For whatever reason we moved off our objective instead of fast roping down into it. The lead pilot had his radio all shot up. With no communication, he came right back over the objective the second time. There was really some withering fire then.

Every airplane was riddled with holes from incoming.

One of the Black Hawks took what was probably an RPG and crashed. The available space over the prison could only hold two birds at once, so the enemy below could focus on each flight.

We got to the runway; the Rangers had dropped in, and assessed the situation. Seems like we sent 18 people back to the Navy ships [as wounded]. I don't think we had anybody killed. Most of the helicopters were ineffective at that point.

Later in the day Delta boarded a transport aircraft and left the island. The Ranger units remained.

Securing The Students

Some things were actually going according to plan. The Ranger mission of securing the True Blue campus had gone smoothly without much opposition and the students were being taken out.

About 10:30 in the morning of the 25th, the Rangers were told there were still students holed up at another medical school campus at Grand Anse. They were not prepared to find students in two different places.

A student at the other campus was in touch with the outside world via HAM radio, while several people in the States were sending messages to Grenada over the airwaves. The student operator hooked up with those in the States and told them where he was and what was happening. The students were trapped in a tower at the Grand Anse campus couldn't get hold of any US troops. The HAM operators, working in concert in different parts of the Americas, were able to connect the necessary military personnel and the students together, affecting a rescue by Rangers.

Ham radio operator Bill Kinsland of Dahlonega, Georgia, was one of those involved.

Bill Kinsland

This interview was done on tape in the Hometown Bookstore in Dahlonega, Georgia, February 19, 2005.

I woke up early in the morning and flipped on the radio, and they had emergency calls out on the 20-meter HAM band. Something was going on and I couldn't figure out quite what at first, but then I realized there was an operation going on down in the Caribbean and they needed HAM radio operators to back it up. I thought, well, that's interesting. Why are they calling on us?

I got to tuning around…there was a Net that normally meets early in the morning, called the International Assistance Traffic Net [IATN]. They operate on 14303 kilohertz and I tuned in there to see if I could pick up anything, and sure enough they were trying to contact somebody on Grenada. There was a lot of concern about students in the medical school.

When Kinsland signed in, he found contact with the students had probably already been made, but two-way commo was not working.

Propagation that day was really mixed up. They could hear them, but they couldn't get back to them. Sometimes you have a lot of atmospheric interference [in HF communication]. I kept listening, and I kept hearing stations down there on [and around] Grenada, so I jumped in and made contact with—I can't remember his call sign, but his name was Mark Barratella—he was a student there at St. George's.

He was really frantic and really sounded scared. He was talking about how there was all kinds of shooting going on. They finally got the students together in this one place and were kind of reluctant to say exactly where that one place was.

They were scared because they were being shot at from all sides. They said bullets were passing through and you could hear choppers going overhead. They were in this tower at the medical school, up in the top, under tables and chairs. You could actually hear it on the microphone coming through.

Whether the students were being targeted, or whether they were in a crossfire zone is unclear, though is no evidence they were being shot at directly except for the students reporting someone was shooting at them. Either way, they were in a bad situation.

Anyway, I jumped in there and they started talking to me and telling me what their situation was. We had this IATN going on and people were getting excited and trying to call in, so I suggested I move them off frequency.

He moved them off frequency about 10 kilohertz and continued to get information from them, leaving the IATN open to manage other traffic.

I tried to get through to the Ranger Camp on the telephone and couldn't.

The American Embassy in Mexico City was on the frequency. It was a HAM radio operator who lived in the Embassy. I relayed information from Grenada to him, and he, through his diplomatic channels I guess, sent it to the Navy Department in Washington. They radioed it back down to their ships off shore at Grenada. They, I guess, got that information to their choppers and Ranger units and whatnot.

Grand Anse

The Rangers made plans to go after the students at Grand Anse using Marine CH-46 helicopters for transport to move elements of Companies A and B of the 1st Battalion to the area. This time there were AC-130 gunships for support, plus two remaining Marine Cobras.

There were to be three waves of three CH-46s each, with A Company arriving first, then B, then C coming in to move the students to waiting CH-53D Sea Stallion helicopters. Of course, few things go entirely as planned and the order of the aircraft was mixed going into the attack. A and B Companies landed out of order, and the first three birds missed the intended LZ all together.

There was some incoming fire from the ground but the main problems were caused by trees, resulting in one bird shutting down in the surf with Rangers piling out when the water intruded.

Another bird was also tree-damaged.

Still, the mission was completed in less than half-an-hour. The students were loaded on the big Sea Stallions and flown out to a waiting ship, the *USS Guam*. The Rangers likewise airlifted out safely, except for 11 men accidentally left behind. Sent out as flankers, the team had not returned by the time of the extraction and was still on the ground. They were notified to move toward "friendly lines" currently occupied by the 82nd Airborne, but they chose instead to go back to the downed CH-47 in the surf line and secure an inflatable boat. Unfortunately, the raft was damaged and didn't support everyone. After a good bit of time in the water, they were picked up near midnight and taken to the *USS Caron*.

Tragedy At Calvigny Barracks

About three miles inland from Point Salines Airfield was a group of buildings called Calvigny Barracks, supposedly a point of housing and training for enemy troops. The small amount of Intelligence available indicated the possibility of a couple of hundred men there.

It was slated as a first-day objective, but one thing and another kept it off the charts until the 27th. By that time the 82nd Airborne was well entrenched and the Rangers of 2/75, supported by elements of C/1/75, were OPCON'd to the 2nd Brigade.

Sixteen Black Hawks headed out to sea carrying the Ranger force, then turned into land. There were gunships, artillery, and Naval fire available for support. Those fires had already devastated the barracks compound and surrounding area.

Companies of the 2nd were to land to the south and southeast of Calvigny Barracks, with B Company taking care of some "Intelligence-said-maybe" anti-aircraft guns. The men of C/1/75 were to hold part of the perimeter and act as a back-up force if needed.

That was the plan.

In a stirring sight, the dark Black Hawks bored in from the sea, flaring upwards to the appropriate height. The first four came in fast in trailing line. The first two set down safely, but the third—which may or may not have been hit—made too much forward progress and plowed into the second bird down. The fourth Black Hawk sheared sharply away and smacked down hard in a ditch. The pilot wouldn't give up and forced the bird to fly, but it was crippled and crashed again not far away.

Bad enough three birds were down in less than half-a-minute, but the debris from those large machines—rotors flying through the air—killed three 2/75 Rangers and injured four others.

Company A, 2nd Battalion, had lost good men in a senseless tragedy, but they got it back together and pressed on. B and C Companies made it down all right, as did C/1/75, and all were ready to take on whatever was present. Oddly enough, the barracks were deserted.

The Rangers spent the night in what was left of the buildings on the site.

Shortly after that night, their missions accomplished, the Rangers were taken home. Nineteen Americans died on Grenada, and about half of them were Rangers.

Perry Doerr

Master Sergeant (ret) Doerr attended Ranger School in March 1981. This interview was conducted via email.

I was the S-3 [Operations] Air NCO for 3rd Brigade/82nd Airborne [as a Staff Sergeant]. I was in Colonel Terry Scott's Assault CP. We arrived on the island on the first plane in on the second day of the invasion. We were the first 3rd Brigade unit in. The Ranger Battalions and the three Battalions of 2nd Bde/82nd went in on October 25.

We got sniped at—not specifically, but in our general area—but no close combat.

3rd Brigade units moved off and took up positions from the 2nd Ranger Battalion. We then began a movement to contact to clear the east shore of the island, with 2nd Bde on our left flank and the sea to our right. We halted short of Calvigny Barracks so the 2nd Rangers could raid it October 27. Several helicopters crashed on landing there, killing or injuring some soldiers. A 2nd Battalion medic received the Silver Star for his actions in treating the wounded under fire.

As the S-3 Air (my officer was new and pushed our units out from Bragg, joining us a few days later), I was Colonel Scott's Air Ops guy. I kept track of the flow of forces in, monitored MEDEVAC aircraft and CAS (close air support; fast movers from the Air Force and the Navy) with our USAF LNOs.

My first impression after getting off the plane was looking at an AC-130 lighting somebody up. That was comforting. But what was not comforting was the fact that we did not control much terrain off the end of the airfield. In order to land C-141s, the planes had to go to the end of the runway and spot-turn around. They would then unload, taking about 20-30 minutes. Problem with this was the terrain rose rather steeply and the PRA/Cubans (People's Revolutionary Army) were only 500-800 meters away on the high ground. I remember thinking one determined guy with a hand-held mortar could have taken out an airplane and then we would have big trouble. We were lucky their heart was not really in the fight.

There were a bunch of students waiting to get on the planes as we got off. This was the first group from the campus right off the end of the airfield, the True Blue site. Later that day 2nd Battalion (Rangers) would go get the rest from the Grand Anse campus near St. George.

By the time I got there the Ranger Battalions and the 2nd Brigade guys had most resistance eliminated. There were only scattered pockets that were just hiding or looking for a chance to give up. They were disorganized and posed a minor threat. As we expanded the movement to contact to gain more secure real estate, the PRA started to strip off uniforms and melt into the population.

SPECIAL OPERATIONS—HOW IT ALL FITS TOGETHER

Lessons learned in Iran in 1979 and Grenada in 1983 gave rise to a much better organized and supported Special Operations effort. The idea was to be able to use all the assets of American Armed Forces Special Operations in one area of interest at the same time—under one command. That command authority is passed down the line through all the various commands until a Ranger puts his feet on the ground along with Special Forces, Air Force commandos, SEALS and others.

The Breakdown

Each branch of the military has its own Special Operations section. Those sections can work independently or together, as the instance may require. Each works under its own command, which in turn can work with other commands under the authority of Central Command (CENTCOM), or the National Command Authority (NCA).

Located at McDill Air Force Base, Florida, the US Special Operations Command (USSOCOM) is the Armed Forces umbrella under which certain elements of the four service arms can unite for joint missions. Those organizations are then termed Joint Special Operations Forces (JSOF) and can be welded into Joint Special Operations Task Forces (JSOTF) for use in such places as Iraq and Afghanistan. The first such use was during the invasion of Panama, December 20, 1989.

The Department of the Army (DA) founded the US Army Special Operations Command (USASOC) on the first of December 1989, to oversee the readiness and capabilities of Army Special Operations Forces (SOF). Additionally, the formation of USASOC helped to simplify the command apparatus of the Army Reserve SOF and greatly enhance the communication and coordination with USSOCOM.

USASOC has its own umbrella, under which the major commands of Army Reserves and National Guard SOF reside. USASOC is responsible for overseeing the National Guard SOF training and readiness capability to make sure they are in line with active force capability.

Army SOF under the auspices of USASOC includes Ranger, Special Forces (also SF-Delta), Special Operations Aviation units (160th SOAR), and Psyops and Civil Affairs people.

Further down the line of command and control are corps and division usage of SOF. Each division must have a contingency plan for coordination with SOF in case they are deployed together.

Since Ranger units can deploy anywhere in a short time, there must be a flexible command structure to insure adequate integration of forces and the necessary logistics and Intelligence to support the unit.

Rangers can be used as an Army-only force, or as part of a JSOTF. Generally, Rangers are the first combat units into an embattled area to secure an area and protect the follow-on forces while landing.

The very first people in are often Pathfinders—only a few—but very necessary.

Once the entry of forces is completed, the Rangers are sometimes placed under operational control of another unit or task force, allowing them to plan for and execute other Special Operations missions.

Since the concept of war has graduated—either upward or downward, depending on your point of view—the size, usage, and placement of forces have also graduated to a new level. Special Operations Command (SOCOM) has been given more and livelier missions and the financial support and equipment to accomplish them.

Defense Secretary Donald Rumsfeld said, "The global nature of the war, the nature of the enemy and the need for fast, efficient operations in hunting down and rooting out terrorist networks around the world have all contributed to the need for an expanded role for the Special Operations Forces."

In 2004, Special Operations troops were on the ground, in the water, or in the air in some 150 countries, chasing terrorists, drug runners, weapons smugglers, and general bad guys.

During the Gulf War in 1991, SOCOM was commanded by General Carl Stiner, who said, "I am so thankful that our nation has these kinds of forces. If we didn't we would be up the creek on the war on terrorism."

THE 75TH RANGER REGIMENT

Formation

General Creighton Abrams brought Rangers back into service in 1974-75 by re-activating the 1st and 2nd Battalions from their WWII stasis. Abrams insisted the units be "the best light infantry unit in the world" and a "standard bearer for the rest of the Army."

In 1983, Operation Urgent Fury—the takedown of Grenada—proved several things to the planners as well as the Brass. For one thing, Special Operations, including Rangers, Delta and SEALS, was going to have to get better organized and integrated under a narrower command structure. The action also showed the need for more Rangers, which resulted in the formation of the 3rd Battalion in 1984. That gave the Rangers enough battalions for the 75th Ranger Regimental Headquarters to be established the same year.

The 75th Ranger Regiment is now part of US Army Special Operations Command, where it can be used to its fullest capabilities. Though Regimental Headquarters is at Fort Benning, Operational Headquarters for the Regiment is at Fort Bragg (Pope AFB), where Joint Special Operations is headquartered.

There is a higher center of control beyond Regimental HQ, but for the purposes of this project, suffice to say "Special Operations."

Mission

The 75th Ranger Regiment is the premiere light infantry strike force of the US Army, with capabilities to launch missions in support of US policy anywhere in the world within a short period of time.

Either in company force or as the Regiment, Rangers specialize in airfield seizure and raids, whether as a singular objective or in support of conventional follow-on forces. Ranger units also deploy in support—the muscle—of SFOD-Delta, and can also be used incrementally for training, recon, or serious guard duty.

For a time, Rangers guarded Saddam Hussein.

Being first and foremost Airborne Light Infantry, the 75th RR can also be called upon to perform infantry-type duties for general-purpose forces in embattled area of operations, including both offensive and defensive postures. Generally, the Rangers are relieved of duty by conventional forces once their objectives have been achieved.

Organization

The Regiment consists of three battalions. The 1st Battalion is at Hunter Army Airfield, Savannah, Georgia, the 2nd Battalion at Fort Lewis, Washington, and the 3rd Battalion is home at Fort Benning, Georgia.

The battalions are organized in identical fashion, consisting of three rifle companies and a Headquarters and Headquarters Company. The battalions are each authorized 580 men, though they are often over strength by 10-to-15 percent to make up for men attending schools or on other assignments.

Regimental Headquarters is made up of a Command Group, a normal staff of S-1 through S-5, a communications detachment, a recon detachment, a Ranger Training Detachment, a fire-support element and a Company HQ.

There is also a team of planners that can be deployed quickly to provide liaison with Special Operations Commands in areas of interest. The team is composed of experienced men who put together contingency plans for overall Ranger missions, including fire support, communications, logistics, and Intelligence. Since the Regiment depends heavily on larger units for in-theater support, coordination and planning cannot be overemphasized, particularly in terms of fire support and Intelligence.

Company Breakdown

    Company Headquarters
    Company Commander—Captain
    Executive Officer—Lieutenant
    Fire Support Chief—Lieutenant
    First Sergeant
    Supply Sergeant
    Tactical Communication Chief—Sergeant
    Fire Support—Sergeant
    Team Leader—Sergeant
    Unit Clerk—Sergeant
    Forward Observer—Sergeant
    Company Aidmen—Sergeant (2)
    Company Aidmen—Corporal (2)
    Armourer—Corporal
    Tactical Commo Systems Operator/Mechanic—Corporal
    Sniper—Corporal
    Fire Support Specialist—Corporal
    Radio Operators—2
    Radio Telephone Operators—3

    Each company has three platoons
Platoon Breakdown
    Headquarters
    Platoon Leader—Lieutenant
    Platoon Sergeant
    Radio Operators—2

Each platoon has three rifle squads and a weapons squad.

Rifle Squad Breakdown

> Squad Leader—Sergeant
> Team Leader—Sergeants (2)
> Automatic Riflemen—Corporal (2)
> Grenadiers—Corporal (2)
> Senior Riflemen—Corporal (2)
> Riflemen—2

Machinegun Squad Breakdown

> Squad Leader—Sergeant
> Machinegunners—Corporal (3)
> Assistant Machinegunners—3
> Ammunition Bearers—3

Weapons Platoon
> Platoon Headquarters
> Platoon Leader—Lieutenant

Hit Hard, But Travel Light

Considering its postion as the top strike force of the Army, the Ranger Regiment must be ready to go at all times. The three battalions take turns being on Ready Reaction Force 1 (RRF1), which means they must be traveling to a mission within 18 hours. One Rifle Company that can deploy in nine hours with battalion command and control maintains even quicker reaction. Rotation of RRF1 from one battalion to another happens about every 13 weeks, though Regimental Headquarters is on high alert at all times.

Battalions on RRF1 cannot train off-post as they must be near their supplies and equipment and mode of transport. They generally wear beepers when on alert.

The other two battalions are free to train wherever needed, but those units must also be ready to deploy quickly, whether to a direct area of interest, or to a staging area either in or out of the US.

To provide the necessary capabilities of such a force, Rangers are highly trained and motivated to conduct raids, seize airfields, recover personnel and equipment, or break down and do conventional light infantry operations. To accomplish any of the above they are able to infiltrate and exfiltrate by land, sea, or air.

Although modern Rangers are being used more to the point of their existence, Ranger history shows plainly that any Ranger unit used in line combat will do better than the regular corps by using better training and a higher degree of aggressiveness.

Still, Ranger units have limitations when it comes to heavy firepower and transportation. Lacking organic support systems, Ranger units must rely on larger in-theater units for heavy fire support and logistics. Typically, a Ranger unit leaves home with just five days' supply.

Although Ranger units are over-loaded with hand-held firepower and machineguns, there is very little anti-armor weaponry, and only the Stinger Missile (shoulder-fired) serves as air defense.

Vehicles are limited to modified Land Rovers, called Ranger Special Operations Vehicles (RSOV), and motorbikes.

Each battalion is authorized 12 RSOVs, primarily used in airfield seizures. The RSOV can carry up to seven men, and boasts a mounted M240 machinegun and either a Mark-19 grenade launcher or a .50 cal heavy machinegun. There is also usually some type of anti-armor weapon on board. The RSOVs can cover distance quickly, as do the 10 authorized 250cc dirt bikes, giving the Ranger Battalion a longer reach with dispersed fire power and greater extension of observation.

In addition, Ranger units in Afghanistan are currently using the eight-wheeled Stryker light armored vehicles to get around. These can be used as gun platforms or for carrying troops, or both. Certain types can carry 105mm cannons and TOW missile launchers.

Through cooperation with other service arms, Rangers can use external fire support for success when their organic weapons are not enough. Fixed-wing and helicopter attacks, Naval fires, and AC-130 gunships add to conventional artillery support to ensure solid coverage of Ranger missions.

Support Elements

Ranger Support Elements (RSE) supply the Regiment with riggers, maintenance staffs, truck drivers and others while the Rangers are on home turf. The RSE is not organic to the Regiment and only go as far as out-loading equipment for deployment. The RSE stays home. On the road Rangers must count on others for support.

Intelligence Gathering—S-2 Section

The Ranger Regiment can be called upon by the Department of the Army for missions anywhere in the world, any time of the year, in any type of climate or terrain. The diverse nature of those missions, as with any military mission, must be thoroughly planned for and directed before the first Ranger sets foot on the ground in enemy territory.

Though the term "military Intelligence" has been jokingly referred to as an oxymoron, MI through the years has saved a lot of lives. Modern requirements dictate the need for as complete a picture of the enemy as possible—his home, training, location, weapons and capabilities. In short, when a Ranger faces his enemy, his knowledge of that enemy is based on hundreds of man-hours of data sifting. Such data comes from many places and in many forms.

Intelligence and Electronic Warfare (IEW) support to the Regiment is non-organic, but the resources run deep and wide. The IEW derives input from several specifically tasked sources.

Types of Intelligence Sources

Human Intelligence—HUMINT
Imagery Intelligence—IMINT
Electronic Warfare—EW
Signals Intelligence—SIGINT
Technical Intelligence—TECHINT

Combat Intelligence—CI

Ranger missions are generally short in duration and limited in scope, but the precise nature of fast attack requires a high degree of accurate Intelligence to back up the firepower. Also, Intelligence assets help to ascertain the proximity of civilians, enemy reinforcements, weather patterns, even the pros and cons of the local political systems.

The Regiment has a fairly large Intelligence system organic to the unit, but outside data is also sent in by various organizations in America and abroad. To that end, the S-2 deploys with the Regiment to give continuous updates and receive on-the-spot information.

The Regimental S-2 section is responsible for gathering and disseminating information from, and to, several components, both military and civilian. Such information comes from several sources and may be given to higher or lower echelons. S-2 also has the authority to task a small unit for Intelligence purposes.

To accomplish this, the S-2 section is made up of several different teams, each with its own directives and manner of Intelligence gathering, all working together to produce a clear picture of an impending battlefield.

The S-2 section functions thusly:

Tactical Intelligence Team—Deploys with the Regiment Tactical Operations Center, but can also be detached to individual battalions. The Tac Team is the manager of incoming Intelligence and maintains a worldwide base of information. It also exposes any shortcomings in the system. Once information is sufficiently gathered, the Tac Team produces summaries and reports. It also produces Intelligence Preparation of the Battlefield (IPB) to illuminate the commander on expected terrain features.

Order of Battle Team—The OB Team is responsible for knowing the enemy's units and capabilities. The team catalogues enemy strength, location, commanders and possible actions. The OB and Tac Teams generally work closely together.

Imagery Team—Known as the IMINT Team, this unit gathers photos, maps, satellite images and other imagery to produce a library of Intelligence used by commanders—including battalion-level—in planning operations. Today's imagery is a far cry from the still photos taken from small planes in WWII.

Combat Intelligence Team—The CI Team works closely with the Tac Team, often in the battle zone. Two main responsibilities are helping support operational security, and acting as liaison with outside Intelligence sources and law enforcement.

Recon Detachment—A combination of LRRPs and Pathfinders, the Recon unit generally operates in small units to do pre-strike tactical surveillance. Specially trained for the task of recognizing and understanding the layout and enemy status on an impending battlefield, the RD also acts as Pathfinders for landing zones and drop zones. All members are rated in free-fall parachuting and swimming abilities. The RD can stay out as long as five days, and is a valuable human Intelligence source.

Military Intelligence Detachment—The MI does a lot of things, including making sure the Regiment is ready to deploy within 18 hours—in itself a huge job. MI also keeps a series of workbooks updated with information on countries, order of battle, and the like for the use of the commander when preparing for deployment. Daily and weekly briefings are given from the Daily Read File and the Weekly Bluebook, and a Top Ten Hot Country List is kept of possible hot spots.

Battalion S-2

Battalion-level S-2 sections augment the Regimental S-2, and can give local support to command decisions on the battlefield in terms of terrain and threat analysis. With the S-3 (operations), the battalion S-2 can task recon missions, and as necessary, Regimental assets can be assigned to a battalion.

More In-House Support

Ranger Psychological Operations

Another important organic asset is the Psyops team. Though Rangers are not normally associated with psychological warfare, they do their share. The Psyops team tells them what to do and how to do it, along with the responsibility of helping to lower the effectiveness of the enemy by working with the local population.

Medical—The Ranger Regiment possesses fine surgeons and medical staff.

Weather—Provided by the Air Force, a staff officer gives pertinent weather information to the commander.

USAF Liaison—At both battlion and regimental level, the Air Force liaison team serves as a vital link to available air assets.

Fire Support—Having little heavy firepower of their own, Rangers use fire support as a valuable tool against the enemy. Fire support coordination takes place at battalion and Regimental level.

Ron Rokosz

I went to 1/509th in Vicenza, Italy as Battalion S-3. I was there two years when Wayne Downing called and said they were going to form a Ranger Regiment at Fort Benning, and he wanted me to come back as his Deputy. So, [my] tour in Vicenza was curtailed by about six months, and I went to Benning.

Downing was already there, with most of his key staff. They had moved into a renovated barracks building. Almost everyone in the headquarters were individuals who had served in either 1/75 or 2/75 previously. 3/75 was being formed at the same time. In fact, the activation ceremonies for the Regimental Headquarters and 3/75 were conducted together—it was one ceremony. Don't exactly recall how long that was after I got there. I remember I was Commander of Troops and the ceremony was done on the parade field in front of Infantry Hall.

At some point, the commander of 2/75 was relieved over a death in a live-fire incident in Honduras. I went out there as acting commander for a couple of months. After that, I returned to Benning and shortly thereafter, the commander of 3/75 was relieved over a personal indiscretion and I went out there as acting commander. Best recollection is that was for a shorter period, maybe a month, or six weeks. A turbulent period.

Keith Nightingale was commanding 1/75 at the time, and he used to joke with me that if he heard I was moving east of Macon, Georgia he was going to send a hit team after me. *1/75 was at Fort Stewart, Georgia.*

Keith Antonia

Rank means very little in the Ranger Regiment. There's a lot of military courtesy, but there's no respect unless you earn it. Leaders eat with their subordinates, live with them in the field, and share their hardships and burdens. Those who can't earn their subordinates' respect, fail. Those who have their subordinates' respect, succeed in whatever mission they're given. Leadership in the Regiment is a privilege—not a right of rank.

Why Rangers Are Elite

All Tabbed soldiers in the Regiment are four-time volunteers: for the Army, Airborne School, the Ranger Regiment, and Ranger School.

It is possible to get into a Ranger unit without a Ranger Tab, but advancement requires it.

Gaining entrance to the Regiment is not as easy as simply volunteering. Prospective members must pass rigid physical, mental and moral tests before admission—and then they must be able to maintain it through all that follows.

Officers and Combat-Arms NCOs must be Airborne and Ranger-qualified, though the lower ranks can apply and be accepted to be trained in-house, and then attend Ranger School. Such men are said to be "born in the Regiment"—termed Batt-boys.

When coming into the Regiment, Ranger-qualified officers and NCOs attend a Ranger Orientation Program (ROP) to help integrate them into the unit and educate them on policy and standards. Enlisted men must go through the Ranger Indoctrination Program (RIP) to ensure their ability to maintain the expectations of the Regiment. Those enlisted soldiers coming in who are not Tabbed must attend a Pre-Ranger course before being slotted for Ranger School.

Rangers live to train and train to live. Training in all types of environments and weather—jungle, frozen tundra, desert, mountain and water—it is all there for a well-rounded education. Training is everything for the Rangers. It is a large part of what separates them from other units.

Standards are high, but they must be met to continue membership in the Regiment, and to continue a raised state of readiness. Rangers are always taught to expect the unexpected.

75th Ranger Regiment Honors

This list does not include the wars in Afghanistan and Iraq, which will certainly add (at least) credit for those campaigns, if not more. There is already at least one Distinguished Unit Citation.

Campaign Participation Credit

World War II

    Algeria-French Morocco (with arrowhead)

    Tunisia

    Sicily (with arrowhead)

    Naples-Foggia (with arrowhead)

    Anzio (with arrowhead)

    Rome-Arno

    Normandy (with arrowhead)

    Northern France

    Rhineland

Ardennes-Alsace
Central Europe
New Guinea
Leyte (with arrowhead)
Luzon
India-Burma
Central Burma

Vietnam

Advisory
Defense
Counteroffensive
Counteroffensive, Phase II and III
Tet Counteroffensive
Counteroffensive, Phase IV, V, and VI
Tet 1969 Counteroffensive
Summer-Fall 1969
Winter-Spring 1970
Sanctuary Counteroffensive
Counteroffensive, Phase VII
Consolidation I and II
Cease-Fire

Decorations
Presidential Unit Citations (Army)
WWII: El Guettar, Salerno, Pointe du Hoc, Saar River Area, Myitkyina
Vietnam: 1966-68
Valorous Unit Awards
Vietnam: II Corps Area, Binh Duong Province, III Corps Area 1969, Fish Hook, III
Corps Area 1971, Thua Thien-Quang Tri
Grenada
Mogadishu
Meritorious Unit Commendations (Army)
Vietnam 1968-69-70
Pacific Area

Keith Antonia—Changes in Regimental Support Forces and Training

When I commanded my company [early 80s] it was 186 [men]. That's a big company. That was the Rifle Company, but we always had our attachments with us. We always had our medics, and I counted them because they were attached to us, and we always had our artillery guys. Maybe the Infantry was 150 or so and the other 30 were attached.

We had an FO [forward observer] and an RTO in each platoon, and then we had a FIST [fire support] team at Company Headquarters. That team was a Lieutenant, a Sergeant, one or two RTOs, and each platoon had a Sergeant and a Specialist, minimum, for artillery.

Rangers have a reputation for making good use of artillery and other fire support. To that end, attached troops train with the Rangers and become part of the group.

That is one reason why Rangers are good with artillery or any kind of fire support. We're talking about helicopter gunships, AC-130 gunships, Naval gunfire, fast-moving fighters and bombers, and artillery and mortars. The artillery guys are actually assigned to Ranger Companies. They were not in artillery battalions and just came down to be trained. They were assigned and trained with the Ranger Companies all the time.

I believe that is still going on.

In the mid-1990s Antonia was first LNO, then S-3 of the Regiment. During that time organic Ranger firepower was increased and other changes were made.

I was S-3 of the Ranger Regiment for two years. Colonel [Stan] McChrystal wanted to make some significant changes to our TO&E. He wanted to consolidate the mortars—we only had 60mm mortars at the time. He wanted to consolidate them at the battalion level and arm them with 60 mike-mikes, 81s, and 120s. So, one of my projects was to change the TO&E, which meant going all the way up through multiple changes of command of Generals to approve all that.

He also wanted other changes. He wanted to form sniper platoons in each Ranger Battalion. In the time before that we had designated snipers in companies, and sometimes some companies had sniper teams attached to their company HQ. He wanted to consolidate all the snipers and create a platoon at the battalion level.

He also wanted to get an armored vehicle —six armored vehicles—and put them in the battalions as a result of Somalia, because you couldn't get across the street without an armored vehicle. We were looking at all different kinds. Wheeled vehicles, we were looking at those little German Weasels that had tracks. We wanted a small armored vehicle so we could move small elements of Rangers through the streets in sniper fire and stuff like that.

"Stuff like that" includes shrapnel and RPGs.

I know that now the Ranger Regiment has Strykers [lightly armored, wheeled troop carrier]. I think they have 18 Strykers in-theater right now [2005]. They were not organic to the Ranger Regiment, but now they are.

We also tried to make other changes, which have happened. We put a Physical Therapist Officer in every single battalion. We did a lot of stuff to change the Ranger Regiment, based on lessons learned in Somalia.

Colonel McChrystal also changed the entire focus of the Ranger training programs. We threw out our training manual—Training Circular 350-1—and completely changed the training so it focused on four things.

One was medical training. He wanted every single Ranger to receive enough medical training to keep his buddy alive until he could get to a medic. While the Rangers were in Somalia they could not move the wounded men to a medic or a casualty collection point for hours and hours.

The second emphasis was physical training [PT]. Every Ranger would foot-march 10 miles a week with a 50-pound ruck, and then do a 25-mile march with a ruck every quarter, and in between those quarters they would do a 30-mile march.

They also had to learn the nine hand-to-hand combat moves that were developed by the Gracie brothers, these ultimate fighters. He paid them to train NCOs in the Regiment on their fighting techniques.

The techniques are heavy on grappling, though there are some deadly strikes. The stealthy removal of sentries is much practiced, and it is not gentle.

The Ranger Regiment is sort of a laboratory where techniques and things are developed. A lot of the standard operating procedures and battle tactics for light Infantry forces came out of the Ranger Regiment. The hand-to-hand combat moves the entire Infantry now trains and teaches.

Now that's doctrine across the Army, but McChrystal started that because he felt that when a Private came into the Regiment, that Private wants to feel like a bad-ass. I don't think McChrystal felt that Rangers would be [much] involved in hand-to-hand combat; instead he used it as a thing to boost confidence and as a PT thing.

The other thing was he had every Ranger fire his weapon at night at least seven nights a month, and to qualify, whether individual or crew-served weapons, at night to the same standard the rest of the Army did during the day.

The fourth emphasis was on small unit battle drills, battle drills, battle drills.

So, we had about a three-page training manual, and if you were doing any other training you were in trouble. This was 1997-98-99.

Performance Oriented Training is the standard in the Regiment and at the training camps, but Antonia said the tasks remained the same, though the focus on training was different.

Regimental Reconnaissance Detachment

All Rangers are taught stealth and surveillance techniques—skills a good recon man should know—however, as loaded with talent and expertise as the Regiment is, Headquarters needed a highly trained recon unit of its own to work directly for the commander.

The Regimental Reconnaissance Detachment (RRD) came into being in October 1984, about the same time as Regimental Headquarters, to which it was assigned. The RRD works only for the Rangers and cannot be under operational control of any other unit.

The small detachment is broken down into three four-man teams that include three scouts and a Team Leader. Headquarters is also a four-man unit consisting of a Recon Platoon Leader, a senior Recon Sergeant, an RTO, and a communications mechanic. The importance of communications to the team cannot be overstated. For that reason, the RRD handles its own burst-transmissions, relays, and receptions.

As of 2006, members of the unit must be E-6 (Staff Sergeant) or above. To be a member of this elite unit—within the ranks of the elite—heavy training over a 20-week period produces a soldier with extra expertise in areas such as navigation, advanced first aid, military free fall techniques and survival. Escape and evasion is also a big part of the extra training, as the teams are often way out ahead of friendly forces and very much on their own until a means of exfiltration is given.

The RRD does much of what the old Lurps did; recon a future strike zone, find the enemy and/or designate a target, and note the terrain. In short, The RRD must be the eyes and ears of the commander by accomplishing one or more of three tasks: Active Reconnaissance, Surveillance, and Direct Action.

However, the Lurps of old and the relatively new LRS Units are tasked for long-term passive reconnaissance in most instances, while the RRD is more of an immediate need player used by the Ranger commander. One or more teams are available to all three Ranger Battalions.

The RRD is not generally used as an assault group, but it can fight if need be, occasionally being tasked to take down selected small targets. Insertion techniques run the gamut from helicopter to SCUBA, and they don't mind HALOs. Even small boats are used, but once inside enemy territory—often deep inside—the team usually has to move by foot, carrying everything they need.

Making good use of night-vision devices of varying kinds, the RRD teams can hang out in an AO for several days, using open eyes as well as several types of sensors and unattended cameras. They can also place navigational beacons and jammers, among other techno-items such as target designation electronics, and report on the weather at the same time. Like the Alamo Scouts in the Philippines, a good recon team can find landing zones, collect Combat Intelligence before and after combat, and above all, stay hidden.

The RRD is being used in Iraq and Afghanistan, and has been deployed to Bosnia, Kosovo, and Haiti.

What does it take to be a Regimental Commander?

Experience—Before taking Regimental Command, a Colonel has been assigned all over the place and done many different tasks. Previous command is a must.

Knowledge—The number of schools a commander has been through makes regular college look easy in comparison. Most commanders also possess Masters' Degrees earned outside the military.

A backbone of iron—Rangers are young and tough. They are extremely aggressive. They have a tendency to jump into heavy combat on a moment's notice. They require excellent leadership.

Ranger Respect—Discipline among Rangers is based on self respect, unit respect and respect for the leader.

Wayne Downing—Bio

General Wayne Downing is a Ranger legend—an icon of the early days of command of Battalion and Regiment. He has risen to four-star heights during his 33 years in military service, and gone on to do good things for the US Government in the fight against terrorism. His lengthy biography is shown in abbreviated form below, followed by his interview.

Downing is a graduate of the United States Military Academy at West Point, Class of 1962, and holds an MBA in Operations Research/Business.

He went through IOBC and the Ranger Course at Fort Benning, 1962-63, and was assigned as a Platoon Leader, B/1/503rd Infantry, 173rd Airborne Brigade, in Okinawa, in April

1963. He took the position of Liaison Officer of the same unit from June 1964 to September, and then in December became the Aide-de-Camp to the Commanding General, 173rd. This lasted until October 1965, during which time the 173rd landed at Vung Tau, Vietnam.

Downing was promoted to Captain in November 1965, and became S-2 (Intelligence), and S-5 (Civil Affairs) Officer for 1st Brigade, 173rd, until April 1966.

He returned to Fort Benning and became an Instructor in Tactics for the Internam Defense and Development Committee, Tactics Group, Brigade and Battalion Operations Department, USAIS, until August 1967.

His first command was Company E, 3rd Battalion, 1st Training Brigade, USAIS, Fort Benning.

From January 1968 to September, he went back to school, taking the IOAC, then was named as Commander, Company A (Counterinsurgency), 2nd Battalion, 14th Infantry Regiment, 25th Infantry Division, back in Vietnam. By December of that year he was S-3 of the 2nd Battalion, which lasted until September 1969, during which time he was promoted to Major.

Still in Operations, Downing was boosted to S-3 of the 2nd Brigade, 25th ID until October 1969. Then, once again he went back to school, spending a couple of years at Tulane University, and then attending Armed Forces Staff College in Norfolk, Virginia until June 1972.

Next were a couple of years as a Senior Operations Research/Systems Analyst for the Office of the Secretary of Defense, which lasted until February 1975.

1st Battalion

Downing came home to the Rangers in March 1975, still a Major, where he was S-3 and later, Executive Officer, 1st Battalion (Ranger), 75th Infantry, at Fort Stewart, Georgia. In June he was promoted to Lieutenant Colonel, but stayed with 1st Battalion until December 1976.

For the next few months he was Commander, Task Force (Alaska), 24th Infantry Division, Fort Stewart, Georgia.

2nd Battalion

By May 1977, he was the Commander, 2nd Battalion (Ranger), at Fort Lewis, Washington, where he stayed until July 1979.

He attended the Air War College at Maxwell AFB, Alabama from August 1979 to May 1980, and then became Secretary to the Joint Staff, United States European Command, Vaihingen, Germany. Late in 1980 he was promoted to Colonel.

In May 1982, he somehow got involved in Armor and became the Commander, 3rd Brigade, 1st Armored Division, Europe.

Regiment

Two years later he was back with the Rangers as Commander of the 75th Ranger Regiment, Fort Benning. Though listed as third commander of the Regiment, many Rangers consider him first.

Special Operations

By November 1985, he had made Brigadier General and was above Regimental command status, becoming Deputy Commanding General, 1st Special Operations Command, Fort Bragg, North Carolina until June 1987.

Then until May 1988, he was the Director, Washington Office, US Special Operations Command (USSOCOM), at McDill AFB, Florida, though his duty station was Washington.

He moved on to become Deputy Chief of Staff for Training, US Army Training and Doctrine Command (TRADOC) at Fort Monroe, Virginia, where he was promoted to Major General in October 1988.

Staying with TRADOC until December 1989, he became Commanding General, Joint Special Operations Command, US Special Operations Command, at Fort Bragg.

He was promoted to Lt. General in August 1991, and was named Commanding General, US Army Special Operations Command, Fort Bragg until May 1993, at which time he was promoted to General Officer and took over as Commander-in-Chief, US Special Operations Command at McDill AFB.

There are 15 decorations and badges listed in his biography. They include:

Silver Star (with Oak Leaf Cluster), Legion of Merit (3 Oak Leaf Clusters), Distinguished Flying Cross (with Oak Leaf Cluster), Bronze Star with V Device (with 5 Oak Leaf Clusters), Purple Heart, Master Parachutist Badge, and of course, the all-important Ranger Tab.

Wayne Downing

This interview with Downing is the result of several emails in June 2004. It is not easy to get an interview with this busy man, and the author is indebted to Ranger William Spies for the linkup. Parts of this interview appear in other places in this project. For example, Downing accepted Noriega's surrender in Panama in 1989. See that section for details.

My questions appear in italics.

As S-3 of the 1ˢᵗ Batt, were you required to learn and be prepared to recite the Ranger Creed along with other leaders?

Absolutely. One of the great things about those battalions was that they were "full participation units." The leaders led from the front. Everyone was expected to do what every other Ranger did. That included PT, road marches, hand to hand, and reciting the Creed.

Would you make a statement regarding your feelings about the Creed?

The Ranger Creed was believed by every man in the unit. We subscribed to its philosophy in every thing we did. It made us unique because it was a living guide to our actions.

Is it true that General Schwarzkopf was going to relieve you if you went into Iraq (1991)? Did you go anyway? What would you have done if you did go?

That is true. He was concerned that we could have a US General captured that Saddam could display as a propaganda victory, and who could possibly disclose the plan.

I did not go. I could do my job better from the Forward Operational Base we were using. Had a tactical situation arisen where my presence was needed, or as operations progressed to a point where we moved our base into Iraq (we were planning this move when the war ended) then I would have gone, and I think he would have supported it. Initially nervous that we would lose a lot of people, he gained confidence in our abilities and let us run. GEN S was very appreciative of the job the troops did and came out after the war and addressed all 1,000 of us.

Was the small group of Rangers in Desert Storm under your command? Were they part of the "SCUD Commandos?"

Yes, it was B/1st Ranger Battalion commanded by Kurt Fuller. The battalion sent a small staff element headed by Ken Keene. Yes, they did one reinforced-platoon-sized raid on a communication facility, and then the war ended.

Were you asked to come out of retirement or was it voluntary?

I was asked to come to the White House and organize a new office, the Office for Combating Terrorism. I became the National Director for Combating Terrorism.

Downing walked away from that office in June 2002, when his "Downing Plan" was rejected in favor of invasion. His plan was to get to Saddam Hussein first, using Special Operations people, air strikes, and indigenous rebels—a plan that may have negated the need for war.

Did you go back to the weapons firm when you resigned as a counter-terrorism advisor?

Since my first retirement, I have always worked for myself. The only exception was when I did the assessment on the Khobar Towers bombing in June 1994, shortly after I retired. That assessment took about four months. I serve on several Boards including Metal Storm, the high tech Australian weapons company.

Tools of the Trade—Modern Era

Rangers carry a lot of firepower—but that is the limitation. They carry what they will fight with to the battlefield, with only five days maximum supplies. The Regiment is dependant on outside assets for support in terms of laying on indirect fire, air support, transportation, and other types of logistical backing.

Still, the amount of organic firepower a Ranger Company can field is awesome and can be overwhelming to ill-trained or protected enemy troops.

In 2005, Strykers (light armored vehicles) were introduced to Rangers in Afghanistan, greatly enhancing their available firepower and mobility.

Standard Weapons Systems per battalion

84mm Ranger Anti-Tank Weapon System (RAWS)—AT-4: 16

60mm mortars: 6

M240B Machineguns: 27

M249 Squad Automatic Weapon (SAW): 54

MK 19 Grenade Launcher: 12

.50 Caliber Heavy Machinegun: 12

Javelin Anti-Tank Weapon: 9

Add to the list personal weapons such as various pistols, knives, Stingers, the M4 (carbine), some sniper rifles, 40mm grenade launchers attached under the barrels of rifles, known as the M203 (not used much any more), and whatever else they can get away with. They will state, however, that only authorized weapons are carried. "Anything else would be illegal, Sir."

At The Armory—Kazziah, Brown, Burkhead

The modern Ranger goes into battle carrying the very best the guys in Army Ordnance will allow. Newer and better weapons to jump from an aircraft, carry through the jungle, or fight in a small house have followed the evolution of the Ranger.

In April 2005, we visited the armory at Camp Frank D. Merrill and got some personal instruction from assistant armourers Sergeant Anthony Kazziah and Sergeant Daniel Brown, and Specialist Brandon Burkhead.

Kazziah: We just went into Iraq and liberated the country and we're finding all these weapons caches and stashes of weapons everywhere. I believe we should be allowed to capture some of them and bring them back and, like our Opfor here at the Ranger Camp, use them as enemy weapons. It just seems more proper to me to have a Ranger student getting shot at by an AK blank than by a SAW [Squad Automatic Weapon] or a 240 [machinegun] because they're used to hearing that sound.

The AK, particularly the 47, has a unique sound that can be distinguished in battle.

There were several SAWs and M240Bs taken apart and some were laid out on the concrete floor.

The armourers said they were so far away from Fort Benning (about 150 miles) that parts were sometimes slow in coming.

Kazziah: Something we're starting to phase out, the old SAW barrels had the removable gas regulators. The new ones aren't removable. I talked to the guys down there [Benning] and they said it was more or less for practical reasons.

That means you can't take it off and clean it.

Brown: A Ranger student out in the field will have a little piece that breaks and he'll bring it in, and if we can't repair it, we've always got a bad SAW, like this one [on the floor in pieces] with a bad mechanism. There is nothing I can do about this one, so what we do is, we use this SAW the whole cycle to fix their weapons.

A question was asked about training for the job.

Kazziah: Technically, what you're supposed to do is go through the Unit Armourers' Course, and he and I just completed that in March. It's a week-long course to be familiarized with basic weapons, where to look in the manuals to find out what's wrong with it, what we can do as an armourer and what we can't do. It's all about the forms. I've been doing this since I was five years old, taking them apart and putting them back together, getting down and dirty with them.

There are a lot of parts in an M240B. I remember watching a frustrated Captain in the Best Ranger Competition trying to put one together in a hurry from a box of spare parts belonging to five weapons. He was bleeding before he finished. Hooah!

Brown: Some of them do have a lot of trouble. It takes time to disassemble and assemble with skill.

Kazziah: There's small tricks to it. There's things you don't want to do out in the field because you might lose a part or something like that. You lose a part and the weapon system is deadlocked. You can't fire it. On top of that, if you take it apart too far in the field you might get a piece of sand or dirt in a bad spot and have a malfunction in a firefight.

How many parts are in one of those things?

Burkhead: Way too many.

Brown: You can break one down into eight basic groups [M249 SAW].

At that point Kazziah and Brown explained just about every component part of the SAW strewn about the concrete floor. They talked about the barrel, the gas regulator, the bolt, the bolt carrier, the firing pin, the piston head, the piston, some of which they "are allowed to operate on," but some are for the armourers are Benning.

Burkhead: This is what replaced the M60 [M240B]. It's a little cleaner-firing weapon. The M60 was originally referred to as the Pig because it makes a mess, it's hard to keep functional, but this is a little more durable. They took one out to see how many rounds they could burn off through it, and they burned about 10,000 rounds. They didn't melt the barrel down at all. Now if you do that the rifling in the barrel will get...[unrifled]...but it still held together for general purpose and still fired.

They have two barrels because if you're doing cyclic rate of fire, which is continuous rounds, you're going to be doing a barrel change every minute. We have mittens [the barrels are hot].

Brown: Actually, we call them oven mitts, but we don't use them up here. You just pop the switch and, barrel off, grab the handle, set it down, other barrel on.

Kazziah: The gunner is pretty much mentally keeping count of how long he's been shooting and when it gets time for a barrel change, he'll say "barrel change," and he'll come up and hit the button, the ammo bearer will. The AG will come up [and use the new barrel], knock it off, let it fall off to either side, and throw it on and lock it down, and the gunner's going. It can actually be done in two seconds.

Brown: If you're in a firefight and you've only got one extra barrel, they're going to stay hot, but they have that minute to cool down.

From there they got into night vision and infrared devices, including laser targeting.

Kazziah: This is what we call an [infra-red laser widget]. This is the newest version [2005] and it is awesome. It has an on-off switch but it can be remote-fired. Your gun team is coming with three people—your gunner, assistant gunner, and ammo bearer.

The device can be activated by either the AG or the ammo bearer while the gunner is busy firing. However, the device also mounts to the side of personal weapons and can be "fired" by the shooter.

When this comes in handy is for identifying targets. This side is like a...laser dot...but it's just infrared and you can't see it [without the infra-red goggles], but this side is like an infra-red flashlight, really like a floodlight. We were on a training exercise down at Fort Benning and we would run this out to the widest fan possible [widest light adjustment], and they would have to have the power cut off in the buildings [they were using for training]. We could sit outside the buildings, probably 100 meters away, and shine that into a window and illuminate the whole room the guys were going into before they went in. The bad guys couldn't see, but our guys could [with night vision].

While wearing night optical devices (NODs) one cannot look directly at an infrared source for long. It is blinding, especially on high settings. The night vision device allows one to see in a dark room fairly well, but the infrared light coming in really brightens things up, even if the bad guys can't see the floor.

During the Vietnam War there was an item called the Starlight Scope, one of the first night-imaging devices for shooters. There were approximately one per battalion, and under lock and key most of the time. The RTB has almost 200 infrared devices and it's just a training unit.

NODs come in monocular and binocular configurations and can be mounted either on a weapon, on a folding hanger on the front of a K-pot (Kevlar helmet), or with a skull-crusher head set worn without headgear.

The statement was made, "The bad guys don't have a chance in the dark." The rejoinder: "That's why we rule the night."

The bad guys are going to be even worse off soon. New technology integrates thermal imaging with the infrared sighting.

Kazziah: They run on AA batteries. You're not going to sit there with this thing on all the time, so they last a while, but night vision goggles, you'll burn up a set of AAs in a night.

While a trigger for the infrared device does mount on the weapon, it was generally agreed that a crew-served weapon like the M240 should make use of the AG. That way the gunner doesn't have his finger near his trigger when his own men are going into a room his weapon is pointing toward.

A question was asked about ammunition storage, especially live rounds.

Brown: Since we're a TDA training unit we get very few live rounds. If someone wanted to try to charge into the armory and take over [gestures], well, maybe not. We've got enough rounds to stop anyone from coming into the arms room.

Without going into detail it can be said that Camp Merrill would not be a good place to invade. The students don't get much, if any, live ammo, but there are a whole bunch of combat veterans with access to whatever they may need. It is, after all, a Ranger installation.

Burkhead: (asked about having AT-4 rockets) No. Different units get them. We're pretty low on the totem pole to be able to get those resources. When I was in Korea [1/506] we had AT-4s, claymores, things you use to train your men on. Then they know what it looks like, how to operate and how to deploy. That way, in combat, they've seen it done.

Brown: I've been here three-and-a-half years, and I think we've only had one live-fire exercise.

Burkhead: It's a matter of resources. They're using them for the war effort. To be honest, we need them for training value for some of the men, but for the most part the men who are assigned here have been to other units and have done it before. You don't get very many brand-new Privates in this camp.

We took a look at the 40mm grenade launcher that attaches to the underside of the M16 and the M4. The old break-in-the-middle M79 "thumper" is no longer in the inventory.

Brown: This is the M203A1, which mounts to the M4. Ranger students take six out per platoon.

Six 203s, six SAWs, three guns [M240], and a couple of AT-4s.

Burkhead: This is the M203 that mounts to the M16. It's a little different.

Sergeant Brown explained the AT-4 while posing for photographs in the firing position. He also graciously volunteered to lie in the mud (it was raining) and demonstrate the correct firing position for the M240, but we found enough dry concrete.

Brown: The AT-4 replaced the LAW [light anti-tank weapon]. You carry it shooting end down. It's one-shot, one-kill. It's an 84mm round, fired from the shoulder. It's one shot, but if you throw it on the ground, one of these guys we're fighting can come up and turn this into a mortar tube. The back blast is 60 meters at a 90-degree angle, so if someone's back there, they're going to get fried.

Differences between the AT-4 and the LAW include amount of firepower and ease of use. The LAW has to be unfolded like a telescope and was not as accurate. However, they are better for jumping because of the size. When the 3rd Ranger Battalion went into Afghanistan they jumped with LAWs.

Sadly, the 5th RTB had no 90mm recoilless rifles (out of favor these days), nor 106mm recoilless, nor the vaunted Carl Gustav weapons system used by the Ranger Regiment.

Brown: This is our M4, our basic peashooter. It has a removable handle so you can mount [a scope] on it, and some have rail systems and some don't. A rail system lets you mounts things, like a sling, and this one also has the gangster grip [a vertical hand hold up front]. It lets you mount all your toys on there [infrared, etc].

Kazziah: It's gas-operated [fires about 650 round in three-round bursts]. It's got a 30-round magazine, although some units have purchased 100-round drums for it.

The question was asked, "Why the M4 instead of the M16?"

Brown: It's lighter and shorter. When people go in to clear rooms and they've got all their RBA [Ranger body armor] and other protective stuff on, with the M16's butt stock fully extended you're going to be out to here [the M4 is about one-quarter shorter].

A Report On Weapons From Iraq

This information comes from the author's personal sources in Iraq and Afghanistan.

US Weapons

M16: Still has a lot of jamming problems.

M4: Popular because of its size, it jams a lot, also.

5.56mm round: Too small, not enough punch, especially on block structures. Hits to the torso do not always put a man down.

M249 SAW (Squad Automatic Weapon): Again, the .556 round, and jamming. Not well liked.

12-gauge shotgun (Mossberg): Used in house-to-house sweeps and clearing. Lots of punch.

M240B machinegun: Fires a better round [7.62mm], which "puts 'em down," and is considered reliable. Also used as a vehicle-mount weapon, like the old M60, which it replaced. The bigger round is effective against a cinder block structure.

M2 .50 caliber heavy machinegun: Everybody wants one.

Beretta 9mm: Not tough enough, but a good weapon in the desert.

.45-caliber pistol (HK and government-issue): Everybody wants one. Used a good bit by Special Operations troops. Torso hits generally very effective.

M14: Old reliable. Being reissued in certain areas. Good sniper rifle with a 7.62mm punch. New models have Kevlar stocks and are lighter.

Barrett .50 caliber sniper rifle: Bang, you're dead at great range. "Hits like a freight train."

Enemy Weapons

Mostly AK47s: The entire country is an arsenal. Works better in the desert than the M16 and the .308 [7.62] Russian round kills reliably. PKM belt-fed light machineguns are also common and effective. Luckily, the enemy mostly shoots poorly. Undisciplined "spray and pray" type fire. However, they are seeing more and more precision weapons, especially sniper rifles.

Fun fact: Captured enemy have apparently marveled at the marksmanship of our guys and how hard they fight. They are apparently told in Jihad school that the Americans rely solely on technology, and can be easily beaten in close quarters combat for their lack of toughness. Let's just say they know better now.

The RPG: Probably the infantry weapon most feared by our guys. Simple, reliable and as common as dog shit. The enemy responded to our up-armored humvees by aiming at the windshields, often at point blank range. Still killing a lot of our guys.

The IED: The biggest killer of all. Can be anything from old Soviet anti-armor mines to jury-rigged artillery shells. A lot found were in abandoned cars. The enemy would take two or three 155mm artillery shells and wire them together. Most were detonated by cell phone, and the explosions are enormous. You're not safe in any vehicle, even an M1 tank. Driving is by far the most dangerous thing our guys do over there. Lately, they are much more sophisticated "shaped charges" {possibly Iranian} specifically designed to penetrate armor.

Fact: Most of the ready-made IED's are supplied by Iran, who is also providing terrorists {Hezbollah types} to train the insurgents in their use and tactics. That's why the attacks have been so deadly lately. Their concealment methods are ingenious, the latest being shape charges in Styrofoam containers spray painted to look like the cinderblocks that litter all Iraqi roads. We find about 40 percent before they detonate, and the bomb disposal guys are unsung heroes of this war.

Mortars and rockets: Very prevalent. The soviet era 122mm rockets—with an 18km range —are becoming more prevalent. One of the Marine NCOs lost a leg to one. These weapons cause a lot of damage "inside the wire."

The Marine base was hit almost daily his entire time there by mortar and rocket fire, often at night, to disrupt sleep patterns and cause fatigue. More of a psychological weapon than anything else. The enemy mortar teams would jump out of vehicles, fire a few rounds, and then haul ass in a matter of seconds.

Bad guy technology: Simple yet effective. Most communication is by cell and satellite phones, and also by email on laptops. They use handheld GPS units for navigation and "Google earth" for overhead views of our positions. Their weapons are good, if not fancy, and prevalent. Their explosives and bomb technology is TOP OF THE LINE. Night vision is rare. They are very careless with their equipment and the captured GPS units and laptops are treasure troves of Intel when captured.

PANAMA

Several good things came out of Operation JUST CAUSE besides the routing of Manuel Noriega and his forces. First, the 75th Ranger Regiment deployed into combat as a unit for the first time. Second, all the various missions were accomplished with excellence, though not always as planned. Third, with Grenada providing valuable lessons about targets, troop deployment and supply, the Rangers were able to add the results of JUST CAUSE to their experiences and exited the conflict much the wiser.

The invasion of Panama on December 20, 1989 was the result of extensive planning over a period of time that tested new guidelines built to ensure better harmony among the various Combat Arms forces. The Goldwater-Nichols Defense Reorganization Act of 1986 called for changes to the US Military Command system at the highest levels. More authority was to be given to the Chairman of the Joint Chiefs of Staff and to the various Commanders-In-Chief. The idea was to streamline the chain of command—to get things done faster and better with less interference from too many high-ranking middlemen in the chain.

Panama was the perfect place to see if the new system worked.

Why Panama?

There were several reasons to take control of the situation in Panama. American interests were large in the small country, and the communist influence was growing along with the drug trade. However, one of the main reasons was to get rid Manuel Noriega—the man allowing it all to happen. Noriega had long overstepped his bounds and had been causing problems for some time. He was becoming a threat to his own people, and to the countries around him. He was a dictator who did not care about his country.

The Players

Over a period of time the players changed a bit, but at the time of the invasion, George H. W. Bush was President, Richard Cheney was SECDEF, and (Ranger) General Colin Powell had just become Chairman of the Joint Chiefs. Ronald Reagan was President when it all started.

General Frederick F. Woerner, Jr, US Army, headed US Southern Command (SOUTHCOM), and was responsible for Panama until interdiction became mandatory. General Maxwell R. Thurman replaced him when things began heating up.

Thurman picked (Ranger) Lt. General Carl W. Stiner, in command of the XVIII Airborne Corps, to head up the operation. Thurman said he wanted Stiner to "be my warfighter."

Major General Wayne Downing, a legendary Ranger, was head of Joint Special Operations Command (JSOC), and so depended on the Ranger Regiment, commanded by Colonel William "Buck" Kernan.

Background

Panama connects Central America to South America at Colombia, about 400 miles from its northern boundary with Costa Rica. An average of about 50 miles wide, Panama contains the Panama Canal—a necessity to inter-ocean shipping. The United States viewed the Canal as a paramount strategic holding and vowed to protect the 52 miles of waterway with a five-mile wide buffer on each side.

Panama was to be granted control of the Canal in 2000, with the provision the US could still defend the passage if necessary. The ability to move Naval vessels from one ocean to the other quickly was one consideration, but economics also played a part in the waterway's importance—that and the ramifications of having a communist country in control of the passage. In addition, US bases in Panama (Quarry Heights, Fort Clayton, Albrook AFB, Howard AFB, and a Naval station) were subject to be attacked, and civilians—both Panamanian and American—were also at risk.

As conditions in Panama went downhill around 1988, Woerner decided to beef up US troop numbers in Panama to make a show of force, hoping to get Noriega to pay attention. For a time the plan went forward, until there were some 13,000 troops in the country. Unfortunately, it took too long and Noriega wasn't intimidated and ignored the warnings.

Noriega

Manuel Antonio Noriega began as an Intelligence Officer under Brigadier General Omar Torrijos—a dictator until his death in 1983. When he died, Noriega took control of the Panama Defense Force (PDF), which included the police.

From the start he burned his candle at both ends, rubbing shoulders with the US government and the Medellin drug cartel, as well as communist-bloc countries. He was warned by the US to cut out the drug cartel, but he did nothing.

In February 1988, two Federal Grand Juries in the US indicted Noriega and several others on drug charges. Noriega responded by taking a firmer grip on his country. He began to harass American citizens and stonewall efforts of the US military to fulfill its obligations and rights in the Canal Zone.

He also began to look elsewhere for the missing help he was no longer getting from the US. Cuba and Nicaragua, in particular, started sending weapons and instructors. With those assets Noriega built new organizations called Dignity Battalions, which were really civilian militia used for population control—and as informants on their neighbors. Oddly enough, a few of those battalions proved surprisingly stubborn during the invasion.

Libya chipped in 20 million to buy the right to use Panama as a staging base for terrorist activities in Central and South America. Things were looking up for Noriega.

Even before the full impact of Cuban and Nicaraguan aid, the Panamanian Defense Force (PDF) contained 19 companies and six platoons, composed of some 14,000 men. However, only about 4,000 were well trained and equipped for combat. For equipment the Panamanian forces were limited to 29 armored personnel carriers, 12 patrol craft, and 28 airplanes for moving troops—hardly enough when confronting firepower-heavy American forces.

In May 1989, Panama held elections and ousted Noriega by electing Guillermo Endara President, despite Noriega's men tampering with the polls and the people. On May 10, Noriega annulled the elections and went after the winners. Endara fled to the Papal Nunciatura, the same place Noriega would soon go.

President Bush had enough at that point and tapped General Thurman—an aggressive warrior-type—to take over SOUTHCOM.

Getting Ready—Early Stage

In 1988, plans went forward to follow General Woerner's proposal of building up US forces in Panama. The idea was to either cause Noriega to back down, or have his own people overthrow him. A second option was to continue the buildup, but more quickly, and to hit Panama with a JTF composed of several branch elements, including Special Operations Forces such as Rangers, SEALS, and Delta.

Brigadier General Marc A. Cisneros was SOUTHCOM J-3 (Operations). Ronald Reagan was President for a while yet.

The mission was to prevent Noriega from doing anything to the 35,000 US citizens in Panama, oppose the Canal, or move elements into the hills to continue fighting guerilla-style. The Panamanian Defense Force (PDF) was in the way and had to be dealt with.

BLUE SPOON

BLUE SPOON was the battle order—one of four operations orders conceived by Woerner and his staff to cover the wresting of control of Panama from the PDF. Using forces already in-country to stop the PDF over an eight-day period, the effort would be supplemented by some 10,000 more troops from the US, plus a carrier battle group.

Included in the troops from the States would be Special Operations Forces (SOF) from SOCOM to carry out missions against Panamanian leadership, Command and Control and airfields. They were also to rescue any hostages, provide recon for the task force, and find Noriega.

BLUE SPOON was originally developed to operate at a slower pace, but as the situation in Panama deteriorated, General Thurman replaced General Woerner. He modified the plan to go forward more quickly—and with a larger punch. To lead the effort, Thurman tapped Lt. General Carl Stiner to command a joint task force of 22,000 soldiers and some 5,000 Marines, sailors, and airmen.

Things were getting out of hand in Panama, but they got suddenly worse in mid-December, 1989, when Noriega named himself Maximum Leader, and the Panamanian National Assembly declared war on the United States.

The Trigger?

In March 1989, Dick Cheney became SECDEF. He and members of the military and the cabinet began actively looking for ways to get rid of Noriega. It was decided to increase control of US installations in Panama and generally make a visible show of force. NIMROD DANCER was part of that move.

General Colin Powell became Chairman of the Joint Chiefs in October and joined Cheney and the others in compressing the timetable of military readiness. The mission would be to eliminate the PDF completely and catch Noriega as soon as possible. World opinion was discussed.

Powell said, "If you're going to get tarred with a brush, you might as well take down the whole PDF...pull it up by the roots."

With the US teetering on the brink of invasion through the fall, only a trigger event of some sort was needed. Such an event occurred on December 17—maybe not enough, but enough—when three American officers in a car were fired upon by the PDF. A Marine Corps

First Lieutenant subsequently died of his wounds. An American Naval officer and his wife were witnesses to the shooting, but were taken into custody by the PDF where they were assaulted.

BLUE SPOON Revisited

General Powell wanted things ready to go as soon as the word came down. Operation BLUE SPOON was rewritten and completed by October 27, calling for more troops going in on a faster schedule—just four or five days to put 27,000 into the small country to join the 13,000 already there. USCINCSO OPORD 1-90 combined elements of the 82nd Airborne, 7th ID, and Special Operations soldiers including Rangers and other Army special units, plus some Navy Special Ops people.

Under the "deliberate" plan, Joint Special Operations Task Force would start the ball rolling with five special ops missions assigned to separate unconventional task forces.

Task Forces GREEN (Army Special Mission Unit) and BLUE (Navy Special Warfare Unit) would go after hostages.

Task Force BLACK (in-theater Special Forces) was to protect opposition leaders.

Task Force WHITE (also Navy SWU) would hit from the sea against Panamanian ports of interest.

Task Force RED was Rangers all the way and would conduct parachute assaults at Torrijos-Tocumen Airport complex in the east and Rio Hato airfield in the west.

There were also to be four conventional task forces, three of which would deploy at H-Hour.

The 193rd Infantry Brigade, designated Task Force BAYONET, was set to take down the Comandancia and PDF holdings in and around Panama City.

Task Force ATLANTIC, made up of elements of the 7th ID (L) and the 82nd Airborne Division, would work in the Canal Zone.

Task Force SEMPER FI was all Marines, and would operate near the Bridge of the Americas and protect Howard Air Force Base.

The fourth conventional group was manned by the 82nd—Task Force PACIFIC. At H+45 PACIFIC would drop in at Torrijos-Tocumen and relieve the Rangers, who would become part of that Task Force. Within a short time, the 82nd was tasked with going after PDF positions at Fort Cimarron, Tinajitas, and Panama Viejo.

Once the initial take down of the PDF was completed, the 7th ID and the 16th Military Police Brigade would begin to stabilize the situation and take over from all other Task Forces.

The finishing touches were added and a new vessel, OPLAN 90-2, was ready by November. That plan contained the details for the tactical operation and was considered ready should President Bush decide to go.

All units taking part were put into rehearsal mode, including the Rangers, who worked out at Fort Benning in the States, and in Panama. Certain units had to prove their efficiency with all weapons in live fire exercises before the invasion, including proficiency at night.

Strict rules of engagement—written and revised by Lt. General Stiner—were set, mandating the troops to use the smallest amount of force necessary to accomplish the mission.

Implementing JUST CAUSE

On December 17, 1989 President Bush was briefed on the final phases of BLUE SPOON. Among several levels of input, it was Powell who told him that even if Noriega could be taken out by Special Operations soldiers, the problem would not be solved because there were "Noriega clones" who would step in and take over. The PDF was corrupt, he said, and must be taken apart completely. The best way to do that was to hit hard with heavy force and dismantle the PDF. Even if Noriega escaped the first net, he would soon be captured, and a hard first strike would limit the ability of the PDF to take hostages and/or set up a guerilla network in the hills.

President Bush listened intently and then made up his mind, saying, "Okay, let's do it. The hell with it!"

Stiner originally set H-Hour for one o'clock in the morning of December 20 so he could get things started at night. Powell told Major General Wayne Downing, JSOTF Commander, to get ready for pre-H-Hour.

So great was US authority in Panama that an advance party of JTF South moved into the country prior to the invasion. That group included General Stiner and members of the XVIII Airborne Corps staff who moved into the forward headquarters base at Fort Clayton.

Several different airbases in the States were the scene of rapid loading of aircraft, including Hunter and Lawson Army Airfields in Georgia—Ranger airfields.

Only one change was made to the operations orders by Cheney, concerning the deployment of F-117A stealth fighter-bombers. Cheney didn't believe the aircraft were necessary, though he changed his mind slightly when given the reasons Stiner asked for them.

Rio Hato, which eventually became a tougher nut than previously considered, was to be covered from the air, as well as La Escondida and Boquete—possible Noriega hideouts. At Rio Hato the PDF's 6th and 7th Rifle Companies—the ones that had rescued Noriega from a previous coup attempt—were known to contain soldiers friendly to the US. The strict rules of engagement meant killing them with overwhelming bombing and aerial fires was not only unwarranted, but also unnecessary. There was no reason to take them all out that way, or any way, and such a move could have caused resentment among the surviving members of the companies and others across Panama, making the Rangers' job of subduing them even harder.

Stiner wanted bombs dropped some 150 yards from the PDF barracks so the soldiers would be stunned and surrender more easily rather than just becoming charcoal.

President Bush said two of the special aircraft could be used against Rio Hato. "They're American troops. Give them what they need."

The name of the operation was changed from BLUE SPOON to JUST CAUSE.

On December 19, the aircraft around the country began to launch. Colonel William F. (Buck) Kernan, Commander of the Ranger Regiment, got his men moving.

Rangers of the 2nd Battalion from Fort Lewis, Washington, were already in Georgia and departed about an hour after noon from Lawson Army Airfield on 13 C-130s. Members of the 2nd had just returned from an exhaustive exercise in north Florida and had to turn around and gear right back up. The other two battalions of Rangers left from Hunter Army Airfield about 2:30 pm. At about 4 pm some 30 C-141s left Charleston Air Force Base full of 82nd Airborne troops.

Twenty more C-141s from Fort Bragg were to carry two battalions of the 82nd together, but icing of the wings delayed the second stage (10 planes) for more than four hours. The order was given to drop the paratroopers when they got to Panama, even if they weren't all together.

Of course, there was no way such a huge movement of aircraft would go unnoticed, though Stiner tried a ruse. CBS newsman Dan Rather commented that evening, "U.S. military transport planes have left Fort Bragg. The Pentagon declines to say whether or not they're bound for Panama. It will say only that the Fort Bragg-based XVIII Airborne Corps has been conducting what the Army calls an emergency readiness measure."

Rather wasn't the only one pricking up his ears. The PDF also knew about the movement, but were not sure exactly what was happening, and so took no heavy precautionary measures. They did institute blackouts in certain parts of the country and put certain units on alert.

Not until quite late in the night of December 19 did messages go out to PDF units from La Comandancia to lock and load, block the runways, and prepare to defend themselves.

Rangers were fired upon as they dropped into Rio Hato, but it wasn't severe. In fact, a general alert wasn't given out until hours after the first drop. To top off the incompetence of the top Panamanian brass, Noriega spent part of the night—not at his command center—but with a prostitute.

Major General Downing made sure air, sea and land forces under him knew what to do if Noriega was located. If he was in the air he would be forced to land or be shot down; if on the ground, the Army Special Mission Unit would go get him with support from the sky.

The night before the invasion the real elected officials of Panama—Endara, Calderon, and Ford—were all invited to dinner at Howard Air Force Base. There they were told of coming events and sworn in to their rightful positions by a Panamanian judge just before midnight.

December 20—D-Day

Panamanian forces nervously awaited what they knew must be coming soon—an invasion by the superior forces of the United States. Superior is the key word in any comparison of the two military contestants. It is hard to imagine what was in Noriega's mind when he decided to push the United States into war. Still, if he doubted the ability of his tiny military, he kept it to himself.

The PDF could field something less than 13,000 troops, but only some 4,000 were trained for the task of combat in a real sense. On the ground there were but two infantry battalions, five light infantry companies, a cavalry troop, and two "public order" companies. Mechanized equipment was composed of 28 armored cars. One thing they did have were French 120mm mortars; a system that out-shot the US 105mm howitzer by two kilometers (13.5 km).

The Panamanian Air Force held about 500 people, but no real danger for the Americans in the form of armed, fighting aircraft. Only 400 souls comprised the "Navy," and they didn't have much to fight with, either.

Added to that small mix of defenders were as many as 18 paramilitary "Dignity Battalions." Rangers were still dealing with them five days later.

The forces were scattered about the country, so there was no large group of defenders anywhere. At Rio Hato Military Airfield the 6th and 7th Rifle Companies held about 400 men. Only 200 soldiers of the 2nd Rifle Company secured the Torrijos-Tocumen Airport, and the rest of the country was held—in places—by 200 men here, 150 there. The command center, La Comandancia, was protected by just 150 men, fragments of several companies fighting together.

American troops, equal in number to the whole of Panama's forces, were already in the country when the shooting started early on December 20. Those forces included the 193rd Infantry Brigade, a battalion each of the 7th ID and the 5th ID (Mech), a couple of Marine Companies, and various other soldiers, airmen, and sailors, totaling some 13,000 in all.

In the early morning of December 20, about 7,000 more US troops dropped in, came by boat or landed in airplanes. Among those were the Rangers and a composite brigade of the 82nd Airborne, along with some SEALs, Delta people, Air Force Special Ops troops, Navy boat units, and psychological teams and Civil Affairs personnel. There were also combat controllers, Pararescuemen, communications teams, and others.

About 7,000 more US troopers would be coming in after H-Hour—that day and over the next several days.

Total US involvement would reach 27,000, with about 22,000 engaged in combat operations.

Special Operations

As the 19th of December flipped over to the 20th, General Stiner was receiving messages about accelerated activity by the PDF. A shooting at the Comandancia, intercepted messages from intra-Panamanian sources, another shooting at Albrook Air Force Station, and other foreboding input prompted Stiner to advance H-Hour by 15 minutes. It wasn't much, but Stiner still hoped to achieve tactical surprise.

To ensure smooth connections between the various Task Forces, Liaison Officers from each unit had been exchanged in advance of operations. The 82nd LNO and Ranger LNO made the trade particularly to ensure there were no problems with challenge and password—different for 1st Battalion and the 82nd DRB, a reaction force held in reserve on the airfield.

Steve Pullen

I was Deputy J-5 for JSOC. My initial mission was to be the Liaison Officer between MG Downing and MG Johnson, Commander of the 82nd Airborne Division during the assault phase. I joined MG Johnson at his headquarters and immediately began providing information from JSOC to both the division G-2 and G-3.

I was on the lead C-141 aircraft with MG Johnson and jumped behind him onto Tocumen International Airport. I remained with the 82nd until the 7th Infantry air-landed at Tocumen. I remained with the 7th Infantry Division until 2 January, when I returned to Fort Bragg.

As I was one of the first jumpers to exit my aircraft, I landed on the leading edge of the main runway near the perimeter fence. As we dropped at 500 feet the jump was very quick. There was a full moon that night so at drop time it was actually very bright. On the run in we could see the fighting in Panama City from the jump door. There was no resistance to our jump.

The 1st Battalion, commanded by LTC Bob Wagner, had jumped before the 82nd and had the mission to clear the PDF from the airfield so that the 82nd could follow. The 1st Battalion engaged and killed several members of the PDF. As I moved to our assembly area following the jump, I heard some small arms firing from the vicinity of the main terminal building. The duration of the firing was very short. The only PDF I saw at the terminal were dead.

First Shots

Many of the Rangers slept on the seven-hour flight to Panama, especially members of 2nd Battalion, who had been on aircraft for many hours already, traveling from Florida to Washington State, and back to south Georgia. Those Rangers, part of the Ready Reaction Force, had been wearing beepers since March. Battalions rotate as RRF, and it was the 2nd Battalion's turn. The men began to wake up about two hours out and make final preparations.

Special Operations forces struck several targets at once. At 0045 a Spectre C-130 gunship and a couple of Apache helicopters opened up on known targets, mostly the 2nd PDF Company positions near Torrijos-Tocumen Airport.

Some 1,300 Rangers then dropped from the sky on two separate targets—Rio Hato in the west (2nd Battalion and A and B Companies of 3rd Battalion and Team Black of Regimental HQ), and Torrijos-Tocumen Airport in the east (1st Battalion plus C Company, 3rd Battalion, and Team Gold, RHQ). Inserted to pave the way for the 82nd Airborne, the Rangers cleared runways and took on any defenses they encountered.

Rangers fell silently through cracking tracer rounds and went to work in two groups. They did what they were trained to do, and succeeded quickly. Very soon, reinforcements arrived and spread out. Roads and bridges were blocked in several places against movement of reinforcements, and the first probing for Noriega began.

Within 45 minutes 2,700 men of the 82nd came floating down to join them. It was the largest Airborne operation since WWII, the first all-jet (C-141) aircraft drop, and probably the lowest mass drop any time. Hitting the silk from 500 feet—300 feet lower than was practiced—some of the men (primarily 82nd troops) were injured on impact, mostly due to not dropping their rucks on the way down and landing too hard. Coming in under fire didn't help matters much, though that was mostly Rangers.

Paratroopers and Rangers were carrying too much weight. The average man was carrying in excess of 100 pounds—so much that it was hard to stand up straight waiting to jump—and the exit was precarious because the extra bulky weight dictated aerodynamics.

The idea of a more mobile, lighter force came a long way toward reality with the lessons learned at Rio Hato and Tocumen. Today's Rangers still carry a lot of gear, but it has become somewhat more streamlined and less overburdening.

Active duty Rangers may argue with the above assessment about less weight on a drop.

The 82nd had some problems getting down in the right places at the right time. Though the division elements were planned to jump 2,288 men, only 2,179 made the drop.

The first eight C-141s dropped long and to the right, 25 minutes late. Two more dropped long and to the right at 3:51 am, three more dropped long and to the right and hour later, and the final seven dropped 26 minutes after that, having had to refuel in flight. The drop plan called for paratroopers to land within 50 meters of the airfield fence, but most dropped outside the fence and some landed in a mangrove swamp. The longest drop was eight klicks too far.

The plan called for 78 HMMWVs (Humvees) to be dropped, though the one carrying SAMs for Stinger missile launchers was lost, and one complete package of Hummers was not dropped at all. Twelve M551 Sheridan light tanks were dropped, and though the Sheridan was so light that heavy machinegun rounds could be a problem, it did sport a 152mm gun. Four 105mm howitzers and a dozen .50 caliber machineguns were also dropped.

The Airborne troops were tasked primarily with isolating Panama City from outside help while internal American forces took control and neutralized the Comandancia (PDF HQ).

Rio Hato

Rio Hato is located a little north of Panama City and contains an airfield. It is far away enough for the Rangers to have to split the Regiment and make two drops, but close enough for the US commanders to worry about the 6th and 7th PDF Companies interceding in the battle for Panama City and the capture of Manuel Noriega.

The 6th Company was motorized, and the 7th, Noriega's favorite, was known as the Macho de Montes. They were well trained.

Several buildings surrounded the airfield, most notably an NCO Academy and the PDF barracks. There was also a bullring. The single runway traces east to west and reaches almost to the shoreline. It is bisected at the eastern end by the Pan-American Highway—in those days, very close to one of Noriega's beach houses.

The plan was to land in force with nearly two battalions, all of 2nd and Companies A and B of 3rd. It was known the two PDF Companies were pretty good, and the Rangers expected a fight.

A few air assets were laid on, and they proved their worth. The mighty Spectre AC-130 was on station, as were a couple of Apache helicopters and AH-6 Little Birds. The Rangers welcomed the fires from the sky, but it was two aircraft of a different type that opened the ball.

Two Stealth F-117s dropped one 2000-pound bomb each near the barracks of the 6th and 7th Rifle Companies at Rio Hato—not on target, but near—killing more than a few who were in the wrong place at the wrong time, already out of the barracks. One bomb landed near a vehicle park behind the barracks, and many PDF soldiers were there to get their "mechanized" force operating.

The idea was to stun with the bombs, have Spectre and the birds open up, then the Rangers would hit the ground shooting. It worked quite well, especially once the Rangers began to find each other in the dark night.

There were, of course, unexpected occurrences, usually resulting in death or capture for the PDF soldiers, but mostly the plan was executed smoothly without excessive casualties. The Rangers lost five killed and several dozen wounded in the short, 500-foot drop and the sharp fight that followed. The men had to sit still and hope for the best on the way in when their aircraft began taking fire before they reached the shoreline.

The Rangers dropped at 0103, a full 18 minutes after the first fireworks began, so the PDF knew something was up and were ready when the Rangers appeared. Anti-aircraft fire was fairly heavy—11 of 13 C-130s took hits during the drop. The Rangers were scattered after the quick jump, but not badly, and began to gather together and begin the takedown of the PDF. Men of different companies and platoon intermixed in the beginning, but their training paid off in their ability to function smoothly together.

Company A was to close on the western edge of the airfield and take down the NCO Academy, while B Company took on the PDF barracks. Company C was technically in reserve. Members of the 3rd Battalion's two companies were to handle the northern area of the airfield.

The plan for Company B was based on how many casualties they took, or didn't take. If the company could take 7th PDF barracks without serious loss, they were to go on to 6th Company's barracks. Since the enemy knew the Rangers were coming, they had left the barracks and set up around the airfield, or melted into the night.

There were several isolated hot spots as the remaining PDF soldiers were located, sometimes by following the path of their incoming tracers. Several machinegun posts were destroyed as the Rangers deployed outward along the runway and into the buildings. A roadblock was set up where the Pan-American Highway bisects the runway just as a group of foolish men in a vehicle careened onto the runway, firing from all windows. Rangers blew the vehicle and the men all over the runway.

There were a few other holdouts among the Panamanians, but after a five-hour fight, most gave up or simply ran away.

The largest single group capture was not of soldiers, but cadets. About 150 cadets had been there for training over the holidays—something of which the Rangers had no knowledge—and were taken intact and unharmed by some quick-thinking young soldiers.

Rangers kept position at the airfield for three days, when 7th ID soldiers relieved them.

There are, of course, some stories. Among the Ranger casualties were one man whose parachute malfunctioned, and another who was ambushed and shot in the head—but survived. There were other jump injuries, and at least one Ranger was hit while still in his aircraft. Sadly, there are reports that a few Rangers were hit by errant fire from a helicopter whose pilot wasn't notified of their movement.

Then there is a great story about a Ranger caught hanging from a tree by his parachute- and taking fire from a PDF soldier below him. Somehow he managed to blow the man up with a frag and survived unhurt.

Originally tasked to the SEALs, Noriega's beach house was instead given to C Company, 2nd Battalion. The 3rd Platoon found some security people there, and needed to gain entrance. A "Ranger key" was used—an AT-4 anti-armor weapon—and the front door was gone.

The best story of Rio Hato can be found in General William Kernan's interview. As leader of the Regiment, he jumped with his men and knows the overall battle well.

After Rio Hato, Company A, 3rd Battalion, was sent with some Delta operatives to secure Penonome Prison. Set to fast-rope in, the order was given to air land because the prison was empty. A second prison on the Isla de Coiba was also secured without action.

Rangers were also dispatched to nearby David Airfield, but found only a lot of civilians.

Torrijos-Tocumen

The Omar Torrijos International Airport is a fairly large area to cover, especially since the Panamanian "Air Force" was also lodged there at adjoining Tocumen. Fortunately, there was only one PDF Company—the 2nd—to deal with for 2nd Ranger Battalion and Company C, 3rd Ranger Battalion.

Battalion Commander Lt. Colonel Robert Wagner headed up that end of Task Force RED, which consisted of the Rangers, a PSYOPS team, a civil affairs team, Air Force combat controllers and Pararescuemen, a couple of AH-6 Apache helicopters, and the "Ranger in the sky"—a slowly circling Spectre C-130.

As H-Hour had been moved up 15 minutes, the birds and Spectre hit at 0045, lighting up the airfield. At 0103 the Rangers made the 500-foot jump into sporadic fire from the ground. Assembling quickly on the ground, the various groups split up to do their jobs. Company A, 1st Battalion, took care of the Panamanian Air Force compound. Many of the aircraft were destroyed in place. Company C, 1st Battalion, made heavy by a platoon of Company B, went after the 2nd PDF Company. There was small resistance as most of the PDF surrendered, but one man, reportedly a West Point graduate, refused to give up and was killed.

The rest of B/1 made use of the dozen gun jeeps and 10 motorbikes to clear the runway and establish blocking positions in and around a complex that covered six kilometers by two.

Company C, 3rd Battalion, commanded by Captain Al Dochnal, was given the job of clearing the airport terminal and the smaller building around it. Separated from a quarter of the men by a scattered drop, Company C went forward. On the way in, they admired the thorough demolition job done on the guardhouse in front of the terminal, courtesy of an Apache.

Inside the terminal were an unexpected 400 civilians, caught there when flights had been cancelled. Two girls had been taken hostage, but when Rangers grew frustrated after nearly a three-hour standoff, they told the gunmen they were coming in, and it was going to be rough. About 10 PDF soldiers made the right decision and gave up.

Also in the terminal, a fight occurred in a men's room—a fair sized airport restroom— with a couple of PDF soldiers literally "holed" up and refusing to come out. When the first Rangers entered the room to clear it, rounds impacted the torso of the lead man, knocking him down. His buddy tried to move him out of the room, but took two rounds to his helmet, and was saved by the Kevlar. Some shooting ensued, but before long a couple of grenades were thrown in. The concussion must have been terrible, but the bathroom stalls shielded the enemy soldiers. That was enough. The Rangers stormed in and shot one man, and threw another out the second story window. The story is, when the enemy soldier hit the ground right next to a Ranger, he went for his pistol and the Ranger killed him.

Once the 82nd Ready Brigade came down, the Rangers combined with them to form Task Force PACIFIC. By 7:30 am the airport complex was cleared, with 50 surviving PDF surrendering.

Members of the 1st Battalion also cleared some citizens out of the Caracul Hotel and escorted them to safety at Howard AFB.

Elements fought through isolated resistance all day, and declared Paitilla Airport secure at about 9:15 that evening. Part of the first attacks at Punta Paitilla Airport, SEALs met more than they bargained for when they came up out of the ocean and put a LAW rocket through Noriega's private jet, then got caught in the open by a few men firing from protected positions. The SEALs lost four men killed and had several wounded in a short, stiff battle that should not have happened. Ironically, the original plan was for Rangers to take Paitilla, but high-rankers wanted to involve the Navy and gave the mission to the SEALs.

The Fox Slips Through

No one knew it at the time, but Manuel Noriega was very near one of the Ranger drop zones when they came floating down. He must not have been too worried about invasion—that is, until he noticed the sky full of parachutes. He and his driver took to the streets only to come upon an American roadblock manned by Rangers. Unfortunately, he was able to get turned around and get away before anyone noticed him.

One concern of General Stiner's was the number of PDF troops who had gotten away. Would they head for the hills and become guerillas under a still-free Noriega? The US Embassy had taken RPG and mortar fire right after the Rangers landed. That could continue if organized resistance occurred, especially if skilled PDF soldiers hooked up with elements of the Dignity Battalions.

The Comandancia defenders put up a good fight, shooting down two Special Ops helicopters and forcing a light observation bird down in the Panama Canal. Hellfire missiles from Apache helicopters and the weapons of Spectre, plus fire from armored vehicles pounded the large structure until Rangers of Company C, 3rd Battalion, came from the airport and cleared the survivors from the building.

Over the next few days the American sphere of influence expanded into the countryside and smaller towns, carrying on its back the new government of Panama.

Rangers often combined with conventional units to reduce strong points or holdouts. Rangers would go forward at night and try to make contact with PDF leadership at such places to ask them to surrender at dawn. The PDF force would be surrounded, and if no surrender occurred at the prescribed time, an attack was either faked or made in a mild way to allow the defenders a face-saving few rounds before giving up. There was no reason to kill a bunch of people at that point, or expose US soldiers to unnecessary risk.

On December 22, newly installed President Endara officially dismantled the PDF, but in several places Noriega supporters fought on, perhaps hoping—he was still at large—that he would return and lead them. One such force was reported north of Rio Hato, at Penonome. Ranger units moved to take them down, as well as a few other holdouts in different places, but by and large they found only empty buildings and uniforms; the PDF were becoming civilians in a hurry.

Finding and Fixing Noriega

Considering an extensive manhunt had been going on since the earliest moment of D-Day, Noriega managed to remain at large for four days. His supporters continued to resist while he was loose, so Stiner and Thurman were pressing hard to find him. They knew there was a plan already designed for Noriega to mate up with remnants of the PDF and paramilitary in the hills and lead them in harassing raids and sabotage operations against Americans and/or the Endara government. Searches of his known residences and offices turned up wads of cash, pornography, and lavish personal items, but no dictator.

A one million dollar reward was posted, but sightings were made before then. Each one was checked out, and a few times it was obvious Noriega and his cronies made it out just in time.

By December 22, General Thurman believed it was possible Noriega would head for the city of David, the capital of Chiriqui Province, where a sizable remnant of PDF were known to be gathered. A combat assault, the last major move of the conflict, was laid on, even though surrender noises were being heard from the leadership of the enemy group. When Rangers got there, nothing much happened.

Noriega was no Custer at Little Big Horn. The little dictator chose not to fight it out, instead running for the safety of the Nunciatura, home of the Papal Nuncio, Monsignor Jose Sebastian Laboa. Ironically, the haven was the same place Noriega's adversary, Endara, fled to after the elections were overturned. Since the US had cordoned off the embassies of Libya and Cuba, but not the Nunciatura, Noriega had little choice. He and a few others slipped quietly into the sanctuary while thousands of Americans scoured the countryside in vain.

General Thurman found out where Noriega was about mid-afternoon on Christmas Eve.

Laboa said he would lift diplomatic immunity by January 4, and there was a huge anti-Noriega rally about to take place. The dictator wasn't dictating anymore.

Major General Wayne Downing took Noriega's surrender at 8:48 pm.

Casualties

The United States suffered 23 killed in action and 322 wounded.

Ranger losses were five killed and 42 wounded.

Panama took it a little rougher with 314 killed and 123 wounded.

US estimates of Panamanian killed and wounded may be a little high due to multiple claims for the same kill on a frantic battlefield.

The Panamanian KIA numbers reflect total losses of both the PDF and the Dignity Battalions. Later figures released by Panama say only 51 uniformed PDF were killed.

Some 200 civilians were also killed.

Such figures are incredibly light for the invasion of a country, but then the strict rules of engagement prevented much death, as did the overwhelming US force that caused a great number of defenders to have second thoughts.

Leader of the Pack—Kernan Biography

William "Buck" Kernan was born in Fort Sam Houston, Texas. He received his Commission from OCS at Fort Benning in November 1968. His first assignment was Liaison Officer, 1st Brigade, 82nd Airborne Division. He would end up leading Airborne troops much of his career.

Kernan was a Winter Ranger, attending Ranger School from November 1968 to January 1969.

He went to Vietnam in August 1969 as a Rifle Platoon Leader for 1/327, and then led the Battalion Recon Platoon (Tiger Force). He was also the Assistant S-3 before rotating back to Fort Bragg, where he commanded a company in 2nd Battalion (Abn), 325th Infantry.

The Infantry Officer Advanced Course came in March 1974, after which he was assigned as Area Commander for the US Army Recruiting Command in Austin, Texas. Two years later he joined the 2nd Ranger Battalion, where he commanded two companies and was Assistant S-3. In the summer of 1978 Kernan attended Command and General Staff College. One year later he was assigned to Military Personnel Center, Washington, DC, and later became Infantry Branch Assignment Officer.

From July 1979 to August 1981 he served as US Exchange Officer (82nd), to the British Parachute Regiment, where he commanded Company C, 3rd Para.

Another Ranger in this project, Colonel (ret) Steve Pullen, also held that position.

Beginning in July 1983, he was first XO, then commander of 2nd Battalion (Abn), 508th Infantry, 82nd Airborne. A few years later, in 1987, he graduated the Army War College and took command of 1st Ranger Battalion at Hunter Army Airfield, Georgia.

He became Deputy Commander of the 75th Ranger Regiment in December 1988, and was promoted to Commander, 75th Ranger Regiment in June 1989.

On December 20, 1989, Kernan jumped with the Regiment into Panama for JUST CAUSE.

In September 1991, the Rangers had to let him go forward to become Assistant Division Commander (Maneuver) for the 7th Infantry Division (Light), at Fort Ord, California.

By July 1993, he had become Director for Plans, Policy, and Strategic Assessments, J-5, USSOCOM, at McDill AFB, Florida.

The next step was a big one, but natural. General Kernan took command of the 101st Airborne Division (Air Assault) from February 1996 to February 1998. In March 1998, he stepped up again, assuming command of the XVIII Airborne Corps at Fort Bragg.

Somewhere during all that he had time to earn a Bachelor's Degree in History and a Master's in Personnel Administration.

Lieutenant General Kernan retired in December 2002, but remains active in military affairs in 2007, including serving as newly-installed President of the Ranger Hall of Fame.

William "Buck" Kernan

A legendary Hall of Fame Ranger, Lieutenant General Kernan allowed a small part of his long history to be printed here. This is one of those extraordinary conversations I only hoped to get, recorded over the telephone January 18, 2007. He began in Vietnam, and then away he went.

I had a rifle platoon in Delta Company first (327th), and went from Delta to Echo and took Tiger Force. I had about 60 men. Our primary mission was to work out in front of the battalion. The basic mission was to find and maintain contact with the enemy and let the battalion pile on if we got into a sizeable fight. That was 1969-70.

Kernan joined the Rangers about three years later when 1st and 2nd Battalions were still getting underway.

I was the Assistant S-3, then I was Headquarters Company Commander, and then I commanded A Company, 2nd Ranger Battalion. That was early '75 to the summer of '77.

How long were you with the Regiment?

I came back and commanded 1st Ranger Battalion after the War College, which was 1987 to December '88. Then I was the DCO, RCO designate (Deputy Commander of Ranger

Regiment), from January to June 1989. Then from June 1989 to August 1991 I was the Regimental Commander.

When orders came down for Panama, did they come from General Downing?

Yes, I got a call on the secure line from General Downing to execute. We worked directly for JSOC. He was my Battalion Commander in 2nd Ranger Battalion, so I knew him well. When I was a Battalion Commander in the 82nd, he was my neighbor, so I knew him socially and professionally for quite some time. There was never any doubt of what he wanted. He was a task, conditions and standards guy. Very well organized. Very focused leader. I found it easy to work for him as a commander. He was a commander's commander.

There was planning long before the invasion, including BLUE SPOON. Did you feel ready when you were called in?

Sure. I was commanding 1st Ranger Battalion when we first got the orders to plan for BLUE SPOON. At that time there two battalions involved—us and 3rd Battalion. We were basically at that point just doing the mission of the seizure of Torrijos-Tocumen and La Commandancia. After the coup in early '89, and the response of the 6th and 7th PDF Companies out of Rio Hato, it was apparent we had to take them down.

Those two companies came to the rescue of Noriega after an in-country coup.

So, we got a change in mission. We reorganized to take on two assault objectives—Torrijos-Tocumen and Rio Hato. Once we reorganized to take down Rio Hato, and they brought that mechanized force in to cordon off the Commandancia, we basically did a mission analysis and did a task-to-troops assessment of what was required. I put a reinforced battalion into Torrijos-Tocumen, which was 1st Ranger Battalion with a company from 3rd Battalion. Then [at Rio Hato] the 2nd Ranger Battalion and the 3rd Ranger Battalion (-) with two command elements, one going to Torrijos-Tocumen and one to Rio Hato. I think we had an appropriate division of labor there.

Lt. Colonel Robert Wagner commanded 1st Battalion, and now heads USASOC. Lt. Colonel Al Maestas commanded 2nd Battalion, and Lt. Colonel Joe Hunt had 3rd Battalion.

We ended up doing a validation exercise literally hours before the execute order came down. In fact, we replicated the time-distance factor across the southeastern part of the United States—the various assault objectives. For us, and the various other special mission units. We executed this thing to make sure we had our timings down, and we were able to validate the plan.

I can remember standing in the hangar doing the "hot wash" with General Lindsey, who was Special Operations Commander at the time. He said, "I don't know if we'll ever do it, but we've validated the plan. We've got a few things we need to modify."

By the time I got back to Fort Benning, things had deteriorated in Panama. I didn't have my 2nd Ranger Battalion redeployed all the way back to Fort Lewis [Washington] when I got the order to execute. As soon as they landed I turned them around and brought them back to Benning.

Bombs Away

There were to be two bombs dropped near the PDF barracks just before the Ranger assault. The size and placement of those bombs, and the reason for using them, has been represented in several ways over the years. General Kernan cleared it up.

It goes back to when the coup occurred, and they had Noriega trapped in the Commandancia. He made a call from the Commandancia to Rio Hato. Those two companies were the most loyal companies he had. Eight minutes from the time of the call they were marshaled on the airfield with their weapons and ammunition, and aircraft were getting ready to move to Panama City to break the siege. So, we knew these people were ready.

When we did the mission analysis and we looked at coming in over the sea, we also looked at how we were going to be able to do this and maintain the element of surprise. There were a number of things done. We put an AC-130 up in aerial watch position. We put some Apaches with our Little Birds (AH-6) behind an island, and I had an LNO with them. It was all time-phased to come in to insure we had adequate protection on the ground and fires from the air to get the assault force on the ground. At 0100 we [were supposed to] drop the first bomb on 6th Company, and one minute later on 7th Company, and one minute later the AC-130 and the Apaches were to open up as we came in to jump.

At the eleventh hour the decision was made to offset the bombs. This was one of those issues that Thurman contested when I briefed him. He did not like dropping the bombs on the two barracks. I was ready to take them out right in their beds if we could. This got debated back and forth and the decision was made between General Thurman, General Stiner, I believe, and General Downing, to offset the bombs. Those bombs were being dropped by F-117s [Stealth], the first time they'd ever been operationally employed. I got the code words they had launched, and I got the code words they were getting ready to execute as we were coming in. Of course, I came off the headset.

Unbeknownst to me, they had decided to offset them 500 meters. Two 2000-pound bombs. If you recall, H-Hour was originally 0100, and they moved it up 15 minutes. Because of that, 6th and 7th Companies had been alerted, and were out of the barracks. Where they offset one of the 2000-pound bombs, hit right behind an area where they had the V-150 and V-300 vehicles. It was also an assembly area for one of the companies. It tore up a number of people that were back there. Had they hit the barracks there probably would have been no damage, because people were out of the barracks.

The AC-130 did a good job on escaping vehicles, and there was a ZBU-23 [anti-aircraft gun] set in the compound between the two companies. I'm sure he couldn't see the AC-130, but he fired in their direction. They put a 105 right in his watch pocket. They next day when I went through there, the only thing you could find was a forearm with a hand on a traversing wheel.

Which Ranger Battalion did you jump with, and where did you land?

We did what we were supposed to do. We looked at where our assembly areas were set up for TOC 1. I was in the middle of the stick, somewhere between 2nd Battalion, which jumped first, and 3rd Battalion. I was looking to land near where the Panamanian Highway bisected the airfield. We were cross-loaded and wanted to land just south, on the sea side of the highway, down one of those keyholes. I actually ended up on the north side of the highway.

Were you scattered out very much when you landed?

It was a pretty good jump. It was great. I remember going to brief the crews before we loaded up. It was cold as hell. I went into Building Four where they had all the crews there, and I briefed them. I told them, "Hey, look. Don't give me an early green, and forget about the red light. We're all going out." I told them I didn't know if we were going to take any fire, but they had to hold it steady so we could get everybody out of the aircraft. We were virtually bingo on fuel. We were going to make one pass and that was it. Had we not executed, we would have compromised the size of the force we were bringing in. The only other place to land was Howard Air Force Base [in Panama].

What was it like coming in?

We started receiving fire before we even got to the shoreline. It was pretty good. It was pretty exciting. I was in the middle of the aircraft, and I didn't see anything come through our aircraft, but I think 13 of the 17 aircraft got shot up.

One report shows 11 of 13 C-130s took hits. General Kernan may be referring to helicopters, too.

I think we had one or two guys shot through the skin of the aircraft, and a couple of guys shot in the air. I remember when I came out there were quite a bit of tracers everywhere, but we jumped at 500 feet, so we weren't in the air very long. Yes, it was exciting.

There was quite a bit of activity everywhere. Of course, we jumped in at 0103, so it was pretty dark. There were a lot of tracers going everywhere. It seemed like there was a lot of control—from our side, anyway. It was difficult to ascertain exactly where everybody was, especially when you're getting your bearings landing.

Hung Up

I actually got hooked up on a light pole that overlooked a bullring. There were lights out all over the place, because my parachute pulled the lights down into the power lines, which caused the electricity to go out right away, which was great. We all had night-vision goggles and they didn't. I knew I was on the lines. I saw that right away. I was just sort of suspended, and I was lucky that I didn't ground out, because it was corrugated tin wall around the bullring. As it turned out—like I said, it was dark—I was probably 18 inches above the ground. Had the easiest landing going.

There was a young RTO landed next to me, and of course I just had my 9mm and my "brick."

The "brick" is a package of orders and other administrative details.

I'd gotten separated from my RTO in the air, and my Sergeant Major was on the other side of the bullring—Sergeant Major Leon Guererro. I told this kid, "You got a radio?" He said yes and I said, "Well, get it up." He said, "Sir, I'm a Platoon Leader's Radioman." I said, "You're mine now! Get your radio in operation." I took his M16 while he set everything up, and he moved with me until I got linked up with my RTO, which took about 15 minutes. I released him to go to his Platoon Leader.

Years later, I'd just taken over command of the 101st at Fort Campbell, Kentucky. We're driving to the reception. I noticed the 3rd Battalion Scroll on his shoulder and I asked him when he was with the 3rd Battalion. He said, "Sir, you don't remember me, do you?" I said I was sorry, but I didn't. He said, "I was the guy that became your RTO that night at Rio Hato." He stayed with me for about a year or so. Great guy.

Into The Night

We immediately encountered a fuel truck that had been going down the Pan-American Highway when we came in. It got shot up by an AC-130 and gasoline was leaking everywhere—

why that thing never went off I don't know. We crossed the highway and there was a Ranger Squad setting up a blocking position, which was part of the plan, right where the highway crosses the airfield. We hadn't brought the aircraft in with our gun jeeps and everything yet. I told them, "Look, I'm moving down in this keyhole, we're going to be moving right in front of you. It's just me, my Sergeant Major, my RTO, and one other individual."

Just as soon as we crossed the Pan-American Highway a vehicle came driving down there at mach speed, shooting out the windows. We hit the deck in the middle of the airfield. It turned in and started shooting everywhere, and I could hear this Squad Leader saying, "Hold. Hold. Hold." Then I heard him say, "Fire!" They hit that thing with machineguns and AT-4s, it flipped all the way up in the air, they just wiped it out. Later on, I asked him what he was saying hold, hold, for. He said, "Sir, I could see you, and I could see the vehicle. We needed to let the vehicle get past where you were so we could engage it." I said, "God bless you."

One of the best stories of that night—there were a bunch of cadets in this NCO Academy. Young, 14-to-18-year-old cadets. We didn't know this at the time. We were told there was nobody there because this was the Christmas holidays, except the 6th and 7th Companies. As it turned out they had brought these cadets in for some kind of training during the holidays. This fire team took down a machinegun position that was in front of one of the barracks in front of where the NCO Academy was. These two young Rangers entered a room and they could hear a bunch of people speaking Spanish, obviously very excited. They didn't fire it up, and they didn't throw a grenade, and they took 140 or 160 of these cadets as prisoners. They weren't armed, but they were all in uniform.

I asked this one young Ranger, "I'm curious. You just took down a machinegun position, you hear all those people speaking Spanish, with no lights on, how come you didn't fire them up?"

He said, "Hey, Sir, the Rules of Engagement said if we're not receiving fire, don't take any unnecessary life." I thought that's pretty dad-gummed disciplined. He was 20-years-old, and because of his actions, those cadets were not harmed at all.

The Rules were pretty strict, but we always had the right of self-protection. We knew we were going to be vulnerable going in. In fact, I had a discussion at a briefing down in Panama before we did JUST CAUSE, with General Thurman right after he took over. We were giving him our missions and course of action review. I gave him my mission, which was to destroy 6th and 7th Companies, and he said, "What do you mean, destroy 6th and 7th Companies?" I said that was my mission.

He said, "I'm not comfortable with that. There's no reason to go in there and take unnecessary casualties or create them. What if they surrender?"

I said, "If they surrender, we'll take them. But, Sir, we're jumping out onto an airfield. We're going to be sticking out there like the balls on a bulldog. We're going in with assault fires. If they want to surrender afterwards, that's fine. We can always throttle down." It was a tough call for everybody to make going in.

We lost five killed and 50-some wounded. I don't remember how many we killed. We captured some of them, but most of them just took off running.

Did you have good contact with the Rangers at Torrijos-Tocumen during your assault?

On the radio. I was talking to the battalion commander and I was talking to my DCO. The next day I flew over there in a Little Bird and met with them.

Why did you choose to make your jump at Rio Hato?

We thought that's where the bigger fight was going to be. I looked at the commanders' analysis as to where I could best be able to influence the operation. I felt very comfortable with my battalion commander and my DCO going in there. Their primary mission was to seize Torrijos-Tocumen, open it up, introduce the Special Mission aircraft, and just to hold that.

The other thing was we had the beach house adjacent to Rio Hato, which was one of Noriega's homes. So, I looked at the mission, looked at the requirements to take down 6th and 7th Companies, and the possibility we may have to do a seizure at Noriega's house, and felt that was the most appropriate place for me to be.

Kernan was asked if the SEALs were part of the beach house takedown, and if Rangers blew the front door off with a LAW.

No, the SEALs didn't take it down. The SEALs didn't come in—we got redirected—they were trying to track him [Noriega] and they lost him. He ended up there in that rest facility or whatever they called it that overlooked Torrijos-Tocumen.

We were in the process of taking down the assault objectives when General Downing called me and told me to go and seize the beach house. I directed the Rangers to go in there and 2nd Battalion actually did that. As they approached the house, there were some security folks there who engaged the Rangers, and they used an AT-4, a good Ranger key, to blow the front door off. The only ones there were the security folks.

The AT-4 is a shoulder-fired weapon like the LAW, but it is not collapsible and packs a little bigger punch.

La Commandancia

Were there Rangers at La Commandancia to clear the building?

We initially had La Commandancia as one of our primary objectives. It was the priority mission for 3/75 so they knew the terrain and composition of the headquarters pretty well.

The Mech unit from the 5th Division had the area sealed off, but La Commandancia had not been cleared. I was given a FRAGO (Fragmentary Order] from JSOC to send an element in there to clear La Commandancia. I tasked Bob Wagner, through TOC II, which was with 1/75+, to send Charlie Company, 3/75 there to conduct the mission, as the company commander was familiar with the original plan. They did a hurried mission brief, immediately started moving to La Commandancia and were literally putting together breaching charges on the move as they attacked to seize and clear the headquarters.

Wayne Downing

General Downing gave several parcels of information during emails. Questions are in italics.

How and when did you get into Panama?

I infiltrated into Panama three days before D-day with parts of our JSOTF.

When Noriega surrendered to you, what was said between you? Can you describe the scene and how you felt?

The only words spoken initially were between Monsignor LaBoa, the Vatican Papal Nuncio or Ambassador in Panama. I asked him if this was him. He said yes. Noriega had lost a lot of weight during his 10 days in the Nunciatura and looked much smaller than I knew him to be. My first thoughts were he might be an imposter while the real Noriega went over the back wall. Of course, we had the other escape routes covered so he wasn't going to get away. Once we got him off the street, two of our largest SF Special Mission Unit guys flexed cuffed him. He resisted, telling me it was beneath his dignity as a captured General. I basically replied tough beans or words to that effect. The boys ignored him and literally picked him up by the arms, walked him [frog-march] about 100 meters to a soccer field, and deposited him in the helicopter. We flew him to Howard AFB, transferred to a MC 130 Combat Talon, and sent him back to CONUS [Homestead AFB, Florida].

Michael Kelso

I was the security leader for Team Black, which was Colonel Kernan's jump TOC [Tactical Operations Center] in Rio Hato.

There were two companies of his [Noriega's] Panamanian Defense Force at Rio Hato. Supposedly some of his better guys. That was also where his beachside villa was. But we jumped on the airfield. There were some pretty good firefights occurred at Rio Hato.

I was on Bird 12. Fourth from the last guy out or something like that. It was pretty crowded. I mean we were full up. During the loading, as I was sitting down my reserve para opened! What a pain in the ass that was getting a new one hooked. Of course, we had combat equipment and so forth.

Before we stood up the Rangers recited the Ranger Creed. It was very inspiring and you knew you wouldn't let your Ranger buddy down. My Ranger buddy for the op was SSG [now SGM] Alan Gibson. He led a company in the drive on Baghdad. A great soldier. As soon as they opened the doors practically, you could hear ack-ack going off, you could see the tracers.

As I recall the last few aircraft coming in were pretty far off the drop zone.

My team was in Rio Hato about a day-and-a-half and then we were relieved by an element of the 7th Infantry Division. We pulled back to Howard Air Force Base in Panama City, where the Regiment conducted follow-on Ops throughout Panama. My security team got back to Fort Benning on Christmas morning at about three in the morning.

Keith Antonia—Grenada To Panama

Lt. Colonel (Retired) Keith P. Antonia left the Army in August 2001 after a tour as Commander, 5th RTB. Though in line for a Colonelcy and most probably at least one star, Antonia opted for the private sector in favor of his family—particularly his children—who would have to move several more times while in school if he continued in the military.

During the time of this recording—July 1, 2005—Antonia was Assistant Director of Cadet Recruiting for North Georgia College and State University, one of the best military schools in the country. This excellent human being was top-ranked in everything he attempted, and his career as a Ranger bears that out. A portion of his career bio is included here.

Other parts of his story are elsewhere in this project, notably in the sections on the Ranger Creed and the 1st Ranger Battalion.

I graduated from the University of Connecticut in 1981, and from there was commissioned as an Infantry Officer. I went down to IOBC [Honor Grad], then Jump School, then to the 82nd Airborne Division where I spent the next three years as a Rifle Platoon Leader, Mortar Platoon Leader, Scout Platoon Leader, and Company Executive Officer.

I went to Ranger School while I was assigned to the 82nd—Class 4-84—in January 1984.

While I was in the 82nd I did Grenada in 1983 as a Battalion Scout Platoon Leader, and I also did six months in the Sinai keeping peace between the Egyptians and Israelis. That's when my first son was born.

Only Rangers jumped into Grenada. We landed on the airstrip. It was pretty much done, all we saw was dead bodies and stuff around the airfield. We went all around the island looking for bad guys. We caught a gas station robber and picked up a few Cubans, but there was no fighting.

The Rangers and Delta had already knocked down most resistance and the students were being rescued. For more details see the section on Grenada.

Then I went to Fort Benning [Georgia] and I went to Pathfinder School. They made me Chief of Pathfinder School for 18 months.

Antonia was then a Captain and became Chief of the school right after his graduation from it, an unusual situation. Once again he was an Honor Graduate.

I was assigned to the 1/507th—back then it was the 4th Airborne Training Battalion—when I came in, Colonel Leonard B. Scott was the battalion commander, and he told me he was going to make me Pathfinder Chief, but first I had to go through Pathfinder School. As Chief, I was responsible for getting Pathfinder Instructors and students through the school. We did Airborne operations, Pathfinder operations, helicopter swing-loads, all that kind of stuff.

After that, I went to the Ranger Department and became the Assistant Chief of the Long Range Surveillance Unit Leader's Course—after going through the course. It's more of a course like Pathfinder School [than like Ranger School]. It's intellectually demanding, but it's not nearly as physically demanding as the Ranger Course. You learn reconnaissance and surveillance techniques, how to identify enemy vehicles, etc. This was 20 years ago, but when I was there we were putting through [mostly] soldiers assigned to LRS Units in division and corps. We had Sergeants mostly, a few Lieutenants, and very few Captains. They were going to be Team Leaders.

There were a sprinkling of others, such as DEA people working in Central and South America, but he doesn't remember any "black" Special Ops types.

Then the Ranger Department became the Ranger Training Brigade while I was there. When [that happened] they made me Commander, Company A, 4th Ranger Training Battalion. I was the first commander of Company A, and my job was to take a bunch of Ranger Instructors and put Ranger students through the City Phase. Before that it was called the Benning Ranger Division [of the Ranger Department]. I did almost two years there.

I left in October of '88 and went straight over to Savannah to the 1st Ranger Battalion. When I got there [the commander] was Buck Kernan. While I was in the 82nd, Kernan was our Battalion XO for Grenada. He was on his way out, but he was there for two or three months. For the bulk of [my time] it was Robert Wagner, now a Lt. General.

I became the S-3 [Air Operations] in October. I was there for four years. [During that time] I commanded Charlie Company, 1/75. But, while I was S-3, we did the invasion of Panama.

[When we found out it was a go] we had about 72 hours. Now, we started planning this thing six months prior. We were involved in top-secret planning exercises to put the initial plan together in May. We worked with all...the "black" Special Operations people and so forth. We put the original plan together and it got nixed and we had to change the whole thing. We started replanning in December. After we replanned everything we did a full dress rehearsal with the entire Ranger Regiment, I think it was December 16. We used the same launching bases, Hunter and Lawson Army Airfield, and we flew down to Eglin Air Force Base [Florida] and we seized two airfields simultaneously. I think one was Duke Field.

We came back home and actually sent 2nd Ranger Battalion back home [to Fort Lewis, Washington] and within hours of them getting back home we were alerted to the actual thing and they had to [load up and fly back to Lawson, in Georgia] and prepare for the night of the 19th, early morning of the 20th.

Back and forth across the continent certainly couldn't have been pleasant, but then Stonewall Jackson once marched his army 177 miles in 10 days through snow and rain on small rations, then had them fight. They won.

So, it was about D-Day, P-Hour [first parachute drop], minus 72 hours when we got the word.

I was a jumping safety on a C-130. Our air package [task organization] going into Torrijos-Tocumen Airport was the entire 1st Ranger Battalion, plus a company from the 3rd Ranger Battalion, which was Al Dochnal's company.

Dochnal was at one point the commander of the 5th RTB.

Our package was 12 C-141s and four C-130s, and of the C-141s, seven were PAX [personnel] birds and five were heavy-drop birds, where we dropped in our jeeps and bikes [dirt bikes] and ammo pallets and supply pallets. We had about 80 Rangers on each of the seven C-141s. So, we had about 700 jumpers.

The scheme of maneuver was that at P-Hour minus five minutes we had an AC-130 come on over the target. He had certain targets he had to service, which included the barracks of the 2nd Rifle Company of the PDF. That was 0100 local on December 20. Then he stopped firing and helicopter gunships came down the runway and took out the Panamanian Air Force communications/staff media area with 2.75-inch rockets. I heard they also took out an anti-aircraft weapon mounted on a jeep or some vehicle.

Then, two minutes later the first 141s started dropping. We had four Soul Two C-141s with Special Ops crews flying them. All the "vanilla" ones would follow the others ones in. Soul Two crews are Air Force Special Operations crews that are trained to do goggle flying at night. They can also fly in much less limited conditions than a vanilla aircraft can.

Special Ops aircraft are considered "black" so the rest are considered "vanilla".

We jumped at 500 feet AGL [above ground level] and that was followed by the C-130s that dropped one minute apart. Those things were crammed.

We out-loaded from Sabre Hall, which is at Hunter Army Airfield. The flight time down to Panama for the C-130s was seven hours and 15 minutes. We had to rig up and load the aircraft about three hours prior to that, so our Rangers were in their parachutes with all of their combat equipment on, stuffed into these C-130s for 10 hours [a lot of men slept on the way down]. I was never so glad to get out an airplane in my life! But, the airborne operation went off without a hitch. I landed exactly where I was supposed to be, nobody landed off base.

I think the figures were that we had one killed in action, a medic on the airfield [1st Batt] and we had four or five who were wounded, but we could never figure out what they were wounded by. It was shrapnel by some sort of explosion. There were also a couple more who were wounded in the Terminal Building, but I think that's all.

What we found was they had probably been alerted—this was four days before Christmas—so when the AC-130 hit its target, the barracks, he pumped 105[mm] rounds into it from one end to the other, then finished up with 40 mike-mike. It was all burned up, but there was nobody in it. I think they got word we were coming and just about everybody left. So, there wasn't a big, huge fight, not like down at Rio Hato where the 2nd and 3rd Ranger Battalions were. They had a fight down there.

So, we finished up a couple of hours of excitement there, and then went into seven or eight days of stark boredom. We went out on patrols, looked for weapons caches, looked for people on the black and gray lists, people we were looking for. We would get Intelligence about where Noriega might be and then we'd launch a patrol to go to the house or location to see if we could find him.

He was actually only a couple of hundred meters from where I dropped in that night. It was in a building right off the airfield, and he was in there with a prostitute. He actually ran into one of our blocking positions and turned around and left.

Duke Durkan—MIA

During the invasion, then Staff Sergeant Brendan "Duke" Durkan was part of Headquarters Company, 1st Battalion, and was supposed to jump in like the rest. However. Durkan was on one of the aircraft that was a little late dropping and some of the people didn't get out of the plane in time. On the second pass it was determined the 82nd was already coming in and no jumps were possible, so Durkan and others were taken to Charleston, South Carolina, still in full combat gear, including grenades and personal weapons.

Durkan reports seeing television there and hearing there was at least on man MIA—and it was him! His wife had been advised her husband was missing during the time Durkan and others were busy securing an Air Force bus to take them back to Hunter Army Airfield in Georgia so they could get back to Panama, which he did early the next morning.

"I took more razzing from my wife than anybody," he said. "The other guys thought I was outside the wire fighting my own private war."

Ed Scholes

Major General (retired) Edison E. Scholes was Chief of Staff of the XVIII Airborne Corps and Joint Task Force South (JTFSO)) during JUST CAUSE. He became the Deputy Commander for the Corps and Fort Bragg in 1991, before commanding US Army Forces at NATO Major Command in Turkey through 1995. Among his other accomplishments, he was Assistant Division Commander of the 82nd Airborne, 1988-89, and farther back, Senior Advisor to a Vietnamese Ranger (Biet Dong Quan) Group in I Corps, 1970-71. His Ranger School graduation was December 1961. Scholes retired in 1996 after 35 years in service.

Scholes is one of several Ranger-qualified officers who figure prominently in the planning and execution of JUST CAUSE, including Wayne Downing, Carl Stiner, Thomas Needham, William Kernan and Colin Powell. Though not a Ranger, General Thurman "could have been."

There were plenty of other Ranger-qualified soldiers scattered through the ranks, both officers and NCOs. Having such an operation run by Rangers is not a bad thing, though Thurman was certainly up to the task.

I met General Scholes at a Vietnamese Ranger Advisors' reunion in Georgia, where he agreed to this telephone interview, conducted May 16, 2006.

I had come that fall to be Stiner's ADC over at the 82nd. I was over there when he turned it over to Jim Johnson and took the [XVIII] Corps. He called me over there to be his Chief of Staff. Then Thurman came in, there had been a big conflict—[General] Woerner didn't want anybody coming down there and messing in his Theater [of Operations—SOUTHCOM].

Some new energy was needed at SOUTHCOM, and General Maxwell Thurman had plenty of it. Scholes said neither Thurman nor his warfighter, General Stiner, slept very much. "You'd see Stiner at Bragg in the basement of his house doing woodwork all night." In truth, Stiner was up for nearly a week during the run-up phase and the initial combat. "He was an outstanding leader, an outstanding commander—great to work for. He'd support you; be right there with you."

All this time we had been alerted to the possibility of going to Panama. We had come up with an OpPlan, we had practiced and practiced, we had gone back and forth to Panama at different times setting up and practicing. War-gaming it. At that point Stiner decided to get in the Sheridans [tanks] and the Apaches and they would exercise them every night to where people would get used to all the sounds.

When we deployed, Downing and I deployed our two assault CPs on the same airplane. We went before the executive order. We went in on the 17th, and Stiner went around briefing everybody and came in on the 19th and mounted the operation.

The ball opened on December 20.

We got in there at two in the morning or so. Delta and JSOC went to their place [won't say where]. At the Task Force HQ we occupied the Army HQ, the operations center. We walked in and said, we're here for another exercise and we're going to take control of the operations center. Thurman, and I think, his G-3, were probably the only people there who knew why we were there. We had done that previously. We started working all the timelines, checking everything, getting all the comms up—the commo officer down there was outstanding.

When Stiner got there around noon on the 19th, we knew it was going down. We got everybody together to brief them and to straighten out any small points that had come up. That's when the people down there knew it and they were sworn to secrecy until later that evening, when they had to get families out of the crossfire and put them in the basement. In particular there was a large officer's quarters that would be caught between the PDF and the air assault that was going in there on the golf course.

We had rehearsed all this numerous times. We knew what to do and what not to do to alert them, and they had seen this activity before. We were certain they knew we were there, but the cover story was that we were having an exercise, which had happened previously.

The first indication we got that he [Noriega] might find out about it [the invasion] was a transmission from Washington. That's when we got together and decided to go a little early—because he was getting frantic phone calls from Washington. I don't think he suspected anything at that point, maybe they should have.

The question was asked if he thought the 15-minute advance in timing was enough.

Oh, yeah. We had 27 operations go down at the same time, but it all depended on Delta getting the CIA agent out of the prison first, and an 82nd trooper being held in a prison [up near the Canal]. The 82nd did that [a little later].

PDF response to Rangers falling from the sky was both more and less than expected, depending on where the action was taking place.

They had a greater response...I guess I sort of expected it...that was a real hot DZ the Rangers went in on Rio Hato. They did a fantastic job there. Second to Delta [mostly Rangers, anyway], they did the best job down there.

We were really concerned about [the Ranger drops being on time and target] because of what their missions were, and we couldn't go short much on their missions because of what they had to do. They were sort of hanging out, particularly down in Rio Hato, on their own. But, it really worked out, primarily because they were being hauled by C-130s out of Pope [AFB] and you're not going to stop those guys up at Pope.

The 82nd paratroopers were dropped long on several runs, through no fault of their own. The Rangers had to be on time, and were.

Once the airfields were secure, elements of the Ranger Battalions were used in support of Delta operations and in other missions, as were other assets put at Commander Downing's disposal as head of Joint Special Operations.

[Largely because of "the tragedy in Somalia,"] when we got down there we assigned a platoon of LAVs [light assault vehicle] with Marines and a platoon of Sheridans with 82nd guys to the Delta force. They belonged to Downing. He could put them anywhere he pleased. They were his. When they were running an operation he would position them where they could always support against anything that happened to Delta. If some sniper started shooting from an upper floor or something like that, you know, one of the Sheridans would just take the floor out.

That would have saved their ass in Somalia.

As with most other Rangers, Scholes directed the conversation toward another soldier, Thomas Needham, the G-3 for Stiner's XVIII Airborne Corps. Needham has since attained the rank of Major General. As head of Operations, Needham was in charge of getting it done in the field.

He is the prime guy. He is the key guy, on the phone to everybody while I was sitting there talking to Thurman's staff and my own staff. Needham was the main staff officer that was constantly monitoring the phones and all that.

The key to doing that [invading from within and without] was the numerous rehearsals that Stiner ran both at Bragg and in-country, and to have moved the Sheridans and the Apaches down there. They got out and ran around every night about midnight so everybody got used to the noise.

Asked if Rangers had trained in Panama just before the invasion, Scholes answered indirectly, saying a lot of units trained there, including a battalion of the 82nd in Jungle Warfare School.

We kept planes busy going back and forth down there, so people knew exactly where they were going to be and what they were going to do—the leaders and all. It was a year-long operation to get ready for it. We never knew exactly when we were going to go.

Dignity Battalions

Our biggest problem became the Dignity Battalions we didn't know about. They were the ones that set fire to the town around the Commandancia [Noriega's HQ], and they were the ones that created all the havoc. They were actually thugs armed with AK47s, M16s...You never knew what size [unit] they were, but they played havoc that first night or so, because we had been told by the CIA there were three, but we found out later on there were 18. They were all over the place. The priests and the people identified them as the ones who were going down the streets throwing grenades into storefronts and setting the fires. There are written statements about that. We had precision fire in all places that would cause no collateral damage. That's a matter of record.

Did they wear uniforms?

No. They were in every garb you could think of. Most of them, because of the suddenness of the operation, most of them were in civilian clothes.

As we got control of the situation we would get a lot of the battalions—which had not surrendered—on the telephone, and we would get a Special Forces translator. We would tell them, if you'll look outside you will see a number of Black Hawks. That is a Ranger Battalion. A little further to the west you'll see a couple of C-130 gunships circling. You have one hour to step out onto the road—in formation—and stack your weapons and surrender. Otherwise, the Rangers and the gunships will prepare for that, and if you watched television last night, you will know what that means. Most of them surrendered after that.

The word went out over the various media connections that anyone caught with a weapon would be treated accordingly. Exchange rewards were set up—$500 for a machinegun, $100 for a rifle, and so on.

In a couple of days we had 50,000 weapons. We put them on ships. We gave the police pistols and shotguns. We got the armored cars, too, about 12 or so.

Taking Noriega

As we got started down there, of course, it was kept very close hold. As soon as the newspapers broke on the morning we were down there, then the US Marshal contingent arrived, the CIA, the DEA was down there, the DI contingent arrived, all those law enforcement agencies, and I said, well, okay, we'll have you here and we'd like to see where you can be worked into the situation. They said, oh, we don't take orders from anybody. I said, fine, get out of the way and stand by.

And so they did and they did not get in the way. I don't know where they went, but 12 days later when we got Noriega out of the Nunciatura—it was at night—we notified the agencies, and I said it'll be up to you all to determine who is the appropriate authority to take Noriega back. There was an MC-130 warming up on the airfield. We evacuated him by Black Hawk to Howard AFB. From there the law enforcement agencies, the DEA, the Marshals—they were primarily the ones making the decision.

We sent two Special Ops doctors with him in order to examine him thoroughly before he took off, in order he could not claim at any time he was beaten or bruised or whatever. Before we turned him over to anybody we wanted a full examination.

They got over to the airport and the two medics waited while they decided who was going to take him. They finally brought him over. He was in an orange jump suit. He had demanded a uniform we had captured the first night.

The doctors said, now, you're going to have to take the leg irons and the cuffs off him. They all looked at one another—nobody had the key. The Spec Ops doc had to pick the lock to complete the examination. Then they asked him to put the leg irons and handcuffs back on him, and he said what's he going to do at 30,000 feet? The doctors went all the way to Miami with him to make sure nothing happened to him.

We almost had him [earlier], but the CIA lost him. The first night of the invasion they were tracking him. He was in a meeting on the other side of the country on the Atlantic side. The CIA were on him, but he left the meeting—apparently he had arranged it—all his people went one way and he went another. As it turned out [where he ended up] was very near where the Rangers were, and they almost got him. They got his uniforms, shoes—and he was, as I recall, with a prostitute. I think they got his red skivvies there, too.

Rangers searched Noriega's beach house near Rio Hato very soon after their drop, plus several buildings containing offices near Tocumen-Torrillos airfield.

A question was asked about Noriega's departure from the Nunciatura.

We had Delta there, and he didn't actually come out. They turned him over and that was a story within itself. [see Wayne Downing's interview]. Delta was in charge of that operation. They had the place surrounded.

The reason we played the music was because the journalists had these high-powered microphones stuck out everywhere. They made fun of us, saying we were using psychological warfare against Noriega, but it wasn't for that purpose at all.

Scholes said he doesn't remember Colin Powell telling Stiner to stop the music. "It was no big deal." Asked who the onsite Delta commander was, he said he had to be careful about such things and refused to name him. Okay.

To demonstrate to the Vatican representatives and personnel there why they should release him, we showed them some of the items captured in his Intel shop. They went back and decided he should leave. Otherwise, they had thought about letting him stay in there. One of the things [found] was a list of what order the priests would be killed under certain circumstances.

The General also talked a little about some videotape that contained some disturbing images. The Nunciatura staff was getting a better picture of just what kind of man they were protecting.

OPERATION DESERT STORM

*B*ravo Company, 1ˢᵗ Ranger Battalion, was the only Ranger unit to serve in the first Iraq War in 1991. Bravo was there to take out a radar installation. That doesn't mean there weren't a lot of Rangers over there sprinkled around in other units.

There was also a small element of LRS soldiers that had been based in Bad Tolz, Germany.

Perry Doerr F/51 LRSC

In 1989, the Long Range Surveillance Unit for VII Corps was F Company, 51ˢᵗ Infantry.

This interview with Ranger Perry Doerr was conducted via email early in 2002.

Headquarters, Department of the Army Ranger Personnel Branch managed all Ranger positions in the 75ᵗʰ Regiment, LRS Units and Light Infantry Divisions. So, as a Ranger-qualified NCO, I was eligible for assignment to any of those units. At the time I reenlisted, I wanted to go overseas again. The only Ranger slots overseas at that time were in the LRS Units.

The concept of force-expanders was at work here. Getting any Ranger-qualified soldiers in any other unit was considered a bonus to that unit.

My understanding is that was exactly the intent of the Ranger NCO management policies at the time.

Our mission was to provide Human Intelligence (HUMINT) in the Corps battle space from 50-150 KM behind the lines, similar to what the LRRPs did in Vietnam. We were organized in three platoons of six teams each, a total of 18 teams consisting of six men each, a commo platoon of about 25 signal soldiers who manned a Company Operations Base (COB) and two Remote Operating Bases (ROB), and a HQ platoon, which had the commander, executive officer, First Sergeant, and Operations Section (S-3 and S-2, plus supply). We were stationed at Ludwigsberg, Germany, at Coffey Barracks. We were attached for admin/log support to the Corps MI [military Intelligence] Brigade, the 203ʳᵈ.

Originally, I was an LNO [Liaison Officer] who normally conducted liaison with the supported unit or the MI Brigade TOC. In LRS units the LNOs are sent from the LRS unit to higher HQ and any supporting unit HQs. These LNOs advise higher HQ, et al, on LRS operations, employment and SOPs, missions (current and planned), and all other facets of LRS operations and support. They are the two-way link between the LRS unit and the unit whose mission we were supporting. We had four LNO positions for E-7s in our LRS Company.

Just before Operation Desert Storm I was given the Operations NCOIC [Non-Com in Charge] job.

In the field I was responsible for four major missions: Planning of all team operations, briefing the Team Leaders and putting together the Target Packets for their mission—Intel, ops codes and procedures, E&E plans, etc—and receiving the team brief-backs along with the CO, so we knew the plans for that team in case of compromise. Inserting and extracting the teams using helicopters, parachute, sea, or ground infiltration, monitoring and forwarding team reports for exploitation, and finally, leading a 20-30-man reaction force that would go to the aid of any team compromised by the enemy.

A COB is the staging and operations base for the LRS Company. Usually the COB was at or near an airfield or LZ to support helicopter operations. Our COB typically had an HQ/ops section (tent), Intel section and briefing area (tent), three platoon CPs, individual team (18 each) tents all isolated from each other for security reasons. That way an individual LRS team could plan for a mission isolated from everyone else in the unit. This was important because we did not want a team's mission to be known by everyone.

We took measures to isolate teams from one another so if a team was compromised (captured), then only one mission was affected. There was no jaw-jacking between soldiers about each other's mission or target. There was concertina wire all over, around each team tent and section, to keep teams and sections isolated and secured with guards.

We were deployed to Saudi Arabia in December 1990. After a few weeks of training in the desert and getting used to the environment, the air war began on January 17, 1991. We set up the COB at Al Quesuma airfield outside of Hafir al Batin in the northeast corner of Saudi Arabia near the border with Iraq.

For six weeks bombs fell all over Iraq while our troops readied themselves.

While this was going on my unit was making final preparations to conduct operations to the Corps front. We moved our teams to the front line positions one week prior to the start of the ground phase of the war via a night ground insertion using HMMWVs. We were to report on enemy positions, troop dispositions and activities from 10 positions in front of the 2nd ACR [Armored Cavalry], and two positions in front of the 1st Infantry Division. These were all located in "no man's land", between the Iraqis and our Corps positions and AA. The decision was made not to insert us very deep in order to not compromise the offensive plan. We would act instead as a "trip wire," providing early warning so that the rest of the Corps could get into position undetected.

We reported Intelligence information from four-man hide sites dug in on the first night. The hides were dug in below the surface, using 2X4s as support for a canvas-covered, plywood roof. The roof and surrounding area were then camouflaged with sand. The teams lived in these hides all day, getting out only at night to stretch out and work out any cramps.

When the ground war began on February 22, my first mission was to move forward...so we could recover our teams out in front of the attack.

I remember sitting in my HMMWV among tanks and armored Infantry fighting vehicles (Bradleys) as far as the eye could see in all directions. It was impossible not to be moved and inspired by the awesome spectacle that I was a part of. A force of 11 divisions total, five divisions and 150,000 soldiers in VII Corps alone, were poised to smash into Iraq, cut off and then liberate Kuwait. The press had been reporting the potential bloody battle that was about to begin, but I somehow did not think that it would be that bad. We were well trained and confident that we could handle the test.

The following is a description of a basic LRSC operation, and details a "hide" used in Operation Desert Storm.

A basic operation was meant to gather Intel, observe major enemy lines of communication (LOC) and installations and activities. Enemy activities were reported via high frequency radio reports to the commander via LRS nets and means.

We normally used six-man teams operating out of hide sites situated along LOCs or near suspected bases or activities. In ODS we went with four man teams because it was easier to hide four men under flat "pool table" terrain of the desert.

The configuration we used was an X-shaped hole dug down three-to-four feet. The legs of the X were about seven-to-eight feet long, and the center of the X held the radio and a camouflaged trap door for observation. Each leg of the X also had a trap door at the foot of it so the team member could get in or out of the hide site or fire his weapon into his sector if that became necessary. This gave a 360-degree observation capability and fighting position configuration to the hide site. The X was then covered with plywood held up by 2x4s. The plywood was covered with burlap that was then covered with white glue so that sand could be applied to it and stick. If the wind blew (as we found out in pre-ops training) that prevented the bare wood from being exposed.

Careful attention still had to be paid to camouflage, specifically ensuring the sand surrounding the site closely matched the sand on the plywood/burlap roof.

The man on observation duty would be in the center of the X looking out the trap door while wearing a "gilly hat" [part of a sniper's camouflage outfit], or a booney cap with a net of burlap strips on it. The observer would then report using the radio.

Gillie hats and suits originated in Scotland, worn by hunters called Gillies.

All other team members would lay low in the site during daylight, facing out from the center of the X into their sector. It was a very effective configuration. I could not find teams even knowing their eight-digit grid coordinates unless someone would come out of the hide site and guide me in.

Rangers In Other Times and Places

Although most of Ranger history can be delineated by large conflicts, there were several instances when men of the Tab went other places without all the fanfare of Grenada or Panama.

In Bosnia and Kosovo Rangers did recon missions—and other things they can't talk about—in small groups, sometimes only one or two men at a time being rotated in and out. There were also a few times when larger elements were used as assault forces.

In Kosovo it is reported that teams were used for whatever they were needed to do, and they weren't washing dishes. The Regimental Recon Detachment (RRD) is liable to show up anywhere, any time.

There was also a mission to Haiti that was cancelled at the last second with Rangers rigged and ready to drop onto the island, plus a mission to Lebanon that never quite materialized.

Areas Rangers worked several times were Central and South America, again doing recon work —and other things they can't talk about. There was some training being done by Rangers for counter-drug and counter-guerilla task forces down there, and perhaps an ambush or two while patrolling the known jungle trails.

Although several stories have come my way during research for this project, I am not willing to break confidentiality rules to tell them.

TASK FORCE RANGER—SOMALIA

Introduction to Insanity

Ranger action in Somalia—October 3-4, 1993—got a lot of attention because of a series of ferocious firefights, fallen birds and multiple US casualties. That vicious battle got all the focus and made it seem—at least to the layman—that the Rangers were there for a short time and did nothing else but get shot up in the Bekaa Market.

These things don't just happen. There are reasons for military missions, and they generally stem from political decisions. America and the United Nations made those decisions based on the ideal of saving lives, first by giving massive aid, then by going after the bad guys who wouldn't let the aid get through. It was house-to-house, Intelligence gathering, searching, much like what has happened in Iraq II—just in a very condensed time frame.

There was only one pitched battle in the entire short-lived conflict, and Task Force Ranger fought it.

Somalia is a small, impoverished, mostly Islamic country in east Africa without much to export, and without money for imports. The country was run for a time in the late 1980s by Siyaad (Siad) Barre. The "President" was actually in control of the country through the favor of a combination of three clans whose names sound vaguely Aztec: Marreexaan, Ogaadeen, and Dhulbahante. As in much of Africa, there was a war going on between rival factions—in this case it was the Isxaaqs.

There were several other clans involved, but there were only two or three serious contenders for power. Barre bowed to the clans in 1991.

This is where the players the Rangers would look for came into focus. Maxamad Faarax (Farah) Aideed was the military commander of the USC force, and figured he had a pretty good chance of taking over. Aideed was a member of the Habr Gidr clan, a very powerful militant group of people who would have gone over the edge had Aideed been killed or captured.

There are at least five different spellings for Aideed's name printed in current literature. I've used the most common offering. As for Habr Gidr, you may pronounce it any way you can.

The clans fought each other and killed innocent bystanders as though life had no value. Over time, young people grew into adulthood knowing nothing but fighting, learning from childhood how to fire a weapon, how to hide, how to kill.

Soon people began to starve. Thousands perished from cruelty and malnutrition. The United Nations took note and attempted to get Aideed and his opponent, Cali Mahdi, to stop shooting.

The UN didn't scare Aideed. He wasn't facing American commanders per se, and new President Bill Clinton had begun to bring Americans home as they were replaced with other UN troops. By mid-year there were fewer than 1,400 combat troops left in-country.

Twenty-four Pakistani soldiers responded to reports of a weapons cache in a radio station and went to investigate. What was probably support for Aideed prompted an ambush and extermination of the Pakistani element in a nasty show of disregard for human suffering.

UN Security Council Resolution 837 proposed to go get Aideed and his henchman in answer to the lawlessness of his supporters.

Who else would get a mission like that but Delta and the Rangers? Two weeks later Admiral Jonathan Howe ordered it done, slapping a $25,000 bounty on Aideed's head. He then requested some Special Operations soldiers to help get things under control.

The Rangers knew they were to be deployed somewhere, and were training hard for it when they were told to stand down. The "idle" time didn't last long. In addition to uncertain deployment possibilities, the Rangers were limited as to the number of men they could have. Another decision of limitation was to withhold C-130 gunship support—a political decision.

Task Force Ranger was formed to do the job under the command of Major General William Garrison, but Howe's request in June wasn't fulfilled until August when the TF deployed to Somalia.

Meanwhile, UN and US troops kept banging away at the Somali militia, increasing the drama of the situation to fever pitch. In July, US helicopter gunships—Cobras—demolished a house with TOW missiles to kill some clan leaders.

In fear for his life, Aideed went underground near the end of the month, but the violence didn't end. During the next three weeks several US soldiers were injured or killed by command-detonated land mines, and there were probes of the UN perimeter.

That was enough. About 440 3rd Battalion Rangers and operatives from C Squadron, 1st Special Forces, Operational Detachment-Delta landed in Mogadishu on August 26, linking up with other members of Task Force Ranger, including SEALS and the all-important air assets.

Task Force Ranger ran six successful missions in Somalia without huge incident before the now-famous seventh, in which 18 men died and about 85 were wounded. Those missions harassed Aideed and took out a number of his ranking supporters.

Figures for the number of US wounded in that battle vary, in part because they are often fragmented by unit structure. For example, Delta's killed and wounded are often included with the Rangers. The number given for Task Force Ranger includes Rangers, Delta operatives, and airmen. There are several accounts that say the Rangers lost 16 or 18 men.

The overall numbers for the full time in Somalia put the number of wounded for TF Ranger over 100. Six of the dead were members of B Company, 3rd Ranger Battalion, 75th Ranger Regiment, and six (seven?) were Delta operatives. The rest were airmen. All were members of Task Force Ranger.

The Battle of Mogadishu

The premise for the mission was simple: fast-rope in from helicopters, capture some bad guys —two Aideed Lieutenants and whomever else was hanging around—and exfiltrate them via vehicle convoy. Such missions had been practiced and accomplished in real time more than once. It should have been fairly straightforward.

The Somali people, armed to the teeth, surprised everybody by falling on the US contingent with everything they had, hundreds of men and women full of hate and mindless rage, bent on the destruction of the Americans in their streets. Instead of the continual frustrating fight between themselves, here was a common enemy numbering more than one hundred men.

Company B, 3rd Ranger Battalion, and Delta lifted off from their compound at Mogadishu Airport at 3:32 on the afternoon of October 3, and were working in the target area 10 minutes later. The ground convoy assigned to pick up the prisoners left a few minutes after the birds flew.

The Rangers were traveling light, considering this was supposed to be a quick snatch done in daylight hours. Heavy combat was not expected. They carried no canteens, for instance, or night-vision devices, believing them unnecessary. Time on target was to be less than 30 minutes.

Delta went in first, four men to a MH-6 Little Bird helicopter, riding outside the bird on small benches. The target building, the Olympia Hotel, didn't hide many secrets as the D-boys flowed inside. Such work is Delta's specialty and they are very good at it. In short order, they had captured 24 Somalis, including the two top men they came after.

Outside, the Rangers got their feet on the ground, set up a defense perimeter, and awaited the coming of the convoy. They were already taking fire. One Ranger fell from his aircraft upon fast-rope insertion when the bird swerved to avoid an RPG and was critically injured. He was first, but not last, and the medics worked to save him.

Incoming fire was building against the Rangers as they held the line for Delta and the prisoners. The convoy arrived and the prisoners were being loaded aboard Hummers and cargo trucks when one of many, many RPGs fired into the air hit a Black Hawk, which crashed three blocks away.

Immediately a six-man team from the Rangers headed that way, along with a Little Bird and a Black Hawk Combat Search and Rescue (CSAR) helo. The Little Bird, arriving ahead of the others, managed to extract two wounded men to safety. The CSAR bird delivered the last of 15 men via ropes just as another RPG hit home, but the pilots were able to get the smoking helicopter back to base.

Had the C-130s been available, the Black Hawks wouldn't have been hanging around being big, slow targets.

RPGs subsequently hit two more Black Hawks. One of them crashed less than a mile from the first downed bird. Two Delta snipers orbiting above volunteered to rope down to the crash site and protect the crew, even though Somalis rushing to the scene were overrunning the area. Those two men, Master Sergeant Gary Gordon and Sergeant First Class Randall Shugart, ended up giving their lives to protect the co-pilot, CWO Mike Durant, who was captured—and returned 11 days afterwards. Durant later said he owed them his life.

Shugart was killed when he ran out of ammunition. Gordon returned to Durant, gave him the last weapon with the last few rounds, and said good luck. Moments later he also lay dead.

Gordon and Shugart were awarded the Medal of Honor posthumously for their efforts. It was the first such since the Vietnam War.

"They weren't doing it to be heroes," Lt. Colonel Danny McKnight said of the two snipers. "They were doing it to take care of each other. That's what they were trained to do."

The prisoners were finished loading and the convoy took off. The Ranger/Delta force on the ground made for the first crash site, taking a beating on the way from intense fire. Casualties were mounting, especially among the Somalis.

Fighting their way into the crash area, beating back the throngs of Somalis, the Ranger/ Delta force set up defensive positions in some buildings to the south and southwest of the downed helicopter and began work to extricate the dead from the bird. The Black Hawk had come down between two buildings and the machine was badly contorted, making it impossible to free the bodies without tearing the bird apart around them.

Meanwhile, the convoy, made up of a 52-man force including Rangers, Delta operatives, and Navy SEALS under the command of Lt. Colonel McKnight, tried in vain to reach the first crash site, but incoming fire was so intense the machines were coming apart under the onslaught. To make matters worse they were being guided by aircraft relaying messages that took too long to receive, causing the convoy to miss turns. At one point they made a complete circle and ended up where they started—only to have to start again.

The convoy couldn't get to the site, so it made for home base, encountering another convoy coming out to reach the downed bird at the second site.

The convoy was out in the open, taking fire from all sides, and there were many casualties, including some of the prisoners. The Humvees were lightly armored with Kevlar and sandbags and mounted either .50 caliber machineguns or Mark-19 grenade launchers, but the amount of incoming was so heavy as to override most safety features. A couple of five-ton trucks were lost, one Humvee was being pushed by a truck, and others were running on flat tires or just the rims.

The second convoy, also unable to traverse the roadblocks and heavy ground fire, stopped long enough to load some casualties and then escorted the first group back to base.

About that time, a company from the 10th Mountain Division tried to reach the second site, but heavy fire pinned them down, too, until they gave up the effort and returned to base with the aid of covering fire from a couple of Little Birds.

The return to base by each separate element was met by a host of personnel, aware of at least parts of the situation and anxious to help any way they could. Some of the command element had been watching much of the action filmed by Little Birds on closed circuit TV and were beside themselves trying to figure out what to do. There was no magic bullet.

The night was not pleasant for anyone on either side. Death continued to pour into and out of the Ranger/Delta holdings near the first crash site. The second site had been overrun.

The Task Force was resupplied by helicopter after dark and told to hang in there. Back at the base the men were almost frantic with concern about their brothers out there in Hell.

Some volunteers for a new rescue force had to be turned down for lack of room in a quickly formed convoy made up of Rangers, 10th Mountain soldiers, SEALs, and Malaysians driving armored personnel carriers (APC). That force ran the gauntlet and made it to the Task Force survivors about two in the morning of October 4. Together they worked to unlock the pilot's body from the bird while fighting off RPG and small arms attacks.

Finally, about daylight, the casualties were loaded onto the APCs and the convoy turned for a soccer stadium occupied by Pakistanis. Not everybody would fit in the vehicles and several Rangers found themselves running "the Mogadishu Mile"—actually a good bit more than a mile—to get out of there.

Incoming fire had slackened, but not stopped. Little Birds were strafing the streets around the convoy. The running Rangers were very nearly alone on the way back.

Let it be said the Rangers—and others—wanted desperately to go back to the city and finish what they started, to give back some of what they had taken from the Somalis, but they were not allowed to go.

President Clinton responded to the fight by adding a bunch of troops on a temporary basis—still not pushing forward, just defending—and pulled everybody out. By March 1994, the remaining UN troops were mainly Asian and African.

Aideed died in August 1995, from gunshot wounds inflicted by his own people.

An excellent book by Tim Bowden, *Black Hawk Down*, and subsequent movie, tried to show the horror of the situation in Mogadishu, and did fairly well in the attempt at transferring reality into a medium of expression. Though some of those in the battle say the book is off on certain small things, it remains the definitive work to date. For instance, the chronicle states some Rangers removed the back plates from their armored vests. Other sources indicate the men were wearing Delta-type vests that contain no back plates, considering they have face-forward missions.

As for whether the raid was a success—hard to call something successful when the casualty rate was so high—the two men being sought were captured, along with 22 others. Mission accomplished. Add to that the successful defense of the perimeter put forward by the Task Force, figure the kill ratio, and consider no man was left behind except the captured Mike Durant—you decide.

WAR IN THE MIDDLE EAST

During the time this book was being written—2001-2007—American soldiers were fighting in Afghanistan and Iraq. The stated purpose by the US administration was regime change.

At the same time, US troops were in the Philippines, Germany, South America, Africa, and several other places, doing a multitude of missions including drug interdiction, pacification, patrolling, and just plain working on an American base somewhere.

The United States Armed Forces were spread pretty thin, and the looming specter of Iran as a nuclear power didn't help matters much. However, the two countries in conflict are on either side of Iran, and full of experienced, well trained and equipped US and Allied soldiers.

It's almost like it was planned that way.

Special Operations Forces (SOF) were needed—and used—more than ever, especially in the lead-in assaults on Afghanistan and Iraq, and the hunt for Osama Bin Laden and Saddam Hussein.

Rangers were among the first assault forces in both countries, taking out airfields and performing raids in their lightning-fast, overwhelming way.

After the "wars" were "won" SOF continued employment in a variety of missions, whether it be SEALs, Special Forces, or Rangers—and a few others.

Unfortunately for historians at this point, Special Operations has gone more-or-less underground. While it is fairly easy to discover what happened in WWII, Grenada, and even Somalia, trying to gather information on current Ranger movements and actions is nearly impossible. Everything they do is classified.

Though it is obvious just from their mission statement that Rangers were involved in primary actions prior to, or at H-Hour in both invasions, there is little information available to the public—or even to a historian such as myself; someone with pretty good access.

So, after all the thousands of words about Rangers of the past, now that the young ones are out there doing their thing, few words are available to be published—with certainty of fact.

There is a small window of information available when Rangers are reported killed. At least one knows where that particular unit—or part of that unit—was located at the time—if the Army is telling the truth. The only other way Rangers make the news is if there is a big battle where some of them get killed, such as the battle of Takur Gar in Afghanistan.

Probably the only people who know what all the Rangers are doing are the commander of the 75th Ranger Regiment and his immediate superiors in Special Operations.

The Long War

Recently, the Rangers—and others—are calling the fight against terrorism the "Long War." Indeed, 10 years has been presented as a possible parameter for planning any future movements.

It has become obvious that the people of Afghanistan and Iraq do not think the same way as those in democratic countries. Changing the leadership has not resulted in immediate change in economics or security for the average citizen. The present leadership is too busy defending its authority to do much else. Very few individual leaders agree with each other about almost anything, leading to constant bickering and stagnation of the process.

Poverty and lack of education play a big part in the ability of insurgents to recruit fighters. In lands where religious affiliation can mean life or death, the idea of a broad-based democratic government is a hard one to promulgate. The family—the clan—is the center of most lives.

In early 2007, the people of Iraq were fighting each other as well as the occupying troops, vying for domination. Bombs continue to explode every day.

Yet, schools are open. Progress is being made in many areas in spite of the fanatics.

In Afghanistan, religious zealots of the Taliban were using the broken promises and restrained authority of the new administration to regain converts. The border with Pakistan is a sieve through which militants travel and move supplies—much the same as Cambodia and Laos during the Vietnam War.

In the United States Congress, people are working hard to thwart President George Bush's drive to succeed—regardless of the consequences of a rapid pullout. It is probable the Rangers are far too busy doing what they do to think much about all that.

What follows are the bare bones of the two conflicts, peppered with the few currently available facts and some pre-war history.

AFGHANISTAN—OPERATION ENDURING FREEDOM

*E*xcerpt of a Reuters article dated October 9, 2004
"This is one of the happiest days of my life," said Sayed Aminullah as he cast his vote at Eid Gah Mosque in the capital.
"I don't care about the result. All I care is that we are having an election. This is a sign that things are improving for Afghanistan."

On September 11, 2001 America suffered her second Day of Infamy at the hands of radical extremists. Those enemies of democracy forgot the lesson of Pearl Harbor—America can be hurt, but not brought down. The United States and some of her allies immediately went to the lock-and-load stage.

General Tommy Franks, who would command US forces in Afghanistan, was on his way to Pakistan to meet with President Musharref about security considerations and counter-terror possibilities when news of the tragedy reached him. His aircraft was rerouted to Tampa, Florida—his command station. All over the world, soldiers began to prepare as Warning Orders went down the line.

The result was American troops once more fighting on foreign soil against an out-of-control government.

In the early morning hours of October 7, 2001 US forces began to pound elements of the controlling factions of Afghanistan known collectively as the Taliban, including members of the then-fledgling terrorist group Al-Qaeda.

In the beginning, attacks were all by air, comprised of heavy strikes from B-1, B-2, and B-52 bombers (all land-based), and many sorties from carrier aircraft such as the F-14 and F/A-18 fighter jets. Added to that mix were Tomahawk cruise missiles slung into the air by US and British ships and submarines.

In all, US Central Command (CENTCOM) forces—air, sea, Special Operations, and conventional ground forces—were deployed from 267 bases. Fifteen different nations hosted some 30 operational sites disgorging military effort.

Technology made this new endeavor somewhat different from those of the past. For one thing, the operation in Afghanistan was controlled and commanded from Tampa, Florida—some 7,000 miles away. The ability to literally "see" the process of taking down the Taliban gave overall commanders a brand-new handle on the situation.

The war in Afghanistan—and later Iraq—is unusual for America for several reasons. Though the beginning phases were very much like the German blitzkrieg of WWII—lightning, overwhelming strikes—there was also a political measure akin to the softer undertakings in Grenada and Panama. For instance, the original name for the operation in Afghanistan was Infinite Justice. That term was set aside in favor of Enduring Freedom because of fear of insulting the Muslim community, which believes only Allah deals in infinite justice.

The Islamic religion—all-pervasive in those parts—contains a fundamental belief in God (Allah) that holds grave sensitivities to any outsiders who do not bear that belief—in that way. The nation of Islam, while supposedly peaceful in intent, had been swayed to the far side by extremists in power to the point where the people of Afghanistan were being held down and exploited by those whose interpretation of the Koran was, to say the least, strict.

Over time Islamic fundamentalists bent their peaceful religion into something focused on hate—and the destruction of the West and all things pertaining to it.

Afghanistan was a lair for terrorists, and President George W. Bush went after them there. His declared intent was to reduce terrorist training camps to rubble, disrupt the Taliban and Al-Qaeda infrastructure and capture the leaders.

America's response to September 11 was swift and sure. There were few thoughts of negotiation or diplomacy. Secretary of Defense Donald Rumsfeld pushed for readiness on September 12, and CENTCOM set to work making plans. Ten days after the twin towers crumbled, General Franks was briefing President Bush on the basic ways and means of taking down the Taliban regime and the Al-Qaeda terrorist network within Afghanistan.

The initial planning was augmented by serious analysis of logistical needs, coalition partner integration, and a long look at the small amount of information Franks had on his target.

By October, he was ready to brief the President again, this time with Rumsfeld's stamp of approval on the plan. Bush gave it the green light, and declared the first bombs should fall on October 7, 2001—just 26 days after terrorist hijackers altered the course of American history—and that of Afghanistan.

Other nations contributed in various measures as part of an international coalition against terrorists. By 2002, the number of coalition partners had grown to 68, of which 27 were represented at CENTCOM. Also present at central headquarters were operatives from a large batch of US government agencies, not to mention liaison people from all the combined US military forces.

Operational requirements included taking down the Taliban infrastructure—unorganized and scattered though it may be, it still controlled some 80 percent of the country—and eliminating as much Al-Qaeda authority as possible. To that end the coalition struck on many fronts at once, after a protracted bombing campaign.

One of the problems with bombing was the terrain. Mountains provide many hiding places, even from the big boys. Another problem was finding the so-called "infrastructure" of the Taliban regime. Their telephone service didn't work very well, if at all, and radio communications were scarce. They didn't possess any large amount of artillery or trucks or have big bases. They were scattered all over the country, seldom in any large numbers, and made extensive use of caves in some areas. In the end, it just didn't pay to use B-52s to kill a dozen Taliban.

The Afghani soldier had been fighting for decades in one war or local conflict or another. They know how it goes. Russia found out the hard way that conquering Afghanistan wasn't easy. For that reason, the US wanted to avoid the stigma attached to "invading" the country.

There was no "war" between America and the country of Afghanistan—the "war" was against Al-Qaeda and the Taliban.

Since relatively small groups of the enemy fought mostly guerilla-style, Special Operations Forces were used in large part to locate and confront them.

Rangers were part of the first strikes in the country, and were combat-hardened later when going after hidden bad guys in the mountains.

The First Drop

On October 20, 2001, about 100 Rangers parachuted onto an airbase on the outskirts of Kandahar to begin ground operations in Afghanistan. They launched in helicopters from *USS Kittyhawk* in the Arabian Sea and returned there after the raid. It was believed Mullah Mohammed Omar, the leader of the Taliban, was there. He was not.

The raid came after two weeks of concerted bombing of Taliban positions. The top dogs had fled.

Later the Taliban said the Rangers had landed on a mountain called Baba Sahib, but were driven off. Other reports said no Rangers or any other US soldiers had the courage to make the attack.

Though the Taliban said the base—a supposed headquarters—was empty, refugees said up to 25 Taliban fighters were killed.

A printed flier with a photograph of firefighters raising the American flag in WTC debris—and the caption "Freedom Endures"—was left behind as a calling card.

Two Rangers were lightly injured during the drop.

Special Forces personnel had been in-country for a week or more before the assault, doing liaison work with Taliban opponents and locating targets. Many SF soldiers also earn the Ranger Tab, so Rangers were on the ground in other capacities, as often happens.

There were other quick assaults on various targets throughout the country around the time of the Ranger attack on the airfield. Hit-and-run ops were also being carried out, and would be for a short time. The small amount of technology the Taliban possessed was mostly destroyed in the first few hours.

The Taliban response to the first attacks were scornful, saying in effect, that since Afghanis didn't really have much of a communication system or any kind of mechanized force, the bombings weren't hurting them very much. They were dug in, like the Viet Cong of old, waiting out the pounding, weapons with them.

Someone had to go in there and get them.

In November 2001, Rangers were sent into northern Afghanistan to work with the Alliance there. The Rangers were to be used in a variety of ways, but principally as target-finders and markers for air strikes against Taliban positions.

Source: NBC: CJCS General Richard Myers

The Ranger Regiment is composed of three battalions, but it was seldom, if ever, those whole battalions were used for a single mission. Small unit actions were the key in Afghanistan. Large areas had to be covered, but major battles were rare—especially once control of the country had been taken from the Taliban, which didn't take long. An interim government was installed just 78 days after the first bombs fell, on December 22.

By that time Special Ops people had linked up with anti-Taliban forces in-country, and were working to target air strikes on enemy positions.

The provincial capitol, Mazar-e-Sharif, fell a few weeks later, followed quickly by Kabul and Jalalabad. Kandahar had fallen in mid-December. The Taliban was finished as a functioning authority in Afghanistan in very short order.

Rangers and Special Forces soldiers learned to work with the people of Afghanistan as much as possible to route out Al-Qaeda figures and Taliban leftovers, especially in the mountains along the border with Pakistan. Sometimes Special Ops soldiers rode horses to get at them.

In mid-summer, 2004 there were about 18,000 US soldiers of all types in Afghanistan.

As of this writing—mid-2006—Taliban and Al-Qaeda members were still fighting isolated battles and chucking rockets and mortar rounds and—a new chilling development—using roadside bombs and car bombs.

Although there are conventional forces in Afghanistan—usually a brigade-sized Army unit, as well as other branches and Allied troops—much of the "probing work" is being still being done by Special Operations troops in what CENTCOM calls "reconnaissance and direct action roles."

On April 31, 2006 Colin Powell pressed his successor, Secretary of State Connie Rice, about how many troops were in Iraq. He said he proposed many more than were originally sent. Bush and Rumsfeld—two civilians—ultimately decided how many to send and keep there.

By late 2006 the idea of sending more troops to help end rising sectarian conflict, or bring troops home either piecemeal or all at once were being pushed against each other in heated debate.

Order of Battle

The initial ground forces arrayed against the Taliban were not large, and they weren't wholly conventional. There was no giant military thrust into the heart of Afghanistan, no multiple divisions grinding forward as in the wars of old.

Instead the conflict was waged largely from the air, but only when the aircraft knew where to put their ordnance. For that, and to work with the people, Special Operations forces were used extensively both for fighting and recon. The main conventional ground force was Marine.

There were, of course, plenty of support personnel and other necessary units. There were two battalions of Engineers and a couple of Explosive Ordnance Companies, some MPs, Civil Affairs people, and a battalion of Field Artillery. There were also a number of Psychological Operations (Psyops) personnel.

The main battle force was made up of two battalions of Marines, plus the 22nd Marine Expeditionary Unit of more than 2,000 men, and the 6th Marine Regiment. There were no full divisions present.

Special Operations was centered in Task Force Angel, which included the 5/19, 1/20, and 1/3 Special Forces Groups, a Naval Warfare Unit, and the 2/75 Rangers—who opened the ground war.

SFOD-Delta was also probably involved, though records of their presence are scarce.

After the main fighting was over, elements of Army divisions rotated through every six months. Those included the 82nd Airborne, 101st Airborne, 10th Mountain Division, and the 25th Infantry Division. Special Ops soldiers continued to work within the country, largely near the border with Pakistan.

Ranger units rotated in and out of Afghanistan on a regular basis in early 2007. Missions were classified, but given the type of training and capabilities of the Ranger Regiment, it is not too hard to figure out the kinds of things they are being tasked to do.

It is a conflict where large troop movements are difficult to perform with any kind of secrecy, and guerilla fighters are the main enemy. Small, fierce actions are the norm. Who better to go after phantoms than soldiers who own the night?

Rangers In Operation Anaconda

Once the initial fighting was over and the Taliban had been rooted out and severely damaged, Operation Enduring Freedom switched from all-out invasion to anti-guerilla warfare. Taliban and Al-Qaeda fighters continued to resist the coalition forces in small groups, doing some physical damage, but mostly disrupting the ability of Afghanistan's fledgling government to bring order. That was especially true in the outlying areas near Pakistan's border.

Increasing attacks by those fighters prompted the US-led coalition to launch a large mission, Operation Anaconda, on March 1, 2002. American soldiers and airmen teamed with Afghan forces and coalition troops in a move to reduce Taliban/Al-Qaeda strongholds in the southeastern part of the country.

Some 1,000 US troops and about 1,500 others descended on several hundred enemy combatants south of Gardez. Elements of the 10th Mountain, 101st Airborne, 160th SOAR, and Special Operations units—including Rangers—were supported by a large air arm that dropped more than a thousand bombs. The airmen also served as close air support in the form of fixed-wing fighters, AH-64 Apache helicopters and AC-130 gunships.

Operation Anaconda continued until late March, succeeding in knocking down the rising enemy element in that area, but not eliminating the threat of continued attacks completely. Since there was no active "army" to combat and dispose of, coalition troops were only able to take down those who fought back, thus marking themselves as the enemy. As with the insurgents in Iraq, Taliban/Al Qaeda fighters don't wear uniforms and can easily throw down their weapons and blend in with the innocents.

Unfortunately, that left a number of enemies free to get away and fight another day.

Takur Ghar

Source: Dept of Defense release, May 24, 2002

The idea behind Operation Anaconda was to push against the Al-Qaeda strongholds from the west (Gardez), and drive the fighters into a blocking force composed of 10th Mountain and 101st Division elements in the east. The mountainous region was home to hundreds of guerillas—or terrorists, depending—and had to be cleaned out for any semblance of order to appear in the region.

Locations in and around the Shah-e-Kot valley were targets. The valley was flanked by tall mountains with numerous routes of infiltration and resupply available to the enemy, as well as well-sited gun positions. During the battle, the enemy was reinforced along a mountain route from the village of Marzak in the southern end of the valley to such an extent the route was dubbed "the ratline."

Task Force MOUNTAIN Commander, Major General Hagenback, planned to push through the valley with US and Afghan conventional troops, but he knew he needed somebody up high to accomplish the necessary recon and target-acquisition. For that purpose he used Special Operations Forces (SOF) in small teams, placed around the mountains in well-concealed hides. In all, SOF included SEALS, Special Forces, Air Force teams, and of course, Rangers. The hidden teams were able to drop fire on massed Al-Qaeda fighters in several locations, using air support.

Although the operation was designed as a "hammer-and-anvil" tactic, the guerillas didn't take the bait and run into the arms of the waiting US troops to the east. For whatever reasons they stood and fought, resulting in a serious firefight on the snow-capped mountain—Takur Gar—a spike driven more than 10,000 feet into the sky and studded with Al-Qaeda.

On March 3, two days after D-Day Anaconda, several MH-47 helicopters from 160th SOAR went aloft carrying SOF soldiers for deployment as recon teams in the mountains. Razor Four went north. Razor Three, holding a SEAL Team and an Air Force Combat Controller (CCT) in its belly, headed for Takur Gar.

Major General Hagenback moved the bulk of his ground troops across the valley to the north end and began a second attack from that direction. Takur Gar recon would give him eyes down into the ratline and into Marzak.

It was at that point things began to go wrong. Bad weather on D-Day and heavy resistance meant not all TF MOUNTAIN troops would get inserted on time. The surprising Al-Qaeda resolution to fight pushed the Afghan troops back into Gardez, eliminating needed support to the troops in the valley. From the start many of the ground troops were under mortar and small arms fire.

To make matters worse, Al-Qaeda had also recognized the significance of Takur Gar and had installed fighters in a fortified position there, supported by a heavy machinegun capable of firing on aircraft flying through the valley below. No one knew of the position until it was too late.

As Razor Three approached its intended LZ in a small saddle near the summit of Takur Gar, people on board began seeing signs of enemy presence in the form of footprints in the snow and castoff equipment. Thus alerted, the occupants quickly discussed aborting the mission, but an RPG struck the bird before action could be taken. The grenade injured one crewman, but it was small arms fire flashing through the craft that did the most damage. Hydraulic lines were severed and the floor of the craft was flooded with slippery fluid; fluid needed to fly the helicopter.

The pilots immediately tried to fling the big Chinook away, the sudden unexpected motion causing a SEAL and a crewmember to lose balance on the wet deck and fall some

10 feet to the rocky snow-covered ground below. That action began the heroic scenes that unfolded on that lonely mountaintop over a period of the next several hours.

Fortunately for the crewman he was tethered to the craft and his mates were able to pull him back aboard. SEAL Neil Roberts got to see the underside of the bird as it staggered away.

Armed with a Squad Automatic Weapon (SAW), Petty Officer Roberts did what SOF are trained to do; he defended himself against overwhelming odds until he could fight no more.

Razor Three had crash-landed a short distance down the mountain, temporarily out of harm's way, but the radios allowed the CCT to bring in an AC-130 gunship to protect them. After making its insertion to the north, Razor Four came back to the fallen ship and evacuated the stranded men, taking them back to Gardez. The pilots of Razor Four were in on the plan with the SEALS to go back and get Roberts.

The AC-130 reported seeing what was probably Petty Officer Roberts surrounded by a half-dozen men on the snow below. Rescue seemed impossible. The brave young man couldn't last against what was now known to be a fair-sized force of Al-Qaeda ensconced on the mountaintop.

Razor Four, five SEALS, and the CCT went anyway.

The main problem was a suitable landing site. There really wasn't one except for the LZ where Roberts was lost. The time it would take to walk up the mountain was unacceptable. It was that LZ or nothing—never mind the last ship was grounded by heavy fire.

Pre-dawn, Razor Four hovered over the 10,000-foot LZ long enough for the six members of the rescue party to get on the ground. The Chinook was holed several times, but managed to get away.

The team moved uphill in the fading darkness until a couple of the enemy were found in a fortified position under a tree. The CCT, TSGT Chapman, and a SEAL opened up and killed both, but the firing brought rounds singing in at them from another bunker about 20 meters from them. Chapman was mortally wounded in the opening burst. The SEALs fired up the bunker and threw grenades, but bullets and grenade fragments caught two men. In a very short time, the expedition of six had lost one killed and two wounded and was seriously pinned down.

With no other option the team disengaged to the northeast—with a wounded SEAL taking point—and called for the big gunship overhead to rain hellfire and damnation on the enemy positions. It is fairly certain that some of the Al-Qaeda fighter perished under the onslaught, but it is very certain that many did not, hidden under the rocks, hoping the ricochets wouldn't find them.

Razors Three and Four and their various occupants had taken some serious hits trying to get established on that mountain top. There was nothing left to do but call in the Rangers.

The Quick Reaction Force (QRF), always a necessity in a spread-out battle, was in this case composed of Rangers located not far away. They were alerted to move forward to a staging area at Gardez, which put them about 15 minutes from the action. Two Chinooks tabbed Razor One and Razor Two, loaded 23 men. There were 10 Rangers in Razor One, plus a Tactical Air Controller (TAC) and a Combat Controller. Also aboard was a PJ—a Pararescueman to help with the wounded. The second bird carried 10 more Rangers.

For whatever reasons, communications were at a minimum, so the rescue party had little knowledge of what to expect at Takur Gar. The SEALs, withdrawing under fire, got through long enough to ask for help, and the QRF was vectored to an "offset" LZ not far from the fight.

They shouldn't go back to the same spot; two birds had already been well ventilated there.

Unfortunately, the radio problems prevented the 160th birds from receiving those instructions, plus essentially negating the communications edge the Ranger Commander should have had.

Without prior knowledge of the situation, the Rangers continued on toward the top of Takur Gar, right where Razors Three and Four were shot up.

Full daylight was fast approaching as the Rangers homed in on the spot they believed the SEAL team still occupied. Instead, a squad of al-Qaeda guerillas were setting up a defense/ambush site, complete with a machinegun. They had already accounted for two Americans. They were ready.

Razor One came floating in, a great big Chinook making a beautiful target for the man on the ground with an RPG. It struck the bird in the right flank and was followed by heavy small arms fire from several directions. The mighty Chinook was shot to pieces and fell heavily about 10feet to the snow.

The Rangers and crew inside took a beating when it fell, but a bullet killed one of the door-gunners outright. Both pilots were badly hurt, one with severe injuries to his hand.

The nose of the big bird was pointing uphill where the main enemy concentration was. Heavy fire came from the bunkers, but it was incoming rounds from behind that did the most damage. The ramp was down and several al-Qaeda fighters were shooting straight into the fuselage.

One Ranger was struck and killed inside the aircraft, and two others died trying to exit the ramp. The rear door-gunner and others fired up the enemy, killing one right away.

With incredible bravery, the Pararescueman and a medic began treating the wounded while bullets flew around them. Rangers started moving forward. With three men down already, the standing men wanted some payback. Two more guerillas went down under rapid fire as the Rangers leap-frogged their way to better advantage.

In true Ranger fashion, the Platoon Leader (of six or seven men) wanted to assault the main enemy bunker—and tried to—but soon found out he needed more men. Again in true Ranger fashion he used his available assets. The Combat Air Controller got on the horn, and within minutes some 500-pounders were mauling the enemy positions. A few of those bombs were very close to the Rangers, the CCT, and eight Chinook crewmen. The aircraft also did some strafing runs, again uncomfortably close. Still, it was worth it. By 0700 the threat of being overwhelmed was past.

The group of Americans moved together and set up a casualty collection point (CCP) at the rear of the helicopter, trying to regroup from the first furious onslaught. Razor Two finally got the message to land at an offset LZ, almost a kilometer away and down the mountain some 2,000 feet. That group of 10 Rangers had an extra SEAL with them and he was able to establish a link with the small unit of SEALs still on the mountain—then about 1,000 yards from the top.

The Special Operations troops were under mortar fire as they clawed their way up the 45-to-70 degree slope, sliding in the snow, held back by many pounds of equipment. It took two hours to reach their brothers, arriving exhausted about 50 yards from the top, knowing they still had to fight.

The Platoon Leader had the extra men, tired or not, and prepared to take the top from al-Qaeda.

Air strikes were called in, and as the last one hit, two Ranger machineguns laid down suppressing fire as seven Rangers assaulted the bunkers, yelling and shooting and throwing grenades as they high-stepped through the knee-deep snow. It didn't take long to maul the enemy position and kill several fighters there.

In order to stay as safe as possible, the leader decided to bring all the wounded to the top of the hill and consolidate his position. Rangers, Army airmen, and Air Force personnel worked together in the super-human task of moving wounded men uphill through the snow. Before all the wounded could be moved an enemy gun opened up on the rear of the helicopter—the CCP —from some 400 yards away. The Pararescueman and the medic were both hit as they worked over the wounded.

Again the men on the ground risked it all to drag the wounded to the relative shelter of nearby rocks while aircraft and Ranger machineguns nailed the distant weapon. Unfortunately, the Pararescueman didn't make it.

When finally in some kind of defendable position the Americans continued to take sniper fire and some mortar rounds. No more daylight rescues were possible—they would have to wait it out.

Al-Qaeda fighters kept trying to get at them, but SOF observers on adjacent mountains could often see them moving around on Takur Gar and were able to use air strikes on them.

It wasn't until a little after dark that four birds from the 160th SOAR were able to move in and extract everybody, including the SEALs working their way down the mountain.

Strykers in Afghanistan

Being Light Infantry, Rangers generally get around on their feet or in Humvees, when not actually flying, fast-roping, or parachuting into a target area. However, Afghanistan has terrific terrain and deadly ambushes to contend with, and the light-skinned Hummers—lacking heavy firepower, armor, and size—can only do so much.

Enter the Stryker, complete with satellite communications and remote control gun turrets. As a try-out, the 2nd Ranger Battalion went into the country with 16 of these fast and deadly vehicles.

The use of the Light Armored Vehicle (LAV) in Afghanistan in 2005 marks a first in Ranger history.

Strykers were named in 2002 after two MOH winners, both enlisted men named Stryker, but unrelated. Made by General Motors and General Dynamics, there are two basic variants of the LAV: Mobile Gun System and Infantry Carrier Vehicle—plus eight variations of those two, including work as a mortar carrier, medevac, and recon vehicle. The weapons platform is anchored by a 105mm gun and a TOW system, but can also be used to fire nuclear, chemical, or biological agents. Of course, there are also machineguns.

The 19-ton vehicle runs on eight massive tires and has a range of 300 miles carrying 11 Infantrymen and the crew. The tires can be inflated or deflated from inside the vehicle, though there are variations of this.

The Stryker is supposed to be deployable by C-130, but necessary armor additions will make it too wide and too heavy. Extra armor will have to be added on site. Some disassembly is needed to fit Strykers on C-130s, taking up to 20 minutes to reassemble.

It has a built-in fire suppression system and self-recovery winch, though with extra armor the winch is insufficient. The Caterpillar power plant and the air-filled tires make the Stryker much quieter than conventional heavy armor, and much faster over roads, though tracked vehicles do better in the sand, mud, or snow.

Experiments with extra armor include "slat" armor, which is essentially a metal birdcage around the vehicle to ward of RPG rounds, and "reactive" armor—used on Bradleys—which explodes outward when struck, nullifying the RPG blast. Regular armor plus some ceramics protects the crew against small arms up to .50 caliber size.

IRAQ

Operation Iraqi Freedom swept Saddam Hussein's forces from the field in a very short time. The combined weight of air and land assault on Iraq's finest crushed them easily. But then, there was never any doubt the might of America could cut Iraq's military into bite-size pieces and consume them.

Starting with attacks by Rangers and Special Forces, the invasion of Iraq went very nearly as planned. It was over quickly, with small losses to Coalition troops. Things seemed—at first—to be a repeat of the first Gulf War in 1991, only this time Hussein was gone.

Then, the real war started.

In the months following the official cessation of hostilities in Iraq in 2003, US servicemen were still dying there. By late 2006, the casualty figure from all sources grew above 3,000 in a resurgence of bombing and sniping by insurgents—some of them from other countries. Anger toward the occupying Allied forces, especially the Americans, grew steadily while planners tried to get the utilities working and a government formed.

Over time, a lot of good was done in terms of getting schools running and propping up the government. Unfortunately, media reports of continued violence and other things gone wrong overshadowed much of the good being accomplished.

Some of the Iraq people welcomed US soldiers, some didn't. At the time of this writing a government of sorts had been formed—after a long time trying—but seemed impotent against rising sectarian violence. Thankfully, the number of Americans being killed and wounded finally began to drop as the Iraqis and other nationals had at each other. Then, that number began to rise again as the insurgents got more organized and began getting some outside help.

Fighting in a land where the enemy—who, without a uniform, looks like any civilian—is willing to take on the Allied Colossus, American soldiers faced the difficult task of keeping the peace while being shot at and blown up.

No large cache of Weapons of Mass Destruction have been found. The idea that Hussein had such WMDs was a big part of why US troops went to Iraq. Members of British and American governments began asking questions. Were WMDs used as a propaganda device to get into Iraq? Was the whole thing carried out to secure Iraq's oil? Does it matter to the soldier on the ground?

Saddam Hussein *was* the Weapon of Mass Destruction. He and his sons and the Baath Party loyalists were no better than thugs. It was time for them to go.

As for WMDs, they're probably still out there somewhere, and may yet be found. But probably they were spirited across various borders, or destroyed just before the invasion, as some say.

In 2006, about 500 artillery shells containing mustard and Sarin gas were found. It is said they were old, but some said still very lethal. Others pointed out that the shells proved the WMDs existed.

What matters is the absence of Hussein, and the emergence of what passes for Democracy.

But, it is not the thrust of this project to second-guess. Let the politicians work it out.

By late 2006, public support for the war had all but vanished. An independent commission filed a report stating flatly that US policy in Iraq had failed. A recent election had ousted many Republicans from office and the Democrats had taken control of Congress. That left President Bush pretty much as a Lame Duck President for his last two years in office.

Policy changes were mandated, but nobody really knew what to do next. The idea of total withdrawal of all troops was called for by some, but most realized the situation in Iraq would only deteriorate further if that happened.

In 2007, President Bush pushed through his plan to control hostilities in Iraq—principally Baghdad—by adding some 21,000 more troops to the mix. He was bitterly opposed by certain members of Congress.

By the time of this writing, it was too early to tell if his "surge" worked. New tactics by the bad guys, such as the use of chlorine gas along with conventional explosives, and new and better weapons to shoot down helicopters, are going to make things harder.

Where does an elite unit such as the Rangers fit in a war of subversion and roadside bombs? The answer is—they don't. Most of the heavy fighting was over in the first few weeks. Rangers—often working in small units—got into some heavy action in the beginning, when there were Iraq military units still functioning, but once they were contained Ranger tasks changed.

Rangers are still very much in the picture, but they are not going house-to-house in Baghdad looking for insurgents. They are out on the borders, looking for certain people, doing recon on border crossings from Iran and Syria, and taking on directed missions against targeted enemy elements. However, information on Ranger movements is highly classified, so there will be few war stories from that direction.

Rangers are all over Iraq working for other units, such as the 101st Airborne (Air Assault) Division, the 10th Mountain Division, and the 82nd Airborne. That is where the war stories will come from.

From Bobby Mayfield, 1/121, 48th Mech Brigade, Iraq, September 2005

First Sergeant Mayfield is a friend of the author's. During his eight months in Iraq we heard from him every day. He knew me as a reporter, and told me I would probably write better stories than the current reporters over there. I said I'd like to go out with the Rangers. He answered, "You don't want to go out with the Rangers. Those guys are CRAZY!"

Tony Torres

A Ranger-qualified Sergeant, Torres served as a member of OPFOR (opposition forces) at Camp Frank D. Merrill before going to Iraq. Though he wasn't with a Ranger unit, his experiences in Iraq help define the situation for all ground troops, and in the end, they help define the Ranger capability.

Torres was deployed to Iraq March 6, 2003 and returned to Camp Merrill on the Army's birthday, June 14.

I was picked to go. It was my birthday weekend, as a matter of fact. The first formation after I came back [from leave] they called two names, mine and Lieutenant [Michael] Browning [also a Ranger, and a West Point graduate]. We were told to go meet up with our First Sergeant afterward. He said, "I need two other volunteers who are going to be going to Iraq". The whole platoon stepped forward, but apparently my name was already picked, and Lieutenant Browning was already picked to go.

As a general rule, training battalion Cadre are not deployable, being too valuable where they are. But OPFOR members are not considered Ranger Instructors per se.

There were a few RIs overseas at the time, but they were there for training purposes. Generally speaking, if you wanted to go to a combat zone you had to get out of the Ranger Training Battalions and into another—deployable—unit.

As far as "volunteering", Torres said this:

They asked me if I wanted to go, and I said, heck yeah, I want to go. I wanted to be there. Just being there to do my part, you know? Feeling like you're useless because all these guys back here are sitting in a non-deployable unit, even though they're Infantrymen, they aren't able to be deployed, and they can't, they won't be. I guess I was an exception, but any one of us would have gone in a heartbeat.

We met up in Fort Benning, they got us ready in CRC, the Readiness Center, we got our shots updated, got all our paperwork straight, met up with all the other soldiers who were picked from units at Fort Benning, flew by civilian plane to El Paso, then from there they flew us on a DC-10, another civilian plane. We had our weapons [and everything], and we went straight from El Paso into Kuwait City.

From Kuwait City we went to Camp Arafjon, and we bedded down for the night. That's where they gave us our separate orders where everybody was split up. The whole group that came from El Paso was a bunch of different MOSs [military occupation specialty], going to a lot of different units. Out of about 169 people, there were only six of us who were Ranger-qualified. The enlisted part of that, which was five of us, went to V Corp LRSU [Long Ranger Surveillance Unit]. All the officers went to the 3rd Infantry Division [as did some other enlisted men] and were used as dismounts [foot patrol].

I was with Echo Company, 51st Infantry. They were based in Dahrmstadt, Germany. We supported V Corp. But now, Foxtrot Company supported the XVIII Airborne [Corps]. They're out of Fort Bragg.

I got sent to Camp Virginia, which is one of the rear camps. It was home for V Corps and all of its Military Intelligence [MI] Battalions. They were handling all the military Intelligence there. Since the main mission for LRS is to gather Intel, they put them closest to the MI folks so info can be passed easier. Everybody else got split up between the other camps.

There were regular six-man LRS teams. There were three platoons, but only two platoons were running missions. The third platoon was running personnel recovery [Combat Search and Rescue—CSAR missions]. They were further up north.

I was originally supposed to go and meet up with those guys in that platoon. They didn't have any spots for me in the 1st and 2nd, because their teams [and tents] were full, but when the war started, we couldn't get up with 3rd Platoon, and I got stuck behind with everybody else.

When Torres got "stuck" he was to become a part of a 2nd Platoon team, but they had just gone into isolation, away from everybody, to assess and plan their mission. So, Torres became a part of 1st Platoon and prepared for something new and different. Inner-city patrols were run in Humvees, six men to a vehicle, with either a machinegun or, in this case, 40mm M19 Grenade Launchers. Average daytime temperatures were 115-to-125 degrees, falling to a balmy 80 or 90 at night. Supply was iffy at times, only two bottles of water a day, he said, and sometimes a day without.

What our team was used for was "presence patrols" for the cities. Since me and one other guy were the only ones with M19 experience, I jumped up behind one and we did patrols.

We did a three-vehicle patrol. The first vehicle had a .50 cal, the second vehicle was the C-2, had all the information, the satellite uplink, and all the commo. The third vehicle was me. There was an LRS team in the first one, and an LRS team in the last one.

So, I was out in the turret with the M19, and we were pulling rear security.

What we would do, we would escort CI [Counter-Intelligence] guys into the cities, and they'd meet with their contacts, and they'd get information from them. When we escorted those guys, we were like their bodyguards. So they'd find out where their bases were, where the bad guys were. Sometimes we'd just do regular presence patrols, just roll up into town and try to find the bad guys.

Torres was asked if they were trying to get someone to shoot at them, since the Hummers made such a good target. His answer started with a grin.

Yeah! You say, look, these are the three worst towns [unnamed except for Balod, an airfield in northern Iraq with two Iraqi Divisions in residence]. Their divisions are humongous, bigger than American divisions. We did the towns around there, and we did Balod. I don't know the names of all the towns, but if you look at where we crossed the Tigris a lot, the towns around there, and in western Baghdad.

Torres spoke of his friends in the 1st and 3rd Ranger Battalions, and said he hadn't been able to talk to them except to visit a couple. He said he'd heard the units had gotten into some heavy stuff. They had. The talk turned to ambushes, particularly from overpasses.

It was common to see that. They're getting a little trickier about their ambushes. Before, they were dropping grenades from overpasses. I know an MP convoy went in just before we did, just ahead of us, and they got hit with a bunch of grenades and Molotov Cocktails—a bottle filled with gasoline and lit with a wick—they'd throw those first, and then shoot some RPGs at them. You saw that a lot. Then they'd run. They'd take off from the overpass and be gone.

Torres was unable to say much about where he had been in Iraq. Though the "war" was over at that point in time, much of the information pertaining to unit deployment was still classified. He was trying to get an idea from his former unit what he could say.

He was asked to tell some part of a mission, but not say where he was at the time, which was about the second or third week into the ground portion of the conflict.

It was pretty scary. There were days when we said, okay, we're going to the three worst towns that surround this airfield. We were helping secure Balod Airfield and all the towns surrounding it. So they say, okay, let's find out [what's happening there], we're going right in, and we're going to see what's wrong with these people, see if there's any outbreaks of any big gangs or anything like that.

So we go into a town, knowing these people don't like us. I'm getting hit in the back [with rocks], because I'm facing the rear [behind the grenade launcher on top of his Humvee]. Little kids, six-year-olds, throwing rocks at me. They're throwing [rocks] from buildings, they're throwing them from the ground, they're throwing from everywhere.

Bullets and RPGs weren't the only problems. The men wore body armor and helmets for several reasons. Those were days before up-armored Humvees, and before the big-time use of IEDs.

I didn't really have a problem wearing armor. It was a definite necessity, and did a good job of keeping all of the rocks from hitting me in the back, since I was always facing the rear. I wore it pretty much every day, after the second week of the war. It was heavier than normal, because I put extra plates in since I was in a turret of the Humvee.

Even up until I left at the end of May, that's what it was like in the towns. It was fifty-fifty. You didn't know what it was going to be like. They either accepted you, or praised you, or they were just really hateful of you. There were no in-between towns.

There's contact we made from rounds being shot through alleys, rounds being shot from around buildings, from the top of buildings they shot.

One of the commo guys had a video camera [an official camera] to see what it was like in the cities, you can probably see the rounds going by his head, two rounds right by his head.

Torres got to use his M19 40 mike-mike grenade launcher when rounds came at them from the top of a building. He said he took it apart. How many rounds, he was asked. "Oh, four or five. All you need is one, Sir."

The question was asked why an LRS unit was doing vehicular patrols in cities?

That's another thing they were worried about when we were there. Why are we still here? Why are we still running missions right now in these towns, doing things MPs are doing. We were doing an MP's job. People over there didn't understand. I didn't care. I wanted to do my part and look for those bad guys.

It's disturbing to know that some of those people over there aren't even informed. They can be really accepting and be really good people, but…to me, it's just going to be guerilla-type [warfare] until we back out or somebody gives up. That's the way it's going to be.

A prophetic statement.

You never know who's who. I saw uniforms dropped in place with ID cards lying next to them. It looks like the guy just ran off naked. You go into a town and you never know. You might be able to tell from a military haircut, but that could be anybody. Now they've changed the Rules of Engagement to [be able to apprehend anyone carrying weapons] a lot of them carry 7.62mm rifles and pistols. That's how a lot of men are dying. Yeah, they might need them to defend themselves against looters, but it's always been like that in that country. Always. They've always had people forming little gangs or fighting for territory. That's how it is over there. There's always been unrest. And now they have all those weapons. Guys are dying standing in the streets directing traffic. It gets you nervous when you go into a town to try to help those people and they think we're there to take them over.

It's a good feeling to see a bunch of kids hanging out of school windows, with the bars open, and hanging out and waving at us, happy to see us there, knowing we can help them out.

Considering Ranger School teaches small-unit ground tactics and does very little vehicular movement or inner-city work, Torres was asked how being a Ranger in that setting helped him.

Using that Ranger training that I got here, it worked out even though I didn't do a lot of ground patrols. I'll tell you what; you just keep in mind that you're a Ranger.

My physical capabilities. This school puts you through so much as far as no sleep, no chow, you're walking miles with 80 or 100 pounds on your back. You say, well, if you can make it through that, you can make it through a lot of stuff. Your body is going to break eventually, but you got to know when that is, and that's what this school does for you, it helps you realize when [that is].

You know when you're over there, that it's a test, but it's really not a test anymore because you're a separate soldier, a different type of soldier. You're a Ranger.

The Deaths of Odai and Qusai

On July 22, 2003, the sons of Saddam Hussein—Odai, the eldest at 36, and Qusai—were discovered in a villa in the northern city of Mosul, about 240 miles north of Baghdad. The ensuing firefight resulted in their deaths.

The spelling of Iraqi and Afghani proper names is a toss-up at times. "Odai" is also spelled "Uday", and "Al-Qaeda" also appears as "Al-Qaida." "Qusai" appears to be one of several possible spellings.

Both Odai and Qusai were highly placed in the Hussein government, with Qusai slated to take over from his father when the time came. Well, it came, but neither Qusai nor his father will be there for the ceremony. Both men were feared by the Iraqi people, with horrible stories of torture and murder corrupting their back trails. Qusai was once head of Iraq's Special Security Organization and commanded the Republican Guard. Odai, nearly killed in an attempted coup several years before the war, is reported to have beaten a man to death during a public gathering, which added but one to the total of those he reportedly killed or had killed.

They were bad guys, and they were just the kids.

Odai and Qusai were numbers two and three on the US list of most wanted Iraqis, with a $15 million reward for information leading to their capture.

Though the short siege on their house wasn't a Ranger operation, there were probably quite a few Ranger-qualified men on the ground in that situation, including members of the 101st and members of special operations troops [Delta] present.

Brad Bonnell, former member of the 2nd Ranger Battalion and Ranger Instructor, was with the 101st Airborne Division at that time as a SFC Fire Team Leader. His platoon, part of the 3rd Battalion, 327th Regiment, was assigned as perimeter guard around the villa and participated in the fight.

This is his account of why and how he got there, how it all came together for the coalition forces—and how it ended for the Hussein brothers.

Brad Bonnell

He begins with his decision to change units and go to the fight. He is one of three Ranger brothers, sons of a Ranger father. He said it was just in his blood to want to go.

Iraq was the big talk at the time. It was the whole planning phase when negotiations were going on, UN inspectors were in-country, and the whole talk was, the invasion's coming, the invasion's coming. If they don't step down, we're going to invade. You know, President Bush…

I joined the Army to fight. That's what I wanted to do. I didn't get the opportunity in the Ranger Regiment. I thought, "I need to hop on this bandwagon before I lose the opportunity and I don't get any combat."

Though he was with the Ranger Regiment for nearly eight years, the only real Ranger combat was the brief, though bloody engagement in Somalia in 1993, and that was a part of the 3rd Battalion, not his 2nd. He came into the Regiment just after Panama. To make matters more difficult for him, he was by then a Ranger Instructor, and therefore, non-deployable.

I was right at three-and-a-half years [at Camp Merrill] and I thought, I gotta get out of here. I told my wife, Jennifer, you might not like my decision, but I'm going to the 101st before this thing's over. I had some Intel; my brother was at the 101st at the time. My oldest brother, Brett, was a helicopter pilot [and a Ranger]. He said, hey, it's coming, it's coming. The tempo is stepping up. You need to get over here as soon as you can.

In November 2002, I left the Mountain Phase.

He didn't go alone. He knows of at least three other men who went to the 101st for the same reason he did—to get to war.

When we got over there, the first day inside Iraq, Day One of the invasion, everybody felt the same way—we're here to do one thing. We're here to get rid of the regime. Everybody had that in their thoughts. That was our mission.

We air-assaulted in. The 101st was part of the largest air-assault mission ever done. It was unbelievable. Chinooks, Black Hawks, all done by rotary-wing.

The first place we landed was Amajef, southern Iraq.

Brad was in-country for a few months before this particular mission came up. By that time he was hardened to the ways of Ira—and to combat.

Saddam's sons, that mission was on July 22. The building was a three-story building [one of which was] a parking garage underground. When you pulled into the front gate of the house you went into underground parking.

At the time my platoon was on QRF [quick reaction force] for the CAG [Combat Applications Group—in this case, Delta trigger-pullers]. We got the call to come up to the TOC [operations center] because we had a planned mission we needed to execute.

They didn't know they]Odai and Qusai] were in there, but they knew somebody was in there. We had been working very closely with the Task Force. When I say Task Force [TF], it's a Special Ops thing.

The group was diverse. In addition to CAG operatives, there were also FBI, DEA, and probably CIA people as well. The men they were seeking warranted all the attention.

We were getting a lot of Intel from the Special Ops community—FBI, and there were a couple of foreign Intelligence sources over there, the British...

We got the mission and got up there 24 hours before the mission kicked off. We were going to do it right from the git-go. The battalion commander briefed us, showed us two pictures. These are the guys we're going after [he said], and he showed us the two sons. We knew who they were.

We had been going on these "ghost missions" for days and days. All of those missions were, yeah we're going after Saddam, he's here, or his two sons, they're here, or one of his high cabinet members. Our battalion was credited with capturing a lot of the "cards."

At that time there was a deck of playing cards featuring 52 of the highest-ranking members of the former Iraqi government, beginning with Saddam Hussein and followed by his sons. Brad's unit had been going after "ghosts" for some time and they felt like this was just another false alarm. At least the false alarms had netted them some bad guys while looking for the top dogs.

We thought he's not in this country. Saddam's in another country. Yeah, yeah, yeah.

Special Ops was part of the briefing and they said we actually have an eyewitness who is a relative of Saddam, and that's his house. He was a cousin of Saddam and he owned the house. This guy was giving Intel to US sources, saying they're definitely there; they're holding my kid hostage.

He said they [Hussein brothers] had been leaving the house every night for a couple of hours, still keeping his son hostage, and he was just tired of it. Well, okay, it was still far-fetched. Then it got postponed just like every other mission. We'd been getting a lot of bogus information from Iraqi people.

It was postponed for, I think, 12 hours. We actually ran it about two hours prior daylight. My platoon was initially planned to do the outer cordon—we made sure no one got into or out of the objective. The main players were the Task Force [Spec Ops], and they were the ones knocking on the door.

I was no more than 50 meters from the house.

The plan was they were going to drive up in an armored SUV [white]. They had armored glass, armored doors, and they were going to drive right up to the front gate. After we got the outer cordon secured, they were going to race up, slam into the front gate, and all pile out.

As they were driving up their vehicle got taken out—I want to say, by an RPK [machinegun]. It hit the engine block.

Bonnell speculated the weapon was probably set up at the front gate when the occupants of the villa noticed the cordon going up. Other witnesses have the weapon placed up on a balcony. Either way, the CAG folks in the SUV un-assed it in a hurry.

I think it was a team of six guys, Spec Ops, and they got in the front gate and down into the parking garage. They got into the lower part of the house, and they started getting fire from the balcony, they had an inner courtyard. They were getting hammered from the inner part of the house. They had to back off. They lost their momentum and their entry plan.

They took three casualties, wounded.

This is where my platoon came in. We started suppressing while they backed up. We gave them a good base of fire so they could pull out. They were pinned down.

They had a drug-sniffing dog with them. The dog got shot and it really pissed them off.

The reason for the drug dog is unclear, although the DEA was present. The CAG soldiers returned to the villa to try again before turning the 101st loose on the house.

They had to regroup. We got them out of there. At the time we had at our blocking positions .50 cals and machineguns [squad weapons]. We had Humvees attached to us, and they mounted .50 cals and Mark 19s [grenade launcher]. My platoon was in charge of those.

Basically it was a free-for-all, shooting 360-degrees all around this building [a fairly large villa].

A question was asked about TOW missiles reportedly used against the house.

That was part of Delta, the TOW Platoons. The TOWs came in later.

The building was sturdily built. Just concrete. Initially, nothing was piercing it. We had Kiowas come in and shoot rockets. They were talking about fast-movers, A-10s, but then they said, ah, that's collateral damage, and that ain't gonna happen.

There were other houses in the area.

They were going to call Apaches in, but there were none in the area. We weren't going to use the TOWs, but then we started thinking...[maybe so].

The word we got was they had an inner bunker, a fortified bunker inside the house. This word was going over the radios, that they had a bulletproof bunker. They had portholes they could sight in on us, but nothing [we had] would pierce the inner bunker. That's when they said, okay; let's start firing TOWs. We started firing them after the second attempt of Spec Ops to go in. They tried it again from the back of the house. We got word they hit one guy, didn't know who it was. It got so hairy—they were getting shot up—they had to get out of there. They were combat-ineffective at that time.

There were four people in the house—the two sons, Odai's [14-year-old] son, and a bodyguard. We got the owner of the house out, and his son. That happened prior to [anything happening].

Bonnell was unclear on how that was accomplished.

My platoon...we started getting fired at from other houses. At one time we were getting fired at from Odai and Qusai's house and from our flanks, the neighbors. They [platoon] returned fire on the buildings; don't know if there were any casualties. Our concentration was on the [Hussein] building at the time. It wasn't any heavy volume coming from those houses. The heavy volume was coming from the objective.

It took a total of eight hours. From start to finish, once we actually got in the house and found out who we had, it was eight hours. When we got in the house, first of all what we saw was a demolished house. We found out there was no fortified bunker inside. The way the construction of the house was, they had enough view where they could shoot at Americans, but they were tucked away way in the back, and nothing was piercing.

They had no fortifications, but they had a bunch of mattresses over them, and furniture. The bodies were not right together. Probably no more than 50 meters apart. They were in two different rooms. It was a big house.

Bonnell said the house occupants were badly torn. "It had to be explosions—the TOWs." Word is a volley of 18 TOWs was used, fired from several directions. Indeed, it took some time to positively identify the mangled brothers.

Rangers Help Rescue POW

PFC Jessica Lynch, a supply clerk for the 507th Maintenance Company, entered the hearts of many Americans the day she was captured in Iraq, a survivor of a March 23 ambush that took the lives of several of her comrades and left her an injured captive.

It was April 1, 2003, when a team composed of Delta operatives, some SEALs, Air Force Pararescuemen, and a security force of Rangers executed a sudden nighttime air assault on a hospital in the city of Nasariyah.

Lynch, 19, was one of several soldiers taken that day. Four of her unit members were later seen on television, though there were at the time about a dozen unaccounted for. Added to that total were 11 bodies found in the same hospital, eight of which turned out to be American.

This type of operation is perfect for Rangers [and maybe Delta and SEALs] and was carried out in typical Ranger style—fast insert, furious assault, and hold position until relieved or evacuated. As usual the Ranger element was standing security for Delta; they tend to go hand-in-hand on such missions. Who better to guard your back?

The whole situation with Lynch has become somewhat controversial in that details change depending on who is telling the story. There was a man named Mohammed, an Iraqi citizen, who reportedly saw Lynch in the hospital and then told some Marines at a checkpoint. The details of his involvement are hazy, but he ended up in the US with a new life.

Also unclear are details of the treatment Lynch was given by the Iraqi doctors. They say it was very good and she doesn't remember any different. There were reports of her being tortured and raped; they appear untrue. The young Private had some broken bones and terrible memories, but thanks to the combined Spec Ops Force, she'll live to fight another day.

It was a good raid, strong in nature and carried off well, but the Rangers didn't have much to do because there was reportedly no resistance. The Iraqi military had been using the building as a staging base, but had left that morning.

Still in all, it was the first POW rescue by Rangers since WWII, and the first ever of a female soldier. A second female soldier, Specialist Shoshanna Johnson, was the sixth American captured after the ambush, suffering bullet wounds in both ankles. Marines rescued her April 22.

How Hot Is Iraq?

The following observation comes from a National Guard soldier, but everybody suffered from the same heat.

Bobby Mayfield, 1SG, C/1/121 Mech, 48th Ga NG

Serious thought and debate went into this analysis. We still don't have as many names for Hot

As the Eskimos do for snow, but we are working on it.

Today it was Mean hot. We have started naming the different kinds of hot. Mean hot is the one that hurts when you walk outside. Beyond that is Ignorant hot and Stupid hot. We decided that being stupid was worse than being ignorant, and that hot like that goes well beyond plain old Mean hot. We are looking forward to the upcoming dust storm today or tomorrow. The dust blocks the sun and keeps the temp down to either Hot hot or Chili hot, depending on how thick the dust is.

After extensive debate, the month of August has taught us that there are at least two previously undiscovered levels of hot that were not included on our last list.

The hottest hot is Thermo-Nuclear Winter hot and the one just below that is Thermo-Nuclear Explosion hot. I am sure you are asking yourself how Nuclear Winter hot can be hotter than Nuclear Explosion hot. The reason we finally decided to put them in this order instead of vice- versa is the fact that in a thermo-nuclear explosion, something survives. In a thermo-nuclear winter, nothing survives. So, in our opinion, that makes the nuclear winter option at the top of the list.

The War Is Over, But Not Over

The following statements come from soldiers' observations, media coverage, and military reports. There is no point to this short section other than to show some of the day-to-day experiences and results of American troops in a very foreign country.

On November 3, 2003 a CH-47 Chinook helicopter was hit by what was probably a Soviet-made ground-to-air missile that uneducated, lightly trained guerillas managed to learn how to operate. Sixteen people died and another 20 were injured.

Earlier in the "war," four or five Americans were being killed every day. The toll on the Iraq civilian population was, as always through such wars, higher than both combatants.

As time passed, the thrust of the insurgency was shifted away from the Allied troops and onto the general population. American deaths began to fall and Iraq deaths climbed dramatically in 2004 and 2005, as the people had at each other in a frenzy of our-clan-and-religion-is-better-than-your-clan-and-religion. Such killings were labeled "sectarian", meaning individual sects were warring with one another in a kind of huge family feud.

Then, in mid-2006-early-2007, American deaths began to rise again.

The favored method of killing Americans is the use of IEDs (improvised explosive devices) that come in all shapes and sizes. The idea is to plant one on or near a road and then either detonate it from a distance using a device such as a cell phone or TV remote, or simply hook it up to a tripwire or pressure switch to explode it on contact.

IEDs can be car bombs, motorcycle bombs, explosives planted inside dead animals or dead people, an artillery shell buried in the road or beside the road covered with trash, or any one of several other things. In the beginning most were not so effective as later—the insurgents have had time to learn how to camouflage things better, and to build shaped charges. It was not unusual for 30 or 40 of them to found in one AO in one day.

Some of them are filled with ball bearings or nails; others have different kinds of metal embedded for shrapnel.

The amount of explosives—usually C-4 or TNT—can fill a car or something as small as a soft drink can. "Pepsi bombs" have been used almost like a grenade. A soda can is filled with explosive and shrapnel, fitted with a short fuse, and thrown over a compound wall or into a crowd.

A new development for finding trip wires is the use of Silly String—a child's toy—sprayed in the air when soldiers enter a building. If the string falls to the ground there are no nearly invisible trip wires strung across the room.

Rocket propelled grenades (RPG) are another big killer. At times, soldiers have reported seeing the air thick with them, coming from all directions. An RPG is bad enough to take out a Humvee or knock down a helicopter, having a bigger punch that the standard hand-thrown grenade. RPGs were also used heavily in Vietnam.

The so-called "Sunni Triangle"—a bad place to be for Americans, and in 2006, for Iraqis—runs from the area around Baghdad west to Ramadhi, then north to Tikrit (Hussein's hometown).

Many foreign fighters went into the Triangle, either as terrorists or mercenaries—and some just to get in on the action.

In western Iraq, early in the war, Rangers dropped onto the runways of an airfield and quickly took down resistance and secured the field. That area, known as H-1, was used by a lot of Special Operations troops for a month or so. Not only was it a staging area of sorts, it was also a POW compound. Raids carried out by Spec Ops netted a lot of bad guys. At one point there were reportedly 200-300 detainees, the majority of which were not Iraqis. Many groups were represented in that bunch; even some al-Qaeda. Members of Hamas, Hezbollah, and Islamic Jihad were also held, among others.

There is a report that Iraqi (or Syrian, or Lebanese, or whatever) fighters are being offered bounties for assaulting military targets. They get so much for a Humvee, so much for a tank, and a bunch for a helicopter.

Getting captured is not considered an option because no one wants to be beheaded on video, or have an electric drill or chainsaw used on them as an instrument of torture.

There is much good being done in the country despite the attacks. Progress is being made in medicine, education, and infrastructure (utilities). A new Iraqi Army is being built, and a national police force was formed. Though there is still trouble between intra-country factions, the government as a whole is slowly becoming a reality, though it seems in 2006 to not have much in the way of authority. Part of the problem is the participants can't quit yelling at one another long enough to make any real progress.

The 504th Airborne (PIR) was given good Intel by a local and were able to locate a very large cache of weapons near Fallujah. They went back the next day and found even more. Seized were 84 anti-tank rounds, 194 152mm artillery rounds, 34 155mm rounds, 45 rockets, and a batch of small-arms ammo.

Apparently, the insurgents have plenty to fight with. The bad part is that is only the tip of the iceberg. Caches of this size are still being found—partly because munitions keep coming across various borders.

Sometimes our medical people do autopsies on dead insurgents just to see what they find. High levels of opiates are a frequent find.

Much of the heavy stuff happens in Anbar Province, which contains Fallujah and Ramadhi. The people who do the bad stuff are very often from other countries, and just want to get in on killing some Americans, or Iraqis, or British...

Al-Qaeda began to show its ugly head, led by al-Zarqawi, but the fearless leader was taken out by air strike. The second man in promised to lead no less effectively. There are still plenty of guys ready to step in and take over, especially since candidates don't have to know much about politics or diplomacy, or even keeping to a budget, relying instead mostly on fiery rhetoric.

Between the Sunni and Shiite militias, Al-Qaeda, and foreign fighters, American forces can be attacked from any quarter, at any time.

It is said that Iran is a big player in Iraq, having infiltrated the ranks long ago. Many of the actual guerilla-type fighters are from foreign hard-core terrorist cells masquerading as Jihadists. To them, killing is no problem. They believe it is an honorable thing to be blown to bits while killing innocent people. What is even more incredible is that their families believe it, too.

Foreign fighters come from Syria, Iran, Egypt, Uzbekistan; literally from all over the Middle East. However, even without them the Iraqi militias are enough.

In the beginning of the occupation, when there were still relatively large numbers of insurgents operating together, they sometimes charged 10 men at US defenses just to see how they did. Armies have used that tactic forever, but only a few are still dumb enough to use it. The Vietnamese, Chinese, and Russians have all done it. But then, these are insurgents, and not an army at all. However, it is reported they are very brave while mindlessly dying.

Also in the beginning, large groups of them tended to hole up in the same place, inviting an air strike. Such places are reportedly sometimes called Allah's Waiting Room.

That was the beginning. In 2006, there aren't so many insurgents left, and they are not exposing themselves any more than necessary. Sectarian militias, some of them in police uniform, are doing much of the killing, and it's now directed mostly at other Iraqis.

Iraqi forces are improving slowly, and they are already taking a heavier load of security work.

Americans are, however, still dying. Recently the fighting has stepped up again.

As in Vietnam, the bad guys can simply drop their gear and mingle with the rest of the crowd to suddenly become Joe Citizen. They don't seem to mind using civilians as breastworks. Murder and terror within a community are used to inspire fear and obedience, thus granting a certain safety to those doing the dirty work.

The difficulty for the Allied troops is convincing the people the bad guys won't hurt them or their families if they help out with information. Often those who help the Allies end up dead, or worse, and in many cases support for the new government carries the same penalty.

Coalition Support

Much was made of the amount of support given by some 35 countries around the globe to US forces fighting in Iraq. Of course, the larger countries such as France and Germany stayed out of things until the money began to flow, but America was joined by a host of smaller countries. Sadly, the total number of soldiers from other countries was far less than the US total of 130,000 in April 2004, just about equaling America's closest supporter, Great Britain, with about 12,000 people in-country. By early 2007, the British were down to about 7,000, and were preparing to remove some of those. Other countries had backed out all together.

American soldiers were backed up by such military powerhouses as Albania (70), Estonia (55), and Mongolia (180). Slightly larger forces were sent by Poland (2,400—said to be good troops), and Italy (3000). South Korean forces began small, but grew to a couple of thousand.

As of mid-2006 the coalition forces were being reduced drastically, and US forces were beginning the long-awaited and very slow withdrawal that depended greatly on how the Iraqi forces were progressing. Word at the time was a draw-down to about 100,000 by year's end.

Right after that sectarian violence went through the roof all over the country, but mainly in Baghdad. Instead of bringing some troops home, more were sent to help quell the rising violence.

RANGER SCHOOL

The Ranger Tab
AR 600-8-22
   25 Feb. 1995
   Section V
8—46. Ranger Tab
   Tabs are awarded to U.S. military and civilian personnel, and foreign military personnel who qualify as prescribed.
   a. Award approval authority. The Commandant of the U.S. Army Infantry School, CG, PERSCOM, and the CG, ARPERCEN, may award the Ranger Tab.
   b. Basic eligibility criteria. The basic eligibility criteria for award of the Ranger Tab is as follows:
   (1) Successful completion of a Ranger course conducted by the U.S. Army Infantry School.
   (2) Any person who was awarded the Combat Infantryman Badge while serving during World War II as a member of a Ranger Battalion (1st—6th inclusive)
   or in the 5307th Composite Unit (Provisional) {Merrill's Marauders}.
   (3) Any person who successfully completed a Ranger course conducted by the Ranger Training Command at Fort Benning, GA.
   DATE APPROVED: The cloth tab was approved by HQDA on 6 November 1950. Authorization to wear the tab was included in Change 2, AR 600-70, dated 23 January 1953. On 25 November 1984, the Army Chief of Staff approved a metal replica of the embroidered tab for wear on the dress mess uniforms.

Origin
   The first Ranger Tabs appeared during the Korean War, when Ranger Infantry Companies (Airborne) were being formed and trained at Fort Benning.
   On November 13, 1950, the first four companies graduated from the six-week course given by the Ranger Training Command, expecting to be awarded an insignia on the order of the white-and-red on black scroll worn by the WWII Ranger Battalions. What they received was the first Ranger Tab, a yellow-on-black arc insignia to be worn on the left shoulder.
   Many of the Ranger graduates took copies of the WWII scroll, removed the BN (battalion) and substituted CO (company).
   Later the yellow on the Tab was changed to the current gold color, and the Tab became a highly prized insignia, which it continues to be today. The scroll has been modified to fit the current situation, and is worn by members of the 75th Ranger Regiment, along with the Tab worn by Ranger School graduates.

The Ranger Training Brigade's Mission

The following is the Mission Statement of the Brigade, with added comments to give a capsule report on why the RTB turns out the kind of soldier who can confidently wear the Ranger Tab.

"The Ranger Training Brigade's mission is to conduct the Ranger, Long Range Surveillance Leader, and Infantry Leader Courses, and to develop the leadership skills, confidence and competence of students by requiring them to perform effectively as small unit leaders in tactically realistic environments."

Though Ranger School is primarily a leadership course, it also prepares a soldier to undertake any and all jobs required in a Ranger unit. Officers and NCOs are treated much the same in the school, and no one wears rank insignia. It is only toward the end of the course that officers are separated out for certain types of training related to command positions, but mostly they all go through together, regardless of prior position.

Some of the students will come in as Private First Class, though once a man earns a Tab he generally becomes a Non-Com. Such men still need leadership training at the squad level.

"The scope of the Ranger Training Brigade's mission extends not only to U. S. Army personnel but also to other services, international soldiers, and to government agencies involved in counter-narcotics operations, such as the Drug Enforcement Agency, Department of Interior, U. S. Customs Service, and others."

Over the years the Ranger course had taught students from Vietnam, Pakistan, Tajikistan, Canada—name the country—as well as bringing interior government people in for all or parts of the course as required by their agencies. To that end, Ranger Instructors sometimes travel to different countries to teach in place, such as in Colombia or Bosnia.

"The Ranger course is designed to further develop leaders who are physically and mentally tough and self-disciplined, and challenges them to think, act and react effectively in stress approaching that found in combat."

The stress is certainly available—but more than once I've heard, "Nothing prepares you for combat."

"The course is about nine weeks (58 days) in duration and divided into three phases: Benning (City) Phase, Fort Benning, Georgia; Mountain Phase, Dahlonega, Georgia; and Swamp Phase, Eglin Air Force Base, Florida."

There have been other places used for training. There is more information in this section on Fort Bliss, Texas, and Dugway Proving Grounds, Utah.

In the three phases the student is taught how to fight in the city, the mountains, and the jungle/swamp. Other times the student will be in Alaska or Colorado in the winter. Where they are, and what they do, is all focused on small unit leadership and the accompanying tactics.

"The Infantry Leader Course is designed to prepare company-level Infantry leaders to lead and train their units in critical skills and selected mission-essential tasks.

The Long Range Surveillance Leader Course is designed to train long range surveillance leaders."

A mission-essential task could be anything from watching from a distance to providing muscle for Delta to overwhelming airfield defenses. Considering the technology of the modern Rangers, the Special Operations connections, and the physical and mental capabilities of the men, a Ranger leader has a great deal to work with when problem-solving to perform a given task.

Why Go To Ranger School?

That's a good question. Men come through from all over the Army—mostly Combat Arms Branches of Infantry, Artillery, and Armor—but the only real requisite for a Ranger Tab is if a soldier wants to be a member of the Ranger Regiment—and that doesn't apply to everybody.

The extreme training schedule of Ranger School is certainly not for the faint of heart, so why would a man volunteer to put himself through the perils, pitfalls, and punishing pain?

Colonel (ret) Steve Pullen went through in 1968, and graduated OCS in 1969.

"You had to be an Airborne Ranger to be an officer in a Combat Arms Unit. The Ranger Tab opened a lot of doors for me. I took command positions over others because of that Ranger Tab [he commanded an Airborne Battalion for the 82nd]. Ranger training gave me confidence. It makes you self-reliant."

Major Barry Blackmon was the Executive Officer of the Mountain Phase in 2002. He said the kind of man going to Ranger School varies, depending on what the Army wants at the time. The Army Chief of Staff sends out a directive delineating what his idea of a Ranger is, and the schools conform to that.

Barry Blackmon

You can't pin it down. Motivation for a 19-year-old is totally different than the motivation for a 28-year-old. Motivation for a 19-year-old enlisted guy that's going to Regiment, hey, he wants to be part of a great unit, wants to be a part of the best unit, and he knows that to be a part of that unit, and go to war, to be ready for war, he has to go to Ranger School and receive that training. My motivation as a 21-year-old 2nd Lieutenant was simple; all officers in the Infantry will be Ranger qualified. I could have been an Infantry officer who maybe wouldn't have gone very far in my career, or transferred out to another branch. In the Combat Arms, if you're not Ranger qualified, essentially you will be discriminated against. There are battalion commanders out there who don't want young Lieutenants who don't have the Ranger Tab. Put it this way, they would rather have a guy who's tried and true, who's been through the rigors and training of the Ranger Course.

General Barry McCaffrey

The following quote is unconfirmed, but it is so good we had to put it in. Whether it is real or not, the sentiment is valid.

As a company commander in combat, crawling around in the mud with an enemy machinegun hammering over my head, the crotch ripped out of my uniform, constipated, hungry, huge bug bites under my eyes, exhausted with days of intermittent sleep, I could always comfort myself by saying it could be worse. I could be back in Ranger School.

Keith Antonia

Already jump-qualified and a veteran of Grenada with the 82nd, Antonia had to wait a while before being given the green light to attend Ranger School. In the meantime he noticed the effect of a Ranger Tab in the decision-making process of other officers.

We were in the Sinai in August of 1983, then went to Grenada in October, then I went to Ranger School a couple of months later [Class 4-84].

I had the number one slot to go to Ranger School coming out of the Infantry Officer Basic Course, where I was the Platoon Honor Graduate. The 82nd was sending a brigade to an exercise, *Bright Star*, in Egypt. There were two battalions going over that they filled up with Lieutenants. What they did was yank me and three already-Ranger-qualified guys out of IOBC after graduation, told us we couldn't go to any schools, and sent us immediately to the 82nd. When we got there the Brigade S-1 took a look at the four of us, saw Ranger Tabs on three shoulders and sent them down with the boys going to *Bright Star*. He sent me to another battalion.

After that I put my packet in to go to Ranger School—twice, the first one got lost or something like that—so six months later I put in another packet, and I finally got approval to go. I had to wait until after Sinai and after Grenada, but then I got to go.

Ed Scholes

As a graduate of North Georgia College (ROTC), Major General (Ret) Edison Scholes was exposed to Rangers at the Mountain Phase camp located in the same county, plus having a "Major Smith" on staff at the college, a man who had been a Ranger in WWII and Korea.

I had such respect for the people in the Ranger camp up there in Dahlonega that [when I joined up] I told them, if you put me anywhere but the Infantry, I will get out.

The leadership confidence and all that course provided you—for young leaders, maybe not Lt. Colonels and people like that—gives you the confidence you need, and to some degree the knowledge. You just don't have time to get all the practice and techniques down—it gives you the knowledge and wherewithal to go forward and do the things you need to do as a leader.

It really gives you the experience of small unit leadership you can't get any other way or any where else.

David Cress

When I was about nine-years-old we would play Army in the woods, and I remember one of the kids had a brochure he got from the Post Office. It was about the Army, and it had a picture of an Army Ranger—mean-looking dude—on the cover. We identified with him.

Life's funny like that sometimes.

I came from Buffalo, New York, and when I got to Basic I was amazed at the thought of risking my life in Vietnam with the guys I was with. So every time they would ask for volunteers for the next level of training I would make sure I was in that group, as I wanted to be with a much tougher group of guys. By the time we got to Ranger School I could see I had thought right as they were all good athletes, and mean-spirited when the occasion presented itself. Kind of like a motorcycle gang that had played on the same professional football team.

Perry Doerr

I spent four years in Italy with the 1/509th ABCT. While I was there I went to Ranger School because I was in the Scout Platoon. Most of the NCOs were Rangers and I was building up a complex. Not really, but I admired and respected them and wanted to attend the school to see if I had what it took. Problem was my unit did not get Ranger School slots. My commander allowed me to attend Ranger School as a re-enlistment payback, but there was a catch…I had to go in a "permissive TDY" status. In other words, since my unit did not get slots, I had to pay my way back to Benning, and then the unit would allow me to go. So I paid to go to Ranger School. Weird, hey?

Steve Bishop

When I was going through the Shake-and-Bake course [1972], we had a Ranger briefing. We actually went to, like a Ranger weekend. This man, I can't remember anything about him, he was the biggest man I'd ever seen in my life. They came up and gave us a briefing about going to Ranger School when we graduated Shake-and-Bake School, if we wanted to.

I realize it's just a piece of cloth, but after I graduated and went to Jump School, went to Vietnam, came back—I always wanted to get that Ranger Tab. I got the opportunity to go and I was not going to be denied. I got it.

What did it do for me? Kept me alive. You put yourself in positions, in my opinion, if you're going to be Combat Arms in the Army you want to surround yourself with the best there is.

Doug Perry

A Grunt might get stopped, might think he's finished, and quit. A Ranger reaches down into his boots and pulls out more guts and fortitude and goes a little farther. Once you've told yourself you've got to go on, that you might die, once you get it in your mind, you can go on.

Ken Bonnell

My Ranger training changed my life. It transformed me from a green farm boy into a young leader and a warrior. My Ranger training gave me a mindset that any hardship can be overcome and that the mission at hand will be accomplished. I have held this mindset even after I left the military.

Pre-Ranger, RIP, and ROP(e)

It seems strange to think that all members of the Ranger Regiment are not Ranger School graduates, yet a rather large component of the men are Privates/PFCs and came into the unit for their first assignment. Other soldiers, particularly officers and non-coms, transfer in from other units after they get their Tab, but must still go through an orientation course. For those incoming soldiers, and those "born in the Regiment" there are a few precursors to actually becoming a part of a Ranger unit.

Though being part of the Regiment earns a man the right to be called Ranger, his buddies know the truth. There are various names for men with Tabs, just the Ranger Scroll, or nothing at all. A "newbie" must undergo not only continuous heavy training, but also nearly continuous heavy hazing from his "peers" until he has proven himself worthy. The hazing can be considered good-natured unless you're on the receiving end. Both the training and the hazing begin immediately upon acceptance to the Regiment and/or Ranger School (including Pre-Ranger, RIP and ROP).

To get to one of those courses a soldier must first have completed Basic (and often Advanced Training—12 weeks), and Ranger-necessary Airborne training (3 weeks).

It is possible to complete Ranger School without being Airborne, but no "Leg" soldier gets in the Ranger Regiment these days because it is first and foremost an airborne force.

Once Airborne-qualified, soldiers who have "signed up" for placement in the Regiment get a little talk from a RIP (Ranger Indoctrination Program) Instructor who explains what will be expected of them. Right then about half of the assembled group quits before they start. The weeding out process has begun.

From more than one source we've heard RIP is designed to make a man quit. A soldier is not pushed to succeed. Either he has it or he doesn't. If he wants to be in a Ranger Battalion he must pass RIP, whether he eventually attends Ranger School or not.

A RIP student has three weeks to learn as much as he can, while surviving the harsh physical realities of Ranger training in the air, on land, and in the water. Among many other things he must learn to kill with a knife or his hands, cross barren ground or mountains in light or dark using his compass and other tools, fast-rope from a helicopter, and live through a Combat Water Survival Test. All the while there are pushups and marching, and running, running, running.

During the three weeks the class size continues to decline as men are injured, quit, or are told to leave because they couldn't hack it.

RIP and Pre-Ranger get rid of the majority of those who have the desire, but not the heart or mind for the grueling process. This keeps valuable time and space in the Ranger Regiment and Ranger School from being filled by someone who probably won't make it.

The success rate of Ranger School—between 60 and 80 percent generally—has gotten higher since these programs were instituted simply because much of the chaff has already been separated from the wheat.

Such a preliminary makes Ranger School sound like the toughest thing going—and it is. Not only are Rangers incredibly knowledgeable, tough, and resourceful on the battlefield, the life of the average Ranger in the Regiment is just that—regimented. Constant training and the call for excellence wears on many a young Ranger and the turnover rate is high.

New RIP graduates are allowed to wear the Ranger Scroll and become recognized as a member of the Regiment. Nevertheless, if they haven't made Ranger School yet, they are not fully accepted. They are Rangers, members of the world's best elite light infantry, yet they are not Tabbed Rangers, and there is a definite distinction.

The term "Battboy" is given to a man who has been "born" into the Regiment, that is, it is his first assignment. A Battboy may or may not ever get to Ranger School, though he may fight all over the world as a Ranger.

Once a man has successfully completed RIP and has become part of the Regiment, he may wait months for a shot at Ranger School. When that finally comes around, he must first pass Pre-Ranger, another three-week course designed to get him ready for the rigors of the three phases of school. Having passed Pre-Ranger he immediately attends Ranger School, a total of 12 weeks of continuous training. If he passes, he is awarded the Ranger Tab to go with the Scroll of the Regiment.

Should a soldier outside the Regiment desire to become part of the unit he must go through Ranger School and get his Tab, but he has no Scroll until he makes it through ROP (Ranger Orientation Program), another three week course designed to integrate him into the world's top infantry strike force.

All in all, it is a wonder the Rangers are able to find 2,000 qualified men to fill the ranks. Apparently there is no shortage of volunteers, considering Ranger School runs full classes year-round. The dropout rate is staggering as the numbers fall during the training process.

Keith Antonia—Ranger Training Elsewhere

[After Ranger School] I went to the Armor Officer Advanced Course at Fort Knox, Kentucky. I was just sent there, I don't know why. I didn't understand that kind of stuff when I was a Lieutenant. I was the Ranger Advisor to Armor Lieutenants who wanted to go to Ranger School. We set up a Ranger training program for them. To prepare these Armor Lieutenants for Ranger School we would take Captains out of the Advanced Course who were Ranger-qualified, and those Captains would develop a Ranger School training program for those Lieutenants.

All Combat-Arms Officers are encouraged to go to Ranger School, although they can opt out.

In addition to the Armor Course we did some Field Training Exercises and some long road marches, waged ambushes, we gave them classes on patrolling and combat orders. We set a severe PT program for them. It was all designed to toughen up their feet, backs, and minds. That was in 1984-85.

Jack Daniel—ROTC Ranger Training

I was assigned as Assistant PMS (Professor of Military Science) at the University of Tennessee, where I organized the first Ranger Training Course for ROTC cadets in a civilian college in the US in January 1962. This unit is still in existence, and is the backbone of the ROTC program at UT.

Only the Ranger Training unit at Virginia Military Institute was organized earlier, in 1961.

The training was intense, offering more training than given to Cadets at West Point. We developed the Achievement Rating System, based on teaching and testing of shooting, moving, communicating, and Ranger history. The students did mountaineering, river crossings, and long and short combat and recon patrols into Knox, Blount, and Sevier Counties.

Luca Bertozzo—Italian Ranger

Since the Vietnam War and maybe before there have been foreign nationals going through the Ranger course. Some come for the prestige, some come to learn. Luca Bertozzo is one of the latter.

I was born on the 17th January 1972 in Montecchio Maggiore, a small town not so far from Vicenza [North East Italy], where the US Army has a base: the EDERLE BARRACKS. I joined the Army in 1992 after the graduation at the Rossi High School in Vicenza. While in service I decided that the Army life style was interesting and could give me the opportunity to do something more. I decided signing remaining in service as a career.

After five years in a regular Alpini unit, the Chief of Staff of the Alpini Corps asked some other comrades and me if we would like to serve in a new battalion: the Airborne Alpini Battalion. I accepted immediately, and in December 1997 I took part with the new unit. It was November 1999 when the Chief of the Staff of the Army realized that there weren't enough Special Operation Forces in Italy. After a short decision process they chose the Airborne Alpini Battalion to start a new project: we had to start the first Ranger unit in the Italian Army. A new challenge was then in front of me: to become a Ranger!

After my graduation as an "Italian Ranger," I quickly realized that it wasn't enough for my aspiration. In 2000, they told me about the US Ranger School, but in that period the course was available only for the officers; so that there was no possibility as an NCO to attempt that course.

In 2002, due to the fact that no officers were available, Sergeant Alessandro GRASSI of the Italian Ranger Battalion, the first NCO, could successfully be graduated in Ranger School.

Something was changing, but after him the Army once again sent officers to the course. I started thinking that it would be only a dream for me, till 2003.

I was on holiday after my deployment in Afghanistan when the phone rang. I was asked to be back to the unit to talk with my commander in Bolzano. The last three Ranger students sent from Italy to the USA failed the course and the Chief of staff of the Army ordered to find an NCO to try to save the situation or "No other Italian would be sent to Ranger School."

At last, after four years it was my turn!

I arrived in the USA in January 2004 [class 05/04] and everything was going in the right way, but while in Dahlonega I had to be recycled due to a fracture in my left foot. During that three weeks long period I could talk a little with the RI's about my job in Italy, finding out that I was only the second NCO in the Italian Army who could attempt the Ranger Course.

The following days during my climbing exercises with the new class at Mount Yonah, I met LTC FLOHR, the BN Commander for the first time. He kindly liked to talk with me because some RI's had told him about my story. After a few minutes, at the end of the meeting, he told me something that I couldn't completely realize at the moment: "If you finish the Ranger Course, I'd like to call you back here as an RI. Are you interested?"

As you can imagine my answer was "yes!" I couldn't believe my ears. Me? A Ranger Instructor? How did it come? I successfully completed the course in May 2004 and I should come back home. But that idea—to be a Ranger Instructor—started to roll in my head.

August 2004, another phone call. "The 5th RTB asked for you in the USA, you must attempt the Ranger Instructor Course!" In October 2004 RIC was completed. I was the first non-American NCO in history to reach that result and to be accepted as part of the Ranger family like no others.

This is shortly my adventure during my 13 years in the Army.

Actually my rank is Master Sergeant and my duty is now training the guys, NCOs and officers that want to be Ranger qualified in Italy. After my graduation as RI, I have to train the personnel that are going to be sent to US Ranger School.

Actually in Italy there are seven US Ranger qualified; 1 trained another NCO that would have to come to the USA next July, and I'm waiting for an officer to send there next October.

Talking about my feelings about the course, the first thing is that through the whole three-phase course a foreign student gets a deep sensation to be part of an elite group. When you think that you have reached your personal limit, the Instructors will teach you how to give and do more and best. I must confess, not only because I served there, the 5th RTB has something more. The mountain phase is the most challenging, due to the terrain and the weight of the special equipment that you must carry. In the other hand, the Instructors are more prepared—everyone is very good in Ranger Course, but as I told you the style of teaching is completely different in Dahlonega. They put attention on more details trying to mentor the students like no others. I could understand more about that point of view during RIC. I mean, I learned more in those three month about training and teaching than in all my military life!

Once in Italy the problem for me was to create "a Ranger mentality" for the possibility to live in a Ranger BN gave me the chance to move deeply inside the American Rangers' mentality. At present I'm able to find out the way to link-up my unit with the US Army units especially while in Iraq, Afghanistan, etc. As you can imagine having good soldiers is not enough if they can't cooperate with their Allies, and to do that we just need to "talk the same language." Well, the Ranger Course is this: a school where you set the soldiers in the same way, disregarding for the unit, the task and at least the nationality. My contribution in my country and how I'm now using my knowledge is basically this: to reduce the gap between the Italian Rangers and the US ones. So that we should be able to create a "Ranger platform" in Italy, which can lead the other units through this kind of mentality: mission first, don't accept the defeat, one hundred percent and then some...

Summarizing the first step is done: a few men in Italy are growing up a new generation of soldiers based on Rangers' mentality. We want to be part of the Ranger family maintaining our particular techniques, but a chance to be fully integrated with the "older brothers" in the USA.

Patrick Corcoran

Corcoran was First Sergeant for HHC at Camp Merrill at the time of this interview (April 2005) and knew Bertozzo fairly well. This was recorded at the USMRA Critter Cookout in the snow and sleet and rain and lots of wind. We were outside. True Ranger weather.

He came through my company, Charlie Company. He comes from his Army where they are standing up their own version of Ranger School. The first time he was in my company he broke his foot and was recycled. We thought for a while there it was his conspiracy to learn a little bit more and be able to take it back as part of his program, but he (really) had a broken foot.

He went all the way through the Benning Phase with a broken foot, and I guess it swelled up enough on him here that he recycled. So, he went back through, did real well here in the battalion, and the commander mentioned to me he talked to him before he left here and gave him an opportunity to come back as a guest Instructor.

He leaves here, goes to Florida [camp], graduates from the course and goes back to [Italy] one of seven Rangers in his country trained through our school. He came here with a great deal of climbing and mountaineering experience and a laundry list of combat experience.

Then he came back here and Colonel Flohr [Commander, 5th RTB] approached me before he returned. He said, "Master Sergeant Bertozzo is coming back here to be a guest instructor, reporting in October. He will go through Ranger Instructor certification exactly as our Instructors have to do. He will teach some patrolling classes, walk some patrols, grade some patrols, and he'll go over and work in operations for the last month he's here."

He's the only one I know, a foreign Cadre Instructor, since I've been here, anyway.

There is pressure put on them to make people succeed. They've got to get them to put out the material and do the re-training if necessary to get people to succeed. It puts them in a unique situation if they're having a hard time communicating with people.

International Rangers

Italian Ranger Luca Bertozzo is not unique as an international Ranger. Other countries have been standing up their own programs for several years, some, but not all, in conjunction with US Army Ranger training.

The following is a partial list of the units overseas:

Philippine Army Scout Rangers
Canadian Rangers
Irish Defense Force Army Ranger Wing
German Jaeger Korps Ranger Corps
Italian Rangers
Swedish Airborne Rangers
Swedish Air Force Rangers

Three Phase Memories

Since Ranger training has changed over the years depending on need, no single set of experiences can speak to that evolution. Still, the fundamental mission of Ranger School is to turn out the very best small unit leader in the world, capable of astonishing feats of endurance and discipline in the accomplishment of whatever task he is given. In short, students get pushed to the absolute limit, and as Howard Denton says, only the strong survive.

"Genuine misery is the one common denominator in all eras."

That fact has not changed since Darby's days, nor is it likely to, making the Ranger Tab a badge of honor and courage like no other.

Denton's personal description of all three phases of Ranger School was originally written for his family. Though there are other accounts of experiences in this history, none are as complete, or as telling, as his.

Denton went through in 1972. After graduation, he became a Rifle Platoon Leader for the 82nd Airborne, as well as being the Company Executive Officer (XO). He also served at the 82nd Recondo School.

He went on to join the 7th Special Forces Group as an A-Team XO, and was the 7th Group HQ S-3 (operations) as a staff officer. An injury in 1975 removed him from jump status. He left the Army as a 1st Lieutenant in 1976, and eventually went into teaching.

"Rangers are the 'apex predators' on any battlefield because they have continued to evolve, change, and adapt to meet the threats of our enemies. I use the term 'Darwinian' not only for its 'only the strong survive, the weak fall by the wayside' message, but also for its implication that not only survival, but also success requires a necessity for adapting to circumstances and accepting change through evolution."
Howard Denton

Ranger School 1972—City Phase

The 4th Ranger Training Battalion, located in a remote corner of Fort Benning, Georgia, hosts the first phase of the Ranger Course.

Howard Denton

The legendary "Rogers' Rangers' Standing Orders" is familiar to every United States Army Ranger. Order number one says, "Don't forget nothing."

Time erodes many memories. But some, chiseled with a tool far sharper than what one finds in a normal life, gouge much deeper into the memory and last longer. While many memories from the distant past are vague, as if only a hallucination, others are clear and crisp, and are remembered as though they were recent events. The tool that chiseled some of these memories so well for me was driven by a sledgehammer called Ranger School.

Order number four demands "Tell the truth about what you see and what you do." I have not always obeyed this one because it goes on to say, "you can lie all you please when you tell other folks about the Rangers, but don't ever lie to a Ranger or officer."

What I write now has no embellishment. It is fact as I remember it to be. Should another Ranger or officer read this, they will know it to be true.

The only other order to which I will refer, number five, admonishes, "Don't ever take a chance you don't have to." I, and every other Ranger, violated this order by the very act of volunteering for Ranger School.

I don't remember sleeping the night before I drove out what was then called 3rd Ranger Company in the Harmony Church area of Fort Benning. Although I had met every requirement to go to Ranger School; physical fitness test, swim test, physical exam, all passed with no problem, the apprehension of what the next nine weeks held kept me awake all night.

In that long night I went over every story I'd heard about the school—nightmare tales of hunger, sleep deprivation, bone-chilling cold rain, endless walking, dismal days and darker sleepless nights of pain and planning for small unit operations that inevitably involved frustrating physical and mental challenges found absolutely nowhere else in the world.

I knew to expect only one C-ration a day when we were in the field. I knew there would be many nights with no sleep, followed with many more nights of only an hour or two of sleep, and I would be wet most of the time. I could also expect senseless hallucinations, cold injuries, and more endless miles to walk. But I wanted the black and gold Ranger Tab, and whatever the Army threw at me, I was willing to take. I knew I was as prepared as I could be.

That first day was hot, and after parking my car in the long-term student parking lot across from Todd Field, I shouldered my duffel bag and began to walk toward an area dominated by WWII-era buildings. After signing in and handing over five copies of my orders assigning me to the school, a young Sergeant wearing a black beret and a black T-shirt with a large Ranger Tab on the front politely reminded me that now, as a Ranger student, I was not to wear any rank or branch insignia on my uniform. I removed the pin-on Infantry Branch crossed rifles and the 2nd Lieutenant bar. Putting them in a pocket, I then looked up to ask this polite Sergeant where I should go next.

From two inches away, with his eyes locked on mine, came his screaming reply. "Get down on your filthy face, you maggot, and knock out 25!" I had just become the feature attraction of a special kind of hell of earth, appropriately called "getting smoked."

He escorted me as I low-crawled and dragged my duffel bag the 75 yards to the barracks, stopping about every 15 yards to do more push-ups. He screamed the entire way. I remember "maggot" being used liberally in his speech, but on later days, vulgar adjectives were added for a more descriptive effect.

Later that day, standing in our first formation as Ranger students, the entire class of more than 300 was told there were far too many of us to graduate, and this problem was going to be taken care of by a simple formula of attrition based on some failing, some quitting, some being injured, and some being run off. I knew they weren't joking.

Then we were introduced to our TAC NCO, a bulldog Vietnam vet named Sergeant Burnell. "Uncle Burnie" had a voice of gravel and one leg of wood from some kind of war injury, and since this special session of hell was now in session, he was called to be the designated demon-miester. He growled that, quite clearly, less than half of this class would graduate. It turned out that far less than half graduated—some through their own ineptitude or by quitting, but many because of bad luck injuries. Sergeant Burnell now occupies an honored place in the Ranger Hall of Fame for his many accomplishments, but in 1972 his job was to serve chaos in large portions to us a Ranger students. I avoided him at all cost then, but would like to shake his hand and thank him now for the high standards he demanded from us at the time. Such is life.

During chow, he informed the student company commander he now wished to be "serenaded by a rock group," and ordered him to "get out of here and go find *Three Dog Night*." The poor student missed that first meal because he kept bringing in Ranger students, three at a time, none of whom could figure out all Uncle Burnie wanted to hear was some Studs sing the hit song, *"Mama Told Me Not To Come."* At the next meal, a trio lucked out and got it right.

Then there was the student, whose real name was Prince Powe, who became for Uncle Burnie a pet named "Prince Bow-Wow", and had to crawl on all fours like a dog during formations, growling and barking at anyone who came near Uncle Burnie.

That first night we scrubbed floors and latrines, made bunks to bounce a quarter from, and sewed "Ranger Eyes" on our patrol caps. We had been told to, "Get what sleep you can, 0530 comes early," by an RI about 2200 that night. Having not slept at all the night before, by 0130 I was very tired and ready to get a few hours sleep before starting the first full day of this school. The bunk felt good. The RI lied.

By 0530 we had already been up two-and-a-half hours. At 0300 we were jolted from our sleep by the sound of a trash can being kicked the length of the barracks, followed by profanity and sharp voices screaming something about maggots again and "one minute to get into formation!"

The black-shirted RIs were all over the place inside our barracks. Within 60 seconds I found myself standing at attention in the dark street, thinking about having slept only 90 minutes in the last two nights.

With red-filtered flashlights as the only light source, we began our first full day of Ranger School at "oh-dark-thirty" with a one-and-a-half mile threat-and-obscenity motivated sprint in combat boots completed in well under 10 minutes, and it seemed to be more like a scene from an unearthly nightmare involving someone named Dante. As it turned out, that run was the high point of the day, and it went quickly downhill from there. I wanted to vomit. Some did.

Then, in a circular sawdust pit, came the physical training (PT). Sit-ups, pushups, side straddle hop in two and four-count styles, squat thrusts, hello-darlings, flutter kicks, leg lifts of various descriptions, windmills, and still more pushups.

All the while we received personal attention from the Instructors. They were everywhere, and there was no way to avoid their gaze. Things began to get uncomfortable. It was still dark after the hour or so when we finished the calisthenics and lined up for chow.

The Mess Hall was little more than a cafe with a chow line, and could not have held more than 70 at most. Because the training schedule allowed only 30 minutes per meal, and our class had well over 300 students, we had a problem. The only solution for serving and eating a meal was simple; eat as you were being served, and if you were at the end of the line shovel it in before the whistle for the next formation.

As we lined up to go in, each student had to take his turn at the chin-up bar for eight good Ranger chin-ups, which if not executed properly earned him a place back at the end of the line. By day two, meals were gulped down whole as we listened to our *Three Dog Night* brothers reminding us that we should have listened to our mothers.

There was a formation after that first breakfast to tell us the next formation would be in 30 minutes, and we had to shower and put on clean fatigues..

The RIs inspected us at that formation, but this time they were worse than before. Anything out of order, including having brown eyes, caused push-ups. No haircut passed, including some whose hair was nonexistent. As the RIs went down the ranks, their bellowing voices from every direction yelled, "Get down," "Drop, you brown-eyed maggot," "Tell him you need a number three haircut, now get out of here," "You need a number one after you give me 25," "Don't you dare look at me, you nasty hippy. After 25, tell the man you need a two. Not a one or a three, a two. If it's not a two when you get back, you'll be thrown out for non-compliance."

Everyone with brown eyes was doing push-ups, and then they joined everyone else running down the street to the barber, as our formation disintegrated in one location and re-formed as a very long line at the barber shop for what I later found to be a ritual with each class.

Everyone had his head peeled that day. Those with brown eyes did push-ups the first day, those with blue eyes the second day, and everyone did push-ups from then on just so no one felt left out.

About this time we were assigned our Ranger buddies. There is no way to explain the significance a Ranger buddy has, no way to describe his importance. My first buddy was from Rockford, Illinois, a bear of a man who could carry any load for days, but was not very good at motivating and leading others when exhaustion set in. He was dropped at the end of the Benning Phase, and I was sorry to see it happen. He could be relied upon to carry extra ammo, canteens, serve as the patrol radio operator (RTO), and carry wounded two at a time, but when it came time to assign chain of command positions, no one wanted him to have any leadership position because he was timid when tired. He was intelligent, likeable and strong as an ox, but he was not someone who could step up and take charge when needed.

Each day, our morning run increased by one mile, so the first mile-and-a-half run became a five-and-a-half mile run on the last day. All runs were made in combat boots, at a pace of a six-minute mile—except for the last, an eight-minute mile.

On the day of the fourth run, as I rolled out of the bunk and my feet hit the floor, the muscles in my lower legs felt like meat on an over-done roast, sliding off the bone. It was the worst pain I've ever had in my legs. It hurt to stand, and it was agony to walk. Now I know I had a bad case of shin splints, but at the time I had no idea what had happed to my legs. I knew it was not good.

As we began the four-and-a-half mile run, I knew two things; one, I would not be able to finish this run, and two, if a student dropped out of two runs, he was out of Ranger School. So I thought, if by some miracle I could finish this run, I might escape the longer run the next day. But if I could not even make this run, then tomorrow…

My shins hurt so badly, I threw up within the first half mile. Knowing I could not finish, I allowed myself to drop out of formation. I had run less than a mile and was picked up by one of the vehicles that always followed to pick up stragglers. Even as I got into the back of the vehicle, the shame I felt was beginning to outweigh the rotting pain I felt in my shins. In a way, the pain in my shins, as bad as it was, was far more tolerable than the shame I now felt for quitting.

We returned to the company area and began grass drills before the rest were finished with their run. It was here I saw the worst side of the Ranger School Cadre. Those grass drills lasted through the rest of the class run, through breakfast, and through the morning formation. The sole purpose of the grass drills was to make us quit, and many did. I just wanted to die, but I had made up my mind it would happen during the last run and not before. For about four hours, we alternated between the grass drills and standing at attention as we were reminded all this would stop if we would just say, "I quit." Two simple words would end the misery. They really did want us to quit, but I wasn't about to, not twice in the same day. Shame was far worse than pain, and I had never been more exhausted in my life, ever. Those of us remaining were finally allowed to join a now smaller class with one run left.

I will never forget that last run, and I will never doubt the power of prayer. The pain in my shins was still there, but it did not seem to matter. Yesterday I was convinced I couldn't finish the run, and I did not. Today, I was prepared to give more than everything to finish. I had found my mental limit yesterday. Today, I needed to know how much farther my real physical limits were.

Sometime later, I looked down at my watch and realized we had been running exactly forty minutes, or five miles. Only one-half-mile to go. I rejoiced.

Then, it hit me. The wall.

I felt as if I had been holding my breath for the last five miles, and within an instant I was out of breath and knew I might not make that last half-mile. I was gasping breath, felt every step, and thought I might only be able to go another 50 yards at best. Before I pass out, I thought, at least I should first finish the run. I could see the lights of the finish line in the distance, about 300 yards, too far to make it, I thought. It's just too far. I had given my best, but I was suffocating.

Just then the man on my right began to stagger and gasped out, "I …can't …make it! Gotta quit!"

Confusion, then anger, entered my mind. He can't quit this close to the line. Not now! He can't be hurting as bad as I am. But then I thought, maybe he is worse off than I am. He needs help to finish. So I reached over with my right hand and grabbed his left arm just as the man on his right helped from that side, and I thought, "Lord, I can't even make it on my own, let alone help him, too. Just get us all over that line and we'll manage from there." The strength that held him up and got us across the finish line did not come from within me. Through those last few hundred yards, with shin splints screaming, gasping for breath and half carrying the man on my right, were the toughest I ran in Ranger School. We made it across, slowed to quick time, and then, gasping, stopped.

The lesson was not lost on me. Changing the focus from my misery to helping the man on my right get through his, with prayer, allowed both of us, all of us, to get through. Too exhausted to vomit or cry, we were now brothers—Rangers. This team is far superior to the sum of its individuals. I could never have finished that run without his lesson, and I am truly blessed for having experienced it.

I now realized my physical limits, wherever they were, had not yet been reached. Those limits were far beyond where I knew or thought they should be, and I was now in uncharted territory. The mind was wrong about what the body could take, and I would draw from this experience more than once before graduating from Ranger School. For those who have experienced this, no explanation is necessary. For those who have never experienced it, no explanation can ever suffice.

In the combatives pit, the round sawdust-filled area also used for PT in the pre-dawn darkness, we learned both self-defense and offense through still more physically degrading activities after the sun was high in the sky. We learned various takedowns, throws, and violent techniques to disarm or kill an opponent. Some students suffered dislocations, broken bones, or torn muscles, any of which caused them to be dropped from the course or recycled into a later class.

After only about a week of this, our numbers dropped by about 50. The rest of us found ourselves packing our gear to go to the next phase to take on the "County Team" at Camp Darby.

On arrival we offloaded, and with the usual yelling, fell into formation. This place was rustic, hot, dusty and miles from nowhere. Our welcoming committee gave us the good news—for the remainder of the course there would be no more PT, but we had to run wherever we went. The bad news, they explained, was there were only 24 hours in each day, and we would be training at least 22 of those from then on. The normally allotted two hours for PT was now ours to enjoy for sleep, socializing, or studying the Ranger Handbook. The rest of every day belonged to them.

We pitched two-man tents within 20 minutes and stowed our gear. After assembling in a primitive classroom, the camp commander officially welcomed us by letting us know we were surrounded by Ranger-qualified combat veterans whose job was two-fold. First, they were to provide us with the finest training in small unit combat and reconnaissance operations in the world, and second, as the hereditary "Protectors of the Tab" they would make sure only the best would graduate.

Our motto became "Prompt Obedience-Self Discipline." I would find out in the coming weeks how difficult that simple motto could become in practice.

No time was wasted in beginning our training. We had classes on everything imaginable for patrolling operations. We learned patrol formation—file, column, etc—forming elements such as security and assault, standardized hand and arm signals for silence, immediate action drills for situations requiring immediate action, actions at the objective, rehearsals, planning and issuing warning orders, fragmentary orders, and the five paragraph operations order (OPORD), which when properly given takes well over an hour to issue. We sharpened skills already learned, such as radio-telephone procedures, encoding and decoding messages, calling for artillery fire or medevacs, how to conduct fire-support coordination with assigned artillery units for pre-planned fire support, arranging for passage of friendly forward lines with guides, challenge and password, and running passwords in case of hot pursuit. If it had anything to do with raids, ambushes or recons, we learned it, the Ranger way.

Then we went into the woods to put into practice what we had learned in the classroom, and that introduced us to one meal a day, and sometimes no sleep at all.

Our first patrol, led by an RI whose no-nonsense approach to issuing a warning order and dividing our eight-man patrol into elements and responsibilities, brought together everything we'd heard in the classes.

His OPORD took fully an hour-and-a-half to give, and covered every contingency imaginable. We had a passage of friendly lines, artillery fire support coordination for primary and alternative routes both to and from our objective, a sand table model of our mission with primary and alternate routes to and from the objective, rehearsals of immediate action drills and actions at the objective. The patrol lasted about 24 hours, dark to dark, and he left nothing out. Halts were called when needed to explain what or why something was being done. As the Patrol Leader, he was responsible for everything the patrol did, and he left nothing to chance. We had a point man, compass man, and pace man, but the RI kept his own pace count and compass check, too. He allowed no margin for error, and for the first time in Ranger School, I began to see these RIs as the true professional soldiers they were. This was the only perfect patrol I saw in Ranger School. We got one C-ration for that entire patrol, and no sleep. As much as I learned from this patrol, fatigue and hunger were beginning to take a toll on our mental abilities and our patience with each other.

There were five significant events remaining at Camp Darby for us to experience.

The first was a two-day student-led patrol where leadership positions were rotated frequently to prepare us for the graded patrols in the Mountain and Florida phases. It was a nightmare of an exercise for some. A few patrols got lost, stayed lost, and roamed all over because the compass man and/or PL were tired, or the pace was off, or somebody misread a map. When that happened, the RIs reverted to their old screaming selves, and some patrols walked almost non-stop for those two days, "just to get the stupid out of their systems."

The eight-man patrol I was with didn't do too badly. The first night we actually got about three hours of sleep. The next night, while we were in our patrol base, I heard in the distance an RI screaming obscenities at his patrol, and then he set off an artillery simulator. Our RI explained, "That's what happens when we catch someone sleeping when they're supposed to be awake. That patrol will walk the rest of the night."

The second event was the toughest mile in the world, by most accounts—the Darby Queen. It is the most difficult obstacle course in the world.

The Queen—featured as part of Best Ranger Competition—winds through thick woods for more than a mile and features many obstacles, some of them 20-30 feet high.

We ran it twice, once for practice and later as a timed event. Complete it in time or fail. I cannot begin to describe it. One must experience it.

The third event was the night land navigation course, a legendary all-nighter that had a time limit requiring students to keep moving fast, with no breaks or rest, or it could not be finished on time. At the start, each three-man team was given a direction and distance (route) to go, say 215 degrees for 1350 meters. At that place you would find three to five stations, each with a different number, about 10-15 meters apart. Only one station was the correct one and had been surveyed for accuracy. The others were wrong. But each of these gave a direction and distance for another cluster of stations, only one of which was right, and so it went all night long, for seven or eight routes to navigate. Some of the distances were just under 1,000 meters, but our longest was around 2,600 meters. This was to be a very long night.

My group of three immediately crawled under a poncho and pulled out our maps and red-filtered flashlights. Our first leg would take us through a ravine that would make it difficult to keep an accurate pace count, so I suggested we pinpoint on the map where that direction and distance should end, and then go to that point by the fastest route. This is basically orienteering, and it worked well. While most other groups were crunching straight through the brush and swamps, we stayed dry, walked a lot farther, but covered the distance faster and more accurately. We worked great together. Our little group of three finished second, but we were the only group to get all stations correctly, and the first group in over two years to max the course.

The fourth of our remaining events involved a night tactical parachute jump onto a tiny drop zone. After landing, we were to conduct a raid against a missile site, and then break into four-man teams and escape and evade across country about 10 miles to King's Pond before sunrise. Our jump was from a CH-47 Chinook helicopter at 1250 feet, in the dark. I was about halfway back in the stick, and after exiting into the windy blackness and counting to 4,000 (one-one thousand, two-one thousand), I felt a tug on the risers and looked around to check for other jumpers, as we had been trained. I had forgotten that "check canopy" comes after counting and before "keep a sharp lookout during descent," so I was puzzled at seeing the dim mushroom shapes of parachutes beneath me now rising rapidly around me. I thought they had caught some kind of updraft that I was somehow missing, and they would have a nice, longer ride down into the black abyss below.

As I watched them drift ever higher above me, I glanced up at my own parachute, and I saw trash. I had a complete malfunction, a "cigarette roll" (also called a "tamale"), and was descending (falling!) at a high rate of speed, stabilized by the streamer above me. I grabbed at my reserve ripcord and pulled it, and the reserve chute deployed immediately, slowing my descent. After hitting the ground not more than five seconds later, I got out of the harness and left the whole tangled mess there for the riggers to figure out. I was having a very hard time getting my rucksack and weapon organized until I realized I was still holding the ripcord grip of my reserve parachute tightly in my right hand. Disgusted with myself, I put it into my pocket and headed for the assembly area. I still have that ripcord grip.

The raid came off without a problem, and we split up into our teams.

By about 0300, we still had almost eight miles to cover cross-country in less than three hours, and a major swamp lay in our path. Our boundaries were a highway to our right and a railroad to our left, and we had been ordered to stay off both. The highway would be heavily patrolled, so we went to the railroad, against orders, and took off. If we were spotted, we agreed to scatter and meet at predetermined rally points farther along. We spent the last few hours of the night jogging on crossties.

We made it in early and linked up with others as they arrived. They were vastly more exhausted and miserable than we. Many were captured—and passed. Some got lost—and failed.

Once all were accounted for, we were required to negotiate the 40-foot rope drop and Slide for Life at nearby Victory Pond.

Mountain Phase Memories

Howard Denton

Denton was already noticing the losses of his comrades when he came to Camp Frank D. Merrill in the mountains of north Georgia.

On that cold, crisp, autumn afternoon, with the winds too high to jump, the Airborne section of my class (the legs went by truck) air-landed at Camp Frank D. Merrill. Located near the Appalachian Trail, high in the Chattahoochee National Forest of northern Georgia, it is without a doubt the most scenic, beautiful, and peaceful area I can imagine in which to train for mountain operations with small units. It also seemed bitterly cold compared to Fort Benning.

After landing at Mosby Army Air Strip, at the back side of Merrill, we secured our gear and moved out to the tree line bordering the school area. At a hasty formation, we were informed the rest of our classmates would be delayed for a while due to an accident involving the trucks carrying them. More than a dozen students were either recycled or put out due to injuries. The class continued to dwindle in size.

We stored our gear in little shacks called "hooches." In these, we could read the names, classes, messages, and other doodles of students from prior classes. Many were legible from years before. I claimed a top bunk because heat rises, and if we were to be fortunate enough to spend nights in this hooch I wanted a little warmth. I, too, carved my initials into the wood and became a small part of "hooch three." One of these, I've been told, is supposed to have been preserved at the Smithsonian Institution.

True. Also a part of one is enshrined in the museum at Camp Merrill. The rest were destroyed in the 1980s, when heated cinder-block barracks were built.

The Mountain Phase was basically two parts—military mountaineering and patrolling operations in mountain environments. Each had its special challenges.

For the first few days we acclimated, we attended classes on mountain operations and spent long hours learning how to tie knots and prepare for rappelling and making rope bridges. We tied knots at a rope corral until our fingers ached, and learned how to build one, two, and three-rope bridges to cross over streams and ravines.

Over 20 knots had to be mastered: square; granny; two kinds of half-hitches; one-two-and-three-loop bowlines; bowline on a coil; bowline on a bight; sheep shank; sheet bend; one-and-two-loop butterfly; clove hitch; round turn with two half-hitches; surgeon's knot; two slip knots; overhand; figure eight; and a couple of others I've forgotten. After mastering them, we would tie them blindfolded, and then had to learn to recognize by feel any knot—as we might have to in the dark. These became timed events, and when we broke into teams it became very competitive to see who could build the fastest two-or-three-rope bridge that held up best as the teams crossed.

We also had classes during this time on patrolling operations. In the planning phase, a warning order must be given to subordinate leaders, and planning begins on the OPORD. The OPORD is given, and later, rehearsals of immediate actions drills, actions at danger areas, and actions at the objective, are undertaken.

Prior to the movement phase, element leaders are briefed of any change in plans, PL (Patrol Leader) insures lead element and flank security understand the routes (primary and alternate), the patrol moves to the ORP (objective rally point), and the PL and necessary element leaders conduct a leaders' recon of the objective and modify plans if necessary.

The objective phase is the meat and potatoes of any patrol, although all phases are of equal importance. When the leader's recon of the objective is completed and the PL and others return to the ORP, last minute changes to the actions at the objective may be given. Then the ambush, raid, or recon is conducted and the appropriate responses for wounded, killed, and POWs are given. Movement to the primary or alternated ORP for dissemination of information, call for artillery, etc., is made.

Another movement phase is then called for, in order to move to the next patrol base where planning begins again for the next mission.

In each of these phases, there are graded leadership positions for the Patrol Leader and for the Assistant Patrol Leader. In addition, spot reports may be given for performance to element leaders and individuals. I've seen students pass patrols and get sunk because of bad spot reports.

[Later] the students went to the old rock quarry on foot to do some rappelling. We rappelled left handed or right handed, regular (backward), "Aussie" (facing downward), and with our buddy strapped to our backs, but the toughest was the "litter rappel." Each student took his turn being bound by rope to a litter, immobile, at the top of the 90-foot high quarry wall. A rope was tied to his litter and he was thrown over the edge with about 15 feet of slack in the belay rope, and fellow students had the sole responsibility of putting the brakes on his free fall. Two other students then escorted the "wounded" student the remainder of the way down, one of either side of the litter. The terror one feels at being thrown over the edge and falling is indescribable, but you do it anyway, and you learn to trust your buddy with your life, literally.

More bonding, the Ranger Way!

Then the graded student-led patrols began. The first was to be a four-day patrol beginning with six men each, and on the evening of the second day we linked up with another patrol to form a 12-man patrol.

We received our mission statement and were assigned positions in the warning order. More detailed than the OPORD, the warning order specifies things like what ammo to bring, who will take what position on the patrol, like RTO, and what type of clothing to wear. I was the RTO (radio operator) for the first planning phase. As such, I assisted the PL in preparing his OPORD and planning the patrol, which was supposed to be a point recon at a place on the Appalachian Trail called Coppermine Gap, a few kilometers west-northwest of Camp Merrill. It was good that I was involved in the planning phase, because later I would need to recall information left out of the first OPORD.

That evening, as our patrol approached the objective, Aggressor Forces ambushed us.

This happened often on patrols. OPFOR are stationed at every training camp.

By that time, I was no longer RTO and was traveling light, about 70 pounds. When they set off the ambush, we heard Aggressors yelling, "Grab one! Get a prisoner!" Several came running at me and a student in front of me, so we each emptied a magazine in our M16s and broke contact fast—ran—and reloaded. As contact was from the front right, we moved quickly to the left and ran in a large semicircle forward through the forest hoping to get around to their rear and hit them. They had vanished.

We stayed quiet and listened for some time, hoping to either counter-ambush them or link up with our patrol, as we had set up on their projected route. It was as if the forest had digested them all. We had done the unthinkable on our first patrol—we had become separated from the rest. In our safety briefing, we had been told what to do if this happened, but we knew if we turned ourselves in it could mean a major adverse spot report. Two of those and you were gone.

I explained to my partner I knew where the next patrol base would be, because I had been the RTO for the planning phase early that morning. Its location had been left out of the OPORD accidentally by the PL, but I remembered where it was to be on the map, at a saddle only about two kilometers west of where we now were. If we moved fast, we might make it before dark. He agreed to go, and within 45 minutes the two of us had "secured" the patrol base as darkness and a crisp, penetrating cold began to set in.

Over and over during interviews, Winter Rangers talked about the cold. Though north Georgia is not New Hampshire, it does get a bit nippy, especially in the higher elevations. Winter Rangers sometimes sew their newly earned Ranger Tabs on with white thread, so others will know they did Mountain Camp the hard way. The practice has tailed off over the years.

On the other hand, former RI Ted Tilson said he used to make his Studs do pushups in a mountain stream, a cold one, before ascending Winding Stair Gap in the summer time. Cuts down on heat injury, he said.

Shortly afterward, the rest of the patrol came in by an alternate route and a new PL began to plan for the next mission. The RI chewed on us some, but said because we took initiative, knew where to go, and got there before the patrol, we would not get the negative spot report.

The next mission was a pre-dawn ambush far away that involved a long night hike. We left the patrol base well before midnight, on what seemed the blackest night I've ever experienced. No moon, no stars, and no light, period. The "Ranger Eyes" on our patrol caps barely glowed, and the rest of the environment was completely ink-black and cold.

Ranger Eyes are fluorescent, vertical stripes on the back of a patrol cap. It gets very, very dark, and tomb-quiet in those woods at night. Anyone out there can hear you breathe. Trying to move quietly in rough terrain in absolute darkness is more than a little difficult.

We shuffled in file formation like blind men, slowly and silently, up and down unknown ridgelines for many hours, without stopping or pausing, trusting our compass man, until we finally halted and heard the whispered "one knee." That compass man, one of my two Night Land Navigation course buddies from Camp Darby, had led us through black ink over 5,000 meters on a crooked route of six or seven legs, keeping his own pace count for each, and had brought us within 50 meters of our ambush site well northeast of Hawk Mountain, just off an obscure trail.

I was surprised to feel frost on the ground as we quietly slipped into a linear ambush position, slightly off that dark trail. Shivering in sweat—now turned ice cold—I prayed for quick action.

The RI must have had radio contact with the Aggressors we were to ambush, for we were in position not more than 15 minutes when seven or eight of them walked into our kill zone. At the PL's signal, we engaged with all the violence an ambush should have. Then, with security placed left and right, at the signal, four of us dashed out to check the bodies for anything of Intelligence value: maps, radios and frequencies, notes, etc. We had 30 seconds to do this, and then we were to move quickly to a preplanned rally point to continue the mission.

As I was searching the "dead," I heard another moaning pathetic obscenities and gasping for breath. With barely enough light to make out the form of a body, we were allowed to use red-filtered flashlights to search. I turned to the groaner, patted him down and felt something wet, slick and large under his shirt that did not belong. Expecting to find maps or some other sweaty junk, I pulled open his shirt. In the dim red light of that freezing dawn, I found intestines, shiny and fully exposed.

This nightmare could have happened only if someone had used live ammo, and had left off the blank adapter for his M16. Horrified, I looked at the man's face, and just as I started to yell to the RI for a medevac, the "victim" grinned and said, "Never fails. Looks real, don't it?"

At the next patrol base, we had about three hours to plan for the next mission, clean weapons, change socks, repack our various loads if needed, and with 50 percent security, catch a few winks. I made a canteen cup of "John Wayne Coffee" from several instant coffee packets, sugar, creamer, and hot cocoa packets I had hoarded. Just as I finished it, we had to move out.

We left in file formation quickly, and had a route of around 15 kilometers to link up with another patrol. About two klicks into the route, the RI called a halt for the purpose of accounting for "sensitive items." These were items, such as weapons, whose loss would be unacceptable. As luck would have it, we were missing a VS-17 panel, an issued item used for aerial resupply or signaling. We had to retrace our route to find it, and located it out in the open back at our old patrol base. The man who'd lost it was not well liked after that, and we had to move fast to make up for the lost time. That PL failed his patrol for not accounting for the panel prior to departure, and for a few other things, and the next PL had even less time to plan for his mission because of the lost time. But link-up was made, and with the other patrol we picked up a Scout Dog Team to work with us. A safety briefing by the dog handler was given to us. "Stay away from this dog."

The next day is hazy, but I remember avoiding that dog. I also remember being told of being trailed by an Aggressor tracking team, and our rear security should be on extra alert. I thought the RI was joking.

After an afternoon phase that seemed endless, we moved into a patrol base just after dark. With special attention to security because of the tracker team allegedly following us, we spiraled into the position in such a way that anyone tracking us would pass across our front on a trail just below us, in what should then become an ambush site.

I don't know who that tracker team was, but not even the dog was alerted to their approach. They were silent and invisible, and they evidently entered our perimeter from downwind. Although the ground was littered with dry autumn leaves, and we should have heard them coming from 200 meters away, the first we knew of their presence was when we heard their M16s open up on us from within our perimeter. Then they vanished.

The RI was livid. We went admin and were lined up, and he demanded to know why, with 50 percent security, had we been breached? And why were we still here and not at a rally point when the signal to evacuate had been given? He sniffed the muzzles of our weapons, and any not having the smell of fresh gunpowder got a major minus spot report. Then he flunked the PL, and he fired the dog, too. He was right, and we were miserable.

After the next mission, the four-day patrol ended. On return to Camp Merrill we cleaned equipment and weapons, enjoyed hot showers, dry clothes, hot meals and warm bunks. We were exhausted, wiser, and still had the six-day patrol to look forward to, but Yonah Mountain was to happen first, and I had heard good things about that place.

We trucked to Mount Yonah, where we learned practical mountaineering over the next few days, and enjoyed a survival meal. Yonah is a large granite outcropping that looks out over north Georgia and is an ideal training area for mountaineering.

Mount Yonah is in Cleveland, Georgia, an area full of mountains rising piecemeal out of the earth. Most have granite outcroppings, but Yonah has a beautiful rock face.

We had an afternoon of survival training with traps, snares, and falls explained to us, followed by a survival meal. At sundown, each two-man buddy team was given a live chicken, an onion, carrot, and potato, and we were told to "enjoy your supper."

Two days later the Studs got their six-day patrol mission at 0400.

We began with 12-man patrols which gave us good firepower and more mission options, and later we linked up to form 24-man patrols, which allowed us to conduct better offensive missions, but made head counts more difficult.

We began with a mid-afternoon helicopter insertion at Bee Bait Knob, a grass-covered mountaintop loaded with Aggressor forces waiting in the nearby tree line. A hot LZ (landing zone) is not a good way to start any patrol. I remember thinking if this were real, we would have been chewed up badly. But, after beginning with that awkward insertion, we proceeded to the point recon of a suspected fuel depot. We then moved to a patrol base where I was up all night helping with an OPORD planning a raid to be made about noon the following day.

Denton rotated from RTO to rear security, losing his buddy.

At a security halt about dawn, I was told by the APL to go back down the trail alone about a hundred meters to provide rear security for the patrol during the halt. I told him, "Don't leave me when we move out," as I could not afford another break in contact. I went down the trail the hundred meters, and in spite of having no sleep in over 24 hours, I was alert and focused. About 30 minutes later, too long for a security halt, I realized I had been left. They had gone on without me!

Again, fortunately, I remembered where the next mission coordinates were. I pulled out my map, found where I was, and saw where the raid was to be. The instructions for "lost students" was very clear; go admin and turn yourself in ASAP. So I humped to the nearest road, several klicks away, and proceeded to the raid site as instructed.

It took about three hours by road to walk directly to the raid site, which was a bridge over a creek with a couple of tents housing Aggressor forces. I entered the first tent and encountered a Circle Trigon Major who was not impressed with my having followed the rules. I was promptly stripped to the waist, bound, gagged, blindfolded, and tied to a tree outside the tent as a POW, to await my rescue during the noon raid. It was very cold.

After the raid, I rejoined my patrol and found out the APL had flunked for leaving me out at that security halt, and the route phase PL had flunked for not taking a head count prior to leaving. I would have been ashamed for contributing to their no-go patrol if I'd fallen asleep, but I hadn't. They had left me, and we all knew never to leave a comrade. There is never an excuse for doing that, whether they are alert at their post, asleep, or dead. If 12 go in, 12 better come out.

It began to drizzle. Another OPORD had to be planned, this time for an ambush in the early morning hours. Staying awake and helping to plan this mission, and keeping the RTO job through the following route phase, I would be awake for about 48 hours. It rained steadily during that route phase, which was exceptionally miserable.

In the cold midnight rain, we left rucksacks and a security force in the objective rally point (ORP) to begin our leader's recon of the ambush site. I still had my ruck with the radio inside. The PL got completely lost trying to return to the ORP after locating the ambush site, and we wandered around for a while. I'll never forget the RI calling us all together and chewing out the PL for getting lost in the rain. He had flunked, and the RI ended his sermon in the dark by telling the PL, "Go 240 degrees for 350 meters." That took us to the exact center of our ORP, and I'll never know how that RI was so accurate.

Then we changed jobs again, and I got rid of the radio and became just another patrol member with the assault element. I was one very cold, soaked and miserable zombie.

Another long walk in the cold rain led to the next patrol base. At that point, Ranger students act on pure instinct, like shipwreck victims making shore after days at sea.

As dawn broke on the third morning of this patrol, the skies cleared and a serious cold snap set in. We were all soaked and eager to start walking. My attitude had improved just a little when I had enough time during the RI changeover to heat a canteen cup of water, dump a packet of sugar in it, and swig it down before leaving the base camp.

Little things mean a lot in Ranger School. My belly was now warm, and the sky was bright, cold, and clearing. I had put on dry socks. The longer we walked, the longer we stayed warm. But there is a trade-off sometimes. The longer we walked, and the colder it was, the more energy we burned and the less reserve we had. I was now going over 50 hours having slept only—at most—one hour, and that was in cold rain, half-submerged.

Sleep deprivation is used as an interrogation tool because of the resulting disorientation and loss of will power. The ability to make good decisions under those limitations is a prime factor.

At a late morning patrol base that third day, we linked up with another patrol, and after the following mission I would become the APL on an easy route phase to another patrol base that was walked mostly in the daylight. Shortly after sundown, the terrain got much steeper and rougher. My only wish was to complete successfully this grade phase and then fall fast asleep, even if I had to sleep while walking to the next objective. I began losing the struggle to remain awake sometime after dark, climbing in rocks, trees and cold.

I used every trick I could think of to stay conscious. Floated along as an alien observer watching someone's dream. Strange to see the students form a perimeter later in some dark woods. Detached and vaguely aware as the RI told a Ranger he was the new PL, and to go get whoever was to be the new APL. Released from duty, the dream continued as I slept on rock ground, wrapped in my space blanket, oblivious to the sub-freezing temperatures settling over the mountains like razor blades through my damp fatigues.

Sometime around midnight the dream ended and the nightmare resumed. We had a dawn raid at a river bend and had to leave now. I was thirsty and pulled out my canteen. The chunk of ice in it wouldn't pour into my mouth. My field jacket was in my rucksack, wet, and all I had on were frozen fatigues. I stuffed the space blanket into my ruck and stood quietly, waiting in the dark, shivering. I would have given a hundred-dollar bill for a hot cup of coffee that night.

It was now day four, three meals eaten, maybe three hours slept total in the past 72, pitch black, and the ground was crunchy with ice coming out in little pillars. I began not to like this place anymore.

At that point, I heard the RI quote poetry, saying, "The woods are lovely, dark and deep, and I have promises to keep, and miles to go before I sleep." I hated him, and through the fog of sleep deprivation, hypothermia, and hunger, I vaguely remembered having heard it somewhere else, and had memorized it at some point. Shivering, I remembered it had been written by, of all names, a poet named Frost. Auditory hallucination?

We walked a long way, crossed a waist-deep, icy river using a one-rope bridge. We all got soaked to our chests from slipping on the submerged rocks, and just before dawn had our raid across the hay field in the bend of the river. As we regrouped after sweeping across the objective, I could clearly smell cooking sausage and bacon, and hot syrup on the breeze. Olfactory hallucination?

Our pants were coated with ice. Thighs, feet, fingers, ears, and cheeks were alternately numb or on fire with cold.

Another hike and we reached another patrol base. Passed, somehow, my earlier APL route phase as a zombie. New RI, then another mission, but I don't remember a thing about it. Then another patrol base in the afternoon. The temperature had warmed up to around 40 degrees. My buddy and I basked in the sun, cleaned our M16s in a mental fog, quietly swapped Marty Robbins lyrics and enjoyed more John Wayne coffee from steaming canteen cups before we each, in turn, took a one-hour nap in this extended patrol base on the south side of a steep mountain. The nap left me no better off mentally.

Later, arriving in another patrol base well after midnight, some events stick out in my memory. One is the decision of our exhausted PL to choose red smoke as the emergency signal to evacuate the patrol base and move to a rally point. The RI jumped all over him and barked, "Ranger, do you really think you can see red smoke in the middle of the night?" The PL apologized and said, "OK, make it yellow smoke."

I won't repeat the RIs response to that, but a "smoking" recalibrated the PL.

That was to be a very rough route phase for me mentally. My thinking and reasoning were scrambled, and although I felt very "in touch," I knew I wasn't. "Losing it" is very scary when you know it is happening. I worried about when the next hallucination would hit, and if I would recognize it as such. Fortunately, there would be no more for me.

Remembering the last run of the "City Phase" and the lesson I'd learned then, I knew my mind would want to quit long before my body had to. I had paid too many dues so far to allow a mental issue to jeopardize my goal of earning the Tab. Prayer worked again.

So, one foot was placed in front of the other, for many miles. Then I slept while walking, dreaming I was walking while sleeping, and later I awoke leaning against a tree at a security halt far from where we started. I had taken a nap while walking. I don't understand how that happened, and I never want to experience it again.

I have no memory of that day or our missions, but I do remember the last night of our six-day patrol. My buddy and I were assigned LP (listening post) duty outside of the patrol perimeter about 200 feet. Our patrol consisted of 24 members, and there were three two-man LPs. Each LP was given a radio (AN/PRC-77) and was told to make a communications check every 30 minutes throughout the night. One of us was supposed to be awake at all times and report anything heard.

We had a plan. As soon as we reached our position, we gathered a lot of dead, dry branches and surrounded ourselves with these to alert us if anyone, especially an RI, tried to sneak up on us. I had a Seiko watch with an alarm buzzer, and after setting it to go off in 30 minutes, I wedged it between my ear and my patrol cap earflaps. We knew we'd be in this position most of the night because our last mission was a big event requiring a lot of planning and coordinating. It was time to catch up on some serious sleep!

Thirty minutes later the first of several commo checks was made. "LP two, over." "Roger two, out," came the brief reply.

So it went through most of the night. Buzzed awake, commo check made, reset alarm, sleep. After two hours I passed the watch to my buddy, and he continue with the 30-minute checks as I slept. I understand one meaning "Seiko" has in Japanese is "success." I agree.

Later the next day, our mission was completed. We returned to Camp Merrill to clean weapons and equipment again, and have a leisurely hot meal in the comfort of a real mess hall. It felt odd eating at a table from a tray, sitting in chairs. Later, after a hot shower, I found a sink and a mirror to use while shaving. About halfway through the shave, I looked closely at my face in the mirror. I, and my buddies, had been changed.

Fatigue, sleep deprivation, and constant cold and hunger had begun to take a very visible toll on us. Our eyes were set deeper in their sockets, and we had creases where there had been none before. We were now two-thirds through with this school, and as I thought of that I smiled wearily. And warily, for one very long third remained: the Florida phase.

Later, we again had the peer rating that knocked out some who had survived the long mountain patrols with passing grades. Some decided to quit. The others were recycled.

There are many other memories of events that happened during the patrols, but I'm not sure where they belong. Some of my favorites are:

Crossing high above a creek on a moss-covered wet log, balancing and hoping not to slip or fall, and all of us making it.

Walking blindly on a dark night in file formation and stepping into black midnight nothingness to tumble headlong down a steep embankment into a crumpled pile of buddies at the bottom, until all were piled up—except the RI—all the while trying to maintain strict noise discipline, and then hearing one finally whisper, "I'm gonna cuss big-time when this $#!+'s over, and it's gonna be real loud!"

From about 20 feet above, the RI told us, "Disregard verticality in your pace count, now drive on!"

The most enduring memory of the Mountain Phase for me is not the bone-penetrating environmental miseries we experienced, nor the individual physical and mental challenges of hunger, stress and sleep deprivation we each had to meet and overcome. It is the quality of sincere dedication to the craft of the US Army Ranger that was demonstrated consistently and constantly by the Instructors we had. They were the definition of the word "professional." Although I could not appreciate it at the time, as had other priorities, such as survival, I would later come to realize it was their uncompromising demands for professionalism and excellence, at all times and under all circumstances, that forged a real change in us.

The Swamp Phase

The 6th Ranger Training Battalion, located at Eglin Air Force Base in northwestern Florida, hosts the third phase of the Ranger Course—known as the Swamp Phase. The original student body is greatly reduced in size, and those remaining are running on adrenaline and determination.

Howard Denton

Our flight to Eglin was a nice nap broken about 30-minutes out by the news that, because of high winds at the drop zone, we would not be making a jump. As we who were Airborne de-rigged, we were glad our class would be together at the start of this phase. On landing, however, we noticed it was a beautifully clear, cool, and calm Florida autumn day, and there were trucks enough for the whole class already waiting at this airstrip. No wind and plenty of trucks added up to two things: this scenario had to be preplanned, and the RIs were up to something. A few students thought we were being paranoid, but then someone asked why we hadn't air-landed at the Florida Ranger Camp instead of on an alternate field requiring transportation to the Florida Ranger Camp (FRC). We soon found out.

About two miles short of the FRC, we were ambushed by the "Holly Gs," a local version of the guerilla forces we would be facing in this phase. No longer opposed by conventional Soviet-styled Aggressor Forces as we had been in the mountains, we were now facing the hit-and-run tactics of unconventional warfare. This was *very* different.

In the classrooms we learned how to reorganize our patrols, tactics, and missions, which were changed from what we had been accustomed to in the mountains, but we understood why and learned quickly.

We shifted to platoon-and-company level Ranger operations in this unconventional environment, and learned recon-in-force (RIF) operations, area recons, large scale raids, and various ambushes. These were named for their shapes: L-shaped, U-shaped, V-shaped, and the familiar linear already used in the mountains. All of these were then practiced in a large, open field where it was easier to understand.

Our rappelling classes were focused on preparing us for actual helicopter rappels from UH-1H and CH-47 helicopters. With loaded rucks and slung weapons, first from towers and later from helicopters, we practiced not just until we got it right—but until we could not get it wrong

We had other classes on subjects we needed to know for the upcoming exercise. Stream crossing techniques, aerial resupply, crossing danger areas, and calling for and adjusting artillery fire were easy refresher courses to those we'd already covered in the mountains and were modified for this environment.

During one of the artillery fire support classes we had, a group of former Rangers—many from WWII—arrived, and were introduced to us by the Instructor. I don't remember what the occasion was, but seeing those older men from a different era gave us a link to our Ranger past we all felt and deeply respected, like meeting previously unknown uncles who had been "the real deal." We held them in awe and silently appreciated their contributions to our great nation. It was an honor to be in the presence of those men.

Then came our introduction to the RB-7, the seven-man rubber boat, inflatable, or as we called it, the LBRB, for "little-bitty-rubber-boat." It was fun to train in. We practiced paddling in straight lines, turning, backing, and had many capsize drills in which we would practice turning over, and then righting the boat. All of this was in the Santa Rosa Sound, a calm body of water between the mainland and the barrier island next to the Gulf of Mexico.

The 13-day patrol was the "mother of all patrols" in Ranger School. It was the most discussed, most dreaded, most anticipated, most "everythinged" experience Ranger School had to offer. To begin with, the experience of almost two weeks of absolutely no contact with the outside world is not normal. Add to that having only one meal a day, walking about 30 miles each day with a heavy rucksack, and then getting only about two or three hours sleep a night, maximum.

Always wet, always whispering, always looking for those looking for us, usually moving, seldom stopping, sleeping, or resting, one mission leads to another and another, and time itself has no meaning except to coordinate and plan for the next mission. The day of the week is unknown and totally irrelevant. For two weeks, our world would be one of plants, streams, sand, swamps, silence, RIs and predatory guerilla forces seeking to cause us to fail this course.

At least the terrain was basically flat. No mountains, just miles of level distance.

By nightfall we were soaked, cold, hungry, and tired. We felt like Ranger students again. On the far side of the swamp we found some higher ground and reached our RON (remain-over-night) position. Pulling into a perimeter, we gathered into our three-man positions, began digging foxholes and working on the night's planning activities.

A three-man foxhole was an arrow-shaped fighting position with a two-man sleeping position on the backside. It allows one man to be alert in the five-foot deep triangular fighting position with his two buddies sleeping, protected from grazing fire, in the 18-inch deep sleeping position attached. If attacked, all three then occupy the fighting position. It looks like a fat arrow, pointing to the outside of the perimeter, and allows one-third security instead of the one-half security we had in the Mountain phase. Translated—more sleep time. Reality—extra sleep time taken up by time required to dig and to prepare. And, it had to be filled in prior to leaving the area.

Many memories of the Florida phase involve sculpting and filling sandy foxholes. I felt like a sugar cookie most of the time, only coated with sand, which is very abrasive.

Long before dawn we were up and had filled in our foxholes. Just prior to the RI changeover, I was counseled on my planning phase of the previous day. The RI had only one question for me. "What do you think you deserve, Ranger?"

Many positive thoughts about that planning phase went through my mind. I'd tried hard. My subordinates had worked well and had done their best, in my opinion. There was teamwork and we'd shared responsibilities. The mission was well planned, well rehearsed, and later well executed as a result of our efforts. But, I still had a nagging problem with his question about being willing to bet lives on the word of a subordinate that orders had been followed without having personally verified it, especially on the first patrol of the exercise.

"I screwed up, Ranger Sergeant," I finally admitted reluctantly, "because I did not personally check up on what my squad leaders told me about their equipment check." I was being honest, but I was hoping he'd cut me some slack for being honest and recognizing the fault.

He said, "They did not do their jobs, and they get a no-go on this patrol. You didn't make them do their job, and you also get a no-go. Men have died because of this on real missions. You're honest, and you won't make this mistake again, I'm sure."

And that was that. And he was right. I couldn't, and didn't, argue. Ranger School is, above all else, about no-excuse leadership. I remembered an earlier comment of his about, "If you are ever my Platoon Leader..." and I became determined to "trust but verify" from that day onward. Especially when it came to the little things.

The only thing I remember about Day Two is walking into a swamp and thinking, "There is no way to stay dry, just do it!" And we walked a long way in water ranging from our waists to our necks, and I was so glad to be over six-feet tall! We discovered the "cypress knees" under water, root projections that banged our shins and tripped us up.

It was surreal wading silently through the swamp. The water was cold and dark. The bottom we walked on was alternately soft under foot or shin busting hard with stumps.

Came time for an airborne insertion. Late one evening we loaded into a C-119 Flying Boxcar for a night jump. I thought those old birds were still in use only in the third world countries. It seemed to take the entire runway to take off, and then only after the plane rattled and shook and sounded like a bucket of bolts. I swore I'd never ride in or jump a C-119 again. We went through the familiar jump commands, then both clamshell doors opened, and when the green light came on we jumped into the night. The jump itself was great. The ride up was not.

About Day Seven a couple of students complained about stolen rations. The RIs were concerned and told us to put the cans in the bottom of our rucks instead of in a side pocket. Sometimes a class has a chow thief or two, one said, and if caught it means immediate dismissal from the course. As hungry as we were, dismissal wasn't going to be the first option we would allow. We decided a lynching would happen first.

Day Ten we were on a "recon in force" operation where we patrolled hoping to make contact with a guerilla force so we could smack them. In three days we would be finished, but each hour seemed to make things harder. We were clearly drawing on our last reserves of motivation, and most of us had lost between 20 and 30 pounds.

Ambushed! Contact right. We went into our immediate action drill for a near ambush and the RIs started tagging students with their walking sticks, saying, "You're dead, Ranger. Lie down and shut up," or "You're wounded, start yelling for help."

The student company commander, who was up for Honor Graduate, then realized we were now being attacked from behind, so he had the lead platoon in the first counter-ambush change to rear security, called for medevacs and fire support, and with dwindling numbers reversed our direction and began to fight out through the second ambush. The RIs kept "killing" students, and then "killed" his RTO.

The student CO dropped his ruck and picked up his RTO's ruck with the radio inside. I was "killed" and got to watch this choreographed ambush come to a finish.

The third ambush, from the right, had a group of about 50 sweep through us on line with at least six M60 machineguns blazing. The RIs had allowed the student CO to be the last man standing just to see what he'd do. His last act was to call in artillery and tactical air strikes on top of our position, as all but he were now "dead." I thought of Custer surrounded by dead men, but with an M60 in one hand and a radio handset in the other, calling in a world of fire as a last act of angry defiance. Then the RIs killed him, too, and they made us lie still for about five minutes. This part was just outstanding.

We heard the guerillas mocking us as they disappeared, then it got quiet. We were dead. The RIs were the only things moving, and they made sure we understood "dead."

We then went "admin", were called into a group, and were told to discuss freely all we had seen, what had happened, what we could have done and should have done, and we were encouraged to speak very freely. That was one of the best learning experiences I've had on tactics. The RIs shared some of their combat experiences, and for about 30-minutes we forgot about our hunger, fatigue, and misery, and focused on Rangering.

This had been a no-win scenario. We had been wiped out by about 200 men from a reinforced Rifle Company of the 101st Airborne Division. Most were combat veterans. Their execution of this ambush was professionally done in every detail. No wonder the RIs were killing us so fast. The student CO passed. Many, they said, froze up and panicked on this mission. Our exhaustion, while a significant factor, could never be allowed to become an excuse for sluggish response and subsequent failure.

Then we walked a considerable distance more and reached another RON site just before sundown. What followed I'll never forget.

On the eleventh day we just walked forever. Knowing we were down to two days did not make it any easier. I remember mumbling, "Only another few hours and then one more day. Just a few hours, then only one day left," and finally, " Just 100 meters more, just 100 meters." But we kept on walking and walking without stopping until well after dark. True exhaustion is both physical and mental.

The eleventh day just about did me in. There really is such a thing as being bone-weary. It's far beyond where anyone thinks it is. I had no reserves left. I was wasted.

Again, as I had done of the fifth run in the City Phase and on the fifth day of the six-day patrol in the mountains, I turned to the Big Ranger for assistance, and I was not left wanting. I remembered again about the mind quitting long before the body had to, and I got the help I needed so desperately. We somehow reached our RON site around midnight, were told to quickly dig foxholes, and then were told we'd be there until well after dawn planning our beach assault for the following night.

It was just after dawn when I awoke to find my buddy several feet above me gathering berries of some sort up in a bushy tree under which we had slept. He quietly whispered, "Huckleberries, hurry up and get some!" Quick math told me I had slept about six hours, and I was groggy but grabbed my canteen cup to help gather berries. We had a feast! I don't know what kind of berry we'd found, but I ate far more than I saved. Prayer works. I had been granted a full belly and more sleep at one time since starting Ranger School.

Then came the OPORD for the culminating exercise. We would have to go down the Yellow River in RB-7s to the East Bay, board a vessel to later rendezvous with a Coast Guard boat to board, be taken eight klicks out into the Gulf, and in the wee hours of the following morning we'd disembark to conduct a beach assault on Santa Rosa Island.

After the OPORD, we walked a short distance to the landing where our LBRBs were, loaded our rucks, and with weapons slung and seven to a boat, began paddling slowly westward down the Yellow River.

Just after dark, we found ourselves leaving the mouth of the river and entering into the bay. The RIs directed us toward a dark hulk a short distance away. Seems like it was an

LST (Landing Ship, Tank) or some other kind of WWII craft. It was very old and smelled of grease, paint, and diesel, but it was good to get out of the LBRBs and have metal under our boots instead of rubber. The LBRBs were towed behind as we lumbered toward the channel leading to the gulf and a rendezvous with the USCG vessel.

By the time we had to transfer to the USCG boat the weather had turned seriously bad. There was a rumor the beach assault would have to be cancelled. Moving onto the larger boat and heading out into the rainy, heaving Gulf made us feel the rumor would be true. Waves were 10-to-12-feet high, and the rain was coming down in torrents. Many began to get seasick and were hanging over the rails.

I think I checked my watch a thousand times during the next couple of hours, hoping somehow to speed up the dawn, but it didn't happen. What did happen, to our surprise, was the order to line up at the rail in boat order to prepare to re-board our LBRBs. A cargo net was draped over the side, just like in the movies, for our use to get into the heaving LBRBs waiting below in the waves.

I stared in disbelief at the little black boats bobbing up and down below. They would appear tiny at one time and in the next instant would rush up and seem close enough to touch. There was plenty of illumination, and the detail of each little inflatable was clear, even in the driving rain.

Climbing down the cargo net and timing the drop into the boat would be difficult, at best. The first student trying to get into our boat made a mistake. As the boat crested just beneath him, he let go of the cargo net and dropped at the same rate as the boat, landing on his back as the boat reached a trough about 12 feet lower. The second student was scooped off the cargo net by the rising boat and rolled ungracefully around in the bottom of it as it was whipped around in the waves. The rest of us learned from this and somehow got into the bucking boats, and our little wet rodeo began.

We all wore life vests, our LBRBs were tied to each other by 120-foot climbing ropes, and we, in turn, were tied to the little boats by our individual 12-foot ropes. Even in Ranger School, safety was an ever-present priority. We were miserable, but safely so!

Eight-clicks out into the Gulf of Mexico on a stormy night, trying to paddle to shore as quickly as possible through torrents of rain and 12-foot waves, is wretched. That's five miles from shore. Five miles. We yelled, cussed, fussed, sang, and even laughed as we paddled continuously northward in the dark rain, drenched, cold, and thinking, God all this would be over, one way or another, in a few hours.

We heard the surf in the distance long before we saw the dunes beyond. Not quite dark, but still not at all light, we found the waves we were riding suddenly getting larger as their energy reacted to the rising bottom. Still lashed to the other boats, ours was suddenly pulled sideways about the same time as we reached the surf, and we were all unceremoniously dumped into the swirling surf as our boat capsized in water well over our heads.

Our capsized boat rode the momentum of the wave into shallower water, dragging us with it. We stood up, dragged and then carried the boat well up beyond the water line, and I have never been more thankful to feel land under my feet. Now on the beach in the dim light, I could see I was surrounded by other sand-coated "sugar cookie" buddies, or more accurately, "sugar prunes." A quick head-count proved all were accounted for, and we formed a hasty defensive perimeter as we began to assemble under a clearing sky.

We were now pressed for time and had landed about two-klicks east of our objective. The sun was almost up. During the brief leaders' recon, the rest of us quickly cleaned the sand and surf from our M16s and prepared for the raid as best we could.

Soon the leaders returned, a few changes to the original plan were disseminated, and our force headed westerly just as the sun came up on a blustery November dawn.

The sunrise at our backs cast very long shadows in the sand toward our objective, just over a mile to the west. We moved fast and with a purpose. Only this mission stood between us and our return to the real world.

I was on the left flank of the attack and was supposed to come around from the beach side with my buddy and others in our squad, and while others were laying down a base of fire, we'd sweep up and over the south side of the objective as other squads came in from the north and east sides with their supporting fire. West of our objective, a blocking force was arranged from another platoon to prevent the Gs from escaping.

The defenders had expected us to come in from the west. They never saw us coming in from the sunrise. As my buddy and I ran up through a draw from the beach side, our others buds were swarming in from the north and sides with covering fire. As we overran a position, one guerilla said, "It's in there, man. Enjoy." We saw food!

My buddy and I had overrun a two-man guerilla position high on a sand dune secluded from view by shrubs, and the Gs we'd just "killed" immediately showed us a bag with about 20 C-rats inside.

We quickly looked around for RIs and saw none. These "dead" guys said they had heard stories about how hungry we'd be and wanted to help. What we saw was simply unbelievable! The first can I pulled out of the bag was labeled "Fruit Cocktail," the second "Date Nut Roll." I wanted to cry for joy.

The "dead" guerillas were laid back having a smoke as we began cramming cans of C-rat chow into our rucks—then it really hit us. This was IT! There were no more missions after this one, no need to hoard chow. We could leave all this and it would not matter at all. It was over!

Later we rated our peers again, and some had to recycle the Florida Phase for getting "peered" or for failing too many patrols. Early the next day, we loaded big commercial buses with soft seats for the ride back to Fort Benning. Like most, I slept the entire way.

"Uncle Burnie" was waiting for us as we disembarked from the buses. We became his "maggots" again, and we felt at home listening to his ranting about having to clean our weapons and all our gear, and how it still was not too late to flunk this school. As soon as we felt our gear was squared away we could turn it in and go to chow. Most of us were rejected many times before our gear passed inspection and we were finally allowed to eat.

Ranger Class 2-73 graduated at 1100 hours on 9 November 1972, on Todd Field. Our guest speaker was Colonel Guy S. Meloy, who in a few months would become my Brigade Commander in the 82nd Airborne Division, and would later become the Commandant of West Point. The Ranger Department Director at the time was Colonel David E. Grange, Jr., for whom today's legendary "Best Ranger Competition" is named.

Although I never saw him, in our class was Second Lieutenant Bradley Holmberg, my roommate in Jump School in August of 1970, when we were both ROTC cadets. Also in the class were Sergeant Bill Acebes, a "Merrill's Marauder Award" winner and later president of the US Army Ranger Association, and Staff Sergeants O'Dell McGee and Fred Weekley, all three of whom I had the privilege of working with later in the 82nd. I've never known finer NCOs. They were *Rangers*.

In our class were students ranging from two-tour Vietnam Special Forces veterans (Prince Bow-Wow) to officers and enlisted men from Singapore, to "cherry" Second Lieutenants (me), to 18-year-old E-4s. The day we signed into Ranger School we became equals. The day we graduated we joined a brotherhood: US Army Rangers.

Rangers Lead The Way

Jack Daniel

A Hall of Fame member and influential Ranger with a long and interesting history, Jack Daniel went through Ranger School in December 1954 to February 1955. He became a Ranger Instructor at the Florida Camp in 1955-56. These are his words, some recorded before a meeting of the Mountain Ranger Association at Camp Frank Merrill and some over the telephone.

The Florida Camp was started in 1952 or 1953, because Bull Simons was the first Camp Commander.

The sequence was different than it is now. From Fort Benning, we went to Florida, and from Florida we went up to the mountains.

The second commander of the Florida camp was Lt. Colonel Harold "Duke" Slater, who had been CO of D Company, 2nd Ranger Battalion, on D-Day. Third came Lt. Colonel Robert Dexter, and that's where Daniel came into the camp as a Lieutenant. First Sergeant Dubrill, a Korean War Ranger, ran the NCOs.

It was the greatest training I ever got in my life. We did small-unit tactics. I learned more about small unit tactics than anybody could. The fact is we were in smaller [than today] patrols. We had recon and combat patrols, of course, but they were not as large. We had about four problems. Operations that were recon, and I think there were two or three combat patrols.

They call the Cadre a company at Fort Benning. I guess we had maybe 30 NCOs and enlisted personnel as Cadre in the Florida Camp. We must have had maybe 20 officers as RIs. It was right after the Korean War, and everything had to be certified by an officer, which was a bunch of bullshit. We only had three or four of our NCOs down there that were what we called Lane Graders (Ranger Instructors). Unless an NCO was in combat in Korea he couldn't be a Lane Grader. It was a waste of personnel.

Daniel said the older NCOs would listen to his critiques and make suggestions. Since he wasn't combat-experienced he had to prove himself before the vets would accept him.

Then we had an Aggressor Company that they sent down. They were from the 29th Infantry.

They spoke Esperanto, or that's what they were supposed to speak. You ever heard of Esperanto? [Yes, Sir, I said, though I had no idea where it came from]. But they really didn't speak that, they just made out like they did.

The question was, is there anything hugely different then than now, excluding technology?

In some ways we were a lot more realistic. Like, for instance, we used to go out and shoot wild hogs and put them in the wire before the students got out there. So when they got out to the OP they could smell the rotten bodies out there [pigs and people smell about the same]. We were a lot rougher on the students than they are now. For instance, the Aggressors would capture some of them. They'd tie them up, blindfold them, and put them in a pit with snakes. Little Pine snakes and like that, non-poisonous.

Such things are no longer done. Is that good or bad?

Jack then talked about "unlimited pushups."

I was at Field Seven, it's torn up, not there anymore. Then I moved to Field Six. It had the old wooden barracks. The Ranger Candidates were separate. They were in, I think, two billets, or three, depending on the size [of the class]. When I went through the course they had tents.

They had a regular mess hall. We had the greatest food in the Army. When we were in garrison we had a ration-and-a-half.

Daniel wrote these quotes in an email, detailing some of the course at the Florida camp.

Field Number Seven—Scouting and Patrolling from the Base. Tactical Problem # 8707; boats down the Yellow River to recon enemy rocket sites on "Whitmire Island," followed by a "rope drop."

Amphibious training and amphibious operation from Gulf Island to Santa Rosa Island, then across the Sound—leave boats and move inland to destroy rocket site. Return, get boats across the Sound, and then portage across island and go out to meet Naval or Air Force vessels.

Later, we conducted the "Island Raid" hitting radar sites—run by Cadre.

During this period—1955-56—we trained the first Vietnamese Ranger Class, and also trained the first class of USMC Recon. The class CO was Major Rice.

Mountain Ranger Students 2004

It is not easy to get to talk to a Ranger student. They are extremely busy during each phase of training, except for the last day before making the transition to another camp, and then they are only seriously busy. On top of that, they are generally so exhausted only a few can make much sense of either questions or answers.

Camp Merrill XO, Major Lange, gave us SFC Daniel Barnes and gave him the list of students we wanted to talk to—a Battboy ("born" in the Regiment), someone with a combat tour, and an officer from outside the Regiment. SFC Barnes got all three.

Since there are three, the questions will be presented along with their answers. The Ranger students—two of whom were already in the Regiment—were PFC Peter James Baker (3/75), E4 George Wines (1/75), and 2nd Lt. Wright (fresh out of IOBC). Both Wines and Baker had already been overseas in combat.

Q: What is foremost on your mind right now?

Wines: The next 10 days in Florida. We're on a very tight schedule, and if anything goes wrong, we won't jump.

Q: Have you got any non-Airborne soldiers in this class?

Baker: Probably about a fourth of them.

Generally the survivors of the Mountain Phase parachute into the next phase—the Florida Camp—but sometimes weather or other factors negate the jump. In any case, the non-Airborne students are usually taken by truck ("a nice four-hour truck ride") to Florida.

A fourth of the students being "legs"—a semi-derogatory slang word for non-Airborne — is not unusual today as it was years back. To be in the Ranger Regiment one must be Airborne-qualified, but many of today's students are from other specialties and do not require jump wings, such as an officer in a tank battalion, or an artilleryman.

Q: Let's talk about RIP (three-week Ranger Indoctrination Program taken when entering the Regiment fresh from Airborne School). Did you also go through Pre-Ranger before coming here?

Wines: First we went to our unit [after RIP]. You've got to spend some time with your unit before they think you're ready for Ranger School. The 75th Regiment puts on a Pre-Ranger program for about three weeks. You complete that; you come right to Ranger School.

That makes 12 weeks of straight training.

Q: When is the last time you slept eight hours?

Wines: [rolls his eyes up] A long, long, time ago.

Q: Private Baker, what was your immediate impression of RIP?

Baker: I'd say my immediate impression was when the Cadre walked out in their black Ranger PTs [shorts and t-shirt for physical training] and that just stood out in my mind, you know, you just knew your chain of command right away. You're just intimidated right away, and initially they just break you down and build you up.

Baker looked to his fellow students for help, and they all did from time to time. The spirit of the Ranger brotherhood was well underway.

Q: How long were you in the Regiment before you went through RIP?

Baker: I was there about three weeks.

Q: Then how long before you went to Pre-Ranger?

Baker: About eleven months.

During that time Baker went and fought for his country as a "Scrolled," but not "Tabbed" Ranger.

Q: What did you do in the meantime?

Baker: I was deployed to Afghanistan.

Q: Can you tell me where you were? [Baker gives a headshake] North or south?

Baker: North.

Q: (to Wines) You were in Afghanistan?

Wines: Iraq twice, Afghanistan once.

Wines, like Baker and many other Rangers, was deployed on missions that took anywhere from a couple of months to two or three weeks. The concept of a "tour of duty" for Special Operations soldiers depends on the duty. Rangers are not occupation troops.

Trying to gain information from recent combat veterans is like asking a teenager what they did last night—besides grimaces, shrugs, and mumbling, you get a whole lot of nothing. Plus, SFC Barnes was sitting right there, listening to every word, making sure of security.

Q: (to 2nd Lt. Wright) Did you go through any kind of pre-course before you came to Ranger School?

Wright: They say IOBC is like a pre-Ranger course. You see a lot of the same things.

Q: Do you expect to deploy when you get out of here?

Wright: I'm going to the 1st ID. They're scheduled to go back to Iraq.

Q: So, where do you go from there? What's your MOS (military occupation specialty)?

Wright: I picked Infantry [11B] so I can switch back and forth; heavy, light, Airborne, I can do it all.

Q: Career?

Wright: Probably.

Q: How about you guys? Career?

Wines: I change my mind about every other week.

Baker: Yes.

Q: You guys who were in combat, when you come to Ranger School, do you feel like you don't really need this, or are they teaching you something new?

Wines: You definitely gain leadership—especially in this phase, maybe not as much as Darby, but this phase seems to be twice as stressful. I felt more stressed-out here than in combat as a Private. You trust your leadership [in the Regiment] so much it's easy to follow them. But here, you're in charge [everybody rotates through leadership positions]. I mean, it's not a combat situation, but you still have to lead men, and when you've never done that before, it can be stressful.

Q: How did you feel as a Private leading the Lieutenant here?

Baker: That's the great thing about the school, there's no rank right away.

Q: Did you know he was a Lieutenant?

Baker: Yeah, you know who the officers are because they're usually the ones writing your operations orders.

Q: (after some general discussion about techniques and methodology) Did you get here thinking you knew what you needed to know?

Wines: I think the techniques you get in this school, you can take them or leave them, but overall they teach you leadership. I think that's the big key. When I came here as a Private, I'm yelling and screaming and telling officers what to do, what direction…it gave me confidence to take on a leadership role. I think that's what you [get most] from the school.

Q: When you guys were deployed overseas did you work primarily in small groups, and did you do any large element stuff?

Baker and Wines: We were in small groups.

Q: You come back here and see them doing a fake IED [improvised explosive device] out here, how does that compare with the real thing?

Baker: I've never been in a live IED. They're not common, well; they're not as common.

By 2006 that had changed.

Baker: They're using det cord to initiate the IED [in training], something loud, but I think in real life it would be twice as shocking to react to.

Wines: I've reacted to one. We got the hell out of there.

Wright: I think when it's real you've really got a lot more chaos, and maybe you've got a guy that's a real-world casualty.

There followed a brief discussion of medical training and it was agreed there was "a pretty good amount for the average line-guy in the Ranger Battalions."

Q: (to Baker) What do you do in the battalion?

Baker: I'm an AG [assistant gunner for the M240 machinegun].

Q: Do they still call them maggots? Heavy weapons people?

Baker: No. We've got ammo bitches and AGs.

Wines: I'm a Gunner/AG. Just depends on the circumstances. Also a 240.

Q: Lieutenant, what were you doing prior to coming here?

Wright: Actually I was a 19-Kilo, a tanker. I agreed [to change to] 11-B [Infantry], go to IOBC, and I've been at Fort Benning since January. Tried to get into the Rangers before, but there were too many people, but I finally got in, and here I am.

Q: How is it?

Wright: How is it? It was cold. A couple of days ago it rained all day.

A discussion followed, including input from SFC Barnes, our PAO, about how cold Florida could be in the winter because the students are often wet. In truth, stories told to the author about the coldest phase often center on Florida and not the mountains, at least in the winter.

Further discussion ascertained all three men have either spent time in, or lived in, mountainous terrain. Lieutenant Wright was already a climber when he got to the Mountain Phase.

Q: How did that affect you here?

Wright: I love the climbing. It's different climbing in military gear. It makes an easy climb a lot more challenging.

Q: How much do you guys hump?

Wines: I guess with guns it's around 60 to 80 pounds.

Baker: If your ruck's wet you can add another 15 to that.

A discussion of ruck/equipment weight from WWII to present ensued, whereupon SFC Barnes said the amount of weight per man depended on the amount of cross-loading. That is, there is a certain amount of unit equipment to carry (ammo, radio batteries, etc) and most of the men "should" be carrying about 90 to 100 pounds, including their weapons and boots. Baker said Assistant Gunners (himself) and RTOs (radio men) carry the most. Nobody argued.

Q: You've been through Pre-Ranger or IOBC, the Benning Phase, and now here. You look like you're about to fall asleep (with Florida to go). Do you think you're going to make it through?

Wines: Yeah. Eventually. I don't really have an option. I've got 10 more days out in the field. Keep my ass out of trouble and I'll be good to go.

Wright: Absolutely.

Baker: I'm going straight through.

Q: How would you rate this school? Did you learn something here? Other than getting a Tab, was it worth coming?

Wines: I guess I really learned leadership.

Baker: You learn a little bit about yourself. I mean, I definitely did on deployment, too, but...

It was generally agreed that the Mountain Phase stretches the breaking point. The question was asked, "How strong are you?" No one cared to answer directly, but all three were headed to Florida.
Bob McMahon

This interview was recorded over the telephone in November 2005. McMahon is a well known retired Ranger, and served at the Mountain Ranger Camp as much or more than anybody.

I joined the Army in January 1953. The main reason was I couldn't get a decent paying job. Every time I tried they'd tell me I was draft age, and they'd get me trained and the next thing they knew I'd be gone. So I said the heck with it, I'll just go in the Army and get it over with.

I went to Basic at Fort Hood, Texas. We were being trained as a "package" company for Korea. But before Basic was finished, the war was winding down and they decided not to send us. Everybody did the original eight weeks of Infantry Basic, and then they took some of us and put us in different places, like commo and medics and transportation for our second eight weeks. I wound up as a Medic and stayed there at Fort Hood. I worked in the pharmacy and as a lab tech.

I put in for OCS to be commissioned as a Medical Services Corp Officer. I finished the first eight weeks, what they called Hell Weeks, and I was having a problem with my map reading, believe it or not. I could not show how I arrived at the answers I could work out in my head, like the grid declination. They wanted me to put it on paper and I couldn't do it. I could work it in my head and get it right.

They were going to recycle me and put me back in the first week, but I said I'd just go see what they had in Personnel.

It is interesting how these men got to be Rangers. In this case it was good for the Rangers because he became an outstanding Instructor of Mountaineering for many years, instead of a Medical Officer.

Personnel wanted to put me in the hospital over there working in the pharmacy. I told them I'd rather have outside work. A Warrant Officer, I'll never forget him. Mr. Celko. He said, "How about working on the [firing] ranges?" I said not really, I didn't care that much for the gunfire. Then he said, "I know what you need. You need to go to the Rangers."

I said, "Rangers? Are they here?" He said, "Yeah, they're over at Harmony Church." He made me an appointment with Colonel Sadler, who was the Assistant Director of the Ranger Department at the time. I had an interview with him and they accepted me.

He explained the [other two] camps to me and asked me where I'd like to go. He also told me if I made the wrong decision that he might change it. I said I came out of north Texas and I hadn't seen the ocean, so I'd like to go down there. He said, "Well, I'm going to send you to the mountains."

That's how I wound up in the mountains [in 1953].

The Benning Phase was 21 days, the guys would leave there and go to Florida, and then they would go to the mountains. But, they had to change that a little later on because when they went to Florida first, they got their feet messed up from being in the water all the time. When they got to the mountains and started climbing and walking those hills, it tore their feet up.

McMahon's first job at the mountain camp in November 1953 was dishwasher.

I was a PV2. I got in a little trouble with the First Cook, and they decided I needed to be out of there because I had a temper. The put me to driving a ration truck between the Ranger Camp and Fort McPherson in Atlanta. We were at Camp Wahsega, the 4-H camp. They had just moved there [from the original camp at Pine Valley] at the beginning of that year. During the summer the 4-H people used the camp, and we lived there during the wintertime. In the summer they moved up to Black Farms where the camp is now and lived in GP Medium tents. They had wooden floors and wooden frames with a tent over it.

McMahon earned his Ranger Tab on March 31, 1955.

Before that happened, SFC Clyde Grizzle and I volunteered for the course. That was in the summer of '54. We finished the Benning Phase and there was an allocation for two people to go Mountain Instructor's Course at Camp Carson, Colorado. We were already in Fort Benning, so they decided we were the two volunteers. We didn't really want to go, but we went anyway, of course. Once we got out there, it was wonderful. It was an instructor's course, lasted eight weeks, and Clyde and I both had a ball out there. The main reason we were picked is because we were from the mountain camp and they wanted to extend, or increase, the mountaineering up there. Until we got back from Carson, the only thing they were doing was mainly rappelling and knot-tying. When we got back, they had us help write the vault files for the training and give classes to the Cadre at the camp on what we learned.

Before we got back, all they had was rope bridges and rappelling, and the bridges were mainly for crossing streams and things. We started [things] like the vertical hauling line, parachute rescue out of trees, basic hand-holds and foot-holds, rock climbing, and advanced rappelling.

We demonstrated some advanced climbing techniques, like tension climbing and stuff like that, but as the years went on we started having them do it, also. We didn't have an area to do tension climbing where there was enough rock. We didn't have a mountain.

That was before they began to practice at Mt. Yonah, as well as in the Lower Mountaineering Area just east of the camp. Tension climbing involves a man holding a line steady from below while the climber ascends a sheer face or goes up under an overhang.

They had the same things they have now as far as different problems. They had the same things to work on. The first thing was daylight recon up to the TVD [Tennessee Valley Divide] and back, then they had an ambush problem, then a combat patrol on the other side of the TVD, where they went in and took out mortar or rocket positions. The last problem was usually when they went all the way to Blue Ridge, where they'd blow the dam or the power plant at the lake.

From what I understand they don't move as far as we used to move, and they don't have all the extra-curricular harassment we had back in the '50s.

He was given orders for Korea in 1956 and became an Instructor at the NCO school there.

I was assigned to I Corps. I had an Instructor's MOS at that time. I was an E-5. I went down and interviewed and got accepted. I had three days of instruction to give. I taught School of Soldier with and without arms, which was mainly Manual 22-5, the drill and ceremonies manual. I did that for six months. The last 12 months over there I was with L

Company, 21st Infantry, 24th Division as a Weapons Platoon Sergeant. We had 60mm mortars and 57mm recoilless rifles.

Still an E-5, I wound up back at the Ranger camp. It was [early] 1959 when I came back. I stayed there until 1962 on the Mountaineering Committee. I taught all the classes we taught there. We broke down into groups and each one of us had our own [specialty] we worked with. I taught handholds and footholds and basic climbing classes.

We were at Black Farms [where the camp is today] at that time. They still had the GP Medium tents. The mess hall was a semi-permanent building. It was wooden. The supply room, orderly room, was two tents put together. Motor pool had a semi-permanent building that was built by Andy Howard and Major Stevens.

After a stint as an E-6 LRRP in Germany, McMahon was sent back to the mountain camp in 1966 where he received orders for Vietnam. More of his story is in that section.

Earl Singletary

The following is an excerpt from a longer interview recorded in Singletary's kitchen in 2005.

When I was an Instructor there [twice], you'd have four platoons, three would be Airborne, and you'd have one platoon that would be 33 guys that were "Legs". We even had Instructors that weren't Airborne—not many—but in order to draw special pay they were either Airborne or Demolition, and they drew Demo pay. We had three or four guys [like that].

Back in those days [mid-late 60's, early '70s] there were something like 1500 enlisted Rangers in the Army. If you take half of those, or almost half, they were in the Ranger Department as Instructors. Scatter the rest of those out in Vietnam and there weren't a lot of them left when they started forming the first battalion.

A lot of Instructors wanted into the 1st Battalion, but the Ranger Schools wanted them to stay put. Premium Instructors were hard to come by.

I worked a deal with the Sergeant Major [CSM Neal] Gentry of the battalion. I said, look, I really want to be in this battalion. He said, "Look, I want you, but we can't touch Instructors. Tell you what we'll do. How long you been there?"

I had been there [Camp Merrill] almost four years. It was time for me to do something else. He said he would get me on orders for Germany, go ahead and clear, then we'll get you a deferment and assign you to the battalion. That's the plan. Well, that happened. We got me on orders for Germany. Sergeant Major found out, Jones, here in the mountains, what was going on, and he got me a deferment and kept me in the mountains.

EVOLUTION OF RANGER TRAINING CAMPS

In the early 1950s there were no Ranger Training Battalions as we have today, but there were groups of Ranger Cadre spread throughout the training system in several places. The current Ranger Training Brigade began in 1950 as the Ranger Training Center, and quickly became the Ranger Training Command on April 5, 1951. Later it was known as the Ranger Department.

The current Ranger student begins his journey through the Ranger Course at Fort Benning (City Phase), travels to north Georgia (Mountain Phase), and then drops into the Florida Camp near Eglin Air Force Base (Swamp Phase). That's now. Various training grounds have been located at Dugway, Utah; Fort Bliss, Texas; Fort Carson, Colorado; Twenty-Nine Palms, California, and other places, but the one constant in Airborne Ranger training is Fort Benning. Ranger classes start at Fort Benning and graduate at Fort Benning.

The original Cadre totaled 29 men—barely a platoon. From there Cadre were organized into companies, and finally, into battalions. However, the battalions field about 250 men—far short of the size of a combat battalion, but bigger than a company.

Class sizes have risen steadily, beginning at a few dozen men and growing to "heavy classes" of 250.

Likewise, training methods have changed with the times according to battlefield need. The first Cadre were Korean War veterans—now they are experienced in Iraq and Afghanistan. The focus of training had changed, and also the methods of measuring the effects of that training. Ranger Instructors are doing more mentoring than yelling these days. Students must not only prove their physical capabilities, but must also excel mentally—hard enough under the circumstances.

The following interviews and histories indicate the changing trends, fashioned to meet changing global threats.

Camp Frank D. Merrill is featured prominently here, mostly because the author lives five miles away. No disrespect is intended to the City Phase or the Swamp Phase, both fine posts. In truth, training standards are the same for all three camps.

How Long At Each Camp?

Time frames looked like this in 2004:

The Ranger Course is 61 days in length, with an average of 19.6 hours of training each day, seven days a week. That amounts to 20-hour days for two months of anguish and pain, and they volunteer for that. At different times the course has run from 58 days to 70.

The City Phase at Fort Benning is 20 days long, conducted by the 4th Ranger Training Battalion, much of it at Camp Rogers and Camp Darby.

The Mountain Phase is 21 days long and conducted by the 5th RTB in Lumpkin County, Georgia at Camp Frank D. Merrill—up north, in the mountains.

The Swamp Phase at Camp James E. Rudder at Eglin Air Force Base in Florida runs 18 days, and is conducted by the 6th RTB. From there the students go back to Fort Benning for graduation.

The idea is for them to parachute in, but sometimes they have to ride back in buses.

Two days of the course are consumed by travel, maintenance, in/out processing and graduation.

Keith Nightingale

Nightingale is featured in several places in this project. Here he talks about the Ranger Training Brigade. He was inducted as a Distinguished Member of the RTB in 2006.

When I commanded the RTB the primary difference was that we had a Desert Phase at Dugway Proving Ground. This was Ken Leuer's [Commander, 1st Battalion] initiative and was primarily designed to inculcate the value/principle of live fire exercises as we learned in the Rangers. It was a great idea and I still believe would have great value. However, the costs associated with airlift as well institutional opposition eventually killed it. I suspect it would receive a better reception now.

As a student, you are unaware of the issues that have to be managed as the RTB Commander. In terms of totality of impact and graduate quality, probably pretty much the same. My issues as the commander centered primarily around attrition issues, insuring quality instruction and soldier safety. I also had the LRSU and Sniper programs to manage, which probably did not exist when I was a student.

The three phases of the Ranger Course are in vastly different environments.

Each location provided a unique and challenging environment, which was very important for both student adjustment as well as Cadre scenarios. Depending on the time of year and weather, any [place] could be a tremendous mental and physical challenge or a break. I have always contended that Ranger School is 90 percent mental and 10 percent physical, though the student would claim the opposite at the time.

Jack Daniel

The beginnings of post-Korean War Ranger training were not always on solid ground.

We almost lost the Ranger Department. If it hadn't been for a guy by the name of John J. Dalton they would have destroyed the Ranger Department. There were so many Regular Army people that wanted to do away with it. It wasn't West Point; it cut across the line. There were plenty of Regular Army West Pointers who were all for the Rangers, then there were others who didn't want to see the Rangers, because they couldn't hack it.

When I went through the Ranger Course I went through as a Winter Ranger, in January and February 1954. The obstacles courses you had to negotiate were done at the respective camps. You had the rope-drop in Florida. We went through the Florida Phase first, then the Mountain Phase. It was white all the way. Nothing but snow. The camp, I think, was at Wahsega [4-H Camp now]. We didn't know where we were. From the time we got on the bus, we were so exhausted. We went from Florida straight up to the Mountain Camp. It was colder than a well digger's rear end in the Klondike.

They didn't have the Slide for Life then. When we went off the Death Slide, they had it on a lake. I've never seen that lake since [it's in Union County]. We climbed up a tree and the wind was blowing it so hard, it was a task climbing the rope ladder up that tree. There was a platform up there. They told us to put our cap in our jacket.

They had this hook, and they told you, if you don't do anything else, drop when you see the red flag. The ice had been broken off that lake. I have never had such a shock of cold. It went straight up my rear end.

Picture a frozen lake with a cable running diagonally above it from the ground on one side to a good height in a tree on the other. Hanging from the cable is a hook connected to a very fast pulley. You hold on to the hook, pick up your feet, and bye-bye. We're told the velocity reached on the trip down can approach the sound barrier. At the appropriate time (before you hit the tree trunk on the other side of the lake) you are given a signal to drop. Sometimes the lake is frozen. Various forms of the slide have been used all over Rangerdom.

Bill Spies—Walking Lanes

Walking Lanes is the same as a Lane Grader, now called a Ranger Instructor. In grading students, we use a Patrol as the organization. Each Patrol has a prescribed lane to stay within. Some lanes may have only one objective to either recon or to attack, snatch a prisoner, or retrieve a hostage. Other lanes may have several objectives. The lanes are control devices for safety and to keep the Patrols separated.

I was never assigned to Florida or the Mountain Camp. In 1963-64 I was assigned to the Patrolling Committee at Benning. Myself and two other officers did "Walk Lanes" (be Ranger Instructors) at all three Ranger Camps during those 18 months I was in the Ranger Department. I walked lanes three times in Benning, twice in the mountains, and twice in Florida. We went to those camps when they were short handed, or had exceptionally large classes.

From August 1973 to March 1976, I was the Operations Officer of the Department. In March of 1976, I was assigned as the Chief of the Benning Phase (now 4th Ranger Training Battalion Commander). Colonel Bowers, the Deputy Director, told me that I would also be his Deputy Director. So, officially I wore those two hats until February 1978.

During this time there was a radical change in the system used to evaluate students.

In that the Army was changing from distributive/norm referenced grading (averaging all scores to pass a course) to criterion referenced testing (Go or No Go), and changing from Lessons Plans and "teaching points" to "Performance Oriented Training" (state the Task, Condition, and pass the Standard), which I had become very familiar with.

Bowers told me that I would "run" the Operations and he'd take care of the admin and supply. Usually the XO/Deputy "ran/supervised" the admin & supply and the Commander "ran" the Operations. Thus, getting all three camps changed over to the new methods fell on me. Bowers resisted/refused to make the change, claiming we could not teach and grade leadership that way. Thus, the Ranger Department was the last of the seven departments to get fully changed over.

For years the Ranger Department, in addition to the three Ranger Camps, had two other Branches—also known as Committees: Patrolling and Combat Conditioning. The three Camps and Patrolling were led by an Lt. Colonel; CCC called for a Major, in my time.

The Patrolling Committee was the largest of the three. In addition to helping put on the Rangers in Action, some of its Cadre, as did I, also walked lanes in the three Ranger Camps when needed. It conducted the Battle Field Infiltration/Indoctrination Exercise where OCS and the Infantry Officer Basic Course (IOBC) Students crawled about 100 yards under live machinegun fire during daylight and again at night.

It taught SERE (Survival, Evasion, Resistance, and Escape) to OCS, IOBC, and the Advance Infantry Officer Course. SERE included classroom work (Code of Conduct as a POW, survival as a POW, and navigation by stars, etc) and the E&E Course (about an 8-mile trek evading "Aggressors"/Opfor with dogs), and if caught the student spent about an hour in a "POW" Compound.

The AIOC students did not run the E&E Course, but were taught in a classroom how to conduct one. The OCS and BIOC classes all spent a week in the woods, organized as patrols, and were graded exactly as Ranger students, only at a lesser level, as the leaders in a patrol during that week. The RIs stayed with the student for the entire week. The students were rotated into leader slots; at least two grades were required, as we do Ranger students.

It was not as physically challenging as the Ranger Course. They got four to six hours of sleep every 24 hours and three meals of C-rations each day. It was a very important week to the students. The grades were weighted very heavy in selecting Distinguished Graduates and one could get recycled, or even denied a commission if his performance was extremely low. Patrolling Cadre did not enjoy the prestige of the Ranger Cadre but they influenced many, many more people, and I feel they had a great impact on the Army. During the Vietnam War, the Patrolling Committee worked in Stewart and Quitman counties, just south of Fort Benning, and it had more Infantry Captains assigned at one time than were in Germany—about 120. That was when the Army had the Instant NCO Courses, about 10 a year, six OCS classes and 16 BIOC classes a year. I do not recall how many AIOC classes came then.

The Aggressors/Opfor soldiers did not belong to the Ranger Department as they now do. They came from "Support Troops" units on Main Post and spent a week with Patrolling, or a cycle with the Ranger Camps. Some were extra good and some were a real headache. Some had good vehicles and equipment; some had trash and were trashy.

The CCC, Combat Conditioning Committee, taught and led OCS, BIOC, & AIOC in Physical Training (the Daily Dozen), Unarmed Combat (Hand-to-Hand), and Fighting with a Bayonet, both by hand and on a rifle. It was the smallest of the three. I am not aware of its Cadre walking lanes as RIs until they were transferred full time to Ranger or Patrolling, and were "murdered" as an RI.

To walk Lanes—be an RI—one had to pass being tested by understudying an RI on a couple classes. Then the committee would act as students and the candidate had to "RI" them through an entire Patrol and grade and council each as if they were students.

All RIs had to pass the "Murder Board" before being allowed to walk lanes.

You'd find it hard to believe the small number of Cadre we had back then in the Camps and in the Department. During Vietnam, we did up to 16 Ranger classes a year, plus 20 IOBC and 10 OCS classes with less than 300 Cadre in the entire Department, except when Patrolling got a big influx of Infantry Captains. Then the Department had about 400.

I was in Patrolling in 1963 and 64. We did 11 IOBC and four OCS Classes a year, plus three of us walked Lanes in all three camps, we provided demonstrators for the Rangers in Action, taught classroom classes, and we had less than 20 Cadre, total, in the committee.

As the Chief of Benning, neither I, nor any of the Camp Commanders were given credit for command time as they now get. We kept requesting it, so it finally did happen. Just before I took Benning, we consolidated all the Benning people under one Lt. Colonel. He had several Majors assigned.

I spent from June 1976 to February 1978 as both the Chief of Benning and the Deputy Director—wearing both hats at the same time. Both jobs were Lt. Colonel slots. I had no other Field Grade to help me, as the Colonel and I were the only Field Grades in the Department here at Benning. I believe I am the only individual, of any rank, to have worn both of those hats at the same time. I am honored to be able to say that.

John Lange

Major John Lange was the Executive Officer of the 5th RTB at the time of this interview, recorded in his office in October 2004.

The 4th Ranger Training Battalion is headquartered at Fort Benning, and they conduct the initial portion of Ranger training, which is largely individual skills and collective skills at the squad level. Collective squad level combat and reconnaissance patrolling—the basics.

It's called City Phase because you're living at Camp Rogers [near a city], but that's RAP week, it's Ranger Assessment week. They go through a series of individual tasks, and that's the initial winnowing process. They do the Darby Queen [huge obstacle course], they do night and day land navigation, they do combat water survival test [CWST], they do a five-mile run, they do a 12-mile timed road march, they do combatives, they do basic Airborne refresher. They do a series of individual soldier tasks that validates their individual level of training before they progress into the squad level collective training.

Then they go out to Camp Darby [on the periphery of Fort Benning, more in the woods] to do field training, and they do much like we do. They have formal instruction in the field environment on techniques, and then they go out and do practical exercises that culminate in a field training exercise where they're actually evaluated.

Ranger School begins and ends at Fort Benning. After Florida the students go back to Benning for graduation. The HQ of the Ranger Training Brigade is there.

For a Ranger student to pass the City Phase and go on to the Mountain Phase, they have to pass all those individual skills, all the physical tests, the Ranger stakes [individual soldier skills, including setting up claymore mines, rappelling, doing radio work, etc.], plus they have to receive at least one "go" on an evaluated position during the FTX.

Typically Ranger students are going to get two opportunities to be in a graded position. It's a "go or no go" standard, and they have to get at least one "go" to come to our phase.

5th Battalion then picks them up, and we focus on mountaineering techniques, and then transition from squad-level combat reconnaissance patrolling techniques to platoon-level collective patrolling techniques. The 22 days a guy spends in the Mountain Phase are broken down [the mountaineering part] into five days of military mountaineering techniques training, some of which is conducted right here at Camp Merrill, at the lower mountaineering training area [the Lowers], and two days spent actively climbing on the cliff face at Mount Yonah. The first goal is to give these guys hands-on experience in techniques that can be used in a variety of situations, not just in the Alps or in the high mountain ranges of Pakistan or Afghanistan. They are techniques that would be useful to an infantry platoon in a variety of theaters.

In 2004 some soldiers from Tajikistan (borders Afghanistan on the north) spent some time at the Mountain Camp, but they weren't impressed by the height of Georgia mountains. They found somewhat belatedly that Ranger School teaches small-unit combat tactics in a challenging environment, and is not intended to replace the Vermont Mountain Warfare Center as a specialty school. In fact, Ranger mountaineering training is very basic—it is not intended to allow a man to immediately transition to a 12,000-foot environment. For that there are several schools abroad that go the full distance with mountaineering training.

The other aspect is especially prevalent up on Mount Yonah. It's a confidence builder. Take a young kid who's never done any rock climbing, have him apply the military mountaineering techniques he's been taught in the last few days, and have him climb 200 feet of open rock face, which is a thousand feet over the surrounding area. When the kid accomplishes that, his confidence shoots through the roof. Will the guy ever climb Mount Everest? Probably not, but he's overcome something he's never done before. That's a critical training effect we hope to accomplish. We don't expect these guys to go and fight on top of Mount McKinley, but hopefully we've given them confidence so when they find themselves in a tough situation somewhere, they can look back and say, "Oh, this is easy. Look at what I've done."

Rangers have told me more than once that Ranger School was a benchmark in their lives, figuring if they could get through that, they could get through anything.

When they come back from Yonah, the students go into combat techniques training right here in camp in our planning bays. They receive instruction, then they do tactical exercise guided by the Cadre, then they do a student-led tactical exercise using various techniques they've been familiarized with. That includes combat patrolling techniques and reconnaissance patrolling techniques, and we've also included the TTPs—techniques, tactics and procedures—that we're learning from overseas.

Students are also shown what is known about IEDs (improvised explosive devices) used in Iraq and Afghanistan.

Some of these guys are coming here right out of training base, the Lieutenants in particular, and they haven't been in the field and seen such operations. This is one of their first opportunities to learn these techniques before they get to their first platoon.

So, there are a variety of techniques, but it's built around teaching them how to conduct raids and ambushes at the platoon level as well as conduct movement and establish patrol bases in between these operations.

Once a new Lieutenant gets to his first platoon, the Platoon Sergeant will continue his education, if he's any good at all.

After combat techniques training they conduct a four-day field training exercise (FTX). They receive an operations order (OPORD), they go through the planning, they deploy to the field, and they conduct four days of continuous operations with multiple raids and ambushes. They come back into this forward operating base—Camp Merrill—and they refit. They get to sleep in the barracks and eat a hot meal.

The Colonel's focus on that refit day is for those students to receive and participate in a very comprehensive after-action review (AAR) of the last four days. The Cadre develops the learning points and they're prepared to guide the discussion, but really we're trying to get the students to provide the input and learn their own lessons.

Hey, this is what we did well; this is what we didn't do so well. The outcome of that AAR is the students and the Cadre make a contract at the end of that thing, and they say, we can't fix everything, but here's the three or five tasks that we all recognize that we're not executing so well, and we're going to focus for the next five days on trying to insure that at least by the time you leave the Mountain Phase, your platoon has corrected those major deficiencies.

The practice of letting the students talk out any problems was used by Ralph Puckett, a new Lieutenant in the Korea War, commanding the Eighth Army Ranger Company. It was considered unusual to allow the lower ranks (or students) to speak unless spoken to, and then they better be answering a question. Puckett, who went on to become an Honorary Colonel of the 75th Ranger Regiment, found the give-and-take sessions rewarding to both officers and enlisted men. Other historical references to the practice can be found in studies of Robert Rogers and James Rudder.

After that refit day they get another **OPORD** that night, and the next morning they doing their planning and everything, and then moving back out to the field. They do five days of continuous operation. They move out from the camp and work their way back into the camp.

Unless you've been in the area around Camp Merrill it's hard to appreciate what "moving out from camp and working back" really means. The camp is on the edge of the Tennessee Valley Divide, and it ain't no pancake. The rough terrain is complicated by the presence of Opposition Forces (OPFOR), members of an imaginary army from an imaginary country who lay in wait for the unwary students, or provide an "enemy" force to raid or ambush.

We've managed to build the scenario so that it makes sense to the Ranger student. If he's really switched on he's going to see that the missions he's executing over that series of days, and the priority Intelligence he's picking up, the maps he finds on the objectives, they may tie into the next day's objective.

The Intelligence and the scenario, and the level of capability of the enemy, we've tried to knit it all together so the student is going to walk away with [the thought] that wasn't just a series of haphazard missions. It all ties into a set of continuous operations.

We're trying, but your average student, once the sleep deprivation and the chow deprivation set in, is he really catching it? No, but the hope is the sharper ones are catching it, because they're going to take those lessons to the field.

Ranger Instructors have to the power to suspend the scenario at any time if they feel the troop isn't properly trained, and cannot, therefore, be graded effectively. The idea is to coach, or mentor the students, but this being the military, there may be the occasional raised voice—with provocation, of course. The RIs are excellent, but even the toughest Sergeant can get frustrated with less-than-ideal circumstances, or students.

Students that complete here are forwarded to Florida, which is the culmination phase [Swamp Phase]. They do get some special technique training with water-borne ops, with rubber boats, and water-crossing operations, and some combat operations in a wet or swampy environment.

Really, that's the "run" phase of Ranger School and they spend most of their time conducting nine days of FTXs there.

Army methodology: crawl, walk, run.

Crawl: I'm going to teach you how to do it; I'm going to show you how it's done. I'm going to describe it, display it, and demonstrate it. In the crawl phase you're learning. In the "walk" phase we're going to physically, the both of us, walk through what I'm trying to teach you. We [5th RTB] are the walk phase, but we're running pretty fast when we leave here because of a number of factors.

[The Ranger Course] culminates in Florida. That's where the most time is spent in field training exercise environment. Very little technique training, mostly teaching, coaching, and mentoring, and them being evaluated.

But, he's running pretty hard when he's here. It's that transition from squad-level collective tasks and individual tasks—we really bring it together. We are training these guys to operate as an Infantry platoon doing combat and reconnaissance patrol techniques.

Ranger School does not evaluate above the platoon level, does not do combined company-level training, however, both in Florida and here we have adjacent platoons working in adjacent areas of operations. We have them doing cross-platoon coordination via radio that replicates that company operation, so they are getting a feel for that.

A Ranger company is essentially two "line" platoons and a headquarters element.

Colonel Flohr assumed command of this battalion and brought a unique vision. He has a definite set of goals he wants to accomplish to enhance what 5th Battalion provides to the Ranger student and our overall role within the Brigade operation—from start to finish the production of a Ranger-qualified combat leader. And what he [Flohr] says time and time again to our RIs, and I think our RIs truly understand is, even a guy who comes to Ranger School and gets to the mountains, but doesn't forward to Florida, for some reason he's dropped from the course—the lessons we're teaching him are every bit as important, because right now what we're seeing in this day and age, a guy that's leaving Ranger School, typically within about 90 days, he's probably in a combat zone somewhere.

The concept of force-expander is at work here. Whether a soldier finishes Ranger School or not, the quality of the training he received up to the point of leaving school (at whatever level he made it to) will work in his favor, and his next unit's favor.

Every bit of training time we have has got to be focused on trying to provide the best training possible because we are sending guys from school into combat. That's the way it's always been, but we think about that every day. It influences everything we do. There is no wasted time up here; there are no half steps. Our instructors are dedicated to maximizing every bit of training opportunity that we possibly can.

Indeed, some of the new students have already been in combat and will be going back.

We have a good mix [of students] with the Army having as many units deployed as we've had, we're seeing lots of guys coming back from an operational theater. Now the time is right for them to go to Ranger School, and they're bringing some lessons learned.

Some few of the combat vets have been known to badmouth certain aspects of Ranger training, feeling perhaps they already know how it's done. Ranger School Cadre would disagree, just as Recondo School Cadre in Vietnam had to deal with experienced men coming out of the bush. By 2006, most of the Cadre were veterans, so the guys coming back from overseas couldn't argue.

We are getting some good feedback from the guys with experience who are students, as well as right now we're very fortunate in 5th Battalion, I thinks it's near 85 percent of our Cadre have operational experience. They go as far back as Panama and Grenada.

Before this book was finished the 5th RTB could boast 92 percent combat veterans as Cadre.

It's interesting when you talk to a 19-year-old Private who has just come back from a deployment where he spent three to six months, and he learned a certain set of techniques, and he comes back and he'll want to tell a Sergeant First Class who's got multiple deployments, "Well, this is crap. What are you guys teaching us?" One of the things we're doing is teaching a standardized doctrine—the basic fundamentals of combat patrolling that are applicable in the arctic, in the swamps, in the desert.

To be sure, new information from recently deployed students and Cadre is always welcome, and assimilated if it serves a purpose.

If we can teach a guy the fundamentals we teach here in the breadth of Ranger School it does make a more flexible and adaptive, critically thinking leader on the ground, no matter what the situation is. He's in the city one day, he's out in the middle of the open desert the next day, if he understands the fundamentals being stressed here he's going to be able to work in the situation, relying on what he's learned here as well as what he's learned in theater.

Mountaineering is a good, specialized aspect of what we do, part of it's for confidence building, but our bread and butter in all three phases of Ranger School is the focus on those combat recon patrol techniques. That's what makes a good, solid combat leader.

Another plus for the mountaineering training is the ability to use ropes and tackle to move not only yourself, but your equipment, too, maybe up the side of a building or across a steep ravine, not to mention rappelling from a helicopter. As Major Lange put it, "We give them some tools for their kit bag." Most Ranger graduates will say the toughest of the three camps was the Mountain Phase (although, oddly enough, Florida is considered the coldest.)

We put equipment on their back and take them out there in a very rigorous set of field training exercises, and they've got to go up and down and around and in and out and climb through the mountain world. The terrain is every bit our coalition partner here in increasing the level of physical and mental challenge. It enhances the training effect.

Since the Ranger Regiment "specializes" in airfield seizures these days, the question was asked about training for such things as part of Ranger School.

They are not learning airfield seizure in Ranger School. That's really a company and battalion-level task. From my conventional experience it's really a battalion-level task. The Ranger Regiment probably has companies for very small operations.

We're focused on the platoon. What they're learning are the building blocks that support a successful company airfield seizure or battalion airfield seizure. They're learning the battle drills that make it possible for a company commander to execute his part of a battlion airfield seizure.

You give me a platoon that can execute battle drills, with soldiers who can execute basic fire-and-movement techniques, basic marksmanship, I can grab a First Sergeant and a company commander, an XO, and they can manage all of the company-level collective "stuff" to do the sexy missions—as long as I've got good solid platoons that know how to do eight or 10 basic battle drills that every platoon has to know to survive on the battlefield. Everything is fundamentally built on those basic platoon-level tasks.

At the end of our interview, Major Lange pointed out the evolution of Ranger training is still at work. The school is more mentally demanding now than even 10 years ago, but certainly still physically challenging in ways unlike any other training. The grading system has changed, also, and students are looked at more thoroughly now under the Go/No Go system.

Daniel Barnes

At the time of this interview in February 2005, SFC Barnes was driving my Lady and I up through the TVD to the Toccoa River to observe a raid by Ranger students. He was acting as Public Affairs Officer for Camp Frank D. Merrill, and had been an RI for some time. He attended Ranger School in 1993, spending a good bit of time with the 82nd Airborne.

Barnes begins by talking about the upcoming raid. The students had two objectives to capture, one of which was across a river. He was asked about the mountaineering aspects crossing over into the raid/ ambush profile for the Mountain Phase.

We're slowly trying to incorporate that, but it's time consuming. We'll have to bounce back and change a lot of stuff, some concepts, to incorporate more and more mountaineering skills. But it's so time consuming I think the Colonel has to make a decision, which is more important—to reiterate or reinforce mountaineering or infantry skills—attacking and raiding.

If you have a whole platoon and you're doing fixed ropes up a mountain face, that's basically the session right there. You don't have time to do that and a raid or an ambush.

[In 1993] they just walked you up and down these mountains until they got bored with you, then they passed you off to the next guy. They got organized some years ago, probably had to do with what happened in '95 in Florida.

There was a tragedy during the Swamp Phase that brought about changes in safety rules.

350-1 [safety guidelines] came rolling through. This modern era, the way things are changing; we kind of got away from the blood and guts.

Safety regulations order # 350-1 covers all Ranger training, and includes classes on hot and cold weather training and classes for RIs. "It makes the guys think of their feet more."

Combined with the extra safety precautions is a change in the overall skills of the students. Leadership has always been stressed, but it is more so today, along with all the new technologies and the placement of Rangers within the Special Operations community.

It's still not an easy course. When I went through I couldn't remember jack. You learned a lot, but you learned it from different aspects. There were no ifs-ands-or-buts about it. I knew exactly what my breaking point was. I knew how other people acted under adverse conditions. You get a guy that doesn't care and you try to get him to go on patrol. They're just thankful their number wasn't called [to lead]. They get you in trouble every five seconds because they're sleeping.

We kind of got away from that, though it's still like that to some degree. We're not focusing primarily just on skinnin' butt; have them all night just running up and down the mountain.

We have guys say they'd like to go back through Ranger School, not as a Ranger student, but just for the classes, because the classes are awesome.

If I could keep myself awake, yeah, the classes were very, very good. When you're not in the classes, and as soon as you're in the woods, it was game on. They really didn't care just how well you could make people function under the most adverse conditions they could possibly raise that were tactically sound. They were just separating the men from the boys, if you will, because they were constantly asking if somebody wanted to quit. If they just felt like making somebody quit, they'd just smoke you, run you up and down the mountain, make you pack and unpack your ruck.

All kinds of harassment, and you still had to try and pass a patrol along the way. But, it was more of an initiation. I've heard that being called that. Like I said, when you got done, you didn't remember squat. It took about a year to recover. I heard somebody say that, and I was always into fitness, but when I got back I couldn't do anything. It takes about a year physically and mentally. I remember for a couple of months I couldn't get it in gear. I asked around, did a little survey within my unit—almost everybody is Tabbed—the general consensus was, yeah, it's going to take about a year to recover.

Barnes was asked what he thought he gained from Ranger School.

It was an accomplishment, as far as an initiation-type thing. As far as learning anything tactical, I wouldn't have remembered anything if I hadn't gone back to a regular unit that does that. Because you're so tired, so smoked.

The question was, "Could you do it in a regular unit when you had to?"

Oh, yeah. Especially the leadership part under extremely adverse conditions. I think that was the intent back then. You know, you get people's heads blown off right next to you, you've been up for a couple of days of fighting and you keep driving into it.

Some years ago that was kind of the focus, to have leaders there under the most adverse conditions, and they just keep pushing forward. You were exposed to so much harassment, harangued so much during the actual course that it would take quite a bit, even in the real world, to shake you up.

As far as having to think on your feet, that really only came into play in a very tight situation. Nowadays, no matter what the situation is, they're [doing] think on your feet more than they're focusing on things going bad. At ground zero guys are expected to think on their feet and make smart decisions on the go.

It's still tough, though, but there is definitely a difference throughout the years.
Doug Perry

The Mountain Ranger Camp (MRC) in the mid-1960s was much different. The students had to leave camp and pass through "friendly front lines" in order to get to their problem sites. There was Opfor (Opposition Forces) out there.

"We'd set up a perimeter. They had to go through it going out and coming in."

Opfor was then called Circle Trigon, posing as enemy forces invading the US. They had two fronts, one at TVD (Tennessee Valley Divide), the other along I-10 in Florida, near Eglin AFB.

"It took a lot of support to run the problems."

Some "leg" units came up from Benning to do the job of Opfor.

"They had Circle Trigon on their jeeps, on their uniforms. Around camp, they stayed separate. They didn't want to come around with that insignia on. They were good."

Circle Trigon at that time was made up a company from 1/58th Infantry or a company of 1/29th out of Benning. These units also supported the Florida Camp, and so were on the move a lot.

"The training was beginning to change."

There was more emphasis on jungle training and Vietnam in particular in the Florida Camp. "They had a village down there. We'd go down and see what they were doing."

MRC pretty much stayed with mountaineering and field exercises in the hills.

"We worked in AOs in MRC."

Training is different now, he said. "In 62-64 we carried a butt-pack and a Ranger buddy-roll, not all this stuff they carry now. I don't see how they move; they're so weighted down. They're in a lot better shape than we were. We didn't have to carry those 65-pound rucks. For us back then it was move, shoot, and communicate. They don't move as fast or as far as we did."

OPFOR (Opposing Forces—Aggressors)

Ranger training could not be complete without an enemy to practice against. Long range surveillance patrols need somebody to sneak up on, and somebody to sneak up on them.

The role of the bad guys falls to the Opposing Forces, also called Aggressor Forces. These young men, mostly E-4 (Corporal) and below—there are also Sergeants, and a Platoon Leader Lieutenant—live on the base with the students, but in separate housing. They can make life miserable for prospective Rangers if they don't stay alert.

Barry Blackmon

Major Barry Blackmon, who ended his tour as Executive Officer at Camp Frank D. Merrill, home of the 5th Ranger Training Battalion (Mountain Phase), in 2001, took the time to describe OPFOR's form and function. This interview was recorded in his office at CFM.

Most of your OPFOR guys, the ones that are here in the Ranger Training Brigade, a lot of them come from the 75th Ranger Regiment. They didn't make it through RIP [Ranger Indoctrination Program] there, therefore were not assigned to the Ranger Regiment, and had to go find themselves another unit. The chain of command says, "Hey, this guy's a pretty good kid, seems to have a good head on his shoulders, he just wasn't physically capable. Can you use him?" We say roger that. We can always use another good OPFOR guy. Bring him on.

At any given point there are about 40. The OPFOR simulates the enemy on the battlefield. They establish objectives; serve as the point for the Ranger student's objective. Usually they man the objective, along with pieces of equipment. If the task to be trained is a raid, they'll patrol around the objective, simulate cleaning a mortar, simulate stacking rounds, basically provide activity on the objective so the friendly forces can report on the activity and figure out how they're going to attack it.

The OPFOR will also drive vehicles so the friendly forces can ambush them. They'll also walk down a trail, or something like that, so the students can ambush them. Usually, between two and five personnel is the picture we're trying to paint. Small unit teams operate within the country of Cortinia. There's a whole Intel picture we paint. It's an offshoot of the Joint Readiness Training Center Intel scenario.

There is a lot of make-believe in Ranger School, which takes the student out of the north Georgia woods and puts him in simulated countries around the world. Cortinia and Atlantica are two such imaginary places, but the problems encountered there are very real. OPFOR must play the part of every different enemy.

In addition to serving as Opposing Forces for raid and ambush, they also pursue the friendly forces during their movement. They'll conduct sniper missions on them, they'll harass them, try to interdict their movement.

The Ranger students will sit in a patrol base, and if the OPFOR locates their patrol base, then they'll attack.

Some of the OPFOR men are very good at what they do, and can give students fits when they track a patrol, remaining unseen until an ambush is sprung. If it wasn't such serious business, it seems like it would be a lot of fun.

Another fun thing is setting up sniper sites, and then looking down the long barrel at students struggling up a steep hillside in the snow. One or two rounds at them is enough to cause the whole group to scatter, then, if the RIs think someone was hit, the students have to figure a way to get the wounded man out of there.

Tony Torres

Sergeant Tony Torres, one of the few Ranger-qualified OPFOR men, came to CFM in July 2000, and went into OPFOR. He went through Ranger School in September 2001.

I was a Regimental Pre-Ranger when September 11 and everything happened. They pulled the 3rd Battalion guys that jumped in first [Afghanistan]; they pulled those guys out of my Pre-Ranger class.

Indeed, when Ranger Battalions began to deploy to Afghanistan, soldiers who had been sent to Pre-Ranger classes were pulled out in the middle of a field problem and sent back to their units to be ready to go. After combat, those men came back and had to continue through Ranger School.

How we get some soldiers here is because when they go through RIP [Ranger Indoctrination Program] they either fail, or they quit themselves, and they get sent up here— they get sent world-wide. So, our RTB will grab a couple of them, because they've already been doing some Ranger training, and have a little bit of that Ranger mentality. So they send them up here for OPFOR. They need Privates; they need Infantrymen.

I'm a team leader. Normally there are four guys on a Rifle Team. Sometimes we have five, depending on how many people are in the platoon at the time. We have a Platoon Sergeant, who runs the platoon, and there are Squad Leaders. There are four squads. First three squads support each company [of the RTB Cadre]. The fourth squad is strictly transportation. They're in charge of Ranger students, driving them to Mount Yonah, picking them up in certain spots if they have to. The Platoon Sergeant takes care of all that, and we have a Platoon Leader [Lieutenant] who handles anything else.

We support Rangers in all ways.

Torres was asked why, as a Tabbed Ranger, he was in OPFOR and not in a Ranger unit?

Basically, I can't be an RI right now because I don't have Rated Squad Leader time, and I'm not a Staff Sergeant. You have to go through certifications to go do that stuff. So they'll keep me over there until I get Rated Squad Leader time. Since I've been deployed [to Iraq], there hasn't been time for me to do that. But, there really wouldn't be anything wrong with having these guys Ranger-qualified, because they've already been through [part of] the school, they already know what it's like. So, when they go out there to play with the actual Ranger students, they've already been there themselves.

We do all kinds of ambushes. We do convex, concave. We do separate three-man or two-man positions, which means we wait for the whole line to come through. We do little harassment pop-shots at them, see how they react to contact, and take off.

The whole idea is to get them to see how they react. They're so tired, and they've already been without food, and they're walking, so, you get into the mode of just walking, without any sense of security over what's going on. [They want to know] how you would react to somebody shooting down on you from a far distance, or if you had 12 of us in one line doing a near ambush, how are they going to react to that?

If S-3 [Operations] wants a certain thing planned or done, what we do is sit one day down with each company and we lay out a plan. We say, hey, who wants us to do what we call "early hits?" If they're due out at 1300, we lay those times down for the whole cycle. Before the Ranger students even get here, we know what days we're going to go out. [We get with each company] so we know we're on the same page. [They'll say] hey, I want two ambushes here, I want three ambushes today, I want you to hit them as soon as they get off the helicopter, I want them in this spot here, in this saddle. We lay it all out ahead of time.

Torres said the S-3 and OPFOR, and even the Commander or the Command Sergeant Major who wants to get out and walk with the students, all get involved in the plan of attack.

The next question dealt with weapons the OPFOR carries.

M14s basically. Mostly older weapons. The idea right now is they're seeing foreign countries with older weapons, though some of them might acquire new ones. We do carry 240s, SAWs, depending on what we planned that day with the company. Maybe during Raid Week we wanted to have a gun position so we brought out a 240 Bravo [the replacement medium machinegun for the vaunted M-60] to build a little bunker around us. When they come running across the objective, how are they going to react to it? A crew-served gun like that, how're they going to react?

When we do our vehicular movements to some of their ambushes during Ambush Week we carry smaller stuff. Some M4s. Sometimes the Team Leader will take an M4. We used to have AKs [Kalishnakov AK47], but we ran out of ammo for that, and they weren't gauged right. It was too much of a safety hazard.

A weapon not gauged correctly can misfire. Torres said some weapons are just too beat up to fix. As for ammunition, everything comes from Fort Benning. A requisition doesn't necessarily mean a delivery. AK47s fire a 7.62mm round, but then so do the M240, M60 and M14.

The question turned to grenades and how they were simulated.

What we'll have is an actual grenade, but it's simulated. It's a dud grenade. Won't go off. We put them on parts of our body, or we're lying on one, so when they go to clear us [gathering Intel after a kill], we might have it lying there. We can say, hey, when you went to clear us, did you do it properly? Because guess what? I had a grenade lying underneath me. It teaches you, you know, a little lesson.

Smoke is good. We throw a lot of smoke to confuse them, especially at night. Sometimes they'll put out an operations order, hey, this white smoke is used for Shift-Signals. So here we come with the white smoke, too, and we throw them at the wrong times, since we don't know when they're doing it, and it confuses them.

We throw grenade simulators sometimes, and we say, hey, if that went off near you guys, you're dead.

We try to keep it safe, really safe.

There are other devices along the way, such as the Hoffman Device, a static simulated explosive that bears the warning "turn your head."

Torres next talked about what it takes to be in an OPFOR unit, which is standard Infantry training. There is no OPFOR School.

The first two classes I was here happened to be the last ones where we stopped tracking them. Two guys would go out; even a PFC would be in charge. [You'd be] building your Land Navigation skills while you were traveling as Infantrymen, looking for Ranger students, looking for signs to see where they're at. You won't know where they're at. [Sometimes they do]. You know there's a grid, a klick grid [a grid square on a map one kilometer across] where they are, but you've got to find them. So, in turn it helps you build your skills, and then when you find them, the Ranger students and the RIs, nobody knows where you're coming from, so it's a surprise to everybody. It was good training right there. I wish we would go back to that, to give these guys more Land Nav. This is beautiful land for navigational skills.

Tracking the students is still done occasionally, but as a coordinated effort.

These days, small-unit tactics and leadership are still the primary thrust of the Mountain Phase of Ranger School, but even there in the Georgia mountains there is a small building that can be transported so the students can practice assaulting and clearing it. Much of the Infantry fighting in Iraq was done in the cities, many of which are surrounded by mountains.

Brian Cunningham

Cunningham commanded the 2nd Ranger Company when it ran the show at Camp Frank D. Merrill—before the up-sizing to battalion.

While at the Mountain Camp we used support troops from the 197th Infantry Brigade stationed at Fort Benning. Each time a new student class arrived, the 197th supplied a contingent of support troops to act as aggressors, and otherwise assist in the training support process. They were referred to simply as Aggressors.

The Circle Trigon was the official insignia of the Aggressor Forces, as prescribed by the Department of the Army at that time.

The insignia consisted of a circle around and touching the points of a solid-filled triangle. The whole thing was a forest green color.

Camp Frank D. Merrill

Camp Merrill is home to the 5th Ranger Training Battalion and the Mountain Phase of the US Army Ranger Training Course. Though CFM has gone through an evolution of infrastructure and personnel, its purpose remains unchanged after 56 years of Ranger training in Lumpkin County, Georgia.

Considering one-eighth of the earth's surface is covered with mountains, the need for troops to operate in that type of terrain could come at any time, particularly in Europe or South America. Almost every war has contained some type of mountain operations.

The first Ranger class began at Fort Benning, Georgia, January 3, 1951. Ranger Instructors from the 2nd Ranger Company and students from the first class conducted 11 days of training in north Georgia, including nine days of patrolling and two days of rappelling at Woody Gap.

Only 47 of 150 students finished the course.

That first class wasn't the beginning of the modern Rangers, however. A few had begun training to be Instructors for the first Cadre in 1949, also at Ft. Benning. Some of those ended up in Lumpkin County, on land owned by North Georgia College in 1952, constructing the bare bones of what was to be the first modest Ranger training facility, the predecessor to CFM.

The first class from the "College Farms" area—now called Pine Valley—began January 1, 1952, with about 15 Cadre.

The first Cadre jump came in September, 1952, when about 20 men left a C-119 twin-tailed "Flying Boxcar" to land in what is now the Parks and Recreation Department, close to the city of Dahlonega, in Lumpkin County.

The College Farms area stayed in business until November 5, 1952, when the Rangers began moving the camp further into the woods and closer to the mountains at Camp Wahsega. That camp was leased from the State 4-H Club nine months out of the year, and afforded the Rangers a wider variety of terrain on which to train.

Between 1959-1960, another move brought the Rangers to their present location in the Black Farms area. As in College Farms/Pine Valley, students were billeted in tents—as were the Instructors up to that time. Hutments were constructed in 1961.

Not until 1987 did things get going in a more modern way, with a consolidated open barracks built for the students, a modern Cadre barracks, and a gymnasium built, plus the Troop Medical Clinic was remodeled.

At that point, the Mountain Ranger Camp was officially designated Camp Frank D. Merrill in honor of the commander of Merrill's Marauders of WWII fame. The Marauders were of the 5307th Provisional (Composite), and became the origin of modern Ranger lineage.

October 1, 1988, the 2nd Ranger Company was reorganized and re-designated the 5th Ranger Training Battalion.

Today CFM has about 250 resident Cadre, and student loads of about 200 per cycle.

Johnny Burt 1948-1953

Staff Sergeant Johnny Burt was a member of the first Instructor Cadre at the Mountain Ranger Camp in Dahlonega, Georgia. The year was 1951, and the earth was cooling as it passed through October and into the serious mountain winter.

Burt was part of the 6th Ranger Company when he and about 10 others came to Lumpkin County and set up shop in the North Georgia College Farms area, now called Pine Valley.

Pine Valley is about seven miles south of Dahlonega on Highway 9.

While at the camp, his designation changed. The Mountain Training Camp was part of the Ranger Department of Fort Benning, and was not attached to a separate unit.

"Ranger Cadre is what we were called."

The first class graduated in January 1952, a task hard enough in itself, but the condition of the camp made it even tougher. Just 36 of 136 made the grade.

The pioneer Instructors were given the task of starting a mountain program from scratch, beginning with shelter for themselves and their students.

"We lived in a damn tent with a wooden floor." Whether in the field or in the un-insulated tents, Burt said, "Our biggest problem was fighting the cold."

The eight-man tents were filled with bunk beds and featured a kerosene heater, but kerosene was sometimes unavailable.

"We burned wood or anything else we could get to burn."

When the first students arrived shortly after the bare bones of the camp were in place, they were billeted in tents also; only most were without benefit of floors.

Burt said eventually the camp could boast a log cabin supply room, a mess tent, and latrine facilities that were "holes in the ground."

There was no place to stack many of the supplies necessary to equip the original 136-man student body, so the ammunition was kept down by a small creek that supplied water to the camp. At least, it did after the Rangers dynamited it.

"Somebody called the Sheriff."

The law came out with the complainant and told him he couldn't do anything about it. "That's the government itself," he said.

One night between cycles, in the pouring rain, somebody noticed the creek was rising toward the exposed ammo. It was already too wet to get a truck close to the site, Burt said.

"We had to get the cooks and everybody out to move it."

Burt thinks today's training is tougher than the early days, but recalls the first classes, besides freezing in their tents and in the field, weren't given much to eat.

The Army gave the camp money to buy a calf every so often, but the Instructors turned them loose and the students had to catch them, kill them, butcher them, and then eat them. During field problems students would scavenge off the land, sometimes raiding gardens or orchards.

"We had two-day, three-day, and four-day problems. It *was* a survival course."

One of the many training mechanisms used by the Rangers was/is the Slide for Life, a scary zoom down a long cable into the water at Rock Creek Lake, near Blue Ridge.

"I helped build it."

To test the safety of the cable, Burt and two other men were made to use at the same time.

"Some of the Instructors were maybe a little too safety conscious for what they were teaching."

The Instructors were a mix in those days, some Rangers, some not. At one point, there were members of the 26th Infantry, just back from Korea, teaching what they had learned. They were not Airborne, nor was the original First Sergeant, Orville Strickland, or the second, Roy Kirby. Burt said there were even PFCs instructing.

"If they had the knowledge, that was it."

Much of training was night action, Burt said.

"The difference [from regular Army training] was when you got out into the company. That's when you had to do the field work."

Though night action was relatively new to some of the men, others were used to it.

"Us old country boys knew that stuff good," he said, referring in part to coon hunting in the darkness.

To get to this paradise, Burt came to Fort Benning from his posting with the 82nd Airborne in Fort Bragg, North Carolina, in November 1949. The Army had a shortage of active soldiers after WWII, and men with enough knowledge, skills, and toughness were needed to form the core of Instructors for the newly-mandated Ranger training.

"They asked for volunteers to train as Cadre."

As there was no precedent for that type of training. The first Instructors, some of them not Ranger qualified, or even Airborne, were taught by whoever had the knowledge to pass along. Burt remembers them as being mostly officers.

"Most of it was classroom, telling us what we had to learn to teach them."

Burt said he volunteered to go through the training in the Harmony Church area so he could be in the first company of Rangers to be formed, but it was not to be.

"I finally talked Van Houten into letting me go into the 6th "

That was in 1950, and Burt went back through training with his new company.

"Just to be on the roster, I guess."

A big man, Burt carried the powerful BAR and used his expertise gained at Armory School to instruct weapons courses at the Mountain Ranger Camp almost two years later.

From there, the 6th was deployed to Germany in January 1951, where members did border patrol, two at a time. Their opposite numbers were two Russian soldiers.

"We had a jeep and they didn't."

Some of the time was spent swapping cigarettes for Vodka through the fence.

"We wouldn't drink it if the bottle was already open."

Some of the company stayed in Germany when the rest were rotated out in October 1951. Some went into Special Operations, and some went as individuals to Korea. Other members went into the 82nd or 11th Airborne. Burt went back to Georgia.

"I came straight back from overseas to Benning, and then up here."

Here is Lumpkin County, where he stayed after his tour as an Instructor was over.

The first Cadre jump took place when "It seems like it was 21 of us" left a C-119 and landed in what are now the Lumpkin County Parks and Recreation Department ball fields.

Burt tells a story on a young man who would become a legend among Rangers, Doug Perry.

"I got my chute gathered up and he came running up to me. He was a little bitty shit back then. He puffed up and said 'I'm going to be a Ranger when I grow up', and he was."

The first jump was about 1,000 feet, Burt said, and as standard as possible.

"You'd better have your static line hooked up."

Burt didn't make a career of the service, but he and the other original RIs opened a path that became the road leading to the formation of a battalion-strength Camp Frank D. Merrill.

He left the first Mountain Ranger Camp January 1, 1953, "the night Hank Williams died," and was discharged February 7, 1953.

Steve Hawk

Steve Hawk was a Ranger Instructor with the 2nd Ranger Company, 1980-83, a TAC NCO, and a member of the newly formed 1st Ranger Battalion in 1974. Leaving the service after eight years as a Staff Sergeant, Hawk chaired the US Mountain Ranger Association as of early 2007, and worked with the Lumpkin County High School JROTC. He has been a huge help during this project.

When I attended Ranger School in the winter of 1975, Doug Perry was one of the RIs I had. We had the Slide For Life Confidence Test at Rock Creek Lake, just over the Tennessee Valley Divide near Morganton. It was February, and it was cold. The temperature never got above 40 degrees while I was in the Mountain Phase.

When we arrived at Rock Creek Lake, the Instructors were using tent poles to break a hole in the ice near the landing point. We crossed the ice-covered dam to get to the other side of the lake. Then we climbed a rope ladder to the top of a large pine tree on the west side of the lake and on the surrounding hillside. At this point, we hooked the pulley onto a cable anchored in the tree and then across the lake to another tree near the water's edge. We were to slide across the lake and watch the signalman for the signal to drop into the lake.

Prior to dropping into the lake, you pull your body into an "L" shape, then your legs and buttocks act like a stone and you can skip across the surface of the water, a lot like skipping a rock. I formed a perfect "L" and just as I came to the last skip, stuck my legs into the bottom of the lake, which at that point was three feet deep. I stood, and was dry from the waist up.

Although I was partially dry, the water was just at 32 degrees, which shocked your body to the point that physical activity was tenuous and difficult. Speech was hampered by the chattering of teeth, and severe shaking of the body to fight the effects of the cold. Each student would then have to report to the NCOIC of the Slide for Life of the successful completion of the task. It went like this: "Sergeant Ranger Hawk has successfully completed the Slide for Life."

However, not many had got it right, and they were punished for their mistakes by a quick swim in the lake. Then they made the attempt to report again. The sadistic Instructors would take advantage of the cold, the stress, and their positions to cause many a Ranger student to return to the water.

I had completed the test with little problem, but as I reported to [RI] Doug Perry, I rendered a hand salute, which was required for reporting. As I did, water on my hand slung into his eyes and across his dry and pressed uniform. As a result of this I was directed back to the lake and ordered to swim to the bottom. I did, which is the Ranger Way, but with hesitation because I was partly dry. After surfacing I was shocked by the cold again and had trouble reporting to Sergeant Perry. Again I was ordered into the lake. It was not until my lips and face were Infantry blue that I was allowed to proceed to the changing tent and dry clothes.

During his time in Ranger School, Hawk was one of the few enlisted men present, most students being from USMA (West Point). He graduated March 13, 1975, Class 6-75, and with the rest of the graduates, sewed his Tab on with white thread to signify a winter passage through Ranger School.

Most Rangers will never forget that class. It was so unbelievably cold. We had to knock the ice off the ropes to rappel on Mount Yonah. There were only 63 graduates out of 260 sign-ups.

In June 1980, Hawk returned to Camp Frank D. Merrill as one of the "sadistic" Ranger Instructors.

There were 43 active Instructors at that time. There were no medics and no OPFOR [they came up from Benning as needed]. There were two blocks of BEQs [bachelor enlisted men's quarters] with 12 rooms in each one, but the majority of men lived off base.

The students stayed in hutments, a semi-permanent structure, but it was home.

Headquarters was a Colonel, and XO, an S-1, and an S-3.

Perry C. Doerr

Doerr was a Sergeant First Class Ranger Instructor at Camp Merrill from January 1987 to September 1989.

He was then Senior RI First Sergeant, B Company, 7th Ranger Training Battalion at Fort Bliss, Texas (Desert Phase, Oct. 1991-May 1994). He later served with 82nd Airborne and F/51 Infantry (LRSC—Long Range Surveillance). Doerr became a Ranger while serving four years with 1/509 ABCT in Italy. He earned his Combat Infantry Badge and two Bronze Service Medals for service in Grenada (1983) and Desert Storm (1991).

In the late 1980's, several things happened to the Ranger group, including re-designation of the 75th Infantry as the 75th Ranger Regiment in 1986, and the elevation of RTBs to battalion size.

The two events were not really tied together, but the Ranger Department Commander at the time, Colonel Mace, did use the re-designation as part of his justification to TRADOC and HQDA to realign the Ranger Department.

TRADOC=Training and Doctrine Command HQDA=HQ, Department of Army

He told us at a meeting with all of the RIs that the realignment was also consistent with other Infantry School initiatives to give departments some sort of historical Infantry lineage and a more tactical flavor. He told us that the intent of having broader officer involvement (mentoring was the big buzz word back then) in training was also consistent with evolving TRADOC policy. We all suspected it would also provide more command positions for officers, so that was attractive for career development purposes.

What were conditions like at CFM during that time?

We, as RIs, were looking at having to undergo significant train-up. Up to that point all RIs were "walker" certified and had to walk at least one patrol per cycle.

We were organized as:

Combat Training Branch, which taught tactical classes, ran practical exercises, and ran the tactical FTXs [field training exercises] where Studs were evaluated on graded patrols. There were five teams (A-E) of about five-seven RIs who all had responsibility for a particular POI [Period or Point of Instruction].

I was on E Team, and we gave the Raid and Link-up classes. Other teams gave the rest of the POI, (ambush, recon, patrol base operations, etc.) all geared toward conducting those ops in a mountainous environment. It is a particular class or groups of sub-classes all related to an operation. For example, all operations related the Objective Rally Point are discussed, as well as composition and actions of various team members.

Mountain Training Branch (about 10-12 "expert RIs"), which taught four days of skills in the "lower" (CFM) area and two days at Mount Yonah.

Desert Branch, run with more RIs from Benning and Florida. We would take the Studs after the Mountain Phase out to Dugway, Utah, for [at that time] a one-week Desert Phase and then jump them into Florida, and return by bus to Dahlonega.

Realignment caused each Instructor to have to be an expert (qualified to teach) all POIs. We would take our companies and platoons through all of the training, so we had to learn and be certified on all classes. Learning the mountaineering classes was a six-week effort that we accomplished during one long cycle break. We had to teach tactical ops, mountaineering ops and desert ops as platoon SMEs (subject matter experts). At first we thought this would degrade training. It was difficult at first, but in the long run made for a better RI. Professionally, I was glad to have gone through it.

To accomplish realignment the Combat Branch teams formed the base of the three companies of 5th RTB. A and B teams became A Co. (1st and 2nd platoons respectively, there were only two platoons to a company then), C team became C Co along with a good number of the Mountain Branch RIs to form the 2nd platoon, and D and E teams became B Co. I was then in 2nd Platoon/B Co. Each company got a few of the old Mountain team RIs to provide quality control on the difficult mountaineering POI and the Desert Branch, which was only three RIs, sent one RI to each company to help with desert training and ops instruction.

There were about 100 RIs and 50 or so support personnel, HQ, Aggressor Forces, medics, commo, etc. Our class size was usually between 200-250. We would get up to over 300 if we had a big class with a lot of recycles. Our platoon sizes were usually around 50, if we had a small class we would keep platoons at 50 and just go with four platoons, giving one platoon of RIs a bit of a break for that class. They would still walk their one patrol with another unit, but would not have to pitch any classes.

The workload while in cycle was pretty high, we would be teaching and assisting for about seven-nine days in a cycle, and we had to have one RI per squad for all instruction. You would usually walk two-three patrols per class depending on what the manning level in your platoon was. Most platoons had five-eight RIs so you were walking patrol or teaching day on, day off, most of the time. You really got to know your class that way.

I think after the first typical resistance to change, the new RTB concept ended up being a good thing. I learned a lot. I think most Studs benefited from seeing the same faces for the entire cycle. There was a better rapport built between RIs and the class. Studs could complain less about "RI Roulette" because in many cases the same RI who taught the class, or was an assistant Instructor during the class PE (practical exercise), was the guy grading a Stud on execution during his evaluation.

Under the old system, the entire class would get instruction from the platform by one RI who was an expert on that class, and often only that class, in a big classroom setting. Now each platoon gets the class from one of their platoon SME RIs, with another three RIs from the platoon assisting. These same RIs see the platoon day in and day out during the evaluation, so you have a good degree of consistency in instruction and evaluation standards.

Doerr said almost half the RIs at the time were Grenada veterans, fairly equally divided between the 1st and 2nd Ranger Battalions and the 82nd Airborne.

Ken Bonnell

I was in Ranger School from January-March, 1969. I believe this was the 25th anniversary of the founding of the US Rangers. I remember that I was young, just out of IOBC, and green as hell. I remember that it was very cold—supposedly the coldest winter in a very long time for Georgia and Florida. We had continuous ice in the Florida swamps. A third of my Ranger Class got frostbite injuries at Benning. It was discovered by the medics at Dahlonega.

My first Ranger Buddy was a very big guy that did not make it through the Florida Phase. I carried him most of the time, and I was half his size! My second Ranger Buddy was Ted Leczo. He and I received our Tabs. He and I had been Cadets at Ohio State University together. After Ranger School, we both were sent to Germany, and both served in the 1st Battalion, 51st Infantry, 4th Armored Division. I have lost all contact with him.

Douglas Flohr and Glenn Legg

This interview was taped June 2, 2004, at West Restaurant, near Mt. Yonah, Georgia, during an early-morning breakfast with the Commander of the 5th RTB, Lt. Colonel Douglas Flohr, and his Command Sergeant Major, Glenn Legg.

The session began with questions regarding the various numbers of students attending the 11 classes a year.

Flohr: It averages between 150 and 250 [students per class—right then they had a class of 240]. I'd say, two classes out of the year we run 250, one class of 200, then the other eight, about 150. [We have] more students in the late spring. I think a lot of units feel a guy has a better chance of success if the weather's better. There's three things that impact on their success as a student. One is Ranger Instructor expertise, which they can't impact on, one way or the other. The second is weather [winter can be rough in the north Georgia mountains], which they can't impact on. The third is their motivation, their morale while they're in the course. They can sustain that, and that will carry them a long ways, but the weather is a huge factor here in the mountains. Probably more than anywhere.

There was a general agreement that Florida could be pretty cold if one was in the water.

The questions turned to types of students, beginning with foreigners. Since the inception of Ranger training, foreign students of many nations have taken benefit.

Flohr: More in the summer time than any other, but I'd say it probably averages between three and five a class. Predominately from the former Soviet Bloc. For example, I'm aware of one in the class right now. He's an Uzbeki. I've found the majority...are from the "Stans." Kurdistan, Kazikstan, Uzbekistan. We're going to have Tajikistan this summer some time.

There are Canadians. They normally come in one batch. They pick the best weather of the year, which was really the last class; class six, the March class. We had five just in that class alone.

They're a mix [of types of unit]. The one that strikes me the most is the PPCLI [Princess Patricia's Canadian Light Infantry]. I see a lot of those guys. A couple of Special Operations guys, but not very many.

There is a Canadian Ranger School, but it's oriented more on survival above the Arctic Circle. I think it's run by the Inuit. It's really long range patrolling and survival above the Arctic Circle. That's been my understanding of it. Eating a lot of seal and that type of stuff.

The questions turned to how rank relates to Ranger School.

Flohr: The only Privates that we allow in—every once in a while somebody will slip in from one of the Regular Army Divisions, but really, the only Privates that are officially allowed in are from the Ranger Regiment. It's hard to discuss the percentages, but I'd say that's about a third. Maybe a little bit less. But, still, it's a substantial client.

Going through the course often brings promotion to the lower ranks, but not always.

Legg: In a regular division that's true, but in the Ranger Regiment they go back and they're E-4s. Specialists. That's an anomaly in the Regiment. In a regular division you're getting a guy, first of all he has to be an E-4 to get here. Most of them are senior E-4s or young E-5s [some of which are promotable anyway], and when they get back they'll go to a promotion board if they're not promotable, and they'll generally get selected for promotion without any problem. They don't have to worry about points because of the way the Army is working the system right now for E-5s. If they are Ranger-qualified and promotable, they'll be promoted [within the Army].

For Rangers, an E-4 passing the course and promoting to Sergeant will probably find a job as a Team Leader in the Regiment, partly due to "the turnover in the Regiment," Legg said.

That's not an issue. People can be performing well, which he obviously is if they sent him to Ranger School...they're going to find a team for him.

The next questions were about Rangers re-enlisting at a higher rate than regular units.

Legg: I personally think it is [higher].

Flohr: I agree. You've got to be a little bit dedicated to come to this school. You have to be more dedicated to stay in this course. A lot of those guys typically have made up their minds. They want a career. They like what they're doing.

I was not planning on staying on as an officer. I was going to make Captain and get out on my first tour and that was kind of the end of it. Ranger School—I don't want to say it brainwashed me—but it changed my attitude, changed my focus for the Army. I just re-upped. I've been indefinite since the day I came in, but it kept me in the Army. I had such a positive experience.

I've got a Bachelor's Degree, a Master's Degree, I've been to Command and General Staff College, and none of those educational experiences has ever had the impact that Ranger School had on me.

Flohr said the War College is probably next, and that he was still a couple of years from making the list for Colonel. He next explained how he got commissioned.

I came through ROTC in West Virginia University and was commissioned a Reserve Lieutenant in May 1985. Finished my last semester of school and received a Regular Army appointment in December and came on active duty, and went straight to Fort Benning.

Actually [Ranger School was in] '87. I went to Ranger School late. I did not come from a military family, my wife was due as I finished up IOBC, and I made a decision not to go then, which was very difficult for a Lieutenant to make, especially when you stand there and tell them you're not going.

Went off to my unit—of course, my wife had the baby there just as we left Benning— and we went up to Alaska. The first thing my brigade commander asked me was, "When are you going to go to Ranger School?" Luckily I had the right answer, which was, "As soon as you'll send me." As soon as he could send me was eight months later. I had already been a Platoon Leader by the time I came to Ranger School. I was at Fort Wainwright, Alaska. General Needham was my brigade commander back then. His nickname was "The Nuke."

The questions turned to the differences in Ranger School over the years.

We didn't eat as much back then. Harry Eikner, who was the Training Analyst for Ranger Training Brigade for 18 years—he didn't start Best Ranger Competition, he picked it up three years after it's inception—but he made it what it is today. Harry said there was a mistake on the calorie count on how much food a Ranger student was supposed to get, and the mistake went for about a four-year period. I went from 185 down to 138. They really didn't feed us enough to sustain us. That was a significant difference.

Another difference was, back then, you could be a rock, at least when I went, I felt you really didn't have to know anything to be successful in Ranger School—you could just muscle your way through it. Now, we feed them more, but we require more out of them. They've got to think, they have to put two and two together. They actually have to do an Intelligence prep of the battlefield. They have to figure out what the enemy is doing. I wasn't capable of anything like that.

The question was, "So you're saying today's Rangers are a lot more academically skilled?"

The wonderful thing about Ranger School, the strength of Ranger School, [it] produces the leaders who can think under stressful situations in the worst climactic conditions. The techniques, you know, how you clear a room, how to conduct a raid, all that stuff may change, but that's not what the strength is. The strength is, we've produced a leader who's going to do a gut check, and he's going to figure a way to accomplish his mission.

The question related to differences between what various ranks are taught.

Flohr: They all learn the same thing. Now, sometimes, towards the end, you'll see officers getting more of the planning phase and the NCOs getting more of the Platoon Sergeant, the execution phase. But that's a few people. The majority of the time everybody has to have the same skills.

Legg: I think one of the unique things about Ranger School, when you're done with it, you've completed it successfully, part of the brotherhood that you have is that you already know what your leader—who has been through Ranger School—is thinking. Even if you're at the team leader level, you know what to expect from a platoon leader who has done the planning, and you know what to expect from the company commander, and all the way up. You've gone through the same training; you've gone through the same thought processes. You can explain and teach your subordinates *how* to think, not *what* to think.

That's important because leaders get killed, they get wounded—somebody has to step up. If you don't teach them how to think, instead of what to think, they're going to get hurt. That's the strength of the American Army, I think. Doesn't matter if you're a Lieutenant or a Sergeant or a PFC, you've still got to be able to accomplish the mission. I think the overall thing about Ranger School is, that really what it's driving toward is getting leaders that understand the mission has to be accomplished. It doesn't matter what your rank is. If you are in charge, then you accomplish the mission. You find a way to do it.

It's more of a mind-set than anything else. The people who come here, who volunteer to come to Ranger School, knowing it's difficult, already have the right mind-set.

During the 5th RTB Open House in early May, 2004, Lt. Colonel Flohr was standing in the shade of the NCO club with people eating BBQ all around him. He was talking with his S-3, Captain Salome, when a Ranger student presented himself. Flohr was overheard telling the student, a recycle, that this was his last chance, and that he'd better stand tall or he'd be gone. My friend witnessed this and was curious, so the question was asked, "Did he make it?" Flohr's answer? "He's still with us today." That exchange led to the following.

Flohr: He had been up in the mountains for two classes. Typically, we put a lot of emphasis on what the RI says. I can give the RIs guidance, but once they hit that wood line, they get out there in the woods, they are the quality control. I can't do enough quality control. I have to trust them. They've got to follow the guidelines and train these guys right. They come back and tell me, "Hey, this guy's not making it."

Well, the first time they do that, they typically say, "He deserves another chance. He's not ready yet, but we can fix him." That happened to Ranger [name withheld] and we gave him another shot. The second time they came back and said, "Sir, he's not learning it. He made the same mistakes." He actually had a negligent discharge—fired his weapon accidentally—the first time. The second time they caught him with his weapon on semi instead of safe. So, he was about to have another negligent discharge. Plus, he [wasn't making it] on patrols.

To be fair, this student was a new officer from a Regular Army unit—not a Ranger unit.

I decided to go ahead and send him to Fort Benning. I can't officially drop a student from the class. The brigade commander has to do that. All I can do is recommend.

But, when I send somebody down to Colonel [William] Kidd, he typically follows my recommendation and sends them on their way. This particular Ranger student went down there and...talked Colonel Kidd into giving him another chance. It's no skin off our nose, the way we look at it. Colonel Kidd decided he'd get a third shot. So, that's why I said this is your last chance.

Recycling a student is not unusual, but a third try at Ranger School is atypical. Every one in the chain of command had given the man a shot, and he wasn't going to get another one.

The CSM went back to an earlier question—is Ranger School better now than when they went through?

Legg: I was a year after him [Flohr—Legg went through in 1988]. What I remember about this phase right here, was Day Two, starting down on Lower Mountaineering, the RIs at the time, yelling and screaming. We did I don't know how many flutter kicks, you know, mass punishment. The mind-set of the RIs has changed dramatically. At that time, you just came to Ranger School and you were tested. You weren't really trained that much.

Flohr: I agree.

Legg: You learned from your peers by making mistakes and things like that, but you really didn't get very many classes that I can recall. You might have gotten it one time. They weren't really that good. You basically showed up, and it was a gut-check for two months, and you either got the Tab or you didn't.

Now, the mentality is more, we're going to teach everything we know, we're going to try and help you learn it, and then we're going to make sure you learned it by proving it to standards. I see a whole lot of patience going on.

Neither man could say exactly when the change took place. The grading system had changed in the 1970s, and Ranger training, per se, has undergone a continuous evolution from Robert Rogers' day. However, there has been a recent, fundamental change in the way students are taught. As the command structure at the three camps rotates, some of the new commanders implement new ideas and the RIs follow suit. Then there are the changes the RIs themselves put forward, changes in training strategies that reflect the changes in today's Ranger.

The gut-check is still necessary, but the battlefield technology has changed so radically that Rangers of today are required to know more and do more.

Flohr: Not a whole lot, but some of it has changed since I came here. That's been my focus from the get-go. It wasn't a dramatic change, but I think we've gotten better at it. That's what I push to these guys, all the RIs, with all the guides [guidelines]. But, I think they've been doing it that way.

I was 1st Battalion S-3, and then I was Brigade S-3, and that was starting in 1999. I don't think it was as good then, but it was certainly was already heading down that road by that time.

Legg: If we don't change Ranger training on a regular basis to keep up with what we see going on in the world, then we're way behind the times, and we're going to be irrelevant soon.

Considering the evolution of training, questions were asked about changes relating to the current conflicts in Iraq and Afghanistan.

Flohr: What we've done is, we've got a new 10-day FTX [Field Training Exercise] that we incorporated for this class. The way you used to train was, you did ambushes and raids up here. You'd get a block of instruction for three days on how to conduct an ambush, then we'd take them out in the woods for four days and they'd do nothing but ambushes. Bring them back in, give them two days of training on raid—and really, the components are relatively the same—then we'd take them out in the field and for five days they'd do nothing but raid. It was lock step. That's what the Army does. It's their methodology. You learn something in class, then you go outside.

What we've done is, we've changed this thing up, so now it's four days techniques training up front. They learn everything. Then a nine-day FTX, with one day in the middle when they come back on the camp and refit and get a big AAR [debrief and analysis] and figure out all the problems they had as a Platoon, and they're given the opportunity to fix those at that point.

The difference is, now a student doesn't know what's going to happen to him from day to day. He may be on ambush one day; he may do a raid the second day. The third day, he has a new mission called the Out Of Sector Mission, where he's going all the way up the Toccoa River, with no rucksack on, he's going to cross the Toccoa River on a rope bridge, hit an objective and come back.

And to get back, he's got to get in a convoy. Then on that convoy he's got to control the movement of the vehicles and watch his route, because somewhere on that convoy there is going to be an explosive device.

So, we've thrown some stuff in that you see overseas, IEDs [improvised explosive device] and that type of thing, without getting rid of the basics, because that's what Ranger School really does—reinforces the basics. It's the building block for a Stud [student] combat leader. We don't want to change that, so we're very careful about what we change.

The subject changed slightly. Asked how much influence he had on mountain training, where Performance Oriented Training is used, he answered this way.

Flohr: I have an amazing amount of influence, and so does the Sergeant Major.

Legg: A lot of people say, why don't you train, since this is mountainous, why don't you just go on an Afghanistan scenario? You can't do that. It's mountainous, but you can't falsify a country where it doesn't fit. We do have to be careful about what we throw in here. You can overwhelm Ranger students, when you take away their chow for an extended period of time and you don't allow them to sleep much, because that's the reality of extended combat. And you put them under as much pressure as you can without shooting at them. When you start throwing in a whole bunch of scenarios in a 10-day period, they're going to get to the point where they don't learn anything. That's the difference in Ranger School [now]. We try to teach them as much as we can.

Does that mean that physical training takes a backseat to teaching?

Flohr: Most of that they go through at Benning. Although, I believe the mountains are really the toughest 22 days of Ranger School. The terrain alone is very, very difficult.

Legg: You don't get PT after Fort Benning. What you get is physical stress from the terrain, and that's what the Mountain Phase is here to teach them—how to deal with the terrain, the thought process that goes into the differences in the terrain between Benning, here, Florida, and there used to be a Desert Phase [Dugway Proving Grounds, Utah].

Flohr: There are some aspects of it that are really physically tougher than when I went through. Charlie Company, for example, has a fixed rope—the terrain is so steep at this one part that there is a rope from tree to tree you have to climb—600 feet straight up. We never had anything like that.

So, some parts are easier and some parts are tougher?

Yes, there's a balance to it. You can't push them to the point where, like the Sergeant Major said, they're not learning.

Knowing they wouldn't say yes, I asked if they were satisfied with the way training was being done, and if they would like to see anything implemented.

Flohr: I'm very happy with what we're doing in our Phase. I have a lot of latitude to guide the staff. I have the ability to go down and ask the Ranger Instructors, "What do you think we ought to do?" and listen to those guys. I bounce stuff off my Sergeant Major, bounce stuff off my staff. We spent the last three months building this new Field Training Exercise and no one's ever told me "no." No one at brigade, even the CG, General Freakley, has told me "no." They allow us the latitude and trust to do what's right for these Ranger students.

Putting together a new FTX is no simple feat. Flohr said the whole battalion took part.

"There are parts of it that young Staff Sergeants figured out, there are parts that some of the Captains put together. But the S-3, Captain Salome, has really been the glue that held the whole thing together. I gave him guidance and he's worked out the details."

Legg: I don't think we'll ever be satisfied. One of the things I'm trying to brainstorm myself is this Phase we're in right here. We've both been to Afghanistan a little bit. I wasn't a Squad Leader there, but if you talk to [the leaders], the challenge is how to move their squad or platoon in terrain like you have in the mountaineering part. How to get resupplied and how to evacuate casualties, and all the realities of that experience over there. What is the validity of upper mountaineering? It has some valid points. How can we make it better? Those are the questions I ask myself as I watch training. I ask people who've been over there. We've got a lot of people who have rotated out of divisions with a lot of combat experience, and have operated in that terrain as a Squad-or-Platoon Sergeant. They've got some ideas and I think they're going to push us in the right track, which is being able to move entire units over that type of terrain, with all their equipment.

All the talk about training excellence and combat veterans led to the question, how many are experienced, and what is the overall quality of today's RI, and today's student?

Flohr: I won't speak for the other RTBs…but you look at this Battalion right here—I'll give you an example of the men we're getting in—I just got four Sergeants First Class, all coming out of Iraq or Afghanistan, and they weren't here a month and they popped on the promotion list for Master Sergeant. They're top performers. Sergeant [Ritemeyer—sounds like], a young Staff Sergeant, just came in from a combat tour, he's Fort Benning's NCO Instructor of the Quarter. We have the TRADOC Officer Instructor of the Year; we have Fort Benning NCO Instructor of the Year, Sergeant Olsen. So, that's the quality of the Ranger Instructors up there.

The advice they're offering is absolutely invaluable.

Flohr and Legg agreed that combat veterans comprised some 75 percent of the Ranger Instructor ranks, and ran about 50 percent for the whole battalion. The RIs have experience in Panama, Somalia, Iraq, and Afghanistan, plus a few other places. There is still at least one man, Sergeant Major Durkin, who fought in Grenada in 1983.

Not since just after the Vietnam War have there been so many combat veterans available to pass their unique wisdom on to the up-and-comers. In 2006 the percentage of vets as RIs was more like 90.

Flohr: They have instant credibility with young soldiers. A lot of these guys—it's not like when we came through Ranger School—you went back to your unit, and the chances of you going to war were slight. You were going to have time to train yourself and get a little bit better. A lot of these young Lieutenants and young E-4s, and young Sergeants, are going to leave here, they're going back to their unit, and they're going straight to Iraq.

We've had a lot of guys from the 101st deploy from Iraq here, get two weeks' leave, go to Ranger School, get two weeks' leave afterward, and go straight back to Iraq.

They [101st] want the experience that Ranger School gives them.

Legg: It's just like an NCO school, ANOC, BNOC, whatever, if you have a guy who wants to come to Ranger School, the fact is it's a career-progression school. As an enlisted guy, especially—as an officer it's almost a requirement that you keep ahead of your peers that way. Especially out in the divisions. Because, quite frankly, they get quotas they cannot fill, not even come close. So, a guys goes to Ranger School, he's a top performer. He's going to go back with that Tab and set a great example for everybody else. He's going to get promoted ahead of his peers at every single look for the rest of his career.

Flohr: When I was a young company commander I walked into my company and I didn't know anybody. Those who had the Tab, you know they had the same experience you do and you know what their baseline standard is. There is an instant relationship there.

There is a Ranger culture out there. I didn't realize it until just a few years ago. I've always enjoyed working with guys who have the Tab.

Guys like General [Petraeus] of the 101st, General Helmick at the 101st; they're pushing their guys to Ranger School. General Petraeus is the one that pulled his division in over there in Iraq and said, okay, I'm going to send guys to Ranger School. Pulled them out of combat and sent them. He realized how much it was worth. There were 20, anyway. He sent them in waves. It was a mix [officers and enlisted]. I would say the vast majority of them were Staff Sergeant and below.

Many of the officers had probably already gone through the course as a matter of career-enhancement. As for the rest of the student body…

Flohr: They're hit-and-miss on the quality. You'll get a class that will be very good and you'll get a class where there will be one Platoon that just can't seem to do anything right. Last class we had, we had 17 soldiers fail the knot-belay test. This class hadn't had any.

I think overall the quality of the American soldier is very, very good. I've been impressed— the first time I was in Afghanistan I was watching this 19-year-old Private out on the gate. In the space of an hour I watched him search people coming through the gate, deal with a local chieftain, deal with senior NCOs and officers coming in and out of the gate, and never drop his security. I thought that's an amazing kid. Fresh out of high school, balancing all these glass balls, and doing well at it.

Legg: You can ask just about any senior guy in the Army that's been to Afghanistan or Iraq with these guys and they'll tell you they probably rival the generation of WWII.

One last question before they went back up Mount Yonah. Why are you a Ranger, and not a SEAL, or Air Force Commando?

Legg: I know why I am. I tried to get in the Air Force. That was my first choice. Showed up for the recruiter and he was late. I thought, well, if the Air Force doesn't have any more sense of urgency than that, I don't want to be any part of it. So, I went over and talked to the Army guys.

Talking with CSM Legg, one gets the impression he would have risen to the top of whatever endeavor he undertook. The Army got a break when the Air Force was late.

Flohr: I was a college student, and paying for school on my own. I took an ROTC class for an easy A. I really enjoyed it. They used to have little Ranger clubs among ROTC students back then, and I got into that thing and enjoyed it. Then I went through my basic course at

IOBC and became an Infantry Officer. I went to IOBC and it was expected that you would go do that.

I went back [to Alaska] primarily, because I knew if I went I'd become the XO. I wanted to be XO of this company. It was the most northern Airborne Company in the free world at the time. The only Airborne Company in Fort Wainwright. They told me, "You get your Tab, you'll be the XO." It sounds like a selfish reason, but that's why I went.

I enjoyed it so much I couldn't imagine doing anything else.

Brian Cunningham

Colonel (Retired) Brian Cunningham graduated Ranger School class 2-70, September 1969. He served a stint with the 1/508, 82nd Airborne, and then went to the 101st Airborne.

Cunningham served with the 101st in Vietnam, half the time in Camp Eagle in I Corps and half in the Cam Rahn sector with C/ 2/327, where he was a Rifle Company Commander.

Back in the States, he served as Assistant G-5, III Corps at Fort Hood, then spent time as S-3 for 3rd Brigade, 1st Cavalry.

He went back to the Infantry School at Benning for nearly a year and ended up as Commander, 2nd Ranger Company, at the Mountain Ranger Camp.

For 20 years after that posting, Cunningham held multiple positions in the US Army Reserves.

There was only one company headquarters assigned to the Mountain Ranger Division (MRD) at that time: 2nd Ranger Company—June, 75-Jan, 77. The company provided all assigned and attached military personnel support, including Headquarters staff from MRD. All Instructors were assigned to 2nd Ranger Company, too.

Contrast that with Headquarters, Mountain Ranger Division, which provided all instruction oversight and doctrinal support. All the instructional staff reported to HQ, MRD, for operational control and 2nd Ranger Company for administrative control.

For me, commanding 2nd Ranger Company was a great honor. Even though my mission at the time was primarily support of the training mission, I also had the opportunity to participate as an Instructor, or Jumpmaster, etc. during training operations.

I got the chance to be associated with some of the finest Ranger Cadre ever to have served at CFM. Many of those who served while I was company commander have gone on to their own greatness. I am proud to have known them. Rangers like Mike Smith, Doug Perry, Lonnie Miller, Danny McKnight, Don Rhodes (Company 1st Sgt at the time), and many others come to mind.

As I recall, the classes ranged in size from about 75-150 or so. Each class had its own personality. Some were more impressive than others, but all had volunteered for this training and that made each special. I seem to recall many of the soldiers going through Ranger School at the time were destined for the 1st and 2nd Battalions.

I think there were about 65 personnel on the CFM staff at that time divided among the command group, patrolling, mountaineering, and other support troops. I estimate about 80 percent were combat veterans.

The company headquarters was located near the dispensary and supply room in the building on the other side of the commissary.

The multi-story barracks buildings were not there at that time. The students lived in green plywood shelters that were called tents and located in generally the same area the student billets are now. I think they really were tents at one time—one of the real old timers can tell you for sure.

See Johnny Burt's interview.

The company executive officer was Danny McKnight. Danny was also an outstanding soldier. He went on to serve a distinguished career. Danny was the ground commander during the operation on Mogadishu [1993, Somalia].

The supply officer was CW4 Bill Weaver. Bill was not a Ranger, but he certainly touched the careers of many Rangers over the years. He is still held in high regard at Camp Merrill.

At the time I was there the organization was thus: all Camp Frank Merrill military personnel were assigned to 2nd Ranger Company for administrative purposes. That included the camp commander (LTC Ken Guillory when I first arrived, later LTC Ray Schuetze) and his staff. This was also true of 3rd Ranger Company at Fort Benning and 1st Ranger Company at Eglin AFB in Florida. The 1st, 2nd, and 3rd Ranger Companies were all under the School Brigade, which was, in turn, under the United States Army Infantry School [USAIS].

Additionally, there was a parallel command structure for the Ranger Training Command. The camp commanders reported to the Ranger Department commander (Colonel Jim Bowers at the time) for operational purposes.

The primary lift support was provided from Fort Benning. Most support was UH-1H Huey helicopters.

During the two summers I spent there, we also received support from a Marine Corps Reserve Squadron. The marines provided both UH-1N and CH-46 helicopters.

In both the above cases, aircraft were used for airmobile operations, airborne operations, and logistical lift support operations.

Cunningham on Kirby

J. D. Kirby has always been an outstanding soldier. I have the highest respect for him. J. D. served as my tactical officer in Ranger Class 2-70. He was my first contact with US Army Rangers. He made a lasting impression on me at that time (July 1969).

Through our membership in the US Mountain Ranger Association, we have since had the opportunity to chat quite a bit about those days.

As a Ranger training tactical officer, J. D. would never cut anybody any slack, and that's the way it should be. You are in Ranger school to be tested—to determine if you are qualified intellectually, physically and emotionally—and at the time, spiritually. If one is to carry on the tradition of excellence, then the test must always be that which upholds the standards in keeping with the tradition of excellence.

Greg Jolin

We took a ride with Ranger Instructor Sergeant Greg Jolin up along the Tennessee Valley Divide outside CFM on February 10, 2003. It was unexpected and informative, mostly because of Jolin himself, a large, heavy-duty Ranger working in S-3 to get things going correctly with the Studs and the OPFOR.

Up in the Divide it was snowing, still a few inches on the ground, and cold.

Jolin was talking about keeping the students safe in that environment of straight-up and straight-down terrain.

"Laying in the snow for nine hours will put a whipping on you."

The terrain and the amount of practiced stealth means traversing some "no-way" terrain that no normal, thinking person would attempt. That is just what they want. Only the best are going up and down that AO without falling out. Looking down an impossible ravine, covered with snow and fallen trees, Jolin says, "That one will put a hurting on you."

Still, he says doing a "hand check" twice a day keeps the frostbite away. This means looking at hands, feet, elbows, knees, even to the point of squeezing student's feet "to check capillary refill."

"Anybody can get hit by a bullet, but we don't want anybody going down for frostbite."

"If a guy goes back to his unit and remembers we checked his feet twice a day, maybe he'll pass that along the other guys in his unit."

Steve Bishop

I came here from Germany in January 1980, and stayed until 1984. I came here as an E7 and started off as a senior Instructor and became an API, one of the staff, then I became a PI, which was a Captain's slot, then I made E8 list. I became NCOIC of Mountaineering, and I was NCOIC of Patrolling when I left here.

We started the Desert Phase at Fort Bliss when I was here. When we started off we had the Benning Camp and the Florida Camp helping us, but then they dropped off and it was just us. We walked 15 klicks a day. Mountaineering walked day one, three, and five, and Patrolling walked days two and four. In those days our five-day FTX was in Florida. They kind-of changed how we did things up here. The students would come up here [CFM] for two weeks and then spend seven days in the desert. We'd leave here on Sunday morning and come back the following weekend. We would jump the students from C-130s into Florida from Bliss, land, unload their stuff down there, fly back to Benning—a lot of times we would jump into Benning, then get on buses and drive back up here.

Only one thing I started when I was an Instructor up here that was different and fun. We were on a five-day FTX patrolling with platoon-sized elements. I said look, these Ranger students, every time you hit them [with OPFOR] they're used to attacking. They always come after you. What if we hit them with the same size unit? What will they do? They have to learn you can't always attack. Sometimes you have to evaluate the situation, and sometimes you have to haul ass.

We had a platoon of RSE [OPFOR] guys and eight Ranger Instructors. We'd take eight machineguns, we all had M14s, and we'd go out and set up L-shaped ambushes. We used TNT, we'd set up stuff like claymore mines, and of course we'd know where they were coming from. We'd hit them, and with all our firepower the Ranger students would always try to attack us. Sometimes I'd even put the RSE guys in formation and do a movement to combat. I'd take a point element of three men and make contact with the Rangers and we'd fall back and shoot like we did in Vietnam, and as we were falling back the Instructors behind us were setting up a big V-shaped ambush on high ground. We would draw the students into this big ambush and just kick their ass. We were trying to teach them something.

The conversation turned to teaching other things.

I tried to teach those kids that when they received an Operations Order from their company commander, when they say "mission," you're writing [everything] down. I taught them how to get there, and that the meat of the mission is operations at the objective. We used to use terrain models, but I'd tell them, what you have to remember is every time you go somewhere, every little stream you cross, every time you pop over a little hill, that has to be in your mind because when a Ranger Instructor puts a map down in front of you and says, "Ranger, where are you?"—they'd put their finger on the map, which covered a whole grid square, and say, "I'm right here, Sergeant." I'd break off a twig and hand it to them and say it again. "Ranger, where are you?" And they'd say, "I don't know, Sergeant."

Well, you have to know. All the time.

Keith Antonia

Antonia commanded a company in the 4th RTB before he commanded the 5th RTB. Not many have held command rank in more than one training camp.

When I was the S-3 for the Ranger Regiment I came out on the battalion command list and my wife said, "Oh, good! Now we get to go somewhere outside of Georgia." Then I got my orders to come to the 5th Ranger Training Battalion in Dahlonega, Georgia. I had to break the news to her. Never having had an overseas assignment, I got...command in Dahlonega.

Antonia was never stationed overseas, though he was across the water for training and short-duration assignments, such as working with the Jordanian Rangers. In May 1989, the entire 1st Ranger Battalion staged a strategic flight to Jordan from Savannah—about 18 hours—but couldn't jump because the wind was too high. For three weeks the 1st Rangers trained with the Jordanian Battalion, doing live-fire exercises and spending time in the desert.

I liked it after I got up here. I didn't like the idea of going to command a training battalion. I would rather have commanded an operational battalion. But, after I got up here, it was zero stress compared to the job I had just come out of. Being S-3 of the Ranger Regiment and of the 82nd (Airborne) were the two hardest jobs I had. I started enjoying my family and myself, and training Rangers was a lot of fun. Coming up here was a huge relief.

The reason why it was stress-free [a relative term] is because of the guys we've got. It is manned with second-time company commanders. They already have command experience before they come up here. It's a smaller company, but it's probably just as much responsibility.

The other thing is you've got all Airborne Ranger NCOs, and they're really good. All you've got to do is keep your thumb on the pace of things, and it's easy. Plus you've got a couple of Majors working for you, and a good staff.

Antonia is being characteristically humble. He was an excellent commander and was highly involved in the training and in liaison with the community, where he still resides.

Fort Bliss, Texas and Dugway Proving Grounds, Utah

Neither place is still used as a standard training ground for Rangers.

Perry Doerr

I got there right after they moved from Dugway. My first cycle was the first Fort Bliss class in the fall of 1991. Some of the Cadre was still moving down when I got there. The reason they moved was the Dugway winters were much harsher with deep snow from October to March, more like cold weather training.

Though it was hot most of the year at Fort Bliss, it got cool from November to March. The worst thing was the temperature difference between night and day—as much as 40 degrees. That and the high altitude really messed with your system.

It was a good assignment. We were actually in New Mexico on a sub-site of Fort Bliss called McGregor Range, about 35 miles north of El Paso. I was the First Sergeant of B Co. All companies followed basically the same training schedule. We would send Cadre back to Fort Benning (we were then the second phase of Ranger School) to pick up the class after they completed the Benning Phase. We then jumped them into Grange DZ [drop zone] to begin the phase. After a short tactical exercise we would bring them to camp for five days of classes. This was the first time the class operated as platoon-sized elements. At Benning they trained as squads. The classes were on raids, ambush, patrol base ops, link-up, desert survival, battle drills, leadership at the platoon level and movement, all focused on the unique desert terrain. We then jumped the class into the tactical (evaluated patrol) period of the phase. They spent eight days conducting raids, recons, and ambushes. After that we had a two-day administration period to process Studs for boards, clean up, maintenance of gear, and movement to the mountains.

Recycles would stay with us for the cycle break and be inserted into the next class. Mountain RIs would come out and pick up the class from us and take any students dropped from the school back to Benning for return to their unit.

Doerr said some RIs were still moving when he got to Bliss in the fall of 1991. He thinks the main reason for the move from Dugway to Bliss was the famed Dugway winter. They were much heavier and had more snow from October to March. He said it was like cold weather training up there.

An interesting anecdote about Fort Bliss involves Colonel Roy Murray, who was a Captain with Darby's 1st Ranger Battalion in WWII, and later commanded the 4th Rangers in Italy. The Colonel was retired out there. He frequently came to be with us, sort of a link to the Ranger historical past. In the summer of 1992, we dedicated Grange DZ to Lt. General (Ret) David Grange. When Lt. General Grange was out there, he and Colonel Murray absolutely had us in stitches during a party/reception at the battalion commander's house with good old WWII stories. It was truly an honor to be in the presence of those two Ranger Legends.
Steve Hawk
For A While, Bliss

Formal training at Bliss wasn't set up until 1980. Hawk was among those who put that together—five years after their first visit. The first class went through in 1983. Bliss is at (near) El Paso, but it also borders New Mexico. Hawk wrote four of the original six classes that were taught in the Desert Phase.

We formulated the plan in 1980. We didn't go out until December to look and see what we had. We had already been given the directive to begin. The four classes I wrote were done at the end of '80 [October-November] and on into '81. On December 26 they sent five of us out there [three Staff Sergeants, a Sergeant First Class, and a Captain] to look at the training sites and see what we were going to have to have. Checked on logistics, looked see how we were going to coordinate.

Most of 1981 was to finish up training, writing classes, coordinating the training, trying to figure out how we were going to move the Rangers from one phase to the desert, where they wanted to stick that phase in—it went in right after Mountain Phase.

At that time, Mountain Phase was the second of three phases, with the Swamp Phase (Florida) at the end. After Bliss, and later Dugway were closed to Ranger training, the three phases resumed in the same order. Today the Mountain Phase is last.

We were looking at Camp Donna-Anna [an outlying camp on Bliss] because we had used it in '75 [when the battalion came out to train in a desert environment]. We kept going back but we changed from Bliss to 29 Palms, California, to the Marine Corps Base. First time we went was 1977. I deployed with them three times, battalion training in the desert. Last time I went out was 1980.

Fort Bliss was chosen, I suppose, because Rangers trained there often.

After a short stint at Dugway, the Rangers returned to Fort Bliss for a time, then both camps were taken off the training schedule.

There were two outlying camps on Bliss that were used by visiting units. They were ideal because they were away from the main post and had training ranges surrounding them. Because of the sheer size of the ranges, fields of fire were not a consideration in any direction. Since a live-fire exercise was part of the program this was ideal.

It was my understanding that the authorities didn't want to support the training because of the money and this is why it was moved to Dugway.

We were given Dugway because no one else wanted to train there, and it met the same criteria as Fort Bliss. However, it was not much of a desert environment as much as it was an "arctic" environment. It was cold!

The Desert Phase [Dugway] was immediately following the Mountain Phase, and the RIs for that phase were taken from the Mountain Phase. There were six original Instructors that developed the Desert Phase and several of them remained in that area to keep the training areas and support ready. However, the original Instructors that went to Bliss to set up the training and train the Instructors were myself, Don Miles, Scott Oswald, a Captain [unknown], and SFC Bertram.

I TAC'd two classes as an RI at the Mountain Camp [4-81 and 8-83].

Tactical NCOs followed a Ranger class from its inception through all phases of training. This practice has since fallen away.

This was unusual as most NCOs only TAC'd one class during their tour. Class 6-82 was the second class to go through the Desert Phase. I would have TAC'd the first class, but we were still training Instructors for the Desert Phase when that class started at Benning.

An Afternoon Raid in North Georgia

In February 2005, Bravo Company of Ranger Class 04-05 was in the mountains near Toccoa, Georgia, getting ready for a raid.

My Lady, Sharon, and I were also there—she as a reporter, me as a lucky man. We were not alone, however. Also present on that occasion were the battalion commander of the 5th RTB, Lt. Colonel Douglas Flohr, and Brigadier General Yarborough, recently named as Assistant Commandant of the Infantry School at Fort Benning. The General was essentially in charge of training all US Infantry troops, including Rangers. He said he was 26 years out of Ranger School and wanted to see what was going on.

The students were probably very pleased to hear that after four days with nine hours total sleep, near exhaustion and starvation from constant stress, they would have a Colonel, a General, a reporter/photographer, and a historian watching everything they did.

It didn't go very well for one platoon—the one the brass was watching—but, in the words of SFC Daniel Barnes, "I've seen worse, believe me."

Barnes was our driver/guide/mentor for the trip and contributed much to this text, both in technical quotes and some great anecdotes.

The General and the Colonel turned right on a muddy path; we turned left. They went to be with the platoon on one side of the Toccoa River, CSM Glenn Legg went to the other platoon across the river.

We were supposed to take photos of that platoon assaulting across the bridge—a great swing bridge built by the forest service and 25 feet off the water—but they had infiltrated across silently before we got there. So, we walked trail until we got to the other objective.

The setup was straightforward. There were two "enemy" positions, one on each side of the river. On the General's side was a "building"—plywood and 4X4s covered with cammo netting—which acted as an observation post for an artillery piece on the other side of the river.

Bravo was split up for the dual raid, which was supposed to happen simultaneously at 4 p.m., about 500 yards apart.

Thick woods thinned to a sort-of clearing with natural berms all around. The little building sat in a shallow bowl with high ground to front and right, a descending trail to the river behind, and a tiny bit of open ground to the left which dropped off a few feet at one end.

Sergeant Barnes cautioned us not to get too close because we might be mistaken for opposition forces. We dropped back about 50 yards and stood our ground. We wanted to be in the middle of it, and we were. Sharon was taking photos from 10 feet away once it got going.

There were four "bad guys"—opposition forces from Camp Merrill—and they were armed well with an M240 machinegun and an M249 Squad Automatic Weapon (SAW), plus some grenades. One of them told us they had already seen the scouts for the Ranger student platoon that was supposed to be doing recon and planning the raid. He called in to the CP and asked if he should tell them they were compromised and see what to do next. Word came back to let them come on—after all, the brass was watching.

Meanwhile the bad guys were conferring and made the decision to set an ambush. Somehow three of them left their camp and went uphill to the right and out of sight. This move was evidently not picked up by the student watchers, because the bad guys circled around behind us and moved past us to our left. There they set up the M240 and the SAW in defilade.

My Lady took their photos from a few feet away, and I asked her why she didn't just jump up and down and whistle. However, the students still didn't pick up on where they were. Granted, there were a lot of trees and brush.

Voices on the radio talked about making sure both platoons hit at the same time.

We waited—and waited—and 1600 hours came and went. Orders came down to fire the "cannon" across the river, to try and get the platoons moving. Mortar-round simulators were blown, a loud bang, followed by the cacophony of the students across the river attacking the "gun."

Still nothing happened on our side. For a moment we all held our breath, knowing what was coming. Then suddenly we were submerged in sound as the security team for the platoon opened up with its own 240s (they had three) on the little building. One bad guy was there, and got behind the building and threw flash-bang grenades and fired his M14.

Ordinarily, the heavy volume of incoming fire would have shred him immediately, but the students were using blanks and, as Sergeant Barnes said, "The bad guys die when they want to. They're pretty much bullet proof."

Once the position was deemed semi-secure, about a squad of students came slowly out of the forest, appearing like magic from the shadowy gloom. They approached the building, weapons ready. Once enough of them were in the open the bad guys to our right hit them with machinegun fire from 30 yards—nearly point-blank—which, in real life would have reduced that squad to nothing almost instantly.

It took the students a couple of beats to realize they were under fire and to pinpoint the source, which was right next to us, and take action to envelope the bad guys. During this time I believe we were killed as being possible bad guys.

The real bad guys, having pulled off a successful ambush, faded away into the woods while the students were still setting up to fight them. Within minutes the students had overrun the empty area and were beginning a sweep to find the ambushers. Unfortunately, the bad guys had circled around and gotten a little elevation, set up their weapons, and opened up on the backs of the students—again, from about 40 yards or less.

The exercise tapered off quickly after that. There were several mistakes being discussed by the RIs in attendance. Their comments: "They are lost in the sauce", and "It's a real soup sandwich."

To be fair, Bravo Company tested out okay in the end of the Mountain Phase, but that day the Colonel and the General and the RIs sat them in a circle after the battle—the whole group looked very much like a thoroughly beaten football team gathered around the coaches.

The difference is death.

Retraining for another try began in that group.

GENERAL RANGER-RELATED INFORMATION

In the myriad bites of information pertaining to the Ranger world there are more than a few items that don't fit anywhere else but here. These are important items—they taste like Ranger. Several significant interviews also reside here.

CSM Kelso—The Top Non-Com of USAIC

Command Sergeant Major Michael Kelso sat just down the hall from Commanding General Benjamin Freakley on the top floor of Building Number Four at Fort Benning. Between the two men control of the giant installation rested easily in 2004.

Both wear the Ranger Tab, as do many other inhabitants of the sixth floor.

What do you have to do to be CSM of Fort Benning's United States Army Infantry Center? A concise version of Michael Kelso's biography follows.

Born March 11, 1956, in Versailles, Missouri

Enlisted in Regular Army, September 1973

First tour with 3rd Btn (Abn), 4th Air Defense Artillery, 82nd Abn Div

Fought with Army of Republic of Rhodesia as a volunteer, 1977

(to get combat experience)

Assigned to 3 Commando, Rhodesian Light Infantry

Served as Troop Medic, machinegunner, and stick leader

Had SIX combat parachute assaults

Again enlisted in Regular Army, March 1979

Served with 1st Ranger Battalion 1979-82

Special Operations Forces Detachment (Europe) 1982-84

3rd Ranger Battalion 1984-87

HHC, 75th Ranger Regiment 1987-92

Co E, 4th Ranger Training Battalion 1992-94

HHC Detachment, Ranger Training Brigade 1994-95

CSM, 4th RTB 1995-96

CSM, 1st Battalion, 501st Parachute Infantry Battalion 1996-99

CSM, Ranger Training Brigade 1999-2002

CSM, United States Army Infantry School March 2002

CSM, United States Army Infantry Center October 2002

CSM Kelso has attended Ranger School, Rhodesian Commando Course, and the Sergeant Major Academy. He also holds a Master of Science Degree in International Relations.

He has earned the Armed Forces Expeditionary Medal with Arrowhead, Rhodesian Operational Service Medal, Master Parachute Badge with Bronze Star (Rio Hato), Ranger Tab, and Expert and Combat Infantryman's Badges. Foreign awards include the Rhodesian, German, British, and Thai Parachute Badges. He was honored as a Distinguished Member of the 75th Ranger Regiment in August 2003.

Michael Kelso

Michael Kelso was Command Sergeant Major of the US Army Infantry Center at Fort Benning, Georgia, at the time of this May 20, 2004 interview. Kelso spoke on several subjects, included here in no particular order. His words were tape recorded in his office on the top floor of Infantry Hall.

On Rhodesia

I was too young to go to Vietnam. I'd wanted to be a combat soldier since I was a little kid. I think what started me on that path was the old TV show "Combat." A great show. That kind of sent me on. All my uncles were either in Vietnam or in Germany during that time frame. My grandfather was in WWI; my dad was in the Korean War. I wanted to be a soldier.

We were fighting communist guerillas [he also called them terrorists] that were trying to overthrow the government. The guerillas were supported by communist countries: Russia, China and Cuba. One operation in Mozambique involved a gunfight with Cubans. They lost! I got six combat jumps in Rhodesia. My Troop Sergeant, Derek Taylor, an outstanding soldier, had over 50! Remember, this war lasted eight years.

Six combat parachute jumps is almost unheard of in the American Army.

Kelso was asked to compare Rhodesian Commando School to Ranger School.

They're not equivalent. [They're not harder, but] they're hard enough. The Rhodesian soldier is as fine a soldier as you'll find anywhere in the world. You have to imagine yourself being surrounded by enemies and surviving for 14 years [a comparison was made with Israel, but it was noted that Rhodesia didn't have the powerful backing Israel has].

The Rhodesians had the frontiersman mentality. Their country was only settled in the late 1800s by English and Afrikaner settlers. This was right before the Boer War.

So they were very, very, bush-savvy. Very hardy—great people.

On Panama

I was the security leader for Team Black, which was Colonel Kernan's jump TOC (Tactical Operations Center) in Rio Hato.

At that time he was the First Sergeant of the Ranger Training Detachment.

There were three or four companies of his [Noriega's] Panamanian Defense Force [PDF] at Rio Hato. Supposedly some of his better guys. That was also where his beachside villa was. Of course the Special Ops, SMU [Special Mission Unit] guys went in there to take that out. But we jumped on the airfield. There were some pretty good firefights occurred at Rio Hato.

I was on Bird 12 [C-130 flown out of Lawson Army Air Field at Fort Benning]. Fourth from the last guy out or something like that. It was pretty crowded. I mean we were full up. During the loading as I was sitting down my reserve para opened! What a pain in the ass that was getting a new one hooked. Of course, we had combat equipment and so forth. Before we stood up the Rangers recited the Ranger Creed. It was very inspiring, and you knew you wouldn't let your Ranger buddy down. My Ranger buddy for the op was Staff Sergeant [now Sergeant Major] Alan Gibson. He led a company in the drive on Baghdad. A great soldier. As soon as they opened the doors, practically, you could hear ack-ack going off, you could see the tracers.

As I recall, the last few aircraft coming in were pretty far off the drop zone.

My team was in Rio Hato about a day-and-a-half, and then we were relieved by an element of the 7th Infantry Division. We pulled back to Howard Air Force Base in Panama City, where the Regiment conducted follow-on Ops throughout Panama. My security team got back to Fort Benning on Christmas morning at about three in the morning.

On Fort Benning, etc.

A question about aircraft led to this information.

There are no aircraft [stationed] here. We get aircraft in as required for Jump School. From all over the country. One day we might have C-130s; the next week we might have C-17s [a relatively new plane]. It's awesome [and large]. It's like sitting in that seat you're in right now [a very comfortable arm chair].

Last week was the last time a C-141 [older model jet] dropped students for Jump School. They're going out of the inventory.

They can land here [without a lot of room left over]. We just did an expansion program for the airfield so we can take C-5s [huge cargo carriers].

Subject change.

We do have some Navy guys here that are Instructors at Jump School. We also have a few Marines here. Then we have a Marine up in the 5th RTB, Gunny Oakes.

Marine Gunnery Sergeant Keith Oakes was a Ranger Instructor at the 5th Ranger Training Battalion in Lumpkin County, Georgia. He participated in the Best Ranger with another RI and the pair won the competition. As if happens, the author wrote the story for the local newspaper "The Dahlonega Nugget" after spending a good bit of time watching the two men train.

CSM Kelso was then asked what influence he wielded at Benning.

I have whatever the CG [Commanding Genera] will allow me to have, and that is quite a bit.

As you know, Fort Benning is a large place. On any given day there are over 30,000 soldiers on the Post. There are some 20,000 permanently assigned here, and then we have some 10,000 in training. Those numbers are going up because of the war. We are getting another Brigade Combat Team, and we are training 8,000 more recruits next year. That's from Privates to Colonels who come to Fort Benning for school.

Throughout this year we will train somewhere in the neighborhood of 65,000 to 70,000 soldiers. Next year over 80,000. Every Thursday and every Friday we graduate companies out on Sand Hill.

We get a fair share of foreigners, but not a great many. We have foreign soldiers come to our officer's courses and our non-commissioned officer's courses.

On Being CSM of USAIC

Succinctly, I am the senior enlisted advisor to the Commanding General on all issues dealing with the enlisted soldier, whether that be training, morale, housing, or discipline.

The day after this interview Kelso spent the day with the Secretary of the Army. Asked if he worked a five-day week he answered this way.

Well, it depends on what you call a five-day week. We come to work at six o'clock in the morning and don't get home usually 'til six o'clock at night. And we're always 24-7. The SecArmy will be here Saturday, too, and we'll be escorting him around.

Our job is more than just soldiering. We also try to maintain camaraderie amongst all the soldiers and families at Fort Benning. We have functions we go to, to try and keep that bond. Last week we had a luau ...sort of like what happens at Mountain Ranger [Association] cookouts, only on a larger scale.

We have a very close relationship with the community outside—Columbus and Phenix City.

He was asked if having been CSM of the RTB and having been a member of the 1st Battalion helped him in his dealings with the 3rd Battalion and Regimental HQ.

My style of leadership is hands-off. I think in the Army today we have great leaders, both officers and NCOs. So, normally, when they know what their mission is, they accomplish it. Very rarely do I have to get involved with the way someone is doing business. They can always come to me for advice and guidance and resources. I go out and visit everybody. I'm not out there to find fault with anything. I just like getting out amongst the soldiers. Unfortunately, this [his office] is my foxhole. I'd rather be out there remembering my youth as opposed to ...

It was observed that he had been on the executive end of things for some time, and that he was unlikely to be allowed back in the field.

It's not a bad thing, but the fire is still there, though. You know, I'm too old [40s], but if they would make me a squad leader tomorrow and tell me I was going to Iraq, I'd be a very happy camper.

On the 75th Ranger Regiment

I came into the Army in 1973 [then got out and went to Rhodesia because the US was pulling out of Vietnam]. I came home in 1978, rejoined the regular Army in 1979, [and went into] the 1st Ranger Battalion. I got to the 1st Ranger Battalion in May or June of '79, and went to Ranger School in July [as an E4].

In those days we graduated on Thursday. That Monday I started the Jump Master Course. We had gotten back to Florida and we were in the barracks and [somebody] said, "Hey, Ranger Kelso, your First Sergeant's on the phone."

The First Sergeant said, "Hey, what are you doing Monday?"

Kelso was to return to the 1st Battalion at Fort Stewart on Friday, but was told instead to stay at Benning and go through the Jump Master Course.

I wanted to say, but First Sergeant, I just got out of Ranger School! But, you can't tell the guy no, so...

When I was with [Bravo Company] 1st Battalion, I ended up as a Squad Leader as a Buck Sergeant. When I left I was a Staff Sergeant. From there, I went to Bad Tolz, did two years there, and fortunately I was back here for the Advanced Non-Commissioned Officers Course. They were filling the brand-new Ranger Battalion [3rd], which was coming on in 1984. This would have been March or April of '84. I was asked if I wanted to come back to the battalion and I said absolutely.

Kelso had to report back to Germany to receive his orders to report back to Fort Benning. You have to admire the way the Army works.

I spent three years with 3rd Battalion and then went to Regimental Headquarters, where I ran RIP [Ranger Indoctrination Program].

We like to say our Non-Coms are the backbone of the Army. We truly believe that. [Poland] ...they're trying to model their Non-Commissioned Officer's Course after ours. I then became First Sergeant of Regiment HQ for 30 months. Serving in the Ranger Regiment was outstanding! They are great soldiers whose patriotism is second to none. There are none better.

On Jumping

Bear in mind this is a man with seven total combat jumps. More than two is rare in the US Army, but Kelso said, "First Sergeant Pippen is over at the Ranger Regiment right now, and he has three stars on his wings {Jump Wings}. He did Panama, Afghanistan, and then one in Iraq."

Of his seven combat jumps, Kelso said, "It's a good news story for me, that I've done those things. But you know the old saying, 'That and a nickel will get you a cup of coffee.'"

Compared to a lot of guys in my situation I don't have all that many [jumps]. I've got about 200.

The question was, "How often do you jump now?"

As often as I want. I mean, I own the Airborne School {big laugh here} so ...

You only have to jump once every 90 days, but the CG and I try to jump at least twice in that period of time.

Everybody lands in the wrong place sometimes. We drop as we reach our release point based upon GPS and that sort of thing, so...if you go to any Airborne operation ever conducted, you're never 100 percent satisfied with where you land. This last June, the 60th anniversary of D-Day, the 507th PIR returned to Normandy for the first time since the war. The CG, BG Freakley and I, were honored to accompany them. He was the first, and I the second jumpers of 650. Awesome! What a great experience for those superb soldiers. All had a super time bonding with each other and the original veteran paratroopers of the 507th.

Several years prior to this interview the author was present at Stringer Drop Zone near Dahlonega, Georgia, when it was reopened after a long closure. The open area is not overlarge and is bordered on all sides by tall trees. Kelso, then CSM for the Ranger Training Brigade, and his commander, Colonel Hazon Barron, jumped in with Lt. Colonel Keith Antonia, Commander of the 5th RTB, and his CSM, Byron Barron.

Somehow the jumpers got out of order exiting the helicopter and no one knew whom the last two were, except that one of them was the Colonel and one was CSM Kelso. The wind was up and Kelso went into the trees. Antonia, thinking it may be his Colonel in the trees, sent everybody who could move toward the tree line.

Kelso was chagrined, but unhurt as he sat with the other three men for a photo taken by the author. He and Antonia were both presented with an enlarged print of the historic occasion.

On Ranger School

For a time Kelso was with Special Forces Operations Detachment in Bad Tolz, Germany.

That was a Special Forces Command in Europe. My little part of that was a Ranger Detachment in Bad Tolz, which was also known as Platoon Confidence Training. We had a two-fold mission. Our primary mission in peacetime was platoons from USARA would come to Bad Tolz and they'd do a 12-day mini-Ranger course with land navigation, mountaineering and patrol.

This was 1982-84. Our detachment wasn't very large, maybe 15 Rangers. We were there for training purposes, but they did have a wartime mission, which they used in Desert Shield/ Desert Storm. I was long gone by then, but as I understand it they served as reconnaissance.

Colonel (Hazon) Barron used to tell a story about what a Ranger was. I don't remember the exact wording, but it was something like, "If someone was to pull up and say NASA needs someone to fly the Space Shuttle, a Ranger would be the first one to raise his hand. He'd say, 'I don't know what I'm doing, but I'll sure give it a shot.'"

I think that's what Ranger School does. It develops an attitude in individuals like, "Might not know what I'm doing, but I'll do the best I can, and keep doing it until I fall down or get it accomplished."

I tell people that there are two occasions in my military career that tell who I am. One of them was serving with the Rhodesian Commandos. I couldn't ask for a better base of experience.

The second biggest positive impact on my career was Ranger School. Coming out of Ranger School, you know, I'd fly that damn Space Shuttle.

There are many great soldiers who are not Rangers. I want to say that first and foremost. But, Ranger School adds to your abilities. We had a SEAL, a Lt. Commander, in here, and he said if you have an affinity for water and you've passed Ranger School, you'd pass SEAL School. He said SEALs have one week, Hell Week, at the end of their training, but Rangers have all nine weeks of school as Hell Week. We get very few SEALs in Ranger School, maybe one a year. Usually if a SEAL comes to Ranger School, it's for punishment.

My brother, Cal, is a retired Navy guy. So, I love SEALs. We do two different things. Quite frankly, I think Ranger School is tougher than SEAL School. Now I'll get phone calls, "So, you want to go to SEAL training?" Well, no, and I don't want to go back through Ranger School, either.

Bonnells—A Family of Rangers

Throughout military history there have been many family ties among troops, including brother-against-brother scenarios in the Civil War, and father-and-son combinations such as General Eisenhower and his son, John, a new Lieutenant, or the contemporary duo of David Grange Jr., and his son, David, both Generals. Many men have followed their fathers or brothers into war, and though some have gone together, it is unusual to have everyone in the same branch, let alone the same units, albeit over time.

All three Bonnell sons were in Iraq at the same time, though in widely scattered places. Tracking the boys was difficult, and they had trouble finding each other over there.

The Bonnell family has Ken at its head, a retired Colonel who fought in Vietnam, and attended Ranger School in the first class of 1967. Ken commanded a company of the 506th Airborne in Vietnam, an element of the 101st Airborne Division.

Like their father, the three Bonnell sons all volunteered for the Army, Airborne School, and Ranger School. They also ended up in some version of the 101st. All three were Eagle Scouts and State Champion wrestlers, showing excellence in every field.

Since all were volunteers there is no restriction placed on them about having the entire second generation in a war setting at once. They chose to be out there where it's happening, as did Ken, twice wounded while commanding Vietnamese Rangers and American Paratroopers during his two tours.

Ken went on to see lots of combat, particularly when he was in command of a small firebase named Khe Gio near the A Shau Valley hotspot. He was awarded two Bronze Stars w/V device, and two Purple Hearts. He later served as S-3 (operations officer) at battalion, brigade, and division level, and commanded a multi-national force as part of CENTAG in Germany.

He retired in October 1990, after four years as Senior Army Advisor at Air Command and Staff College at Maxwell AFB.

Ken went into the Army as a commissioned officer after graduating ROTC at Ohio State University. Two of his sons, Brett and Bryon, followed him and began their careers as butter-bar Lieutenants. Both are now Majors.

Brett made Ranger School in the summer of 1987, while still an ROTC Cadet at OSU. He was commissioned in 1988, and was an Infantry Platoon Leader with the 101st during Desert Storm in 1991. He became a helicopter pilot and went on to command an aviation unit of the 1st Cavalry Division in Korea. That led to command of an aviation maintenance company of the 101st as part of Operation Iraqi Freedom.

Bryon also went through Ranger School while still an ROTC Cadet at OSU, graduating in 1989 as Distinguished Honor Graduate of his Ranger class, possibly the only ROTC cadet to ever do so. He was commissioned in 1990, and became an Infantry Platoon Leader in the 7th ID, and later commanded two different companies in the 101st.

He served with the 2nd ID in Korea, and was the Assistant G-3, 3rd ID, in Iraq. He returned State-side in the winter of 2003, and became S-3 of a Mechanized Infantry Battalion, part of the 3rd ID at Fort Stewart, Georgia.

Brad, the youngest, was delivered of his mother, Bonnie, while his father was guarding a bridge in Vietnam.

I finally caught up with Brad in north Georgia in October 2004, and taped some of his history. For more of his story see the section on the deaths of Saddam Hussein's sons. Brad was part of that. What follows here is the lead-up to that action in Iraq.

He has been on drug missions in Mexico and Peru, gone to Haiti and Honduras, and taken part in operations he can't talk about. Rangers in general are not big men—though some are very big—and Brad is one of the former. Shorter than average, he is an earnest young man built like a fireplug and looks as if he could rip the door off your car.

Brad Bonnell

We [my brothers and I] are three years apart from each other.

He was in high school when his middle brother, Bryon, went into the Army. Brad said going into the Army was almost a foregone conclusion.

I knew it. We were set from young ages, you know, you were either going to join the Army or...[laughs]. It was kind of bred into us. Not that we hated it. At very young ages we were playing the old cowboys and Indians and army stuff out in the woods. We lived around it all our lives as kids.

Brett and Bryon, Brad's older brothers, both went to Ohio State and were commissioned as officers, but Brad went in right out of high school.

My Dad came to me in my junior year in high school. It really hit me. He said, son, the most respected men in the Army are the NCOs. He said, I know your brothers are officers, I was an officer, but, if you want to really make something out of your life and be respected, you've got to be an NCO. He said he had more respect for his NCOs than his officers, and he said, "You'll be a great NCO."

I never had the drive to go to college. I could have gone athletic-wise for football or wrestling, but I never [really wanted] to do it.

I went through Ranger School in March 1992, class 9-92. I graduated on the fiftieth anniversary of Ranger School, and I graduated on my Dad's twenty-fifth anniversary of graduating Ranger School.

Now, that's something.

I joined the Army in August '90, and I went to 2nd Ranger Battalion up in Fort Lewis, Washington.

That makes him a Battboy, "born in the Regiment."

I was there for about six months, just after the JUST CAUSE [Panama] operation, and they came to me and asked, "Are you ready to go to Ranger School?" and I said, yeah, I want to go. So, I packed my stuff and the next thing I know I'm in Benning.

I was a Private, E-2. I went through Basic, then I went through Airborne School, then I went to through RIP [Ranger Indoctrination Program] that's held down in Benning, and then they assigned me to the 2nd Ranger Battalion.

That's a lot of tough schooling just to get to the Ranger Regiment, where the training really begins. Asked if he thought twice after going through the heavy-duty RIP, he said no, because he'd known all along that he was going to be a Ranger, whatever it took. With a father and two brothers already walking that road, he just naturally took it for granted.

For more on RIP and Pre-Ranger, see the chapter with that name.

They had Pre-Ranger back at Benning, and I had to go to that, and right after I graduated that I went to Ranger School.

I went through in March. It was cold. It snowed on us in Fort Bliss [Texas].

I did two tours with 2/75. I got there in '90 and I left in '96. Then [for a break] I went to the LRS Unit on post, at Fort Lewis. Foxtrot, 52nd. It was considered I Corps LRSU.

The training was about the same, but we didn't have much money, that the Regiment had. They get the best of everything. They also have soldiers that want to train, that want to be there.

I consider the quality of soldiers you've got in the Regiment—they went that extra mile [four-time volunteers].

[LRSU people] volunteer, but the quality of the soldier is not the same. You've still got the soldiers that, you know, "Yeah, I'm here, but half the time I'm here because I was put here." An LRS Unit is not all volunteer.

Brad ran a few missions with the LRS Unit along the Mexican border. He also went to Jungle Warfare School in Panama four times—three times with the 75th. "They were really active in those days." One more trip came with the LRSU.

I was with them for almost two years. Primary mission was recon and surveillance. Hide sites, surveillance sites.

We went to Haiti. I went with the Rangers. We went to Gitmo [Guantanamo, Cuba] first. We staged out of there. We had our full company, Alpha, 2/75. We spent almost a month on the USS George Washington—aircraft carrier—and that was our portion, we were going to assault off of that into Haiti. Our mission was to take down a barracks complex. The invasion got stopped, they said, hey, let's get them off the ship, they sent us all back to Gitmo.

Though not usually acknowledged as a Ranger action, the unrest in Haiti had a large force waiting to pounce when they were recalled—all but a few.

The other two battalions got diverted back to home base. They were ready to jump in at the time. The whole Regiment was mobilized.

It was mentioned that the 75th Regiment could likely have taken the whole of Haiti by itself.

On the USS George Washington, we had Alpha Company, and we had a platoon from 1st Battalion that we picked up in Savannah, we had CAG, I think two teams. We had DEA agents that were flying Little Birds. We had the Air Force, the 160th, with us, and we had some Navy SEALS.

CAG is the acronym for Combat Applications Group—in this case, Delta. The 160th is the Air wing Delta and the Rangers use. Little Birds are two-seat observation helicopters with teeth.

We actually did four missions in Haiti, just A Company. We went into a city and did some presence patrols. Just a show of force, with platoon-sized elements. Special Forces were pulled out, so it was just us in the area at the time. Some shots were fired, but I don't think they were directed at us. We knocked down a couple of doors looking for [certain people].

The comment was made that the Rangers wanted to get into something.

You're going to find if you talk to Rangers—they join the Rangers because they like that mentality. They're going to look for a fight. The old "break contact" is not in their vocabulary.

That was '94? It's kind of funny because we—A Company, 2nd Ranger Battalion, we were the first unit to work on aircraft carriers. They had a concept they were talking about to deploy the US Army off aircraft carriers. Get the whole air-sea-land aspect. We did a lot of training with the Navy operating off of carriers.

This was all rotary-wing transport.

My Ranger Company Commander at the time, [then] Captain Rick Carlson, is my battalion commander now in the 101st. I'm in the 3rd of the 327th, 1st Brigade. Our heritage goes back to the old glider battalions.

The way I look at it, the 101st is probably the closest to being like the [Ranger] Regiment, although everybody's not Airborne-qualified.

Most of them are jumpers, but the 101st is no longer considered a fully Airborne Division. Now it's an Air-Assault Division, much like the old 1st Cavalry Division in Vietnam.

As far as the quality of the soldiers, that's probably the closest you'll get to a Ranger unit.

I went back to the 75th in the middle of '97. I was a Weapons Squad Leader. We had the 240 Bravos and the 240 Golfs.

The M240 took up where the M60 left off as the "heavy" hand-held or mounted machinegun. Also capable of firing from a bi-pod, the 240 uses a belt-fed 7.62mm round, and is considered a crew-served weapon. For more information, see the section on modern weapons.

I was a Team Leader, but I was also a Sniper Squad Leader for a while. The way they used us was not like the old conventional Vietnam…snipers. We were used more as a recon element, but we had the ability to take out key targets if we had to. We trained anywhere from 800 meters on in. The farthest I shot with an M24 was right at a thousand meters.

Brad said he was the first man to "jump" a Barrett .50 caliber sniper rifle, broken down and carried in a WWII-vintage bag. The snipers also used the M24 (7.62mm), the Army version of the civilian Remington 700, and even the old M14 was in their armory. Sometimes the armourers fool around with weapon mechanics, resulting in some use of magnum rounds.

I did numerous overseas deployments with them, training exercises. With the Regiment I've been in Belgium, Canada, Jordan twice, Germany, and Thailand. When we go over there [Thailand] we usually train with their elite soldiers, like their Special Forces and Royal Marines.

They don't match up to what we have, but probably for that country, yes [they're pretty good].

I was with the 2nd/75th the second time until '99. Then I got orders that I needed to become a Ranger Instructor. At that time I thought, okay, change of pace, spend some time up here. I spent three-and-a-half years out there at the Mountain Camp. I was part of the Mountaineering Team. Also, I walked patrols. I was with Charlie Company the whole time.

From Camp Frank D. Merrill, home of the Mountain Phase of Ranger Training, Brad made the jump to the 101st in order to see combat.

Mike Martin Marches On

Martin is a well-known Ranger with vast experience. This interview was recorded over the telephone in 2006.

I left Vietnam in 1966 and went straight back to Germany, to the 509th. I had made E-7 in Vietnam, so they made me the First Sergeant of the 1/509.

First Sergeants are generally ranked E-8.

They'd bring in a regular hard-stripe First Sergeant and he wouldn't last two months, so they'd put me back in as First Sergeant. They put me up running the S-2—they didn't have an officer for that—and I did that for about a year, with three NCOs under me.

I guess my claim to fame—they had the Niemegen March over there. It was a 100-mile march. You marched 25 miles a day. The Colonel called me in and said I want you to take this thing, but I'm putting a Lieutenant with you. We decided we would do fancy drill and all that stuff the whole march. We did, but we trained every day. The Lieutenant wouldn't come to training. All he had to do was carry a saber. The first day of the march he started falling out, so he and I had a little confrontation. He was a big guy, but I said, Lieutenant (no name), we practiced six months for this thing and you're not going to hold us down. I said, I'm going to stomp your ass if you don't get in there and march.

With a little help from his teammates, Martin was able to persuade the Lieutenant to march. "It almost killed him, but he made it." It doesn't pay to argue with a Ranger senior NCO.

Out of 50 nations, we came in first. We did it for two years and were first every time. Then they wanted us to go all over Europe. We [509th] were called the Black Hawk Marching Team.

Germany to Vietnam to the Mountain Camp to Korea

Martin did a second tour in Vietnam beginning in 1968.

I left there [Vietnam] in December 1969, and came back to the States and was assigned to Fort Benning. I went in for an interview with Sergeant Major [Theron] "Bull" Gergen at the Ranger School, and he assigned me up to the 2nd Ranger Company at the Mountain Camp.

Lt. Colonel Shalikashvili commanded the camp at that time, and was succeeded by Edward "Moose" Yon before the end of Martin's tour. Yon had been the XO of Martin's company in the 504th in Germany. The linkage between Rangers is very extensive. Sometimes it seems as if they all know each other, or have at least heard of each other.

I got there and they said, with all your experience with mountaineering, we're going to put you in mountaineering.

Sounds logical, but there was already an E-7 in place and he would have remained in charge even though Martin outranked him as a senior E-7.

I said not if I outrank him. So the Sergeant Major said, well, you'll be the Patrolling NCOIC [Non-Com in charge]. I stayed there until about six months before I left the Mountain Camp. They jumped me up to operations for the last few months.

Martin and Mike Smith went up to Washington for family business (Smith's mother lived there) and ended up going to the Pentagon. Martin found the right Sergeant Major and volunteered to go back to Vietnam. The Sergeant Major pulled his records and said he needed to some overseas time, and that he was going to Korea. At that point Martin had nine years in Germany and two tours in Vietnam. "I need overseas time?" He told the man he hated the Koreans, having worked with them in Vietnam, and that there might be trouble if he went there. He went, anyway.

The Black Beret

When a civilian thinks about soldiers, he or she likely envisions a person wearing a steel helmet. True enough, most of the time in battle, soldiers wear protective headgear. However, there are many versions of headgear the general public understands little about.

Head coverings have long been used to signify identity on the battlefield or the parade ground.

Function is not necessarily a part of the importance of a particular head covering, but some are purely functional, and without insignia.

Current Rangers wear the tan beret now, as opposed to the black beret they wore for many years. The black beret now belongs to everybody in the Army.

US Army Chief of Staff, General Eric Shinseki, spoke on October 17, 2000.

Among other things, he said, "Effective 14 June, 2001, the Army's first birthday in the new millennium, the Army will don its new headgear. The black beret will become the Army standard."

On January 27, 2001, more than 2,400 soldiers of the 75th Ranger Regiment took off their black berets for the last time, replacing the revered cover with a newly authorized tan version. The black beret was to become headgear for the rest of the army, spreading the trademark widely enough to lose all significance.

Though Ranger Officers tried to put a good face on things, the change was not well received.

Throughout the ranks, both active and retired, protests were heard. Even politicians got involved in the "Save Our Beret" campaign. Governor of Georgia, Zell Miller, a former Marine, wrote to General Shinseki on February 21.

"First and foremost, I am convinced this will have a detrimental effect on morale within the Army's Ranger units. I believe it is inadvisable to take this symbol of achievement from an important and proud component of the Army like the Rangers. Second, I do not believe the black beret alone will promote unity or esprit de corps in the Army. I encourage substance over a symbol."

Colonel Hazen Baron, then the Ranger Training Brigade Commander, was given the mission of defending (explaining) the change.

"The Army uses distinctive head gear to show that an organization performs a unique mission for the entire Army. It doesn't defy the Army's goal of unit. We're all in the same Army. It simply distinguishes a particular unit with a particular mission, and today, historically, the tan beret symbolizes the mission of the Ranger. The training brigade is the Rangers' credential agency. We've graduated 50,000 Rangers since 1951. More than 14,000 are on active duty. The Chief of Staff has decided to award distinctive headgear—the tan beret—to the Rangers. It all starts here. The Army and the Rangers look to us to provide role models."

The History of the Ranger Black Beret By Robert Black

Bob Black is one of the foremost authories on the subject of the black beret, an issue that continues to plague the hearts of Rangers. This piece appeared on the Korean War Rangers website, but is only published in print in this document. I asked Bob if he would write a short piece for this book, and the following are excerpts of what he gave me. Permission was given via email December 13, 2003.

History does not care about "authorization." History is concerned with what happened.

The red, white and black scroll insignia designed and worn by the World War II Rangers was not an authorized insignia during World War II, and did not become so until after the Rangers parachuted into Grenada in 1983. Thus it was with the Ranger Black Beret. It was not authorized when it began. It was something the troops wanted.

Berets were a European headgear, primarily used by French and English troops.

In the spring of 1951, while lower numbered companies were fighting in Korea, in Germany, or training replacements at Benning, the third training cycle, consisting of the 10th, 11th and 12th Airborne Ranger Companies, was training at then Camp Carson, Colorado. To be a paratrooper was just part of the training to be an Airborne Ranger, and the men wanted a headgear that was distinctive from the "overseas cap" with its red, white and blue parachute hat patch and sky blue piping, designating infantry. The Rangers wanted something "Ranger." At least 50 percent of Ranger training was conducted at night. Thus Captain Charles Spragins, Commander of 10th, and

Captain Rudolph M Jones, commanding the 11th Ranger Company, gave their approval to the purchase of black berets, the black signifying the color of the primary operational time of the Rangers. These berets were worn when the company photographs of both 10th and

11th Companies were taken. Passes were issued permitting men to wear the black beret, and stating that it was part of the Ranger uniform.

There is no headgear that so clearly says "Airborne Ranger" as the 1951 Ranger Black Beret.

Companies 1, 2, 3, 4, 5 and 8 were fighting in Korea, and few of them had knowledge of the black beret concept. At Fort Benning, Colonel John Van Houton, Commanding Office of the Ranger Training Center, supported the black beret movement. He assigned Lt. Colonel Wilbur "Coal-bin Willie" Wilson as Project Officer. Wilson outfitted Sergeant John Roy of the 7th Rangers, not only in black beret, but also in black boots—in a brown shoe army. Carrying a paper of authority from his commanders, Sergeant Roy traveled about Fort Benning conducting the test Colonel Van Houten wanted. Again the troops were delighted, but those in authority outside the Rangers were not. With the disbandment of the Rangers in 1951, the concept did not reach Department of the Army level.

When war erupted in Vietnam, many of the Rangers who fought in that long and bloody war reached back into history and began to wear the Ranger Black Beret. It was still unauthorized, but clearly a Ranger tradition was established. The men wore it with pride. Some left notice that they wanted to be buried with their beret.

By Army Regulations 670-5, dated 30 January 1975, the black beret became an authorized headgear for the Rangers, and it would remain that way for 25 years.

On October 17, 2000 Army Chief of Staff General Eric Shinseki, in a speech before the Association of the United States Army (AUSA), made the announcement that starting in June of 2001, the black beret would become the Army standard. The Chief of Staff has the authority to take such action but he has a responsibility to act wisely and in the best interest of the soldiers.

The Chief of Staff of the Army is not beyond criticism. As Americans, we have the right to question the actions of leaders. General Shinseki had many options, including leaving the Rangers with their tradition and using another color, such as time-honored Army khaki, for the remainder of the troops. He would not do this. The serving Rangers were forbade talking about the change, and requests from Ranger Associations of World War II, Korea and Vietnam to meet with the General were ignored.

A lady from Army public relations told this writer the color black was chosen because of "fashion." An Army report said that giving the black beret to all soldiers was about "our excellence as soldiers, our unity as a force, and our values as an institution." How a hat can do all that was not explained. You cannot pull an army out of a hat.

To the embarrassment and anger of many, black berets for United States soldiers were purchased from communist China, where seven Chinese firms were involved in production. Millions of dollars were wasted as Congress forbade their use and the communist-made berets were warehoused.

General Shinseki's action may have been pleasing to him, but it tore a Ranger family apart in ways that will likely never be totally healed.

An Army Chief of Staff has great power for good or ill. General Eric Shinseki ignored our requests to choose another course of unity, or even another color beret. He would not even meet with men who had given 100 percent and then some to earn that headgear.

The Korean War Ranger Association supports the serving Rangers in meaningful ways. Soldiers must do what they are ordered to do. We veterans were not, and are not, under the orders of Eric Shinseki or any member of the Army. We stand by our tradition of the Ranger Black Beret and we wear it as it was worn in 1951. It does not prevent us from raising funds and supporting serving Rangers. We need not wear the same beret or the same underwear to be close and supportive of the serving Rangers—the veteran Soldier of World War I did not have to wear the uniform of the soldier of World War II in order to be of support—he had his own tradition.

Just How Many Rangers Are There?

The total number of living Ranger-qualified individuals in the year 2004 is hard to quantify, but the best efforts of researchers indicate there are about 15,000 retired, living, Tabbed Rangers —active duty Rangers are a different thing.

Not all Rangers are members of a Ranger Association, and not all are members of the Army any more. Though the Ranger School now produces about 1200-1500 newbies a year (15,000 in 10 years), where they end up is about as cohesive as a shotgun blast, and no accurate roles are kept of the number of surviving members dating back to WWII. The Ranger Battalion Association of WWII listed barely more than a thousand members in 2006.

We asked all kinds of Army bureaus and members of the statistical brotherhood and came up with these numbers to reflect the current number of active duty *officers* in the Army only. There were 76,140 active duty Army officers as of the summer of 2002, of which 8,800, or 11.5 percent, are Ranger-qualified. Taking into account there are only 5,282 Infantry officers, that means there are a bunch of non-Infantry officers out there with Ranger training, some 3,518 of them.

To break it down further, consider the roughly 50 percent of Company Grade officers wearing the Tab, while Field Grade officers comprise nearly 90 percent of their peer group. As of this writing in 2003, there were 299 Generals (0-7 to 0-10) wearing the Tab.

As they saying goes, "If you want to climb the ladder, you'd better be wearing a Ranger Tab."

These numbers do not reflect the Tabs worn by members of other branches (Marines in particular), nor the large group of non-commissioned officers out there. The Regiment is Sergeant-heavy, as are the Training Battalions.

Now then, consider Darby's Rangers (1st, 3rd, 4th Battalions of WWII) to be the first of the batch, include Rudder's 2nd and 5th Battalions, the 6th Battalion in the Philippines, Merrill's Marauders (who were technically not Rangers at all, but were given Tabs), all the Korean War companies, Vietnam Rangers, and those who wore the Tab in peacetime, plus the graduates of Ranger School from 1971 onward, and you have a great big bunch of guys who share the title.

However, of all those thousands, there are just 2,300 (or so) in the 75th Ranger Regiment, which is all three go-to-war battalions, including HQ and support elements. About 1,300 of them are field-soldiers. The Ranger Training Battalions comprise another 700 or so. The rest of the Tabbed Rangers are scattered throughout the US Armed Forces, mostly in Combat Arms.

An interesting fact is that about 40 percent of the 75th is populated by non-Tab-wearing Rangers. They are the Privates; the grunts. They have earned the name "Ranger" by virtue of being in the unit, but not the Tab. When the Private goes through Ranger School, he is promoted to Buck Sergeant, and there can only be so many Sergeants in the Regiment. Sometimes getting the Tab gets you right out of the Regiment because there are only so many TO&E slots to fill. Still, they are counted as Rangers, wherever they end up.

So, how many Rangers are there? Our best guess is about 80,000 men, total, who still live, and who have earned the right to be called Rangers. Now, if you want to add the Lurps...

BIBLIOGRAPHY

There are many, many, printed words about Rangers. Sifting through them was both educational and fun. If you read two books about Ranger history, you will find a few conflicts in the details of the text. Still, though details can be skewed, the overall picture remains whole and undamaged—the concept of a Ranger organization remains valid.

This is most of what I read, not counting the wide, though dubious, offerings of the Internet. Sadly, a computer crash in 2005 robbed me of some 20 percent of the bibliography. I have reconstructed it as best I could, but some of the printed input is missing.

The Internet supplied me with maps and dates and biographies, but I passed on any written histories unless I recognized the author. I learned that most of the better, first hand histories are not available in an on-line format. For those, you have to go to the bookstore, or have a good friend with a great library—both of which I did.

It should be noted that the mass of information represented here is only part of my education. Dry history aside, the best stories about Rangers come from Rangers.

In the nine years of spending time with Rangers, both active and retired, I've come to know them well. Information comes from a lot of different sources, and it's amazing what a person can learn by just standing there, watching and listening.

Raiders Or Elite Infantry?
David Hogan
Greenwood Press, 1992

75th Ranger Regiment Information Booklet
2001

General Ranger/Army History sent from 5th RTB, Dahlonega, Ga

An Illustrated Guide to Modern Elite Forces
Max Walmer
Arco Press

A Concise History of US Army Lineage
Geoffrey T. Barker

Rudder's Rangers
Ronald L. Lane
Ranger Associates Press

Lead The Way, Rangers
Henry S. Glassman
Also Chapter 10 by Lt. Raymond Herlihy

US Army Special Operations in World War II
David W. Hogan, Jr.
Center of Military History
Dept of the Army 1992

Seven Firefights In Vietnam
John Cash, John Albright, Alan Sandstrum
Office of the Chief of Military History
US Army 1985

Phantom Warriors (Volumes One and Two)
Gary A. Linderer
Ballantine Publishing

The Eyes of the Eagle
Gary A. Linderer
Ballentine

Eyes Behind The Lines
Gary A. Linderer
Ivy Press

Infantry In Vietnam
Small Unit Actions in the Early Days: 1965-1966
Edited by LTC Albert N. Garland
The Battery Press

A Distant Challenge
The US Infantryman in Vietnam 1967-1972
Edited by Infantry Magazine
The Battery Press

Incursion
(The move into Cambodia)
J D Coleman
St. Martin's Press

The Stilwell Papers—not all of them, certainly
Joseph W. Stilwell
Edited by Theodore H. White
William Sloane Associates, Inc., N.Y.

The Marauders
Charlton Ogburn, Jr.
Harper & Brothers, NY

Darby's Rangers
We Led The Way
William O. Darby
William H. Baumer
Presidio Press

Darby's Rangers
Mir Bahmanyar
Osprey Publishing

Sid Saloman
2nd Ranger Battalion Booklet

After-Action Report
5th Battalion
D-Day to D+4

Rangers Lead The Way
Col. (ret) Thomas H. Taylor
Turner Publishing Company
1996
Paducah, Kentucky

The Fool Lieutenant
The story of Robert Edlin
Moen and Heinen

Eighth Army Ranger Company
August 1950—March 1951
Narrative Compilation
Eighth Army Ranger Association

US Army Ranger
1983-2002
Mir Bahmanyar
Osprey Publishing

Black Hawk Down
Tim Bowden

America Takes Over
Boston Publishing Company
Edward Doyle, Samuel Lipsman and Editors of BPC
Part of a series—The Vietnam Experience

The Black Tigers
Compiled and Edited by CSM Michael Martin and Lt. Col. McDonald Valentine
Harmony House Publishers—Louisville

A Bright And Shining Lie
(John Paul Vann and America in Vietnam)
Neil Sheehan
Random House/NY

The LBJ Tapes
Taking Charge 1963-64
Edited by Michael Beschloss
Simon & Schuster

Winged Sabers
The Air Cavalry in Vietnam
Lawrence H. Johnson III
Stackpole Books

Into Laos
The Story of Dewey Canyon II/ Lam Son 719
Keith William Nolan
Presidio Press

Green Berets At War
Shelby L. Stanton
Presidio Press

Special Forces At War
An Illustrated History, Southeast Asia 1957-1975
Shelby L. Stanton
Howell Press

SOG
The Secret Wars of America's Commandos in Vietnam
John L. Plaster
Simon and Schuster

11ᵗʰ Annual Ranger Hall of Fame Brochure
Fort Benning, Georgia
August 2003

The Dahlonega Nugget
Bonnell article
Black Beret article

The Sun
Marysville, Ohio
April 23, 2003
Iraq/Bonnell article

Rangers In Korea
Robert Black
Ballentine Books

Rangers in World War II
Robert Black
Ballentine Books

Behind The Burma Road
William R. Peers
Dean Brelis
Little, Brown, and Company

History of WWII, 2ⁿᵈ Ranger Battalion HQ Company
Compiled by George M. Clark, William Weber, Ronald Paradis
Edited and Published by James W. Eikner 1946

The Rangers At Hwachon Dam
Martin Blumenson
Army Magazine (copyright Dec. 1967)
Based on interviews done in 1951 Korea

The Guts To Try
Colonel James H. Kyle, USAF (Ret.)
Orion Books/Crown Publishing

Recondo
Larry Chambers
Ivy Books

The Raid
(Updated version of Son Tay)
Benjamin F. Schemmer
Ballantine Books

Ripcord
Screaming Eagles Under Siege, VN 1970
Keith W. Nolan
Presidio Press, Inc.

Diary Of An Airborne Ranger
A LRRP's Year in the Combat Zone
Frank Johnson
Ballentine Books

LRRP Company Command
The Cav's LRP/Rangers in Vietnam 68-69
Kregg P. J. Jorgenson
Ballentine Books

D-Day
The Climactic Battle of WWII
Steven E. Ambrose
Simon and Schuster

The Enemy Within
Casting Out Panama's Demon
Focus Publications (Int), S. A.

Stolen Valor
B.G. Burkett and Glenna Whitley
Verity Press, Inc.
Dallas, Texas

1. James Michael Johnson, *Militiamen, Rangers, and Recoats: The Military in Georgia* (Macon: Mercer University Press, 1992), 10-12.

9. Robert S. Davis, Jr., *The Wilkes County Papers* (Easley, SC: Southern Historical Press, 1980), 25-26, 38-43; Revolutionary War pension claim of Shadrach Nolen, GA/Sc S-4622, National Archives and Records Administration; Lachlan McIntosh, "The Papers of Lachlan McIntosh," *Collections*, 12: 24; Johnson, *Militiamen*, 93. For rosters of the Georgia rangers see "The Georgia Provincial Rangers," *Georgia Genealogical Society Quarterly* 18 (1982): 139-51 and Davis, *The Wilkes County Papers*.

The Bay State Monthly, Vol. 2, Issue 4
January 1885, Boston
Article on Robert Rogers by Joseph B. Walker

Article on Rangers by Larry Ivers
Colonial Wars of North America, 1512-1663
An Encyclopedia
Editor Alan Gallay
Garland Publishing, Inc
1996

Article—Rangers, Scouts, and Tythingmen
Larry Ivers
Published in Forty Years of Diversity
Essays on Colonial Georgia
University of Georgia Press, 1984

Robert Rogers' Journals

Mr. Bertil Haggman, LL.M.
Member, Swedish Authors Association
Research Works, Civil War

Ronald H. Cole
Joint History Office
Office of the Chairman of the Joint Chiefs of Staff
Washington, D.C. 1995

History of Invasion of Panama
Corps Historian's Personal Notes Recorded During The Operation
Source: 870-5a Organizational History Files, XVIII Airborne Corp, 1989-90, Operation
JUST CAUSE, Corps Historian's Notes, Notebook #1. PERMANENT

Army News Service Press Release
Dec. 21, 1999
By SSG Amanda C. Halford
Army Marks Tenth Anniversary of JUST CAUSE

American Edition
Edited by Dr. F. B. Hough
J. Munsell's Sons, 1883

From Savannah to Yorktown: the American Revolution in the South
Henry Lumpkin
Paragon House, 1981

Internet Disclaimer

There are many, many incursions into cyberspace for data research and some retrieval. The main function of the Internet in this project has been to crosscheck facts, such as "Where is Cowpens?" or to view maps or documents. The Internet is notorious for posting misleading or wrong information put out by anyone with a website, so cruising for information was often tedious while trying to home in on specifics.

In short, the Internet is a great source of information—but it is not first-source material except for certain things such as maps, brief biographies and histories—used in the learning phase of this project—and contact with libraries and Ranger organizations.